STRATEGIC
SUSTAINABILITY

Strategic Sustainability examines how organizations can implement environmental sustainability science, theories, and ways of thinking to become more competitive. Including examples and ideas implemented in various countries, it is based on known scientific principles about the natural world and organizational principles focusing on the work domain. The intersection of these two realms of research creates a powerful and new approach to comprehensive, seemingly contradictory issues.

Daniel S. Fogel draws from disparate fields and creates a story about organizations, their future, and how people are part of the problem and, more importantly, part of the solution. Readers will find ways to take action to improve organizations and avoid denigrating our natural environment, learning to be mindful of the urgency we should feel to improve our impact on the world. The focus on the natural environment provides a powerful focus for creating value in organizations and addressing the major challenges we all face.

Advanced sustainability students, working professionals, board members, managers, and legislators responsible for governing organizations or implementing public policy will find this book useful. A companion website features an instructor's manual with test questions, as well as 38, 10-minute videos for classroom use.

Daniel S. Fogel is the Graduate School Research Professor in Sustainability and Director of the Master of Arts in Sustainability at Wake Forest University, USA. He has been recognized for his work consulting for organizations such as General Electric, Bank of America, and Raleigh City Government, and has published widely in behavioral studies, education, health care, psychology, sociology, economics, and management journals and books. He is Chairman of EcoLens, Chairman of The EcoLens Network, and Chairman and CEO of SP3.

"*Strategic Sustainability* offers a comprehensive coverage of firm-natural issues related to the environment, ranging from critical drivers to strategic options at hand. The book is well-structured and well-illustrated with practical and more theoretical cases in a global context. Each chapter challenges the reader critically to think, reflect, and apply key insight from the chapter."

John Parm Ulhøi, *Aarhus University, Denmark*

STRATEGIC SUSTAINABILITY

A Natural Environmental Lens on Organizations and Management

Daniel S. Fogel

Routledge
Taylor & Francis Group

NEW YORK AND LONDON

First published 2016
by Routledge
711 Third Avenue, New York, NY 10017

and by Routledge
2 Park Square, Milton Park, Abingdon, Oxon OX14 4RN

Routledge is an imprint of the Taylor & Francis Group, an informa business

Library of Congress Cataloging in Publication Data
Names: Fogel, Daniel S., author.Title: Strategic sustainability : a natural environmental lens on
    organizations and management / Daniel S. Fogel.
Description: New York, NY : Routledge, 2016. | Includes index.
Identifiers: LCCN 2015038703| ISBN 9781138916555 (hbk) | ISBN 9781138916579 (pbk) |
    ISBN 9781315689531 (ebk)
Subjects: LCSH: Management—Environmental aspects. | Sustainable development—Management. |
    Strategic planning—Environmental aspects.
Classification: LCC HD30.255.F64 2016 | DDC 658.4/012—dc23
LC record available at http://lccn.loc.gov/2015038703

ISBN: 978-1-138-91655-5 (hbk)
ISBN: 978-1-138-91657-9 (pbk)
ISBN: 978-1-315-68953-1 (ebk)

Typeset in Galliard LT
by Swales & Willis Ltd, Exeter, Devon, UK

CONTENTS

ACKNOWLEDGMENTS

One person, alone, does not develop a book. So many people have helped me on this journey. I wanted to acknowledge the institutional support beginning with the University of Pittsburgh, Katz School of Business and especially some of my colleagues there—Ravindranath Madhavan, in particular; Wake Forest University's Schools of Business; and the Teaching and Learning Center and the Asia Pacific Centre for Sustainable Enterprise at Griffith University in Australia (which all provided financial support). Special recognition goes to Wake Forest University's Center for Energy, Environment and Sustainability. Without this team, I could not have even conceptualized some of the material in this book: Miles Silman (the Center's Director), Alan Palmiter, Abdou Lachgar, Jon Clift, Ashley Wilcox, Bob Browne, DeDee DeLongpré, Emily Waklid, and Michelle Klosterman. Thanks for your support and collegiality. Mike Aper did a great job providing research support. .

So many students have contributed to my development and discussion of ideas. In particular, the brave souls in the summer of 2012—and beyond—who took my electives and slogged through the book's drafts: Sumit Agarwal, Chris Barius, Harry Byrd, Tina Carper, Alex Espinoza, Rob Hink, Matt Howard, Kristin Kenyon, Jenny Kichler, Brennan Lewis, John Lintner, Chris McMillan, Kelly Meany, Cynthia Redwine, Meg Ruschmann, Stephan Schlesinger, Katie Spearman, and Bryan Sprayberry. Special mention needs to go to those who traveled with me to Germany and Spain (to learn of the European solutions for renewable energy) as well as to several U.S. cities: Leigh Boone, Louis Brotherton, Jennifer Coates, Emilie Collins, Brad Daniel, Shridhar Dasu, Simon Everett, Harris Falb, Clayton Forbes, Manabu Hoizumi, Robin Hood, Suresh Janardhanan and Elizabeth Romano (both of whom braved several experiences with me), Ed Jazee Johnson, Nishith Kholia, Dan McKenzie, Chuck Marckeardt, Mark Montes, Matt Needham, Andy Place, Ivan Regueira, Nick Tuite, Don Ware, and Eugene Young (in addition to the students named above). Thanks to some of my partners in consulting, especially Rich Pandullo and Peter Marsh; the Carnegie Mellon University Tepper School of Business Executive Education people; and the many clients who were kind to me as I explored this material.

To the unmentioned (yet not forgotten) students and colleagues who supported me, provided ideas, and gave me inspiration—thank you so much.

And to the Beckmann family, Rachael Clapp, Roopali Bahal, Pasquale Quintero, Kaitlin Dunnevant, Jill Westfall, Kristyn Eske and Rachel (Carter) Hutchings for fantastic administrative support.

My wife, Susan, was amazingly patient with me through this process—my love for her cannot be defined and grows every day. My daughters Cathy, Cristene, and Jessica, and their spouses Rob, Ed, and Brian were sources of support and provided the ultimate inspiration for me; my grandchildren (in order of age)—Tyler, Matthew, Haley, Samantha, and Cooper—may the solutions and ideas in this book make for a better world for them and all people wherever they choose to live!

ACRONYMS AND ABBREVIATIONS

AASHE	Association for the Advancement of Sustainability in Higher Education
ACUPCC	American College and Universities Presidents' Climate Commitment
AEA	Atomic Energy Act
AEC	Automotive Electronics Council
AFNOR	French Industrial Standards Authority
ANSI	American National Standards Institute
ASC	Aquaculture Stewardship Council
ASM	available seat mile
BLM	Bureau of Land Management
BPA	bisphenol A
BREEAM	Building Research Establishment Environmental Assessment Method
BSI	British Standards Institution
BTU	British Thermal Unit
CAC	Command and Control
CAFE	Corporate Average Fuel Economy
CAR	Climate Action Reserve
CASBEE	Comprehensive Assessment System for Building Environmental Efficiency
CBBA	Climate, Community, and Biodiversity Alliance
CCAR	California Climate Action Registry
CCS	carbon capture and sequestration
CDP	Carbon Disclosure Project
CEJAPA	Clean Energy Jobs and American Power Act
CEO	Chief Executive Officer
CERCLA	The Comprehensive Environmental Response, Compensation, and Liability Act
CEV	Corporate Ecosystem Valuation
CFC	chlorofluorocarbons
CII	Confederation of Indian Industry
CITES	The Convention on International Trade in Endangered Species of Wild Fauna and Flora
CLA	Clean Air Act
CO_2	carbon dioxide
COO	Chief Operating Officer
CPSA	Consumer Product Safety Act
CPSC	Consumer Product Safety Commission
CRS	Creative Recycling Systems
CSR	Corporate Social Responsibility
CSRC	Corporate Sustainability Report Coalition
CWA	Clean Water Act
DCF	Discounted Cash Flow
DEFRA	Department of Environmental Food and Rural Affairs

DEPA	Danish Environmental Protection Agency
DGNB	Deutsche Gesellschaft für Nachhaltiges Bauen (German Sustainable Building Council)
DJSWI	Dow Jones Sustainability World Index
DOE	U.S. Department of Energy
DOT	U.S. Department of Transportation
EAs	Environmental Assessments
EBIT	Earnings Before Income Tax
EDF	Environmental Defense Fund
EEI	Edison Electric Institute
EHS	environment, health, and safety
EIA	Energy Information Administration
EIS	environmental impact statements
EIS Act 2007	Energy Independence and Security Act of 2007
EPA	Environmental Protection Act
EPA	Environmental Protection Agency
EPCRA	Emergency Planning and Community Right-to-Know Act
EPP	environmental preferable purchasing
EPR	Extended Producer Responsibility
EPRI	Electric Power Research Institute
ES	Ecosystem Services
ESG	environment, social, and governance
EU	European Union
EU ETS	European Union Emissions Trading Scheme
FCPA	Foreign Corrupt Practices Act
FDA	U.S. Food and Drug Administration
FEED	front end engineering design
FERC	Federal Energy Regulatory Commission
FICCI	Federation of Indian Chambers of Commerce and Industry
FIFRA	Federal Insecticide, Fungicide, and Rodenticide Act
FLO	Fair Trade Labeling Organizations International
FSC	Forest Stewardship Council
FTF	Free Trade Federation
FTSE	Financial Times Stock Exchange (United Kingdom)
FWS	U.S. Fish and Wildlife Service
GDP	Gross Domestic Product
GEIS	Global Equity Index Series
GEO	Global Environment Outlook
GEOSS	Global Earth Observation System of Systems
GHG	greenhouse gas
GIS	Geographic Information System
GNP	Gross National Product
GRI	Global Reporting Initiative
GW	gigawatt
IAU	International Association of Universities
ICLEI	International Council of Local Environmental Initiatives (rebranded as Local Governments for Sustainability)
IEP	International Electricity Partnership
IETA	International Emissions Trading Association
IFC	International Finance Corporation
IISD	International Institute for Sustainable Development
ILO	International Labour Organization

IMF	International Monetary Fund
IPAT	Human Impact (I) on the environment equals the product of P = Population, A = Affluence, T = Technology. This describes how our growing population, affluence, and technology contribute toward our environmental impact.
IPCC	Intergovernmental Panel on Climate Change
ISO	International Standards Organization
KPI	key performance indicator
LCA	life-cycle assessment or analysis
LEED	Leadership in Energy and Environmental Design
LEPC	Local Emergency Planning Committees
LNG	liquid natural gas
MD&A	Management Discussion and Analysis
MIC	Metlakatla Indian Community
MNC	multinational corporation
MPRSA	Marine Protection, Research, and Sanctuaries Act
MSC	Marine Stewardship Council
MSCI	Morgan Stanley Capital International
NAAQS	National Ambient Air Quality Standards
NAFTA	North American Free Trade Agreement
NEPA	National Environmental Policy Act
NGOs	non-governmental organizations
NGPA	Natural Gas Policy Act
NHTSA	National Highway Traffic Safety Administration
NIOSH	National Institute of Occupational Safety and Health
NOAA	National Oceanic and Atmosphere Administration
NOP	National Organic Program
NPV	net present value
NRC	Nuclear Regulatory Commission
NSA	non-state actors
NWF	National Wildlife Foundation
NWFA	National Wood Flooring Association
NWPA	Nuclear Waste Policy Act
NYSERDA	New York State Energy Research and Development Authority
OCSLA	Outer Continental Shelf Lands Act
OECD	Organization for Economic Co-operation and Development
OFPA	Organic Foods Production Act
OMB/OIRA	Office of Information and Regulatory Affairs
OPA	Office of Price Administration
OPEC	Organization of Petroleum Exporting Countries
OSHA	Occupational Safety and Health Administration
OXFAM	Oxford Committee for Famine Relief
PCW	PricewaterhouseCoopers
PET	polyethylene terephthalate
PPM	parts per million (PPB = parts per billion)
PPP	purchasing power parity
PR	public relations
PRTR	Pollutant Release and Transfer Registry
PURPA	Public Utilities Regulatory Policy Act
R&D	research and development
RCRA	Resource Conservation and Recovery Act
RDECOM	U.S. Army Research, Development, and Engineering Command

REC	renewable electricity credit
ROCE	return on capital employed
ROE	return on equity
ROI	return on investment
ROIC	return on invested capital
RONA	return on net assets
RPM	revenue passenger mile
RPS	renewable portfolio standards
S&P	Standard and Poor's (U.S. Stock Index)
SASB	Sustainability Accounting Standards Board
SC	Stakeholder Council (within the GRI)
SCR	Selective Catalytic Reduction
SEC	Securities and Exchange Commission (USA)
SFI	Sustainable Forest Initiative
SG&A	selling, general, and administrative expenses
SLEEP-AT	Social and Demographic, Legal, Economic, Environmental, Political, Administrative, and Technological
SME	small and medium sized enterprises
SPOTA	Sustainable Painting Operations for the Total Army
SRI	socially responsible investing
SSE	Sustainable Stock Exchanges Initiative
STARS	Sustainability Tracking, Assessment, and Rating System
SWF	Sovereign Wealth Fund
TNA	total net assets
TNS	The Natural Step
TSC	Toxic Substances Control
UNEP	United Nations Environmental Programme
UNFCC	United Nations Framework Convention on Climate Change
USDA	United States Department of Agriculture
USFC	United States Forest Service
VCS	Verified Carbon Standard
VOC	volatile organic compound
WBCSD	World Business Council for Sustainable Development
WCED	World Commission on Environment and Development
WFTO	World Fair Trade Organization
WHO	World Health Organization
WRI	World Resources Institute
WTO	World Trade Organization
WWF	World Wildlife Fund

INTRODUCTION

This is a book about organizations, and how they can implement environmental sustainability science, theories, and ways of thinking to become more competitive. The information is based on known scientific principles about the natural world *and* organizational principles focusing on the work domain; the intersection of these two realms of research creates a powerful and new approach to comprehensive, seemingly contradictory issues.

Basic Assumptions

The book approaches sustainability in three key ways. First, the text broadly focuses on how we use the planet's resources, incorporates a brief history of human behavior, explores existing unsustainable practices, and develops a vision and means to change these practices.[1] The sustainability field of study is then defined as satisfying current needs without sacrificing future well-being through the balanced pursuit of ecological health, economic welfare, and social welfare.[2] This culminates in a set of likely outcomes, which includes the attainment of a sustainable world with resilient economies, societies, and natural environments.[3]

Certain assumptions affect the approach and presentation of this material. For example, I approach this subject matter as if we are in the Anthropocene era (i.e., a world we have indelibly and irreversibly changed with respect to practical timescales). Anthropocene means that we have entered a new geological era with humans influencing environmental outcomes at least as much (if not more) than non-anthropogenic forces. While we are capable of reversing many of these trends, I believe that the structure of society currently has some design flaws preventing us from creating a sustainable future (e.g., how we manage waste and fossil fuels). Thus, many challenges we face are *design challenges*; this should give us confidence that we can find ways to restructure the way we do things, today, to create a more sustainable world for tomorrow.

Among the major assumptions in this book is that we can redesign society (including organizations) to become more responsive to these needs and challenges. Also, the science we use assumes *politics of the possible*, certain discourses, and a precautionary approach.

Politics of Constraints and the Politics of the Possible

One way to envision disparate design outcomes is to compare and contrast the *politics of constraints* with the *politics of the possible*.[4] The difference is presented in the book *Break Through*;[5] its authors argue that we have seen recent changes in perspective in terms of what will achieve a sustainable world. The previously prevailing view (i.e., *politics of constraints*) relies on expert judgment, market and government solutions, and, largely, on the efficacy of conservation and the preservation of natural resources. This perspective assigns "limits to growth," and advocates that the ways to build a sustainable society are those of constraining our use of resources.[6]

In contrast, *politics of the possible* advocates balance among environmental, social, and economic outcomes. Sometimes this idea is labeled "ecological modernization" (i.e., environmental adjustment of economic growth and industrial development, which is an effective adaptive process). The Green Parties (common in many European countries) promote political solutions to balance other societal interests; this view advocates a healthy management of natural resources over restriction of resources.

So, these two discourses differ in terms of how they describe the challenges, consider the environment, identify relevant agents and their motives, use metaphors, generate solutions (e.g., prosaic vs. imaginative), and their breadth of focus. To further illustrate the differences between these two viewpoints, Table I.1 juxtaposes the philosophies of two books: *Silent Spring* by Rachel Carson, and *Natural Capitalism: Creating the Next Industrial Revolution* by Paul Hawken, Amory Lovins, and L. Hunter Lovins. One supports the politics of constraints; the other favors the politics of the possible. The tone of the two books is different, as are their assumptions. Both books' authors believe that we can somehow control nature, an assumption that has been challenged by many authors.[7]

Sustainability Discourses

Different views on environmental sustainability can lead to different conclusions and assumptions,[8] since environmental issues rarely present themselves in well-defined boxes. For example, global climate change (due to build-up of carbon dioxide and other greenhouse gases [GHG] in the atmosphere from burning fossil fuels) relates to air pollution in local contexts and, as a result, also becomes an issue of transportation policy. Additionally, these issues lead to the destruction of ecosystems (e.g., tropical forests), which normally act as "carbon sinks" (absorbing carbon dioxide from the atmosphere); this leads to issues of fossil fuel dependence and depletion, which have necessitated a growing use of alternative sources of energy (e.g., wind and solar power).[9] This change is related to the promotion of social policies focusing on the pricing of resources. So, there are myriad discussion areas that can seem daunting and imprecise, based on a single issue like GHG build-up.

Table I.1 Two Books Indicative of These Views

Book	*Carson*, Silent Spring[1]	*Hawken, Lovins, and Lovins*, Natural Capitalism[2]
Principles	• Forging weapons from the insect's own life processes. "Only by taking account of such life forces and by cautiously seeking to guide them into channels favorable to ourselves can we hope to achieve a reasonable accommodation between the insect hordes and ourselves."[3]	Four principles: 1 Radical resource productivity 2 Biomimicry 3 Service and flow economy 4 Investing in natural capital
Assumptions	• Humans and nature are separate, and humans should be subordinate to nature. • Nature is harmonious and in balance. • Humans should not control nature; humans should live in harmony with it. • Sets up several generations of writing about our eco-tragedy imagining humans as living in a fallen world—we must return to harmony.	"Natural capitalism recognizes the critical interdependency between the production and use of human-made capital and the maintenance and supply of natural capital."[4] "Our focus is to bring about these changes in the human side of the economy that can help preserve and reconstitute these systems, to try and show for now and all time to come that there is not true separation between how we support life economically and ecologically."[5]
Critique	Tends to support constraints and that humans are the main problem to be solved—to stop using chemicals and other harmful elements. Nature is an objective fact.	Supports a positive approach that we can learn from nature, and use that knowledge to grow and live more productively. Nature has multiple meanings.

Notes

1 R. Carson, *Silent Spring* (Boston: Houghton Mifflin, 1962).

2 P. Hawken, A. Lovins, and L.H. Lovins, *Natural Capitalism: Creating the Next Industrial Revolution* (New York: Little, Brown and Co., 1999).

3 Carson, 296.

4 Hawken, Lovins and Lovins, 3–4.

5 Ibid., 21.

It is often useful to clarify the assumptions behind the arguments since some of the main views are relatively nuanced. For example, one view is that we have moral and economic rationales for exploiting natural resources, assumes nature has no intrinsic value, and holds that human prosperity depends on nature's exploitation and development (and that human inventiveness and technology can transcend any resource problem).[10] Alternative strategies include placing human power, growth, and development at the center of politics; developing new kinds of nature; and clarifying societal aspirations and how we can attain them.[11] Still other views are based on a pollution paradigm (i.e., we should limit ourselves through conservation and regulation, stop nature's destruction, and go back to living in harmony with nature).

I take a reformist, imaginative approach in this book. I assume that the core environmental problems are relatively straightforward; can be identified, discussed, and addressed; and that caring for the environment is just as important as caring for economic viability and social justice. Through modern science, we know a great deal about human impacts on our natural environment; my opinion is that we must quickly redesign myriad systems to meet modern-day environmental challenges. To do so, we can draw from nature, *and* organizations, inventions and innovations.[12] Furthermore, if we can show people the harm to the natural environment in a manner that is powerful and personal, they will require action.[13]

Finally, most of the material in this text invokes the precautionary principle (i.e., we act even in the face of scientific uncertainty). I accept sustainability science, which considers forecasts as sufficient grounds for action to ensure global sustainability. Consider Table I.2 as an illustration of the precautionary principle related to global climate change and global warming. Assume that the science is flawed, and we take actions to mitigate the negative impacts of climate change. We incur unnecessary costs and possibly a global depression from ill-invested money. If the science is flawed and we do not act, then we get to use the money for other purposes.

Yet, what if the data are correct (which is the core assumption in this textbook)? If we act, we get a chance to mitigate the harmful effects of global warming before the impacts are too extensive. If we do not act, we will face devastation.[14] Given this simplistic illustration, I believe we must act. The disadvantages of being wrong are too salient; negative economic growth is much more manageable than devastation to human existence.

You might consider developing a clear idea of your dominant discourse and beliefs since these fundamental assumptions are critical to your evaluation of the material presented in this book as well as other information you may read. While you might find this task difficult, you will obtain knowledge in this book to assist you. As you develop your own discourse and list of assumptions, you should consider certain concepts and questions:

- What is the focus of your attention (e.g., firms, individuals, species, the world)?
- What assumptions are you making about humans and their relationship to the natural world? For example, *weak sustainability* assumes that human-made capital can effectively substitute for natural capital and services provided by ecological systems; however, if natural systems are limited and there is little substitution between different types of natural and human-made capital stocks, then per capita consumption might not be sustainable in a world with a growing population. Weak sustainability advocates that the substitution of human-made capital for exhausted natural capital is justified so long as the increase in productive capacity of human-made capital more than offsets the loss in productive capacity from natural capital (e.g., the decline in wetlands may be offset with constructed wetlands). *Strong sustainability* advocates emphasizing the ecological imperatives of carrying capacity, biodiversity, and biotic resilience.[15] Vital services, provided by ecological systems, cannot effectively be substituted by human-made capital.[16]

Table I.2 Risks with Addressing Global Climate Change

	Action taken?	
Outcome	Yes	No
False	Cost; global depression	The world is okay; used money for other issues
True	Cost; mitigate impacts	Catastrophe

- What agents are included in your perspective, and what are their motives? For example, does your discourse include all living things or only humans?
- What is meant by sustainability?
- What are your key metaphors and other rhetorical devices? A common one for the politics of the possible is a triple bottom line (i.e., recognizing that balance is related to three outcomes: economic, social, and environmental).
- What are your politics associated with the chosen discourse? Do you think we should advocate command and control or market solutions? (Chapter 3 will explain these distinctions.)
- To what extent do you think that humans can engineer their way to a more sustainable world?
- Do you adhere to the precautionary principle?

In summary, keep in mind core assumptions I have made in this book. They affect the topics included in this text. Also, having clarity about your own core assumptions will make for a richer experience as you read.

How the Chapters Fit Together

I use a core model (see Figure I.1) in every chapter to maintain continuity over the material. This model has four main sections. At the start of each chapter, I highlight part of the model to signify the sections included in the chapter.

The model's *first* section describes the pressures on firms (i.e., ones they are recognizing and trying to understand in the context of their business) from the natural environment, society, and regulatory bodies. The *second* section is core strategy information (i.e., the concept of strategy, how it is formed, and different types of strategies); this section anchors the *third* section's recommendations about core actions firms could use to increase competitiveness. The *third* section focuses on the myriad actions firms may implement to increase competitiveness; these actions are functions within a firm (e.g., marketing and operations), and processes (e.g., reporting and lifecycle analysis). The *fourth* and final section shows the information's relevance to specific situations (such as entrepreneurship) and contexts (e.g., universities, municipalities, and emerging markets).

The first three chapters of this book explain why firms need to apply an environmental sustainability lens to their strategies, and describe the pressures they are feeling (or will be feeling) as environmental and social demands become more and more powerful. These pressures are calling for responses from companies as they continue to use natural and other resources. Specifically, Chapter 1 addresses the current state of the natural environment as it relates to business; changes in the natural environment will call for firms to be responsive to maintain access to these resources (or control resource costs). Chapter 2 describes the pressures on firms from social movements, social justice concerns, and social responsibility; these pressures impact a firm's reputation and license to operate. Chapter 3 focuses on government regulations (mainly of business), and their impact on organizational competitiveness; regulations are rapidly changing and legislative design is utilizing some market-based solutions to control organizational behavior (e.g., the use of cap-and-trade systems prevalent in Europe, California [U.S.], and Australia). Together, these three chapters present a compelling argument for firms to prioritize management of their environmental footprints and the role of the natural environment in their strategies.

Chapters 4 through 7 introduce the conversation about strategic thinking in organizations. They include core strategic theory, apply this theory, and demonstrate how sustainability can inform strategic thinking. Chapter 4 begins the conversation on strategies, and organization-specific practices that help firms respond to environmental, social, and regulatory pressures; this chapter presents environmental sustainability as a lens for a firm's strategy. Chapter 5 continues the discussion on strategy, defines a sustainable organization, and illustrates how to analyze factors external to a firm. Chapter 6 bridges external analysis with internal analysis by looking at a firm's general competencies and those specific to sustainability. Chapter 7 presents information on firms' thinking about businesses or groups of businesses within one firm. This chapter explains how firms compete with one another through their cost advantages and unique value offerings to customers.

Chapters 8 through 11 take a deeper look at company practices derived from environmental sustainability strategies. Chapter 8 includes information on the expansive area of reporting and sustainability measurements. Chapter 9 introduces marketing considerations (e.g., relevant guidelines for pricing products and

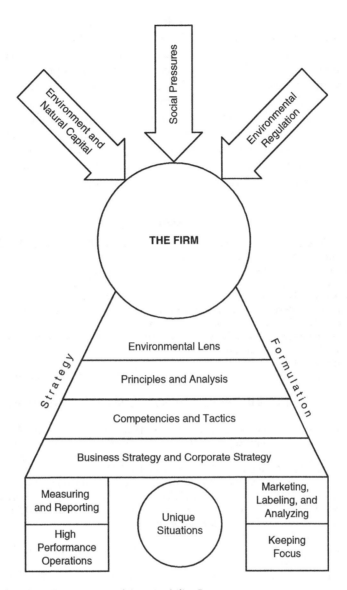

Figure I.1 Strategy Model with an Environmental Sustainability Lens

labeling green products). Chapter 10 discusses high-performance operations (including a pivotal conversation on location analysis and supply chain management). Chapter 11 outlines the ways firms can maintain focus as they implement their strategies, and includes discussions on organizational culture and flexibility.

Chapter 12 is based on myriad inquiries from entrepreneurs (and students) about business start-ups and environmental sustainability. Often these start-ups are in the clean-tech sector. This chapter presents a framework for gathering relevant information and offers pertinent questions to consider when pursuing an idea for a new business. Also, this chapter applies some of the book's material to different contexts (e.g., governments and municipalities, NGOs, universities, and emerging geographic markets). Each of these contexts calls for a unique organizational approach to environmental sustainability.

In each chapter, I have worked to provide useful and applicable real-life examples of the principles being discussed. For example, you will find several profiles and case examples in each chapter. Using sound research methods and my background in organizational theory and practice, the material is decidedly global yet there is a bias toward U.S. examples to maintain continuity and clarity of the material.

I support the arguments whenever possible with valid scientific and social research (as opposed to opinion and speculation). Environmental sustainability is still an understudied area of research, and requires greater understanding to legitimize its value in global and organizational discussions. I agree with one author justifying sustainability as a legitimate area of study that "scientists seeking to promote a sustainability transition have needed to tap into, and indeed engage in, cutting-edge research in areas ranging from complex systems, theory of cultural and political ecology."[17] If we use this breadth of material and science, then we can move forward in improving environmental risks and opportunities that impact all of us.

This book draws from disparate fields and creates a story about organizations, their future, and how we, as humans, are part of the problem—yet more importantly, *part of the solution*. My hope is that you will find ways to take action to improve organizations and avoid denigrating our natural environment. As you read this material, be mindful of the deep sense of urgency we all should feel to improve our impact on the natural world.

Notes

1 R. Guha, *Environmentalism: A Global History* (New York: Pearson, 1999); R. Allitt, *A Climate of Crisis: America in the Age of Environmentalism* (New York: Penguin, 2014).

2 Adapted from the Brundtland Commission, *Report of the World Commission on Environment and Development: Our Common Future* (New York: World Commission on Environment and Development, 1987), 15.

3 United Nations, *The Future We Want* (New York: Resolution adopted by the General Assembly on 27 July 2012 (66/288)), http://sustainabledevelopment.un.org/futurewewant.html (accessed July 16, 2014).

4 J. S. Dryzek, *The Politics of the Earth: Environmental Discourses*, 2nd ed. (New York: Oxford University Press, 2005); T. Nordhaus and M. Shellenberger, *Break Through: From the Death of Environmentalism to the Politics of Possibility* (New York: Houghton Mifflin Company, 2007).

5 Nordhaus and Shellenberger, *Break Through*.

6 D. H. Meadows, J. Randers, and D. L. Meadows, *Limits to Growth: The 30-Year Update* (White River Junction, VT: Chelsea Green, 2004).

7 For example, see D. Jamison, *Ethics and the Environment: An Introduction* (New York: Cambridge University Press), 75.

8 Dryzek, *The Politics of the Earth*, 8–13.

9 See the recent Intergovernmental Panel on Climate Change (IPCC) report for a complete picture on climate change impacts on our world. Fifth Assessment Report (2014). The report has four components: (1) The Physical Science Basis; (2) Impacts, Adaptation and Vulnerability; (3) Mitigation of Climate Change; and (4) Synthesis Report, http://www.ipcc.ch/report/ar5/index.shtml (accessed July 16, 2014).

10 R. J. Brulle, *Agency, Democracy, and Nature: The U.S. Environmental Movement from a Critical Theory Perspective* (Cambridge, MA: MIT Press, 2000); Dryzek, *The Politics of the Earth*; C. Harper, *Environment and Society: Human Perspectives on Environmental Issues*, 4th ed. (Upper Saddle River, NJ: Pearson, 2008); P. Hawken, *Blessed Unrest: How the Largest Movement in the World Came Into Being, and Why No One Saw It Coming* (New York: Viking, 2007); Nordhaus and Shellenberger, *Break Through*.

11 A. R. Edwards, *The Sustainability Revolution: Portrait of a Paradigm Shift* (Gabriola, BC: New Society Publishers, 2005) and Hawken, *Blessed Unrest*.

12 P. Hawken, A. Lovins, and L. Hunter Lovins, *Natural Capitalism: Creating the Next Industrial Revolution* (Boston, MA: Little, Brown, 1999).

13 Nordhaus and Shellenberger, *Break Through*.

14 These states are often referred to as Type I and Type II errors. In statistics a Type I error is when the null hypothesis is true yet it is rejected. A Type II error is when the null hypothesis is false and one fails to reject it.

15 S. C. Hackett, *Environmental and Natural Resources Economics: Theory, Policy, and the Sustainable Society*, 4th ed. (Armonk, NY: M.E. Sharpe, 2011), 362–367.

16 For the various arguments for and against these concepts see E. Neumayer, *Weak Versus Strong Sustainability: Exploring the Limits of Two Opposing Paradigms* (Cheltenham: Edward Elgar, 2003). Also see "The Shaky Ground of Sustainable Development," in D. Worster, *The Wealth of Nature: Environmental History and the Ecological Imagination* (New York: Oxford Press, 1993), Chapter 12.

17 W. C. Clark, "Sustainability Science: A Room of Its Own," *Proceedings of the National Academy of Sciences of the United States of America*, 106, no. 6 (2007): 1737–1738.

Part I

PRESSURES ON THE FIRM

1

THE ENVIRONMENT AND
NATURAL CAPITAL

Coca-Cola Watches over Troubled Waters

Water is a unique issue because of its local nature, immediate and obvious impact, and direct tie to human health and development. This makes any action toward water-challenge solutions much more compelling. Of course, water is also critical for countless organizations. For example, beverage businesses rely on water for agriculture, manufacturing, and the safety and taste profile of their products; therefore, they must ensure a consistent supply of this critical resource.[1]

When Greg Koch, Coca-Cola's Director of Global Water Stewardship, Environment & Water Resources, joined Coca-Cola in 1996, the company had already developed a strong focus on water efficiency within manufacturing and had launched wastewater management programs. However, as Coca-Cola and the world began to see growing water challenges, the company sought to expand its understanding of, and actions regarding, water issues (e.g., pollution, improper management, uneven distribution, and non-universal access). Koch's team, located at Coca-Cola's corporate headquarters in Atlanta set the company's global strategic direction on water, established policy and requirements, formed and managed key partnerships (with such organizations as the World Wildlife Fund and the U.S. Agency for International Development), and played a governance role related to these efforts throughout the company.

As of end of 2014, Coca-Cola and its bottling partners were operating in 206 countries and had about 1,000 production facilities.[2] Operating on a global scale, they have experienced a diverse array of water challenges, which would only be exacerbated by further global population growth and climate change.[3] In 2003, they were among the first corporations to disclose to shareholders that regional water quality and quantity posed a material risk to its business. The degree of risk was perhaps like that of no other business, given Coca-Cola's well-recognized brands, corporate size, geographic scope, non-diversification, and perhaps most critically, its local business model.

Coca-Cola distributes its products within close proximity to its plants in almost all of its manufacturing locations. It is not an export business (i.e., it does not make products in one location and ship them vast distances or even across borders). Therefore, Coca-Cola is interested not only in water quality and quantity, but also in the health and sustainability of the ecosystems and people comprising their markets and employee bases. Koch stated, "Our business can only be as sustainable (in every facet of that term) as the sustainability of communities where we exist."[4]

Coca-Cola conducted a qualitative, and then a quantitative, risk assessment of its global business that led to the formation of Koch's role. This assessment report led to the creation of a global water stewardship strategy[5] that included plant-level performance objectives, watershed protection, community engagement, and a drive to increase global awareness of the need for action and collaboration on water resource sustainability. Koch commented,

> *The most important thing I've learned through my work on water at Coca-Cola is that our business requires three licenses to use water, everywhere we do business: the physical license (sustainable quantity and quality of water resources), the regulatory license, and the social license encompassing the social and political acceptance of our use of water.[6]*

Chapter Overview

The purpose of this chapter is to introduce the environmental challenges facing companies; the broader discussion will include information on ecosystems, climate, and natural resources. This chapter also contains the core definition of sustainability and explores how this definition can guide company action. At the end of this chapter, you should be able to:

1 define, in your own words, sustainability and its core assumptions;
2 define natural capital and demonstrate how it adds value to organizations;
3 model the core challenges for water, energy, and climate change;
4 state at least two impacts of each challenge on firm strategy.

Figure 1.1 shows the overall model for this book and highlights some of the pressures firms are facing. These pressures are compounded by environmental uncertainty (e.g., unusual weather events), and the increasing challenge of ensuring supplies of critical resources (e.g., water).

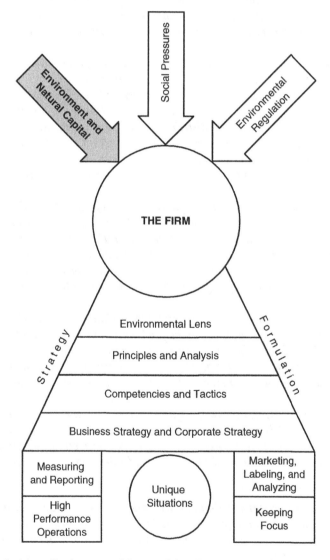

Figure 1.1 Strategy Model with an Environmental Sustainability Lens

The Value of Natural Capital

Analysis of how the natural environment impacts a firm's strategy can be a highly effective way to understand its means of creating value. This analysis may call for new ideas and concepts. For example, consider six types of capital:[7]

1 *human* (in the form of labor, intelligence, culture, and organization);
2 *financial* (consisting of cash, investments, and monetary instruments);
3 *manufactured* (including infrastructure, machines, tools, and factories);
4 *social* (in the form of social networks and relationships);
5 *intellectual* (intellectual property rights, patents, and codified knowledge);
6 *natural* (resources, living systems, and ecosystem services).[8]

Natural capital is "all the familiar resources used by humankind (e.g., water, minerals, oil, trees, fish, soil and air). But it also encompasses living systems (e.g., grasslands, savannas, wetlands, estuaries, oceans, coral reefs, riparian corridors, tundra, and rainforests)."[9] Ecosystems are dynamic entities composed of the biological community and abiotic environment.[10] An abiotic environment is characterized by the absence of life or living organisms, and the abiotic and biotic composition and structure of an ecosystem are determined by the state of a number of interrelated environmental factors. Changes in any of these factors (e.g., nutrient availability, light intensity, temperature, species population density, and grazing intensity) will result in dynamic changes to the nature of these systems. For example, a fire in a temperate deciduous forest could kill large trees and most of the mosses, herbs, and shrubs occupying the forest floor. As a result, nutrients stored in the biomass would be released into the soil, atmosphere, and hydrologic system, resulting in destruction of the forest.[11] However, after a short recovery time, the ecosystem would then become a system of grasses, herbaceous species, and tree seedlings. Therefore, the resources offered by this system would *change*, affecting how a firm uses inputs from the ecosystem or where it makes investments.

Ecosystems, which provide the resources necessary to our existence, are critical to our survival. Yet, they are often overlooked when organizations consider the risks and strategies of their operations. Nevertheless, the value of ecosystems becomes evident when considering available scientific evidence:[12]

1 Ecosystem services such as providing food, soil formation and recreation, are provided by natural ecosystems and essential to civilization.[13]
2 Ecosystem services operate on such large scales and in such intricate and little-known ways that most cannot be replicated by technology.
3 Many of the human activities modifying or destroying natural ecosystems may cause deterioration of ecological services; the value of those services, in the long term, usually dwarfs any short-term economic benefits.
4 Considered globally, large numbers of species and populations are required to sustain ecosystem services.
5 Human activities are already impairing the flow of ecosystem services on a large scale.
6 If current trends continue, humanity will dramatically alter nearly all of the planet's remaining natural ecosystems within the next 50 years.

Given these trends, firms can enhance their competitiveness by taking steps to assess the value of ecosystems to their businesses. To grasp the value of these systems, consider that natural ecosystems perform countless services that, in many cases, could not easily be supplanted by technology (if at all) in a sustainable manner. For example:[14]

- provisioning services such as water, timber and fish;
- regulating services (e.g., mitigation of droughts, floods and climate change);
- cultural services (e.g., aesthetic and recreational benefits);
- supporting services (i.e., fundamental processes such as carbon cycling and photosynthesis).

Organizations could enhance their competitiveness by taking into account this natural capital. A focus on natural—as well as human, financial, manufactured, and social—capital results in placing a value on the natural resources that businesses often take for granted; these systems have been surprisingly robust, so we have little experience imagining what we would do without them. However, recent attention to, and evidence of, the destruction of ecosystems is forcing firms to take natural capital into account when strategizing.

Developing strategies for preserving natural systems is difficult and imprecise because many of the services we receive from living systems have no known substitutes (e.g., photosynthesis and water). Also, just as machines cannot provide substitutes for human intelligence, knowledge, wisdom, and organizational abilities, technology cannot always replace our planet's life-supporting systems. The World Bank's *Wealth Index* description makes this point as the Bank describes the value of natural capital to the development of nation states. The introduction in a 2011 report states:

> This volume asks a key question: Where is the Wealth of Nations? Answering this question yields important insights into the prospects for sustainable development in countries around the world. The estimates of total wealth—including produced, natural, human and institutional capital— suggest that human capital and the value of institutions (as measured by rule of law) constitute the largest share of wealth in virtually all countries. *It is striking that natural capital constitutes a quarter of total wealth in low-income countries, greater than the share of produced capital* [emphasis added].[15]

This quote suggests that better management of ecosystems and natural resources will be key to sustaining development while these countries build infrastructure as well as human and institutional capital. For example, cropland and pastureland comprise 70 percent of the natural wealth of poor countries; this obviously argues for a strong focus on efforts to sustain soil quality. Yet challenges abound. For example, salt water increasingly is penetrating Vietnam's Mekong Delta, impacting rice fields and farms and the quality of soil along the delta. Many areas have no fresh water and soils that are not conducive to growing crops.[16]

This new approach to capital also provides a comprehensive measure of changes in wealth, which is a key indicator of sustainability. There are important examples of resource-dependent countries, such as Botswana, that have even used their natural resources to underpin impressive rates of growth. In addition, research finds that the value of natural capital per person actually tends to rise with income when we look across countries; this contradicts the common wisdom that development necessarily entails depletion of the environment.[17]

Therefore, we must take into account these important sources of wealth, especially as we consider how to increase the value of companies. This focus demands that we pay attention to the state of natural resources and their ecosystems in environments where firms operate. Firms do these analyses so that these resources can be taken into account as we mount organizational strategies that are responsive to the environment, and to protect these resources. The following sections describe some of the resources (and implications of the resources) in terms of a firm's strategy and in creating a sustainable world.

What Is Sustainability?

Throughout history, we have seen complex human societies die out as a result of growth-associated impacts on ecological support systems. For example, ecological hypotheses of the Maya collapse include population growth, epidemic disease, deforestation, and hillside erosion from human uses of the land, causing drought and climate change. According to this theory, these conditions, coupled with human failure to recognize the need to change societal practices, led to this civilization's dramatic downfall. This evolution of events implies that modern industrial society, which continues to grow in scale and complexity, may similarly collapse if resources are mismanaged and abused.[18]

Sustainability, on the other hand, is characteristic of a process or state that can be maintained at a certain level indefinitely. In recent years, public discourse has led to a use of this term in reference to how long human ecological systems can be expected to be usefully productive. In its environmental usage, "sustainability" refers to the potential longevity of vital human ecological support systems (e.g., the planet's climate, agriculture, forestry, fisheries, and various natural systems on which these processes depend). Of course, the implied preference is for systems to be productive indefinitely (e.g., "sustainable agriculture" is defined by certain well-known practices such as crop rotation, biodiversity, and the use of nonpolluting fertilizers and pesticides).

One of the first and most often-cited definitions of sustainability is the one created by the Brundtland Commission, led by former Norwegian Prime Minister Gro Harlem Brundtland. According to the Organisation for Economic Co-operation and Development (OECD), the term "sustainable development" was introduced in 1980 and popularized in the 1987 report of the World Commission on Environment and Development (the Brundtland Commission). The Brundtland Commission report defined sustainable development as "development that meets the needs of the present without compromising the ability of future generations to meet their own needs."[19] This definition implicitly argues for the rights of future generations to raw materials and for vital ecosystem services to be taken into account.

The Commission's definition contains two key concepts—"needs" and "limitations"—and they can be further defined as follows:

> In this context, *needs* means "in particular the essential needs of the world's poor" and *limitations* means "limitations imposed by the state of technology and social organization on the environment's ability to meet present and future needs."[20]

The Brundtland Commission report contributes to a better understanding of the meaning of sustainability. But how to practically act on this meaning is much harder to grasp, especially when it comes to organizations. Operationalization of the term "sustainability" begs a quantitative definition that sets achievable sustainability goals. Organizations must know whether their efforts add value to their bottom lines or not, so they must know what to measure if they are to achieve a sustainable state.

Recent attempts to operationalize "sustainability" have produced metrics for items such as GHG emissions and their reduction. For example, some analysts believe that fossil fuel use should be measured because of its production of climate-altering emissions. Other analysts have measured climate neutrality as it is relatively easy to measure; thus, it is a reasonable proxy metric for overall sustainability. (Chapter 9 provides extensive information about these metrics for companies.) The good news is that many institutional sustainability programs prioritize becoming climate neutral at the top of the list of sustainability goals.[21]

Table 1.1 Several Sustainability Definitions

Sustain: to cause to continue (as in existence or a certain state, or in force or intensity), to keep up, especially without interruption, diminution, flagging, etc.; to prolong.[22]

"Sustainable Seattle follows the United Nations Brundtland Commission's definition of sustainability as 'meeting the needs of the present without compromising the ability of future generations to meet their own needs.' Bruntland Commission on Sustainable Development. We agree with U.N. Secretary-General Kofi Annan that 'sustainable urban development is one of the most pressing challenges facing the human community in the 21st century. In practice, we seek to balance concerns for social equity, ecological health, and economic vitality to create a livable community today while ensuring a healthy and fulfilling legacy for our children's children.' Our flavor of sustainability comes directly from the people of the Central Puget Sound and is neatly summed up by the sustainability indicators, goals, data, and actions that are a product of participatory action research fundamental to Sustainable Seattle."[23]

A thing is right when it tends to preserve the integrity, stability, and beauty of the biotic community. It is wrong when it tends to do otherwise.[24]

Actions are sustainable if:

- there is a balance between resources used and resources regenerated;
- resources are as clean or cleaner at end of use as at beginning;
- the viability, integrity, and diversity of natural systems are restored and maintained;
- they lead to enhanced local and regional self-reliance;
- they help create and maintain community and a culture of place;
- each generation preserves the legacies of future generations.[25]

Business operations that positively impact the environment and the company's reputation while enhancing bottom-line profit opportunities.[26]

Figure 1.2 Peterhead Power Station. Courtesy of Scottish and Southern Energy

Table 1.1 is a compilation of a few diverse approaches to the definition of sustainability by various groups or organizations. As can be seen through these various definitions, the ultimate goal of any attempt to support a sustainable world is to maintain the productivity of nature and the environment (as well as immaterial gains in their utility) for as long as possible.

Profile: High and Low Cost Abatement Approaches[27]

Figure 1.9 shows that full-scale gas carbon capture and storage (CCS) projects are among the most expensive ways to abate CO_2 emissions. In 2008, the United Kingdom passed the world's first legally binding climate-change target entitled The 2008 Climate Change Act. This act aimed to reduce UK GHG emissions by at least 80 percent from their 1990 emissions baseline by 2050.[28] To comply with their 2050 target, the UK made £1 billion in capital funding available through the UK Electricity Market Reforms for CCS. The capital funding was made available to:

- *generate learning that will help to drive down the costs of CCS;*
- *test and build familiarity with the CCS regulatory framework;*
- *encourage industry to develop suitable CCS business models;*
- *contribute to the development and early infrastructure for CO_2 transport and storage.[29]*

In 2012, the CCS Peterhead Project in Aberdeenshire, Scotland was granted the UK's first license for permanent geological storage of CO_2 under the seabed.[30] In 2013, a subsidiary of Royal Dutch Shell, Cansolv Technologies Inc. captured the first tonne of CO_2 at Shell's Aberthaw Power Station in South Wales which is also the world's first integrated SO_2/CO_2 capture plant.[31] In 2013, the UK announced its two preferred bidders for the £1 billion Carbon Capture and Storage Commercialisation Programme Competition: the Peterhead Project and the White Rose Project in Yorkshire, England.[32] In 2014, Shell UK Ltd. cosigned an agreement with the UK Secretary of State which granted funding for the Peterhead Project. In order to meet its operational deadline of 2019, Shell UK Ltd. has partnered with Scottish and Southern Energy:

> *The Peterhead Project aims to design and develop a CCS system for capturing emissions post combustion at one of its existing three 385MW combined gas cycle turbines. The CO_2 would then be transported to the Shell-operated Goldeneye gas field in the North Sea using existing pipeline infrastructure.[33]*

The project's scope involves a six-month contractual timeline that includes developing a landfall solution at the Peterhead Power Station (PPS); designing a new CO_2 export pipeline from PPS to a subsea tie-in (2.5 km beneath the seabed) with the existing Goldeneye pipeline.[34] After funding was appropriated for the project by the UK, Shell UK Ltd. and Scottish and Southern Energy awarded Wood Group Kenny the front end engineering design (FEED) contract for the subsea and pipeline elements. Ultimately, the project aims *to capture 90 percent of the CO_2 prior to transporting it to its permanent storage location 100 km offshore beneath the North Sea.*[35]

Diving Deeper

How do we evaluate this approach? Consider the McKinsey Abatement Cost Curve in Figure 1.9. CCS is shown as one of the most expensive methods for carbon abatement. Yet, could a company justify this approach because of its effectiveness? What technical and economic criteria would you suggest to compare and contrast abatement approaches?

The State of Resources

Now, let us consider a few natural environmental resources that are critical to businesses. Table 1.2 outlines various environmental issues alongside current trends and challenges; I will only discuss the first three because they adequately illustrate the challenges that firms face. These challenges pressure firms to create responses that do not compromise their competitiveness.

Table 1.2 State of Resources: A Summary[36]

Major Environmental Issue	Trends and Challenges
Energy	A carbon-constrained future requires a shift toward new energy strategies, sources, and technologies. The sources of energy and availability of energy are of concern as demand increases and supply sources are being depleted and challenged.[37] Difficult to balance reliable, affordable, and environmental requirements.
Climate change	Warming of the Earth; CO_2 levels are increasing. The build-up of GHGs threatens to lead to global warming and accompanying rising sea levels, changed rainfall patterns and increased intensity of storms.[38]
Water	Availability; quality; license to operate;[39] impacts on energy and food.
Deforestation	Loss of acres; unsustainable timber harvesting; soil erosion; flooding.[40]
Desertification	Warming; Dry Earth.[41]
Nitrogen	Excessive amounts of nitrogen fixation in oceans.[42]
Acidification; air Pollution	Acid rain; smog particulates; volatile organic compounds pose a risk to public health; toxins in the air.[43]
Waste	Disposal and recycling of solid waste and toxic waste; how to handle toxins;[44] amount in developing economies.
Ozone layer	Warming; natural protection eroding.[45]
Biodiversity; land use	For the most recent 10,000 years, man has been the greatest factor impacting biodiversity, with adverse impacts occurring at an accelerating pace since the Industrial Revolution, including habitat destruction, habitat fragmentation, overexploitation, and pollution.[46]

Energy

One widely discussed issue—related to public policy, firm competitiveness, and the state of our environment—is our energy future. The demand for energy is rising, the supply of certain fuels is being depleted, and the environment is variously impacted by resources used and how they are processed.[47] Several organizations have developed scenarios to understand the range of possible outcomes. For example, Shell Oil developed two scenarios to assist in thinking about our energy future with similar outcomes in terms of environmental impacts (mainly climate change and GHG) and the range of solutions. The recent scenarios are labeled mountains and oceans.[48] Mountains is a status quo with stability being the preferred outcome which results in some societal rigidity. Oceans refer to compromise as the preferred outcome with competing interests accommodated and societal change causes some disruption and immediate market forces gain prominence. In the first of the previous scenarios—called "Scramble"—policymakers pay little attention to more efficient energy use until supplies are tight, and they do not seriously address GHG emissions until there are major climate shocks. In the second scenario—"Blueprints"—growing and immediate local actions begin to address the environmental challenges of economic development, energy security, and pollution. A price is applied to environmental outcomes, providing a huge incentive for companies to develop clean energy technologies (e.g., CO_2 capture and storage as well as energy-efficiency measures). The result of these actions is much lower CO_2 emissions.

These scenarios help Shell test their strategic options against a range of possible developments over the long term. They believe that Blueprints' outcomes offer the best hope for a sustainable future. Former Shell Chief Executive Officer Jeroen van der Veer stated:

> I am convinced they [Blueprint scenarios] are possible with the right combination of policy, technology and commitment from governments, industry and society globally. But achieving them will not be easy, and time is short. We urgently need clear thinking, huge investment, and effective leadership.[49]

In the Scramble scenario, society is scrambling to make up for lost time when responding to environmental outcomes. To understand these outcomes, this section will summarize energy demand and supply trends, and explain why these trends are of concern to organizations. I will discuss the ways firms can mitigate and adapt to these trends in later chapters.

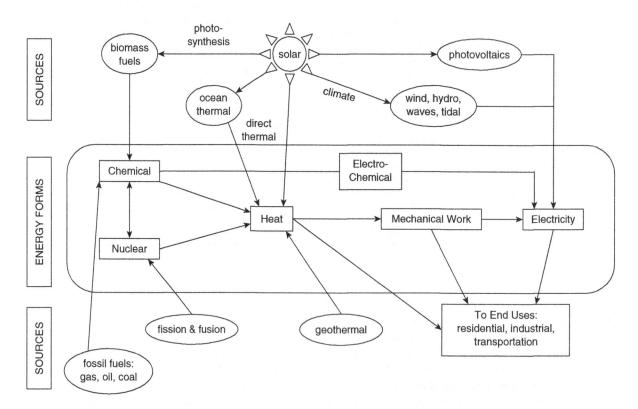

Figure 1.3 Sources of Energy[50]

Sources of Energy

Figure 1.3 shows a diagram of energy sources and conversion processes featuring renewable and nonrenewable sources of energy as well as various forms of energy (e.g., the energy we use in our homes, businesses, and cars). The origins of familiar energy sources have differing time scales for both development and depletion. For example, a single growing season of a few weeks is long enough for photosynthesis to convert CO_2, H_2O, and solar energy to biomass (e.g., plants); however, it takes millions of years for the biogeochemical production of coal. All common forms of energy utilized on Earth can be traced to ongoing or defunct cosmic processes (e.g., tides from lunar cycles and geothermal magma from the survival of deep subterranean molten material).

Some of these sources are considered renewable, meaning that the source (e.g., solar power or wind energy) is available continuously without depletion or degradation. Renewable sources have less significant emissions, health hazards, and involve fewer social injustices than other energy sources.[51] Nonrenewable sources (e.g., natural gas and oil) are those that can be depleted, and they generally have significant emissions with impacts on our environment.

Strictly speaking, we do not consume energy; we convert it from one form to another.[52] Also, very few countries are self-sufficient in power; this makes energy a top priority for the future of an ever-expanding world population. For example, many countries need to import energy sources from other countries; the United States imports more than 12,000 barrels of oil per day. The top five sources of U.S. crude oil imports in September 2011 were Canada (2,324,000 barrels per day), Saudi Arabia (1,465,000 barrels per day), Mexico (1,099,000 barrels per day), Venezuela (759,000 barrels per day), and Nigeria (529,000 barrels per day).[53] The U.S. did not even make the top 20 importing countries of crude oil or petroleum in 2015 which means that it is approaching a point of self-sufficiency in energy production. Energy affects economic growth and is integral to the economic viability of all countries. It also has an impact on a country's security since it can be converted into weaponry (e.g., atomic bombs).

A major change in the state of U.S. energy sources from 2011 to 2015 has been the previously undiscovered sources of natural gas; this has been described as a "game changer" by most energy utility executives.[54] The U.S. Energy Information Administration (EIA) expects natural gas marketed production will grow at an average rate of 1.3 percent in 2015. This increase in production has drawn commentary about the energy independence of the U.S. For instance, an increase in domestic production over the last several years has partially replaced pipeline imports from Canada and has resulted in increased exports to Mexico. The EIA expects these trends will continue through 2017.[55] Some commentators suggest that the U.S. will increasingly reach energy independence based on the identified gas reserves.

Worldwide energy consumption increased twentyfold during the 20th century (see Table 1.3). To put this point in perspective:

> Aggregate energy used worldwide equals the physical work of 306 billion human beings (as of 2008). It is as if every man, woman, and child on the planet each had a crew of 46 people working for them. In the United States, every person has 238 such hypothetical workers.[56]

Table 1.3 Energy Consumption, 2000–2014 (in million tonnes oil equivalent)[57]

Country (top energy consumers)	2000	2005	2010	2014
United States	2,269	2,320	2,217	2,224
China	1,161	1,774	2,526	3,034
Russia	619	651	703	751
Japan	519	521	499	437
India	453	540	722	872
Germany	336	336	328	307
Canada	251	271	252	251

Developed nations (e.g., the U.S.) have become increasingly dependent on the use of energy, and they have invested much and developed newer ways for energy use to support economic growth. Therefore, we ask: How can we create a sustainable future? Do current supply and demand conditions compromise our future?[58]

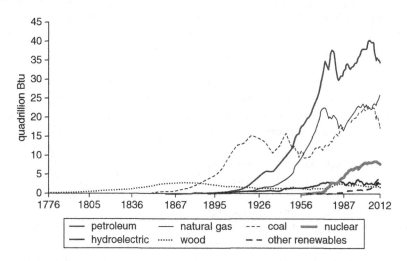

Figure 1.4 History of Energy Consumption in the United States (1776–2012)[59]

The United States' energy history is one of large-scale change as new forms of energy have emerged (see Figure 1.4). Wood served as the primary form of energy until about 1885 when it was surpassed by coal. Despite its tremendous and rapid expansion, coal was overtaken by petroleum in the middle of the 20th century. In the second half of the 20th century, natural gas experienced rapid development, and coal began to expand again. Late in the 20th century, still other forms of energy (e.g., hydroelectric power and nuclear electric power) were developed and supplied significant amounts of energy.

The EIA's Annual Energy Outlook 2014, which assumes current laws and regulations will remain unchanged, projects that fossil fuels will continue to provide most of the energy consumed in the United States over the next 25 years. However, the EIA predicts that fossil fuels' portion of overall energy use will decline as the role of renewable forms of energy grows. Non-hydroelectric renewable energy is projected to double in use by 2035.[60] Also, growing domestic production of natural gas and crude oil will continue to reshape the U.S. energy economy, with crude oil production approaching the historical high achieved in 1970 of 9.6 million barrels per day.[61]

Global investment in renewable energy worldwide was about $270 billion, half of which was in the developing world.[62] Predictions abound about the world's energy use and future. Renewables, excluding large hydro-power, account for 10 percent of global power generation. Estimates are that this amount will be 20 percent by 2030.

Figure 1.5 shows energy flows in the United States in 2011, illustrating three important points. First, coal is a major source of power and, by all accounts, will continue to dominate our system for generating electricity, at least over the short term.[63] Second, the U.S. imported about 30 percent of our energy supply, especially petroleum, although recently this amount dropped dramatically. This energy dependence concerns some policymakers, particularly in regard to national security issues and foreign policy. Third, the major use of energy in the United States is in transportation; this means that any major energy policy must include changes to our transportation system, including taxes paid, types of vehicles used, and how we develop public transportation.

Figure 1.6 reveals that renewable energy sources are versatile in their applications. They are mainly used for electric power (50 percent), yet can be used in residential, commercial, industrial, and transportation applications. This versatility and environmental friendliness are why so many people are trying to develop renewable sources, which remain underutilized and comprise less than three percent of U.S. energy sources.

Figure 1.7 and Table 1.4 show world energy consumption. Noticeable in this chart and table is the prediction that non-OECD countries—including Brazil, India, Russia, and China (the so-called BRIC countries)—are projected to consume dramatically more energy and represent a larger percentage of world

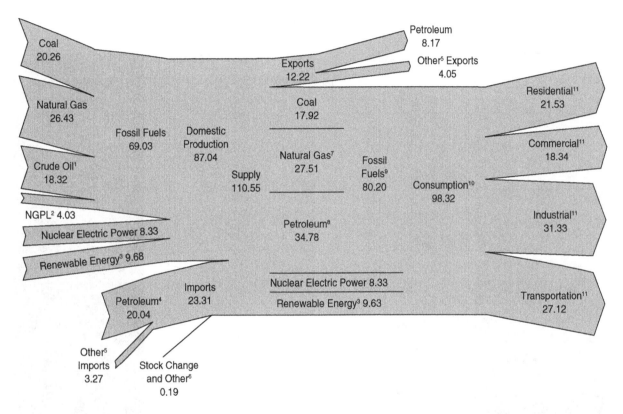

Figure 1.5 U.S. Energy Flow, 2014[64]

Source: U.S. Energy Administration, *Monthly Energy Review* (March 2015) Tables 1.1, 1.2, 1.3, 1.4a, 1.4b, and 2.1.

Notes: Data are preliminary. Values are derived from source data prior to rounding for publication. Totals may not equal sum of components due to independent rounding.

1 Includes Lease condensate.
2 Natural gas plant liquids.
3 Conventional hydroelectric power, biomass, geothermal, solar- photovoltaic, and wind.
4 Crude oil and petroleum products. Includes imports into the Strategic Petroleum Reserve.
5 Natural gas, coal, coal coke, biofuels, and electricity.
6 Adjustments, losses, and unaccounted for.
7 Natural gas only, excludes supplemental gaseous fuels.
8 Petroleum products, including natural gas liquids, and crude oil burned as fuel.
9 Includes –0.02 quadrillion Btu of coal coke net imports.
10 Includes 0.16 quadrillion Btu of electricity net imports.
11 Total energy consumption, which is the sum of primary energy consumption, electricity retail sales, and electrical system energy losses. Losses are allocated to the end-use sectors in proposition to each sector's share of total electricity retail sales. See Note 1 "Electrical Systems Energy Losses" at the end of the U.S. Energy Information Administration, *Monthly Energy Review* (March 2015), Section 2.

consumption. This growth is shown in Figure 1.7 from 2007 through 2035 and in the brief time between 1998 and 2007 (as shown in Table 1.4). Figure 1.8 shows the average growth in energy-related CO_2 emissions. This chart shows that increased energy usage will come at a distinct price, with non-OECD countries (in light grey) representing increasing percentages of CO_2 emissions whereas the OECD countries will be relatively flat (in dark grey).

These changes have resulted in many discussions about who is responsible for climate change and for cleaning up our world. The next section explores the climate-change issue and demonstrates how climate change will affect businesses.

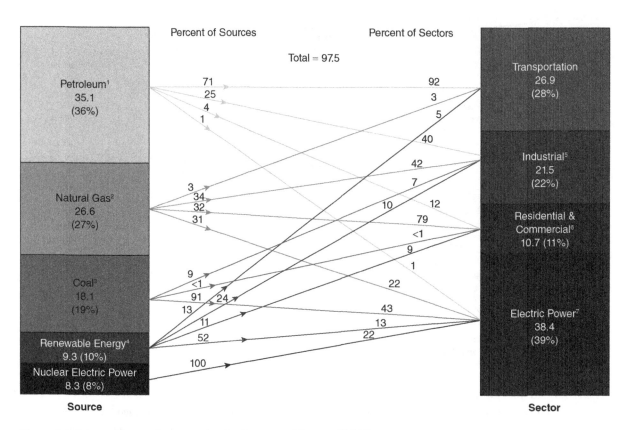

Figure 1.6 Primary Energy Consumption by Source and Sector, 2013[65]

Sources: U.S. Energy Information Administration, *Monthly Energy Review* (May 2014). Tables 1.3, 2.1–2.6.

Notes: primary energy in the form that is first accounted for in a statistical energy balance, before any transformation to secondary or tertiary forms of energy (for example, coal is used to generate electricity). Sum of components may not equal total due to independent rounding.

1 Does not include biofuels that have been blended with petroleum—biofuels are included in "Renewable Energy."
2 Excludes supplemental gaseous fuels.
3 Includes less than –0.1 quadrillion Btu of coal coke net imports.
4 Conventional hydroelectric power, geothermal, solar photovoltaic, wind and biomass.
5 Includes industrial combined-heat-and-power (CHP) and industrial electricity-only plants.
6 Includes commercial combined-heat-and-power (CHP) and commercial electricity-only plants.
7 Electricity-only and combined-heat-and-power plants whose primary business is to sell electricity, or electricity and heat, to the public. Includes 0.2 quadrillion Btu electricity new imports not shown under "Source."

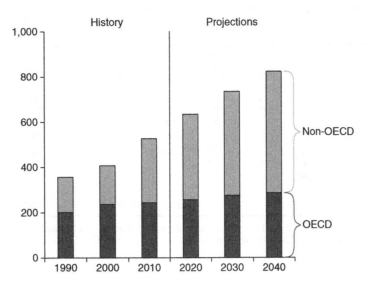

Figure 1.7 World Energy Consumption 1990–2040 (quadrillion Btu)

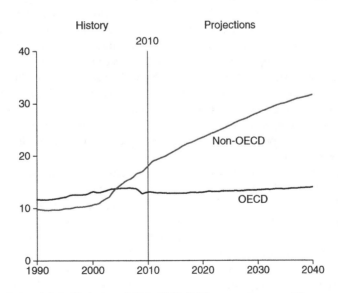

Figure 1.8 World Energy-Related CO_2 Emissions 1990–2040 (billion metric tonnes)[66]

Table 1.4 World Energy Consumption by Country Groupings 2010–2040 (in quadrillion Btu)[67]

Region	2010	2015	2020	2025	2030	2035	2040	Average annual percent change 2010–2040
OECD	242	244	255	263	269	276	285	0.5
Americas	120	121	126	130	133	137	144	0.6
Europe	82	82	85	89	91	93	95	0.5
Asia	40	41	43	44	45	46	46	0.5
Non-OECD	282	328	375	418	460	501	535	2.2
Europe and Eurasia	47	50	53	57	61	65	67	1.2
Asia	159	194	230	262	290	317	337	2.5
Middle East	28	33	37	39	43	46	49	1.9
Africa	19	20	22	24	27	31	35	2.1
Central and South America	29	31	33	35	39	42	47	1.6
World	524	572	630	680	729	777	820	1.5

For consistency, OECD includes all members of the organization as of September 1, 2012, throughout all the time series included in this report. For statistical purposes, Israel is reported as part of OECD Europe in IEO2013. See Appendix M for the complete list of regional definitions used in IEO2013.

Climate Change

Climate change impacts people and the environment, and it is becoming an increasingly salient issue for organizations. Unfortunately, many organizational leaders do not address climate-change impacts despite obvious consequences to their operations, strategies, and bottom lines.[68] Also, views on the theory of climate change are varied; some question the science behind its conclusions.[69]

In his 2009 book, Brian Fagan traces the history of climate change and shows that from the 10th to the 15th centuries, the Earth experienced a rise in surface temperatures that changed the climate worldwide. This is a preview of today's global warming.[70] In some areas (such as western Europe), longer summers brought bountiful harvests and population growth that led to cultural thriving. Vastly different cultures, such as those of the Arctic Inuits and the Norse, were able to make connections and trade together by traveling thousands of miles since the ice was broken apart. Yet, during this same period, in many parts of the world (including North and Central America), people experienced famine and drought. The impact of this historical warming suggests we could be underestimating the power of climate change to disrupt our lives.

Not all societies or politicians support global warming trends as human-caused (and the implications that we should act now to mitigate the effects). Journalist Nigel Lawson, former Chancellor of the Exchequer and Secretary of State for Energy in the United Kingdom, calls for a "cool look" at global warming. Among other things, he concludes that reports are deeply flawed (e.g., the Stern Review), global warming is not the devastating threat it is widely alleged to be, and some of the remedies currently being proposed would be worse than the threats they are supposed to avert.[71] For example, halting production of fossil fuels would have devastating economic implications.[72]

Australia is an example of how whimsical some countries can be toward climate change. Australia is responsible for about 1.5 percent of global carbon emissions. On a per capita basis, this amount makes Australia one of the world's highest polluters. It was once a leader in carbon abatement including an innovative cap-and-trade system which used market prices to provide incentives for organizations to reduce carbon emissions (Chapter 3 explains this type of system in more detail). Yet, it completely changed its approach with a government change from the Labour Party to the Conservative Liberal Party.[73]

Some scientists have based their recommendations for adaptation and mitigation on a specific target with respect to climate-change metrics (e.g., 350 parts per million (ppm), representing atmospheric CO_2 amounts; this means that 0.035 percent of the molecules in the air would be CO_2).[74] These advocates believe that 350 ppm is the limit for a safe operating boundary.[75] Thus far, humans have caused CO_2 to increase from 280 ppm in 1750 to over 397.01 ppm in 2014.[76] The implication of this concentration is that we have reached a dangerous tipping point in warming our climate, which is resulting in harmful changes. If we cannot cause the CO_2 in the atmosphere to drop below the 350 ppm target, some scientists say that the damage we are already seeing from climate change will continue and, worse yet, accelerate.

Some authors think the models tell us little, if anything. Scientists have used many models to estimate the social cost of carbon and evaluate alternative abatement policies. The authors believe these models to have crucial flaws such as arbitrary discount rates, unclear theoretical foundations, and an imprecision in the calculations that make for arbitrary results. These authors state that the models tell us next to nothing about the likelihood and nature of catastrophic outcomes.[77]

Despite some of the different points of view, this book takes the stance that climate change is a real and present risk. This assertion is based on the scientific evidence cited in the next section. The strategic impact of climate change on business relates mainly to potential influences on competitiveness. These impacts are on costs of operations; costs of compliance; physical, fiduciary, and reputation risks; changes in demand (as markets shift toward low-emission, low-impact products); and the development of new technologies that could render core competencies obsolete. Greater energy efficiency and new technologies hold promise for reducing GHGs, protecting the environment, and for solving these global challenges. Achieving this efficiency requires both significant investments from private sector organizations as well as public policy changes. The following review summarizes some of the science of climate change and then delineates how some organizations may respond to these issues.

A startling fact is that the median time between an emission and maximum warming is 10.1 years with a 90 percent probability range of 6.6 and 30.7 years. The contributing factors to this impact are the carbon cycle, climate sensitivity, and ocean thermal inertia.[78] Avoiding CO_2 emissions and therefore avoiding climate damage is manifested within the lifetimes of those who released the emissions. This is the issue to confront. Emissions impacts is not a trans-generational issue, it is our issue!

The Science

Climate change is defined as "any systematic fluctuation in the long-term statistics of climatic elements (e.g., temperature, pressure, or wind) that is sustained over several decades or longer. Such an occurrence usually has significant societal, economic or environmental consequences."[79] The main concern of late has been that human impacts on the climate, which are causing increasingly ill effects on our world, appear to be harmful to human existence.[80]

The process of collecting and interpreting environmental indicators (e.g., temperature, precipitation, sea level, and GHG concentrations in the atmosphere), over a given area and specified period of time, plays a critical role in our understanding of climate change and its causes. Key findings on climate change in the United States are often classified in terms of weather and climate; water, snow, and ice; GHGs; oceans and other environments; and society and its relationship to ecosystems. Appendix 1.1 summarizes the key findings in each of these areas.

As with any field of scientific study, there are uncertainties associated with the science of climate change.[81] However, these uncertainties do not imply that scientists lack confidence in all aspects of climate science. Some aspects of the science are known with "virtual certainty" because they are based on well-known physical laws and documented trends. Here are the Environmental Protection Agency's (EPA's) comments on what is known and what is uncertain.[82]

WHAT IS KNOWN

Scientists know with virtual certainty that:

- The increase in GHG levels (e.g., CO_2), and its impact on the composition of the Earth's atmosphere, has been understood and well-documented since pre-industrial times.
- The atmospheric build-up of CO_2 and other GHGs is largely the result of human activities (e.g., the burning of fossil fuels and ecosystem degradation). "Human influence on the climate is clear."[83]

The evidence for human influence has grown since AR 4 (AR 4 is the previous Intergovernmental Panel on Climate Change (IPCC) report).[84]

- Increasing GHG concentrations tend to warm the planet.
- An "unequivocal" warming trend of about 1.0 to 1.7 degrees Fahrenheit occurred from 1906 to 2005. Warming occurred in both the Northern and Southern Hemispheres as well as over the oceans.[85] This trend will continue.[86]
- The major GHGs, emitted by human activities, remain in the atmosphere for periods ranging from decades to centuries. It is therefore virtually certain that atmospheric concentrations of GHGs will continue to rise over the next few decades.

WHAT IS VERY LIKELY

The IPCC has stated: "Most of the observed increase in global average temperatures since the mid-20th century is very likely due to the observed increase in anthropogenic (i.e., human-caused) greenhouse gas concentrations."[87] In short, a growing number of scientific analyses indicate, but cannot prove, that rising levels of GHGs in the atmosphere are contributing to climate change (as theory predicts). In the coming decades, scientists anticipate that, as atmospheric concentrations of GHGs continue to rise, average global temperatures and sea levels will also continue to rise, and precipitation patterns will change. "Each of the last three decades has been successively warmer at the Earth's surface than any preceding since 1850."[88]

The IPCC is an important organization in terms of climate-change research and policymaking.[89] Comprised primarily of an international body of scientists, it was established by the United Nations Environmental Programme (UNEP) and the World Meteorological Organization in 1988. The body provides a scientific view of the current state of knowledge with regard to climate change and its potential impacts.[90]

WHAT IS NOT CERTAIN

Important scientific questions remain about how much warming will occur, how fast it will occur, and how it will affect the rest of the climate system, including precipitation patterns and storms. Answering these questions will require scientific knowledge advances in a number of areas, including:

- an improved understanding of natural climatic variations, changes in the Sun's energy, impacts of changing humidity and cloud cover, and so on;
- a determination of humankind's relative contribution to climate change (e.g., via burning fossil fuels, and detrimental land-use changes) vs. natural causes;
- better projections of GHG emissions, and how the climate system will respond;
- an improved understanding of climate changes at local levels;
- an improved understanding of the potential for rapid or abrupt climate change.[91]

The EPA and various other national governmental agencies conduct climate economic analyses to estimate the economic and environmental effects of potential domestic climate-change mitigation programs and strategies. Given the complexity of the economic and environmental interactions underlying the issue of climate change, models vary in terms of target questions, methodologies, and policy recommendations.[92]

The implications of this information are widespread for firms receptive to it. Organizations will further attempt to control carbon emissions produced by their production facilities and other assets (e.g., infrastructure, data centers, factories, power stations, and various forms of transportation). New businesses will spring up that reward suppliers and end users, in the power and transport sectors, for consuming less energy.[93] Firms will also need to manage their regulatory environment to shape public policies benefitting the environment and their businesses.

The investment community is also responding. We will likely see an increase in the volume of requests from investors for companies to disclose GHG data, climate strategies, and progress in reducing emissions.[94] Later in this book, we will discuss the new approaches demanding such disclosure.[95]

Some companies will compare and contrast mitigation and adaptation strategies.[96] McKinsey and Company's Greenhouse Gas Abatement Cost Curve provides a quantitative basis for discussions about the actions most likely to generate emissions reductions, the potential costs, and it provides a global mapping of opportunities to reduce emissions of GHGs across regions and sectors. Figure 1.9 shows the global GHG abatement cost curve. The curve presents an estimate of the maximum potential of all technical GHG abatement measures below €60 per tCO_2 if each lever were pursued aggressively.

These data do not forecast what role different abatement measures and technologies will play; however, they do give an idea of the likely strategies that firms will use to offset impacts of climate change on their businesses.[98] For example, according to this curve, companies are more likely to choose energy efficiency and lighting retrofits instead of new sources of energy, absent incentives and regulations.

Companies such as Microsoft, Coca-Cola, and General Motors recently joined the Obama administration to invest over $140 billion to lower anthropogenic carbon. Above these investments the companies pledged to bring over 1,600 megawatts of new renewable energy on line, reduce water use by 15 percent, and target reductions in deforestation in their supply chains. These moves by the private sector are critical to achieving any meaningful goals of carbon reduction.[99]

The abatement approaches have many challenges. The approaches do not take into account the implementation challenges. For example, organizations vary in their ability to implement even simple approaches. The

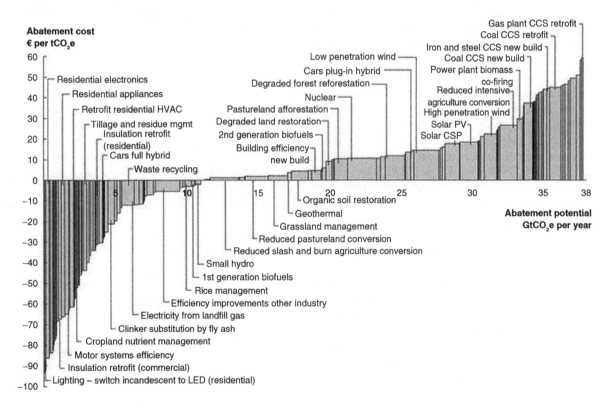

Figure 1.9 High Cost and Low Cost of Abatement Approaches[97]

Source: Global GHG Abatement Cost Curve v2.0

Note: The curve presents an estimate of the maximum potential of all technical GHG abatement measures below €60 per tCO_2e if each lever was pursued aggressively. It is not a forecast of what role different abatement measures and technologies will play.

Abatement Curve uses simple pay back methods, not considering the present value of the investment. Some investments such as physical facilities retrofits can provide benefits for very long periods of time, whereas soil restoration may vary quickly within a few years. One could also ask whether end of life costs should be included in the calculations.

A few other issues are the potential market failures that could influence viable technologies. Also, a big factor in every technology is uncertainty about regulatory support. These issues were not considered in the curve.

Energy is a critical factor in our environment. Other resources matter critically, as well. The next section contains information about water, an increasingly visible and concerning resource.

Water

As illustrated in the introduction, Coca-Cola is one example of a company that understands the important relationship between water and humanity. However, with 83 million more people on the planet each year, water demand will continue to increase, unless we change how we use it. Almost 96 percent of the planet's freshwater resources are stored in groundwater, half of which straddles borders. Also, nearly 70 percent of the world's freshwater is locked in ice. Most of the remaining 30 percent is in aquifers that we are draining much more quickly than the natural recharge rate. UNESCO, a United Nations body, estimates that 273 aquifers are shared by two or more countries. Groundwater provides about a fifth of the planet's water needs and half of its drinking water.[100] Two-thirds of our water is used to grow food.

Water supply is often drawn from surface waters (e.g., lakes, groundwater, or even desalinated saltwater). For example, if you live in Tokyo, your water comes from reservoirs; Beijing uses groundwater pumped from the northern province of Hebei. Riyadh (Saudi Arabia's rapidly growing capital) depends on desalinated seawater drawn from the Persian Gulf. Factory-bottled water and local tap water (repackaged in bottles or plastic bags) are the primary sources of drinking water for more than 10 percent of urban consumers worldwide; in countries like the Dominican Republic, this amount could be as much as 90 percent.[101]

Americans use about 100 gallons of water at home each day; however, millions of the world's poorest subsist on fewer than five gallons a day. As of 2010, 46 percent of the world's people did not have water piped to their homes, and women in developing nations walked an average of 3.1 miles to get water. By 2025, 1.8 billion people are expected to live in regions with severe water scarcity.[102]

These statistics mean that one in eight people lacks access to clean water. Each year, 3.3 million people die from water-related health problems. Data also suggest that water may well become our most challenging natural resource, and the topic of more conversations than our energy future.

Table 1.5 shows the cost of water to a consumer by municipality per 100 gallons, assuming roughly 4,000 gallons per month usage in 2009.[103]

So if water becomes scarce and its cost increases, what does this mean for business? If water were increasingly scarce in a location, would businesses relocate to obtain this precious resource? Also, what implications do water trends have for leisure businesses?[104] For example, U.S. vacationers rank going to the beach or a lake as their favorite outside activity; more Americans fish than play tennis and golf. The U.S. recreational boating industry generated about $33.6 billion in 2009. In Florida, 3,000 gallons are used to water the grass for each golf game played. U.S. swimming pools lose 150 billion gallons to evaporation each year.

Lack of water is a cause of concern in the western part of the United States and has resulted in a search for other water sources. California experienced a three-year drought from 2011 to 2014 that is considered the worst in 500 years, and it continues to-date. As a result, farmers have been forced to sell cattle and other livestock; public officials asked citizens to voluntarily cut their water usage by 20 percent. Most outcomes of this

Table 1.5 Cost of Water per Consumer by Municipality

Copenhagen	*$3.43(USD)*
Cork, Ireland	$0.00
San Diego, CA	$1.65
Memphis, TN	$0.30
Singapore	$0.61
São Paulo, Brazil	$0.65

Note: Price variations are caused by several factors (e.g., public policy, water availability, and the existence [or lack of] infrastructure).

situation are clearly negative for the affected populations and economies, though some unusual business opportunities have emerged (e.g., modern-day prospectors sifting through flecks of gold in slow-running waters).[105]

The issues we are facing are a combination of quality and quantity. We may meet these challenges with technical solutions (e.g., desalination plants). Yet in some locations, freshwater will become scarce, resulting in price increases. As evidenced by cases such as Coca-Cola, some industries (e.g., beverage businesses), view water as their key resource (vs. money and other materials) for manufacturing their end products. Global food and beverage companies have created tools to measure and abate this use of water. For example, the Inter-American Development Bank, backed by some corporate sponsors, funded a modeling tool Hydro-Bid, that is for water planners in worldwide communities. This tool builds on other existing tools, such as Aqueduct, by the World Resources Institute, and offers "what-if" assessments and risk assessments.[106]

Chapter Summary

This chapter's information defined a set of natural environmental pressures that firms are facing. I established how natural capital is valuable to a firm's competitiveness, and its ability to be sustainable (i.e., to, at least, maintain itself at a certain level indefinitely). Three major environmental pressures are critical to most organizations: energy sources and uses, climate change, and water demand and supply. The main point in each discussion was that our natural environment is critical for our economic well-being and much more. The environment is changing dramatically; these changes call for unique organizational-level action. Ultimately, companies that take action are more likely to be sustainable and competitive.

Case Revisited: Coca-Cola Case Response

Many businesses can go a long way in helping the United States lower its emissions and meet the challenges of evolving resource availability and quality (e.g., as Coca-Cola is doing with water).[107] Coca-Cola and its bottlers have spent nearly $2 billion to reduce their water use and improve water quality and engage civil society and governments on shared challenges in watersheds and communities.[108] Businesses can take a lead role in identifying and studying resources to optimize their competitiveness. Reducing GHG emissions and air pollution and preserving water can be accomplished by reducing materials used in products, implementing operational efficiencies, and effectively managing the supply chain—all topics discussed in this book.

Implementing these changes will save money, improve productivity, protect the environment, and increase the nation's energy and resource security. Leading companies that pursue comprehensive GHG management strategies, energy efficiency, and pollution prevention stand to gain a competitive edge over firms failing to make these changes, especially because most evidence indicates that increasing regulations will force such changes in the near future.

An increasing number of private firms now see significant opportunities in addressing resource availability, just as Coca-Cola is doing. Mondelez International, the maker of Oreos, plans to invest over $400 million (all dollar values refer to US dollars throughout the book) from 2014 to 2024 to help cocoa farmers manage the ill effects of climate change.[109] Thousands of companies are profiting from energy-efficiency improvements in their facilities and operations via cost savings and the production of new products and services. Thousands more are positioning themselves to be ready for new markets in energy-efficient products and renewable energy technologies. At the same time, companies such as Coca-Cola are educating themselves, their customers, and their suppliers on possible impacts of future climate change and resource availability.[110] Additional and active information-sharing will expand the base of ideas, opportunities, and solutions for everyone.

Leading businesses and corporations are evaluated on many aspects of their performance (e.g., product quality, ethical standards, and reputation in the community). These leaders can provide powerful examples of how to promote GHG reduction strategies through corporate incentives; one example is providing financial assistance to employees using public transportation, carpooling, and even telecommuting. Other "green" practices (e.g., recycling, purchasing recycled materials, and being a good steward of resources such as freshwater) also contribute to emissions reductions and **environmental sustainability**. Corporate policies, involving employees and day-to-day operations, can have positive impacts on sustainability.[111]

Profile: Geoengineering Coral Reefs

Coral reefs have experienced lots of major challenges. The following lists show some of the man-made and natural stresses on coral reefs.[112]

Man-made stresses include: population increases; fish depletion; poisons and unsustainable fishing methods; ship-based pollution; coral and coral sand mining; urban construction near coastal regions; and excessive non-point pollution. Natural stresses include predators, tropical storm damage, wave actions, flooding, and warmer ocean temperature resulting in bleaching.

These stresses have resulted in the loss of over 19 percent of coral reefs in recent years and some estimates are that worldwide 60 percent of the coral reefs are in danger of extinction.[113] As one stark example, more than a third of all coral reefs near coastal areas around Thailand have been destroyed by sediment from land developments to build hotels, resorts, and private homes.[114]

One solution to the coral reef destruction is to create artificial reefs which are man-made underwater environments that encourage marine life and increase fish stocks.

Several unsustainable solutions have already been tried: shopping carts, old cars, rubber that has broken apart and floated away, and all sorts of other refuse. Some better solutions have been leaving old oil rigs in place.

Recently several other solutions have been suggested including these two:

1   *Concrete units or reef balls, positioned to promote photosynthesis and for plankton to drift into the inner surfaces. The concrete contains microsilica to strengthen the material. Over 500,000 of these balls have been placed in the waters of over 60 countries. They are expected to last about 500 years.[115]*
2   *Steel reinforcing bars anchored on the sea floor with a constant flow of electricity. Sea water in contact with the electricity crystallizes on the metal. This approach, called Biorock, is stronger than concrete and cheaper to make.[116]*

Yet, a question remains. Should we be putting man-made objects into the sea instead of spending money on preserving the natural habitat? Are we ultimately doing more damage to the ocean and coral reefs by putting concrete, metal, and other materials into the sea that become part of the marine ecosystem?

Terms to Know

Climate change: any systematic fluctuation in the long-term statistics of climatic elements (e.g., temperature, pressure, or wind) that is sustained over several decades or longer

Environmental sustainability: the potential longevity of vital human ecological support systems (e.g., the planet's climate, agriculture, forestry, fisheries, and various natural systems on which these systems depend)

Natural capital: resources, living systems, and ecosystem services that are used by humankind

Sustainability: a characteristic of a process or state that can be maintained at a certain level indefinitely

Questions and Critical Thinking

1   The book follows an anthropomorphic (i.e., human survival) perspective. Consider your perspective on sustainability. To what extent do you share this human-centered view of sustainability?
2   Consider particular resources (e.g., water, energy sources such as fossil fuels), potential impacts of those resources, and a specific target organization, such as LG, TATA in India, Wal-Mart, Nokia, AmBev, or Bank of America. Try to draw relationships between the *resource* and *impacts* on an organization. (Consider the example of Coca-Cola and its need for water as a context for thinking about this relationship.)
3   Read several publications on environmental sustainability and determine their core assumptions. An example of this analysis can be found in Table I.1. Read also the Introduction to this book and answer the questions posed in that Introduction as related to your core assumptions. Once you have determined

the assumptions, identify how they influence the presentation of the material. What is included or not included in the readings? What effect would changing the assumptions have on the conclusions reached?

4   Compare and contrast adaptation and mitigation responses to the challenges presented in this chapter. For example, if a firm is located in an area that has high energy costs, and if energy is a large percentage of production costs, what could the firm do to adapt to this situation? What could it do to mitigate the situation? Can you think of situations that might exist when adaptation is a firm's only viable tactic?

5   Obtain a copy of the *International Energy Outlook 2013*, published by the U.S. Energy Information Agency.[117] Consider one of the special topics in the report: "Will carbon capture and storage reduce the world's carbon dioxide emissions?"

6   The pursuit of greenhouse gas reductions has the potential to reduce global coal use significantly. Because coal is the most carbon-intensive of all fossil fuels, limitations on CO_2 emissions will raise the cost of coal compared to the costs of other fuels. Under such circumstances, the degree to which energy use shifts away from coal to other fuels will depend largely on the costs of reducing CO_2 emissions from coal-fired plants (vs. the costs of using other low-carbon or carbon-free energy sources). The continued widespread use of coal could depend on the cost and availability of carbon capture and storage technologies that capture CO_2 and store it in geologic formations. To what extent do you think this technology will offset the pending challenges that firms will experience with energy source supply?

Appendix 1.1. Key Findings Related to Climate Change[118]

Environmental issue	Scientific findings
Greenhouse gases	
GHG indicators characterize the amount of GHGs emitted into the atmosphere through human activities, the concentrations of these gases in the atmosphere, and how emissions and concentrations have changed over time.	• *U.S. greenhouse gas emissions.* In the United States, GHG emissions caused by human activities increased by 14 percent from 1990 to 2008. CO_2 accounts for most of the nation's emissions and most of this increase. Electricity generation is the largest source of GHG emissions in the United States, followed by transportation. Emissions per person have remained about the same since 1990.
	• *Global greenhouse gas emissions.* Worldwide, emissions of GHGs from human activities increased by 26 percent from 1990 to 2005. Emissions of CO_2, which account for nearly three-fourths of the total, increased by 31 percent over this period. As in the United States, the majority of the world's emissions are associated with energy use.
	• *Atmospheric concentrations of greenhouse gases.* Concentrations of CO_2 and other GHGs in the atmosphere have risen substantially since the beginning of the industrial era. Almost all of this increase is believed attributable to human activities.
	• *Climate forcing.* Climate or "radiative" forcing is a way to measure how substances, such as GHGs, affect the amount of energy that is absorbed by the atmosphere. An increase in radiative forcing leads to warming, while a decrease in forcing produces cooling. From 1990 to 2008, the radiative forcing of all GHGs in the Earth's atmosphere increased by about 26 percent. The rise in CO_2 concentrations accounts for approximately 80 percent of this increase.
Weather and climate	
Weather indicators include temperature, precipitation, storms, droughts, and heat waves. These indicators can reveal long-term changes in the Earth's climate system.	• *U.S. and global temperature.* Average temperatures have risen across the lower 48 states since 1901 with an increased rate of warming over the past 30 years. Seven of the top 10 warmest years on record for the lower 48 states have occurred since 1990, and the last 10 five-year periods have been the warmest five-year periods on record. Average global temperatures show a similar trend, and 2000–2009 was the warmest decade on record worldwide. Within the United States, parts of the North, West, and Alaska have seen temperatures increase the most.

(continued)

(continued)

Environmental issue	Scientific findings
	• *Heat waves.* The frequency of heat waves in the United States decreased in the 1960s and 1970s, but has risen steadily since then. The percentage of the United States experiencing heat waves has also increased. • *Drought.* From 2001 through 2009, roughly 30 to 60 percent of the United States' land area experienced drought conditions at any given time. However, the data for this indicator have not been collected for long enough to determine whether droughts are increasing or decreasing over time. • *U.S. and global precipitation.* Average precipitation has increased in the United States and worldwide. Since 1901, precipitation has increased at an average rate of more than 6 percent per century in the lower 48 states and nearly 2 percent per century worldwide. However, shifting weather patterns have caused certain areas (e.g., Hawaii and parts of the Southwest) to experience less precipitation than they used to. • *Heavy precipitation.* In recent years, a higher percentage of precipitation in the United States has come in the form of intense single-day events. Eight of the top 10 years for extreme one-day precipitation events have occurred since 1990. The occurrence of abnormally high annual precipitation totals has also increased.
Oceans The world's oceans have a two-way relationship with climate. The oceans influence climate on regional and global scales, while changes in climate can fundamentally alter certain properties of the ocean. These findings examine trends in ocean characteristics that relate to climate change (e.g., acidity, temperature, heat storage, and sea level).	• *Tropical cyclone intensity.* The intensity of tropical storms in the Atlantic Ocean, Caribbean, and Gulf of Mexico did not exhibit a strong, long-term trend for much of the 20th century, but has risen noticeably over the past 20 years. Six of the 10 most active hurricane seasons have occurred since the mid-1990s. This increase is closely related to variations in sea surface temperature in the tropical Atlantic. • *Ocean heat.* Several studies have shown that the amount of heat stored in the ocean has increased substantially since the 1950s. Ocean heat content not only determines sea surface temperature, but it also affects sea level and currents. • *Sea surface temperature.* The surface temperature of the world's oceans increased over the 20th century. Even with some year-to-year variation, the overall increase is statistically significant, and sea surface temperatures have been higher during the past three decades than at any other time since large-scale measurement began in the late 1800s. • *Sea level.* When averaged over all the world's oceans, sea level has increased at a rate of roughly six-tenths of an inch per decade since 1870. The rate of increase has accelerated in recent years to more than an inch per decade. Changes in sea level, relative to the height of the land, vary widely because the land itself moves. Along the U.S. coastline, sea level has risen the most, relative to the land along the mid-Atlantic coast and parts of the Gulf Coast. Sea level has decreased relative to the land in parts of Alaska and the Northwest. • *Ocean acidity.* The ocean has become more acidic over the past 20 years, and studies suggest that the ocean is substantially more acidic now than it was a few centuries ago. Rising acidity is associated with increased levels of carbon dioxide dissolved in the water. Changes in acidity can affect sensitive organisms such as corals.
Snow and ice Climate change can dramatically alter the Earth's snow- and ice-covered areas. These changes, in turn, can affect air temperatures, sea levels, ocean currents, and storm patterns. These findings focus on trends in glaciers, the extent and depth of snow cover, and the freezing and thawing of oceans and lakes.	• *Arctic sea ice.* Part of the Arctic Ocean stays frozen year-round. The area covered by ice is typically smallest in September, after the summer melting season. September 2007 had the least ice of any year on record, followed by 2008 and 2009. The extent of Arctic sea ice in 2009 was 24 percent below the 1979 to 2000 historical average. • *Glaciers.* Glaciers in the United States, and around the world, have generally shrunk since the 1960s, and the rate at which glaciers are melting appears to have accelerated over the last decade. Overall, glaciers worldwide have lost more than 2,000 cubic miles of water since 1960, which has contributed to the observed rise in sea level.

- *Lake ice.* Lakes in the northern United States generally appear to be freezing later and thawing earlier than they did in the 1800s and early 1900s. The length of time that lakes stay frozen has decreased at an average rate of one to two days per decade.
- *Snow cover.* The portion of North America covered by snow has generally decreased since 1972, although there has been much year-to-year variability. Snow covered an average of 3.18 million square miles of North America during the years 2000 to 2008, compared with 3.43 million square miles during the 1970s.
- *Snowpack.* Between 1950 and 2000, the depth of snow on the ground in early spring decreased at most measurement sites in the western United States and Canada. Spring snowpack declined by more than 75 percent in some areas, but increased in a few others.

Society and ecosystems

Changes in the Earth's climate can affect public health, agriculture, energy production and use, land use and development, and recreation. Climate change can also disrupt the functioning of ecosystems and increase the risk of harm or even extinction for some species. This chapter looks at just a few of the impacts that may be linked to climate change, including heat-related illnesses and changes in plant growth. The EPA looks forward to expanding this chapter in future reports as the science evolves and the capacity to report on these types of indicators is broadened.

- *Heat-related deaths.* Over the past three decades, more than 6,000 deaths across the United States were caused by heat-related illness such as heat stroke. However, considerable year-to-year variability makes it difficult to determine long-term trends.
- *Length of growing season.* The average length of the growing season in the lower 48 states has increased by about two weeks since the beginning of the 20th century. A particularly large and steady increase has occurred over the last 30 years. The observed changes reflect earlier spring warming as well as later arrival of fall frosts. The length of the growing season has increased more rapidly in the West than in the East.
- *Plant hardiness zones.* Winter low temperatures are a major factor in determining the plants that can survive in a particular area. Plant hardiness zones have shifted noticeably northward since 1990, reflecting higher winter temperatures in most parts of the country. Large portions of several states have warmed by at least one hardiness zone.
- *Leaf and bloom dates.* Leaf growth and flower blooms are examples of natural events that are quite responsive to climate change. Observations of lilacs and honeysuckles in the lower 48 states suggest that leaf growth is now occurring a few days earlier than it did in the early 1900s. Lilacs and honeysuckles are also blooming slightly earlier than in the past, but it is difficult to determine whether this change is statistically meaningful.
- *Bird wintering ranges.* Some birds shift their range or alter their migration habits to adapt to changes in temperature or other environmental conditions. Long-term studies have found that bird species in North America have shifted their wintering grounds northward by an average of 35 miles since 1966, with a few species shifting by several hundred miles. On average, bird species have also moved their wintering grounds farther from the coast, consistent with rising inland temperatures.

Notes

1 The Coca-Cola Company, "Water Stewardship," *Reasons to Believe: 2010/2011 Sustainability Report* (Atlanta, GA), 19–25, https://www.coca-colacompany.com/content/dam/journey/us/en/private/fileassets/pdf/2012/11/ TCCC_2010_2011_Sustainability_Report_Full.pdf (accessed December 15, 2015).
2 Ibid.
3 While water, the basis of life, is an infinitely renewable resource, freshwater is increasingly unavailable to humans and other life forms in many parts of the world.
4 Personal correspondence with G. Koch, May 15, 2011.
5 Ibid.
6 Ibid.
7 P. Hawken, A. Lovins, and L. Hunter Lovins, *Natural Capitalism: Creating the Next Industrial Revolution* (Boston, MA: Little, Brown, 1999), 2.
8 R. Eccles and M. Krzus, *The Integrated Reporting Movement* (Hoboken, NJ: Wiley, 2015), 192–194.

9 Hawken, Lovins, Lovins, *Natural Capitalism*, 3.

10 M. Pidwirny, "Organization of Life: Species, Populations, Communities, and Ecosystems," in M. Pidwirny and Scott Jones, *Fundamentals of Physical Geography*, 2nd ed. (PhysicalGeography.net, 2006), chap. 9, pt. (d.), www.physicalgeography.net/fundamentals/9d.html (accessed December 19, 2011).

11 H. John Heinz III Center for Science, Economics, and the Environment, *The State of the Nation's Ecosystem 2008: Measuring the Lands, Waters, and Living Resources of the United States* (Washington, DC: Island Press, 2008). Also see UN Environment Programme (UNEP), "Millennium Ecosystem Assessment," www.unep.org/maweb/en/Index.aspx (accessed December 19, 2011).

12 G. C. Daily et al., "Ecosystem Services: Benefits Supplied to Human Societies by Natural Ecosystems," *Issues in Ecology* 1, no. 2 (Spring 1997): 1–18.

13 Ibid.

14 G. Daily, ed., *Nature's Services: Societal Dependence on Natural Ecosystems* (Washington, DC: Island Press, 1997); G. Heal, *Nature and the Marketplace: Capturing the Value of Ecosystem Services* (Washington, DC: Island Press, 2000); *Millennium Ecosystem Assessment, Ecosystems and Human Well-Being: Synthesis* (Washington, DC: Island Press, 2005), 7, http://www.millenniumassessment.org/documents/document.356.aspx.pdf. (accessed December 15, 2015).

15 World Bank, *Where Is the Wealth of Nations? Measuring Capital in the 21st Century* (Washington, DC: World Bank, 2006).

16 Salt Water Increasingly Attacks Vietnam's Mekong Delta, *Tuoi Tre News*, July 29, 2015, http://tuoitrenews.vn/society/29503/salt-water-increasingly-attacks-vietnams-mekong-delta (accessed December 18, 2015).

17 L. Palumbo, "A post-GDP Critique of the Europe 2020 Strategy," *Procedia-Social and Behavioral Science*, Vol. 72 (February 5, 2013): 47–63.

18 J. Diamond, *Collapse: How Societies Choose to Fail or Succeed* (New York: Penguin, 2005).

19 World Commission on Environment and Development (now known as the Brundtland Commission), *Our Common Future: From One Earth to One World* (Oxford: Oxford University Press, 1987).

20 Ibid.

21 Wal-Mart is an example of one such business.

22 *Webster's New International Dictionary* (Springfield, MA: Merriam-Webster, 1986).

23 Sustainable Seattle, "About Us," http://www.sustainableseattle.org/about-us/ (accessed December 18, 2015).

24 A. Leopold, *A Sand County Almanac, and Sketches Here and There* (New York: Oxford University Press, 1949).

25 D. McCloskey, Professor of Sociology, Seattle University.

26 M. Chenard, email correspondence with author, December 15, 2008.

27 Co-authored by Michael Aper, Master of Arts in Sustainability candidate at Wake Forest University.

28 U.K. Department of Energy & Climate Change, "Policy: Greenhouse Gas Emissions," https://www.gov.uk/government/policies/reducing-the-uk-s-greenhouse-gas-emissions-by-80-by-2050 (accessed January 15, 2015).

29 U.K. Department of Energy & Climate Change, "UK carbon capture and storage: government funding and support," https://www.gov.uk/uk-carbon-capture-and-storage-government-funding-and-support (accessed January 15, 2015).

30 Carbon Capture and Sequestration Technologies @ MIT, "Peterhead Project Fact Sheet: Carbon Dioxide Capture and Storage Project," http://sequestration.mit.edu/tools/projects/peterhead.html (accessed January 15, 2015).

31 Shell United Kingdom, "Peterhead CCS Project," http://www.shell.co.uk/gbr/environment-society/environment-tpkg/peterhead-ccs-project.html (accessed January 15, 2015).

32 United Kingdom, "Preferred bidders announced in UK's £1bn CCS Competition," https://www.gov.uk/government/news/preferred-bidders-announced-in-uk-s-1bn-ccs-competition (accessed January 15, 2015).

33 Carbon Capture and Sequestration Technologies, "Peterhead Project Fact Sheet: Carbon Dioxide Capture and Storage Project," MIT, http://sequestration.mit.edu/tools/projects/peterhead.html (accessed January 15, 2015).

34 "WGK awarded FEED contract by Shell for world-first CCS pipeline," Link2 Portal, October 16, 2014, http://www.link2portal.com/wgk-awarded-feed-contract-shell-world-first-ccs-pipeline (accessed January 15, 2015).

35 "Peterhead CCS Project," Shell United Kingdom, http://www.shell.co.uk/gbr/environment-society/environment-tpkg/peterhead-ccs-project.html (accessed January 15, 2015).

36 P. Marber, *Seeing the Elephant: Understanding Globalization from Trunk to Tail* (Hoboken, NJ: John Wiley & Sons, 2009): 95–136 (ch. 3, Energy: Twilight of the Hydrocarbons?), and 249–290 (ch. 7, Environment: The Hidden Cost of Everything); Frontline, especially the following videos: Watching Our World Change; Fossil Fuels: The Engine of our Lives; Ten Years to Reverse Course; America's Addiction to Coal; Cars: Second Largest Source of Carbon Emissions; Big Oil; Two Instructive Lessons from the Past; Carbon Free Power; Will America Summon the Political Will? L. R. Brown, *Plan B 3.0: Mobilizing to Save Civilization* (New York: W.W. Norton, 2008); J. Diamond, *Collapse: How Societies Choose to Fail or Succeed* (New York: Viking, 2005); T. L. Friedman, *Hot, Flat, and Crowded: Why We Need a Green Revolution, and How It Can Renew America* (New York: Farrar, Straus, and Giroux, 2008); J. G. Speth, *The Bridge at the Edge of the World:Capitalism, the Environment, and Crossing from Crisis to Sustainability* (New Haven, CT: Yale University Press, 2008); H. John Heinz III Center for Science, Economics, and Environment, *The State of the Nation's Ecosystems 2008*; *Millennium Ecosystem Assessment, Ecosystems and Human Well-Being* (5 vols.) (Washington, DC: Island Press, 2005).

37 U.S. Energy Information Administration, http://www.eia.doe.gov/ (accessed December 19, 2011).

38 "Climate Change," EPA, http://www.epa.gov/climatechange/; "Adapting to a Changing Climate," America.gov, http://www.america.gov/climate_change.html; "Global Warming: A Way Forward: Facing Climate Change," National Geographic, video, 07:43, http://video.nationalgeographic.com/video/player/environment/global-warming-environment/way-forward-climate.html (accessed December 19, 2011).

39 "Water: Our Thirsty World," Special Issue, National Geographic, April 2010. http://ga.water.usgs.gov/edu/gwdepletion.html (accessed December 19, 2011).

40 "Deforestation," National Geographic, http://environment.nationalgeographic.com/environment/global-warming/deforestation-overview.html (accessed December 19, 2011).

41 "Desertification," FAO, http://ngm.nationalgeographic.com/2010/04/table-of-contents (accessed December 19, 2011).

42 "Ocean Nitrogen Fixations: New Findings Blow a Decade of Assumptions Out of the Water," ScienceDaily, January 11, 2007, http://www.sciencedaily.com/releases/2007/01/070110181230.htm (accessed December 19, 2011).

43 "Ocean Acidification," EPOCA, http://oceanacidification.wordpress.com/ (accessed December 19, 2011).

44 "Wastes," EPA, http://www.epa.gov/osw/ (accessed December 19, 2011); "Global Warming: A Way Forward: Facing Climate Change," National Geographic, video, 07:43, http://video.nationalgeographic.com/video/player/environment/global-warming-environment/way-forward-climate.html (accessed December 9, 2014).

45 "Ozone Resources," NASA Advanced Supercomputing Division, http://www.nas.nasa.gov/About/Education/Ozone/ozonelayer.html (accessed December 9, 2014).

46 "Biodiversity," The Encyclopedia of Earth, http://www.eoearth.org/article/Biodiversity?topic=49480 (accessed December 19, 2011).

47 "More Complicated Than You Think," *The Economist*, October 30, 2010, 87. Millennium Project, *2020 Global Energy Scenarios* (Washington, DC), www.millennium-project.org/millennium/scenarios/energy-scenarios.html (accessed December 21, 2011).

48 Shell International, BV, "New Lens Scenarios," www.shell.com/global/future-energy/scenarios/new-lens-scenarios.html (accessed September 9, 2014).

49 J. van der Veer, Foreword to Shell International, *Shell Energy Scenarios to 2050* (The Hague: Shell International BV, 2008), http://www.shell.com/energy-and-innovation/the-energy-future/shell-scenarios.html (accessed August 15, 2012).

50 Adapted from J. W. Tester, E. M. Drake, M. J. Driscoll, M. W. Golay, and W. A. Peters, *Sustainable Energy: Choosing Among Options* (Cambridge, MA: MIT Press, 2005), 17.

51 D. J. C. MacKay, *Sustainable Energy: Without the Hot Air* (Cambridge, UK: UIT Cambridge Ltd., 2009).

52 University of California–Davis, ChemWiki, "1st Law of Thermodynamics," http://chemwiki.ucdavis.edu/Physical_Chemistry/Thermodynamics/Laws_of_Thermodynamics/First_Law_of_Thermodynamics (accessed July 2, 2014).

53 U.S. Energy Information Administration, "Crude Oil and Total Petroleum Imports Top 15 Countries," November 29, 2011, Crude Oil Imports table, www.eia.gov/pub/oil_gas/petroleum/data_publications/company_level_imports/current/import.html (accessed June 19, 2012).

54 Keith Trent, executive vice president of Duke Energy, presentation at the Working Professional Programs at Wake Forest University (December 2013).

55 U.S. Energy Information Agency, *Short-Term Energy Outlook* (released May 6, 2014), www.eia.gov/forecasts/steo/report/natgas.cfm?src=Natural-b1 (accessed December 15, 2015).

56 P. Marber, *Seeing the Elephant: Understanding Globalization from Trunk to Tail* (Hoboken, NJ: John Wiley & Sons, 2009), 96.

57 "Total Energy Consumption, 2010," in Enerdata, *Global Energy Statistical Yearbook 2011* (Grenoble: Enerdata, 2011) http://yearbook.enerdata.net/2010/2010-energy-consumption-data.html.

58 U.S. Energy Information Administration, *Annual Energy Outlook 2011*, Report No. DOE/EIA-0383(2011), December 16, 2010, www.eia.doe.gov/oiaf/aeo/graphic_data.html (accessed December 19, 2011); BP Energy Lab, "Energy Usage and Carbon Emission Calculator," www.bp.com/en/global/corporate/sustainability/bp-energy-lab/calculator.html.

59 U.S. Energy Information Administration, *Energy Sources have Changed throughout the History of the United States*, Today in Energy, http://www.eia.gov/todayinenergy/detail.cfm?id=11951# (accessed July 21, 2015).

60 U.S. Energy Information Administration, *Annual Energy Outlook 2014*, DOE/EIA 0383, 2014. www.eia.gov/forecasts/aeo/pdf/0383(2014).pdf (accessed December 15, 2015).

61 Enerdata, *Global Energy Yearbooks 2015*, https://yearbook.enerdat.net/ (accessed July 21, 2015).

62 "Not a toy," *The Economist*, April 11, 2015, 56.

63 J. Fallows, "Dirty Coal, Clean Future," *Atlantic Magazine*, December 2010, www.theatlantic.com/magazine/archive/2010/12/dirty-coal-clean-future/308307/ (accessed December 1, 2012).

64 U.S. Energy Information Agency, "Energy Flows," http://www.eia.gov/totalenergy/ (accessed August 6, 2015).

65 U.S. Energy Information Administration, "Primary Energy Consumption by Source and Sector, 2013," http://www.eia.gov/totalenergy/data/monthly/pdf/flow/css_2013_energy.pdf (accessed July 21, 2015).

66 U.S. Energy Information, *International Energy Outlook 2013* (Washington DC, U.S. EIA, 2013), 171, http://www.eia.gov/forecasts/ieo/pdf/0484%282013%29.pdf (accessed October 24, 2014).

67 U.S. Energy Information, *International Energy Outlook 2013* (Washington DC, U.S. EIA, 2013). Page 21 http://www.eia.gov/forecasts/ieo/pdf/0484%282013%29.pdf (accessed October 24, 2014).

68 S. Dunn, "Down to Business on Climate Change: An Overview of Corporate Strategies," *Greener Management International*, 39 (2002): 27–41; A. Kolk and J. Pinske, "Business Responses to Climate Change: Identifying Emergent Strategies," *California Management Review*, 47, no. 3 (Spring 2005): 6–20; A. C. Jones and D. L. Levy, "North American Business Strategies Towards Climate Change," *European Management Journal*, 25, no. 6 (December 2007): 428–440; C. Okereke and D. Russel, "Regulatory Pressure and Competitive Dynamics: Carbon Management Strategies of UK Energy-Intensive Companies," *California Management Review*, 52, no. 4 (Summer 2010): 100–124; Y. Schreuder, *The Corporate Greenhouse: Climate Change Policy in a Globalizing World* (London: Zed Books, 2009); G. Friend, *The Truth About Green Business* (Upper Saddle River, NJ: FT Press, 2009).

69 See, for example, Peter Singer, "Does Helping the Planet Hurt the Poor?" *Wall Street Journal*, January 22, 2011, C8–C9.

70 B. Fagan, *The Great Warming: Climate Change and the Rise and Fall of Civilizations* (New York: Bloomsbury Press, 2009).

71 N. Lawson, *An Appeal to Reason: A Cool Look at Global Warming* (London: Gerald Duckworth & Co., 2009).

72 B. McKibben, "Global Warming's Terrifying New Math," *Rolling Stone*, August 2, 2012, 5, http://www.rollingstone.com/politics/news/global-warmings-terrifying-new-math-20120719 (accessed July 2, 2014).

73 "Australia and Global Warming: Stranded," *The Economist*, November 22, 2014, 37.

74 B. McKibben, "Keystone XL Back on Obama's Desk," 350.org, December 23, 2011, www.350.org/en/node/27997 (accessed December 25, 2011).

75 J. Rockström et al. "A Safe Operating Space for Humanity," *Nature* 461 (September 24, 2009): 472–475. An updated analysis of planetary boundaries is W. Steffen, K. Richardson, J. Rockström, S. E. Cornell, I. Fetzer et al., "Planetary Boundaries: Guiding Human Development on a Changing Planet," *Science*, 347 (2015): 1–10.

76 National Oceanic and Atmospheric Administration, Earth System Research laboratory. "Trends in Atmospheric Carbon Dioxide, 2014," www.esrl.noaa.gov/gmd/ccgg/trends (accessed October 24, 2014).

77 R. Pindyck, "Climate Change Policy: What do the Models Tell Us?" (*NBER Working Paper* No. 19244, July 2013).

78 K. Ricke and K. Caldeira, "Maximum Warming Occurs About One Decade After a Carbon Dioxide Emission" *Environmental Research Letters* 9, No. 12 (2014), http://iopscience.iop.org/1748-9326/9/12/124002/article (accessed December 8, 2014).

79 J. Moran, *Climate Studies: Introduction to Climate Science* (Boston, MA: American Meteorological Society, 2010).

80 J. Hansen, *Storms of My Grandchildren: The Truth About the Coming Climate Catastrophe and Our Last Chance to Save Humanity* (New York: Bloomsbury U.S.A., 2009), xi.

81 "The Clouds of Unknowing," *The Economist*, March 20, 2010, 83–86.

82 The EPA used the term "virtual certainty" (or virtually certain) to convey a greater than 99 percent chance that a result is true. Other terms used to communicate confidence include "extremely likely" (greater than 95 percent chance that the result is true), "very likely" (greater than 90 percent chance that the result is true), "likely" (greater than 66 percent chance that the result is true), "more likely than not" (greater than 50 percent chance that the result is true), "unlikely" (less than 33 percent chance that the result is true), "very unlikely" (less than 10 percent chance that the result is true), and "extremely unlikely" (less than 5 percent chance that the result is true). These judgmental estimates originate from the IPCC: "1.6 The IPCC Assessments of Climate Change and Uncertainties," in S. Solomon et al. (eds.), *IPCC Fourth Assessment Report: Climate Change 2007: Working Group I Report, "The Physical Science Basis,"* (Cambridge, UK: Cambridge University Press, 2007), www.ipcc.ch/publications_and_data/ar4/wg1/en/ch1s1-6.html (accessed December 25, 2011).

83 IPCC, "Summary for Policymakers in Climate Change 2013: The Physical Science Basis. Contribution of Working Group 1 to the Fifth Assessment Report of the Intergovernmental Panel on Climate Change," eds. T. F. Stocker et al. (Cambridge University Press, Cambridge, UK and New York, U.S.A., 2013), 15.

84 Ibid., 17.

85 Ibid.

86 Ibid.

87 Ibid.

88 Ibid., 5.

89 Ibid., 8.

90 For a description of the IPCC's work, see www.ipcc.ch/ (accessed September 1, 2015).

91 S. Solomon et al. (eds.), *Climate Change 2007: The Physical Science Basis* (Cambridge, UK: Cambridge University Press) http://www.ipcc.ch/publications_and_data/publications_ipcc_fourth_assessment_report_wg1_report_the_physical_science_basis.htm (accessed September 1, 2015).

92 The EPA uses various modeling tools and data. For more information about these modeling tools, see "Climate Economic Modeling" at www.epa.gov/climatechange/EPAactivities/economics/modeling.html (accessed August 25, 2015).

93 P.-A. Enkvist, T. Nauclér, and J. M. Oppenheim, "Business Strategies for Climate Change," *The McKinsey Quarterly*, no. 2 (2008): 24–33.

94 A. J. Hoffman, *Getting Ahead of the Curve: Corporate Strategies That Address Climate Change* (Arlington, VA: Pew Center on Global Climate Change, October 2006); see also F. G. Sussman and J. R. Freed, *Adapting to Climate Change: A Business Approach* (Arlington, VA: Pew Center on Global Climate Change, April 2008).

95 U.S. Securities and Exchange Commission, "SEC Interpretation: Calculation of Average Weekly Trading Volume under Rule 144 and Termination of a Rule 10b5-1 Trading Plan, 17 C.F.R. pts. 211, 231, 241" (2001) www.sec.gov/rules/interp/33-8005a.htm (accessed December 15, 2015).

96 T. Nauclér and P.-A. Enkvist, *Pathways to a Low-Carbon Economy, Version 2 of the Global Greenhouse Gas Abatement Cost Curve* (New York: McKinsey and Company, 2009).

97 McKinsey and Company, *Impact on the Financial Crisis on Carbon Economics*, Version 2.1, 2010, 8.

98 Nauclér and Enkvist, *Pathways to a Low-Carbon Economy*.

99 V. Volcovici, "U.S. Private Sector Vows to Ante Up on Climate Finance" (*Reuters*, July 27, 2015) http://www.reuters.com/article/2015/07/27/us-usa-climatechange-business-idUSKCN0Q127B20150727?feedType=RSS&feedName=everything&virtualBrandChannel=11563 (accessed August 5, 2015).

100 "Deep Waters, Slowly Drying Up," *The Economist*, October 9, 2010, 86–87.

101 C. Fishman, *The Big Thirst: The Secret Life and Turbulent Future of Water* (New York: Free Press, 2011).

102 "For Want of a Drink," *The Economist*, May 22, 2010; P. Rogers and S. Leal, *Running Out of Water: The Looming Crisis and Solutions* (New York: Palgrave, 2010); "Deep Waters, Slowly Drying Up," *The Economist*.

103 "For Want of a Drink," *The Economist*; P. Rogers and S. Leal, *Running Out of Water*, 1–17.

104 *National Geographic*, "Water: Our Thirsty World," 217, no. 4 (April 2010): 114–115.

105 "Pepsi Co Backs New Tool to Predict Water Risks." (GreenBiz, September 9, 2014). www.greenbiz.com/blog/2014/09/05/could-new-tool-help-predict-water-risks (accessed September 1, 2015).

106 P. Clark, "A World Without Water," *Financial Times*, July 14, 2014, 1.

107 G. Koch, Correspondence, December 5, 2014.

108 P. J. Newcomb, "Innovation for Sustainability." Alfred University Symposium on Sustainable Business. November 7, 2014.

109 *The Wall Street Journal*, "How Oreos Hopes to Maintain Its Chocolate," April 9, 2014, http://online.wsj.com/articles/SB10001424052702303532704579481511940626956 (accessed November 20, 2014).

110 This work does not guarantee that Coca-Cola will be profitable. The company has struggled in the recent past where operating margins have fallen to 11.4 percent in 2014 from 20.7 percent in 2009. The company expects that it will not turn a positive return on its U.S. bottling investments until after 2020. October 2014 the company started to cut costs by $3 billion by 2019 and cutting jobs of at least 1,600 white-collar jobs globally. M. Esterl, "Coca-Cola to Sell Nine U.S. Plants," *The Wall Street Journal*, September 25, 2015, B3.

111 *L'APPEL À L'ACTION . . . CONTINUE* (United Nations Commission on Sustainable Development: International Coral Reef Initiative, October, 2013) http://www.icriforum.org/sites/default/files/ICRI_Call_to_Action_FR_2013.pdf (accessed January 6, 2015).

112 Ibid.

113 Biorock Technology, http://www.biorock.org/content/thailand-third-coastal-reefs-destroyed-sediment (accessed January 6, 2015).

114 "Watery Dwellings," *The Economist Technology Quarterly* (December 6, 2014), 4.

115 Biorock Technology, http://biorock.net/Technologies/index.html (accessed January 6, 2015).

116 "For Want of a Drink," *The Economist*, 3–5.

117 A. Nagourney and I. Lovett, "Severe Drought Has U.S. West Fearing Worst," *New York Times*, February 2, 2014, A1, A18. U.S. Energy Information Administration, *International Energy Outlook 2013*, Report No. DOE/EIA-0484(2013) (Washington, DC: EIA, July 2013) http://www.eia.gov/forecasts/ieo/pdf/0484%282013%29.pdf (accessed June 3, 2014).

118 Ibid., 58. This table is largely taken from the U.S. EIA website and report.

2

SOCIAL PRESSURES ON ORGANIZATIONS

E+Co Faces Its Social Challenges

Phil LaRocca and Christine Eibs-Singer, E+Co founders, were convinced that small and medium-sized energy enterprises held tremendous potential to simultaneously address energy power and waste.[1] So, when this duo founded E+Co (pronounced "E and Co") in 1994, they explained their company's mission as empowering "local small and medium-sized energy enterprises to supply clean and affordable energy to households, businesses, and communities in developing countries through a combination of capital investment and business development support."

The founders encouraged local solutions to energy poverty and energy waste, tailored to the needs and means of each community. They argued that grassroots entrepreneurs were the missing link between local needs and global investment so E+Co trained local entrepreneurs within developing countries who had an interest in starting clean-energy businesses. E+Co offered seed capital (ranging from $25,000 to $1,000,000) along with a range of enterprise development services.[2]

The company was technology neutral with an eye on moving people "up the ladder" of modern practices. For example, if a household used firewood, the goal would be to use that resource more efficiently (e.g., by installing a more efficient, wood-burning stove or substituting firewood with agricultural residue). The long-term goal would be to transition a household off a resource, like firewood, entirely. Eventually, homeowners could use renewable and environmentally beneficial resources, such as solar energy, to heat their homes. Entrepreneurs collaborating with E+Co would have the technologies to enable households to use these types of energy.

This model of empowering local entrepreneurs, through a focus on improving energy power and energy waste, enabled E+Co to help over 250 small but growing clean-energy businesses.[3] In turn, E+Co was a major participant in supplying clean energy to over five million people, reducing carbon dioxide emissions by four million tons, generating thousands of jobs, and garnering millions of dollars in income and financial returns for the employees and companies of E+Co's partners. This vast impact is particularly noteworthy as the firm's projects are located mainly in northern and southern Africa, Central America, Brazil, Peru, Cambodia, and southern rural China—all regions of the world with limited resources for developing clean and sustainable energy.

One of their particularly important case studies involved a company in Ghana called Toyola. Black carbon, caused by cooking over open fires, is linked to the spread of toxic air over much of the developing world, and scientists recognized it as a significant contributor to climate change.[4] In Ghana, two entrepreneurs—Suraj Wahan and Ernest Kyei—developed an energy-efficient cook-stove business to respond to this environmental and social need; their cook stoves produce 40 percent less black carbon emissions than traditional cook stoves. Working with an initial loan of $70,000 from E+Co (and with the ongoing support of E+Co's staff in Ghana), Toyola expanded beyond their initial market coverage in urban centers, increased sales by 500 percent after one year of operation, and has become a major success story for E+Co. The Toyola case study also illustrates how to successfully engage potential competitors as business partners.

Today, Toyola has launched a "purchase on credit" consumer option, expanded into commercial distribution, employs over 200 people, and is evaluating the implementation of a franchising infrastructure. The company responded to certain social needs (i.e., employment and health) by developing a business related to environmental sustainability; E+Co continues to partner with it through two additional loans of $100,000 and collaboration to create carbon offsets, bringing the benefits of carbon finance to local African markets.

E+Co now needs to consider how it will scale its operations to grow throughout Africa and other parts of the world, and it will feel more and more pressure to act as a good corporate citizen. How will it balance these demands as it struggles to maintain its growth?

Chapter Overview

Chapter 1 demonstrated the challenges that companies face from depleting resources and eco-services. This chapter presents another set of pressures on companies from *social movements* and *social challenges*. These pressures often take the form of *environmental activism* and *social justice*, which require firms to consider: (1) their definitions of "stakeholders" and (2) their responsibilities to the environment and society. E+Co is an example of how these pressures can be addressed, and even yield new business opportunities, in places where businesses were not historically profitable or feasible.

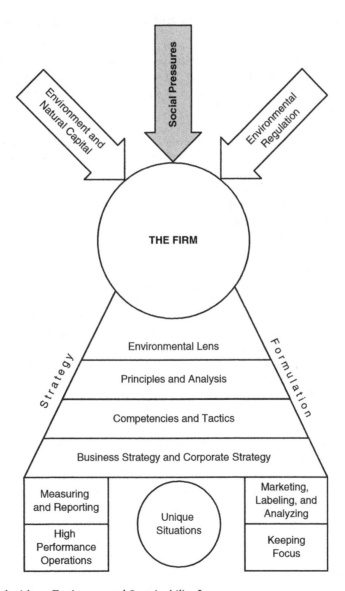

Figure 2.1 Strategy Model with an Environmental Sustainability Lens

Evidence is mounting that companies are becoming more sensitive to social pressures and desires to adhere to Corporate Social Responsibility (CSR) principles.[5] This chapter will begin exploring various complexities of these pressures and the rising role of CSR. Later in the chapter, two key examples—*fair trade* and *population change*—will be discussed to further understand the connections among social pressures, the environment, and business.

At the end of this chapter, you should be able to:

1 specify what a stakeholder is and identify important stakeholders for a particular firm;
2 define and discuss various views toward CSR;
3 define fair trade and analyze its benefits in a market economy;
4 specify major social pressures on firms (e.g., population growth, consumer preferences, and attempts to create social justice).

The Dawn of Companies and Environmental Activism

Limited Brands is a U.S. apparel firm with sales of over $9 billion, more than 2,600 specialty stores carrying the brand's title, and over 700 other locations selling several alternatively branded products (e.g., Victoria's Secret). The firm was the target of a 2004 campaign by ForestEthics, an advocacy group, which pressured the company to print its catalogs on paper produced from sustainable sources.[6] Limited Brands responded with a multi-pronged strategy; the company:

- partnered with its paper supplier to convert four of its mills to Forest Stewardship Council (FSC) standards;
- eliminated all pulp supplied from the Boreal Forest (Alberta's Rocky Mountain Foothills) and Inland Temperate Rainforest (in British Columbia);
- shifted its catalogs to 10 percent post-consumer waste (during 2007);
- committed to phase out use of endangered forests;
- allocated $1 million to research and advocacy (to protect endangered forests and ensure environmental leadership in the catalog industry).

The company also committed to continuously improving environmental attributes of catalog paper and overall paper use. (Progress is audited by an independent third party and made public.) In April 2008, Tom Katzenmeyer, vice president of investor relations at Limited Brands, met with government representatives from the Canadian province of Alberta to discuss their concerns about threatened caribou habitats in forests that Limited Brands was deforesting; the meeting led to new enthusiasm for working with government agencies to help solve environmental problems and was an indicator that earlier social pressures had forced a strategy change and reshaped the company's overall outlook toward the natural environment. This type of collaboration (between companies and environmentally focused organizations) has occurred elsewhere. These relationships are often called cross-sector alliances and will be discussed in detail in Chapter 12. For example:

- Wal-Mart has worked actively with several non-governmental organizations (NGOs) to help realize its three sustainability goals: creating zero waste, offering the most environmentally friendly products on the market, and using 100 percent renewable energy sources.[7]
- IKEA has joined with the Rainforest Alliance and World Wildlife Fund (WWF) to promote forest certification in China using the FSC's certification of wood products.[8]
- General Motors, Rio Tinto, and Conoco Philips collaborated with environmental groups (e.g., the World Resources Institute [WRI]) to form the U.S. Climate Action Partnership, which called upon the U.S. government in 2008 to order reductions in greenhouse gas emissions.[9]

The original environmentalism movement offered something very important: It inspired an appreciation for the nonhuman world, focused attention on future generations (and responsibilities toward them), and called upon people to limit their use of resources and focus on overcoming ecological degradation.[10] However, early environmentalism was also an albatross, supporting "the politics of limits which seeks to constrain human ambition, aspiration and power rather than unleash and direct them."[11] In focusing exclusively on nonhuman worlds that have been lost (vs. the human world), environmentalists tended to feel more resentment than gratitude (or partnership) toward the prior environmental efforts of companies.

The current dominant attitude of NGOs and companies has changed to one of *cooperation*. Organizations are starting to work together to solve environmental problems, each using its distinct competencies to contribute to solutions.[12] This change in attitude provides hope that we will be able to address all sorts of environmental and social issues by bridging people and organizations with varied views.

Social Justice as Part of Environmental Sustainability

One such social issue is *social justice* (and its relationship to the conditions of the natural environment). Social justice issues are complex; the relationship between poverty and racism to environmental sustainability is often overlooked. Here we will explore the impact on human rights of caring for (or neglecting) the environment. This focus is often referred to as *ecojustice*,[13] and can be global and local, intragenerational and intergenerational, and often spans various aspects of a person's existence.[14]

> *Environmental justice* is the fair treatment and meaningful involvement of all people regardless of race, color, national origin, or income with respect to the development, implementation, and enforcement of environmental laws, regulations, and policies. This is the goal of the U.S. Environmental Protection Act (EPA) for all communities and persons across the United States. It will be achieved when everyone enjoys the same degree of protection from environmental and health hazards and has equal access to the decision-making process to ensure a healthy environment in which to live, learn, and work.[15]

Businesses will sometimes decide to place hazardous industrial facilities in areas inhabited by economically disadvantaged populations; these facilities may victimize a specific subset of society.[16] This type of decision by for-profit organizations is an example of why **environmental justice** is such an important issue. Harmful activities (e.g., improper management and disposal of toxic chemicals) contribute to the victimization of entire communities. Since companies might not feel responsible for them (and all too often experience little resistance from these communities), they often do not see their actions as problematic.

Consider a contemporary and major issue with the production of palm oil, a $30 billion (USD) business. This growing business demands large labor pools and often operations are in economies with somewhat lax labor laws and vested government interests. For example, Malaysia is often cited as a place with forced labor in the palm oil fields. Malaysia ranked Tier 3 (the lowest rank) for alleged insufficient efforts to stop human abuses.[17] Felda Global Ventures was set up by the Malaysian government and is one of the largest palm oil producers. It sells large quantities of palm oil to Cargill, a U.S. company, who then sells to companies that produce food products, such as Nestlé SA.[18] Only about 20 percent of the palm oil is certified by the Roundtable on Sustainable Palm Oil, an organization that certifies palm oil on environmental and social criteria. This lack of certification leaves the companies and consumers to make purchase decisions based on these important criteria, especially social justice criteria.[19]

One of the most provocative aspects of environmental injustice is its focus on future generations (i.e., intergenerational impacts of present neglectful and harmful practices). Consider, for example, environmental and health impacts of noxious substances; many have only begun to be understood by scientists. This concern was the basis of the Brundtland Commission's statement that "sustainable development is development that meets the needs of the present without compromising the ability of future generations to meet their own needs." This definition contains two key concepts:

1   the concept of "needs," in particular the essential needs of the world's poor, to which The Commission said overriding priority should be given; and
2   the idea of limitations imposed by the state of technology, and how societies are organized based on our ability to meet present and future needs.[20]

This area of concern includes the right of all people to have access to water, air, and property rights. Large segments of Africa, for example, are exposed to the impacts of climate change as a result of more droughts, desertification, and abusive land use policies. Many wealthier nations are pledging support to help Africa. Yet some of this support is not substantial. U.S. President Obama followed his 2015 trip to Kenya with a pledge of $140 million to help mitigate ill effects of climate change on 11 African nations benefitting over 11 million households, a relatively meager $12.75 per household.[21] Industrial development and exposure to harmful substances can produce unlivable conditions for society's most vulnerable populations (including the socioeconomically disadvantaged).

Thus, some researchers have proposed that companies should use certain principles to develop programs preventing victimization; they might include:

1 the right to protection from environmental degradation;
2 the prevention of harm (i.e., the elimination of the threat before harm occurs);
3 shifting the burden of proof so that the polluters (vs. impoverished victims) bear the burden of costly litigation;
4 obviating the proof of intent (as most corporate polluters cite reduced costs and other reasons for their choice of location);
5 redressing inequities when these occur.[22]

These principles are similar to U.S. Executive Order 12898, establishing environmental justice as a national priority.[23] The EPA enforces this order to ensure that grave environmental degradation cases do not occur in areas where impoverished groups reside. In response to public concerns, in 1992 the EPA created the Office of Environmental Justice and implemented a new organizational infrastructure to integrate environmental justice into the EPA's policies, programs, and activities. The office provides leadership to ensure that environmental justice is incorporated into agency operations; the most active group is the Environmental Justice Coordinators Council, which ensures policy input, program development, and implementation of environmental justice through the agency. This new structure has established a commitment to making environmental justice a priority, starting with the EPA's senior management and including all personnel throughout the agency.

In contrast, little progress has been made on the international front in terms of social justice. International issues are the same as domestic ones (i.e., relatively powerless populations are victimized by those polluting their communities). Some have proposed the formation of a *world environmental organization* or a *world environmental court* to address these injustices, similar to the World Trade Organization (WTO) or International Monetary Fund (IMF).[24]

In today's world, an increasing number of companies are developing strategies to address social and environmental justice issues. In some cases, companies initiate these changes on their own; however, they often occur because of the influence of outside groups or organizations. In these cases, an outside entity becomes an invested part of the company. This investment often makes these groups *stakeholders* in a company.

Profile: Cities vs. Suburbs

Many researchers point to a shift of population from the countryside to the city. The United Nations estimates that, worldwide, 5.2 billion will be located in urban areas by 2020. A recent commentary suggested, however, that "people may be moving towards cities, but most will not end up in their centres."[25] They wind up in suburbs.

Suburbs have been around since Ancient Roman times, when the word was coined. The growth of suburbs came with the growth of transportation modes, mostly the car. Families wanted to get more land at affordable rates to live in less dense environments and to control better who were their neighbors. They wanted easier living and quieter locations. Others viewed the suburbs as uniformed housing that was located in a boring place creating a homogeneity that was based on conformity rather than individuality. The suburbs make people travel too much, contributing to environmental degradation.

Which create a more sustainable world – cities or suburbs? As you can imagine, research is conflicting. For example, one study showed that

> *despite the lower environmental impacts associated with less car use, inner city households outstrip the rest of Australia in every other category of consumption . . . . In each state and territory, the centre of the capital city is the area with the highest environmental impacts, followed by the inner suburban areas. Rural and regional areas tend to have noticeably lower levels of consumption.[26]*

Another study showed that "cities are the most sustainable social design we have in the modern world."[27]

To resolve these ideas, consider that the context might not be the best basis of comparison. A better approach might be to look at the consumption habits of inhabitants within each context and the processes used by the locations. Some locations are more sustainable because they have certain characteristics. Consider one such list:

1. *__The Connected City__: Both growing technological enablement and traditional social connectivity provide opportunities for greater awareness, trust, and collaboration among stakeholders.*
2. *__The Decisive City__: Cities often have the urgency, remit, and accountability to act decisively—for example, on mitigation and adaptation efforts related to climate change.*
3. *__The Adaptive City__: Cities are among the most adaptable structures in society.*
4. *__The Collaborative/Competitive City__: The healthy tension between peer-to-peer collaboration and economic and brand competition among cities has potential to drive precompetitive sustainable innovation and rapid diffusion of solutions.*
5. *__The Visceral City__: Urban living is shaped by numerous real and potential feedback loops. As urbanization and its impacts rise and become more visible, awareness and urgency become more acute.*
6. *__The Personal City__: The influence of shared identity and values—in cities and elsewhere—is a particularly powerful driver of individual and collective action.*
7. *__The Experimental City__: Cities have inherent advantages to experimentation, like complementary ecosystems for R&D and low barriers to entry for nontraditional actors.[28]*

So what do you think? While each context may have its sustainability challenges, do we stand a better chance making cities more sustainable than suburbs? What are your criteria for a sustainable location—what principles should locations live by and what processes would produce the best outcomes?

Stakeholders

Stakeholders are often thought of as individuals or groups affecting (or being affected by) the achievement of business objectives. Increasingly, stakeholders include those interested in the environment and environmental outcomes. One view is that companies would perform better (and be more sustainable over the long term) if they paid more attention to all of their stakeholders. This view is intended to help managers improve organizational performance by being responsive to the interests, demands, and needs of stakeholders who could influence (or be influenced by) organizational performance.[29]

Companies generally view their stakeholders in one of two categories. *Primary stakeholders* are typically shareowners, customers, employees, and suppliers. These groups constitute "the firm"[30] (i.e., all the components necessary to complete the cycle of business). *Secondary stakeholders* are typically communities, governments, and NGOs. Primary and secondary stakeholders can be viewed in terms of three variables: power, urgency, and legitimacy.[31] (Primary stakeholders get high marks in all three categories.)

Primary and secondary stakeholders might have some power over a firm; however, a firm will often have power over certain stakeholders, as well. For example, firms employ people; thus, they have some ability to dictate certain employee-related actions. On the other hand, consumers can influence firms through product feedback, based on ethical principles (e.g., justice and fairness) or on utility (e.g., cost-benefit analysis or principles of character and reputation). Environmentally focused NGOs might place demands on organizations to improve environmental performance and disclose environmental practices.

Also, another perspective on the meaning of "stake" is that stakeholders have taken some sort of risk or made an investment in an organization, expecting a return or desired outcome (e.g., communities can make such a claim because they provide the physical and social environment that companies rely on to exist). Additionally, stakeholders may change position (i.e., from secondary to primary and vice versa). An example of this can be seen in the case, *United States* v. *Microsoft*.[32]

In the Microsoft case, the federal government sued Microsoft for antitrust concerns. By doing so, it moved from a secondary stakeholder (with no impact on Microsoft's business strategy) to a primary stakeholder (with significant impact on strategy).[33] Many related lawsuits against Microsoft are ongoing. As a result, Microsoft has changed its products and methods of operations and now has a large government affairs department.[34]

Some U.S. Department of Interior initiative projects are related to environmental justice and stakeholders. For example, the Metlakatla Indian Community (MIC) Environmental Justice Demonstration Project, held on the Annette Islands Reserve in Alaska, brings together federal, tribal, and local organizations and government agencies to find ways to improve polluted areas. The MIC has been impacted by high unemployment (which has soared as high as 85 percent). This unemployment has been caused by the closure of their timber mill. The MIC is trying to find other employment opportunities for its members.[35]

Natural resource-dependent organizations, such as extraction industries, consider the natural environment as a primary stakeholder. Others, such as service companies, consider it a secondary stakeholder.[36] Additionally, groups and entities that represent the environment but have no relationship to a company (e.g., ForestEthics working with the Limited Brands) can become secondary or even primary stakeholders. These complicated relationships are increasingly becoming part of both for-profit organizations and community conversations.

Environmental activists frequently dispute a company's actions (e.g., the Yadkin Riverkeeper's relentless legal battles with Alcoa;[37] the Riverkeeper organization questioned Alcoa's deposits of waste into the Yadkin River). These types of inquiries give a voice to the natural environment and a platform for engagement on sustainability issues. This give and take between firms and their stakeholders is often viewed in contrast to neoclassical economic theory (which argues that the sole purpose of a corporation is to maximize wealth for shareholders). However, the neoclassical theory seems narrow in view of the stakeholder perspective, which maintains that multiple stakeholders are critical to a corporation's ability to make a profit and sustain itself. The stakeholder perspective is more robust because it understands that the corporation functions as a result of multiple stakes in the firm. The support of communities, governments, and other entities is critical to a firm's existence and its ability to be profitable; they might not only constitute part of its customer base, but they also potentially have the power to slow or shut down operations if they find a reason to do so.

Firms often struggle with reconciling interests of disparate stakeholders. Polluting the environment to optimize profits and laying off employees for efficiency, for example, pose difficult issues when multiple stakeholders are considered; pleasing one stakeholder might mean hurting another. For this reason, business leaders spend considerable time to fully understand the roles of their stakeholders, and current and future leaders might want to view the environment as a significant stakeholder. In response to multiple stakeholders and their competing demands, the business world has developed the concept of *social responsibility*.

Social Responsibility of the Firm

CSR (also known as corporate responsibility, corporate citizenship, or building a sustainable corporation) reflects a company's policies and procedures that respond to the social needs of various stakeholders. The term has become a new corporate disclosure and is showing up in stock indexes, internal and external reports, and community actions. Companies want to tell the world about their good citizenship; they are discussing their responsibility at public forums, on their websites, and in case studies used at major universities. One study showed that the amount of attention given to CSR has increased dramatically in just the last few years.[38] Another study concluded that CSR "is often misguided, or worse. But in practice, few big companies can now afford to ignore it."[39]

Government and quasi-governmental organizations are showing a growing interest in the CSR of companies. In 2006, Britain passed the UK Companies Act, requiring public companies to report on social and environmental matters,[40] and the United Nations promotes CSR around the world through its Global Compact (a set of principles defining how companies can be considered high-quality corporate citizens).[41]

There are three primary reasons for the growing interest in CSR. First, scandals and economic turmoil have caused many to question the integrity of some business organizations. Second, a proliferation of associated rankings and ratings are putting pressure on companies to report non-financial performances; these assessments are increasingly spotlighting associated practices that can affect their brands and generate increased scrutiny. However, concerns over climate change and environmental degradation have probably been the most significant drivers of the growing interest. In a survey of company leaders, many reported that society now expects businesses to take on more public responsibilities.[42]

This increase in interest has caused investors to take note of organizations' CSR activities. The Dow Jones has developed indexes measuring CSR within and across firms.[43] One index, the Dow Jones Sustainability Group Index, is a resource for potential investors that tracks the performance of investments in companies with sustainable practices. This index includes around 200 companies and claims to represent the top 10 percent of firms committed to sustainable practices. It recognizes the importance of integrating economic, environmental, and social factors in business strategy.

Tools like the Dow Jones Sustainability Index help society and investors assess the sustainability practices of companies and help companies develop ways to assess their own levels of sustainability practices. Many analysts view CSR as a multistage process with escalating commitments. The lowest level is compliance (i.e., determining whether a company meets the legal requirements for reporting and disclosure of information about its impact on the environment and society). The next level is philanthropy (i.e., funding certain community activities with pre-tax profits). A more involved level involves using CSR as a risk-management tool.

Many companies are becoming more aware of their statements and actions, are increasingly focusing attention on the impacts of their business practices on communities, and are generally required to integrate CSR into their strategies following environmental disasters (e.g., the Bhopal pesticide factory explosion and the Exxon, Valdez, and BP oil spills).[44] Still, few company executives can determine the full effectiveness of their CSR activities. A review of more than 165 studies over the past 40 years concluded that there is a positive link between companies' social and financial performance; however, this link is weak.[45]

Although results show that CSR activities do not destroy value, there is still minimal incentive for firms and investors. Scholars have argued that enhanced social performance can lead to obtaining better resources,[46] higher-quality employees,[47] better marketing of products and services,[48] and that it might even lead to the creation of unforeseen opportunities.[49] Unfortunately, the gap between scholarship and practice is still wide. Until companies fully grasp their social responsibilities, more significant linkages between action and profit will be hard to find. But for the companies that have begun to grasp this vision, there are several different methods they can utilize to develop robust and accountable CSR policies and practices.

Methods Companies Use to Support CSR

When it comes to implementing CSR, companies focus on two primary activities: *measurement* and *creation* of outcomes. One major measurement technique is the Global Reporting Initiative (GRI), which is the main format for reporting on environmental sustainability issues within organizations (and is covered in Chapter 8). *Philanthropy* is a popular method for supporting CSR goals; this method usually takes the form of issuing grants or supporting projects related to a firm's strategy and brand. Examples are numerous, such as Duke Energy Inc.'s giving in 2011, which included $16.5 million through its Duke Energy Foundation; 66 percent of those funds went towards community vitality projects. A few companies go as far as making CSR the core of their business models and strategies; others develop processes to ensure that certain social responsibility principles are enforced. Some companies partner with NGOs that develop CSR processes for companies. For example, Starbucks has relied on Conservation International to create more economically, environmentally, and socially sustainable coffee.[50] Another level of CSR involves integrating it into the fabric of the company; some companies even develop explicit processes to ensure that social issues and emerging social forces are part of their overall strategic conversation. (This process includes educating and engaging boards of directors, designing metrics for measuring outcomes, and outlining critical social issues that mesh with company strategy.)[51]

In support of their CSR goals, some companies will actively manage their implicit social contracts; this might include transparent reporting, changes in regulatory approaches, and the development of voluntary standards of behavior.

Unilever has gained visibility through its CSR program, especially its focus on sustainability. The company has refocused its 400+ brands "on the good the product can do." The counter argument to these efforts comes from their investors who saw their returns drop over several years.[52]

Another example is the carpet industry's development of environmental standards; some companies are also working to create products that are healthier for consumers and the environment. Best-in-class companies *shape* debates on social issues. CEOs are storytellers about their companies; their role in society is to set standards, not only for themselves but also for other companies. Whole Foods CEO Walter Robb regularly discusses the actions his company is taking and actively engages in conversations with industry participants and consumers about healthful food.[53] Companies, like Whole Foods, do not just create CSR strategies; as industry leaders, they pave the way to better living.

Arguments against CSR

Some company managers argue that CSR should not exist. They believe that CSR encroaches on what should be the proper work of governments, that CSR is simply a public relations (PR) ploy that takes away money from shareholder returns, and that CSR diverts attention from establishing enforceable rules that advance the common good (e.g., laws that help prevent oil spills or protect humans around the world). This argument centers around the claim that companies are repackaging work they do anyway, but in ways that are more socially acceptable.

Nike is often cited as an example of this argument.[54] A flurry of news stories in the mid-1990s described labor abuses (i.e., underage workers, safety violations, forced overtime, and generally poor conditions) in independently owned factories in China and Indonesia producing apparel and shoes for the Nike Corporation, while Nike concurrently claimed that it was socially responsible.[55] Nike, at first, argued that it had no responsibility for the labor conditions in its supply chain; they were not alone in their attitude among apparel retailers and brand name companies.[56] However, Nike changed as a result of their missteps and the resulting attention; they now have one of the most advanced and admired CSR departments and set of CSR practices of any company in the world. Morgan Stanley rated Nike best-in-class for its environmental, social, and governance behavior among all other apparel companies. This rating was part of their Sole Responsibility Index.[57]

Over the next several years, companies' attitudes toward their suppliers changed radically. Levi Strauss & Co. became the first U.S. apparel company to create and enforce a code of conduct for its suppliers; under extreme consumer and social pressure, other companies followed their lead[58] and required their suppliers to commit to various fair labor practices.

These actions can be viewed as purely PR ploys to gain good favor with the media and consumers. After all, as U.S. economist, professor, and author Milton Friedman famously declared, the sole business of managers of publicly held companies is to maximize the value of outstanding shares. For him, any effort to use corporate resources for purely altruistic purposes is a misuse of fiduciary responsibility.[59] While this free market attitude may be compelling, companies are being pressured to engage in CSR and demonstrate CSR behaviors in their actions and annual reports.

Current authors are equally firm in their messages. Former U.S. Labor Secretary Robert Reich argues that companies focused on CSR divert their attention from their primary responsibility—return to shareholders. Why do we want companies to make moral decisions by allocating shareholder money to social causes? Reich argues that companies should provide maximum returns to shareholders and then let shareholders allocate their money to these causes. If society wants companies to act in a certain manner then they need to enact legislation and capital incentives to do so.[60]

Politicians and advocates praise companies for acting "responsibly," and they condemn them when they fail to do so. However, the praise and blame are often disconnected from laws and rules defining responsible behaviors. Their messages (that companies are "moral beings" with social responsibilities) divert public attention away from their tasks of establishing laws and rules to protect citizens, consumers, and the environment; they are also generally soon forgotten, barely affect the behavior of consumers or investors, and leave the real democratic process to companies and industries seeking competitive advantages.[61]

Yet, despite Friedman's and Reich's comments, many companies appear to be changing their behaviors regardless of cost. Ultimately, as societal attitudes are increasingly favoring a more socially responsible business world, companies are increasingly being forced to participate in CSR. This is especially true when consumers begin demanding certain types of products. For example, the conversation about *free trade* vs. *fair trade* has become particularly important and instructive for understanding an organization's behavior.

Fair vs. Free Trade

Fair trade refers to corporate practices toward suppliers and guarantees that these suppliers receive fair prices (i.e., market average prices) for their goods. The practice originated from work completed by the Oxford Committee for Famine Relief (OXFAM) in the United Kingdom and the Mennonite Central Committee in Canada in the mid-20th century.[62] These organizations bought goods at fair prices directly from poor regions of the world and sold them in industrialized nations. These philanthropic efforts led to a larger movement with the intention to reform trade; it was supported by a number of organizations (e.g., the Fair Trade Labeling Organizations International [FLO], the World Fair Trade Organization [WFTO], the Network of European World Shops [NEWS], and the Fair Trade Federation [FTF]).

Several principles seem to guide this movement: (1) direct trade between importers and producers, (2) the establishment of long-term trading relationships, (3) minimum pricing, and (4) premium pricing to support social outcomes.[63] *Direct trade* increases producers' market access since they do not have to use middlemen (who decrease producers' margins). *Long-term relationships* ensure stability in producer–supplier relationships. *Minimum pricing* (the hallmark of the fair-trade movement) establishes fair prices that reflect an acceptable living wage for producers and their workers. *Premium pricing* is often a result of purchasers contributing to community and business social development projects, and it is not directly tied to product performance. Fair-trade standards also usually contain environmental requirements (e.g., resource management, compliance with progressive laws and regulations, and sustainable practices).

Prior to the fair-trade movement, farmers in developing nations had low visibility to sell their goods in more mature nations; many also had a tendency to engage in practices that Western purchasers deemed inappropriate. For example, developing-nation farmers would pay low wages and provided unsafe working conditions; some farmers would engage in unsustainable practices (e.g., exploiting fishing areas by using unsafe pesticides and not considering replenishment rates). Fairtrade Canada is one organization that sets standards defining what fair-trade products are, and it provides Canadians with a way to know whether those standards have been met and these unacceptable practices are occurring. The intent is to clarify practices of "fair trade" and "instill confidence in the public that it is not about empty promises."[64]

There are myriad examples of companies supporting the fair-trade movement. For instance, The Body Shop, a division of L'Oréal, buys 20 natural products from small producers (e.g., aloe from Guatemala and shea butter from Ghana).[65] Whole Foods, under its Whole Trade program, uses ingredients (in products like EcoPath Biodynamic soaps) that come from producers protecting the environment and workers' rights.[66] Mars candy bars use cocoa sourced from farms certified by the Rainforest Alliance (which also protects the environment and workers' rights).[67] Starbucks, one of the first companies to take a fair-trade stance, sources espresso beans for most of its drinks in the United States (and all of its drinks in Europe) from farmers in places such as Mexico and Indonesia who receive guaranteed minimum prices for their products. Additionally, Starbucks teamed with NGOs (e.g., TransFair USA and FLO) to help small-scale coffee growers develop sustainable farming practices.[68]

NGOs are also important in this effort. Groups such as the Fairtrade Foundation and Rainforest Alliance certify that suppliers are farming with minimum impacts on forests and broad ecosystems, and that they are paying workers fairly (among other certifications). More than 5,000 companies sell products with either a Fairtrade or Rainforest Alliance logo.

The global market for certified sustainable agricultural products was worth $64 billion in 2012 (up from $42 billion in 2008);[69] these agricultural products are obviously in profitable markets that are staged to expand. Even though this market is poised for growth, cautionary tales should be heeded. Aveda (a unit of Estée Lauder) sells its Uruku line of lipsticks, eye shadows, and facial bronzers made using a plant called "urukum"—a spiky fruit found in Mutum, Brazil, among the Yawanawa indigenous people. Aveda can charge a premium price for these products because they appeal to customers as beauty products *and* help save the rainforest's environment and cultures by giving the tribe a sustainable livelihood.[70] Aveda has had a two-decade relationship with the Yawanawa; this tests the idea that big firms can profit and also help the planet through such relationships.

Investigations have shown that the Yawanawa do not produce much of the urukum and delivered none of it to Aveda between 2008 and 2010. Also, urukum is really not so exotic (as Aveda portrays it). Best known as *annatto*, it is an inexpensive food coloring grown commercially around the world; it actually gives products such as Kraft Macaroni & Cheese an orange hue. Investigations further revealed that Aveda gives the Yawanawa about $500 per year for the product, which is not nearly enough to support the 700 villagers.[71] In this case, Aveda uses terms such as "fair trade" and "exotic" to entice consumers to pay for products that appear to be more socially responsible. Due to examples like this, the fair-trade movement has been strongly criticized.

Aveda is not the only company to knowingly misrepresent a product; some argue that the fair-trade movement, in general, is ineffective and needlessly increases the costs of doing business. Fair-trade practices also make up only a small fraction of total trade. In the coffee industry (the poster child for this movement), fair trade accounts for only 5 percent of total coffee sales.[72] Also, the practice of fair trade is inefficient since it requires some production practices that do not improve product quality (e.g., building housing for workers and providing schools for children improves the communities in which companies operate, but is money not invested to increase shareholder wealth through new products and processes). Finally, some fair-trade practices may include national agendas (e.g., requiring trade based on human rights issues). Some even argue that the United States should block trade with certain nations not adhering to basic human rights.

The criticism of this practice is that *free trade* (vs. *fair trade*) is the best means of facilitating change.[73] Free trade is probably the most agreed-upon principle among all economists. The argument is that unimpeded trade is wealth enhancing for every nation engaging in trade. Market prices are more reflective of efficient prices if trade among nations is allowed to occur without tariffs, quotas, and other government interventions. Here is how Adam Smith, in *The Wealth of Nations*, stated the idea:

> It is a maxim of every prudent master of a family, never to attempt to make at home what it will cost him more to make than to buy. The tailor does not attempt to make his own shoes, but buys them of the shoemaker. The shoemaker does not attempt to make his own clothes but employs a tailor . . . .

> What is prudent in the conduct of every private family can scarce be folly in that of a great kingdom. If a foreign country can supply us with a commodity cheaper than we ourselves can make it, better buy it of them with some part of the produce of our own industry employed in a way in which we have some advantage.[74]

These ideas have been transformed into theories stating that nations open to trade can attain greater production efficiencies and higher living standards by specializing in products and services with comparative advantages (i.e., it will benefit by producing goods and services yielding the highest margins compared to other producers). This free-trade idea can be tested; tests can look at whether or not open economies enjoy greater prosperity. A second approach is to study what happens when closed economies open their economies (e.g., in Central and Eastern Europe in the late 1980s). A third test is to measure the impact of trade on a nation's growth. All three approaches have shown that Adam Smith was right; openness to international trade has been shown to promote economic growth.[75]

Consumers play a large role in confronting companies and in making purchase decisions that cause firms to make changes in their business practices, including their sustainability practices. Chapter 8 contains information on the role of consumers in the demand for environmentally friendly and socially responsible products.

Some think the *fair-trade* movement's primary benefit is its ability to provide information to consumers and establish standards of practice to help organizations create effective and efficient sustainable practices and to help consumers make informed choices. At a minimum, it provides a means of bringing new producers into markets and establishing best practices in nations lacking access to world markets and consumers. Yet, there are still many societal and environmental challenges that fair trade does not address. One such challenge is overpopulation, a complicated mixture of interactions that put pressures on firms and how they do business.

Population and the Environment

Anthropogenic environmental change (i.e., change caused by humans) is as old as civilization.[76] Herodotus and William the Conqueror both wrote of this relationship. It is also the basis of the well-known Malthus hypothesis that "geometric (exponential) growth in population would outstrip the arithmetic (linear) growth in the means of subsistence."[77] Over time, population has been linked to economic, social, and environmental outcomes, and our understanding of its impact has grown significantly through scientific investigation and technology.

Table 2.1 World Vital Events per Time Unit, 2015[78]

Time unit	Births	Deaths	Natural increase
Year	134,034,782	57,179,795	76,854,987
Month	11,169,565	4,764,983	6,404,582
Day	367,219	156,657	210,562
Minute	255	109	146
Second	4.3	1.8	2.4

Population—its size and changes—affects the environment. Also, these impacts differ in developed vs. developing nations. And while population models are far from simple, we see some clear environmental outcomes of population change (e.g., population growth in arid climates uses up water before it can be replenished; this usage results in poorer water quality and a lower water supply). Thus, population growth can have a significant relation to the quality and availability of natural resources.

As of 2015, the world population was around 7.3 billion, a net increase from 2000 of 2.4 people per second. The number of births far outweighs the number of deaths (see Table 2.1).

Also, more than 98 percent of the world's population growth in 2014 was occurring in developing nations.[79] Predictions estimate that even though the percentage of growth is expected to slow by 2050 (see Figure 2.3), the overall population will continue to grow (see Figure 2.2)—probably due to the use of technology to keep people alive longer.

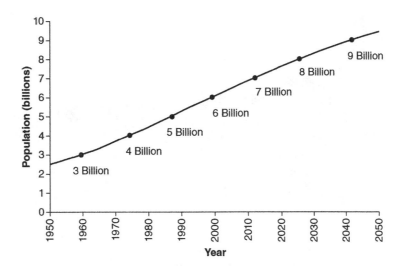

Figure 2.2 Projected Population Growth[80]

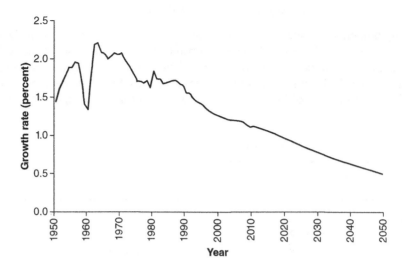

Figure 2.3 Percentage of Projected Growth[81]

Population size is only one of several important variables impacting the natural environment. Other related dynamics include changes in population *migration* and *density*. All of these factors have a big impact on the environment. *Population density* can impact resources such as air, water, and land. For example, we see high levels of ozone in densely populated areas.[82] (Ground-level ozone is the principal component of smog, which is produced from the action of sunlight on air contaminants and chemical reactions from sources such as automobile exhausts.) *Population migration* to cities is high, and there is a continuing trend toward

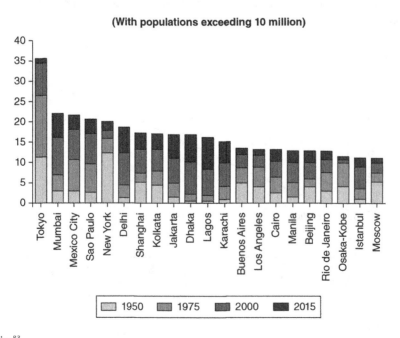

Figure 2.4 Megacities[83]

ever-larger urban agglomerations. As of 2000, 261 cities in developing countries had populations over 1 million (vs. 213 cities in the mid-1990s). In 1994, there were 14 so-called megacities worldwide (defined as cities with at least 10 million inhabitants); as of 2015 this number had reached 24 cities, and the number of people living in slums and squatter settlements is projected to double to over 3 billion by 2030. The development of megacities is most prevalent in emerging markets; this growth will intensify the environmental impacts in those nations.

The causes of population growth are varied and include a lack of accessible education in some areas (which influences literacy and fertility rates),[84] a need for financial security in old age (which means that children are sometimes considered economic assets), a lack of contraceptives, child mortality, the status of women in some societies, and other social dimensions (e.g., national policies and religious beliefs). Declining infant mortality rates are often attributed to better nutrition due to increased agricultural production and better methods of food distribution and storage. Also, clean drinking water, improved sanitation, mass inoculations, and better medicine have led to an overall decrease in mortality rates.

Population changes in the developing world have different influences than in the developed world. Hans Rosling illustrated these differences during a talk at the 2010 Technology, Entertainment and Design (TED) salon in Cannes, France.[85] His core message was that the most significant results of population changes (e.g., social, economic, and environmental) are dependent upon how the developed world handles the poorest people in the world. His reasoning was that richer nations have the means for opening up societies that are less capable of trading (providing opportunities for economic growth), and that the world would be better off if all nations grow and prosper.

While a link between the environment and the state of the population is obvious, the theories behind the link between population and environment are varied and far from clear. The most popular and well-known model is:

Environmental Impact = population size × (affluence + consumption patterns) × level of technology of the society.[86]

This "Impact, Population Size, Affluence and Technology" (IPAT) formulation fits well with the concept of carrying capacity.[87] *Carrying capacity* is how many people the planet can accommodate so that human life on earth remains sustainable. The formula links environmental impact to wealth; thus, as emerging markets' middle classes develop, so will negative environmental impacts. At the same time, as middle classes create wealth, technology will develop to offset negative environmental outcomes.

One alternative to this model shows refinements in the following terms:

Environmental Impacts = population × consumption × technology resource use × technology waste management × amount by which the environment changes in response to a given amount of resource extraction or pollution.[88]

This model is more refined because it makes distinctions in use patterns and mitigation tactics.

A third version of the link between population and environment is the pressure-state-response model.[89] This model is a systems theory showing pressures (e.g., population, consumption, and technology) that affect the environment and create outcomes through scarcity, hazards, and loss of amenities (e.g., the loss of biodiversity). Natural systems are influenced by filters (e.g., legal and economic systems) leading to societal responses such as changes in behavior and regulatory retorts.[90] Figure 2.5 shows some projections about population growth which would indicate that more and more environmental pressures will be evident in the next 50 years. Figure 2.6 shows some important relationships between population levels, growth, and various outcomes of these relationships (including outcomes on the environment).

Most theorists agree that human impacts on the natural environment are a product of population size and flows, consumption per person, and technology. These impacts are measured by how many resources are used and how much waste or pollution is produced for each unit of consumption. Throughout history, humans have enhanced their survival rates, population sizes, and lifespans by doing certain things that other living

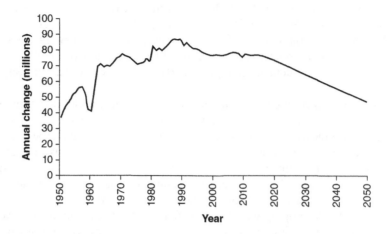

Figure 2.5 Projected Population Growth in Millions of People. Annual Change Data[91]

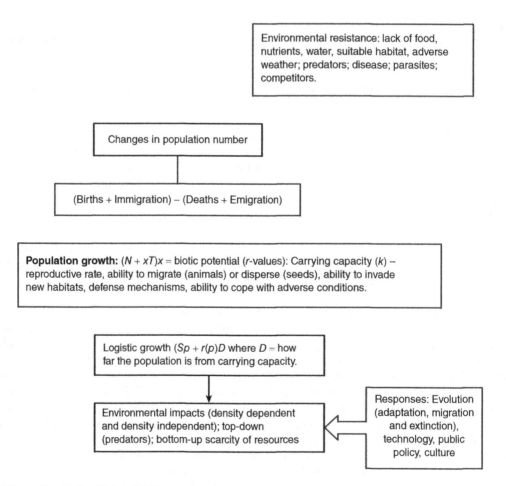

Figure 2.6 Some Population Relationships

beings cannot, for example, the recovery of fossil fuels has given us new sources of energy to improve our life conditions and medical breakthroughs have lowered child mortality. Humans have the ingenuity to solve crises and problems with new and innovative processes and products.

Some researchers believe that technological impacts are infinite and that we should not be concerned with how population affects the environment;[92] these people believe that the primary value of the natural environment is its capacity to be a resource for humans. Thus, humans may increase their carrying capacity in the short term while potentially making trade-offs that will not pay off in the long term.[93] Others believe that the earth is finite and that our natural systems are being pushed to an ever-closer limit that will compromise human existence.[94] One paper concluded that the planet's carrying capacity is 7.7 billion people,[95] a limit we are likely to exceed in the next few decades.

Developed vs. Developing Nations

Developed countries are defined as industrial and industrially advanced countries. They are sometimes defined as countries with a large stock of physical capital, with most people undertaking highly specialized activities[96] and possessing relatively high incomes and standards of living. Developing countries, according to the World Bank classification, are countries with low or middle levels of Gross National Product (GNP) per capita and include five, high-income, developing economies: Hong Kong (China), Israel, Kuwait, Singapore, and the United Arab Emirates. Despite their high per capita income, they are classified as "developing" because of their economic structure or the official opinions of their governments.[97]

We can compare and contrast these two types of countries using the following model:

Environmental Impacts = population × consumption × technology resource use × technology waste management × amount by which the environment changes in response to a given amount of resource extraction or pollution (Table 2.2).[98]

Table 2.2 shows differential trends of each part of the third model in each type of nation. For example, population growth is greater in *developing* nations than in *developed* nations. Interestingly, responses to resource depletion are uncertain because developed and developing nations have differential responses to this situation. Some developing nations (e.g., Brazil) are sensitive to the need to conserve precious resources (e.g., water) and to replace fuel types with nonpolluting resources. Other countries are less sensitive (e.g., the United States is relatively insensitive to fossil-fuel use).

Although fertility rates have declined in most world areas, population growth in some places continues to be fueled by high levels of fertility (particularly in Asia and Africa). Some nations have an especially high average number of children per woman, e.g., Niger, where the number is as high as 7.5 children. Even in areas where fertility rates have declined to near replacement levels (2.1 children per couple), population continues to grow because of "population momentum," which occurs when a high percentage of the population is young.[99]

Table 2.2 Comparison of Developing and Developed Nations Using the I = P × A × T Model

	Developed	(Greater or less)	Developing
Population size		<	
Population growth		<	
Fertility rates		<	
Death rates		<	
Consumption		>	
Technology resource use		>	
Technology waste management		>	
Amount by which the environment changes in response to a given amount of resource extraction or pollution		?	

The higher the population size, the more we can expect to reach limits on global resources (e.g., arable land, water, forests, fisheries, and fossil fuels). Decreasing farmland contributes to a growing concern about the limits of global food production. Global water consumption rose six-fold between 1900 and 1995, more than double the rate of population growth. This rate will continue. Developing nations will feel the negative impact of population size more than developed nations because these resources tend to be less available in developing nations. Therefore, more people will have access to fewer of the resources. Figure 2.6 shows the consequences of population explosions in developing countries.

The distribution of population impacts the environment in three key ways. First, less-developed regions cope with a growing share of population pressures and dwindling resources; per capita availability of resources declines as population increases. Second, migration shifts differentially impact the local environments, alleviating the strain in some areas and worsening problems in others. For example, as people migrate to the cities, rural areas' natural environments improve and those of cities potentially become worse. Third, urbanization (particularly in less-developed nations) frequently outpaces the development of infrastructure and environmental regulations (leading to haphazard and large environmental impacts).

The composition of population also has an effect on the environment. Overall, our world has the largest segment of young people (age 24 and under) and the largest proportion of elderly (age 65 and over) in history.[100] Migration patterns vary by age. Young people are more likely to move; thus, we can expect increasing levels of migration and urbanization by this group along with intensified urban environmental concerns. This migration pattern is most noticeable in developing nations where workers generally move from agricultural employment to cities, seeking higher-paying jobs and a better quality of life.

The relationship between economic development and environmental pressure resembles an inverted U-shaped curve. Middle-income nations (i.e., most developing countries) are likely to have the most powerful negative effects on the natural environment. The least-developed nations have rather insignificant impacts; highly advanced countries, like the United States, can mitigate environmental impacts by using technology and efficiencies.

Technology, policy contexts, and cultural factors in mature economies (e.g., the United States) mediate the relationship between population and the environment. For example, learning to extract and utilize fossil fuels increased the use of those types of fuels and also increased environmental challenges (e.g., pollution). The current trend toward the use of natural gas in the United States is similar to what is going on with fossil fuels; the technique of hydraulic fracturing or "fracking" to obtain gas is a controversial process.[101] Cultural variables are also important. For example, attitudes toward the environment, conservation, population control, and myriad other factors are culturally based. *Culture* primarily determines how societies resolve issues that are common to all humans. Developed and developing nations tend to have different views, in addition to nation-specific characteristics.[102] These differences in worldview often complicate or inhibit finding common solutions to current challenges.

There are myriad other impacts of population on the environment:

- Effects on climate change vary between developed and developing nations (Figures 2.7 and 2.8).
- High-density populations with more wealth create a large environmental footprint (e.g., a U.S. citizen places at least 20 times the demand on the planet's resources as does a person in Bangladesh). As developing nations increase their wealth, we can expect greater environmental challenges.
- Developed nations are more likely to practice environmental stewardship of resources.
- Wealthy nations can pass on their environmental problems to developing nations (e.g., moving waste to these countries and relocating pollution-emitting production facilities; some developed nations have actually bought land in developing nations to use as waste-dumping grounds).[103]
- Rapid population growth in developing nations influences the need for food production and, consequently, the need for land. For example, as developing nations increase in population, families subdivide their land; this action makes growing an adequate food supply difficult because there is less land for each new family. Also, new land for agriculture might not be well-suited and could be prone to soil erosion, deforestation, and loss of biodiversity.
- Increases in nonpoint water source pollution and irrigation become problematic with rises in population. (Nonpoint source water pollution affects a water body from sources such as polluted runoff from agricultural areas draining into a river, or wind-borne debris blowing onto a body of water.)

- Seventy percent of the world's water use is for irrigation. If food production continues to increase in the developing world, more water will be used for food production; therefore, less will be available for direct human consumption.

In sum, the relationship between population dynamics and environmental impact is important and complex. These effects create pressures on businesses. Many firms locate to cities to attract labor (especially employees with specific skills); however, this concentration of workers causes environmental challenges. For these reasons, some firms will more consciously locate their facilities; they see beyond just customer responsiveness and employee attraction and consider the mitigation of environmental pressures.

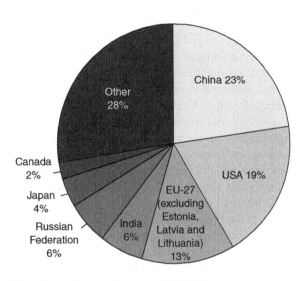

Figure 2.7 Percentage Carbon Dioxide for Various Countries (2007)[104]

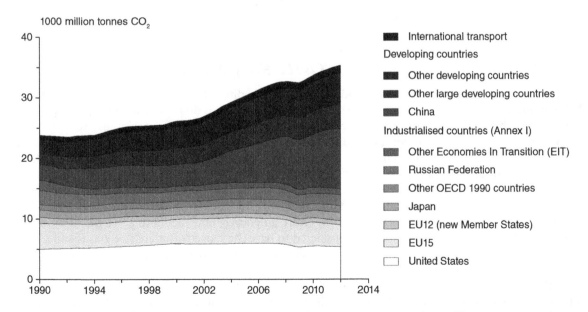

Figure 2.8 Global CO_2 Emissions per Region from Fossil-Fuel Use and Cement Production[105]

47

At the very least, population dynamics will be one important variable in the planning equation as firms decide where and how to create a sustainable world. Later chapters will include information on how businesses handle these pressures.

Chapter Summary

Pressures on companies come from social movements, other outside sources, and a sense of duty (to be good stewards of the environment). Often, that responsibility means navigating social movements (e.g., fair trade) or simply preparing their businesses to cope with social changes (e.g., challenges brought on by population fluctuations). Evidence is mounting that companies are becoming more sensitive to these social pressures and choosing to adhere to CSR principles.

Advocacy groups, governments, and the public can place significant pressures on companies to consider environmental impacts; however, the environment is unique in that it is not obvious who is responsible for speaking on its behalf. Also, companies must be accountable to various stakeholders; environmental groups are just one of these stakeholders. Some companies engage in CSR to increase their responsiveness to stakeholders and ensure their reputational capital. Some companies take CSR a step further and adopt the attitude that they are part of a larger ecosystem and if they are not engaged in larger societal issues, they will not be relevant in the long run. Companies use various methods to respond to these social pressures (e.g., partnering with NGOs, setting up CSR offices, and engaging communities through philanthropy).

Businesses with supply chains connected to other countries are increasingly aware of the use of fair-trade practices, such as paying fair prices for goods and providing access to the supply chain to companies that otherwise would be excluded from trade opportunities.

An important issue (not often on the agendas of corporations) is the relationship between population and environmental degradation. Some researchers believe that the largest environmental challenge to companies is the result of this relationship. The world's population passed the 7 billion mark in 2011; some scientists believe that within 50 years, the planet will be at its maximum carrying capacity. If this occurs, we could see mass starvation and poverty. In this case, organizations will be challenged to support communities in unprecedented ways. Regardless, population changes will always have an effect on resource availability, environmental quality, and other areas of the environment, profoundly influencing companies' abilities to attain, create, and sell products. For this reason, the relationship between population and the environment will be part of every company's planning process.[106]

Case Revisited: E+Co Has Many Opportunities

The E+Co case presents some interesting ideas for understanding organizations and their relationships to their communities. E+Co is responding to a social need; however, it is doing so with a for-profit governance structure. At this point, it might want to scale up its operations to gain efficiencies and remain competitive; given its mission and operations, it is likely to increase its scale through partnerships. E+Co has forged partnerships with like-minded organizations (e.g., Greenpeace International and the Bill & Melinda Gates Foundation). But at this point, it might need to also join with more traditional organizations (e.g., franchising or partnering with larger energy companies). Some would argue that such partnering would be a bad decision because E+Co would then be dominated by the larger companies; however, its power is in its expertise and network. Thus, it might be able to create an entirely new model to serve the "bottom of the pyramid" (i.e., those that are generally not considered to have the capacity to purchase goods and services in world markets). Also, it could look to other successful organizations that share certain commonalities (e.g., Teach for America).[107]

As E+Co develops, its social responsibility values could serve it well. For example, it might find certain opportunities and financial support because it adheres to its social values. Yet, it struggled with maintaining its capital structure and in 2012 restructured as Persistent Energy Partners located in New York City.

Profile: Hannah Jones[108]

Not long ago Nike was nearly synonymous with low wages and poor working conditions. Throughout most of the 1990s, Nike was on the defensive against countless allegations and reports of worker abuse. In 1998, at the National Press Club, Nike CEO Phil Knight discussed the company's plan to improve its labor practices and its image. In the speech, Knight announced that the company had begun using water-based cements in sole manufacturing, would meet all Occupational Safety and Health Administration (OSHA) standards for indoor air quality, had raised the minimum age of factory workers to 18, acknowledged the need for independent monitoring, expanded their education programs to include middle and high school equivalency tests for all of their workers, increased its support of the company's micro-enterprise loan program, and would fund university research and open forums to explore issues related to global manufacturing.[109]

That year a socially minded, change-agent would join the company. Prior to joining Nike, Hannah Jones had worked for BBC radio and CSV, a European NGO, where she coordinated social action campaigns ranging from AIDS/HIV awareness to racism.[110] Upon joining Nike, Jones immediately began to broker dialogue between policymakers, civil societies, and trade unions across Europe.[111]

In her early years with Nike, Jones began to realize:

> *An environmental solution could actually become a worker rights solution too. I was asked to step into the role of VP of Corporate Responsibility in late 2005. In 2009, we did a business redesign and set ourselves up as the Sustainable Business and Innovation Team (SB&I).*

The SB&I team has since fostered new capabilities in Nike's center of excellence to leverage the company's 36,000 employees and innovate new ways to make decisions based on their overarching sustainability strategy. Today, Jones is Nike's Chief Sustainability Officer and VP of the Innovation Accelerator team. As part of the company's overarching sustainability strategy, the company has devised six major impact areas:

- *Waste—Find innovative ways to use any material purchased anywhere in their supply chain that does not ultimately end up as a useful component or product, or cannot be reused at the end of product life.*
- *Energy/Climate—Understand, track, and decrease energy use and greenhouse gas emissions.*
- *Labor—Focus on long-term, strategic suppliers that demonstrate a commitment to worker engagement and well-being.*
- *Chemistry—Make products in ways that protect workers, consumers, and the environment.*
- *Water—Design products from materials that require less water to produce as well as help material vendors and contract factories reduce their water-related impacts and eliminate hazardous substance from discharging into water.*
- *Community—Leverage the power of their employees, brands, consumers, and partners to support organizations and collaborations that create positive long-term changes that expand access to sport, empower adolescent girls in the developing world, and support the communities in which they live, work, and play.[112]*

Becoming a Change-Agent. Figure 2.1 shows how external pressures influence the firm and shape its foundation. In what ways did the social pressures that Nike faced during the 1990s influence their strategy formulation? How can effective strategy formulation mitigate the external pressures the firm may face?

Terms to Know

Corporate social responsibility: method of corporate self-regulation incorporated into a business model, which assumes responsibility for not only returns to shareholders but also such things as impacts on the environment

Environmental justice: the fair treatment and meaningful involvement of all people regardless of race, color, national origin, or income with respect to development, implementation, and enforcement of environmental laws, regulations, and policies

Fair practices: corporate practices toward suppliers (guaranteeing that these suppliers receive fair prices for their goods)

Stakeholders: individuals or groups that affect (or are affected by) the achievement of business objectives

Questions and Critical Thinking

1 To what extent do you think stakeholder theory and neoclassical economic theory are at odds? For example, doesn't neoclassical economic theory suggest that one way to maximize shareowner wealth is to respond to important stakeholders?

2 What processes should companies enact to ensure they are getting accurate information about the social pressures on their firms? For example, some firms form partnerships with NGOs to gain information and insights. At the same time, giving power to these NGOs may cause problems and unnecessary exposure to criticism.

3 Does helping the planet help or hurt the poor? Should we aim at development that does no further damage to our ecosystems, wilderness, or endangered species? Or should we prioritize previous economic outcomes? For example, our fossil-fuel economy has created opportunities across the world, lifting millions out of poverty.

4 Who speaks for the environment? Who are the environment's stakeholders? Who has legitimate obligations to protect these areas?

5 To what extent do we, as a society, need to address population growth in certain areas? (Some believe that without control, our world's population will grow so large that we will see mass starvation and poverty.) Should we restrict population growth? To what extent do you see a relationship between population growth and environmental degradation?

6 Recent attention in China has focused on Beijing's pollution, which has been rated more than 255 levels above the highest level on the Air Quality Index, which is used to report daily air quality (in Beijing, it hit 755 on January 12, 2013, moderate levels are around 100).[113] A new study suggests the situation is even worse.[114] For the first time, Beijing has a plan to restrict construction and industrial activity, curb vehicle use by government officials, and order schools to limit outside activity. Should the Chinese government pay businesses subsidies to help them become more environmentally friendly (given severe situations like the one in Beijing)? Or should the Chinese government use regulations and restrictions? Or both?

Notes

1 O. Branzei and K. McKague, *E+Co: A Tipping Point for Clean Energy Entrepreneurship (A)* (London, ONT: Richard Ivey School of Business, 2007), 1.

2 EnergyAccess, "E&Co—Case study," http://energyaccess.wikispaces.com/E%26Co+-+Case+Study (accessed January 7, 2014).

3 D. Bank, "E+Co Avoids Liquidation, Barely, and Emerges Persistent," *The Huffington Post*, December 12, 2012, http://www.huffingtonpost.com/david-bank/eco-avoids-liquidation-ba_b_1932503.html (accessed December 18, 2015).

4 K. Connolly, "Environment: Turning Carbon into Cash with Offsets." *Newsweek*, December 14, 2009. www.newsweek.com/environment-turning-carbon-cash-offsets-75863 (accessed December 1, 2014).

5 D. S. Siegel and D. F. Vitaliano, "An Empirical Analysis of the Strategic Use of Corporate Social Responsibility," *Journal of Economics and Management Strategy* 16, no. 3 (2007): 773–792.

6 ForestEthics, "ForestEthics and Victoria's Secret Reach Pact on Environmental Stewardship," press release, December 7, 2006, http://www.greenbiz.com/news/2006/12/06/forestethics-and-victorias-secret-reach-pact-environmental-stewardship (accessed May 4, 2011); "Strange Bedfellows," *The Economist*, May 24, 2008, 8–9.

7 Wal-Mart, "Environmental Sustainability: Our Three Sustainability Goals," http://corporate.walmart.com/global-responsibility/environment-sustainability (accessed November 15, 2012).

8 IKEA, *The IKEA Group Approach to Sustainability: How We Manage Sustainability in our Business*. http://www.ikea.com/ms/en_US/pdf/sustainability_report/group_approach_sustainability_fy11.pdf (accessed December 18, 2015).

9 U.S. Department of State, *U.S. Climate Action Report 2010* (Washington, DC: Global Publishing Services, June 2010), 2–8, http://unfccc.int/resource/docs/natc/usa_nc5.pdf (accessed November 10, 2012).

10 D. H. Meadows, J. Randers, and D. L. Meadows, *Limits to Growth: The 30-Year Update* (White River Junction, VT: Chelsea Green, 2004).

11 T. Nordhaus and M. Shellenberger, *Break Through: From the Death of Environmentalism to the Politics of Possibility* (Boston, MA: Houghton Mifflin Co., 2007), 10.

12 M. Tereck and J. Adams, *Nature's Fortune: How Business and Society Thrive by Investing in Nature* (New York: Basic, 2013).

13 L. Westra, "Environmental Justice," *Law and Politics of Sustainability*, vol. 3 in K. Bosselmann, D. S. Fogel, and J. B. Ruhl (eds.), *Berkshire Encyclopedia of Sustainability* (Great Barrington, MA: Berkshire Publishing, 2010), 352–355.

14 A. R. Lucas, W. A. Tilleman, and E. L. Hughes (eds.), *Environmental Law and Policy* (Toronto: Emond Montgomery, 2003); see also L. Westra, *Human Rights: The Commons and the Collective* (Vancouver, BC: UBC Press, 2012).

15 U.S. Environmental Protection Agency, "Environmental Justice," www.epa.gov/oecaerth/environmentaljustice/, last updated March 20, 2014.

16 R. Bullard, *Dumping in Dixie: Race, Class and Environmental Quality* (Boulder, CO: Westview Press, 1990).

17 S. Zain Al-Mahood, "Palm-Oil Migrant Workers Tell of Abuses on Malaysian Plantations: Global Palm Oil Industry Contributes to Human Trafficking, Rights Advocates Say," *The Wall Street Journal*, July 26, 2015, http://www.wsj.com/articles/palm-oil-migrant-workers-tell-of-abuses-on-malaysian-plantations-1437933321 (accessed August 17, 2015).

18 Ibid.

19 Ibid.

20 World Commission on Environment and Development (now known as The Brundtland Commission), *Our Common Future: From One Earth to One World* (Oxford: Oxford University Press, 1987).

21 A. Pashley, "'Forgotten' forests need climate cash to halt emissions," ClimateHome, May 27, 2015, http://www.climatechangenews.com/2015/05/27/forgotten-forests-need-climate-cash-to-halt-emissions (accessed December 15, 2015).

22 R. D. Bullard, "Decision Making," in L. Westra and B. Lawson (eds.), *Faces of Environmental Racism: Confronting Issues of Global Justice*, 2nd ed. (Lanham, MD: Rowman & Littlefield, 2001), 3–28.

23 Exec. No. Order 12898, Federal Actions to Address Environmental Justice in Minority Populations and Low-Income Populations, 59 Fed. Reg. 7629 (February 11, 1994).

24 F. Biermann and S. Bauer (eds.), *A World Environment Organization: Solution or Threat for Effective Environmental Governance?* (Surrey, UK: Ashgate, 2005); A. Postiglione, *Global Environmental Governance: The Need for an International Environmental Agency and an International Court of the Environment* (Brussels: Bruylant, 2010).

25 "A Planet of Suburbs," (*The Economist*, December 6, 2014), 49.

26 *Consuming Australia: Main Findings*, Australian Conservation Foundation, 2007, p.10, http://www.acfonline.org.au/sites/default/files/resource/res_Atlas_Main_Findings.pdf (accessed December 16, 2014).

27 *Citystates: How Cities are Vital to the Future of Sustainability.* (Washington, DC: SustainAbility), 17–37.

28 Ibid.

29 R. E. Freeman, J. S. Harrison, and A. C. Hicks, *Managing for Stakeholders: Survival, Reputation, and Success* (New Haven, CT: Yale University Press, 2007).

30 M. B. E. Clarkson, "A Stakeholder Framework for Analyzing and Evaluating Corporate Social Performance," *Academy of Management Review* 20, no. 1 (January 1995): 92–117.

31 R. K. Mitchell, B. R. Agle, and D. J. Wood, "Toward a Theory of Stakeholder Identification and Salience: Defining the Principle of Who and What Really Counts," *Academy of Management Review* 22, no. 4 (October 1997): 853–886.

32 *United States* v. *Microsoft Corp.*, 253 F.3d 34 (D.C. Cir. 2001); for case history, see U.S. Department of Justice, Antitrust Case Filings, "United States vs. Microsoft Corporation," www.justice.gov/atr/cases/ms_index.htm (accessed December 20, 2011).

33 The plaintiffs, the U.S. Department of Justice and 20 U.S. states, alleged that Microsoft had abused its monopoly power with respect to Intel-based personal computers; the central issues were whether Microsoft was allowed to bundle its flagship Internet Explorer web browser software with its Windows operating system. The government argued that Internet Explorer was a distinct and separate product that did not need to be tied to the operating system. Ultimately, Microsoft had to change some of its practices related to its supply chain and product bundling.

    The European Union filed a similar lawsuit against Microsoft. Both suits, together, are estimated to have cost Microsoft over €1.6 billion (about $2.13 billion) in fines since 2004. EU Commission inquiries also included compatibility issues affecting Microsoft's servers, its Office software, and the bundling of its RealPlayer media system.

34 S. Arnott, "Microsoft Reaches Deal over Internet Browsers," *Belfast Telegraph*, December 17, 2009, 36.

35 EPA, "Environmental Justice Collaborative Model: A Framework to Ensure Local Problem-Solving," http://www3.epa.gov/environmentaljustice/resources/publications/interagency/iwg-status-02042002.pdf (accessed December 18, 2015).

36 S. Waddock, "Stakeholder Theory," *The Business of Sustainability*, vol. 2 in K. Christensen, D. S. Fogel, G. Wagner, and P. J. Whitehouse (eds.), *Berkshire Encyclopedia of Sustainability* (Great Barrington, MA: Berkshire Publishing, 2011), 422–426.

37 A. D. Braun, "Yadkin Riverkeeper Plans to Sue Alcoa," *The Business Journal*, November 9, 2011, http://www.bizjournals.com/triad/news/2011/11/09/yadkin-riverkeeper-plans-to-sue-alcoa.html (accessed November 11, 2011).

38 "Global Business Barometer: A Survey Conducted by *The Economist* Intelligence Unit on Behalf of *The Economist*," *The Economist*, November–December 2007.

39 "Just Good Business," *The Economist*, January 19, 2008, 3.

40 G. L. Clark and E. R. W. Knight, "Implications of the UK Companies Act 2006 for Institutional Investors and the Corporate Social Responsibility Movement" (unpublished paper), http://works.bepress.com/eric_knight/1 (accessed May 12, 2011).

41 United Nations, "What Is the UN Global Compact?" www.unglobalcompact.org/ (accessed May 12, 2011).

42 Economist Intelligence Unit, *Doing Good: Business and the Sustainability Challenge* (London: Economist Intelligence Unit, February 2008).

43 Mallenbaker.net, "The Dow Jones Sustainability Group Index," www.mallenbaker.net/csr/CSRfiles/djsgi.html (accessed May 12, 2011).

44 Pearson Education, InfoPlease, "Oil Spills and Disasters" (2007), www.infoplease.com/ipa/A0001451.html (accessed May 12, 2011). See also Edward Broughton, "The Bhopal Disaster and Its Aftermath: A Review," *Environmental Health* 4, no. 6 (2005): 1–6.

45 A. Ullman, "Data in Search of a Theory: A Critical Examination of the Relationship among Social Performance, Social Disclosure, and Economic Performance of U.S. Firms," *Academy of Management Review* 10 no. 3 (1985): 540–557.

46 P. L. Cochran and R. A. Wood, "Corporate Social Responsibility and Financial Performance," *Academy of Management Journal* 27, no. 1 (March 1984): 42–56; S. A. Waddock and S. B. Graves, "The Corporate Social Performance-Financial Performance Link," *Strategic Management Journal* 18, no. 4 (April 1997): 303–319.

47 D. B. Turban and D. W. Greening, "Corporate Social Performance and Organizational Attractiveness to Prospective Employees," *Academy of Management Journal* 40, no. 3 (June 1997): 658–672; D. W. Greening and D. B. Turban, "Corporate Social Performance as a Competitive Advantage in Attracting a Quality Workforce," *Business & Society* 39, no. 3 (September 2000): 254.

48 M. R. Moskowitz, "Choosing Socially Responsible Stocks," *Business & Society Review* 1, no. 1 (1972): 71–75; C. J. Fombrun, *Reputation: Realizing Value from the Corporate Image* (Boston, MA: Harvard Business School Press, 1996); C. J. Fombrun, "Building Corporate Reputation through CSR Initiatives: Evolving Standards," *Corporate Reputation Review* 8, no. 1 (Spring 2005): 7–11.

49 C. J. Fombrun, N. A. Gardberg, and M. L. Barnett, "Opportunity Platforms and Safety Nets: Corporate Citizenship and Reputational Risk," *Business & Society Review* 105, no. 1 (Spring 2000): 85–106.

50 J. Craves, "Starbucks and Conservation International," (*Coffee and Conservation: Are your Beans for the Birds?* January 12, 2006) http://www.coffeehabitat.com/2006/01/starbucks_and_c/ (accessed August 17, 2015).

51 I. Davis, "The Biggest Contract," *The Economist*, May 26, 2005, 69–71; M. E. Porter and M. R. Kramer, "Strategy and Society: The Link Between Competitive Advantage and Corporate Social Responsibility," *Harvard Business Review* 84, no. 12 (December 2006): 78–92.

52 *The Economist*. "In Search of the Good Business," *The Economist*, August 9, 2014: 55–56.

53 Several personal conversations with Walter Robb at Wake Forest University, April 2012.

54 D. L. Spar and J. Burns, *Hitting the Wall: Nike and International Labor Practices* (Boston, MA: Harvard Business School, 2000), 15.

55 P. Rivoli, *The Travels of a T-Shirt in the Global Economy*, 2nd ed. (Hoboken, NJ: John Wiley, 2009), 125–126.

56 A. Hale and J. Willis (eds.), *Threads of Labour: Garment Industry Supply Chains from the Workers' Perspective* (Malden, MA: Blackwell, 2005).

57 Morgan Stanley, "Branded Apparel and Footwear," *Sustainable and Responsible* (August 20, 2015): 3.

58 E. Bonacich and R. P. Appelbaum, *Behind the Label: Inequality in the Los Angeles Apparel Industry* (Berkeley: University of California Press, 2000).

59 H. G. Manne, "Milton Friedman Was Right," *Wall Street Journal*, November 24, 2006.

60 R. B. Reich, *Supercapitalism: The Transformation of Business, Democracy, and Everyday Life* (New York: Alfred A. Knopf), 207–208.

61 Ibid.

62 R. D. Thrasher, "Fair Trade," *The Business of Sustainability*, vol. 2 in K. Christensen, D. S. Fogel, G. Wagner, and P. J. Whitehouse (eds.), *Berkshire Encyclopedia of Sustainability*, 218.

63 A. Nicholls and C. Opal, *Fair Trade: Market-Driven Ethical Consumption* (Thousand Oaks, CA: Sage, 2005), 33–34.

64 Fair Trade Canada, "What is Fair Trade?" http://web.fairtrade.ca/en/about-fairtrade/what-fair-trade (accessed December 15, 2015).

65 "The Body Shop Values Report 2007," The Body Shop, www.scribd.com/doc/11569837/The-Body-Shop-Values-Report-2007 (accessed January 8, 2012).

66 A. Lomax, "Fair's Fair at Whole Foods," *The Motley Fool*, April 2, 2007, www.fool.com/investing/general/2007/04/02/fairs-fair-at-whole-foods.aspx (accessed June 15, 2011).

67 *Dark Armadillos of the Soul, Daily Kos,* "Did You Hear About the Tainted Candy?" blog entry by Jaxpagan, October 27, 2011, www.dailykos.com/story/2011/10/27/1027941/-Did-You-Hear-About-the-Tainted-Candy (accessed May 1, 2012).

68 "Starbucks and TransFair USA Enter into Breakthrough Alliance to Promote Fair Trade Certified Coffee," Business Wire, April 10, 2000, www.thefreelibrary.com/Starbucks+and+TransFair+USA+Enter+into+Breakthrough+Alliance+to . . . -a061391661 (accessed November 1, 2011).

69 EcoAgriculture Partners, www.ecoagriculture.org/ (accessed May 10, 2011). "Ecoagriculture" is a term coined in 2000 by Jeffrey A. McNeely and Sara J. Scherr in *Common Ground, Common Future: How Ecoagriculture Can Feed the World and Save Wild Biodiversity* (Collingdale, PA: Diane Publishing, 2001) www.ecoagriculture.org/greatest_hits_details.php?id=867 (accessed December 1, 2012). H. Willer and L. Lernoud eds., *The World of Organic Agriculture. Statistics and Emerging Trends 2014* (BiBl-IFOAM Report, Bonn, Germany, 2014): 13. https://www.fibl.org/fileadmin/documents/shop/1636-organic-world-2014.pdf (accessed October 29, 2014). Ecoagriculture is a conservation strategy and a rural development strategy.

70 J. Lyons, "Skin-Deep Gains for Amazon Tribe," *Wall Street Journal*, May 5, 2011, A1, A14.

71 Ibid.

72 M. Sidwell, *Unfair Trade* (London: Adam Smith Institute, 2008) www.adamsmith.org/sites/default/files/images/pdf/unfair_trade.pdf (accessed November 1, 2011).

73 J. E. Stiglitz and A. Charlton, *Fair Trade for All: How Trade Can Promote Development* (New York: Oxford University Press, 2005).

74 A. Smith, *An Inquiry into the Nature and Causes of the Wealth of Nations*, ed. Edwin Cannan (London: Methuen & Co., 1904/1776), I.11.47–I.11.52, http://www.econlib.org/library/Smith/smWN5.html#I.11.47.

75 Ibid. See also J. D. Sachs and A. Warner, "Economic Reform and the Process of Global Integration," *Brookings Papers on Economic Activity* (Washington, DC: The Brookings Institution, 1995): 3, http://www.brookings.edu/~/media/Projects/BPEA/1995%201/1995a_bpea_sachs_warner_aslund_fischer.PDF (accessed December 15, 2015).

76 T. Dietz and E. A. Rosa, "Rethinking the Environmental Impacts of Population, Affluence and Technology," *Human Ecology Review* 1, no. 2 (Summer 1994): 277–300.

77 Herodotus, *The History of Herodotus*, vol. 6 of *Great Books of the Western World*, trans. G. Rawlinson (Chicago: Encyclopedia Britannica, 1952), 1–341; J. R. Weeks, *Population: An Introduction to Concepts and Issues*, 3rd ed. (Belmont, CA: Wadsworth, 1986); T. R. Malthus, *An Essay on the Principle of Population*, ed. A. Flew (New York: Penguin Classics, 1985/1798).

78 U.S. Census Bureau, "International Data Base World Events," https://www.census.gov/population/international/data/idb/worldvitalevents.php (accessed June 9, 2015).

79 A "population" is a group of members of the same species living together in an area; a "community" is composed of populations of different species living together in an area.

80 International Programs. International Database. Census.gov Midyear Population. The population estimate is for July 1 of the given year, http://www.census.gov/population/international/data/idb/informationGateway.php (accessed August 17, 2015).

81 L. M. Hunter, *The Environmental Implications of Population Dynamics* (Santa Monica, CA: Rand, 2000).

82 See AirNow.gov for local air quality indexes (AQI) and forecasts.

83 National Geographic. Rare Video: Japan Tsunami, http://video.nationalgeographic.com/video/news/japan-tsunami-2011-vin (accessed July 15, 2014).

84 The World Bank, "Adolescent Fertility Rate (Births Per 1,000 Women Ages 15–19)," table, http://data.worldbank.org/indicator/SP.ADO.TFRT (accessed December 20, 2011).

85 H. Rosling, "Global Population Growth, Box by Box," TED: Ideas Worth Spreading, video, June 2010, www.ted.com/talks/hans_rosling_on_global_population_growth.html (accessed December 20, 2011).

86 R. T. Wright and D. F. Boorse, *Environmental Science: Toward a Sustainable Future*, 11th ed. (Boston, MA: Benjamin Cummings, 2011), 201.

87 Carrying capacity is the maximum population of a species that a given habitat can support without being degraded over the long term.

88 American Association for the Advancement of Science, "The Theory of Population-Environment Links," in *AAAS Atlas of Population & Environment* (Los Angeles: University of California Press, 2001), http://atlas.aaas.org/index.php?part=1&sec=theory (accessed December 19, 2011).

89 Ibid., 10.

90 L. M. Hunter, *Population and Environment: A Complex Relationship.* Population Matters Policy Brief RB-5045 (Santa Monica, CA: Rand Corporation, 2000), http://www.rand.org/pubs/research_briefs/RB5045/index1.html, accessed December 19, 2011.

91 Ibid.

92 J. L. Simon, *The Ultimate Resource* (Princeton, NL: Princeton University Press, 1981).

93 J. E. Cohen, *How Many People Can the Earth Support?* (New York: Norton, 1995).

94 National Academies Press, *Population Summit of the World's Scientific Academies* (National Academies Press, 1993), http://www.nap.edu/openbook.php?record_id=9148 (accessed December 19, 2011).

95 J. C. J. M. van Den Bergh and P. Rietveld, "Reconsidering the Limits to World Population: Meta-analysis and Meta-prediction," *BioScience* 54, no. 3 (March 2004): 195.

96 According to the World Bank classification, these include all high-income economies except Hong Kong (China), Israel, Kuwait, Singapore, and the United Arab Emirates. Depending on who defines them, developed countries may also be middle-income countries with transition economies, because these excepted countries are highly industrialized. Developed countries contain about 15 percent of the world's population. They are also sometimes referred to as "the North." See definition of "Developed countries (industrial countries, industrially advanced countries)" in "Glossary," T. P. Soubbotina, *Beyond Economic Growth: An Introduction to Sustainable Development*, 2nd ed. (Washington, DC: IBRD/The World Bank, September 2000), 132–133, www.worldbank.org/depweb/english/beyond/global/glossary.html (accessed December 19, 2011).

97 Several countries with transition economies are sometimes grouped with developing countries based on their low or middle levels of per capita income; sometimes, because of their high industrialization, they are grouped with developed countries. More than 80 percent of the world's population lives in the more than 100 developing countries. "Glossary: Developing countries," ibid.

98 American Association for the Advancement of Science, "The Theory of Population-Environment Links."

99 Hunter, *Population and Environment*.

100 Wright and Boorse, *Environmental Science*, 210–216.

101 Union of Concerned Scientists, "EPA Findings on Hydraulic Fracturing Deemed 'Unsupportable,'" www.ucsusa.org/scientific_integrity/abuses_of_science/oil-extraction.html, accessed December 20, 2011; The Center for Media and Democracy, Source Watch, "Fracking," www.sourcewatch.org/index.php?title=Fracking (last modified March 21, 2014).

102 This is evidenced by world organizations such as the World Bank, UN, WTO, and others classifying these nations into developed and developing nations.

103 T. Granger, "Study Shows E-waste in Developing Countries Is on the Rise" (Earth911.com, May 11, 2010), http://earth911.com/news/2010/05/11/study-shows-e-waste-in-developing-countries-is-on-the-rise/ (accessed December 20, 2011).

104 Global Greenhouse Emission Data, CO_2 Emissions Per Country, EPA (EPA Climate Change, 2007), accessed September 20, 2015.

105 European Commission, "Trends in Global CO_2 Emissions," Joint Research Centre, PBL Netherlands Environmental Assessment Agency, 2013 Report, http://edgar.jrc.ec.europa.eu/news_docs/pbl-2013-trends-in-global-co2-emissions-2013-report-1148.pdf (accessed July 21, 2015).

106 Persistent Energy Partners. About. http://www.persistentenergypartners.com/about/ (accessed December 3, 2014).

107 See Teach For America, www.teachforamerica.org/ (accessed November 1, 2011).

108 Co-authored by Michael Aper, Master of Arts in Sustainability candidate at Wake Forest University.

109 "Nike In the Global Economy," C-Span, May 12, 1998, http://www.c-span.org/video/?105477–1/nike-global-economy (accessed on January 21, 2015).

110 "Hannah Jones," LinkedIn ®, https://www.linkedin.com/pub/hannah-jones/4/430/6b2 (accessed January 21, 2015).

111 "How She Leads: Hannah Jones of Nike," GreenBiz, February 6, 2012, http://www.greenbiz.com/blog/2012/02/06/how-she-leads-hannah-jones-nike (accessed January 21, 2015).

112 Nike Inc., "About: Sustainability," http://about.nike.com/pages/sustainability (accessed January 21, 2015).

113 W. Ma, "Beijing Pollution Hits Highs," *Wall Street Journal*, January 12, 2013, A10.

114 "Mapping the Invisible Scourge," *The Economist*, August 15, 2015: 40.

3

ENVIRONMENTAL REGULATION AND ITS IMPACT ON ORGANIZATIONS

Duke Energy Merges with Progress Energy

Historically, public utilities were privately owned yet controlled by public entities, which is a practice that has carried over to modern times. Modern public utility regulation originated with ferries, sewers, mills, bridges, and railroads, which were often privately owned in early America as well as in England.[1] This is also how Duke Energy and Progress Energy are regulated. These two companies provide electricity to several southern states and charge customers rates for electricity according to the state's public utility commission agreements. Based in Charlotte, North Carolina, Duke Energy owns 58,200 megawatts of base-load and peak generation in the United States, which it distributes to its 7.1 million customers. It has approximately 33 percent of the market share in North Carolina.[2]

The U.S. Supreme Court has increasingly allowed governments to regulate a wider range of businesses, and this has coincided with the development of new technologies for generating and distributing energy. Common-law rules applying to public utilities are:

1 Service to the public. *A public utility operates a business that is thought to provide a service to the public.*
2 Monopoly power. *A public utility has the legal (or de facto) authority to prevent other businesses from competing with it.*
3 Fixed territory. *A geographical boundary is defined for providing service.*
4 Technological limits. *As technology changes, the nature of a business's monopoly may be narrowly construed.*
5 Duty to serve. *The business has a duty to serve all members of the public (but only the specific service defined by the monopoly status).*
6 Reasonable prices. *Rates charged by public utilities, which common law requires be reasonable, may be regulated by the legislative branch.*

On July 1, 2012, Duke Energy and Progress Energy merged; the merger had been in process for more than two years. The Federal Energy Regulatory Commission (FERC), which is the main federal regulatory body over the electric utilities, had to approve the merger and associated plans along with each affected state. On the day of the merger, customers of now the largest utility company in the United States got a big surprise. The new CEO, Bill Johnson, was fired and received a severance package of more than $45 million. Jim Rogers, the previous Duke Energy CEO, took over (despite his previous announcement that he would retire).

This surprising change in leadership created a firestorm. The North Carolina Utility Commission quickly scheduled a hearing, called several Duke employees and board members to testify about what had happened, and worked to determine if any illegal activity occurred during or after the merger. Citizens called for reversing the merger. Many felt deceived by the Duke board; they wanted the board to be held accountable. The public utility commission also came under scrutiny. Duke Energy argued that it had responsibilities to the shareowners, and that the public utility commission could not dictate how the company operated.

Chapter Overview

This chapter examines regulatory pressures on firms within U.S. jurisdictions, including U.S. firms operating in global marketplaces. The focus, here, is mainly on how to classify environmental regulations and understand their varied impacts on firms. Also, this chapter discusses how firms respond to regulations and court decisions.

At the end of this chapter, you should be able to:

1 identify some of the market failures that may harm environmental efforts;
2 compare and contrast command-and-control (CAC) and market-based regulatory efforts;
3 compare and contrast the costs and benefits of legislation;
4 specify how companies typically respond to regulations.

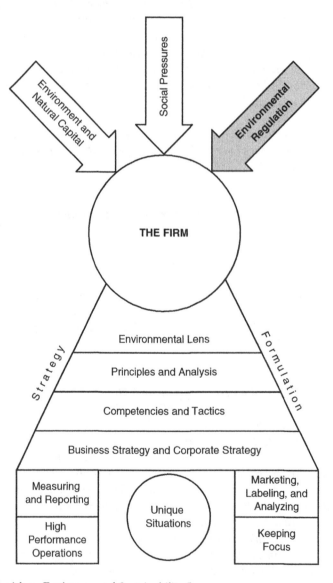

Figure 3.1 Strategy Model with an Environmental Sustainability Lens

Many Americans believe that government regulation is necessary for ensuring that businesses consider and address environmental issues, and polls show the positive sentiment of U.S. citizens toward governmental regulations protecting the environment. When asked: "Would you favor or oppose Congress passing new legislation this year to regulate energy output from private companies in an attempt to reduce global warming," 56 percent of Americans responded that they would favor such an idea, and 40 percent said they would not.[3] The Pew Research/National Journal Congressional Connection Poll found that 56 percent of Americans favored protecting the environment in response to this question: "Which one of the following do you think should be the most important priority for U.S. energy policy: keeping energy prices low or protecting the environment?"[4]

However, the relationship between businesses and lawmakers remains complex and involves numerous factors for consideration by both parties. This chapter seeks to outline some of these complexities and offers suggestions for improving environmental regulations that will satisfy some of the concerns of both companies and citizens. This chapter focuses on legal regulations and issues in the USA. This focus helps to keep the conversation consistent.

Market Failure Can Cause Market Distortions

Most economists and analysts believe that markets are relatively efficient. It is believed that for any initial allocation of resources, a competitive process of exchange among individuals via input or output markets will lead to economically efficient outcomes. A competitive system (i.e., built on the self-interested goals of consumers and producers and transparent pricing) will achieve an efficient allocation of resources for all parties in the market.[5] However, these outcomes might or might not be equitable.

In truth, competitive markets often fail for several reasons. For example, they can fail to include important information about products, services, and unaccounted "costs" in the pricing of products and services. These failures are critical to our conversation about environmental sustainability because market failures often occur when natural resources are not properly considered in business strategies (i.e., the use of resources is not taken into account when prices are calculated).

I will discuss, here, the most prominent reasons for market failure related to environmental sustainability. After outlining the reasons, I will suggest a few tactics that can offset these failures. Later in this chapter, I will explain how government regulation plays a role in this equation.

Incomplete Information Can Cause Market Distortions

If consumers do not have complete information about a product or service, they cannot make good decisions. In the current mature market, there are some regulations related to what companies must disclose about their products, but there is much information (e.g., environmental footprints and certain nutrition facts) that companies are not obligated to disclose. PepsiCo has been reengineering some of its snack foods; their program "Performance with Purpose" is attempting to design foods that are healthier, tastier, and more profitable for Pepsi with lower quantities of such ingredients as sugar and salt.[6] Much of this information is communicated only on standard labels that do not usually reflect the innovations companies such as Pepsi are implementing. Similarly, firms such as Wal-Mart and Nestlé are considering labeling that shows the environmental impacts of their products so consumers can make informed choices. These labels would have information different from the standard nutritional facts on current labels.

Incomplete information leads to *adverse selection* when products of different qualities are sold for a single price because buyers and sellers are not sufficiently informed to determine the true value. A company's reputation is critical when there is incomplete information; a lack of information forces consumers to trust the seller. An obvious example of this is when you hire a plumber or electrician; you generally would not know whether they complete work at a high standard until you can test the functionality of the finished work. Because most individuals do not want to wait until the work is done to ensure quality, they must rely on reputation. Reputation is also important when buying products because we often buy a particular product based on what we know or feel about a company. So *branding* is a critical tool companies use to communicate their reputations (by presenting promises to consumers about a product's quality). In this way, it becomes a means for overcoming market failure due to incomplete information.

When firms cannot market themselves based on reputation, they tend to use other means of letting customers know about their products, such as standardization. Creating standard ways to present a product or using common sales techniques, such as guarantees, helps consumers gain confidence that a product's price accurately reflects its value. Also, sellers use market signals (e.g., quality seals). We will discuss the use of this technique further when we take a closer look at quality seals for environmental goods and services (see Chapter 9).

Externalities: Unaccounted Costs

Another reason for market failures is what economists call *externalities* or *unaccounted costs*. Sometimes market prices do not reflect activities of either producers or consumers. This occurs when a consumption or production activity has an indirect effect on other consumption or production activities not reflected directly in market prices; the cost is then absorbed external to the market that caused the cost. One of the most obvious examples of *unaccounted costs* impacting the environment is pollution. A chemical plant may dump waste into a stream causing recreation sites downstream to be unsuitable for recreation; the producer does not bear the true cost of this impact absent regulation.

There are many tactics for combating pollution that ultimately cut down on unaccounted costs. An emission standard, created usually by federal governments, provides a legal limit on how much pollution a firm is allowed to emit; if the firm exceeds it, it can face monetary or even criminal charges. The firm could install abatement equipment and procedures (or change inputs and production materials) as long as the fines and penalties are higher than the cost of abatement. Otherwise, they may delay expenditures to avoid unnecessary costs. Another technique is the federal and state governments charging *upfront fees* that force companies to make environmentally friendly choices.

Different countries have different preferences as to how to make firms absorb these costs. The United States tends to use standards; countries such as Germany and Spain tend to use fees. The U.S. EPA has most often provided specific pollution standards for various industries and provides incentives to buy renewable energy. (I will provide an in-depth explanation of one such U.S. system at the end of this chapter.) The German government, on the other hand, provides energy resource providers with incentives via a *feed-in-tariff*

Table 3.1 Regulatory Foci and Corporate Environmentalism in the United States[7]

Focus	Approximate dates	Sample legislation and agencies
Operating line function for environment within companies; ancillary to company strategy	1960–1970	
Command-and-Control (CAC), focused on conservation and ecology, technology-based standards, companies focused on compliance and created separate functions within organizations to focus on compliance	1970–1980	Environmental Protection Agency established; Safe Drinking Water Act; Toxic Substances Control Act; Resource Conservation and Recovery Act Superfund
Criminal enforcement; forced disclosures; social responsibility more prevalent among organizations; organizational environmental protection—cost, liability, public scrutiny and impact on regulations	1980–1990	Pollution Prosecution Act of 1990
Market-based incentives; some evidence of companies considering environmental issues in a strategic manner	1990–2000	Deposit Fund Systems for Recycling; Marketable Permit Systems
Global-based solutions, change to cooperative stance, NGO involvement in companies, communities	2000–present	Kyoto and beyond, Stimulus Fund in the U.S., EPA becomes stronger

(i.e., energy distributors are required to pay a premium to renewable energy producers and purchase the energy source). The feed-in tariff is like a tax to encourage energy providers to use renewable energy sources.

Each technique depends on the ability of regulators to set accurate standards and balance the costs of compliance with the costs of noncompliance. When a government has limited information about the costs and benefits of pollution abatement, a standard *or* a fee could be preferable; a standard would be preferable when the marginal social cost curve is steep and the marginal cost curve is relatively flat (i.e., money spent per unit of emissions increases rapidly when the level of emissions increases, yet the marginal costs to producers does not change very much when the level of emissions changes).

Company responses to environmental regulations vary and are covered at the end of this chapter. First, however, consider why regulation exists at all.

Regulation and Environmentalism

The focus of government regulation has changed dramatically over the last 50 years. Major changes have mirrored public sentiment about why regulation is important. Table 3.1 summarizes some of these changes.

The history of environmental regulation is well documented in various sources;[8] a few generalizations about regulation, its history, and the types of regulation will explain how we arrived at our current state of regulation in the early 21st century. While the regulatory focus may have changed over the years, many earlier laws are still in effect and important to organizations as they try to comply with mandates and the agencies enforcing regulations (see Appendix 3.1 and Appendix 3.2 for a summary of major environmental laws influencing companies).

Environmental laws and regulations seek to protect, restore, and preserve, natural capital working throughout the atmosphere, hydrosphere (i.e., oceans, seas, lakes, ponds, rivers, and streams), and the lithosphere (the outer, solid part of the Earth, including the crust and uppermost mantle). Chapter 1 demonstrated that the world has interrelated cycles involving such resources as water, carbon, oxygen, nitrogen, phosphorous, and sulfur. Any system disturbances can disrupt other parts of a cycle or system. This fact is at the core of the creation of environmental laws.

Environmental protection laws have two primary goals: preventing irreparable environmental damage and forcing the consideration of environmental values into private and commercial activities.[9] These foci became important in the United States around 60 years ago when large groups of people began recognizing that environmental protection was imperative to preserving social and cultural values and the planet's natural resources. The National Environmental Policy Act of 1969 was established to provide "all Americans safe, healthful, productive, and aesthetically and culturally pleasing surroundings."[10] This Act resulted in additional legislation (e.g., the Clean Air Act and Clean Water Act).

The concern of most companies is that new political administrations, public sentiment, and global impacts tend to make environmental legislation a somewhat whimsical and hard-to-hit target. This lack of clarity causes companies to be hesitant about investing in environmental improvements (e.g., 2013 and 2014 EPA regulations have been unclear about how companies should comply with the reporting of CO_2 emissions; this uncertainty has delayed firms' investments in new technologies [e.g., carbon capture]).

Regulators tend to be more consistent and have several structural options to achieve the two primary goals for environmental protection. *Prescriptive regulation* or *CAC* focuses on regulating the behavior of individual facilities and plants rather than providing incentives. One characteristic of this approach is that it requires firms to use particular pollution abatement technologies (e.g., in the United States, the Clean Air Act Amendments of 1990 required new electric power plants to install large scrubbers to remove sulfur dioxide from the flue gases). Another prescriptive characteristic is to impose *performance standards* (e.g., a ceiling on a firm's emissions), capping how much pollution can be emitted from a plant. Regulators sometimes combine these approaches to get the best available regulatory outcomes, and they consider various factors, especially the costs of monitoring and enforcing their standards.

Other methods of regulation include *market-based* or *incentive-based instruments*. These instruments are more contemporary, incorporate market principles into government policies, and are much more decentralized than CAC mechanisms, focusing instead on aggregate or market-level outcomes (e.g., total effluents in water).

Allowable trading is a characteristic of market-based regulation and is sometimes referred to as *cap and trade*. The usual process of cap and trade is that the government establishes a total allowable quantity of pollution (the cap) for a group of firms. It then allocates allowances to regulated firms, with each allowance corresponding to a unit of pollution. At the end of a period of time (usually a year), a firm must retire one allowance for each unit of pollution they have emitted during that period. Firms having difficulty meeting their allowance limits can buy allowances from other firms and reduce their pollution at a lower cost. The total amount of pollution allowed is fixed by regulation; however, allocation of that pollution among firms is left to the market.

Cap and trade has many variations in how allowances are allocated initially, distributed, and priced. Programs vary as to whether firms can save their excess allowances and what industries are included and not included in the regulation. Figure 3.2 explains the European Union Emission Trading Scheme (EU ETS), the largest cap-and-trade system in the world.

Figure 3.2 shows that the Kyoto Protocol is the impetus for the EU ETS. The Kyoto Protocol is an international agreement linked to the United Nations Framework Convention on Climate Change (UNFCC). The Protocol's major feature is that it set binding targets for 37 industrialized countries and the European Union (EU) for reducing GHG emissions. The major distinction between the Protocol and Convention is that the Convention encourages industrialized countries to stabilize GHG emissions; however, the Protocol *commits* them to do so.[11]

EU companies try to comply with the Kyoto Protocol through a cap-and-trade system, using offsets or other mechanisms to attain reductions. Market participants are varied and include operating firms, carbon funds, and offset aggregators; each of these entities uses a variety of emission commodities to trade on markets or to verify their emissions levels. The EU trading scheme is of great interest to all nations around the world as it is the largest and most complex attempt to use markets to solve environmental challenges. Unfortunately, the world's largest carbon market has been a "mess."[12] In Europe, the EU ETS carbon spot price was below €5 (about $6.65) in early 2013, causing concerns among European policymakers that without further government support, the market would collapse.

Another technique, which has gained popularity in the last 15 to 20 years, is simply providing more information to consumers; this effort not only helps firms better comply with regulations but also addresses one of the market failures discussed earlier. *Right-to-know laws* require the information provision by private firms (e.g., the EPA has recently required firms to release information on CO_2 emissions).[13] *Eco-labeling* and *certification programs* fall under this technique and inform consumers about how various products were manufactured or the environmental characteristics of certain assets (e.g., the building where a firm operates). Many programs providing certifications are run by NGOs and therefore tend to be voluntary rather than mandatory. Regardless, firms adopting this approach are beginning to address information gaps in the marketplace. (Chapter 9 includes more information on eco-labeling mechanisms.)

Enforcement behind various types of CAC or market-based regulation can be either governmental organizations or NGOs. Both exert pressure on companies to obtain a certain level of environmental stewardship. In the United States, the EPA is the most important and prominent government agency for environmental regulation, created by Congress in 1970 (during the Nixon administration), and administers nine major environmental statutes that were passed by Congress between 1969 and 1980:

- Clean Air Act (CAA);
- Comprehensive Environmental Response, Compensation, and Liability Act (also known as the Superfund) (CERCLA);
- Federal Insecticide, Fungicide and Rodenticide Act (FIFRA);
- Federal Water Pollution Control Act (also known as the Clean Water Act);
- Marine Protection, Research and Sanctuaries Act (MPRSA);
- Noise Control Act of 1972;
- Safe Drinking Water Act;[14]
- Solid Waste Act, known as Resource Conservation and Recovery Act (RCRA);
- Toxic Substances Control Act (TSCA).

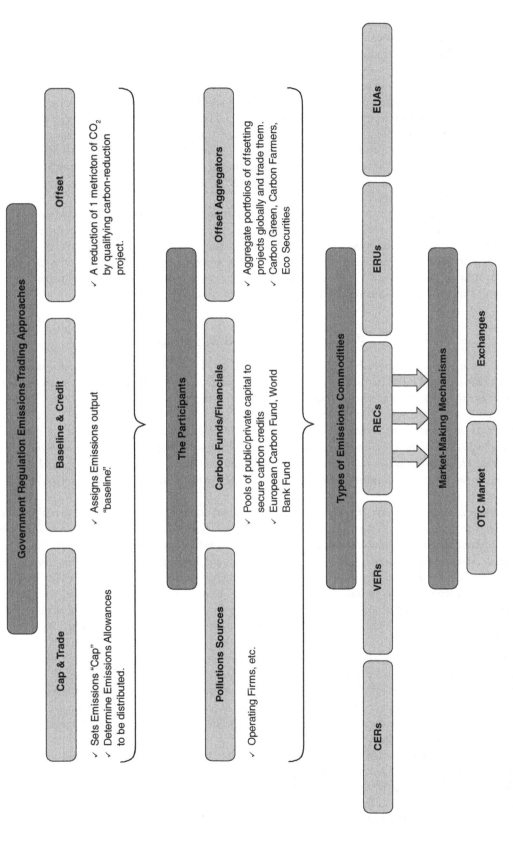

Figure 3.2 European Union Emissions Trading Scheme

The executive action creating the EPA transferred existing executive branch functions from other agencies to the EPA. The EPA establishes and administers pollution-control regulations in the absence of an enumerated, comprehensive federal environment strategy. Thus, each Act includes administrative mandates that the EPA must carry out.

In 2011, the EPA began to regulate CO_2 and other GHG emissions. Several news articles stated that this move represented an unconstitutional power grab that would kill millions of jobs.[15] Congressional and business leaders are trying to overturn the EPA's proposed GHG regulations.[16] The House of Representatives Committee on Oversight and Government Reform asked trade associations and businesses to disclose the proposed or existing regulations that bothered them the most. The organizations had a litany of complaints; however, they cited the EPA most frequently. Among the most-cited complaints was the EPA's role in regulating GHGs, emissions from industrial boilers, pollutants in Chesapeake Bay, coal ash, ground-level ozone, and nutrients in Florida water.[17]

Thus, the relationship between government regulation and companies is still strained even after 50 years of policymaking and regulation. It is a conflict rooted in the endless debate over whether the responsibility to protect the environment should be left up to capitalistic companies or governments. While the government will clearly remain a key player in protecting the environment, both companies and the government must figure out how to analyze costs and benefits to create effective policies to protect the environment. The next section will explain the relationship between costs and benefits.

Profile: Advocacy and Bill McKibben

Bill McKibben is an author and environmentalist recognized for his activist stance on climate change. He designed his book The End of Nature *in 1989 for a wide audience interested in climate change or for those uninformed about the pending dangers of increased and human-induced CO_2 into our atmosphere.[18] He founded 350. org, a planet-wide, grassroots climate change movement.[19] His is currently the Schumann Distinguished Scholar in Environmental Studies at Middlebury College and a fellow of the American Academy of Arts and Sciences. He won the 2013 Gandhi Prize and the Thomas Merton Prize, and holds honorary degrees from 18 colleges and universities. He has other accolades; for example,* Foreign Policy *named him in their inaugural list of the world's 100 most important global thinkers,[20] and the* Boston Globe *said he was "probably America's most important environmentalist."[21]*

McKibben is one of many activists who travel the world advocating that we must stop using fossil fuels to prevent a pending disaster from climate change. For example, he wrote "Global Warming's Terrifying New Math."[22] McKibben presents three numbers in this article: 2° Celsius (limit of warming before disaster hits), 565 gigatons ("scientists estimate that humans can pour roughly 565 more gigatons of CO_2 into the atmosphere by mid-century and still have some reasonable hope of staying below two degrees"); and 2,795 gigatons ("The number describes the amount of carbon already contained in the proven coal and oil and gas reserves of the fossil-fuel companies, and the countries (think Venezuela or Kuwait) that act like fossil-fuel companies. In short, it's the fossil fuel we're currently planning to burn. And the key point is that this new number—2,795—is higher than 565. Five times higher.").[23]

McKibben's amazing dedication to a cause is not without criticism. Some view activists such as McKibben as not being objective about the science of climate change. Other activists, such as Vandana Shiva, who advocates for non-GMO foods,[24] have been criticized for ignoring data counter to her arguments.[25] Her response to the criticism does not further the GMO science but appears like a defense of her character.[26] Other people such as James Hansen, former NASA scientist, have created this bridge between public policy and science for climate change regulation and have been equally criticized.

Finally, several authors stated that America's environmental problems have been manageable problems and that alarmists have caused a distortion in our policy conversations.[27]

What do you see as the positive and negative outcomes of having people do both science and policy advocacy? Is this dual work necessary to create the changes we need to have more positive environmental outcomes? Or is this dual role one that distorts science and policy?

Weighing Economic Efficiency and Environmental Protection

Imagine that you have been asked to evaluate ways of reducing pollution in your community. You decide to take the approach of focusing on net benefits (an approach most regulators would also take). For example, the difference between the total benefits of cleaner air and the total costs of reducing emissions would yield the best "net" policy to pursue.

The efficient level of pollution abatement achieves the greatest possible net benefit. The net benefit from a given level of pollution control is measured by the vertical distance from the benefit curve down to the cost curve. At low levels of pollution control, net benefits are small. As abatement increases, benefits increase more rapidly at first (vs. costs), so net benefits increase. As more and more abatement is done, however, the benefits rise less rapidly, while the costs of abatement increase. Eventually the benefits increase more slowly than costs, and net benefits fall as more abatement is done.[28] This information demonstrates that there is a stage when the cost of protecting the environment begins to outweigh benefits from protecting it.[29]

We find that the economic efficiency level of pollution control is *not* zero; this means that, at some point, the gains are not worth the extra costs. Most economists would advocate moving toward marginal benefits equaling marginal costs. Therefore, the efficient level of pollution control is where extra benefits of the last unit of abatement equal its extra cost. Beyond that, additional costs of any further abatement outweigh the benefits.

Cost-and-benefit equations apply to a wide range of environmental issues (e.g., water pollution, biodiversity preservation, endangered species protection, air quality, and the management of natural resources such as fisheries and forests). Therefore, we must understand how to measure the various costs and benefits of environmental actions.

Measuring Costs

True costs are *opportunity costs* (i.e., what you give up by doing one thing instead of another). The true value of electricity, for example, includes capital to pay for the construction of electricity-generating plants and money that could have gone into alternative investments. Therefore, when companies dedicate resources to pollution control, there is less money to spend on other things. While corporations generally pay for the initial costs of such things as pollution control, consumers bear the burden in the end because a corporation's costs are reflected in the end prices of products and services (e.g., electric utilities typically recover much of the cost of pollution control by charging higher rates for electricity). This pricing process for recovering costs is a cycle because the consumption of goods or services by the consumer causes pollution in the first place.

A firm measures the costs of pollution, or it uses data on revenues and production costs to estimate lost profits or diminished productivity associated with environmental protection (assuming that profits forgone are equivalent to costs incurred). These types of costs often stretch beyond the obvious (e.g., some companies might bear the cost of endangered species protection, which includes preserving habitats, enforcement, and public education). These types of actions affect a company's bottom line as well as the consumer's pocketbook.

Measuring Benefits

The value of a product can be determined by what consumers are willing to pay for it (i.e., their *willingness to pay*).[30] As we analyze willingness to pay, we might see better decisions being made about what actions to take. We would know the reasons consumers would pay one amount over another. Some people might be willing to preserve a parcel of land because they visit it, others because it backs up to their property and preserves their quality of life, and others because they want to preserve land for future generations. People who will visit the land are said to have *use-values* since they use the land for their enjoyment; those who want to preserve the land because it backs up to their property or for the future *have non-use-values* (i.e., they derive benefits from the existence of an environmental amenity but not from its direct use).

This distinction is key when policymakers decide whether to charge for use of a particular environmental amenity. In the marketplace, measuring benefits can be straightforward (e.g., simply observing the prices people pay for goods); however, environmental goods are typically not traded in markets. Thus, viable techniques might include *revealed preference*, which is the observation of behavior in *related markets* and use of that information to infer willingness to pay for environmental quality. For example, the amount someone is willing to pay to travel and enter a park may disclose that person's revealed value for that environmental condition.

Querying people about what they would be willing to pay to protect the environment requires some degree of certainty that they are telling the truth; thus, researchers collecting data have many methods for testing for true preferences (e.g., presenting two different options). Ultimately, analysts try to get to the *marginal benefit* (what people are willing to pay for incremental improvement in the environment). Policy designers are constantly trying to find the marginal benefits of pollution control and species protection.

Putting Costs and Benefits Together

An effective measurement of costs and benefits can lead to informed policy decisions; in theory, decision making is relatively simple once we know the costs and benefits. An analysis can be carried out for multiple policies/perspectives; from these data, we can decide on the optimal policy (e.g., Policy A is more efficient and preferable to Policy B as the net benefits are greater under Policy A).

In reality, policy work is much more complicated. Cost-benefit analysis omits important political and moral considerations. What if we consider guaranteeing every person's basic human rights at any cost? Or that a particular region will not be disadvantaged when locating polluting industries? Then we have a different analysis vs. just a cost-benefit analysis. Also, if we discount benefits that will occur in the future, current generations are privileged over future ones.[31] Even the valuation of an ecosystem tends to be seen as cheapening the resource (e.g., putting a price on water, which cannot be replaced). Finally, the emphasis on efficiency does not take into account distributional equity since there will be winners and losers. So while the cost-benefit analysis yields clarity, these other equity considerations must be taken into account before a government decides on a policy. One author phrased these equity and choice issues as "ultimately humanity's course will be determined less by iron laws of nature or by unbounded market powers . . . neither biology nor economics can substitute for the deeper ethical question what kind of world do we want to live in?"[32]

A cost-benefit analysis is how most legislation is created; companies and NGOs can play a role in this lawmaking by providing data to legislators so that they can better calculate costs and benefits. The enforcement of new laws is passed on to agencies (e.g., the EPA) that are responsible for creating and implementing regulation. Firms must also navigate pressures from the court system, which upholds, abandons, or clarifies laws created by Congress (and enforced by agencies).

Common Law in Environmental Cases

The role of the courts is not limited to ruling on disputes over legislation; the court system also impacts companies by ruling on cases considered common law. In these cases, there is a conflict between two parties that does not arise from a statute. *Common law* has the advantage of being decentralized; remedies can be tailored to individual circumstances (and include monetary damages and injunctive relief).[33]

Nuisance is the most frequently pled common-law tort action in environmental litigation.[34] Nuisance law has traditionally protected the rights of landowners to use and enjoy their properties. There are two forms of nuisance laws: public and private. Under both types, the plaintiff must prove that the defendant's activity unreasonably interferes with the use or enjoyment of a protected interest and has caused the plaintiff substantial harm (including potential harm). One difficulty in nuisance cases is proving a connection between the interference and a polluter's acts. For example, China's air pollution has caused enormous concerns in California as pollution evidence has been traced to China's factories. How solid would this evidence be if California were to sue Chinese factories? How could they attribute the pollution to specific sources? How could they attribute the pollution to specific health impacts?[35] Complications can also arise because of the long time periods and complicated manner in which pollutants (including air pollution) cause harm.

There are various other types of common law related to environmental torts. *Trespass* is a direct physical invasion or intrusion. *Negligence* cases require the plaintiff to demonstrate that (a) a legal duty exists requiring the defendant to conform to a certain standard of conduct for the protection of others against an unreasonable risk, (b) the defendant has breached that duty, (c) a reasonably close causal connection exists between the conduct and resulting injury, and (d) the defendant's conduct resulted in an actual injury to the plaintiff. *Strict liability* is a less burdensome standard on the plaintiff since it involves an abnormally dangerous activity (e.g., drilling in unusually hazardous conditions). The *public trust doctrine* is based on the principle that certain resources are unique and valuable when privately owned, yet they must also be available for public use (e.g., air, running water, the sea, and shorelines).

In sum, companies can be subject to statutes or common law and, as a result, may be held liable for the environmental outcomes of their actions. Executives have become concerned, in recent years, about civil penalties assessed by federal environmental agencies; criminal prosecution is also now a key component of environmental enforcement.

Renewable Energy Portfolio Standards

Recently, many states and the federal government have created incentives for people to opt for renewable energy as a source of household power, and some states are experimenting with a set of standards for electric utilities to generate a certain amount of electricity via renewable energy sources. Most standards are in the form of *renewable portfolio standards* (RPS); this requires utility companies to have a set percentage of renewable or alternative energy sources by a certain date.[36] RPS are usually measured in absolute terms (e.g., kilowatt hours) or as a percentage share of retail sales. Generally, these resources include wind, solar, geothermal, biomass, and some types of hydroelectricity; however, in less common instances, they may also include such sources as landfill gas, municipal solid waste, ocean thermal, and tidal energy. Many states have found unique ways to implement RPS. For example, Massachusetts requires utilities to generate 15 percent of their electricity from renewable or alternative energy sources (with a 1 percent increase each subsequent year until the mandated 15 percent goal is reached). The North Dakota legislature passed HB 1506 in March 2007, establishing a voluntary renewable portfolio objective of 10 percent by 2015.[37]

RPS legislation is not new; there is evidence that RPS started in the United States around 1983 (with the first serious effort in California in 1995); associated standards were implemented in 2002. Only two RPS regimes have been enacted by regulatory channels (Arizona and New York) and two through voter approval (Colorado and Washington); the rest have been government mandated. Other countries that have used this policy mechanism include Australia, Belgium, Canada, China, India, Italy, Japan, Poland, Sweden, and the United Kingdom.[38]

Figure 3.3 shows the various U.S. states that have adopted RPS (as of June 2012). The U.S. government predicts that their RPS goals will be fully implemented by around 2030, and that RPS mandates will cover 56 percent of total U.S. retail electricity sales (requiring that a percentage [an average of about 17 percent] of those sales be met with renewable energy sources). Some states will have additional capacity on a voluntary basis.

Of the more than 37 gigawatts (GW) of nonhydro-renewable energy capacity added from 1998 through 2009 in the United States, roughly 61 percent (23 GW) occurred in states with active or impending RPS obligations.[39] In total, existing state RPS policies will require roughly 73 GW of new renewable capacity by 2025 (representing roughly 6 percent of total U.S. retail electricity sales in that year and 30 percent of projected load growth between 2000 and 2025). If these states increase their renewable energy targets (or if additional states adopt RPS policies), the total set of state RPS policies would result in an even greater quantity of new renewable energy.[40]

Another important feature within some states' policies is a *renewable electricity credit* (REC) *trading system*. This mechanism allows electricity producers that generate renewable electricity to trade or sell certificates of generation to other electricity suppliers that do not generate enough RPS-eligible renewable electricity to meet their RPS requirements. This REC trading system is designed to minimize overall costs of compliance with the RPS. Thus, in regions with few or expensive renewable resources, electricity suppliers can comply with generation mandates at lower costs by purchasing RECs rather than being required to use only local resources or investing in their own renewable generation facilities. The flexibility provided by this trading

States Renewable Portfolio Standards

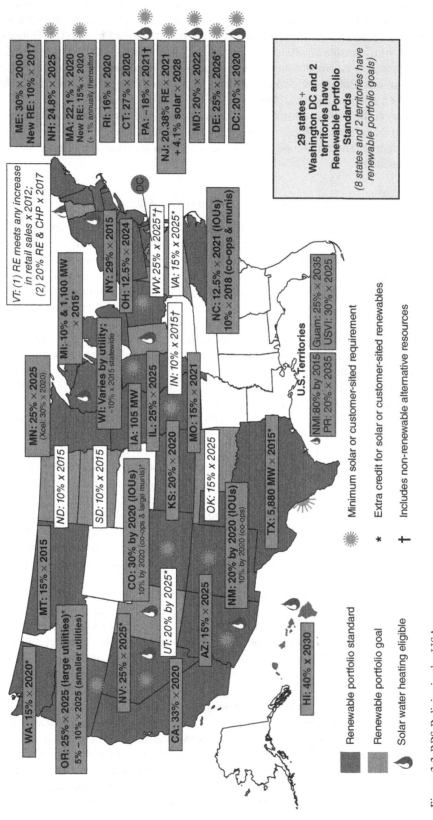

ME: 30% × 2000
New RE: 10% × 2017

NH: 24.8% × 2025

MA: 22.1% × 2020
New RE: 15% × 2020
(+ 1% annually thereafter)

RI: 16% × 2020

CT: 27% × 2020

PA: ~18% × 2021†

NJ: 20.38% RE × 2021
+ 4.1% solar × 2028

MD: 20% × 2022

DE: 25% × 2026*

DC: 20% × 2020

29 states +
Washington DC and 2
territories have
Renewable Portfolio
Standards
(8 states and 2 territories have
renewable portfolio goals)

VT: (1) RE meets any increase
in retail sales × 2012;
(2) 20% RE & CHP × 2017

NY: 29% × 2015

OH: 12.5% × 2024

WV: 25% × 2025*†

VA: 15% × 2025*

MI: 10% & 1,100 MW
× 2015*

WI: Varies by utility:
~10% × 2015 statewide

IN: 10% × 2015†

NC: 12.5% × 2021 (IOUs)
10% × 2018 (co-ops & munis)

MN: 25% × 2025
(Xcel: 30% × 2020)

IA: 105 MW

IL: 25% × 2025

MO: 15% × 2021

ND: 10% × 2015

SD: 10% × 2015

MT: 15% × 2015

CO: 30% by 2020 (IOUs)
10% by 2020 (co-ops & large munis)*

KS: 20% × 2020

OK: 15% × 2025

TX: 5,880 MW × 2015*

WA: 15% × 2020*

OR: 25% × 2025 (large utilities)*
5%–10% × 2025 (smaller utilities)

NV: 25% × 2025*

UT: 20% by 2025*

NM: 20% by 2020 (IOUs)
10% by 2020 (co-ops)

AZ: 15% × 2025

CA: 33% × 2020

Hi: 40% × 2030

U.S. Territories

NMI: 80% by 2015 | Guam: 25% × 2035
PR: 20% × 2035 | USVI: 30% × 2025

✺ Minimum solar or customer-sited requirement

* Extra credit for solar or customer-sited renewables

† Includes non-renewable alternative resources

■ Renewable portfolio standard

■ Renewable portfolio goal

⬨ Solar water heating eligible

Figure 3.3 RPS Policies in the USA

Source: Database of State Incentives for Renewables and Efficiency (DSIRE) RPS Policies summary map, March 2013

mechanism is helpful in limiting costs because diverse sources of renewable energy are spread throughout the United States. Also, RECs can offset the costs of utilities that buy renewable energy.

Current Impacts of RPS

In general, states with RPS policies have seen an increase in the amount of electricity generated from eligible renewable resources. However, some states *without* RPS policies have also seen significant increases in renewable generation over the past few years; this is most likely a result of federal incentives, state programs, and market forces. The most important federal incentive may be the *production tax credit*, which awards tax credits to entities that generate electricity using eligible renewable technologies. Increases in renewable generation have often been most significant when: (1) an RPS mandate was in effect, and (2) a production tax credit was available to electricity producers.[41]

Currently, there is no RPS program at the national level, and programs vary widely by state in terms of program structure, enforcement mechanisms, size, and application; a large range of policies are under the RPS umbrella. In general, an RPS program specifies the renewable energy resources eligible to satisfy the generation requirement; often, the selected eligible resources are tailored to best fit a state's particular resource base. Some states also set electricity generation targets for specific types of renewable energy to encourage use of that renewable resource.

Some data show the total amount of electricity that is expected to be generated from this program from 2003 to 2030. Biomass (including wood) and wind are the two renewable fuels expected to show tremendous growth in the future, partly as a result of RPS programs.[42] (Keep in mind this potential growth when we discuss clean-technology entrepreneurship in Chapter 12.)

Federal Programs

The U.S. EIA has examined several proposed federal RPS standards. One proposal (analyzed in 2007) called for 15 percent of U.S. electricity sales to be generated from eligible renewable resources by 2020; this included an REC trading program allowing electricity suppliers to choose between generating renewable electricity and purchasing RECs toward compliance. It also awarded triple credits for electricity produced from distributed resources (i.e., produced at a non-central generating station, such as from a rooftop solar photovoltaic system). This program, similar to RPS, would provide incentives for energy producers to use renewable sources of energy. With these proposed standards, EIA's analysis showed a tripling of electricity generated from biomass (and large increases in wind and solar photovoltaic generation) by 2030; this increase could displace coal generation and some nuclear and natural gas generation.

Challenges of RPS

Some analysts believe that RPS policies have done little to support growth in renewable energy supplies and that growth has come at high costs.[43] Also, there are concerns about the ability of RPS programs to support long-term contracts (that renewable energy generators require), the willingness of policymakers to enforce renewable energy purchase obligations, the complexity of crafting well-designed programs, the challenges of minimizing windfall profits for some generators, the need to enact supporting policies beyond the RPS, and whether alternative policies might deliver comparable social benefits at lower costs.[44] Additionally, smaller energy producers face significant challenges under the RPS due to significant transaction costs and risks.

Another RPS challenge is that standards were supposed to be technology neutral (meaning that competition would result in the most economically attractive technologies); however, most state policies have mandated percentages for different technologies (e.g., solar and wind). Some analysts have shown that certain technologies will be favored with a federal policy;[45] this could cause monopolies and hamper competition and innovation. Thus, the United States might want to adopt a federal policy that includes not only RPS but also cap and trade and, in some areas (especially for emerging technologies), feed-in-tariffs.[46] This approach is comparable to a comprehensive federal energy policy (similar to what is occurring in other countries) and should allow the market to decide on the most efficient technologies. This approach is challenging; many companies will claim that increased costs will lead to decreased competitiveness.

The Effectiveness of Regulation

In 2011–2012, the EPA moved aggressively on its regulatory agenda to control GHG emissions and hazardous pollutants from utilities, power plants, and other sources. The EPA implemented the GHG-tailoring rule, which required permits and the best available control technology to reduce GHG emissions from large sources. Many business leaders and legislators have questioned the effectiveness of these actions, which have influenced other environmental legislative areas as well. Opponents have cited a study claiming that regulation has an annual cost of $1.75 trillion;[47] public-opinion surveys have indicated that U.S. citizens do not favor this kind of spending.[48] (However, when the same people were asked about specific regulatory initiatives [e.g., limits on GHG emissions and strict regulations on oil drilling], most were supportive of the regulations.)[49]

Another study shows, among other outcomes, that regulatory benefits exceed regulatory costs by seven to one for significant regulations.[50] As an example, the regulatory benefit of the Clean Air Act exceeds its costs by 25 to 1;[51] other studies show this ratio at 22 to 1.[52] Many retrospective evaluations of regulations by the EPA and Occupational Safety and Health Administration (OSHA) have found that the regulations remain necessary; regulatory agencies have reduced fatalities, injuries, illnesses, and environmental damages in the 40 years since Congress enacted health, safety, and environmental protection. Some studies also find that they *do not* produce significant job losses or have adverse economic impacts on regulated industries.

One study in particular showed that high regulatory costs are not responsible for slowing economic recovery and job growth. The study reasons that claims by opponents of regulation fail in three ways: (1) the claims focus mostly on costs rather than balancing benefits, (2) the money spent on regulation spurs economic activity in the form of goods purchased and services rendered, and (3) many claims are based on unreliable data.[53]

Several recent studies found that the economic effects of environmental policies depend mostly on how strict those policies are. Strictness is a difficult concept to measure. One set of studies calculated an index based on "the explicit or implicit price of green policies."[54] If the prices are explicit, such as traded permits, the researchers assumed the most stringent measures are in place. They calculated stringency scores for 24 OECD countries for 1990 to 2012.

They found that the strictest policies are in Nordic countries and the laxest ones are in Greece; the USA is near the middle. All said, they found that an increase in stringency of environmental policies as measured by their index does not harm productivity.

One could explain these results in several ways such as: (1) the damage from environmental regulation is not powerful enough to change the needle of overall productivity; (2) the policies did as much good as harm—for example, firms are encouraged to invest in innovation and therefore one could argue that policies do more good at the firm level than to the economy.[55]

Profile: The RITE Project[56]

This chapter discusses the effectiveness of regulation. Shapiro et al. found that regulatory benefits exceed regulatory costs by seven to one for significant regulations.[57] Further, an aggregate study done by Shapiro et al. found that regulations do not produce significant job losses or have adverse economic impacts on regulated industries.[58] In New York City, RPS funding is gathered through a surcharge on each kilowatt-hour sold by investor-owned utilities.[59] The New York State Energy Research and Development Authority (NYSERDA) manages the RPS fund which is separate from and in addition to the state system benefits charge.[60]

Among the main-tier priorities for New York RPS are ocean and tidal power. Upon adoption of RPS, New York based companies began to strategically adapt to regulatory events. In one example, Verdant Power began

Figure 3.4 Midtown Skyline. Photo Credit: Scott McCullough, Master of Arts in Sustainability candidate, 2015

to adapt to the changing regulatory landscape by coupling emerging technology developers with utility industry veterans who had advanced experience in constructing and operating electricity generation facilities.[61]

In 2012, the FERC issued a pilot commercial license for the RITE Project. The license was issued after testing a demonstration of grid connected tidal turbines for three years. During the testing, the turbines provided electricity to New York City businesses.[62] In 9,000 turbine-hours of operation, the turbines provided 70 megawatt hours of energy to the participating commercial end-users.[63] The license authorizes the installation of up to 30 Generation 5 turbines in the East River. The Gen5 turbines have a rotor diameter of five meters and are composed of mild steel, stainless steel, cast iron, and reinforced plastics.[64] Although wave energy will not become competitive with fossil fuels and other renewables in major markets until 2025, the tidal power industry was able to adapt expertise from the conventional hydroelectric industry[65] and may become cost competitive much sooner.

Ebb and Flow*. Figure 3.3 shows that renewable energy sources are projected to grow 3 percent by 2040 whereas coal is supposed to decrease 7 percent. Since 2009, the Department of Energy has spent about $6 billion in clean coal and President Obama has approved $2 billion in tax credits for carbon capture in the 2016 budget.[66] However, in February of 2015, the federal government announced that it was walking away from FutureGen, a clean coal project in Illinois that was expecting $1 billion in stimulus money. Knowing the projected RPS outcomes, in the next 20 years, do you think that the federal government should focus on subsidizing the high initial costs of clean coal carbon capture or focus on incentivizing smaller-scale renewables, like tidal power, that won't be competitive for another ten years?*

How Companies Respond to Regulation and Ratings

Governments worldwide have expanded regulatory interventions for private economic activities. Also, economic relationships are increasingly integrated across national borders and are governed by a growing number of international regulations;[67] a key objective is to correct negative externalities and market failures interfering with the behaviors of firms and environmental health. However, it is difficult for businesses to anticipate and prepare for many new regulations.[68] Table 3.2 shows typical firm-level responses to regulatory and legal pressures (i.e., *avoid*, *reduce*, *adapt*, and *disregard*) to regulatory events. Firms may use all of these responses throughout their existences. Determining the correct response is dependent upon myriad factors (e.g., executive perceptions, company capabilities, and past experience with similar events).

Uncertainty generally causes firms to withdraw from commercial activities, engage in countermeasures (when they perceive an uncertainty as a threat), and resolve uncertainty by participating in trade associations and lobbying. Research suggests that firms perceiving a high degree of uncertainty associated with a CO_2 emission regulation, for example, will generally cope by taking the least costly (and sometimes least effective) routes of compliance.[69] Thus, a regulation may cause firms to do the opposite of the intent behind it.

Table 3.2 Strategic Responses to Regulatory Events[70]

Strategy	Tactic	Description
Avoid	Postponement	Defer decisions and wait for more certainty[71]
	Stabilization	Increase predictability through implementation of standard procedures or establishment of long-term contracts[72]
	Withdrawal	Exit business in uncertain markets and focus on predictable environments[73]
Reduce	Influencing	Manipulate determining circumstances or actors that constitute uncertainty[74]
	Investigation	Collect additional information; draw on professional expertise to be applied in decision-making process[75]
	Simplification	Reduce number of uncertain factors considered in decision-making process[76]
Adapt	Cooperation	Collaborate with suppliers, customers, or competitors in research or production; engage in trade associations[77]
	Flexibility	Enlarge range of strategic options, e.g., through diversification[78]
	Imitation	Examine and copy strategy of successful competitors[79]
	Integration	Restructure business portfolio through mergers and acquisitions[80]
	Internal design	Change organizational design by establishing modular structures, low degree of formalization or decentralization[81]
Disregard	Business as usual	Pretend that uncertainty does not affect decisions[82]
	No-regret moves	Execute activities associated with uncertainty that are advantageous regardless of how uncertainty resolves itself[83]
	Substitution	Replace uncertain decision criteria with assumptions derived from comprehensive consideration or detailed analysis[84]

Studies are mixed in terms of how executives manage such uncertainties. They might withhold investing, develop a proactive environmental strategy, reorganize to adapt, or they might try to get more data. Some firms might even avoid highly uncertain environments, as they may lack the skills necessary to adapt.[85]

Additionally, companies now have to navigate *environmental ratings*, which is a ranking awarded by independent agencies. Research has shown the positive impacts of these ratings on consumers and investors, but it has not been as clear about the impacts on companies. We know that firms do pay attention to these ratings; poorly rated firms tend to respond by implementing practices aimed at improving their standings with independent agencies.

One study looked at the environmental ratings from KLD Research & Analytics Inc. (KLD), which is the largest multidimensional corporate social performance database available to the public.[86] KLD informs the Russell 100 Index, S&P Index, and Domini Social 400 Index. TIAA-CREF uses these ratings for choosing equities included in its Social Choice Equity Fund, and this rating scheme has been referred to as "the de facto research standard" for corporate social responsibility ratings.[87] They found that firms receiving poor KLD ratings subsequently improved their environmental performances more than other firms. This difference was driven by firms in highly regulated industries, with more low-cost opportunities to exploit. Thus, firms respond to stakeholders.[88]

Firm behavior can also be influenced via information disclosure. This is usually accomplished by making transparency and independent ratings critical to stakeholder knowledge. This method of regulation is probably more effective (or at least as effective) as behavior control and punishment.[89]

Common Pool Resources

Governments provide public enterprise goods (e.g., mail service) and "pure public goods" (e.g., court systems and national defense); the difference between the two (when provided by noncompetitive methods) is that public enterprise goods are excludable (i.e., some people can be excluded from using the good via non-payment). Pure public goods (e.g., national defense and court systems) do not require direct payments to use or consume. Still other common goods—*common pool resources* (commons)—are finite yet non-excludable. For example, fishing grounds are *commons* since fishing by one boat reduces future catches; however, it is difficult to exclude fishing boats from going where they please. The problem with *commons* is they tend to be overused and depleted; in some situations, users support the destruction of the very resource on which they are depending (i.e., *tragedy of the commons*). Rational users make demands on such resources until expected benefits equal expected costs; however, individual decisions can cumulate to tragic overuse and the potential destruction of *commons*.[90]

As a result, some *commons* have already been taken over by national, state, or local governments, and research (over the last 50 years) has indicated there are myriad other solutions to these problems. It is not clear, for example, that the government should provide mail service given that private enterprises (e.g., UPS, DHL, and Federal Express) may do so more efficiently. Also, people do observe community rules and regulations designed to control natural resource use. Thus, we might be able to design processes to stabilize local *commons*. Here are a few possible design principles:

1   clearly define boundaries so that effective exclusion of external and untitled parties is known;
2   develop rules regarding the appropriation and provision of *commons* that are adapted to local situations;
3   develop collective-choice arrangements that allow most resource appropriators to participate in decision-making processes;
4   develop a process of monitoring by those who are part of (or accountable to) the appropriators;
5   create a graduated scale of sanctions for resource appropriators who violate community rules;
6   create inexpensive and easily accessible mechanisms for conflict resolution.[91]

Chapter Summary

This chapter revealed a key pressure on firms: regulation. In an ideal world, companies would be able to perfectly balance utilizing and protecting various forms of capital while maintaining a strong profit and managing competitors. Because it is not an ideal world, the market often fails due to issues such as incomplete information and unaccounted costs. These failures are often damaging and cause some stakeholders to be misinformed about how a company is affecting the environment. Thus, regulation becomes necessary; it compensates for market failures.

Although many oppose government control, one study showed that high regulatory costs are *not* responsible for slowing economic recovery and job growth (as is often believed). Regulation is simply a complex process and often requires the consideration of myriad factors to determine an optimal course of action. As such, there are several methods of regulation (e.g., CAC *and* market-based). Regulators most often weigh costs and benefits to assess the efficacy of a regulation; however, some research has shown that this method has major faults (e.g., costs are often overestimated and benefits are underestimated). Regulation is a complicated matter. U.S. firms also face a lot of uncertainty in this type of regulatory climate, can find it hard to plan for (and predict) upcoming regulations, and can become indecisive as a result. The court system assists in defining, establishing, and enforcing policies and laws associated with regulation and protection of the environment.

RPS is a regulated means of impacting the adoption of renewable energy sources for the purpose of weaning the United States off fossil fuels. The effect of this regulation is still unknown and contrasts somewhat with solutions in other countries.

Case Revisited: Duke Energy

Duke is facing many interesting challenges as a result of its merger with Progress Energy. One challenge is whether it will comply with North Carolina's Public Utility Commission's (PUC) possible mandate to terminate Jim Rogers.[92] The PUC may ask Rogers to resign, and Duke may refuse the PUC's mandate; this refusal might come with a backlash against Duke on other issues, such as requests for rate increases. Also, given that the Utility Commission is one of Duke's key stakeholders, it may want to be cautious in taking too hard of a stand.[93]

Terms to Know

Common law: also known as case law or precedent, it is law developed by judges through court decision and similar tribunals

Economic efficiency: every resource is optimally allocated to serve each person in the best way

Regulation: mandates of the government that are legally binding

Questions and Critical Thinking

1   Agriculture has a privileged place in environmental law. While it is considered a major polluter, uses unusual amounts of resources such as water (almost 70 percent of available water worldwide), and sometimes overuses fungicides, it escapes many of the laws and penalties that other industries are assessed on. Do you think that agriculture should be treated differently from other industries (given its central role in our existence)?

2   Until recently, the regulation of electricity in the United States did not reflect its full social costs. Pollution caused by electric utilities was historically unregulated (which allowed utilities to avoid the costs of controlling it). Under traditional utility regulation in the United States, utilities had no incentive to adopt energy efficiency and demand response programs (e.g., time-based pricing). In fact, utilities had incentives to build more power plants since their rates are calculated partially based on capital investments (i.e., their profits were largely based on the amount of electricity used). Utilities, however, have had recent changes in their regulatory environment (such as cap-and-trade proposals), which have increased pressures to use renewable energy sources. Do a little background research on these changes and then comment on whether or not these regulatory changes are likely to raise prices for consumers.

3   Conflicts related to water pollution, and the rights to use water, have led many regulators to be concerned that they are not regulating water to its fullest extent. For example, review the following article on hydraulic fracturing: S. Hargreaves, "Fracking Blowback Spooks Energy Industry," CNNMoney, April 11, 2011, http://money.cnn.com/2011/03/11/news/economy/fracking_natural_gas_oil_water/index.htm. How should regulators handle the water issues mentioned in this article?

4   One way to control industrial pollution is to educate the public (e.g., via labeling and public service announcements) about company products and actions resulting in higher levels of pollution. To what extent would this information help decrease hazardous environmental outcomes of company actions? To what extent do you think consumers would take into account environmental impacts when they purchase goods? What could be done to increase consumer awareness and provide incentives for them to take the environment into account when purchasing goods and services?

5   Consider the case, *Hanley* v. *Kleindienst*, 484 F.2d 448 (2d Cir. 1973). The National Environmental Policy Act (NEPA) requires the submittal of environmental impact statements (EISs) for all major federal actions; this information can affect how easily companies receive permits and agency approvals for work to be completed. In the *Hanley* case, a party is trying to construct a jail and an office building. The Second Circuit found that the mere fact that a project is important in a community does not trigger the need to prepare an EIS. Instead, there must be more than opposition before the EIS must be prepared. Do you think this EIS process should occur for all projects?

Appendix 3.1. U.S. Environmental Laws and Critical Events

Name	Date	Authority	Agency	Summary
Atomic Energy Act (AEA)[94]	1946	42 U.S.C. §§ 2011	EPA, DPE, NRC	Established the Atomic Energy Commission (AEC) to promote the utilization of atomic energy for peaceful purposes consistent with common defense, security, and with the health and safety of the public. Since the abolition of the AEC, much of the work of the AEA has been carried out by the Nuclear Regulatory Commission (NRC) and the U.S. Department of Energy. When the EPA was formed, however, the AEC's authority to issue generally applicable environmental radiation standards was transferred to it. Other federal and state organizations must follow these standards when developing requirements for their areas of radiation protection. The EPA also received the Federal Radiation Council's authority under the AEA, which is to develop guidance for federal and state agencies with recommendations for developing radiation protection requirements to work with states and to establish and execute radiation protection programs.
Federal Hazardous Substances Act[95]	1960	15 U.S.C. §§ 1261–1278	CPSC	Requires that certain hazardous household products ("hazardous substances") bear cautionary labeling to alert consumers to the potential hazards that those products present and inform them of the measures they need to protect themselves from those hazards. Any product requires labeling that is toxic, corrosive, flammable or combustible; an irritant; a strong sensitizer; or that generates pressure through decomposition, heat, or other means—if the product may cause substantial personal injury or illness during (or as a proximate result of) any customary or reasonable foreseeable handling or use (including reasonable foreseeable ingestion by children).
National Environmental Policy Act (NEPA)	1969	42 U.S.C. §§ 4321		Ensures that all branches of government give proper consideration to the environment prior to undertaking any major federal action that significantly affects the environment. Environmental assessments (EAs) and environmental impact statements (EISs), which are assessments of the likelihood of adverse effects from alternative courses of action, are required from all federal agencies.
Occupational Safety and Health Act	1970	29 U.S.C. §§ 61		Ensures worker and workplace safety. Requires employers to provide workers with a place of employment free from recognized hazards to safety and health (e.g., exposure to toxic chemicals, excessive noise, mechanical dangers, heat or cold stress, and unsanitary conditions). Created the National Institute for Occupational Safety and Health (NIOSH).
Clean Air Act	1970	42 U.S.C. §§ 7401	EPA	A comprehensive federal law that regulated airborne emissions from area, stationary, and mobile sources. Authorized the EPA to establish national ambient air quality standards (NAAQS) to protect public health and the environment.
Federal Insecticide, Fungicide, and Rodenticide Act (FIFRA)	1972	7 U.S.C. §§ 135		Provides federal control of pesticide distribution, sale, and use. Gives the EPA authority not only to study the consequences of pesticide use but also to require users to register when purchasing pesticides.

(continued)

(continued)

Name	Date	Authority	Agency	Summary
Endangered Species Act	1973	7 U.S.C. §§ 136, 16 U.S.C. §§ 460		Provides a program for the conservation of threatened and endangered plants and animals and their habitats. The U.S. Fish and Wildlife Service (FWS) and the Department of the Interior maintain the list of endangered species and threatened species. Anyone can petition the FWS to list a species or prevent some activity that might endanger a species. The law prohibits any action (administrative or real) that results in a "taking" of a listed species or adversely affects habitat. Likewise, importation, exportation, and interstate and foreign commerce of listed species are all prohibited.
Safe Drinking Water Act	1974	43 U.S.C. §§ 300f		Protects the quality of drinking water. Focuses on all waters actually or potentially designated for drinking use, authorized the EPA to establish safe standards for purity, and required owners and operators of public water systems to comply with standards.
Toxic Substances Control Act (TSCA)	1976	15 U.S.C. §§ 2601		Enacted to test, regulate, and screen all chemicals produced in (or imported into) the United States. Requires that any chemical destined to reach the consumer marketplace be tested for toxicity prior to commercial manufacture.
Resource Conservation and Recovery Act (RCRA)	1976	42 U.S.C. §§ 321		Gave the EPA authority to control hazardous waste (including the generation, transportation, treatment, storage, and disposal of hazardous waste). The 1986 amendment enabled the EPA to address environmental problems that could result from storage of petroleum and other hazardous substances in underground tanks. Amended by the Hazardous and Solid Waste Amendments of 1984 (HSWA), which required the phasing out of land disposal of hazardous waste.
Clean Water Act	1977	33 U.S.C. §§ 121		An amendment to the Federal Water Pollution Control Act of 1972. Gives the EPA the authority to set effluent standards on an industry-by-industry basis (technology-based) and continued the requirements to set water quality standards for all contaminants in surface waters. The CWA makes it unlawful for any person to discharge any pollutant from a point source into navigable waters without a permit. (Amended 1987.)
Consumer Product Safety Act (CPSA)[96]	1978			Established the Consumer Product Safety Commission (CPSC), defines its basic authority, and provides that when the CPSC finds an unreasonable risk of injury associated with a consumer product, it can develop a standard to reduce or eliminate the risk. The CPSA also provides the authority to ban a product if there is no feasible standard, and it gives the CPSC authority to pursue recalls for products presenting a substantial product hazard. (Generally excluded from the CPSC's jurisdiction are food, drugs, cosmetics, medical devices, tobacco products, firearms and ammunition, motor vehicles, pesticides, aircraft, boats, and fixed-site amusement rides.) For assistance viewing the act, see below.
Chlorofluorocarbon (CFC) Ban	1978			
Comprehensive Environmental Response, Compensation, and Liability Act (CERCLA or Superfund)	1980	42 U.S.C. §§ 9601		Provides a federal Superfund to clean up uncontrolled or abandoned hazardous waste sites as well as accidents, spills, and other emergency releases of pollutants and contaminants into the environment. Grants the EPA the power to seek out parties responsible for releases and ensure their cooperation in the cleanup. The EPA cleans up "orphan" sites when potentially responsible parties cannot be identified or located (or when they fail to act). The EPA also recovers costs from financially viable individuals and companies once a response action has been completed.

Act	Year	Citation	Description
Nuclear Waste Policy Act (NWPA)[97]	1982	42 U.S.C. §§ 10101	Supports the use of deep geologic repositories for the safe storage and/or disposal of radioactive waste. The Act establishes procedures to evaluate and select sites for geologic repositories and for the interaction of state and federal governments. It also provides a timetable of key milestones that federal agencies must meet when carrying out the program. NWPA assigns the Department of Energy (DOE) the responsibility to site, build, and operate a deep geologic repository for the disposal of high-level waste and spent nuclear fuel. It directs the EPA to develop standards for protection of the general environment from offsite releases of radioactive material in repositories. The Act directs the Nuclear Regulatory Commission (NRC) to license the DOE to operate a repository only if it meets the EPA's standards and all other relevant requirements.
Emergency Planning and Community Right-to-Know Act (EPCRA)	1986	42 U.S.C. §§ 11011	Introduced as Title III of the Superfund Amendments and Reauthorization Act of 1986 (SARA). Helps communities safeguard public health and safety and protect the environment from chemical hazards. Requires each state to appoint a State Emergency Response Commission (SERC), which divides states into Emergency Planning Districts and names a Local Emergency Planning Committee (LEPC) for each district.
Shore Protection Act[98]	1988	33 U.S.C. §§ 2601	Prohibits the transportation of municipal or commercial waste within coastal waters by a vessel without a permit and number (or other marking). Permits are not to run beyond renewable, five-year terms and terminate when the vessel is sold.
Marine Protection, Research, and Sanctuaries Act (MPRSA)[99]	1988	16 U.S.C. §§ 1431 and 33 U.S.C. §§ 1401	Prohibits (1) transportation of material from the United States for the purpose of ocean dumping; (2) transportation of material from anywhere for the purpose of ocean dumping by U.S. agencies or U.S.-flagged vessels; (3) dumping of material transported from outside the United States into the U.S. territorial sea. A permit is required to deviate from these prohibitions. Under MPRSA, the standard for permit issuance is whether the dumping will "unreasonably degrade or endanger" human health, welfare, or the marine environment. The EPA is charged with developing ocean-dumping criteria, to be used in evaluating permit applications. The MPRSA provisions, administered by the EPA are published in Title 33 of the U.S. Code. The MPRSA provisions that address marine sanctuaries are administered by the National Oceanic and Atmospheric Administration and are published in Title 16 of the U.S. Code.
Oil Pollution Act (OPA)	1990	33 U.S.C. §§ 2702–2761	Streamlined and strengthened the EPA's ability to prevent and respond to catastrophic oil spills. A trust fund financed by an oil tax is made available to clean up spills when the responsible party is incapable or unwilling to do so.
Pollution Prevention Act	1990	42 U.S.C. §§ 13101, 13102; §§ 6602	Focused industry, government, and public attention on reducing pollution via cost-effective changes in production, operation, and raw materials use.

(continued)

(continued)

Name	Date	Authority	Agency	Summary
Federal Actions to Address Environmental Justice in Minority Populations and Low-Income Populations[100]	1994	E.O. 12898		Its purpose is to focus federal attention on environmental and human health effects of federal actions on minority and low-income populations with the goal of achieving environmental protection for all communities. The executive order (E.O.) directs federal agencies to identify and address the disproportionately high and adverse human health or environmental effects of their actions on minority and low-income populations, to the greatest extent practicable and permitted by law. The order also directs each agency to develop a strategy for implementing environmental justice. The order is also intended to promote nondiscrimination in federal programs affecting human health and the environment, as well as provide minority and low-income communities access to public information and public participation. In addition, the E.O. established an Interagency Working Group (IWG) on environmental justice chaired by the EPA Administrator and comprised of the heads of 11 departments or agencies and several White House offices.
National Technology Transfer and Advancement Act[101]	1996	15 U.S.C. §§ 3701		Requires federal agencies and departments to use technical standards, developed or adopted by voluntary consensus standards bodies, if compliance would not be inconsistent with applicable law or otherwise impracticable.
Federal Insecticide, Fungicide, and Rodenticide Act[102]	1996	7 U.S.C. §§ 136	EPA	Provides for federal regulation of pesticide distribution, sale, and use. All pesticides distributed or sold in the United States must be registered (licensed) by the EPA. Before the EPA may register a pesticide under FIFRA, the applicant must show, among other things, that using the pesticide according to specifications "will not generally cause unreasonable adverse effects on the environment."
Protection of Children from Environmental Health Risks and Safety Risks[103]	1997	E.O. 13045	EPA	The order applies to economically significant rules under E.O. 12866 that concern an environmental health or safety risk that EPA has reason to believe may disproportionately affect children. Environmental health or safety risks refer to risks to health or to safety that are attributable to products or substances that the child is likely to come into contact with or ingest (e.g., the air we breathe, the food we eat, the water we drink or use for recreation, the soil we live on, and the products we use or are exposed to). When promulgating a rule of this description, the EPA must evaluate the effects of the planned regulation on children and explain why the regulation is preferable to potentially effective and reasonably feasible alternatives.
CAFE Standards	1975		NHTSA	The National Highway Traffic Safety Administration (NHTSA) regulates CAFE standards and the EPA measures vehicle fuel efficiency.
Poison Prevention Packaging Act			CPSC	
Food, Drug, and Cosmetics Act[104]			FDA	

Name	Year	Citation	Agency	Description
Actions Concerning Regulations that Significantly Affect Energy Supply, Distribution, or Use[105]	2001	E.O. 13211		It applies to any significant energy action as defined by the E.O. A significant energy action is one that promulgates (or is expected to lead to the promulgation of) a final rule that is: a significant regulatory action under E.O. 12866 and likely to have a significant adverse effect on the supply, distribution or use of energy or is designated by the Administrator of OMB/OIRA as a significant energy action.
Federal Food, Drug, and Cosmetics Act[106]	2002	21 U.S.C. §§ 301	EPA	Authorizes the EPA to set tolerances (or maximum residue limits) for pesticide residues on foods. In the absence of a tolerance for a pesticide residue, a food containing such a residue is subject to seizure by the government. Once a tolerance is established, the residue level in the tolerance is the trigger for enforcement actions. That is, if residues are found above that level, the commodity will be subject to seizure.
Energy Independence and Security Act (EIS Act 2007)[107]	2007	Public Law 11–140		Aims to: move the United States toward greater energy independence and security; increase the production of clean renewable fuels; protect consumers; increase the efficiency of products, buildings, and vehicles; promote research on and deploy GHG capture and storage options; improve the energy performance of the federal government; increase U.S. energy security; develop renewable fuel production; and improve vehicle fuel economy. EIS Act 2007 reinforces the energy reduction goals for federal agencies put forth in E.O. 13423, as well as introduces more aggressive requirements. The three key provisions enacted are the Corporate Average Fuel Economy Standards, the Renewable Fuel Standard, and the appliance/lighting efficiency standards.

Appendix 3.2. Global Laws and Critical Events

Name	Date	Summary
Brundtland Report	1987	This report was published by the United Nations World Commission on Environment and Development (WCED). The report is credited with the establishment of an influential definition of sustainable development: "development that meets the needs of the present without compromising the ability of future generations to meet their own needs."
NAFTA	1994	This agreement will remove most barriers to trade and investment among the United States, Canada, and Mexico. Under the NAFTA, all non-tariff barriers to agricultural trade between the United States and Mexico were eliminated. In addition, many tariffs were eliminated immediately, with others being phased out over periods of five to 15 years. This allowed for an orderly adjustment to free trade with Mexico, with full implementation beginning January 1, 2008.
Convention on International Trade in Endangered Species of Wild Fauna and Flora	1973	CITES (the Convention on International Trade in Endangered Species of Wild Fauna and Flora) is an international agreement between governments. Its aim is to ensure that international trade in specimens of wild animals and plants does not threaten their survival. CITES was drafted as a result of a resolution adopted in 1963 at a meeting of members of IUCN (The World Conservation Union). The text of the Convention was finally agreed upon at a meeting of representatives (which included 80 countries) in Washington, DC on March 3, 1973. On July 1, 1975, CITES entered in force. CITES is an international agreement to which countries adhere voluntarily. States that have agreed to be bound by the Convention ('joined' CITES) are known as Parties. Although CITES is legally binding on the Parties (in other words they have to implement the Convention); it does not take the place of national laws. Rather, it provides a framework to be respected by each Party (which has to adopt its own domestic legislation to ensure that CITES is implemented at the national level). For many years, CITES has been among the conservation agreements with the largest membership (with now 175 Parties).
Montreal Protocol on Substances that Deplete the Ozone Layer	1987	The Montreal Protocol on Substances that Deplete the Ozone Layer is a landmark international agreement designed to protect the stratospheric ozone layer. The treaty was originally signed in 1987 and substantially amended in 1990 and 1992. The Montreal Protocol stipulates that the production and consumption of compounds that deplete ozone in the stratosphere—CFCs, halons, carbon tetrachloride, and methyl chloroform—are to be phased out by 2000 (2005 for methyl chloroform). Scientific theory and evidence suggest that, once emitted to the atmosphere, these compounds could significantly deplete the stratospheric ozone layer that shields the planet from damaging UV-B radiation. UNEP has prepared a *Montreal Protocol Handbook* that provides additional detail and explanation of the provisions.

Basel Convention on the Control of Transboundary Movements of Hazardous Wastes and their Disposal	1989	The most comprehensive global environmental agreement on hazardous and other wastes. The Convention has 175 Parties and aims to protect human health and the environment against the adverse effects resulting from the generation, management, transboundary movements, and disposal of hazardous and other wastes. The Basel Convention came into force in 1992. During The Present Decade (2000–2010), the Convention will build on this framework by emphasizing full implementation and enforcement of treaty commitments. The other area of focus will be the minimization of hazardous waste generation. Recognizing that the long-term solution to the stockpiling of hazardous wastes is a reduction in the generation of those wastes (both in terms of quantity and hazardousness), Ministers meeting in December of 1999 set out guidelines for the Convention's activities over the next decade.
International Code of Conduct on the Distribution and Use of Pesticides	1985	Worldwide guidance document on pesticide management for all public and private entities engaged in, or associated with, the distribution and use of pesticides. It was adopted for the first time in 1985 by the Twenty-fifth Session of the FAO Conference. The Code is designed to provide standards of conduct and to serve as a point of reference in relation to sound pesticide management practices, in particular for government authorities and the pesticide industry. In November 2002, the 123rd Session of the FAO Council (with the authorization of the 31st Session of the FAO Conference) approved the revised version of the International Code of Conduct on the Distribution and Use of Pesticides by Council Resolution 1/123.
Kyoto Protocol to the United Nations Framework Convention on Climate Change	1997	The Kyoto Protocol is an international agreement linked to the UNFCC. The major feature of the Kyoto Protocol is that it sets binding targets for 37 industrialized countries and the European community for reducing GHG emissions. These amount to an average of 5 percent against 1990 levels over the five-year period 2008–2012.

Notes

1 F. Bosselman, J. B. Eisen, J. Rossi, D. B. Spence, and J. Weaver, *Energy, Economics, and the Environment: Cases and Materials*, 3rd ed. (New York: Foundation Press, 2010), 26–27.

2 *State & County QuickFacts: North Carolina*, U.S. Census Bureau, http://quickfacts.census.gov/qfd/states/37000.html, last revised June 11, 2014.

3 PollingReport.com, "USA Today/Gallup Poll, June 11–13, 2010: Would you favor or oppose Congress passing new legislation this year that would do the following?," www.pollingreport.com/prioriti2.htm (accessed August 22, 2010).

4 "Right now, which ONE of the following do you think should be the more important priority for U.S. energy policy: keeping energy prices low or protecting the environment?" Pew Research/National Journal Congressional Connection Poll, PollingReport.com, June 10–13, 2010, http://www.pollingreport.com/enviro2.htm (accessed April 17, 2011).

5 J. Buchanan, *Liberty, Market, and State* (New York: New York University Press, 1986); J. M. Buchanan and V. Vanberg, "The Market as a Creative Process," in J. M. Buchanan, *Federalism, Liberty, and the Law*, vol. 18 (Indianapolis: Liberty Fund, 2001), 289–310.

6 J. Seabrook, "Snacks for a Fat Planet," *New Yorker*, May 16, 2011, 54–71.

7 *Source:* Adapted from A. J. Hoffman, *From Heresy to Dogma: An Institutional History of Corporate Environmentalism* (San Francisco, CA: New Lexington Press, 1997), and S. Ferrey, *Environmental Law: Examples and Explanations*, 5th ed. (New York: Aspen, 2010).

8 For example, see J. R. Neill, *Something New Under the Sun: An Environmental History of the Twentieth Century World* (New York: W.W. Norton, 2000); R. N. L. Andrews, *Managing the Environment, Managing Ourselves: A History of American Environmental Policy*, 2nd ed. (New Haven, CT: Yale University Press, 2006); D. J. Fiorino, *The New Environmental Regulation* (Cambridge, MA: MIT Press, 2006); N. Vig and M. E. Kraft (eds.), *Environmental Policy: New Directions for the Twenty-First Century*, 7th ed. (Washington, DC: CQ Press, 2010).

9 S. Ferrey, *Environmental Law*, 5th ed., 80.

10 Ibid., 81.

11 United Nations, Framework on Climate Change, "Kyoto Protocol," http://unfccc.int/kyoto_protocol/items/2830.php (accessed June 2, 2012).

12 "ETS, RIP?" *The Economist*, April 20, 2013, 75–76.

13 EPA's new law on CO_2. See Ryan Tracy and Deborah Solomon, "EPA Orders Deep Cuts in Emissions," *Wall Street Journal*, December 22, 2011, B3.

14 The EPA also exercises some responsibility over four other environmental statutes. And it operates under the restraints of the Administrative Procedure Act, the National Environmental Policy Act (NEPA), and various federal constitutional principles. The Departments of Interior, Commerce, Transportation, and Labor and the Council on Environmental Quality and others have primary responsibility for administering numerous other environmental laws, including the following: Coastal Barrier Resources Act; Coastal Zone Management Act; Deepwater Port Act; Endangered Species Act; Environmental Programs Assistance Act; Environmental Quality Improvement Act; Federal Land Policy and Management Act; Fish and Wildlife Coordination Act; Fishery Conservation and Management Act; Marine Mammal Protection Act; Marine Protection, Research and Sanctuaries Act; National Environmental Education Act; National Environmental Policy Act; National Forest Management Act; National Park System Mining Regulation Act; National Wildlife Refuge System Act; Occupational Safety and Health Act (OSHA); Oil Pollution Act of 1990; Outer Continental Shelf Lands Act Amendments of 1978; Pollution Prevention Act; Pollution Prosecution Act; Radon Gas and Indoor Air Quality Research Act; Shore Protection Act; Soil and Water Resources Conservation Act; Surface Mining Control and Reclamation Act; Water Resources Conservation Act; Wild and Scenic Rivers Act; and Wilderness Act.

15 F. Upton and T. Phillips, "How Congress Can Stop the EPA's Power Grab," *Wall Street Journal*, December 28, 2010, A13, http://online.wsj.com/article/SB10001424052748703929404576022070069905318.html (accessed January 15, 2011); J. M. Broder, "Greenhouse Gas Rule Delayed," *New York Times*, September 15, 2011; J. A. Dlouhy, "State Officials Clash with EPA over Greenhouse Gas Rules," *Houston Chronicle*, February 9, 2011.

16 R. Tracy, "House Votes to Stop EPA from Regulating Greenhouse Gases," *Wall Street Journal*, April 7, 2011.

17 L. Radnofsky, "Business Groups' Target: EPA," *Wall Street Journal*, February 7, 2011, http://online.wsj.com/article/SB10001424052748703989504576128132645791552.html (accessed January 15, 2011).

18 Bill McKibben bio, http://billmckibben.com/bio.html (accessed January 19, 2015).

19 350.org, http://350.org/ (accessed January 20, 2015).

20 R. Matthews, "An Homage to Leading Environmentalist Bill McKibben," *Wall Street Journal*, December 26, 2014, http://globalwarmingisreal.com/2014/12/26/homage-leading-environmentalist-bill-mckibben/ (accessed January 20, 2015).

21 B. Moran, "The Man Who Crushed the Keystone XL Pipeline," *Boston Globe*, January 22, 2012, http://www.bostonglobe.com/magazine/2012/01/22/bill-mckibben-man-who-crushed-keystone-pipeline/HkXTD01Z6bXLvibbf8piGK/story.html (accessed January 20, 2015).

22 B. Mckibben, "Global Warming's Terrifying New Math," *Rolling Stone*, July 19, 2012, http://www.rollingstone.com/politics/news/global-warmings-terrifying-new-math-20120719 (accessed January 19, 2015).

23 McKibben, 2012.

24 Seed Forum, http://vandanashiva.org/ (accessed January 19, 2015).

25 M. Spencer, "Seeds of Doubt," *The New Yorker*, August 25, 2014, http://www.newyorker.com/magazine/2014/08/25/seeds-of-doubt (accessed January 20, 2015).

26 V. Shiva, "Seeds of Truth: Vandana Shiva and The New Yorker," *Independent Science News* (December 17, 2014): 26.

27 P. Allitt, *A Climate of Crisis* (New York: The Penguin Press, 2014), 333. See H. P. Shabecoff, *A Fierce Green Fire* (*PBS*, Washington, DC, October 1, 2013); A. Rome, *The Bulldozer in the Countryside and the Rise of American Environmentalism* (Cambridge, UK: Cambridge University Press, 2001).

28 N. O. Keohane and S. M. Olmstead, *Markets and the Environment* (Washington, DC: Island Press, 2007), 21.

29 N. O. Keohane and S. M. Olmstead, *Markets and the Environment* (Washington, DC: Island Press, 2007), 135.

30 S. J. Buck, *Understanding Environmental Administration and Law*, 3rd ed. (Washington, DC: Island Press, 2006).

31 This point has been the basis of criticizing the Brundtland Commission's definition of sustainability.

32 P. Sabi, "Betting on the Apocalypse," *The New York Times*, September 8, 2013, SR5.

33 Judicial authority can resolve legal problems and does not involve judgments for money. *Tort actions*, by individual plaintiffs, can attack problems with a specificity that generic regulations may overlook.

34 S. J. Buck, *Understanding Environmental Administration and Law*, 3rd ed., 35–39.

35 J. Lin, D. Pan, S. J. Davis, Q. Zhang, C. Wang, D. G. Streets, D. J. Wuebbles, and D. Gua, "China's International Trade and Air Pollution in the United States," *Proceedings of the National Academy of Sciences* 111 (February 4, 2014): 1736–1741.

36 Center for Climate and Energy Solutions, "Renewable and Alternative Energy Portfolio Standards," www.c2es.org/us-states-regions/policy-maps/renewable-energy-standards (accessed December 19, 2011); U.S. Energy Information Administration, "Most States Have Renewable Portfolio Standards," February 3, 2012, www.eia.gov/todayinenergy/detail.cfm?id=4850 (accessed December 18, 2015).

37 Renewable Energy Portfolio Standard (RPS) & Alternative Energy Portfolio Standard Programs (APS). http://www.mass.gov/eea/energy-utilities-clean-tech/renewable-energy/rps-aps/ (accessed December 18, 2015); Center for Climate and Energy Solutions, "North Dakota RPS," www.c2es.org/_taxonomy/term/1542/0 (accessed December 18, 2015).

38 R. Wiser, G. Barbose, and E. Holt, "Supporting Solar Power in Renewables Portfolio Standards: Experience from the United States," *Energy Policy* 39, no. 7 (July 2011): 3894–3905.

39 H. Yin and N. Powers, "Do State Renewable Portfolio Standards Promote In-State Renewable Generation?" *Energy Policy* 38, no. 2 (February 2010): 1140–1149.

40 Wiser and Barbose for Berkeley Lab, http://emp.lbl.gov/sites/all/files/REPORT%20lbnl-3984e.pdf (accessed December 18, 2015).

41 K. Cory and B. Swezey, "Renewable Portfolio Standards in the States: Balancing Goals and Rules," *The Electricity Journal* 20, no. 4 (May 2007): 21–32.

42 U.S. Partnership for Renewable Energy Finance, "Ramping Up Renewables: Leveraging State RPS Programs amid Uncertain Federal Support," http://uspref.org/wp-content/uploads/2012/06/Ramping-up-Renewables-Leveraging-State-RPS-Programs-amid-Uncertain-Federal-Support-US-PREF-White-Paper1.pdf (accessed September 20, 2015).

43 International Energy Agency, *Deploying Renewables: Principles for Effective Policies* (Paris: IEA, 2008); see also N. H. van der Linder et al., *Review of International Experience with Renewable Energy Obligation Support Mechanisms*, LBNL-57666, ECN Publication ECN-C–05-025 (Energy Research Centre of the Netherlands, May 2005).

44 Ibid.

45 A. Kydes, "Impacts of Renewable Portfolio Generation Standards on US Energy Markets," *Energy Policy* 35, no. 2 (February 2007): 809–814.

46 L. Butler and K. Neuhoff, "Comparison of Feed-In-Tariff, Quota and Auction Mechanisms to Support Wind Power Development," *Renewable Energy* 33, no. 8 (August 2008): 1854–1867.

47 S. Shapiro, "Do Regulations Cost $1.75 Trillion? Not Exactly," *The Huffington Post*, February 9, 2011, www.huffingtonpost.com/sidney-shapiro/do-regulations-cost-175-t_b_820311.html (accessed December 18, 2015).

48 F. Newport, "Americans Leery of Too Much Gov't Regulation of Business," Gallup, February 2, 2010, www.gallup.com/poll/125468/americans-leery-govt-regulation-business.aspx (accessed October 23, 2011).

49 J. Dick, "Support for Addressing Climate Change Holds Firm," *National Journal*, August 2, 2010, http://congressionalconnection.nationaljournal.com/2010/08/support-for-addressing-climate.php (subscription required) (accessed August 23, 2011).

50 S. Shapiro, R. Ruttenberg, and J. Goodwin, "Saving Lives, Preserving the Environment, Growing the Economy: The Truth About Regulation" (White Paper #1109, Center for Progressive Reform, Washington, DC, July 2011).

51 Ibid.

52 Shapiro et al., "Saving Lives, Preserving the Environment, Growing the Economy"; U.S. Office of Management and Budget, Executive Office of the President, 2011 Report to Congress on Benefits and Costs of Federal Regulation

and Unfunded Mandates on State, Local, and Tribal Entities (Washington, DC, 2011), www.whitehouse.gov/sites/default/files/omb/inforeg/2011_cb/2011_cba_report.pdf (accessed November 2, 2011).

53 Shapiro et al., "Saving Lives, Preserving the Environment, Growing the Economy."

54 "Environmental Regulations May Not Cost as Much as Governments and Business Fear," *The Economist*, January 3, 2015, 62.

55 A. Dechezleprêtre and M. Sato, "The Impacts of Environmental Regulations on Competitiveness" (Grantham Research Institute, 2014) http://www.lse.ac.uk/GranthamInstitute/publication/the-impacts-of-environmental-regulations-on-competitiveness/ (accessed August 16, 2015). S. Albrizio, E. Botta, T. Koźluk, and V. Zipperer, "Do environmental policies matter for productivity growth? Insights from New Cross-Country Measures of Environmental Policies" (OECD, 2014). http://www.oecd-ilibrary.org/economics/do-environmental-policies-matter-for-productivity-growth_5jxrjncjrcxp-en (accessed August 15, 2015).

56 Co-authored by Michael Aper, Master of Arts in Sustainability candidate, 2015.

57 S. Shapiro, R. Ruttenberg, and J. Goodwin, "Saving Lives, Preserving the Environment, Growing the Economy: The Truth About Regulation" (White Paper #1109, Center for Progressive Reform, Washington, DC, July 2011).

58 Ibid.

59 North Carolina University, "Database of State Incentives for Renewables and Efficiency," http://www.dsireusa.org/incentives/incentive.cfm?Incentive_Code=NY03R (accessed February 15, 2015).

60 North Carolina University, "Database of State Incentives for Renewables and Efficiency," http://www.dsireusa.org/incentives/incentive.cfm?Incentive_Code=NY03R (accessed February 15, 2015)

61 Verdant Power, Inc., "About Us" (New York, 2015), http://www.verdantpower.com/about-us.html (accessed February 15, 2015).

62 Verdant Power, Inc., "RITE Project" (New York, 2015), http://www.verdantpower.com/rite-project.html (accessed February 15, 2015).

63 Ibid.

64 Verdant Power, Inc., http://www.verdantpower.com/uploads/2/4/7/6/24768638/khps-t5m.png (accessed February 15, 2015).

65 J. Hunt and D. Cardwell, "Experimental Efforts to Harvest the Ocean's Power Face Cost Setback," *New York Times*, Energy & Environment, April, 2014, http://www.nytimes.com/2014/04/28/business/energy-environment/experimental-efforts-to-harvest-the-oceans-power-face-cost-setbacks.html?ref=topics&_r=0 (accessed February 15, 2015).

66 J. Snyder, M. Drajem, and M. Philips, "The White House Walks Away from Clean Coal" (BloombergPolitics, Energy, February, 2014), http://www.bloomberg.com/politics/articles/2015-02-14/the-white-house-walks-away-from-clean-coal (accessed February 15, 2015).

67 A. M. Rugman and A. Verbeke, "Environmental Policy and International Business," in A. M. Rugman and T. L. Brewer (eds.), *Oxford Handbook of International Business* (New York: Oxford University Press, 2001), 537–557.

68 V. H. Hoffman, T. Trautmann, and M. Schneider, "A Taxonomy for Regulatory Uncertainty-Application to the European Emission Trading Scheme," *Environmental Science & Policy* 11, no. 8 (December 2008): 712–722.

69 R. A. Leone, *Who Profits: Winners, Losers, and Government Regulation* (New York: Basic Books, 1986).

70 Adapted from C. Engan and V. H. Hoffmann, "Corporate Response Strategies to Regulatory Uncertainty: Evidence from Uncertainty About Post-Kyoto Regulation," *Policy Sciences* 44, no. 1 (March 2011): 57.

71 L. J. Bourgeois and K. M. Eisenhardt, "Strategic Decision Processes in High Velocity Environments: Four Cases in the Microcomputer Industry," *Management Science* 34, no. 7 (1988): 816–835; A. A. Marcus, "Policy Uncertainty and Technological Innovation," *Academy of Management Review* 3 (1981): 443–448; B. Wernerfeldt and A. Karnani, "Competitive Strategy under Uncertainty," *Strategic Management Journal* 8, no. 2 (1987): 187–194.

72 R. M. Cyert and J. G. March, *A Behavioral Theory of the Firm* (Englewood Cliffs, NJ: Prentice Hall, 1963); B. Lev, "Environmental Uncertainty Reduction By Smoothing and Buffering: An Empirical Verification," *Academy of Management Journal* 18, no. 4 (1975): 864–871; J. D. Thompson, *Organizations In Action* (New York: McGraw-Hill, 1967).

73 L. R. Jauch, R. N. Osborne, and W. F. Glueck, "Short Term Financial Success in Large Business Organizations: The Environment-Strategy Connection," *Strategic Management Journal* 1, no. 1 (1980): 49–63; K. D. Miller, "A Framework for Integrated Risk Management in International Business," *Journal of International Business Studies* 23, no. 2 (1992): 311–331.

74 H. Courtney, J. Kirkland, and P. Viguerie, "Strategy under Uncertainty," *Harvard Business Review* 75, no. 6 (1997): 67–79; W. J. Heinsz and A. Delois, "Following the Herd and Sleeping with the Enemy: Strategies for Managing Policy Uncertainty," *Academy of Management Proceedings* (2004): M1–M6.

75 Heinsz and Delois, "Following the Herd and Sleeping with the Enemy"; J. G. March and H. A. Simon, *Organizations* (New York: Wiley, 1958); D. Miller and P. H. Friesen, "Strategy-Making and Environment: The Third Link," *Strategic Management Journal* 4, no. 3 (1983): 221–235; D. Miller, M. F. R. Kets de Vries, J.-M. Toulouse, "Top Executive Locus of Control and Its Relationship to Strategy-Making, Structure, and Environment," *Academy of Management Journal* 25, no. 2 (1982): 237–253.

76 Bourgeois and Eisenhardt, "Strategic Decision Processes in High Velocity Environments"; F. E. Emery, "The Next Thirty Years: Concepts, Methods and Anticipation," *Human Relations* 20, no. 3 (1967): 199–237; D. A. Levinthal and J. G. March, "The Myopia of Learning," *Strategic Management Journal* 14, no. 8 (1993): 95–112.

77 N. M. Carter, "Small Firm Adaptation: Responses to Physicians' Organizations to Regulatory and Competitive Uncertainty," *Academy of Management Journal* 33, no. 2 (1990): 307–333; B. J. McNeeley, "The Relationship of Regulatory Uncertainty and Coalition Formation within Marketing Channels," *Journal of Marketing Management* 5, no. 1 (1995): 47–61; Thompson, *Organizations in Action.*

78 A. A. Marcus, "Policy Uncertainty and Technological Innovation"; B. Mascarenhas, "Coping with Uncertainty in International Business," *Journal of International Business Studies* 13, no. 2 (1982): 87–98; Wernerfeldt and Karnani, "Competitive Strategy under Uncertainty."

79 C. R. Anderson and F. T. Paine, "Managerial Perceptions and Strategic Behavior," *Academy of Management Journal* 18, no. 4 (1975): 811–823; Bourgeois and Eisenhardt, "Strategic Decision Processes in High Velocity Environments."

80 D. D. Bergh and M. W. Lawless, "Portfolio Restructuring and Limits to Hierarchical Governance: The Effects of Government Uncertainty and Diversification Strategy," *Organization Science* 9, no. 1 (1998): 87–102; Cyert and March, *A Behavioral Theory of the Firm*; Thompson, *Organizations in Action.*

81 T. Burns and G. M. Stalker, *The Management of Innovation* (New York: Oxford University Press, 1961); J. R. Galbraith, *Designing Complex Organizations* (Reading, MA: Addison-Wesley, 1973); P. R. Lawrence and J. W. Lorsch, "Differentiation and Integration in Complex Organizations," *Administrative Science Quarterly* 12, no. 1 (1967): 1–47.

82 Emery, "The Next Thirty Years."

83 Courtney et al., "Strategy under Uncertainty."

84 D. Collis, "The Strategic Management of Uncertainty," *European Management Journal* 10, no. 2 (1992): 125–135; Wernerfeldt and Karnani, "Competitive Strategy under Uncertainty."

85 C. Engan and V. H. Hoffmann, "Corporate Response Strategies to Regulatory Uncertainty: Evidence from Uncertainty about Post-Kyoto Regulation," *Policy Sciences* 44, no. 1 (March 2011): 53–80.

86 J. R. Deckop, K. K. Merriman, and S. Gupta, "The Effects of CEO Pay Structure on Corporate Social Performance," *Journal of Management* 32, no. 3 (June 2006): 329–342.

87 S. Wadock, "Myths and Realities of Social Investing," *Organization & Environment* 16, no. 3 (September 2003): 369–380.

88 C. Eesley and M. J. Lenox, "Secondary Stakeholder Actions and the Selection of Firm Targets," draft paper (Durham, NC: Fuqua School of Business, Duke University, May 30, 2005), http://faculty.darden.virginia.edu/LenoxM/pdf/stake_wp2.pdf (accessed March 15, 2011).

89 A. K. Chatterji and M. W. Toffel, "How Firms Respond to Being Rated," *Strategic Management Journal* 31, no. 9 (September 2010): 917–945.

90 G. Hardin, "The Tragedy of the Commons," *Science* 162, no. 3859 (December 13, 1968): 1243–1248.

91 E. Ostrom, J. Burger, C. B. Field, R. B. Norgard, and D. Ploicansky, "Revisiting the Commons: Local Lessons, Global Challenges," *Science* 284, no. 5412 (April 9, 1999): 278–282; A. R. Poteete, M. A. Janssen, and E. Ostrom, *Working Together: Collective Action, the Commons, and Multiple Methods in Practice* (Princeton, NJ: Princeton University Press, 2010).

92 P. Barrett, "Jim Rogers: The CEO Who Wouldn't Leave," *Bloomberg Businessweek*, September 20, 2012, http://www.businessweek.com/articles/2012-09-20/jim-rogers-the-ceo-who-wouldnt-leave (accessed December 4, 2014).

93 In July 2013, the Duke board of directors named Lynn J. Good, formerly the executive vice president and chief financial officer of Duke Energy Ohio, to the post of president and chief executive officer of Duke Energy.

94 U.S. Environmental Protection Agency, "Summary of the Atomic Energy Act," www2.epa.gov/laws-regulations/summary-atomic-energy-act (accessed August 24, 2012).

95 U.S. Consumer Product Safety Commission, "Federal Hazardous Substances Act," August 12, 2011, www.cpsc.gov/PageFiles/105467/fhsa.pdf (accessed March 15, 2012).

96 U.S. Consumer Product Safety Commission, "Consumer Product Safety Act," August 12, 2011, www.cpsc.gov/PageFiles/113852/cpsa.pdf (accessed August 22, 2012).

97 U.S. Environmental Protection Agency, "Summary of the Nuclear Waste Policy Act," www2.epa.gov/laws-regulations/summary-nuclear-waste-policy-act.

98 U.S. Environmental Protection Agency, "Summary of the Shore Protection Act," http://www2.epa.gov/laws-regulations/summary-shore-protection-act (accessed September 1, 2015).

99 U.S. Environmental Protection Agency, "Summary of the Shore Protection Act," www2.epa.gov/laws-regulations/summary-shore-protection-act (accessed August 30, 2012).

100 U.S. Environmental Protection Agency, "Summary of Executive Order 12898—Federal Actions to Address Environmental Justice in Minority Populations and Low-Income Populations," www2.epa.gov/laws-regulations/summary-executive-order-12898-federal-actions-address-environmental-justice (accessed September 3, 2012).

101 U.S. Environmental Protection Agency, "Summary of the National Technology Transfer and Advancement Act," www2.epa.gov/laws-regulations/summary-national-technology-transfer-and-advancement-act (accessed September 3, 2012).

102 U.S. Environmental Protection Agency, "Summary of the Federal Insecticide, Fungicide, and Rodenticide Act," www2.epa.gov/laws-regulations/summary-federal-insecticide-fungicide-and-rodenticide-act (accessed September 3, 2012).

103 U.S. Environmental Protection Agency, "Summary of Executive Order 13045—Protection of Children From Environmental Health Risks and Safety Risks," www.epa.gov/laws-regulations/summary-executive-order-13045-protection-children-environmental-health-risks-and (accessed September 3, 2012).

104 U.S. Food and Drug Administration, "Federal Food, Drug, and Cosmetic Act," www.fda.gov/regulatoryinformation/legislation/federalfooddrugandcosmeticactfdcact/default.htm (accessed September 15, 2015).

105 U.S. Environmental Protection Agency, "Summary of Executive Order 13211—Actions Concerning Regulations That Significantly Affect Energy Supply, Distribution, or Use," www.epa.gov/laws-regulations/summary-executive-order-13211-actions-concerning-regulations-significantly-affect (accessed September 15, 2015).

106 U.S. Environmental Protection Agency, "Summary of the Federal Food, Drug, and Cosmetic Act," www.epa.gov/laws-regulations/summary-federal-food-drug-and-cosmetic-act (accessed September 15, 2015).

107 U.S. Environmental Protection Agency, "Summary of the Energy Independence and Security Act," www2.epa.gov/laws-regulations/summary-energy-independence-and-security-act (accessed September 16, 2015).

Part II

STRATEGY FORMULATION

4

STRATEGY WITH AN ENVIRONMENTAL LENS

Patagonia in 2015

Patagonia—founded by Yvon Chouinard, a world-class climber—is a designer, marketer, and distributor of high-performance outdoor wear. Chouinard originally named the company Chouinard Equipment, and it soon evolved into the firm now named after a wild and rugged region of southern Argentina and Chile. In the 1980s, the company expanded its brand to include accessories (e.g., hats, children's outdoor wear, and surf wear) and through successive organizational iterations, sales and profit margins grew rapidly (although not smoothly) through the 1980s and 1990s. By 2010, Patagonia was a highly recognized name.

The company's strategy hinges on four pillars—quality, design, environment, and the core customer[1]—and it has been highly praised for its product quality and design. Patagonia's core customer is called a "Dirtbag" (i.e., someone who prefers the human scale to the corporate, vagabonding to tourism, the quirky and lively to the toned down and flattened out, temporary jobs, tribal travel following the seasons, and a rugged lifestyle indicative of the most dedicated climbers and outdoors people).[2] These four pillars have positioned Patagonia as a high-quality producer of clothing and related equipment.

Still, the company has its challenges despite wide recognition in their market (e.g., the Dirtbags are aging and competitors have been duplicating some of Patagonia's quality techniques). However, it has received myriad accolades because of its close work with suppliers, its production of small-batch sizes, and its innovative approach to product design. Patagonia is well known for selling clothing systems (as opposed to one-off pieces of clothing), and its environmental commitment influences its decision-making throughout the business (e.g., supplier choices, retail store construction and location, and product design). For example:

- *Patagonia has supported environmental groups through grants and in-kind contributions.*
- *In 1985, Chouinard implemented an "Earth Tax" program, which included a donation of either 1 percent of sales or 10 percent of pretax profits (whichever was greater) to environmental groups.*
- *Patagonia seeks to resolve conflicts between business and environmental commitments by minimizing the environmental harm of its products and processes.*
- *Patagonia challenges other firms to meet its environmental commitment; its environmental focus is renowned among like-minded organizations and individuals.*

From the beginning, Chouinard did not want the company to grow rapidly; he felt it would lose its focus. The side effect of its slow growth and environmental focus is that the returns on products did not seem to cover the added costs of the company's philosophy and practices. For example, it charged a premium on its popular Alpine clothing yet this premium might not be enough to cover the product's costs. Other competitors were able to produce approximate clothing systems with higher margins, and a company study found that 45 percent of its customers are unaware of its environmental contributions.

Over the years, the competitive pressures have continued to rise, and they reached a breaking point in 2010. The company began to weigh their values against their bottom line and were forced to consider changing their practices. Also, Chouinard was getting older and needed to confront his succession. He retired as CEO, hiring Rose Marcario. Rose was Patagonia's COO and CFO; led M&A at Capital Advisors; was SVP and CFO of Apple spin-off *General Magic*.[3] Thus, with competition and costs rising, the company was forced to consider changing its focus without losing its core values.

Chapter Overview

Like Patagonia, organizations are often faced with developing strategies for success that can conflict with core values. For this, they often draw upon the latest business literature featuring concepts that are often over-simplified into algorithms or formulas for success that fly in the face of sound, time-tested principles of management. The danger of these new theories and practices is that they may prohibit effective *thinking* about complex problems (e.g., strategic thinking). This is the focus of this chapter.

A key goal throughout this book is to overcome the temptation to provide formulaic solutions to difficult organizational challenges; instead, you should develop new yet sound and tested skills and perspectives. No formula can fully prepare you for every situation; instead, you will need a worldview that will allow you to fully see the risks and benefits and attain a solid grounding in strategic thinking.

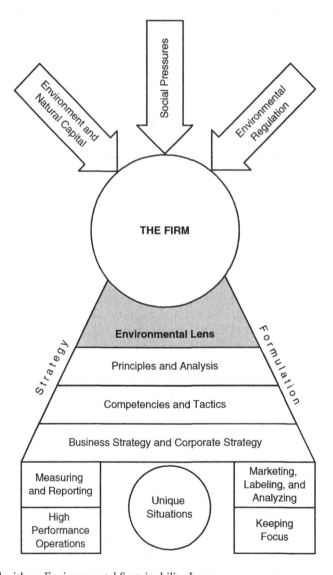

Figure 4.1 Strategy Model with an Environmental Sustainability Lens

Defining Strategic Thinking

Strategic thinking is a process of critically analyzing an organization's past and present-day situations to make decisions about future actions. Most of the analytical techniques analysts and managers use to think strategically are frameworks that enable us to identify, clarify, and understand principal factors relevant to setting the future course of an organization. Such frameworks are invaluable for helping us to come to grips with an organization's complexities.

Oftentimes, the value of strategic thinking is that analysts and managers engage in a guided process that organizes disparate information into a format that can be discussed among managers across an organization's operations. Strategic thinking helps companies focus their attention and set goals so that organizational members know what to emphasize in their daily activities. Also, every organization has finite resources, so allocating among competing investments is a constant (and often difficult) process of making tradeoffs. Without clear, active, and effective strategic thinking, these decisions are that much more difficult and potentially unproductive and wasteful.

Executives and analysts study strategies to understand sustained differences in organizational performances. I place high value on strategy and understand it as the essence of an organization's existence. It is the closest to a determinant of success as is possible; thinking strategically helps organizational members gain control over their activities and futures by setting and agreeing upon paths they should follow.[4]

Myriad aspects of strategic thinking must be understood before you can master the process of creating strategy. For example, the creation and implementation of strategy involves allocating finite resources to achieve and sustain competitive advantages. A *competitive advantage* is defined as obtaining unusual returns or outcomes compared to competitors.

When deciding on a strategy, organizational members take into account various sources of information (e.g., market behavior, the environment's macroeconomic conditions, and the organization's competencies). The creation and implementation of any plan will be hindered by various types of uncertainties and risks (e.g., macro conditions change frequently and new competitors or political influences enter markets suddenly). As decisions are made, correlating strategies must reflect an organization's approach to these inevitable risks.

As organizations begin making decisions, organizational members must remain cognizant of potentially missing information, the difficulties inherent in the decision-making process, and the politics involved in the implementation of decisions; this keeps them critically mindful about strategy and what informs this strategy.[5] Strategic decisions are relatively long term, include commitments that are not easily changed, typically involve risk, and are often adventures into the unknown.[6] Hence, you should not be so surprised by the big failures you see in the newspapers and among investors. While some authors have found that certain failures can be predicted, others view failures as a set of circumstances that cannot easily be foreseen by analysis.[7]

Strategy *content* and strategy *process* are two sides of the same coin, creating a symbiotic relationship to help decision makers think and act strategically as the organization evolves over time. All of these factors (in one way or another) rely on natural resources and create environmental impacts. The major bias in this presentation (and what makes it different from other presentations about firm-level strategy) is the focus on environmental sustainability. In this chapter, I will add to our earlier definition some of the nuances of sustainability.

The Institutional View[8]

Exposure to various theories about the conduct of organizations will help you learn how to describe organizations, evaluate and predict their behaviors, and prescribe what they should do to increase competitiveness. The most widely accepted views of an organization are the *economic view* and *behavioral view*. The purpose of this section is to suggest yet a third view (i.e., the *institutional view*). The institutional view is particularly useful when examining why performance differences exist across countries and why these differences matter in strategic assessment.

Three Views of the Organization

The *economic view* emphasizes that organizations are players within an industry and compete with a well-defined set of competitors to obtain scarce resources. This view assumes that an organization's behavior is rational and a product of its economic incentive structure. Thus, organizations are analyzed using concepts such as costs, revenues, demand and supply, industry structure, economic value-added, and resource scarcity. The ultimate goal of the organization, according to the economic view, is to produce a competitive return for the shareholder.

The behavioral view assumes that the logic of the organization differs from the logic of the marketplace. Organizations are viewed as being led by managers with values and attitudes that impact the motivation of others. The behavioral view analyzes the organization through the lens of human resources, leadership, motivation, decision-making processes, and bounded rationality.[9] Unlike the economic view, rationality is not assumed. The behavioral view emphasizes the manager's role in directing participant behaviors to achieve goals.

The *institutional view* is a third perspective on organizations.[10] An institution is a set of cognitive, normative, and regulative structures and activities that provide stability and meaning to social behavior. Table 4.1 shows a list of institutions that typically influence business organizations by providing definitions of what is (or is not) legitimate behavior. Table 4.2 shows some questions addressed from the perspective of the institutional view. Organizations then choose various strategies to comply, modify, or not comply with these pressures.

Some Assumptions of the Institutional View[11]

Analysts adopting the institutional view make various assumptions about an organization and its environment. Among the more important assumptions are:

1 *Organizations are products of their environments* and are influenced by interactions occurring within close proximity (e.g., with customers, suppliers, employees, shareholders, and regulatory agencies). Other interactions are historical or otherwise removed (e.g., the way it was founded, the way other organizations in the industry act, and society's cultural assumptions).
2 *The organization is a product of its own history*, which passes on accumulated knowledge from one period to the next. It is viewed as a bundle of technical, organizational, and economic routines that act as a repository for the experience and knowledge that it has accumulated. Once an organization's identity is shaped, it defines the organization and how it does things.[12]

Table 4.1 Eleven Typical Institutions That Influence Business Organizations

Institution	How it may influence business organizations
Property rights	Guarantees (or defines) what organizations can buy or sell without intervention
Capital markets	Provides a means for exchanging assets
Other factor markets	Provides a means for obtaining labor or materials as inputs to production
Universities	Sources of research and labor for organizations
Securities and Exchange Commission	Regulation of capital markets, guaranteeing transparency in trades and protection from unfair practices
Taxing authorities	Means of obtaining resources from organizations in exchange for the maintenance of public institutions that protect and provide for organizations
Banks	Provide a source of capital (and services related to capital) for organizations and consumers
Rule of law	Means of arbitration for disputes among organizations and individuals
Industry recipes, fads and associations	Provides a basis for sharing information and imitating competition or best in class
Competition	Means of evaluating who is *us*, who is *them*, and the results of an organization's work
Balance sheets; income statements	Continuity and consistency in the way information is shared

Table 4.2 Typical Questions Addressed by the Institutional View

---

Why do organizations of the same types (schools, hospitals, steel companies, or consulting companies), located in widely different locations, so closely resemble each other?

To what extent is an organization's behavior shaped by conventions, routines, and habits?

Why is it that the behavior of organizational participants so often departs from the formal rules and stated goals of the organization?

To what extent are our interests culturally constructed?

Why do certain organizational innovations take hold and others do not?

Why are some organizations viewed as excellent in some cultures and not in others?

Why do organizations have so much difficulty changing their behavior event in the face of compelling reasons to do so?

How do institutions develop? Why do institutions exist such as The Environmental Protection Agency, independent government councils, and the World Trade Organization?

---

3   The institutional view assumes that *organizations are guided by procedures and not goals*. The organization is viewed as a complex, multi-layered, constantly interacting entity that has some agreed-upon procedures to coordinate its activities. These procedures define and motivate the organization—more than its goals.

4   The institutional view assumes that *organizations take on characteristics of key people, events, and units within and outside of the organization*. Organizational behavior is guided by moral beliefs, normative obligations, and regulative expectations. Organizations act in accordance to laws, industry norms, and their own definitions of appropriate behavior.

Legitimacy

Analysts who use the institutional view assess whether or not an organization is legitimate. By legitimacy, one could mean that the organization is established and operated in accordance with relevant legal or quasi-legal requirements. Also, the organization may be considered legitimate when it adheres to a deeper moral base (e.g., expected values or desired behaviors). Finally, an organization is legitimate to the extent that it adopts a common frame of reference (or definition of a situation).

Three sets of factors shape organizational legitimacy: (1) the environment's institutional characteristics, (2) the organization's characteristics, and (3) the process by which the environment builds perceptions of the organization.[13] In sum, the ability of an organization to be perceived as legitimate is a product of three factors—the environment, organization, and process by which the two interact.[14]

Analytical Emphases in the Institutional View

Various authors emphasize different themes, methods, and concepts within the institutional view. Here are three related emphases for analyzing organizations.

1. Regulative Emphasis

Institutions constrain and regulate organizational behavior through rule setting, monitoring, and sanctioning activities. Institutions consist of formal written rules as well as unwritten codes of conduct. When the rules are broken, sanctions are levied against offenders. Ultimately, a third party must enforce rules through the involvement of a court or arbitration mechanism. For example, U.S. public companies conform to the Securities and Exchange Commission (SEC). All organizations are expected to conform to applicable local, national, and international laws.

2. Norms and Values

Institutions also have norms and values (e.g., desirable ways of acting); conformity provides legitimacy. Norms act to define performance criteria and legitimate ways to pursue those standards. An organization's

91

actions should seem reasonable in terms of institutional social rules and behavioral guidelines (e.g., investors have certain expectations of organizations before they invest in companies, and employees expect certain conditions of employment).

3. Cognitive

The cognitive emphasis focuses on how organizations interpret institutions. What an organization does is largely a function of how managers, employees, and other stakeholders perceive the organization; organizations understand themselves only to the extent that they interact with other organizations and institutions and develop meaning from this. They develop categories or labels (e.g., suppliers and competition) to understand the various interactions and experiences they have. To change an organization, one must change the meaning it ascribes to itself and its environment.

How to Analyze Institutional Influences

I will cover two analyses to identify institutional influences on an organization (Table 4.3). These include:

1 analyze the relationship of the organization to its institutions;
2 compare organizations to each other.

One can compare organizations to the institutions that influence them. For example, local, state, and federal governments influence most organizations. Community groups, industry associations, and unions are other examples of institutions influencing organizations. Institutions can also reside in laws and common practices.[15] Thus, the analyst asks:

- "How do these institutions influence an organization?"
- "Are the organizational structures, policies, practices, and routines similar (or influenced by) the organization's institutions?"

The more you can establish a link between an institution and organization, the more likely the institution influences the organization. Additionally, the organization can influence the institution. For example, many analysts argue that long-established organizations will set expectations for newer organizations' structures, strategies, and systems.

Another way to determine an institution's impact on an organization is to compare organizations to each other. If an organization has practices different from others (e.g., those in the same industry), then one can assume that the organization has not been as influenced by its institutions as other organizations. Organizations imitate each other's practices (particularly those with whom they associate over time).[16]

Generic Strategies Organizations Use to React to Institutions

Although all organizations are subject to the effects of institutional forces, they do not all respond in the same manner to these pressures. Table 4.4 presents five generic strategies used by most organizations.

Table 4.3 Determining Institutional Influences on Organizations

Analysis	Example
Compare organizations to their institutions	Regulated organizations take on some of the practices of their regulatory agencies; thus, organizations take their institutions into account when designing strategy.
Comparison of organizations to each other	Many large organizations have similar structures.

Table 4.4 Generic Strategies Organizations Use to React to Institutions[17]

Strategy	Example
Acquiescing	The organization changes its policies to comply with government regulations or industry practices
Compromising	Explaining to a government agency that the organization is complying with regulations (even if it looks as if it is not)
Avoiding	Creating a government affairs office to influence legislators to support the organization and not allowing regulatory agencies to influence the organization
Defying	An organization breaking with common industry practices to maximize its benefits
Manipulating	Developing methods for changing the institution (e.g., Wal-Mart changing the practices of its suppliers as described in Chapter 1)

Organizations might *acquiesce* to the institutional impact. For example, organizations have a tendency to imitate other organizations like themselves. They tend to adopt organizational structures or practices that they perceive as successful and aligned with common practice. Thus, they sometimes reduce uncertainty by imitating the ways of others. A study found that highly profitable organizations serve as role models for all organizations.[18] Could Patagonia serve this purpose, influencing all organizations to act more environmentally responsibly?

Avoidance is when an organization disguises its nonconformity or attempts to buffer parts of the organization from the impact of institutional demands. Organizations try to avoid the demands of institutions if these institutions impose conflicting requirements (e.g., that impede organizational objectives, rules, and technical requirements). Organizations may engage in illegal activities yet try to disguise these from regulatory bodies. Also, organizations might form boundary units within their organizations to give the appearance that they are conforming but buffer the rest of the organization from institutional impacts (e.g., a sustainability department might make it appear that a firm cares about the environment, but it does not involve people throughout the organization).

Defiant organizations not only resist institutional pressures to conform, but they do so in a very public manner. Defiance is likely to occur when the norms and interests of organizations diverge substantially from those attempting to impose the requirements. Some organizations take their fight to the public (e.g., against government regulations or new requirements from regulatory agencies). Defiance occurred when the EPA announced its intent to regulate carbon output by U.S. companies.[19]

Organizations attempt to defend themselves and improve their bargaining power by developing linkages to improve their sources of power. One could argue that the reason many multinationals have local joint venture partners in emerging markets is because these local partners have powerful connections and are perceived as legitimate organizations. Organizations try to adopt impression management techniques to improve their reputations or legitimize their acts.

Questions to Ask When Analyzing Organizations

Table 4.5 presents a list of analytical questions one could ask when employing the institutional view.

Table 4.5 Analytical Questions When Applying the Institutional View

1	What are the key institutions impacting the organization?
2	What are the key institutional pressures on the organization? Analyze the regulative, normative, and cognitive pressures and expectations for legitimacy.
3	How similar is an organization to others in its context? To what extent is the organization different from other organizations?
4	What must an organization do to be seen as legitimate?
5	What strategies does the organization use to respond to institutions? Are these strategies effective?
6	To what extent is the organization legitimate (i.e., complying with laws, acting as it "should," and fitting within common definitions of an organization)?

Summary of the Institutional View

Institutions are formal and informal rules (and associated enforcement mechanisms) that provide structure for economic actors:

1   Institutions reduce uncertainty by establishing a stable (although not necessarily efficient) structure for economic actors and by limiting choices.
2   Institutions are important because they affect firm performance.
3   Institutions determine opportunities that are available in society; organizations take advantage of these opportunities to gain competitive advantages.
4   Organizations seek legitimacy; legitimacy provides differential access to resources.
5   Firms look alike because they are forced (or coerced) to act alike, or they imitate other organizations.
6   Firms are different because they react to institutions in different ways using unique strategies.
7   Certain circumstances, such as firms operating in multiple settings, present conflicting mandates for strategy formulation.

The institutional point of view helps to see why strategy making is so important. It provides a rich context to use a set of concepts that help managers think strategically. Organizations respond to the environment in which they operate. Thus, strategy must be responsive to these contexts and is a primary reason why I recommend that analysts do extensive external analysis to inform strategic choices. This chapter and Chapter 5 will explain these external analyses.

Strategic Thinking

This material is organized around a few central ideas (see Figure 4.1). To understand the concepts about strategy, consider some underlying assumptions:

1   Organizations are purposeful, boundary-maintaining, and socially constructed systems of human activity[20] that are created to achieve some purpose. For our purposes, I assume that the role of organizations in society is very meaningful; this assumption is important as you consider why two organizations in the same industry or doing similar work make very different choices in terms of strategic direction. Also, this purposeful behavior and deliberate design are what make organizations different from other social collectives (e.g., families and social groups).
2   Organizations must find a balance between competing and cooperating with other organizations. Organizations are not self-sufficient; they interact with external entities and associated cultures. Therefore, organizations, industries, and institutions influence individual and group behavior. This assumption applies to the dynamic relationships existing between entities engaged in competition and cooperation (e.g., when Apple developed its new iPhone with HTC, Google was not far behind in developing its phone with HTC; thus, HTC was working with two industry leaders). Rapid competitive responses often create partnerships among competitors and suppliers.
3   Business organizations spend a great deal of time and effort *positioning* themselves within markets. (Positioning refers to offering unique benefits that increase the customer's willingness to purchase a product or service from a firm.)
4   Organizations have activity systems (i.e., certain routines, resources, and capabilities)[21] that are just as important to a successful strategy as the positioning of the firm.
5   The principles in this chapter can apply to various types of organizations including non-government, government and for-profit businesses. This chapter's discussion is biased towards for-profit business success.
6   You can discover principles related to competitive advantage through theory, research, and practice.

I will build on these assumptions to describe important principles for developing and implementing strategy. An effective strategy is one that:

- has a clear focus and direction;
- is informed through analyses of external forces;
- is informed through analyses of the organization;
- can be implemented.

These criteria help organize your strategic thinking and analytical tools to gain and use data. Also, the effective strategist has the necessary analytical and behavioral skills and knowledge to carry out every stage of the strategy formulation and implementation. These factors increase the probability that the strategist will allocate resources to create organizational value.

Profile: Tech Giants and Changing Climates[22]

Table 4.6 lists key questions that help the firm begin developing a sound approach. The first two questions ask the firm, "What global trends might influence your organization?" and "What can you learn from the macro environments in which you do your work?" From an environmental lens, many firms in the past focused solely on social pressure and responded by creating sustainable initiatives in hopes of improving their corporate image. However, today, the prior questions stir deeper discussion about the role of risk mitigation and financial predictability in enterprise value analysis.

In particular, global firms are increasingly confronted with the risk of extreme storms, water scarcity, and material supply shortages.[23] Further, compounding those challenging cost calculations are the introduction of social unrest and political instability in environments where firms do business. Tech firms are among the most globalized firms in the world and they are taking climate change very seriously. In fact, their investment efforts are so significant they are forcing reluctant, adjacent industries not only to acknowledge climate change, but also to respond to it. In the same week of February 2015, Google and Apple both announced the launch of major renewable energy projects.

Google announced that the firm will buy power from wind farm Altamont Pass. In partnership with NextEra Energy, Google will own 770 wind turbines, replacing 48 of them to produce enough energy to power 100 percent of the Googleplex.[24] Apple announced their $850 million agreement to buy power and build a 280-megawatt solar farm in Monterey County, California. Seemingly not to be outdone, in the following week, Google announced yet another project; this time a $750 million fund in partnership with SolarCity for investment in residential solar projects.[25]

The Answer, My Friend, Is Blowin' in the Wind. Tech firms are looking at the macro environment and responding with a sense of urgency by creating renewable energy and green data programs. The goal is to mitigate risk and predict the financial implications of future climate change. At a Goldman Sachs conference, Apple CEO Tim Cook said, "We expect to have significant savings because we have a fixed price for the renewable energy, and there's quite a difference between that price and the price of brown energy." What are some of the potential implications these major investments will have on utilities companies located adjacently to these tech giants? How can changing their corporate culture to better align with Google and Apple's benefit their bottom line?

Organizations and Strategy

Why do firms exist?

One reason is to coordinate and motivate people's economic activities to achieve goals. Markets promote this coordination and motivation; they provide opportunities for individuals to pursue self-interested behaviors and guide those choices via pricing. A well-functioning market leads to interdependent behaviors (i.e., one person's choices and actions impact other people). When markets are functioning efficiently, no other arrangement of economic activity would be preferred.[26]

However, sometimes the market fails. A study of market failures is critical to understanding when a firm should be the best mechanism to coordinate and motivate people. For example, firms maintain memories about clients, their needs, and how best to serve them. NGOs fill in where businesses and government do not address a societal need. This type of knowledge is not available via the general market (or at least not in a cost-effective manner). This type of analysis involves understanding risk management, specific types of contracts and assets, and whether business is best done inside or outside a firm (via outsourcing and market transactions). Answering these questions influences a firm's strategy.[27]

Table 4.6 Questions about the Basic Elements of a Strategy

External Conditions:

1   What global long-term trends might influence your organization?[28]
2   What can you learn from the macro environments in which you do your work?
3   What can you learn from a strategic analysis of your industry or industries, the marketplaces, competitors, and other key players and stakeholders who influence your organization?[29]
4   Where will you be active and with how much emphasis? What are the organization's boundaries?
5   Who are your core customers and stakeholders and what trends do you see for them?
6   What are your core products and services?[30]
7   What are your key success factors?[31]

Internal Conditions:

8   What are your resources and capabilities (activities)?[32]
9   To what extent are these resources and capabilities rare, relevant, durable, and connected?[33]
10 To what extent do the resources and capabilities fit with the organization's administrative history, structure, systems, culture, and management style?
11 What can you do to enhance the returns from your resources and capabilities?
12 What are your core metrics?[34]

Focus:

13 What do you want to achieve? What are your fundamental purpose, values, mandates, targets and objectives; why are you in business?
14 Where are the growth opportunities: core, adjacencies, breakthrough, white spaces, and blue oceans?[35]
15 How can you be different compared to those with whom you compete or cooperate for resources? What are your points of parity and difference?
16 Will your strategy beat the market?
17 What are your strategic imperatives and initiatives?

Implementation:

18 What can you achieve?
19 What moves should you make to achieve your purpose? Goals?
20 What will be your speed and sequence of the moves?
21 What is a realistic action plan given the tradeoffs in priorities, timing, and politics?
22 How do you balance commitment and flexibility?
23 How will you obtain returns? What are your best business models?[36]
24 How do you know you are achieving your purpose?

Analytical and Process Skills for Content Awareness and Content-in-Use (these questions relate to the necessary base knowledge needed to do strategy and the organizational processes to do strategic thinking):

25 What is your starting point for the strategy? What change management challenges do you have?
26 What data do you consider most important for your strategic thinking?

27 What are the key concepts, theories, models, and methods for understanding strategy?[37]
28 How can you act to gather relevant information and to make decisions?
29 Is your analysis granular enough to gain specific data to make decisions?
30 How should you phrase your strategic alternatives and your strategic direction?
31 How do you manage inevitable biases and internal political influences on decisions?
32 Who should be at the table and how does each member perform a role in the process?
33 How does one behave to create a sense of perspective, urgency to act, to make changes and to convince others that these changes are organizationally appropriate?
34 What are the internal and external processes for innovation?

Note: Each of these questions is answered using analysis frameworks and methods that specify data for the organization and help the analyst make strategic decisions.

Therefore, there are many questions that need to be answered before a strategy can be agreed upon within a firm. Table 4.6 lists questions that serve as the basis of strategic thinking; they address the four success criteria for effective strategy plus necessary processes for strategy making. Strategy, ultimately, is about being different from others and deliberately choosing a different set of activities to deliver a unique mix that offers value. The questions in Table 4.6 help to define and implement an organization's strategy to create this difference.

Apple Inc. is a company with unique positioning in the technology markets. In particular, Apple has unique attributes that heighten its position (e.g., its stores, image, and celebrated founder). It has also presented itself as an environmental leader.[38] Apple states that its MacBook computers are the world's greenest family of notebooks; that its product displays are free of mercury and arsenic; that its iPhone 5 is free of BFRs, PVC, arsenic, mercury, and is powered by an adapter that outperforms the strictest global energy efficiency standards;[39] and that it designed its iPods and iPhones to be free of polyvinyl chlorides and brominated flame retardant.

Greenpeace International's *Guide to Greener Electronics* aims to push the electronics sector to reduce its environmental impact, energy use, emissions (throughout its supply chain), and use of unsustainable materials. The *Guide* also pushes companies to use their influence in support of stronger environmental legislation.[40] Greenpeace's *Guide to Greener Electronics* ranked Apple in sixth place in 2012 (which was down one position from 2011 but up from 14th in 2008). Apple received the point reduction in 2012 for its lack of transparency in reporting its use of renewable energy;[41] Apple refuses to provide key details on its manufacturing processes.

These facts indicate that Apple's image as "green" might not be as straightforward as many consumers believe, which raises questions about Apple's strategies and tactics. Should Apple have an environmental focus as part of its core strategy and positioning? Is this really a major activity consumers should know about? Many feel Apple is guilty of using "green" as a marketing ploy (i.e., "greenwashing"). Greenwashing is often levied against firms who do a bare minimum to save resources or use environmental sustainability to offer products. For example, Huggies had a small piece of cotton on its diaper and Proctor and Gamble marketed the diaper as supposedly natural.

Positioning the Firm

If there were one ideal position for all organizations, there would be no need for strategy and strategic thinking. Companies would face simple destinies that would be defined by formulas; operational effectiveness would differentiate them and *not* positioning. Most firms would probably earn the cost of capital rather than gain a competitive advantage. Yet, the world of business does not work this way; there are various ways to play the game, handle positioning, and engage in activities to support it.[42]

As you study an organization's strategy, consider that strategy occurs at various organizational levels. Most important for our discussion are three levels of analysis: business, corporate, and functional. *Business* or unit strategy refers to the positioning and set of activities for a single line of business in a single market or industry, and it defines how an organization competes in this market. *Corporate* strategy refers to an organization's strategy for multiple units or lines of business (defining the various markets in which a firm competes and how these multiple lines are coordinated). *Functional* strategy refers to strategies specific to functions within a business (e.g., marketing, operations, and finance). Ideally business, corporate, and functional strategies mesh to form coherent stories (or theories) about how organizations should attain and sustain competitive advantages.

When an organization's strategy adheres to the four criteria for success (i.e., specific knowledge about a firm's competitive advantage), it increases the likelihood that the firm can communicate a compelling story to all stakeholders. To tell this story, analysts and managers alike have to be confident that the developed strategy is effective. To be effective, a strategy must have focus, take into account external and internal data, and be implementable.

Every organization has a strategy; it allocates resources regardless of whether or not this allocation is purposeful. Some organizations work to put their strategies into words whereas other companies' strategies are more haphazard or intuitive. The purpose of learning about the analytical tools behind forming a strategy is so that organizations can be purposeful in their actions. The more a strategy is defined and informed by analysis, the less an organization's actions will be impacted by power battles, individual whims, fads, and wishful thinking.

Identifying a Company's Strategy

Where do you look to find a company's strategy?

It can actually be found in several places (which might or might not yield consistent information). The firm's *executives* are generally responsible for articulating strategy and putting it into action. Also, strategy is enacted through a firm's *decisions* (e.g., a specific strategy for targeting a segment of the population is revealed through marketing choices). And observers and analysts use systematic *frameworks, theories,* and *tools* to discover components of a firm's strategy; this chapter contains descriptions of some of these decision-making tools.

The organization's strategy is evident in various places. First, organizational analysts watch the moves of organizations, for example. They watch how organizations respond to external pressures to understand more about the strategy. They might find detailed information in annual reports and other company documents which disclose important information. These disclosures are required for public firms. Many organizations will disclose strategies so that they can inform investors, customers, and employees. While some details may be missing from these disclosures, the expressions of focus are often informative.

The majority of literature describing strategy fails to mention the impact of the natural environment on strategy development. My perspective argues that prominent external factors influencing organizational behavior include the natural environment (and individuals or groups that pressure companies to have concern for the environment) because so many of an organization's resources come from the natural environment. Thus, environmental factors must be considered when developing organizational strategies. Organizations can increase their competitiveness or effectiveness (and achieve a more positive impact on the environment) by incorporating principles and practices for environmental sustainability in their strategies. One set of research found that environmental perspectives, woven into a company's values, assumptions, and beliefs, are partial determinants of its behavior towards the environment. Thus, a company's beliefs are viewed as determinants of its environmental performance.[43]

I assume that managing the environment precedes environmental performance. *Environmental management* consists of efforts to minimize the negative environmental impacts of a firm's products and conduct.[44] *Performance* then represents a more advanced level of environmental sustainability, which results from a firm's actions. Thus, the desire to treat the environment well must start with core, company-wide values, assumptions, and beliefs. These factors form part of a firm's focus.

If an organization integrates environmental concerns into its values and beliefs, this integration enables an environmentally focused strategy. When organizations incorporate environmental issues into core strategies, they are more likely to explore how this important area can increase their competitiveness and effectiveness.

Interestingly, you are at a time in history when political and social environments are receptive to this way of thinking. As a result, the view of an organization's role in sustaining the environment is shifting (i.e., firms assuming this responsibility are often regarded more favorably than their peers).

Here is an example of how some would phrase this change:

> Environmentalism has offered something profoundly important to America and the world. It inspired an appreciation for, and an awe of the beauty and majesty of, the nonhuman world. It focused our attention on future generations and our responsibility toward them. And it called upon people to take valiant risks, from saving rain forests and whales to inventing wondrous new technologies that will help us overcome the ecological crises we face. . . .
>
> But environmentalism has also saddled us with the albatross we call the politics of limits, which seeks to constrain human ambition, aspiration, and power rather than unleash and direct them. . . .
>
> Today, you have new choices to make. You must choose between a politics of limits and a politics of possibility; a focus on investment and assets and a focus on regulation and deficits; and a discourse of affluence and a discourse of insecurity. And, most of all, you must choose between a resentful narrative of tragedy and a grateful narrative of overcoming.[45]

The authors quoted above refer constantly to the "death of environmentalism" to signal a need to be more proactive and positive about what we can invent together. They are suggesting that environmentalism should not be viewed as just a movement; it should be part of everyday thinking. Thus, environmental issues should be core to strategy.

One way that organizations can create this incorporation of an environmental lens is to use analytical frameworks and certain questions that challenge them to obtain and analyze information. I presented Table 4.6 earlier in this chapter and it contains a set of questions that can be effective in this endeavor and support the model presented in Figure 4.1. Table 4.6 is divided into four sets of "criteria" along with a final section with analytical questions.

Focus

The first two questions from Table 4.6 are two of the most fundamental questions, but they cannot be fully answered without working through the subsequent questions. Some work can be done on these questions before collecting market data or analyzing internal activities; however, the organization's "focus" is a product of in-depth analysis of external and internal conditions. The following are questions from Table 4.6 about *Focus:*

- What do you want to achieve? What are your fundamental purposes, values, mandates, targets, and objectives? Why are you in business?
- How can you be different from competitors? What are your points of parity and difference?

A firm operates in the interests of its owners through maximizing their returns, which implies maximizing the value of the firm's investments. Thus, thinking strategically implies creating organizational purpose and unifying the energy and creativity of organizational members in pursuit of that purpose. To accomplish this, firms develop missions, values, and vision statements (i.e., statements that help identify the character and essential values of an organization and desired outcomes of organizational work). For example, 3M's mission states, "to solve unsolved problems innovatively."

Most important is that statements are clear, can be used to guide organizational behavior, and provide a sense of a firm's purpose beyond profit; after all, maximizing shareholder wealth is to a business as breathing is to life (i.e., breathing is essential, but it is not the purpose of life). Also, they establish how a firm is different from competitors. Again, competitive strategy is about being *different*; it means deliberately choosing a different set of goals and activities to deliver value.

External Conditions

The next set of questions is about the external focus of a firm. Among the more important questions are:

- What can you learn from the macro environments in which you do your work?
- What can you learn from a strategic analysis of our industry (or industries), marketplaces, competitors, and other key players in our competitive set?
- Where will you be active and with how much emphasis? What are the boundaries of your organization?

The key with this analysis is attaining a complete understanding of the structure of an industry and the competitive dynamics among industry players. A simple (yet powerful) means of completing this analysis is to gather information about the activities of competitors, potential entrants (or substitutes), customers, suppliers, and other factors influencing the industry (e.g., the economy and public opinion). The goal is to understand a firm's boundaries, which means identifying the correct market, players in this market, and what powers have influence on the business.

After this kind of data is gathered, a firm must consider possible, reasonable strategic moves and existing or potential players. Several techniques and frameworks are commonly used to help identify these various external factors. The two most popular tools are: Michael Porter's Five Forces Analysis and the Value Net.[46] Five Forces include information about direct competitors, suppliers, substitute products, and customers. The Value Net analysis is a variation on this analysis including complementors such as government regulation and other partners. These analyses are often fine-tuned to look at competitors, industry profitability within specific market segments, dynamics of markets (including product lifecycles), and unique industry characteristics. (Chapter 5 details these analyses.)

It is also important to consider how the age and location of a company (or industry) can impact strategy. Strategic thinking is very different within young, immature industries; they tend to have much more uncertainty (e.g., about key players and how the industry will evolve). Mature industries tend to squeeze profits from process innovations rather than new product innovations. Firms operating in international venues are obligated to think about unique institutional arrangements influencing their behaviors (e.g., many countries do not have clear property rights laws or effective capital markets). These differences influence firms' conduct and the viable strategies available to them.

Ultimately, an effective external analysis informs a firm about the viability of certain strategic moves and positioning within certain markets. This type of analysis helps a firm understand the boundaries of its activities and the dynamics of players within those boundaries. Thus, high-quality strategic thinking can inform business leaders about specific tactics to overcome strategic disadvantages or how to exploit strong market positions.

Internal Conditions

The next questions help build strategy by gathering information about a firm's internal capabilities:

- What are your organization's resources and capabilities?
- Does the organization possess the necessary resources and capabilities to yield competitive advantages?
- What managerial actions can managers and organizational leaders take to increase returns on these resources and capabilities?

These questions primarily address a firm's activities and are often referred to as *operational effectiveness*. Operational effectiveness is about achieving excellence in individual functions within an organization. Strategy is about combining these activities into a coherent, well-functioning whole.

For example, one well-cited example is Southwest Airlines, highly regarded for its rapid gate turnarounds (i.e., the very short timeframes between the arrivals and departures of flights).

Southwest Airlines Co. operates Southwest Airlines and AirTran Airways, passenger airlines that provide scheduled air transportation in the United States and near-international markets. Southwest principally provides point-to-point, rather than hub-and-spoke, service. AirTran principally provides hub-and-spoke, rather than point-to-point, service, with approximately half of AirTran's flights originating or terminating at its base of operation in Atlanta, Georgia. Southwest's rapid gate turnaround, which allows greater use of aircraft, is essential to its high-convenience, low-cost positioning in the airline industry. Southwest achieves this positioning through well-paid gate and ground crews; their productivity is enhanced by flexible labor rules (e.g., allowing employees to make rapid decisions on their own). With no meals, no seat assignments, and no baggage transfers with other airlines, Southwest avoids having to perform activities that increase costs. It selects airports and routes to support its operating strengths (e.g., it uses the Boeing 737 for all flights). All of these activities are interconnected to form a coherent whole; individual activities, performed efficiently and effectively, mutually reinforce others.

The key activities for Southwest are:

- limited passenger service;
- talented ground and gate crews;
- low ticket prices;
- reliable, frequent departures;
- efficient aircraft utilization;
- short-haul, point-to-point routes between midsize cities and secondary airports.

These core activities are supported by other activities (e.g., no seat assignments, no baggage transfers, and flexible union contracts).[47] These internal activities allow the company to be as efficient as possible and maintain low prices. Through developing this strategy, Southwest is able to develop a niche in the airline industry. While this strategy does limit its offerings and qualify its customer base, they can offer what many other airlines cannot (e.g., lower prices and greater efficiencies). As such, Southwest excels at using strategy to differentiate itself from competitors. These unique characteristics do not last forever and current industry competitors such as Spirit Airlines and Virgin Air can copy what Southwest does. Southwest is now challenged to innovate and offer something new and unique to its customers.

Implementation

The *implementation* and *formulation* of strategies are of equal importance. Companies discover a great deal as they implement their plans. Competitors respond, new data become evident, and company employees (and other stakeholders) react (and provide new insights), which impact a firm's strategy. Thus, managers generally want to maintain their commitment to a course of action yet remain adaptable to inevitable changes in competitive conditions. (The topic of metrics for measuring progress is addressed in Chapter 8.)

Analytical and Process Skills

Strategy formulation and implementation involve analytical and process skills for content awareness and content-in-use. Some firms strictly rely on data for all key decisions; other firms (e.g., Apple and Google) look to leaders' personal opinions for direction. Also, strategic thinking involves many different types of theories and perspectives. Some firms take a strictly economic point of view, looking for efficiencies and incentives; others realize that they are operating in an institutional environment and are sensitive to how their strategic moves will impact perceptions among various stakeholders. Other firms take a hybrid view. (See the earlier section in this chapter on the institutional view.)

Finally, strategic thinking is a competency within an organization. It is developed over time and involves transparent processes and guiding principles. Organizational members that do not have a clear idea about how they think, strategically, will have strategies lacking coherence and clarity.

Summary of Strategic Thinking

At this point, you should be able to review a firm's strategic documents and formulate some questions about a firm's strategy. As you ask yourself the basic questions in Table 4.1 (to enrich your strategic thinking), consider the following points:

1   When adopting a strategy, recall the criteria for effective strategy (i.e., a clear focus and direction, effective external/internal analysis, and implementation ability).
2   Each criterion suggests a framework (i.e., analysis techniques) to help managers and analysts think strategically. In addition to the criteria for effective strategy, consider that organizational members develop analytical and behavioral skills necessary to support critical strategic thinking.
3   An effective strategy is as much about *positioning* as it is about *adopting activities* to support this positioning.
4   The desire to grow is a trap; your goal is to achieve the organization's purpose so that it can maximize shareholder wealth. While growth might provide returns to shareowners, it could also be expensive to achieve and take value away from the firm.
5   Many disciplines contribute to strategic thinking; also, strategy is as much about what you *will* do as what you will *not* do.

In sum, strategy is much more than a single planning process; instead, it is an ongoing process. Many analysts think effective strategy comes from a single, good, strategic planning system. While planning may be important, continual strategic thinking is key. Organizations use various planning systems. Organizations use at least four types of approaches for conceptualizing strategy: *strategy as perspective*, *strategy as positioning*, *strategy as experimenting*, and *strategy as planning*. Thus, to think strategically, strategists (i.e., consultants, managers, individual contributors, or other stakeholders) think about the purpose and perspective of the organization: *How should it be positioned within its markets? What are its main activities or competencies? How will it implement its strategy?*

This four-fold approach to thinking strategically is instructive; it suggests that organizations that think strategically are considering all four criteria discussed earlier (see Table 4.6). Additionally, the pressures discussed in the prior chapters also impact firms' strategies; thus, consideration of these pressures should always be present in strategic discussions and further demonstrate the need for continuous reevaluation. Therefore, due to the ever-changing nature of strategy, a key characteristic for successful companies is *adaptability* (a topic discussed in Chapter 11).

An interesting example of adaptability comes from a 132-year-old company that remade itself, using environmental principles and practices as a basis for product innovation. Tennant is a mid-sized company that makes commercial floor scrubbers. The company often referred to itself as a nonresidential floor maintenance company; however, it then changed its mission to an environmental solutions company, focusing on multiple surfaces (not just floors) and environmentally friendly products. This change resulted from a need to find viable growth opportunities and respond to pressures for improved environmental outcomes. Tennant developed a new cleaning device, ec-H_2O (called ec-water), using only tap water as the cleaning agent. The machine adds oxygen to the water and uses electricity to create two safe-to-touch streams of ions (one acidic and one basic). The solution breaks up dirt, suspends it, and carries it back to the machine. The inspiration for the new device came from a new mission statement, new leadership, a need for new markets, and a trip to Japan where Tennant executives saw hospital personnel using ionized water to clean wounds.[48] Tennant's openness to new strategies and tactics allowed it to make changes and explore new possibilities. The result was a revitalization of the company's position in the market.

The next chapter further explores how environmental sustainability impacts strategic thinking and provides a new way of thinking about this subject as it relates to strategy.

Chapter Summary

The purpose of this chapter was to introduce principles for strategic thinking. *Strategic thinking* is a process of critically analyzing a firm's past and present-day situations in order to make well-considered decisions for the future. This process enables a firm to create a position in a market (or several markets) that is supported by multiple activities. For example, firms positioning themselves as the low-cost provider manage closely the efficiency of their processes and constantly look for lower-cost inputs.

Positioning refers to defining a unique market space for servicing customers. Effective strategic decisions require organizations to develop a clear focus, direction, and support their decisions with analyses of external forces, internal organizational activities, and effective implementation. *Strategic decisions* are relatively long-term and include commitments that are not easily changed.

To stimulate strategic thinking, this chapter presented questions categorized according to *focus, external conditions, internal conditions, implementation*, and *analytical* and *behavioral* skills. These questions are part of a Strategic Thinking Model (see Figure 4.1). Since the focus of this book is on environmental sustainability principles and practices, this impacts our analysis of external conditions, internal firm conditions, and suggests a unique implementation process and certain analytical and behavioral skills.

Current thinking has changed about the role of firms in providing solutions to environmental challenges. Broadly defined, this is a change from the *politics of limits* to the *politics of possibility*.

How Patagonia Overcame 2015

The Patagonia case reflects several issues that have been addressed in this chapter. First, its positioning is supported by four pillars (i.e., quality, design, environmental concerns, and the target customer). These pillars guide the company in all of its decisions. Patagonia matches many of our criteria for effective strategy: (1) it has a clear focus that guides employee behavior, (2) it is informed by its internal competencies and values, and (3) it has a sense of the external environment. Patagonia has influenced industry practices with respect to sustainability. It has spent its corporate money on educating customers and suppliers, created grant programs for communities, and created standards by which others could become like Patagonia. You can learn from Patagonia that not only can a firm act in a sustainable manner, but it can also act in a way to influence others to do the same.

Terms to Know

Business strategy: the positioning and set of activities for a single line of business in a single market or industry; business strategy defines how a firm competes in this market

Competitive advantage: the means for obtaining unusual returns (compared to competitors)

Corporate strategy: an organization's strategy for multiple lines of business, defining the various markets in which a firm competes

Functional strategy: refers to strategies specific to functions within a business (e.g., marketing, operations, and finance)

Operational effectiveness: achieving excellence in individual functions or activities within an organization

Strategic thinking: a process of critically analyzing a firm's past and current situations to make decisions for future actions

Profile: Can Concrete Be Environmentally Friendly?

If you want to make your own concrete to build a building, you will need to start with calcium carbonate (the main ingredient in limestone).[49] Add some rock containing silicate, a combination of silicon and oxygen, found almost everywhere in the form of clay. Now the tricky part. Heat the mixture with water at temperatures about 1450 °C (about twice as hot as a coal or wood fire). You will now get calcium silicate which will cool down as a powder called cement. Now you can make concrete by adding water and small stones in the right proportions—a useful structural material.[50] *Getting it wrong will result in either a slushy mess or structural defects in your building. Sometimes you will combine concrete with steel which helps with cracks and structural integrity.*

This material is cheap compared to other building materials. It can be formed into molds and is amazingly resilient in terms of shapes and places it can work. It also needs maintenance as water seeps into it and causes cracks or rusts the reinforcing steel within structures.

This maintenance is one area where innovations create a more sustainable material—a self-healing concrete made by mixing the bacterium B. pasteurii, along with calcium lactate as a food source, into the concrete when it is made. Scientists found that the bacterium could excrete calcite.[51] *Normally dormant, these bacteria come alive when cracks form and, when combined with water, they look for food. The excreted calcite builds up to span the crack, sealing it up. Scientists find that this method can recover 90 percent of its strength.*

Filtercrete is another innovation. It is a porous concrete. "The pores in the concrete allow water to flow through it, reducing the need for drains, while the bacteria inside the concrete purify the water by decomposing oils and other contaminants."[52] *One can even find a textile version of this concrete called concrete cloth.*

Finally we can find self-cleaning concrete which contains titanium dioxide particles. These particles sit on the surface of the concrete, not changing the appearance, yet when they absorb UV light from the Sun, the particles create free radical ions, which break down any organic dirt that comes into contact with them. When washed or exposed to wind, the remains are removed.[53] *"The white concrete of the new Jubilee Church in Rome is expected to stay clean for the ages thanks to a photocatalytic additive to the concrete."*[54] *The practice even has a new name "concrete décor."*

Questions and Critical Thinking

1   Table 4.6 contains some questions analysts ask to define a firm's strategy. Take a core set of these questions and suggest at least one means by which you would obtain data (e.g., from a company's annual report). Also, how would you interview an executive to tease out this information?

2   To what extent can the analytical tools and theories applied to firms also be applied to individuals or countries? Do individuals have strategies over their lifetimes? Do countries have strategies?

3   When do the applications of tools and frameworks begin to fail as firm-level strategies are applied at different levels of analysis?

4   We are focusing on environmental sustainability in this book. Refute the comments I have made about this being a unique and separate focus within the study of strategy.

5   Many analysts believe that a firm's strategy should be established prior to taking action. Yet, experience and data show that strategy has an emergent characteristic (i.e., as a firm acts, it further clarifies and changes its strategy). Can you suggest ways that a firm might control this emergent characteristic so that it does not lose focus yet is adaptable to change?

Notes

1   F.L. Reinhardt, R. Casadesus-Masanell, and D. Freier, "Patagonia," Harvard Business School Case 703–035, March 2003 (revised January 2010).

2   Organic Consumers Association, "Patagonia," www.organicconsumers.org/sponsors/patagonia/ (accessed July 15, 2010).

3   D. Sachs, "Patagonia CEO Rose Marcario fights the fights worth fighting," Creative Conversations, February 2015, http://www.fastcompany.com/3039739/creative-conversations/patagonia-ceo-rose-marcario-fights-the-fights-worth-fighting (accessed February 18, 2015).

4   J. Pfeffer and R. I. Sutton, *Hard Facts, Dangerous Half Truths and Total Nonsense: Profiting from Evidence-Based Management* (Boston, MA: Harvard Business School Press, 2006), 135–157.

5   Effective strategic thinking always has emergent and design characteristics. That is, we can set a direction but also constantly review this direction for potential revisions.

6   Chapter 11 will explain how organizations use real options and other techniques to overcome this bias towards big bets.

7   R. Repetto (ed.), *Punctuated Equilibrium and the Dynamics of U.S. Environmental Policy* (New Haven, CT: Yale University Press, 2006).

8 The following people provided helpful feedback on earlier drafts: Professor John Prescott, Gaurab Bhardwaj, Bongjin Kim, Balajai Koka, and Alexandre Lopes. Of course, the author bears responsibility for the content of this Instructional Note.

9 This view of the organization stems from J. March and H. Simon, *Organizations* (New York: John Wiley, 1958).

10 The institutional perspective is a relatively new view of the organization. It has been used to study mostly the evolution of certain professional societies and the impact of regulations and regulatory agencies on society. More recently, the view has been applied to organizational behavior and has extended the idea that the economic rational choice model of the organization may be a special case of this institutional view. See P. Abell, "The New Institutionalism and Rational Choice Theory," in W. Richard Scott and S. Christensen (eds.), *The Institutional Construction of Organizations: International and Longitudinal Studies* (Thousand Oaks, CA: Sage, 1995), 3–14.

11 The primary sources for these include Abell, "The New Institutionalism and Rational Choice Theory," and W. Richard Scott, *Institutions and Organizations* (Thousand Oaks, CA: Sage, 1995).

12 P. Selznick, *The Moral Commonwealth: Social Theory and the Promise of Community* (Berkeley: University of California Press, 1992); P. Selznick, *Leadership in Administration: A Sociological Interpretation* (New York: Harper and Row, 1957); P. Selznick with the collaboration of P. Nonet and H.M. Vollmer, *Law, Society and Industrial Justice* (New York: Russell Sage Foundation, 1969).

13 R. C. Hybels, "On Legitimacy, Legitimation, and Organizations: A Critical Review and Integrative Theoretical Model," *Academy of Management Proceedings* 1995 (meeting abstract supplement), 241–245; J. G. Maurer (ed.), *Readings in Organization Theory: Open-System Approaches* (New York: Random House, 1971).

14 J. W. Meyer and B. Rowan, "Institutionalized Organizations: Formal Structure as Myth and Ceremony," *American Journal of Sociology* 83, no. 2 (September 1977): 340–363.

15 Note that the institutional view subsumes stakeholder analysis, since institutions can reside in practices, laws or cultures in addition to specific stakeholders. Also, the institutional view has a theoretical basis to support it as a theory of the organization.

16 M. S. Kraatz, "Learning by Association? Interorganizational Networks and Adaptation to Environmental Change," *The Academy of Management Journal* 41, no. 6 (December 1998): 621–643.

17 Adapted from C. Oliver, "Strategic Responses to Institutional Processes," *The Academy of Management Review* 16, no. 1 (January 1991): 145–179.

18 H. A. Haveman, "Follow the Leader: Mimetic Isomorphism and Entry into New Markets," *Administrative Science Quarterly* 38, no. 4 (December 1993): 593–627.

19 M. Yglesias, "Reactions to the Proposed EPA Rules on Carbon Emissions" (*WonkWire*, June 2, 2014) www.wonkwire.rollcall.com/2014/06/02/reactions-proposed-epa-rule-carbon-emissions/ (accessed December 4, 2014).

20 H. Aldrich, *Organizations Evolving* (Thousand Oaks, CA: Sage, 1999), 2.

21 R. R. Nelson and S. G. Winter, *An Evolutionary Theory of Economic Change* (Cambridge, MA: Belknap/Harvard University Press, 1982); B. Levitt and J. G. March, "Organizational Learning," *Annual Review of Sociology* 14 (1988): 320.

22 Co-authored by Michael Aper, Master of Arts in Sustainability candidate at Wake Forest University.

23 L. Hepler, "Apple, Google and the evolving economics of energy," GreenBiz, February 11, 2015, http://www.greenbiz.com/article/google-inc-apple-inc-wind-solar-fossil-fuels-renewable-energy-economics (accessed March 30, 2015).

24 M. O'Brien, "Google buys Altamont wind energy to power Googleplex," GreenBiz, February 11, 2015, http://www.mercurynews.com/business/ci_27503195/google-buys-altamont-wind-energy-power-googleplex (accessed March 30, 2015).

25 BusinessGreen Staff, "Google makes biggest renewables bet yet on $750 million SolarCity fund," GreenBiz, March 2, 2015, http://www.greenbiz.com/article/google-makes-biggest-renewables-bet-yet-750-million-solarcity-fund (accessed March 30, 2015).

26 J. Roberts, *The Modern Firm: Organizational Design for Performance and Growth* (New York: Oxford University Press, 2004), 88–103.

27 R. H. Coase, "The Nature of the Firm," *Economica* 4, no. 16 (November 1937): 386–405.

28 Obtain a discussion about global trends such as "National Intelligence Council Global Trends 2030: Alternative Worlds" (December 2012). http://publicintelligence.net/global-trends-2030/ (accessed January 20, 2015).

29 This analysis is best accomplished with a structural analysis of an industry such as the Value Net and Five Forces analysis. At the least, specify boundaries, players, and the relationship among players.

30 In some businesses these may be core platforms or core programs, such as within military suppliers who define programs including various technologies, products, and services.

31 Key success factors are answers to two questions: (1) What do customers want? and (2) What do we need to do to compete?

32 R. M. Grant, *Contemporary Strategy Analysis.* 8th ed. (West Sussex, UK: John Wiley and Sons, 2013).

33 Ibid.

34 P. Fitzroy, J. M. Hulbert, and A. Ghobadian, *Strategic Management: The Challenge of Creating Value* (New York: Routledge, 2012), 547–591.

35 M. W. Johnson, *Seizing the White Space: Business Model Innovation for Growth and Renewal* (Cambridge, MA: Harvard Business Press, 2010).

36 A. Osterwalder and Y. Pigneur, *Business Model Generation: A Handbook for Visionaries, Game Changers, and Challengers* (Hoboken, NJ: John Wiley and Sons, 2010).

37 Fitzroy et al., 2012; D. Besanko, D. Dranove, M. Shaley, and S. Shaefer, *Economics of Strategy*, 6th ed. (Hoboken, NJ: John Wiley and Sons, 2013).

38 B. Charny, "How Green Is Apple?" *The Wall Street Journal*, December 31, 2008.

39 "Apple and the Environment: The Story behind Apple's Environmental Footprint," www.apple.com/environment/our-footprint/ (accessed December 19, 2011).

40 Greenpeace International, "FAQ about the *Guide to Greener Electronics*," www.greenpeace.org/international/en/campaigns/climate-change/cool-it/Campaign-analysis/Guide-to-Greener-Electronics/FAQ/ (accessed December 15, 2015).

41 Greenpeace International, "Apple—6th Position, 4.5/10," *Guide to Greener Electronics* 18 (November 2012), http://www.greenpeace.org/international/en/Guide-to-Greener-Electronics/18th-Edition/APPLE/ (accessed December 15, 2015).

42 Operational effectiveness is performing similar activities better than rivals perform them. Operational effectiveness is necessary but not sufficient to effective strategy. Strategic decisions are important, involve a significant commitment of resources and are not easily reversible. These decisions are deliberate attempts to influence the firm and its environment to increase competitiveness.

43 D. A. Vazquez Brust and C. Liston-Hayes, "Environmental Management Intentions: An Empirical Investigation of Argentina's Polluting Firms," *Journal of Environmental Management* 91, no. 5 (May 2010): 1111–1122.

44 M. A. Hajer, *The Politics of Environmental Discourse: Ecological Modernization and the Policy Process* (New York: Oxford University Press, 1995); D. Sayre, *Inside ISO 14000: The Competitive Advantage of Environmental Management* (Delray Beach, FL: St. Lucie Press, 1996).

45 Ibid., 16–18.

46 M. E. Porter, *Competitive Strategy: Techniques for Analyzing Industries and Competitors* (New York: Free Press, 1998); A. M. Brandenburger and B. J. Nalebuff, *Co-opetition* (New York: Doubleday, 1997).

47 M. E. Porter, "What Is Strategy?" *Harvard Business Review* (November–December 1996): 73.

48 *R&D Magzine*, "Electrolysis powers these scrubbing bubbles," September 25, 2008, www.rdmag.com/Awards/RD-100-Awards/2008/09/Electrolysis-Powers-These-Scrubbing-Bubbles/ (accessed December 19, 2011).

49 Limestone is a rock formed from compressed and fused (by heat and pressure) layers of living organisms over millions of years.

50 J. E. Gordon, *Structures: Or Why Things Don't Fall Down* (New York: Penguin, 1978).

51 A. Forty, *Concrete Culture: A Material History* (London: Reaktion Books, 2012). D. Zamarreñol, R. Inkpen, and E. May, "Carbonate Crystals Precipitated by Freshwater Bacteria and Their Use as a Limestone Consolidant," *Applied and Environmental Microbiology* 75, no. 18 (September 2009): 5981–5990.

52 M. Mindownick, *Stuff Matters: Exploring the Marvelous Materials that Show Our Man-Made World* (New York: Houghton Mifflin Harcourt, 2014), 68.

53 C. Goguen, "How precast concrete buildings can clean themselves and our air," http://precast.org/2013/04/its-a-wash/ (accessed January 6, 2015).

54 M. Chusid, "Self-cleaning concrete!" *Concrete Décor*, 5 no. 4 (2005). http://www.concretedecor.net/decorative concretearticles/vol-5-no-4-augustseptember-2005/self-cleaning-concrete/?resetapplication (accessed January 6, 2015).

5

STRATEGY PRINCIPLES AND ANALYSES TO INFORM STRATEGY

Wal-Mart Becomes Environmentally Friendly

Today, Wal-Mart's "economy" is actually larger than Ireland's (with a 2014 market capitalization of $244.17 billion).[1] However, back in 2005, Lee Scott (the CEO at the time) felt that Wal-Mart was in trouble. The company's growth was stagnant, it was receiving pushback from various stakeholder groups, and its international expansion was not very successful. The company was also engaged in numerous lawsuits, received an enormous amount of bad press for failing to provide a living wage and healthcare to over half of its employees, and was being accused of gender discrimination and the destruction of local economies.[2] Sales growth had slowed in previously prosperous stores, and its stock price (after rising 1,205 percent during the 1990s) had fallen 30 percent since Scott took over in 2000.[3]

Scott was looking for ways to improve the company's performance and reputation.[4] He decided to focus on environmental sustainability, using the company's supply chain management as the target for increased profitability. This supply chain focus was nothing new to Wal-Mart, yet it was new in terms of what demands it would place on the chain. In October 2005, in an auditorium in Bentonville, Arkansas, Scott announced to the company's 1.6 million "associates" (Wal-Mart's name for employees) that the company would be taking on three aspirational goals: "to be supplied by 100 percent renewable energy; to create zero waste; and to sell products that sustain our resources and the environment."[5]

The audience wasn't expecting this.

Wal-Mart had been a defensive player when it came to environmental issues and had previously viewed sustainability as a compliance challenge. However, the company realized that it was the largest private user of electricity in the United States, emitted more than the equivalent of 2.8 million households in terms of carbon (28 million households if you counted their supply chain),[6] and that it could work with several outside groups on this new effort. Key consultants included Blu Skye, Conservation International, and the Environmental Defense Fund (EDF). These organizations helped Wal-Mart identify products and processes (e.g., within production and shipping) that would have the greatest environmental impact if altered.

Wal-Mart decided on five analysis areas: GHG emissions, air pollution, water pollution, water use, and land use across 134 product categories.[7] For each of these product categories and impact areas, the Union of Concerned Scientists estimated an environmental impact score per $1 spent by a consumer (e.g., GHG emissions in tons of CO_2 equivalents per $1 spent on electronics). These data (and other information) led to a focus on energy, waste, and products.[8]

The company established eight principles to green its supply chain:

1   *identifying goals, metrics, and new technologies;*
2   *certifying environmentally sustainable products;*
3   *providing network partner assistance to suppliers;*
4   *committing to larger volumes of environmentally sustainable products;*
5   *cutting out the middleman;*
6   *restructuring the buyer role;*
7   *consolidating direct suppliers;*
8   *licensing environmental innovations.[9]*

The company defined the specific sustainability projects to drive environmental improvements. This work led to 14 sustainability "value networks" (or projects): Global Greenhouse Gas Strategy; Alternative Fuels; Energy, Design, Construction, and Maintenance; Global Logistics; Operations and Internal Procurement; Packaging; Textiles; Electronics; Food and Agriculture; Forest and Paper; Chemical Intensive Products; Jewelry; Seafood; and China. Every network had a team that looked at current impacts, use of resources, potential reduction or improvements in resource use, potential for innovation, synergies across areas, assurance in the supply chain, and risk mitigation.

This work led to myriad programs that were designed to improve Wal-Mart's environmental footprint (e.g., Wal-Mart and the WWF designed a requirement for fish supplies to help manage fishing and avoid overfishing in some areas). As soon as 2012, Wal-Mart claimed that it had year-to-year improvements toward its three goals:

- *Globally, the company saw a 10.61 percent reduction in GHG emissions (from its 2005 base) by the end of 2009.*
- *One hundred and nineteen factories in China have demonstrated greater than 20 percent improved efficiency (compared to a 2006 baseline).*
- *Wal-Mart USA redirected 81 percent of waste in California compared to its 2006 baseline.*
- *Plastic bag waste was reduced by 47.95 million pounds (or approximately 3.5 million bags) globally since 2006.*
- *Wal-Mart China successfully drew more than 470,000 farmers into their Direct Farm program in 2010 (bringing the total number of farmers in the program to just over 757,000).*[10]

Chapter Overview

The way that organizations formulate competitive strategy has changed over time; they now incorporate more considerations into decisions, including ones about the natural environment as it impacts their thinking and strategy creation in various ways (e.g., many companies have conducted environmental assessments, planning, and project implementation to offset negative environmental outcomes).[11] Organizations have also increased their reporting of environmental information,[12] and they have used environmental principles and practices to reengineer everything from products and services to core business models (used to increase firm value).[13] Analysts can no longer simply consider natural environmental impacts of corporate actions as "externalities" (i.e., results of business activities that are not priced into goods and services).[14] For many organizations (e.g., Wal-Mart and WWF), using the natural environment as a strategic focus has become a source of *competitive advantage*.[15] This chapter should help you understand why this concept is so important.

The first half of the chapter will explain how environmental sustainability creates a competitive advantage; the second half focuses on the fundamental components for building strategy. A firm must know its core principles and be able to conduct external *and* internal analyses before it can develop solid strategies (see Chapter 4). Although some of these analyses are not specifically focused on environmental sustainability, they are useful for determining where a company stands and foreseeing where it should move in the future. If a company integrates environmental sustainability into its core business, analyses should assist it in achieving organizational outcomes.

At the end of this chapter you should be able to:

1　specify the reasons businesses should apply environmental sustainability as a lens on strategy;
2　specify a firm's resources and competencies as sources of competitive advantage;
3　understand the value of developing core principles for guiding a company;
4　use at least one method of industry analysis to identify strategic opportunities.

I will continue to use the strategy model introduced in Chapter 1. In this chapter, I will focus on *competitors*, *suppliers*, *customers*, and the *strategy formulation process*. This chapter focuses on business organizations. Yet, the principles and concepts in this chapter apply to not-for-profit and government organizations. Most of these applications are described in other chapters, especially Chapter 12.

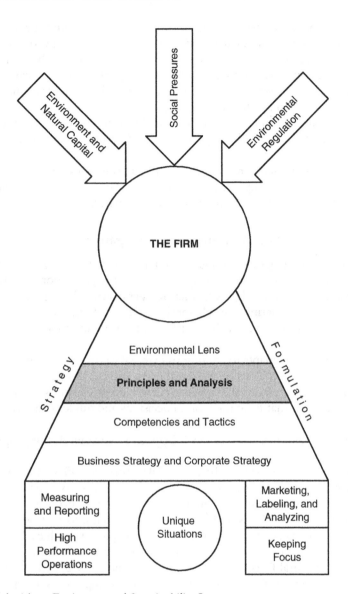

Figure 5.1 Strategy Model with an Environmental Sustainability Lens

The Resource-Based View of the Firm: An Introduction

A resource-based view of a firm argues that the major source of competitive advantage is found *within* a firm (i.e., in its resources and how those resources are used). **Resources** are tangible and intangible assets that enable a firm to perform and support its positioning in markets. For example, a firm's brand (and its use) may enable it to charge a premium on products and services. However, the brand by itself is of little consequence if the company does not use it to enhance product and service offerings.

This view suggests that each firm is unique and defined by its personal history, set of resources, and capabilities. Each brand, for example, is a unique result of specific actions taken by a firm. Firms achieve superior performance by identifying, acquiring, and using the appropriate resources necessary for the production of products and services. This chapter introduces the foundational components for creating *resource-based strategies* and explains how this perspective can help you understand how to use environmental sustainability principles and practices.

Although this view is concerned with resources utilized by companies, proponents of this view have not traditionally included the biophysical environment within the scope of the conversation. Thus, I take the traditional resource-based view a step further by advocating that a focus incorporating the natural environment (which provides new pressures and opportunities for firms) will ultimately lead to a more favorable positioning and outcome.[16] This perspective also provides a more holistic view because natural environmental changes may alter the importance of certain resources[17] (e.g., as water becomes scarcer, production capabilities might favor less water-intensive ways to produce products). Also, the possession of resources is not necessarily valuable; it is their use or exploitation that creates superior economic value.

When resources are brought together in unique combinations, they can be used to achieve sustainable competitive advantages. So this management challenge involves recognizing, developing, and nurturing appropriate bundles of resources (including natural resources) within internal and external constraints.[18]

What Is a Sustainable Organization?

The sustainable organization is defined as an organization that operates today without compromising its own future well-being (or society's).[19] This definition recognizes that organizations are designed to achieve goals and create foundations for the future. The **sustainable corporation** has many facets, one of which is the natural environment. When considering the relationship of the natural environment to corporate strategy, there are several characteristics to recognize. The sustainable corporation has:

1 *resiliency,* which means that it adapts to conditions external to the firm (such as those outlined in the first three chapters), utilizes and develops relevant resources and capabilities (described in this and the next chapter), and evidences an operational excellence (described in Chapters 8–11);
2 a set of *principles* and *values* that form the basis of decisions and guide organizational behavior (discussed in this chapter);
3 a *focus* based on external and internal analyses (discussed in Chapter 4, this chapter, and Chapters 6–8).

One example illustrates the points above. In 2011, IBM turned 100 years old. Over the years, it has endured tremendous challenges and an ebb and flow in its ability to generate profits; yet, it built its organization to be resilient, respond to contemporary issues, and its evolution has demonstrated the key characteristics described above. IBM was built around the idea that information was going to be important in the 20th century,[20] and it has tried to keep true to its principles and values despite the challenges it has faced. Even in hard times, the company conducted relentless external and internal analyses, confronting what one author calls "the brutal facts."[21] In the late 1990s and early 2000s, IBM remade itself, adapting to new markets and to the new reality that hardware was not going to sustain its development; however, services would. Also, it realized that its customer relationships, as they changed, informed it about how it needed to change.[22] Thus, IBM (through its resiliency and ability to adapt) is a noteworthy example of sustainability. You will see similar examples of firms adhering to these principles; some have targeted environmental sustainability particularly well along with others (like IBM) that demonstrate an overall competency for sustainability.

The remaining chapters build on these three characteristics by explaining their importance, how to analyze them, and how they help identify ways to incorporate environmental sustainability into the core of a firm's strategy. This chapter provides a rationale for why environmental sustainability should be at the foundation of an organization's strategy, a set of core principles that can guide a firm's strategy, and analysis tools that are valuable components of any strategy development.

Profile: A Bright Future[23]

Table 5.2 shows a summary of the ways that environmental sustainability can enhance a firm's competitiveness. BrightSource Energy, based out of Oakland, California, is also showing how it is done. The firm leverages the sun's incoming energy by focusing the sunlight onto mirrors which then reflect the light onto 2,200-ton boilers built 339 feet in the air.[24] The extremely hot steam then powers turbines to generate electricity. In 2013, the Ivanpah Solar Electric Generating System went live on the grid in Nipton, California where it produces 377 megawatts of power supplying about 140,000 homes.[25] The firm also reports that the plant reduces the U.S. carbon-footprint by 400,000 tons per year.[26]

The firm has contracts with Southern California Edison and Pacific Gas and Electric to build 14 plants across the Southwestern United States by 2017.[27] Among other investors, BrightSource has attracted VantagePoint, BP, Morgan Stanley, and Google.[28] Along with its U.S. operations, the firm operates in China, Europe, Israel, and South Africa, managing over 20 gigawatts of solar, wind, and conventional power worldwide;[29] an energy amount equivalent to roughly 40 coal-fired plants.

One of the major challenges for renewable energy in connecting to the traditional grid is their ability to provide base load power. Traditional sources provide start and stop power quickly, at any time of day, and any day of the year. Photovoltaics are less attractive in many places for those very reasons. Often times, scalability isn't feasible in conjunction with the high initial costs. In the case of BrightSource Energy, adhering to numbers 7 & 8 of the Hannover Principles has served the firm well. Photovoltaics and solar thermal both rely on natural energy flows. However, converting solar energy into electricity requires a solar inverter which converts the incoming DC into usable AC. Often times, solar inverters are among the most expensive components. By understanding the limitations of design, BrightSource Energy investors saw the industrial-scale solar thermal technology as an opportunity to exploit the weaknesses of their potential renewable competitors.

Get Your Shine On. *Economies of scale would suggest that with each solar thermal plant built, the firm's initial costs would be driven down by repetition and improved practices. The firm's first industrial-scale solar thermal plant was built in Rotem, Israel in 2008.[30] In 2011, the firm filed an Application for Certification with the California Energy Commission to build in Inyo County, CA while also piloting a project, in partnership with Chevron, using solar thermal energy to enhance oil recovery in Coalinga, CA. Ivanpah began operating in 2013. The firm has an opportunity to dominate the industrial solar thermal market in California; however, expired federal subsidies and delayed permitting have slowed their advancement. Should the firm stay and pursue cross-sector alliances in California or move the bulk of their operations overseas where the market is more accessible, but potentially less stable?*

The Value of Natural Systems

Everyone depends on ecosystems for goods and services; thus, they might be considered "natural capital" and on a par with other forms of capital that we rely on for productive economic activity.[31] Ecosystems are also models of sustainability. For example, the sun energizes the processes of energy flow and nutrient cycling, and humans make use of the energy that flows through natural ecosystems. Consider this:

- To produce food, we have converted almost 11 percent of the Earth's land area from forest and grassland biomes to agricultural ecosystems.
- Grasslands sustain our domestic animals for labor, meat, leather, and milk.
- Forest biomes provide us with 3.3 billion cubic meters of wood annually for fuel, building materials, and paper.
- Some 15 percent of the world's energy consumption is sourced from plant material (e.g., firewood and peat).[32]

Table 5.1 shows a partial list of the ecosystem services we use. These services and goods are not priced into products and services so we tend not to recognize how important they are to our everyday lives.

Calculations of the total annual value of ecosystems, referred to as *global net primary production of land ecosystems*, range around 120 pentagrams of dry matter (including agricultural and other natural

Table 5.1 The Value and Functions of Ecosystem Services[33]

Number	Ecosystem service	Ecosystem functions	Examples
1	Gas regulation	Regulation of atmospheric chemical composition	CO_2/O_2 balance, O_3 for UVB protection, and SO_x levels
2	Climate regulation	Regulation of global temperature, precipitation, and other biologically mediated climatic processes (at global or local levels)	GHG regulation, dimethylsulfide (DMS) production affecting cloud formation
3	Disturbance regulation	Capacitance, damping, and integrity of ecosystem response to environmental fluctuations	Storm protection, flood control, drought recovery, and other aspects of habitat response to environmental variability (mainly controlled by vegetation structure)
4	Water regulation	Regulation of hydrological flows	Provisioning of water for agricultural (e.g., irrigation) or industrial (e.g., milling) processes or transportation
5	Water supply	Storage and retention of water	Provisioning of water by watersheds, reservoirs, and aquifers
6	Erosion control and sediment retention	Retention of soil within an ecosystem	Prevention of loss of soil by wind, runoff, or other removal processes; storage of silt in lakes and wetlands
7	Soil formation	Soil formation processes	Weathering of rock and the accumulation of organic material
8	Nutrient cycling	Storage, internal cycling, processing, and acquisition of nutrients	Nitrogen fixation, N, P, and other elemental or nutrient cycles
9	Waste treatment	Recovery of mobile nutrients and removal or breakdown of excess or xenic nutrients and compounds	Waste treatment, pollution control, detoxification
10	Pollination	Movement of floral gametes	Provisioning of pollinators for the reproduction of plant populations
11	Biological control	Trophic-dynamic regulations of populations	Keystone predator control of prey species, reduction of herbivores by top predators
12	Refugia	Habitat for resident and transient populations	Nurseries, habitat for migratory species, regional habitats for locally harvested species, or overwintering grounds
13	Food production	That portion of gross primary production extractable as food	Production of fish, game, crops, nuts, fruits (by hunting and gathering), subsistence farming, or fishing
14	Raw materials	That portion of gross primary production extractable as raw materials	The production of lumber, fuel, or fodder
15	Genetic resources	Sources of unique biological materials and products	Medicine, products for materials science, genes for resistance to plant pathogens and crop pests, ornamental species (pets and horticultural varieties of plants)
16	Recreation	Providing opportunities for recreational activities	Ecotourism, sport fishing, and other outdoor recreational facilities
17	Cultural	Providing opportunities for noncommercial uses	Aesthetic, artistic, educational, spiritual, and/or scientific values of ecosystems

ecosystems).[34] Humans appropriate about 30 percent of this total production for agricultural, grazing, forestry, and human-occupied land.[35] These estimates indicate that humans are using a large percentage of the ecosystems.

Our impact on the Earth is even greater since we convert many materials and agricultural lands into housing, highways, factories, and the like canceling out another 7–8 percent of potential primary production. *Primary production* is the production of organic compounds from atmospheric or aquatic carbon dioxide and may occur through the process of using light as a source of energy (photosynthesis) or using the oxidation or reduction of chemical compounds as a source of energy (chemosynthesis). Almost all life on Earth is directly or indirectly reliant on primary production; thus, we have become the dominant biological form on Earth despite representing only 5 percent of its biomass.[36]

So, how much are natural ecosystems actually worth to us?

Several researchers have tried to calculate the incremental value of each type of service provided by the natural world to determine how changes in the quality of these services or goods might influence human welfare (e.g., we can calculate the economic value of removing a forest based on the fact that it would no longer provide lumber, CO_2 sequestration, or promote the hydrologic cycle). According to various calculations, the total value of services from ecosystems amounts to $41 trillion as of 2010.[37] Compare this with the same year's global GDP of $74.54 trillion.[38] This means that the world's governments would have to spend *over half* of their gross income just to pay for all of the natural resources used in a year.

Others have tried to calculate the cost-benefit consequences of converting ecosystems to more direct human uses (e.g., converting a wetland into a rice field). Researchers found that, in every case, the value of the transfer was a *loss*. So why do we continue to convert ecosystem services to services that are less valuable? The main reason is that most ecosystem services are simply not priced into our decisions.[39] However, these figures make it quite apparent that companies ought to practice environmental sustainability. The next section outlines this case along with the assumption that natural capital is valuable to everyone and, in many cases, irreplaceable with other capital forms.

The Case for Corporate Environmental Sustainability

Up until this point, it has been stressed that firms seek sources of competitive advantage to increase firm value, and that environmental sustainability should be recognized as a method for increasing this value. Of course, there are other ways firms can try to increase their value. For example, they can position themselves within attractive industries to gain high returns on investments; however, data show that firms do not have the bandwidth to keep changing industries. Also, industry factors account for only a small portion of inter-firm profit differentials.[40] Thus, this type of positioning produces lower profits than those produced from specific company actions. Even if firms could rapidly transition into different industries, they would tend to adopt similar strategies since they would lack the necessary competencies to do otherwise.

Another means of gaining competitive advantage could be profit arising from market power (e.g., monopoly profits). Firms could gain these profits by being protected from competition through regulation or property rights (e.g., patents). However, most firms are active participants and face competition; thus, they strive to find ways to continuously innovate by using their resources and capabilities to gain advantages. In essence, they spend most of their time figuring out how to play *within* an industry instead of *where* to play.

The approach, in this book, is that every firm is unique, the key to profitability is to exploit this uniqueness, and that establishing a competitive advantage involves formulating and implementing a strategy to exploit these unique strengths. Environmental sustainability is a powerful way to enhance a firm's competitive advantage and to promote long-lasting value creation; thus, it can become a strength if its potential is properly harnessed.

The utilization of environmental sustainability principles and practices focuses a firm on adapting to the natural environment. Recall the discussions in the first three chapters about the pressures firms are facing with respect to the natural environment. This adaptation was the basis of the institutional view discussed in Chapter 4. They must respond to these pressures; however, organizations can increase their returns by simply adopting this mindset on a daily basis. For example, when they price natural capital and their competitors do not, the innovating firms are internalizing others' costs and creating advantages for themselves.

Also, the previous section explained the value of natural capital to firms. Since each organization uniquely utilizes ecosystems and responds to pressures, firms have the potential for using these resources to creatively position themselves in markets. This means firms can move *beyond* compliance with regulation and use environmental sustainability as a way to *create new products and services, new business models, and new platforms*.[41]

Table 5.2 The Value (Business Case) for Environmental Sustainability as a Source of Competitiveness

Area	Example
Compliance	License to operate
	Legal liability decreased
	Response to pressures from regulatory bodies
Increase top-line and bottom-line outcomes	Meet customer preferences
	Productivity improvements
	Decrease in cost of capital
Ways to be unique	Reputation and brand equity
	Unique resources and capabilities
	Preserve natural resources
New platforms and business models	Sources of innovation
	New products and services

Environmental sustainability, managed correctly, can be a means of creating revenues and cutting costs. Goldman Sachs reported that companies with cutting-edge environmental, social, and good governance policies have outperformed the Morgan Stanley Capital Investment (MSCI) world index of stocks by 25 percent since 2005.[42] Seventy-two percent of companies on the list outperformed their industry peers, were financially healthier, and achieved enduring value.[43] From 2006 through 2007, companies on the Dow Jones Sustainability World Index performed 10 points above the Standard and Poor's 500 (the general standard for the stock market).[44] Another study stated similar results and that the worst-performing companies were not likely to have anybody in charge of sustainability.[45] Several other studies found similar results.[46]

Table 5.2 lists the value gains from using environmental sustainability as a source of competitiveness. Firms that want to embed environmental sustainability[47] in their strategies should adopt certain principles and practices; this topic is covered in the next section.

The Importance of Developing Clear Principles

A critical component of any strategy is an organization's guiding principles that determine how it will operate and make decisions. This determination is part of the external analysis. These principles contribute to a firm's uniqueness, culture, and decision making. While we expect firms to be responsive to their environments (and utilize their resources and capabilities), guiding principles tend to be a more permanent basis for formulating strategy.

One researcher presents nine principles of sustainability performance, stating that "increasingly companies have recognized that sustainability values and principles are important for long-term corporate profitability and are using them to define their sustainability strategies."[48] Broader (yet similar) lists of principles have been proposed by other authors.[49] You can find a list of the major frameworks for developing principles in Appendix 8.1.

The Natural Step's Framework for Strategic Sustainable Development is used globally by many organizations to guide their sustainability efforts. This framework uses a systems approach to create an open-source methodology organized by The Natural Step, which is a nonprofit research, education, and advisory organization dedicated to sustainable development. Our focus is on The Natural Step's principles that provide guidance for how an organization can move toward sustainability and become part of a sustainable society. The Framework for Strategic Sustainable Development states that we must eliminate our contributions:

1 to the progressive buildup of substances extracted from the Earth's crust;
2 to the progressive buildup of chemicals and compounds produced by society;
3 to the progressive physical degradation and destruction of nature and natural processes;
4 to conditions that undermine people's capacity to meet their basic human needs.[50]

Advocates of this framework suggest that the key guiding question is, "What do you want our company to look like in the future?"[51] The Natural Step's principles have been used by many organizations seeking to become more sustainable (including well-known sustainability advocates such as IKEA, McDonald's, Interface Carpet, and Nike). Even the Whistler Blackcomb Resort (the site of the 2010 Winter Olympics) developed its strategic plan using these principles.[52]

The Hannover Principles is a similar framework, which has been widely used and is named after the city of Hannover, Germany. These guidelines have been used primarily for the built environment and were precursors of other well-known guidelines (e.g., LEED™ [Leadership in Energy, Environmental Design],[53] CASBEE [Comprehensive Assessment System for Building Environmental Efficiency],[54] BREEAM® [Building Research Establishment Environmental Assessment Method],[55] and Cradle-to-Cradle). The nine original Hannover Principles were:

1 Insist on rights of humanity and nature to co-exist
2 Recognize interdependence
3 Respect relationships between spirit and matter
4 Accept responsibility for the consequences of design
5 Create safe objects of long-term value
6 Eliminate the concept of waste
7 Rely on natural energy flows
8 Understand the limitations of design
9 Seek constant improvement by the sharing of knowledge.[56]

The principles proposed in this book build upon The Natural Step and the Hannover principles. These new principles strive to help companies marry strategic focus and unique positioning with natural environmental sustainability. I will provide a brief definition of each principle and an example of how each principle might be applied to a strategy creation.

Principle 1

Do no harm by finding ways to decrease concentrations of substances extracted from the Earth's crust and those produced by society. Firms adhere to this principle by seeking ways to decrease fossil fuels and finding more renewable sources of energy.

Principle 2

Identify ways to facilitate and build upon the productivity of natural systems. Ecosystem services can offer excellent sources of competitiveness and services that are duplicated by man-made structures. For example, agricultural firms that use natural crop rotation and natural processes for pest control have been shown to be more productive than those that artificially control crops.[57]

Principle 3

Offer biologically inspired production models and materials; look for biological insights that suggest innovative ways to produce and use the planet's resources. One way firms can facilitate and build upon natural systems is to use biomimicry (i.e., imitating biological processes to innovate product and service design) as a basis of production. For example, architects and builders are discovering ways to design buildings that decrease the need for artificial substances (e.g., paint and lighting fixtures); the designs mimic nature's designs. This methodology is discussed more extensively in Chapter 9.

Principle 4

Advocate decreasing the degradation of our world by physical means. The less we build, the more we can develop a more sustainable world. Do we really need so many new housing developments, strip malls, and lengthy commutes to work? Reducing our footprint on the world will increase productivity and decrease our impact on the environment.

Principle 5

Do not expose people to conditions that systematically undermine their capacities to meet their needs. This principle addresses human-capital needs and helps firms consider waste, working conditions, pay, and all interactions between an organization and those providing supplies to the organization.

These five principles enable organizations to meet the three characteristics of a sustainable organization (resiliency, set of principles and values, and a focus). These principles also provide a method for developing a competitive advantage while still honoring the natural world. A sustainable organization that uses these principles would effectively respond to the environmental, social, and regulatory pressures it is experiencing with strategies based on the principles. These principles can guide company actions and help managers determine how to make specific investment decisions.

At this point, I will begin to introduce several analytical tools to help develop a viable strategy, guided by the five principles described above. As discussed in Chapter 4, a viable strategy is based on external and internal analyses to create clarity of focus and high-quality implementation.

Types of Analysis

I will discuss two major external analysis tools in this chapter—broad, macro categories of impact and industry analysis—and include some additional analysis tools for consideration. In Chapter 6, I will build on these tools and describe how to assess a firm's resources and capabilities. Once these analyses are described, you will have the major methods to frame a strategy and make decisions about generic strategies (e.g., low cost or differentiation [the focus of Chapter 7]). I will then expand our conversation to discuss how firms develop strategies for multiple product lines that are within various markets (also in Chapter 7). These discussions consistently illustrate how strategy formulation and implementation are informed by a natural environmental lens.

Impact Categories

"Impact" analysis tools enable companies to look at factors impacting them (and may not be industry-specific). A simple (yet powerful) impact tool to describe macro conditions is called "SLEEPT-AT" (Social-Cultural [S], Legal [L], Economic [E], Environmental [E], Political [P], Administrative [A], and Technological [T]), which analyzes a set of factors used in the contextual scanning component of strategy formulation. With each of these factors, companies are looking for at least two outcomes: (1) *trends* in each category and (2) the *risks* of doing business as a result of these trends. For example, if a firm finds that a certain country is creating the rule of law and is enforcing this rule of law (an example of the "political" factor), the risk of doing business in that country may lessen as the new rule of law would enable more transparent business processes. The following is a description of each of these factors.

Sociocultural Factors

Sociocultural factors include the sociocultural aspects that may affect companies including *health consciousness, demographic factors* (e.g., population growth rate and age distribution), *cultural attitudes*, and *emphasis on safety*. Trends in social factors affect the demand for a company's products and how that company operates (e.g., cultural factors may impact a product's desirability). Companies may change various management strategies to adapt to these social trends.

Legal Factors

Legal factors include the legal system within a country, laws that impact workers and consumers, legal requirements for firms, and health and safety laws. These factors can all affect how a company operates, its costs, and the demand for its products (as described in Chapter 3). Also, some legal requirements may cause a company to enter a market using certain techniques such as joint ventures (a common legal requirement in emerging markets).

PRINCIPLES AND ANALYSES TO INFORM STRATEGY

Economic Factors

Economic factors include economic growth; exchange, interest, and inflation rates; output; and monetary and fiscal policies. These factors have major impacts on how businesses operate and make decisions as well as the economic conditions under which certain strategies might or might not incur additional risk (e.g., interest rates clearly impact a firm's cost of capital, and inflation relates directly to pricing and investments).

Environmental Factors

Environmental factors (the focus of this book and described initially in Chapter 1) include ecological and environmental conditions (e.g., resource availability, weather, climate, and climate change). Several industries are impacted dramatically by environmental conditions (e.g., farming, insurance, and tourism). Environmental conditions can also create competitive opportunities for firms that use any type of natural resource.[58]

Political Factors

Political factors (which include fiscal and monetary policies and procedures, administrative structures for enforcing the law, trade policies and procedures, and political stability) are how and *to what degree* a government intervenes in the economy (as well as the type of political system under which a business operates). Governments have great influence on myriad important institutions (e.g., education, health, and infrastructure).[59]

Administrative Factors

Administrative factors include laws, policies, and institutions that typically emerge from a political process and are mandated (or enforced) by governments, international contracts among nations (including treaties), and international organizations. Companies often assess colonial ties, memberships in regional trading blocs, and the use of a common currency (e.g., certain contexts require firms to implement extensive liaisons with government agencies, increasing their costs of doing business in those contexts).

Technological Factors

Technological factors include aspects such as research and development (R&D) activity through independent technology companies, technology incentives, and the rate of technological change. These factors may determine the quality of innovation as well as the rates of adoption in consumer markets.

The "SLEEP-AT" model's factors will vary in importance to a given company (based on its industry and the goods it produces). For example, consumer and business-to-business companies tend to be more affected by social factors, while global defense contractors (e.g., Lockheed Martin) would tend to be more affected by political factors. Risk is likely to increase the volatility in these factors; thus, large multinational companies (MNCs) that have a corporate strategy (e.g., Procter & Gamble) may find it more useful to analyze one department at a time with the "SLEEP-AT" model rather than try to analyze the company as a whole.

Industry Analysis

The first three chapters presented several external influences impacting a firm's decisions and performance. To analyze these influences, managers and analysts often organize information according to the source of the influence (e.g., political, social, or economic), or they focus on sources more immediate to their specific competitive environment using an industry analysis. **Industry analysis** provides an assessment of an industry, the firm within the industry, and identifies key factors affecting performance in vertical trading relationships and horizontal competitive relationships to determine how changes in the business environment will impact firm performance (and ultimately to determine viable strategic moves that will increase a firm's performance).

Therefore, the core of an organization's environment revolves around the relationships it has within its industry or set of stakeholders. The simplest starting point for this analysis is to look at:

- who the customers are
- the value of the products and services to customers;
- the intensity of competition;
- the competitiveness of the products or services provided by suppliers.

Industries vary in terms of *outcomes* and *descriptive characteristics* (e.g., their average return on equity, their concentration, entry and exit barriers, product differentiation, and available information [see Table 5.3]). For example, consider two extremes of industry-structure conditions: *perfectly competitive* and an *oligopoly*. An industry with *perfect competition* (the theoretical ideal in a capitalist society) has many firms, no barriers to entry or exit, generally a homogeneous product, and no impediments to information flow. Contrast this type of industry with airline manufacturers, which tend to be *oligopolies* with significant barriers to entry and exit, only a few firms, minimal product differentiation, and an imperfect availability of information.

The purpose of this section is to offer a few ways to analyze an industry, especially as industries tend to exist within varying conditions (Appendix 5.1 has a detailed outline for doing this kind of analysis).

Table 5.3 The Profitability of 10 U.S. Industries in 2000 to 2010 and Returns of Largest Companies in the Industry 2015[60]

Industry	Median ROE 2000–2010 (%)	2015 ROE (%); ROIC (%)	Leading U.S. Companies
Aerospace and Defense	23.14	23.45; 37.18	Boeing; United Technologies; Lockheed Martin; Honeywell International Inc.; General Dynamics; Northrop Grumman; Raytheon; Textron Inc.; L-3 Communication Holdings Inc.; Precision Castparts Corp.; Huntington Ingalls Industries, Inc.; Spirit AeroSystems Holdings, Inc.
Airlines	23.49	3.84; 9.50	American Airlines, Delta Air, United Continental, Southwest, JetBlue, Alaska Air, SkyWest, Hawaiian, Spirit Airlines
Automotive Retailing	8.29	32.34; 2.59	AutoNation, Murphy USA, Penske, CarMax, CST Brands, Group 1 Automotive, AutoZone, Sonic Automotive, TravelCenters of America, O'Reilly Automotive
Energy (General Utilities)	8.29	11; 6.62	PG&E, Consolidated Edison, Sempra, Public Service Enterprise, CenterPoint Energy, Integrys Energy
Wholesalers, Healthcare	15.75	11.23; 16.05	Abbott Laboratories, Medtronic, Baxter International, Stryker Corporation, Becton Dickson and Company, Boston Scientific, Zimmer Holdings, CareFusion, CR Bard, Varian Medical Systems, Alere, DENTSPLY International, Hologic
Hotels	10.05	5.77; 8.61	Carnival, Las Vegas Sands Corp., Marriot International, MGM Resorts, Caesars Entertainment, Royal Caribbean Cruises, Hilton Worldwide, Wynn Resorts
Household and Personal Products	66.11	19.31; 30.38	Jarden Corp., Newell Rubbermaid, Tupperware Brands, Blyth, Libbey, Lifetime Brands, EveryWare Global, CSS Industries, Q.E.P Co, CTI Industries, OurPet's Company, AeroGrow International, As Seen On TV, Proctor & Gamble, Kimberley-Clark

Insurance (Property and Casualty) (stock)	14.96	12.41; 11.99	Allstate, The Travelers Companies, Progressive, The Chubb Corporation, CNA Financial, Fidelity National, W.R. Berkley, Erie Indemnity Company, Old Republic International, Markel Corp., The Hanover Insurance Group
Internet Services and Retailing	13.9	N.A.	Amazon; Google; Liberty Media; eBay; Yahoo
Oil/Gas Production and Exploration	19.5	6.25; 11.84	ConocoPhillips, Chesapeake Energy, EOG Resources, Anadarko Petroleum, Apache Corp., Marathon Oil, Murphy Oil, Noble Energy, California Resources Corporation, Pioneer Natural Resources, Continental Resources, Southwestern Energy

The first analysis step is to draw industry boundaries, which is a difficult task and dependent on the questions you are seeking to answer. In general, I suggest you use **segmentation** (i.e., a process of disaggregating industries into specific markets). Starting with *buyers* allows for clear identification of all other industry players.[61]

Some people use published sources to identify industry boundaries.[62] This is a standard used by federal statistical agencies to classify businesses for the purpose of collecting and analyzing data. While this method is useful, analysts for specific firms tend to need more focused data. The purposes of segmentation are to: identify attractive segments, select strategies for different segments, and determine how many different segments the company should serve. I will demonstrate two approaches to segmentation used by analysts when they look at a specific firm: *horizontal* and *vertical*.

Horizontal Segmentation

Horizontal segmentation involves looking at the various industry segments into which a product can be sold and identifying possible segmentation variables (e.g., raw material, geography, or a customer's industry). For example, one could differentiate the provision of a simple product such as cereal, according to the target supermarkets, hypermarkets, and specialty stores. Each of these segments might or might not call for specific analyses. Once the analyst identifies these variables, he or she forms a segmentation matrix, analyzes segment attractiveness, identifies key success factors, and then decides on strategic moves. The real difficulty in this analysis is identifying the most strategically significant segmentation variables by identifying the most meaningful divisions in the market and the requirements of these segments.

Let us consider, for a moment, the energy industry. We can segment the industry according to the characteristics of buyers (e.g., commercial, residential, and industrial). Also, energy segmentation may vary by source characteristics (e.g., renewable and nonrenewable) and pricing may vary based on these groups. However, all of this segmentation might not call for different strategies, as competitiveness within this industry tends to be low (since energy companies are usually local monopolies). As energy markets are deregulated, however, these industry factors take on more significance. Competitors will be introduced; thus, customers would have additional options.

Vertical Segmentation

We could also use vertical segmentation (or what is known as profit pool mapping).[63] *Vertical segmentation* traces various elements of a product from manufacturing through its various uses. For example, we could break up the U.S. automobile industry into auto manufacturers, new car dealers, used car dealers, auto lenders, lending, insurance, aftermarket parts and repair, and rentals.

Bain Consulting Company suggests four steps to do this analysis:[64]

1 *Define boundaries*: What is the range of activities that add value? Analysts look upstream and downstream beyond conventional industry boundaries (see Appendix 9.1 for a discussion about value chains).
2 *Estimate size*: Total industry profit can be estimated by applying the average margin earned by a sample of companies to an estimate of industry total revenues.
3 *Estimate profit from each value chain activity*: Gather information about pure play companies (i.e., those specializing in the single value chain activity) and disaggregating data for those performing multiple activities.
4 *Compare profits*: Compare the aggregation of profits in each activity (Stage 3) with the total for the industry (Stage 2).

This analysis provides a means of comparing and contrasting where value is created and destroyed in an industry chain of companies.

Another powerful analysis to represent vertical segmentation is *strategic group analysis* (i.e., grouping firms together by the same or similar strategies along strategic dimensions).[65] These dimensions could be product type, pricing, geography, or a number of meaningful factors that group firms. These dimensions are usually positioned in a bivariate map (such as those in Figure 5.2).

By selecting the most important strategic dimensions and locating each organization in the industry along them, one can identify groups of companies that have adopted more or less the same competitive approaches. This analysis is most useful in identifying strategic niches within an industry and the strategic positioning of different firms. It may even help anticipate when a firm might make an aggressive move into another market space.[66]

Figure 5.2 shows a strategic group map for the education industry. The two dimensions are geographic scope and cost. While all of the organizations are in the education business, this analysis shows the dramatically different strategies they use. Community Colleges serve small geographic regions and tend to be lowest cost solution for education. Comprehensive four-year and Tier 1 universities are more geographically dispersed (attracting students from various locations) and tend to price themselves at a premium.

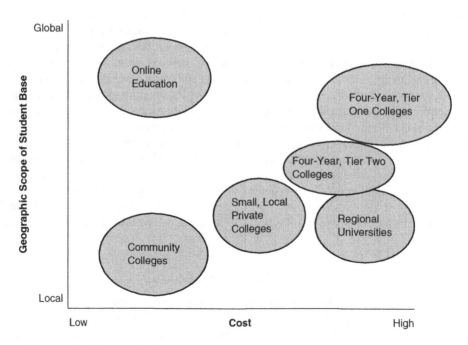

Figure 5.2 Strategic Map for the Education Industry

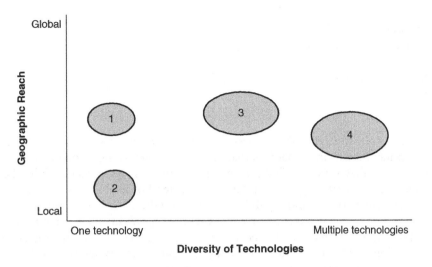

Figure 5.3 Strategic Group Map or Energy Technologies

Figure 5.3 is a hypothetical example for the renewable energy industry and firms that play in this industry. It shows the various strategies; the size of the circles relate to revenue of that grouping. Group 1 may find opportunities to move geographically while using its same, single technology, or it could move into new technologies (taking advantage of existing manufacturing or customer bases). Group 4 could move globally, competing with weaker competitors in foreign markets. This hypothetical strategic group map is very simplified; however, it demonstrates how this kind of mapping can give a company insight into the position of its competitors and potential opportunities for its future.

Other Areas of Analysis: Five Forces Model and More

Once industry boundaries and customers have been identified through segmentation, the next step is to analyze industry players and their relationships; this analysis includes suppliers, potential entrants, and substitutes. Here, we generally use a Five Forces model;[67] this analysis will show the ways in which industry factors are related to each other and provide a format for describing an industry's structure. I will describe this model and suggest ways to improve it by using a clearer analysis format.

A firm's profitability (as indicated by the rate of return on capital relative to the cost of capital) is partially determined by industry factors. The Five Forces model includes sources of *horizontal competition* (e.g., substitutes, entrants, and established rivals) and sources of *vertical competition* (e.g., suppliers and buyers). Appendix 5.1 has a format for this analysis, and this is a general description of the Five Forces approach.

The *availability of substitutes* influences the prices that customers are willing to pay for a product or service. For example, some businesses traditionally have not had much competition because of their excellent locations relative to target markets; as a result, they have been able to charge higher prices for their products. However, the Internet began enabling consumers to often (and easily) find competitive products and substitutes. Travel agencies, telecommunications providers, and even art galleries have suffered from online competition; many have lost their location advantages. The propensity of buyers to *substitute between alternatives* also influences prices. Some buyers value their time and/or comfort and are willing to pay premiums; however, the more complex the product or service, the harder it is for consumers to identify substitutes. Many industries have companies earning in excess of the cost of capital; this situation attracts others to enter the market. Yet, in most industries new entrants cannot enter on equal terms with incumbent firms as a result of *barriers to entry* (i.e., the unit cost disadvantage faced by would-be entrants). The principal sources of entry barriers are:

- capital requirements;
- economies of scale;
- product or service differentiation;
- cost advantages;
- access to distribution channels;
- government or legal barriers;
- retaliation.

In line with our view of the firm, the effectiveness of barriers to entry depends on the *resources* and *capabilities* of potential and incumbent firms. Barriers that are effective against new companies might be ineffective against established firms that are diversifying from other industries (e.g., Microsoft has been able to enter many new markets due to its market power and ability to extend products).[68] At the same time, incumbent firms might have excellent resources and capabilities to ward off diversified firms and government regulations can become significant hindrances (myriad global firms are finding this in emerging markets across borders).[69]

Rivalry among competitors is probably the most powerful determinant of dynamics in an industry, and thus the industry's profitability. The severity and activeness of competition is determined by certain conditions; among the more important are the concentration (i.e., size and number) of firms competing within a market, diversity of competitors, product differentiation, production capacity, and cost conditions (mainly from scale economies and the ratio of fixed to variable costs). For example, if excess capacity exists, high prices will drop—but how far? When fixed costs are high relative to variable costs, firms will take a marginal business at any price that covers variable costs. This philosophy (i.e., taking business at any price) happened in the recent financial crisis following 2008, when large engineering firms took on business they would normally not have considered. The implications of these actions were that smaller firms (either incumbents or new entrants) had difficulty winning business and making a profit because more established, reputable firms were taking on less desired jobs to keep their businesses profitable.

Buyers and suppliers have complementary impacts on industries; when either is concentrated, for example, it has more power to influence industry firms. The more important an item is to a buyer, the less power. A good example of this is patented drugs; individuals are willing to pay a lot more to get a drug they need. (Note that firms often play the role of both buyer *and* supplier as they buy products that they turn around and sell to other buyers or consumers.) Suppliers might have unique resources so their power will increase relative to buyers of their goods.

These are some of the dynamics that cause players to obtain variable levels of margins in their industries. The Five Forces model is definitely a helpful way to organize information that leads to the analysis of industry attractiveness, viable strategies, and key success factors; however, it does have several limitations. First, it does not help analyze factors impacting demand for products and services. While it accounts for the availability and prices of substitutes or complementary products, it ignores changes in consumer tastes, income, and moves firms can make to increase demand (e.g., increases in information through product certifications and advertising).

Second, it does not account for some of the pressures we discussed in the first three chapters—especially government. Third, it tends to be qualitative, and analysts are hard pressed to quantify factors (e.g., the probability of entry by a new firm). Fourth, it is based on an assumption that firms' strategies are to obtain margins *away* from other industry players. This is a narrow view of strategy.

To help correct some of these flaws, researchers have tended to change some of the framework's assumptions and alter the analysis focus. One alternative is the Value Net analysis that puts the target firm at the center of the analysis and classifies industry players as competitors, customers, suppliers, and complementors.[70] This method brings added value to the Five Forces model because it includes *complementors*. Competitors include existing rivals, substitutes, and entrants. *Complementors* are influences on profitability that are not directly within the industry analysis. For example, doctors are clearly influential on branded drug purchases in the United States, yet they are not suppliers, customers, or rivals of the pharmaceutical companies. So, they are classified as *complementors*. Software and hardware are related in the computer industry, yet they are not often addressed in the same Five Forces analysis.

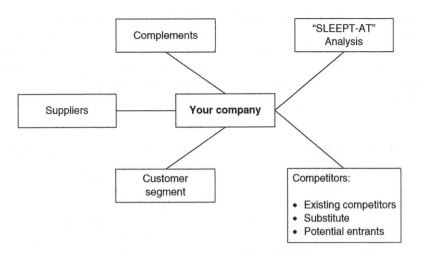

Figure 5.4 Analysis Format for External Conditions to Inform a Firm's Strategy

Another benefit of the Value Net analysis (Figure 5.4) is that it emphasizes the many strategic opportunities that can come from cooperative interactions that bring benefit to all players. For example, competitors can promote favorable regulations and legislation, such as when soft-drink companies promote water standards[71] or consumer product companies and associations are suggesting environmentally friendly product standards.[72]

Analysis vs. Action

Analysts are often overwhelmed by the vastness of collecting data and using those data to suggest strategies to a firm. To help with this complexity, Appendix 5.2 contains some suggestions for organizing one's thinking about how to develop and communicate about a complete strategy. Table 4.6 from Chapter 4 helped to develop strategy by asking you to answer specific questions related to the success criteria of internal analysis, external analysis, focus, and quality implementation.

While many analysts want to develop a strategy before any resources are allocated to implement the strategy, reality dictates otherwise. Most managers know that the strategy formulation process is influenced heavily by their firm's *actions*; thus, this dynamic between detailed a priori analysis and learning from implementation is fundamental to a firm's success. For example, few could have predicted the massive recession, beginning in late 2007, and its impact on firms in all industries. The ability to respond to these changes (and to adapt one's planned strategy) is a subject we will cover in Chapter 11. As we move forward, it should become clearer how analysis, strategy, and action can work together to make companies successful.

Chapter Summary

This chapter was an introduction to the development of core principles (and use of) analysis tools in developing business strategy. This approach (to both principles and analysis) is rooted in a resource-based view of the firm. Additionally, this chapter presented the case for corporate environmental sustainability as a lens on a firm's strategy. The core support for this case was that firms are experiencing pressures from changes in the environment, customer requirements, and regulatory mandates. These pressures are coupled with tremendous opportunities to use this way of thinking for increased competitiveness. Two major analyses are the basis of strategy formulation—*external analysis* (including macro conditions) and *industry structure analysis* and *internal analysis* (mostly assessments of a company's resources and capabilities). We focused on external analysis in this chapter using the SLEEPT-AT model for macro-conditions descriptions and the Five Forces and Value Net methodologies for industry analysis.

The goal of this chapter is to lay the groundwork for what must precede successful corporate environmental sustainability. Firms must see the natural environment as a resource and an asset and, through this perspective, integrate this asset into their core principles. From this point, firms can conduct their external and internal analyses as usual with their core principles guiding their analysis. This chapter has provided some of the most useful tools for external analysis; with this progression in mind, the following chapters will dig deeper into developing strategies and show how environmental sustainability can easily fit into the core strategies of all firms. The next chapter will discuss effective internal analysis.

Case Revisited: Wal-Mart as a Model Company for Environmental Sustainability

The story of Wal-Mart illustrates many of the principles and practices discussed in this book (especially within this chapter). The company chose a few principles and goals to guide its actions. The company's environmental focus enabled it to realize key goals, maintain its profitability, and increase its reputation. (Note that it took the CEO's commitment, employee involvement, and lots of help from outside organizations to realize these outcomes.) Wal-Mart not only illustrates the key points of this text about creating strategies, but it is also an example of the dedication and perspective it takes to be successful at implementing environmentally sustainable strategies.

Wal-Mart updated its approach over the years. For example, it changed its number and types of networks, increased the sophistication of its supplier data and requirements, and tended to increase the number of people involved in its sustainability effort as the evidence grew that its reputation was increasing in a positive manner. Wal-Mart continues to invest a significant amount of time, money, and effort into measuring sustainability and tracking progress toward its goals.[73]

Figure 5.5 Sylvia Earle Speaking at Wake Forest University, 2015. Photo Credit: Scott McCullough[74]

Also, Wal-Mart has looked at its competitive environment and decided that its road to competitiveness was with the environmental sustainability principles and practices it adopted. This decision was based on how it could distinguish itself from competitors; its external analysis revealed these opportunities. As you will discover in the next chapter, it also realized that it had the competencies to support this new strategy.

Terms to Know

Industry analysis: method of external analysis related to a specific firm. At the least, *industry analysis* identifies the power of key industry players

Resource-based firm: the major source of competitive advantage is based within the firm (i.e., in its resources and how those resources are used)

Resources: tangible and intangible assets that enable a firm to perform and support its positioning in markets

Segmentation: the process of disaggregating customers according to specific characteristics

Sustainable corporation: a company that operates today without compromising its own or society's future

Profile: Sylvia Earle[75]

Chapter 5 outlines five principles for the firm through an environmental lens. Although about 71 percent of Earth's surface is covered by ocean,[76] it is often a source of natural capital that is neglected by conservation measures and undervalued economically. The principles that build upon The Natural Step and Hannover Principles strive to help companies marry strategic focus and unique positioning with natural environmental sustainability. Principle 4 advises the firm to advocate decreasing the degradation of our world by physical means. Often times implementing this principle begins with a foresighted, unique individual who sets a precedent of character and gives firms data that can be used to develop strategy models giving them a competitive advantage for future economic growth.

There are over 267 known marine species that have been negatively impacted by entanglement or ingestion of oceanic plastic debris including seabirds, turtles, seals, sea lions, whales, and fish.[77] The negative impacts from plastic pollution can cause adverse effects known as trophic cascades which are indirect interactions that control entire ecosystems, limiting the density and behavior of their prey.[78] These tangibles directly affect economic drivers such as fisheries, tourism, and recreation. For example, the Great Barrier Reef in Australia, which is deteriorating from oceanic pollution and negative trophic cascading, added a total economic contribution of $5.7 billion (with employment) to Australia in 2012.[79] Without the life's work of individuals like Sylvia Earle, who expand the firm's environmental lens, these economic figures would be largely neglected by business-as-usual.

Sylvia Earle has been a director of over 12 corporate or nonprofit organizations and is the former chief scientist of NOAA; during her career she has logged over 7,000 underwater hours, setting a world record in 2012 by solo diving at 1,000 meters depth.[80] Her research has focused on the importance of marine ecosystems which provide basic life support systems enabling stability and resiliency in today's global economic system. Her data, which include over 190 scientific, technical, and popular publications have contributed greatly to the development of strategy models worldwide.

With the five principles outlined in this chapter, who are some burgeoning individuals today that will provide competitive data to help firms develop effective strategy models for future success? How can these data be used to improve the strategy model's foundation, i.e., measuring and reporting, marketing, labeling, and analyzing?

Questions and Critical Thinking

1   We have discussed industry analysis and how to analyze an organization; however, we could identify many other entities to analyze (e.g., supply chains, networks, and regional groups). To what extent do these other analyses matter for developing strategy? For example, consider a group of organizations located together (e.g., in Silicon Valley or in other industrial parks throughout the world). How would an analysis of these groups add to a particular firm's strategy?

2   Is it possible for a firm to survive forever and does it really matter if it survives? Maybe firms will come and go, yet the lessons learned will be carried forward. Could we consider this knowledge transfer as a source of sustainability?

3   Critically analyze the suggested principles for developing strategy using environmental sustainability as the lens. Take each principle suggested in this chapter and discuss its ability to inform a firm's strategy. What are the positive aspects of using each principle? What other principles would *you* add?

4   Take one industry and analyze two different firms within that industry. Now consider changing your boundaries and determine what might happen to the industry analysis and firm strategy as a result. For example, take a boundary condition of domestic only (e.g., the United States) and then change the boundary to include another region in the world.

5   Coffee bars, mutual funds, transportation using existing infrastructure (e.g., Uber), home video rentals, and social networking are relatively new industries in the past 20 years. What industries might evolve in the next 20 years? (Consider that most new industries evolve using existing technologies and are a result of incumbent firms or start-ups.)

Appendix 5.1. Industry Analysis

Industry analysis helps managers and analysts to:

* assess industry and firm performance;
* identify key success factors affecting performance in vertical and horizontal relationships;
* determine how changes in a business environment may impact performance;
* identify opportunities for strategic moves (for a firm or its competitor).

Step 1. Vantage Point

Decide on a vantage point. Are you a supplier, competitor, buyer, substitute, potential entrant, or complementor?

Step 2. Defining the Market

Start with segmentation analysis. Decide on your boundaries.

Step 3. Players

Who are the players? The analyst will have decided some of these when defining the boundaries and customers; however, now the analyst needs to decide on a complete list of players.

Step 4. Structural Analysis

Conduct a structural analysis; below are some questions to consider for this. For each question, designate the current state of affairs and future trends.

Rivalry

Each factor is analyzed as to what extent the category erodes or enhances profitability for a typical firm in the industry.

EXISTING COMPETITORS

- Degree of seller concentration? (Prices are lower when there are many firms in the market.)
- Rate of industry growth? (Stagnant or declining industries intensify competition.)
- Significant cost differences among firms?
- Excess capacity? (Firms with excess capacity may be under pressure to boost sales and can expand easily to take sales from rivals.)
- Cost structure of firms; what is the sensitivity of costs to capacity utilization?
- Degree of product differentiation among sellers? Brand loyalty to existing sellers? Cross-price elasticity of demand among competitors? (When products are undifferentiated and switching costs are low, firms tend to cut prices to generate sales.)
- Buyer's costs of switching from one competitor to another? (If high, then initial customer acquisition is critical.)
- Are prices and terms of sales transactions observable?
- Can firms adjust prices quickly?
- Large or infrequent sales orders? (Competitors might fight harder for each sale.)
- Use of facilitating practices (e.g., price leadership and advance announcements of price changes)? History of cooperative pricing? In the absence of price leadership price announcements (or other facilitating practices), firms might be unable to find the mean industry price. Some firms send signals that they will match price cuts.
- Strength of exit barriers? (Could prolong price wars.)
- High industry price elasticity of demand? (When consumers are price sensitive, non-price competition can threaten industry profits.)

POTENTIAL ENTRANTS AND BARRIERS TO ENTRY

- Economies of scale? (Entrants may incur high costs to get to this point.)
- Importance of reputation or established brand loyalties in purchase decisions?
- Entrant's access to distribution channels, raw materials, technology, favorable locations, and its know-how? (These factors, when protected, can be strong barriers to entry; incumbents can overpay to protect these factors, giving entrants an advantage.)
- Experience-based advantages of incumbents? (A steep curve puts entrants at a cost disadvantage.)
- Entrants' perceptions about expected retaliation by incumbents and the reputation of incumbents for toughness? Does the incumbent have a reputation for predatory pricing in the face of entry?
- Network externalities demand-side advantages to incumbents from large, installed base? (Large, installed base favors incumbents.)
- Government protection of incumbents? (Laws and administrative regulatory practices may favor some firms over others.)

SUBSTITUTES AND COMPLEMENTS

- Availability of close substitutes?
- Price-value characteristics of substitutes?
- Price elasticity of industry demand? (Useful measures of the pressure substitutes place on an industry. When the industry-level price elasticity is large, rising industry prices tend to drive consumers to purchase substitute products.)
- Availability of close complements?
- Price-value characteristics of complements?

Suppliers

- More concentrated than the industry it sells to?
- Are purchases relatively small volumes (relative to customer of suppliers)?

- Few substitutes for supplier's inputs?
- Do firms make relationship-specific investments to support transactions with specific suppliers?
- Do suppliers pose credible threat of forward integration?
- Are suppliers able to price-discriminate among prospective customers according to ability/willingness to pay for input?

Buyers

- Is a buyer's industry more concentrated than the industry it purchases from?
- Do buyers purchase large volumes? Does a buyer's purchase volume represent a large fraction of the typical seller's sales revenues?
- Can buyers find substitutes for an industry's products?
- Do firms in industry make relationship-specific investments to support transactions with specific buyers?
- Is price elasticity of demand of buyer's product high or low?
- Do buyers pose credible threat of backward integration?
- Does product represent significant fraction of cost in buyer's business?
- Are prices in the market negotiated between buyers and sellers on each individual transaction, or do sellers post a take-it-leave-it price that applies to all transactions?

Step 5. Key Success Factors

These tend to come from a summary of analysis to better understand two key questions: (1) What do customers want? (2) How does the firm survive competition? (See Chapter 6.)

The key success factors can suggest needed core competencies within the firm. Some examples of key success factors:

- technology;
- manufacturing;
- distribution;
- marketing;
- human resources;
- organizational;
- others.

Step 6. Industry Attractiveness

What is the current industry attractiveness? What is the future of industry attractiveness?

Step 7. Potential Moves

What are the potential moves that each player could make?

Appendix 5.2. Presentation of a Strategy

This brief outline will help you present a company's strategy in a manner that is concise yet informative for your audience. This format builds on information presented throughout this book. Before you begin, consider two important areas:

1. Analytical Skills for Content Awareness and Content-in-Use

These questions relate to necessary base knowledge needed to do strategy.

1   What data does the analyst consider most important in our strategic thinking?
2   What are the key concepts, theories, models, and methods in use today for understanding strategy formulation and industry dynamics?

3   What are the key strategic issues facing an organization today and in the future?
4   What constraints does the organization face, given our priorities, timing, and internal politics?

2. Behavioral Skills for Developing and Implementing the Strategy

These questions relate to how the organization processes data and makes decisions and changes; it also addresses the planning processes the organization uses.

1   How can the organization act to gather relevant information and make decisions? How does each organizational member perform his or her role during the strategy process?
2   How should the organization phrase its strategic alternatives and our strategic direction?[81]
3   How do organizational members create a sense of perspective, disciplined thought, disciplined people, and disciplined action?

Questions to Consider for the Presentation

1   What are the expectations for this presentation? For example, is the presenter trying to persuade his or her audience on a strategic move that can increase the company's value? Is he or she trying to inform organizational members about the company's strategy? Can the presenter state the purpose clearly and *adapt the presentation to the purpose.*
2   What contextual factors influence the company and how? (Consider the SLEEP-AT analysis.)
3   Where should the organization play? (This section describes the company's positioning for its products and services.)
4   Analyses to increase value—use four criteria for effective strategy:

a   *Internal*: costs, resources, and capabilities (see Chapters 6–7). What are the resources and capabilities? To what extent do these resources and capabilities lead to competitive advantages? Are they connected? Are they sustainable? And do they fit with the organization's administrative history, structure, systems, culture, and management style? What can the firm do to enhance the rents from our resources and capabilities?

b   *External*: boundaries, costs, relationships among players, points of difference, points of parity (see Chapters 1–3 and 5). What can we learn from the macro environments in which we do business (including key success factors)? What can we learn from analyses of our industry or industries, the marketplaces, competitors, and other key players in business? Where will we be active and with how much emphasis? What are the boundaries of our firm?

c   *Focus*: mission, vision, timeframe, low cost and differentiation, niche. What do we want to achieve? What do we consider our fundamental purpose, values, mandates, targets and objectives? Why are we in business? How can we be different compared to those with whom we compete or cooperate?

d   *Implementation*: What can we achieve? What moves should we make to achieve our purpose? What will our speed be (and the sequence of the moves)? What is the timeframe for our strategy? How will we obtain returns? What is our business model? What measurements will we use?

- Look for places to gain greater alignment; relationships within the industry; strategic groups (including mobility opportunities); brand analysis.
- Consider existing competitors and potential entrants and the potential moves they would make (given any move you or others can make).

5   Strategic alternatives

a   What are the scenarios for the future?
b   Consider various perspectives in arriving at value; this way, the chosen strategy (positioning and activities) will yield greater margins, increased revenues, decreased investments, and lower cost of capital. Specify risks and how to mitigate risks.

    c   Is the strategy clear, informed by data, and does it differentiate the firm?

    d   Could the organization take options on more than one strategy?

    e   In summary, what are our strategic imperatives or intents?

6   How is the organization to be managed? (See Chapter 6–11.)

    a   What can management do to increase operational effectiveness?

    b   Does the organization have characteristics of excellence?

    c   Is management implementing effectively, with clear information, decision rights, and a clear structure?

    d   Any special issues?

    e   Does the organization have a clear business model?

7   Value creation. Specific references to margins, revenues, investment in fixed and working capital, cost of capital, special considerations (e.g., leases and contracts). How will organizational members measure my progress in terms of performance, sustainability, and impact?

Notes

1 http://www.wikinvest.com/stock/Wal-Mart_(WMT)/Data/Market_Capitalization (accessed December 4, 2014).

2 M. Gunther, "The Green Machine," *Fortune*, August 7, 2006, 46; D. Nassar, "Why Wal-Mart Does Not Strengthen Our Economy," *The Huffington Post*, April 30, 2008, www.huffingtonpost.com/david-nassar/why-wal-mart-does-not-str_b_99463.html (accessed 2 December 2015).

3 Gunther, "The Green Machine."

4 E. Humes, *Force of Nature: The Unlikely Story of Wal-Mart's Green Revolution* (New York: HarperCollins, 2011).

5 E. L. Plambeck and L. Denend, "Wal-Mart's Sustainability Strategy," Stanford Graduate School of Business Case No. OIT71, April 17, 2007, 1–2.

6 Ibid.

7 P. Engardio, "Beyond the Green Corporation," Bloomberg Businessweek on NBC News.com, January 19, 2007, www.msnbc.msn.com/id/16710668 (accessed June 27, 2011).

8 M. Bower and W. Leon, *The Consumer's Guide to Effective Environmental Choices: Practical Advice from the Union of Concerned Scientists* (New York: Three Rivers Press, 1999).

9 Endnote: E. Plambeck and L. Denend, "The Greening of Walmart's Supply Chain," *Supply Chain Management Review* (July/August 2007): 18–25.

10 Wal-Mart, *Building the Next Generation Walmart . . . Responsibly: 2011 Global Responsibility Report* (Bentonville, AR: Wal-Mart Stores, Inc., 2011), http://walmartstores.com/sites/ResponsibilityReport/2011/ (accessed June 27, 2011).

11 R. Sroufe, "Effects of Environmental Management Systems on Environmental Management Practices and Operations," *Production and Operations Management* 12, no. 3 (September 2003): 416–431.

12 M. Delmas and M. W. Toffel, "Stakeholders and Environmental Management Practices: An Institutional Study," *Business Strategy and the Environment* 13, no. 4 (August 2004): 209–222.

13 R. Handfield, R. Sroufe, and S. Walton, "Integrating Environmental Management and Supply Chain Strategies," *Business Strategy and the Environment* 14, no. 1 (January/February 2005): 1–19.

14 Millennium Ecosystem Assessment, *Ecosystems and Human Well-being: Opportunities and Challenges for Business and Industry* (Washington, DC: World Resources Institute, 2005).

15 E.g., M. J. Epstein, *Making Sustainability Work: Best Practices in Managing and Measuring Corporate, Social, Environmental and Economic Impacts* (San Francisco, CA: Berrett-Koehler, 2008); C. Laszlo and N. Zhexembayeva, *Embedded Sustainability: The Next Big Competitive Advantage* (Stanford, CA: Stanford University Press, 2011).

16 S. Hart and M. B. Milstein, "Creating Sustainable Value," *Academy of Management Executive* 17, no. 2 (2003): 56–69; S. L. Hart, *Capitalism at the Crossroads: The Unlimited Business Opportunities in Solving the World's Most Difficult Problems* (Upper Saddle River, NJ: Wharton School, 2005), 38–44.

17 D. Collis and C. A. Montgomery, "Competing on Resources: Strategy in the 1990s," *Harvard Business Review* 73, no. 4 (July–August 1995): 118–128; R. Amit and P. J. H. Shoemaker, "Strategic Assets and Organizational Rent," *Strategic Management Journal* 14, no. 1 (1993): 33–46.

18 M. T. Lucas, "Understanding Environmental Management Practices: Integrating Views from Strategic Management and Ecological Economics," *Business Strategy and the Environment* 19, no. 8 (December 2010): 543–556.

19 Adapted from World Commission on Environment and Development (now known as The Brundtland Commission), *Our Common Future: From One Earth to One World* (Oxford: Oxford University Press, 1987), chapter 2.

20 *The Economist*, "The Centenarians Square Up," June 9, 2011, 65.

21 J. Collins, *Good to Great: Why Some Companies Make the Leap—and Others Don't* (New York: Harper Business, 2001), 65–89.

22 *The Economist,* "1100100 and Counting," June 9, 2011, 67.

23 Co-authored by Michael Aper, Master of Arts in Sustainability candidate 2015 at Wake Forest University.

24 D. Cardwell and M. L. Wald, "A Huge Solar Plant Opens, Facing Doubts about Its Future," Energy and Environment, *The New York Times,* February 13, 2014, http://www.nytimes.com/2014/02/14/business/energy-environment/a-big-solar-plant-opens-facing-doubts-about-its-future.html?_r=0 (accessed April 12, 2015).

25 D. Cardwell and M. L. Wald, "A Huge Solar Plant Opens, Facing Doubts about Its Future," Energy and Management, *The New York Times,* February 13, 2014, http://www.nytimes.com/2014/02/14/business/energy-environment/a-big-solar-plant-opens-facing-doubts-about-its-future.html?_r=0 (accessed April 12, 2015).

26 BrightSource Energy, Inc., "Ivanpah," 2015, http://www.brightsourceenergy.com/ivanpah-solar-project#.VSxY5dzF8-A (accessed April 12, 2015).

27 A. Aston, P. Engardio, and J. Makower, "25 Companies to Watch in Energy Tech," Bloomberg Business, Bloomberg L.P., 2015, http://www.bloomberg.com/ss/09/07/0714_sustainable_planet/6.htm (accessed April 12, 2015).

28 A. Aston, P. Engardio, and J. Makower, "25 Companies to Watch in Energy Tech," Bloomberg Business, Bloomberg L.P., 2015, http://www.bloomberg.com/ss/09/07/0714_sustainable_planet/6.htm (accessed April 12, 2015).

29 BrightSource Energy, Inc., "Company," 2015, http://www.brightsourceenergy.com/company#.VSxGC9zF8-A (accessed April 12, 2015).

30 BrightSource Energy, Inc., "SEDC," 2015, http://www.brightsourceenergy.com/sedc#.VSxaUdzF8-A (accessed April 12, 2015).

31 P. Kareiva, H. Tallis, T. H. Ricketts, G. C. Daily, and S. Polasky (eds.), *Natural Capital: Theory and Practice of Mapping Ecosystem Services* (New York: Oxford University Press, 2011), 3.

32 R. T. Wright and D. F. Boorse, *Environmental Science: Toward a Sustainable Future,* 11th ed. (Boston, MA: Benjamin Cummings, 2011), 123.

33 *Source:* R. Costanza et al., "The Value of the World's Ecosystem Services and Natural Capital," *Nature* 3, no. 87 (May 15, 1997): 254 (Table 1). We include ecosystem "goods" along with ecosystem services.

34 1 pentagram equals 1 billion metric tons.

35 P. Vitousek, P. R. Ehrlich, A. H. Ehrlich, and P. Matson, "Human Appropriation of the Products of Photosynthesis," *BioScience* 36, no. 6 (June 1986): 368–373.

36 N. Ramankutty, A. T. Evan, C. Monfreda, and J. A. Foley, "Farming the Planet: 1. Geographic Distribution of Global Agricultural Lands in Year 2000," *Global Biogeochemical Cycles* 22, no. 1 (March 2008): GB1003.

37 One way to organize thinking about valuation methods is to use the following outline:

Total Economic Value of Ecosystem Services (ES):

A Market Values (the dollar value people pay for ES)

   a Use values: when people use the resource in some way and directly pay to use it.

      i Direct use extractive (e.g., buying lumber); non-extractive (e.g., fee paid to enter a park)
      ii Indirect use values such as volunteering

   b Non-use values such as paying to protect a park that the person will never visit.

B Non-market values (ES is not directly purchased on the market)

   a Use values: classic commons

      i Direct use values—extractive such as picking flowers you don't pay for
      ii Indirect use such as flood control

   b Non-use values—altruistic or bequest

Sample valuation methods can include:

Market methods such as paying for a resource, decreased productivity or earning lost from ecosystem damage or defensive or preventive expenditures such as the purchase of a water filter; replacement costs such as remediating an ecosystem; ecosystem service that enhances the value of an asset such as availability of water in a location.

Non-market methods such as revealed preference (travel costs to go camping); premium one would pay for a house on a lake; avoided costs such as not having to pay for a water filter given the quality of water.

38 Central Intelligence Agency, "World: Economy," *The World Factbook Online,* www.cia.gov/library/publications/the-world-factbook/geos/xx.html (accessed June 15, 2011).

39 A. Balmford et al., "Economic Reasons for Conserving Wild Nature," *Science* 297, no. 5583 (August 9, 2002): 950–953; National Research Council, *Valuing Ecosystem Services: Toward Better Environmental Decision Making* (Washington, DC: National Academic Press, 2005).

40 R. Schmalensee, "Do Markets Differ Much?" *American Economic Review* 75, no. 3 (June 1985): 341–351; R. P. Rumelt, "How Much Does Industry Matter?" *Strategic Management Journal* 12, no. 3 (March 1991): 167–185; A. M. McGahan and M. E. Porter, "How Much Does Industry Matter, Really?" *Strategic Management Journal* 18, no. S1 (July 1997): 15–30; G. Hawawini, V. Subramaniam, and P. Verdin, "Is Performance Driven by Industry- or Firm-Specific Factors? A New Look at the Evidence," *Strategic Management Journal* 24, no. 1 (January 2003): 1–16; V. F. Misangyi, H. Elms, T. Greckhamer, and J. A. Lepine, "A New Perspective on a Fundamental Debate: A Multilevel Approach to Industry Corporate and Business Unit Effects," *Strategic Management Journal* 27, no. 6 (June 2006): 571–590.

41 D. Fogel, *The Future of Business Organizations and Their Attention to Environmental Sustainability*, Asia Pacific Work in Progress Research Paper Issue 13 (Queensland: Griffith University, April 2013).

42 The Goldman Sachs Group, *Introducing GS Sustain* (New York: Goldman Sachs, June 22, 2007), www.unglobal-compact.org/docs/summit2007/gs_esg_embargoed_until030707pdf.pdf (accessed October 25, 2011).

43 M. Alderton, "Green Is Gold, According to Goldman Sachs Study," *CR: Corporate Responsibility Magazine*, July 20, 2007, www.thecro.com/node/490 (accessed October 21, 2011).

44 S. Smith, "S&P Dow Jones Indices formed from merger of S&P Indices and Dow Jones Indexes," *ETF Strategy*, July 3, 2012, www.etfstrategy.co.uk/sp-dow-jones-indices-formed-from-merger-of-sp-indices-and-dow-jones-indexes-47812/ (accessed December 15, 2012).

45 D. Mahler et al., *"Green" Winners* (Chicago, IL: A. T. Kearny, 2009) www.atkearney.com/documents/10192/6972076a-9cdc-4b20-bc3a-d2a4c43c9c21 (accessed October 15, 2011).

46 IDC and Atos Origin, *The Business Case for Environmental Excellence Is Real* (New York: IDC, 2009) www.natcap-solutions.org/business-case/IDCbusiness_case.pdf (accessed October 2, 2011).

47 Laszlo and Zhexembayeva, *Embedded Sustainability*.

48 Epstein, *Making Sustainability Work*, 41.

49 E.g., Laszlo and Zhexembayeva, *Embedded Sustainability*, 115.

50 B. Nattrass and M. Altomare, *The Natural Step for Business: Wealth, Ecology, and the Evolutionary Corporation* (Gabriola Island, BC: New Society, 1999), 23.

51 A. Thompson and R. Blume, "The Natural Step Framework," in K. Christensen, D. S. Fogel, G. Wagner, and P. J. Whitehouse (eds.), *Berkshire Encyclopedia of Sustainability*, Volume 2: *The Business of Sustainability* (Great Barrington, MA: Berkshire Publishers, 2011), 351.

52 Resort Municipality of Whistler 2010 Winter Games Office, *Resort Municipality of Whistler 2010 Olympic and Paralympic Winter Games Strategic Framework*, Version 1 (October 2006), https://www.whistler.ca/images/stories/PDF/Admin/Strategic_Framework_Version_1_October_2006.pdf (accessed December 21, 2015).

53 U.S. Green Building Council, "LEED," www.usgbc.org/leed (accessed June 8, 2011).

54 Japan GreenBuild Council and Japan Sustainable Building Consortium, "An Overview of CASBEE," www.ibec.or.jp/CASBEE/english/overviewE.htm (accessed June 8, 2011).

55 BRE Global, "What is BREEAM?" www.breeam.org/about.jsp?id=66 (accessed June 8, 2011).

56 William McDonough & Partners, *The Hannover Principles: Design for Sustainability* (Charlottesville, VA: William McDonough & Partners, 1992) http://www.mcdonough.com/wp-content/uploads/2013/03/Hannover-Principles-1992.pdf (accessed December 22, 2015).

57 H. Blatt, *America's Food: What You Don't Know about What You Eat* (Cambridge, MA: MIT Press, 2008), 33.

58 M. Funk, *Windfall: The Blooming Business of Global Warming* (New York: The Penguin Press, 2014).

59 K. G. Palepu and T. Khanna with R. J. Bullock, *Winning in Emerging Markets: A Road Map for Strategy and Execution* (Boston, MA: Harvard Business Press, 2010), 14.

60 Adapted from Damodaran Online, "The Data Page," http://pages.stern.nyu.edu/~adamodar/New_Home_Page/data.html (accessed July 15, 2015). *Note:* This table shows the profit variation among industries. In general, the analyst is likely to find greater variation within industries than across industries.

61 Note that we designate industry competitors as those that supply a market. For example, we tend to think of the U.S. automobile industry as composed of automakers located in the United States and other countries. Some authors may disagree with this approach—see S. S. Mathur and A. Kenyon, *Creating Valuable Business Strategies* (Boston, MA: Elsevier/Butterworth-Heinemann, 2007).

62 U.S. Census Bureau, "Introduction to NAICS," www.census.gov/eos/www/naics/ (accessed June 20, 2012).

63 O. Gadiesh and J. L. Gilbert, "How to Map Your Industry's Profit Pool," *Harvard Business Review* 76, no. 3 (May 1998): 139–147.

64 Ibid.

65 J. McGee and H. Thomas, "Strategic Groups: Theory, Research and Taxonomy," *Strategic Management Journal* 7, no. 2 (March/April 1986): 141–160.

66 K. G. Smith, C. M. Grimm, G. Young, and S. Wally, "Strategic Groups and Rivalrous Firm Behavior: Towards a Reconciliation," *Strategic Management Journal* 18, no. 2 (February 1997): 149–157.

67 M. E. Porter, *Competitive Strategy: Techniques for Analyzing Industries and Competitors* (New York: Free Press, 1980).

68 G. S. Yip, "Gateways to Entry," *Harvard Business Review* 60 (September 1982): 85–93.

69 Khanna and Palepu, *Winning in Emerging Markets*, 42–43.

70 A. M. Brandenberger and B. J. Nalebuff, *Co-opetition* (New York: Doubleday, 1996), 17.

71 For example, see The Coca-Cola Company, *Live Positively: 2009/2010 Sustainability Review* (Atlanta, GA: The Coca-Cola Company, 2010).

72 For example, ASTM International, "Consumer Product Evaluation Standards," www.astm.org/Standards/consumer-product-evaluation-standards.html (accessed December 1, 2012).

73 E. Plambeck and L. Denend, "The Greening of Walmart's Supply Chain . . . Revisited," *Supply Chain Management Review* (September/October 2011): 16–23.

74 Scott McCullough, Master of Arts in Sustainability candidate at Wake Forest University.

75 Co-authored by Michael Aper, Master of Arts in Sustainability candidate at Wake Forest University.

76 United States Department of Commerce, National Oceanic and Atmospheric Administration, "Ocean," http://www.noaa.gov/ocean.html (accessed February 3, 2015).

77 M. Allsopp, A. Walters et al., "Plastic Debris in the World's Oceans," United Nations Environment Programme, Greenpeace International, 2012, http://www.unep.org/regionalseas/marinelitter/publications/docs/plastic_ocean_report.pdf (accessed February 3, 2015).

78 B. R. Silliman and C. Angelini, "Trophic Cascades Across Diverse Plant Ecosystems," *Nature Education Knowledge* 3, no. 10 (2012): 44, http://www.nature.com/scitable/knowledge/library/trophic-cascades-across-diverse-plant-ecosystems-80060347 (accessed February 3, 2015).

79 Deloitte Access Economics, "Economic Contribution of the Great Barrier Reef," Great Barrier Reef Marine Park Authority, March 2013, http://www.environment.gov.au/system/files/resources/a3ef2e3f-37fc-4c6f-ab1b-3b54ffc3f449/files/gbr-economic-contribution.pdf (accessed February 3, 2015).

80 National Geographic Society, "Explorers," 2015, http://www.nationalgeographic.com/explorers/bios/sylvia-earle/ (accessed February 3, 2015).

81 M. E. Porter, "What Is Strategy?" *Harvard Business Review* 61 (November 1996): 61–78; D. J. Collis and M. G. Rukstad, "Can You Say What Your Strategy Is?" *Harvard Business Review* (April 2008): 82–90.

6

COMPETENCIES AND TACTICS TO
SUPPORT STRATEGIES

The Struggle over Cape Wind

Cape Wind Associates is proposing the first U.S. offshore wind farm on Horseshoe Shoal in Nantucket Sound, off the coast of the U.S. state of Massachusetts approximately 30 miles long and 25 miles wide. The project would have 130 wind turbines, covering 24 miles. Each turbine would be about 285 feet tall and would produce up to 420 megawatts of energy and could provide about three-quarters of the Cape Island's electricity needs.[1] The proposed location is attractive because of the available wind, ability to mount the windmills in relatively shallow water, high electricity demand, and the project's location in federal waters (which affords some freedom from some state regulations). The wind project would eliminate the risk of potential oil spills, create an energy independence from foreign oil imports, and offset over 1 million tons per year of CO_2 (as well as 1.8 tons of nitrous oxide and 4,000 tons of sulfur dioxide [by avoiding the use of fossil fuels]).

The project has garnered support and resistance. Support has come from several regional towns; Greenpeace USA; the National Resources Defense Council; Bill McKibben, an environmental author; and the Boston College Environment Action Coalition. Opposition has come from Senator Edward M. Kennedy (and several other politicians), several regional towns, tourism agencies, International Wildlife Coalition, and a group of citizens called the Board of Alliance to Protect Nantucket Sound.

Opponents emphasize the environmental challenges, public safety concerns for recreational and commercial boats and aircraft, the negative impacts on fish populations, and the wind farm's adverse visual impact (which might impact tourism and the local economy). Also, some have commented that the project could have enormous costs.[2] The Cape Wind organization has spent over $30 million on scientific research, geotechnical exploration, Doppler oceanographic studies, avian research, socioeconomic studies, community outreach, and litigation. (The only other serious U.S. offshore wind project was planned for Long Island, and it was cancelled.) Many of the project's investors have grown concerned: the project will potentially exceed $1.6 billion in costs, it originally started over 10 years ago, and many have also questioned its efficacy. And while they remained convinced that the technical issues were viable, the political problems have seemed insurmountable.

Thus, the project's investors and managers began to realize the benefits of extensive analysis related to all stakeholders impacted by the project. In fact, one of the major challenges was to satisfy these stakeholders and understand their impacts on the organization. This industry analysis (i.e., looking at the external conditions within which the company operates and the impact of all external stakeholders) was critical to Cape Wind's understanding of its own strategy.

Chapter Overview

What should managers do with the external analysis once it is complete? How does industry analysis impact an organization's strategy? Ultimately, the answers are discovered during the process of identifying sources of competitive advantage; additionally, research on firm excellence has indicated that the only sustainable source of competitive advantage is the ability to consistently create *new sources of competitive advantage.*[3]

Thus, a major use of external analysis is to find these sources and decide on how to implement them. External analysis can help a firm identify (1) where competitive advantages can be gained and (2) what strategic elements should be emphasized. (For example, Cape Wind increasingly discovered that it had not addressed concerns of powerful people and regional organizations.)

This chapter offers advice for one major source of competitive advantage: *resources and capabilities* (including innovation, flexibility, and responsiveness to changes in external conditions). *Resources and capabilities* are often the least understood sources of competitive advantage. This is where the notion of internal analysis becomes important; it is not enough for a firm to understand the external environments impacting it; a firm must also understand its own "DNA." This chapter focuses on the part of the firm's "DNA" that is *resources and capabilities.*

I will cover key success factors that result from industry analysis and show how certain resources and capabilities, developed by firms, meet industry requirements. Finally, we will look at some common tactics firms can use to uphold the environmental sustainability view of the firm. At the end of this chapter, we will discuss how a firm can create new market spaces by altering an industry's key success factors.

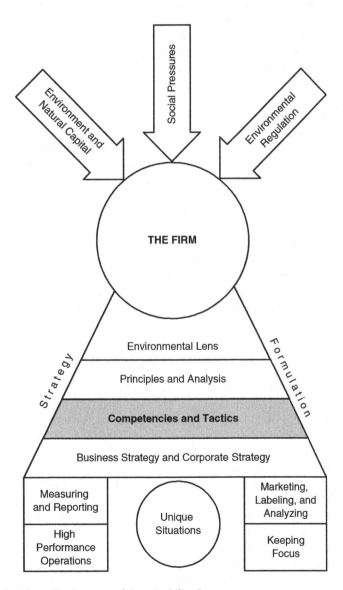

Figure 6.1 Strategy Model with an Environmental Sustainability Lens

At the end of this chapter, you should be able to:

1 specify how a firm can identify sources of competitive advantage;
2 explain various methods for evaluating resources and capabilities;
3 identify specific tactics and activities related to environmental sustainability and firm competitiveness;
4 demonstrate how firms can invent new businesses using key success factors.

Resource-Based View of the Firm

Strategic thinking includes matching a firm's *resources and capabilities* to *opportunities arising in the external environment*; increasingly, firms are recognizing the role of resources and capabilities (i.e., the resource-based view) as the *basis of strategy*. As contemporary industries are generally unstable (due to the fact that information flow is increasing, industry practices are more easily shared, and the efficiency of capital markets allowing for companies to flow in and out of industries), internal resources and capabilities are viewed as more of a secure basis for formulating strategy. Also, resources and capabilities are excellent sources of competitive advantage because they enable flexibility when positioning an organization within market spaces.

The greater the rate of change in an organization's external environment, the more likely it is that internal resources and capabilities (rather than an external market focus) will provide a viable foundation for long-term strategy. When faced with changing markets, firms ask whether or not they should serve the same basic customer needs or deploy their capabilities and resources in other markets; with this view, a firm is not tied down to a specific market. Also, some researchers have shown that using existing resources and capabilities can create "blue ocean" opportunities (a term for investing in new opportunities to attract new customers).[4]

I define *competitive advantage* as when one of two firms, competing within the same market, earns (or has the potential to earn) a persistently higher rate of return on capital. Note that this is a dependent variable (i.e., competitive advantage is an outcome of activities that firms use to support a market position). *Thus, we are trying to identify the resources and capabilities that will yield extraordinary returns for companies.*[5] Establishing competitive advantage by developing, using, and protecting resources and capabilities will be a sustainable basis for survival.

This approach differs from industry selection, emphasizes the uniqueness of each company, and suggests that the key to profitability is differentiating from other firms; therefore, establishing a competitive advantage involves formulating and implementing a strategy that exploits a firm's unique strengths (in this case resources and capabilities). The following sections explain resources and capabilities, analyses for identifying resources and capabilities with competitive advantage in mind, and ways for gaining and sustaining resources and capabilities.

Resources and Capabilities

To start our conversation, consider the distinction between (1) *resources* and (2) *capabilities*. *Resources* are productive assets owned by a firm. *Capabilities* are what the firm can do. Resources can be tangible (e.g., a physical plant), intangible (e.g., technology, patents, reputation, or culture), human (e.g., skills, know-how, capacity for communication and collaboration, and motivation), and natural (e.g., land and water). Resources—tangible or intangible, human or nonhuman—are relatively easy to identify and value. For example, labor markets help to value labor rates through transparent supply and demand, and we have methods that help to match those rates against a firm's needs and current labor pool. Also, marketing professionals have developed sophisticated ways to understand the nature of brand loyalty and how this loyalty is developed. Brands are resources. This same sophistication is available in terms of how new technologies are developed and their value in the market. I mentioned earlier that natural capital is harder to value.

Capabilities reflect the actions of firms, how firms handle their resources, and their processes for using resources. When discussing capabilities, there is not as much confidence about methods for analysis and ways to value them; however, we do have some information on how capabilities might develop and their relationship to resources. For example, firms emphasizing environmental sustainability may take existing assets and ask what opportunities exist for economizing on their use (e.g., water or energy use). Several research studies show that the mindset of management toward environmental sustainability has an impact on how successfully a firm uses environmental sustainability principles and practices for competitiveness.[6]

Resources are not productive on their own; they must be used. This is why resources are paired with capabilities. To perform a task, a group of resources must work together. Thus, we can define *organizational capability* as a firm's capacity to deploy resources for a desired end result. Our primary interest is in capabilities that can provide a basis for competitive advantage *and* that are simultaneously environmentally sustainable.

Some authors describe the activities that an organization does particularly well (relative to competitors) as *distinctive capabilities*. Others call them *core competencies* (to distinguish the capabilities fundamental to a firm's strategy and performance).[7] Core competencies provide a basis for entering new markets. (Note that I will use the terms *capability* and *competence* interchangeably.)

The first step to discover sources of competitive advantage is to use analyses to identify a firm's resources and capabilities. The next section will discuss key success factors, which is one process for identifying resources and capabilities and linking them to specific markets. (The ultimate goal is to determine why some firms are more successful than others and the resources and capabilities that support these success factors.)

Profile: The Start of Smart[8]

Chapter 6 discusses the important role industry analysis plays in developing a successful strategy model. In order to understand what the firm needs to compete, successful firms analyze and adapt to their competitive field and customer wants. Early in May 2010, 16 people worked diligently in a garage.[9] Industry recipes had caused blind spots providing an opportunity for Nest, the Palo Alto based start-up. By December of that year, the team had built their first thermostat prototype. Founder and CEO of Nest, Tony Fadell, and his team sought to reinvent the thermostat, a device that had long waited in the periphery of information technology.

According to Fadell, Americans change the temperature in their homes about 1,500 times each year. He also estimates that about 10 million thermostats are sold annually in the U.S.[10] In a blog announcing Google's acquisition of Nest in 2014, Fadell stated:

> *Starting a business focused on the lowly thermostat seemed like a crazy idea at the time, but it made all the sense in the world to us. That little device that went unnoticed and unchanged year after year on the walls of our homes was a lost opportunity to save energy and money.[11]*

Nest's thermostat offers cutting-edge capabilities that include cloud-based analytics to pre-cool homes and Wi-Fi capabilities that allow customers to adjust their thermostat via smartphone. The thermostat also tracks energy usage and makes efficiency recommendations based on customer preferences.

Google Ventures led the last two major rounds of financing and the company has been collaborating with Nest since 2011. Google's involvement has piqued interest in the utilities industry and has major implications for facilities investment. Google, like other information technology leaders, is looking to the horizon in what is now being called the Internet of Things. Firms everywhere are positioning themselves competitively as the pull toward rethinking objects as computers that can send and receive data increases. For example, a jet engine with remote sensors could notify manufacturers when it needs preventative maintenance or an HVAC services company could use remote diagnostics to identify where problems are occurring without having to inspect all the equipment each month.[12]

Hot Competition. *Information technology firms everywhere including Samsung, Apple, and Microsoft are also collaborating with and acquiring start-ups that connect objects like homes and appliances to the Internet. In such a fiercely competitive market, competencies determine which firms survive and prosper. One unique tactic for firms to stay competitive is for a radical shift from goods and products to an economy focused on services and flows.[13] When thinking about the Internet of Things, can you think of any sustainable goods- or products-based companies that might be uniquely attracted to this growing market?*

Key Success Factors and Competencies

Industry analysis yields a great deal of useful information, including some basis for success in the industry and identifying resources and capabilities (see Chapter 5). To survive and prosper in an industry, a firm could answer two questions: (1) What do customers want? and (2) What does a firm need to do to compete? The answers to these two questions yield a list of industry key success factors, which are useful to a firm when it decides on the resources and competencies that it wants to develop to support its positioning.

To answer the first question, analysts look closely at an industry's target customers. They are trying to identify specific attributes of these customers and what factors attract and cause them to buy a firm's products. For example, if customers choose apparel (e.g., Patagonia) based on a company's environmental sustainability policies and practices, then environmentally sound product design might be a key success factor for a clothing company. As such, customer analysis usually looks at the *demand characteristics* that are the basis of consumers' purchase decisions.

The second question requires an analysis of industry competition; key questions include:

- Who are the existing competitors?
- Who else might enter the competitive field?
- How intense is this competition?

It might not be enough for some firms to offer environmentally friendly products that match competitors; they might need to exceed those standards to attract customers. Thus, firms that want to gain a competitive advantage are constantly looking for ways to exceed competitors' offerings.

Many analysts use a four-part framework for predicting competitor behavior:[14]

1 *Competitor's current strategy.* How is the competitor competing at present? What is the company saying about its strategy? What actions and commitments of resources are indicative of its strategy?
2 *Competitor's objectives.* What is the competitor trying to achieve? (Some companies are focusing on gaining market share; others seek to gain more profitability from current operations.) The more a company is satisfied with its current performance, the more likely it is to continue with its present strategy. With lower profitability, a firm is likely to adopt a new strategy.
3 *Competitor's assumptions about the industry.* Assumptions are guided by the beliefs that senior managers hold about their industries and the success factors within them. Evidence shows that not only do these belief systems tend to be stable over time, but they also tend to converge among firms within an industry (what can be referred to as *industry recipe*s).[15] These recipes may cause blind spots and opportunities for other firms to compete with incumbents.
4 *Competitor's resources and capabilities.* If a rival has a massive investment in environmental sustainability, it would probably be unwise for a company to unleash a marketing campaign to show how a commitment to environmental sustainability exceeds the competitor's. Identifying a competitor's resources and capabilities could help us understand what that firm can defend if challenged.

Key success factors are an important step in identifying competitive advantage. They link the market or external conditions with internal resources and competencies. This process is foundational; however, there are myriad other methods analysts utilize to identify the unique and advantageous qualities of a firm. Below, I will discuss several of these methods.

Methods for Identifying Competencies

DuPont Model

A means of identifying core competencies is to model a firm's profitability using the DuPont Model.[16] This model asks what drives a firm's relative profitability within an industry. Analysts can disaggregate return on capital employed into its components, which then indicate the main drivers of superior profitability. Figure 6.2 shows this analysis format.

The analyst looks for areas where unusual contributions have been made to the return on capital employed (ROCE).[17] *Return on Capital* is a measure of how effective an organization is at obtaining returns on investments in specific projects. There are multiple ways to create an ROCE. Some firms have an ability to cut costs and use a low-cost strategy (which will be discussed in Chapter 7). Other firms create unusual value by increasing a customer's willingness to purchase goods (referred to as a differentiation strategy [also described in Chapter 7]).

In many industries (e.g., the airline, steel, and supermarket industries), key success factors (i.e., what drives profitability) are more obvious than in emerging industries. The DuPont Model can assist in identifying these factors and in recognizing when they are changing (within a changing industry). For example, steel customers want low prices, consistent production, and supply reliability; specialty steel customers sometimes also want technical specifications met for a particular application. These differences in key success factors impact what supply firms do for their customers.

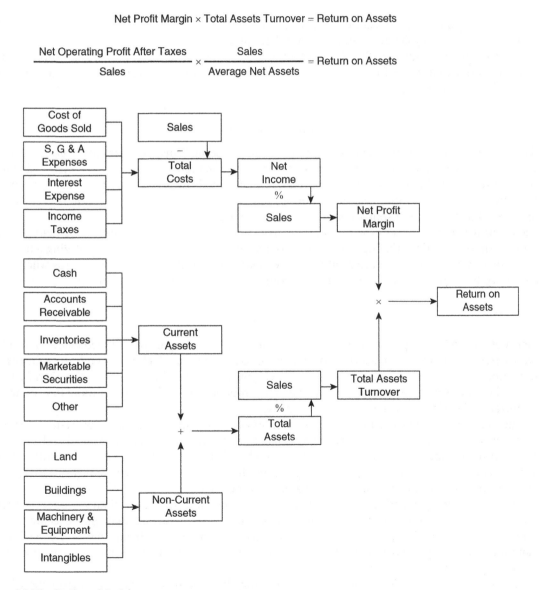

Figure 6.2 The DuPont Model

As an industry becomes more globalized, some key success factors change to respond to new competitors and customers. Competitors tend to produce commodity products, and they have high fixed costs, excess capacity, high exit barriers, and cost efficiencies. Thus, the key success factor is *cost efficiency*, requiring large-scale plants, low-cost locations, and rapid capacity adjustment.

Airlines measure profitability by operating income per available seat-mile (ASM), which is determined by:

1   *Yield*: total operating revenues divided by the number of revenue passenger miles (RPMs).
2   *Load factor*: ratio between RPMs and ASMs. Load factors are influenced by competitiveness of prices, efficiency of route planning, building customer loyalty through quality of service, frequent flyer programs, and matching airplane size to demand for individual flights.
3   *Unit cost*: total operating expenses divided by ASMs (expenses/ASMs are influenced by wage rates and benefits levels, fuel efficiency of aircraft, productivity of employees, load factors, and level of administrative costs).

The airline industry and its organizations are instructive as the key success factors demonstrate how a specific firm can focus on a few key factors to monitor and determine how well it is operating.

However, despite its many benefits, the DuPont Method has some disadvantages. It is a short-term measurement and looks at profits before taxes. It does not link directly to cost of capital so it is hard to know the true costs of a firm's activities.

Value Chain Analysis

Another method is to look at *functions* of a firm. For example, some firms do a particularly good job of managing their finances, so much so that they are able to gain unusual returns from this organizational function even though their main business might be in production of a good. Apple's design capability, GE's management abilities, and Mercedes' engineering are renowned examples of how functions within organizations can include core competencies and sources of competitive advantage.

A value chain analysis separates the activities of a firm into a sequential chain and can be helpful in determining if a firm has functions that operate as core competencies (see Appendix 9.1). Analyzing a firm's value chain can identify places where unusual value is generated; however, it can also identify areas where competencies cannot be found. (These areas can then become viable candidates for outsourcing.)

Routines

Another method—which is probably the most powerful means of identifying competencies—is to identify *routine behavior*. A routine is a repeated performance in some context, which has been learned by organizational members in response to selective pressures.[18] Organizational routines represent the *actual pattern of work* that takes place within the organization and is an appropriate locus of inquiry for more fully understanding organizational performance and organizational learning.[19]

Routines differ from systems in important respects. *Systems* (and standard operating procedures) are formal and explicitly formulated patterns of behavior, which are directly under managerial control and can be easily copied by a firm's competitors.[20] In contrast, *routines* are largely informal and less directly controlled by management.[21] (For example, a planning system may specify the deadline for submitting plans to management, but the corresponding routine might suggest that it is acceptable to be late by a few days.)

Routines have various functions. They serve as a way to maintain organizational knowledge, they provide a balance between political interests, and are managerial targets (i.e., organizations must execute them reliably[22] and consistently).[23] Thus, routines are organizational resolutions to problems that have been faced over time, and they are the key competencies that firms have to implement strategy (because strategy must become routine for employees to carry it out).

One of the less-discussed aspects of routines is that they have both *functional* and dysfunctional consequences on organizations. For example, routines can function to create decision-making efficiencies; however, they can also cause decision-making rigidities. As a result, organizational members might refrain from using new analysis that does not fit into their routines.

In contrast to the dominant monolithic approach, routines can be divided into different classes (which are distinguished by the interrelationships that influence the process of learning new routines).[24] To function effectively, *meta-routines* must be consistent and coherent.[25] The different classes of meta-routines are:

1   *Assessment routines.* These are sequences of coordinated actions aimed at assessing and evaluating operating routines; as in any assessment function, they are the supporting infrastructure designed to facilitate and evaluate the performance of operating routines (e.g., monitoring adherence to procedures [in the case of airline pilots] or routines for ensuring a person's performance is at expected levels [performance reviews]).
2   *Maintenance routines.* These are sequences of coordinated actions aimed at keeping operating routines in a functional state (e.g., the ways in which firms bring in new employees or conduct their training).[26]
3   *Development routines.* These are sequences of coordinated actions aimed at updating operating routines when warranted; this involves making minor adjustments to a routine when performance lags. There is a sense that drastic change is needed, and a firm evaluates (or imports) new routines from outside (e.g., strategic planning and adopting a new approach to teaching could both be aimed at changing operating routines).[27]

This type of framework shows that operating routines are only the "immediately observable tip of the iceberg"; operating routines draw upon meta-routines, which serve to manage, maintain, and develop them. Therefore, any attempted change to operating routines should be seen in the context of its relationship to meta-routines. For example, operational routines are relatively easy to identify; however, their importance to organizational performance is minimal. Development routines (which are critical to organizational innovation) are more difficult to identify; as a result, they are hard to change. Meta-routines (e.g., development routines) offer greater leverage. This leverage can be functional (helpful to innovation) or dysfunctional (misguiding responses to implement strategy).

Explicitly conceptualizing routines as multilevel phenomena helps clarify how organizational activities become sources of competitive advantage. *One of the core tenets of the resource-based view of strategy is that for organizational capabilities to contribute to a firm's sustainable competitive advantage, they should be inimitable[28] valuable, rare,[29] and possess isolating mechanisms.[30]*

- *Inimitable* refers to not being able to copy the resources and capabilities.
- *Valuable* means they are valuable in terms of supporting the market positioning of the firm.
- *Rare* means that not many (if any) other firms possess the resources and capabilities.
- *Isolating mechanisms* are ways firms embed and use capabilities (such that other firms cannot easily understand or use them).

Over the years, this tenet has resulted in broad acceptance of the idea that organizational activities and routines represent "sticky" (i.e., non-tradable and inimitable) resources. Under this view, a firm is heterogeneous with respect to the bundle of resources it controls and uses.[31] A multilevel framework of routines helps explain why this is the case: routines constitute interdependent systems, which are difficult to replicate piecemeal.

Table 6.1 shows that the interfaces between levels of routines are critical for explaining *causal ambiguity* (i.e., the idea that managers themselves are often unable to explain why their strategies work). Levels of routines might be relatively easy to describe and explain in isolation; however, the secret to managing the interfaces (and developing a successful integration among all routines) is often tacit. This could be why many successful firms (e.g., Whole Foods) are reputed to follow sustainability principles guiding *all* activities within the firm. Activities are integrated and transparent (even to competitors). The company is secure in the knowledge that its source of competitive advantage lies in the way *all* components are tied together (not in any one component); thus, they are not easily copied by competitors.

Table 6.1 Routines within Organizations

Observable repeated action sequences	• Do you notice that people in the organization do the same things in the same order? • Do you notice that people in the organization do the same things in the same order in response to similar situations?
Increasing reliability	• Do the same people do the same sequences of behaviors more than once? • Do you feel confident that the people can do this sequence even if some key people were to leave the organization?
Increasing speed	• Do the sequences of behavior take less and less time to perform? • Do people in the organization devote less time to this routine? • Does it take less and less supervision to perform the routine?
Perform suboptimally at times	• When confronted with a problem, do you use the same ways to solve problems?
Found in formal and informal behavior	• Do sequences of behaviors occur as formal rules and regulations as well as agreed-upon ways of doing things?
Have identifiable use of concepts and linkages	• Do people use the same language for describing sequences of behaviors?
What is the object of the routine?	• Operational or meta?

This description of operating and meta-routines may also help us understand the intricate tradeoff between *ease of routine change* and a routine's potential for *sustained competitive advantage*. A tightly coupled set of routines and meta-routines is an effective barrier to imitation by other firms.[32]

Finally, the routine view helps managers to best decide on centralized and decentralized actions. *Centralized actions* (i.e., those controlled by top management) may best be made when interfaces of routines are involved. *Decentralized actions* (with various control centers) may best be made when specific routines need to change. This view helps in various types of managerial actions (e.g., assisting multinational firms with determining when local knowledge and practices should influence corporate practice). Global integration is probably best carried out for routine interface decisions; specific operating routines and meta-routines are best suited for local decision-making. One approach does not work without the other; both centralized *and* decentralized actions must work together to achieve the same goal-directed behavior.

Evaluating the Importance and Strengths of Competencies

I have outlined a few methods for identifying resources and competencies. We have discussed a model for identifying profit drivers, the value of identifying core functions, and the importance of identifying routines. Once resources and competencies are identified, analysts can evaluate them according to two criteria:

1 *Importance*: Which resources and capabilities are most important in conferring sustainable competitive advantage? Can you make money from them (e.g., through property rights, relative bargaining power, and embedding the resources and capabilities within the organization)?
2 *Strength*: What is the relative strength and ability to confer competitive advantage? What are a firm's resources and capabilities' strengths and weaknesses (vs. a competitor's)? How scarce are they and how relevant to the business? What is the durability of the resource and competence and can it be replicated? (If it can be replicated, it will not be strong or unique for a long period of time.)

To identify and evaluate the importance and strength of a company's capabilities, managers can look both inside and outside the firm. Internal discussions (between employees and departments) may be valuable in terms of sharing insights, gathering evidence, and building consensus regarding an organization's resources and capability profile. Evidence derived from a firm's history can reveal when the company performed well, periods when it performed poorly, and ongoing patterns throughout its history.

Another way of appraising the importance and strength of capabilities is by evaluating the accessibility of key resources as they relate to the external environment. If a resource or capability is widely available within an industry, it might be essential to compete; however, it will *not* be a sufficient basis for competitive advantage. For example, if all companies have access to water and fuel sources, those resources may be essential; however, the strength of those resources (to set firms apart from competitors) would not be very significant. Also, a resource or capability might be readily available to a firm but not have high value in terms of the most important functions of an industry. When determining sources of competitive advantage, it is best when a resource or capability is highly relevant to key success factors in the market.

Benchmarking is another powerful, external tool for the qualitative assessment of performance relative to competitors; therefore, it is helpful in determining the most valuable resources and capabilities. *Benchmarking* is a process of identifying, understanding, and adopting outstanding practices from organizations worldwide to help an organization improve its performance.[33] Performance is inescapably tied to the efficient and strategic use of resources and capabilities. Benchmarking offers a systematic framework and methodology for identifying particular functions and processes and then for comparing the performance of these functions and processes with other companies. McKinsey & Co. suggests that a quality benchmarking process should have five stages:

1   Decide on what to benchmark.
2   Identify partners or those to benchmark.
3   Establish benchmarking metrics.
4   Gather data.
5   Do the analysis.[34]

Enthusiasts of benchmarking often neglect to take into account interdependencies (while critics of benchmarking often overemphasize them); however, some routines are indeed importable (to the extent that they are modular). Benchmarking efforts focused on such modular routines are worthwhile.[35] For example, if a firm does an excellent job at customer service this capability may be tied to important organizational cultural factors not easily detected or duplicated.

The process of assessing the importance (and strength) of resources and capabilities has to do with more than understanding what makes a company unique; it is also closely tied to a firm's long-term financial success. For example, profits earned from resources and capabilities depend not just on their ability to establish competitive advantage but also on how long that advantage can be sustained; this depends on whether resources and capabilities are durable and whether or not competitors can imitate the benefits they offer. Resources are *imitable* if they are transferrable or replicable. (Therefore, something once considered valuable might not always remain so for the organization.)

If a competency is of high importance and strength, managers will want to protect it. One method is to ensure that a firm gains the maximum benefit from a competency; otherwise, money will be spent on a competency that does not confer value to the organization. Important in this analysis of returns is the *recipient* of the returns. We usually expect the owner of the capability to acquire the return; yet, ownership is not always clear-cut. Consider universities, which are dependent on human capital to generate returns; highly regarded faculty often have significant bargaining power, might get unusual returns for their employment (e.g., large salaries), and might receive a percentage of returns on their inventions. However, who actually *owns* that intellectual capital? The professor? Or the university who pays him/her to produce the capital? We see similar struggles in the press with respect to CEOs; there is often debate over CEO pay and the associated individual's true value within the organization. Unfortunately, much of the research on the relationship between CEO pay and returns to share owners shows a low correlation between the two.[36]

Another way of protecting resources is by investing in (or retaining) resources that are highly durable. Some resources are more durable than others; durable resources have a more secure basis for competitive advantage. The increasing pace of technological change is shortening the useful lifespan of many resources (e.g., capital equipment and proprietary technologies); however, brands can show remarkable resilience and may only need refreshing as trends change.

What if a firm needs to develop a capability? An easy way to obtain a resource or capability is to transfer it from one firm to another. The ability to buy a resource or capability depends on its transferability (i.e., the extent to which it is mobile between organizations). Some resources (e.g., cash and raw materials) are easily transferable and can be bought and sold with little difficulty, whereas some natural resources are *not* easily transferable (e.g., water and clean air).

If a firm cannot buy a resource or capability, it must develop it. Some resources and capabilities are easily replicable (e.g., store layout), whereas some capabilities are not (e.g., Disney's service capability has proven surprisingly difficult to replicate by other companies). Identifying resources and capabilities (and evaluating their importance and strength) is an involved process; however, with this information, a firm can move into the strategy development phase.[37]

After reviewing the data from these analyses, the analyst could begin to form strategic conclusions by answering a few key questions:

- How do we exploit our key resources and competencies most effectively?
- Can we de-emphasize superfluous resources and capabilities?
- Can we find ways to deploy them to greater impact?

These decisions are not easy ones since they always involve tradeoffs among competing outcomes. Yet, one core decision should always be to ensure that important resources and capabilities are used to their fullest. This focus is discussed in the next section.

Gaining and Sustaining Competitive Advantage Using Resources and Capabilities

Successful firms develop their capabilities over significant periods of time. In many cases, we can trace the origins of a core competency to the circumstances that prevailed during the founding and early development of a firm; therefore, in some cases, organizational capability is *path-dependent*. For example, the world's largest oil and gas companies have nearly identical products and similar strategies; however, they display very different capability profiles. Exxon-Mobile and Royal Dutch Shell illustrate these differences. Exxon-Mobile is known for its outstanding financial management capabilities (exercised through rigorous investment controls and unrelenting cost efficiency); Shell is known for its decentralized, international management capability, which allows it to adapt to different national environments and become an insider wherever it does business.

These different origins explain the companies' capabilities, which are still evident today. This history is often embedded in routines, which organizations often follow without conscious awareness. Several factors contribute to organizational members' efficiency and effectiveness at performing such activities (e.g., they must have contact with each other [to learn and cultivate a culture], communicate, and share important information about how a culture operates).

If capabilities develop over long periods of time and are embodied within organizational structure and culture, they can also impede a firm's ability to change. The more highly developed an organization's capabilities, the narrower its repertoire (and the more difficult it is for the organization to adapt them to new circumstances). Thus, *core capabilities* can become *core rigidities*, which inhibit a firm's ability to access and develop new capabilities.[38]

Fortunately, many firms are surprisingly adaptable; this quality is important for overcoming rigidity. Thus, it might be much more rare to have rigid capabilities than is commonly thought. Many companies are able to adapt to changing circumstances by integrating, building, and reconfiguring internal and external competencies to address rapidly changing environments.[39]

What if a firm does not have this adaptability or needs new capabilities? How do companies develop new capabilities? *Capabilities* can be acquired through mergers, acquisitions, and alliances; the major rationale for an alliance is to combine different capabilities so that a market can be served and firms can make large profits. Another means is via internal development (by focusing attention on needed resources and capabilities and ensuring that routines are developed for using resources effectively). Last, some companies develop new capabilities by finding unique ways to enter a market. All of these methods will be discussed in the following sections.

Entry and Exit Tactics

Industries are dynamic, the interaction among firms is dynamic, and firms leave and enter industries on a regular basis. *Entry* is pervasive in many industries; it occurs when a new firm (or an existing firm that wants to diversify) enters a new market. *Exit* is the opposite of entry and occurs when firms withdraw products or services from a market by closing down, selling off associated products or services, or focusing on other markets. Research on entry and exit demonstrates certain consistencies:[40]

1   Within 10 years, the composition of a typical industry will vary. Thirty to 40 percent of the industry will be new firms with combined sales of about 10–15 percent of the industry total. Thirty to 40 percent of incumbents will exit. About half of the firms will be diversified firms and half will be new firms. About 40 percent of exiting firms will be diversified firms (which may still operate in other markets).
2   Entrants and exiting firms tend to be smaller than established firms.
3   Most entrants do not survive 10 years; however, those that do, grow rapidly.
4   Entry and exit rates vary by industry.
5   Entrants are often successful in apparel, lumber, infrastructure, and fabricated metals; less movement is seen in tobacco, paper, chemicals, primary metals, and coal.
6   Conditions that encourage entry also foster exit.

Therefore, industries are often dynamic. Managers can expect most new ventures to fail quickly unless they can secure capital to support needed growth.

Incumbent firms often mount strategies to deter entrance (whether against new firms or diversifying firms); Table 6.2 shows these tactics. In many industries, incumbents have the advantage. For example, surveys in Britain and the United States in 2011 suggested that 7–9 percent of the population used Twitter, compared to almost 50 percent for Facebook.[41] At the time of the survey, Twitter was only a few years old, demonstrating that even in an industry with seamless connections, new companies struggle to gain the popularity of incumbents. Additionally, social media is an example of how new industries often rely on older industries.

Facebook and Google will typically originate news. Most of the news for these outlets comes from traditional news media websites (e.g., CBS News, ABC News, New York Times, Washington Post, and CNN); new entrants may repackage the news and make it available to new users, yet traditional news outlets still have a major role to play in the industry. While Twitter and Facebook have quickly established themselves as the de facto social networks across almost every major industry for adult users, these platforms, while still popular, certainly are not necessarily going to be used by the younger demographic.[42] Image-led social channels, such as Tumblr, Instagram and Snapchat, are rapidly growing in popularity among 13–19-year-olds, and it might be at the expense of their more established, but increasingly less cool, older brothers. Sixty-one percent of teenagers cited Tumblr as their favorite social media site, ahead of Facebook (55 percent) and Twitter (22 percent). Almost as many chose Instagram (21 percent) and Snapchat, which launched in 2011, is already being used by 13 percent of teenagers.[43] One could have a difficult time predicting entry and exit with these dynamics.

Table 6.2 Possible Entry Deterrence Tactics

Entry barriers	Most effective when firms have proprietary intellectual property or regulatory support
Production and distribution barriers	Economies of scale and scope; superior access to critical inputs, location, patents, or government subsidies; few channels that are used by incumbents
Sunk costs	Incumbent has incurred costs that cannot be recovered, and the entrant has not made this investment
Reputation	Long-standing relationships with suppliers and customers; high brand equity
Pricing tactics	Entrants are unsure about demand or costs when incumbents use prices to distort market information; incumbents may compete actively by reducing prices to protect market share

Most firms do not make entry and exit decisions very often; when they do, they are based on diverse factors (e.g., costs, exiting competitor responses, and alternative investments available to the firm). An entry or exit decision can be very costly and significant for a firm (e.g., an entry mistake can be expensive and create long-term impacts on the ability of a firm to make decisions in the future). Firms tend to have assets that do not move as easily as selling a stock in a company.

Once firms enter markets, they tend to use certain tactics to increase competitiveness. The next section focuses on tactics related to environmental sustainability.

Unique Tactics and Activities

Firms have unique ways to compete. I will cover some major ones here; Chapters 9–12 contain more specific applications of these tactics. The ones I emphasize are derived from our focus on environmental sustainability. As we explored in previous chapters, these tactics are untapped ways for firms to gain competitive advantages since they can often decrease the amount of waste in the value chain and offer unique products to consumers. Applying these tactics may not only make the use of natural resources more effective and efficient, but it also has the potential to propel a firm to a place above its competitors.

Radical Resource Productivity

Radical resource productivity is a more effective use of resources, and it has several benefits. It slows resource depletion at one end of the value chain and lowers waste at the other. The deletion of waste lowers organizational costs for firms and society. In *Natural Capitalism*, the authors state:

> Nearly all environmental and social harm is a product of uneconomically wasteful use of human and natural resources, but radical resource productivity strategies can nearly halt the degradation of the biosphere, make it more profitable to employ people, and thus safeguard against the loss of vital living systems and social cohesion.[44]

This tactic helps firms obtain the same amount of utility (or work) from a product or process while using less material and energy. This economizing plays out in various organizational functions. For example, companies are developing ways to make natural resources (e.g., energy, metals, water, forest, and biodiversity) more productive. Resource productivity improves quality of life in addition to saving resources and money. When we improve the use of resources, we improve air and water quality.

A growing number of companies are thinking strategically about natural resources from extraction to use. Air Canada has set out to radically improve its profitability through cutting costs; its fuel costs per year are currently over $3 billion and recent changes in the EU ETS will result in a carbon tax for Air Canada as of 2014. To increase the efficiency of its use of natural resources, the company established a department focused on fuel savings and carbon emissions reductions; this department is exploring how to use biofuels to help the airline meet its reduction target.[45]

Biomimicry

Biomimicry is innovation inspired by nature (i.e., the conscious emulation of life's genius).[46] Janine Benyus championed the idea in her groundbreaking book, *Biomimicry*.[47] The book explores nine of nature's laws, strategies, and principles that might be helpful for human innovation:

1   runs on sunlight;
2   uses only the energy it needs;
3   fits form to function;
4   recycles everything;
5   rewards cooperation;

6   banks on diversity;
7   demands local expertise;
8   curbs excesses from within;
9   taps the power of limits.

In a subsequent video presentation, she described 12 strategies for acting on the "laws" of nature (which she outlines in her original work). These 12 strategies help professionals, such as product designers, design better (i.e., more productive and environmentally friendly) products or services based on nature's lessons.[48]

For example, diversity is critical for sustaining a healthy ecosystem. Benyus points to some research by James Drake and Stuart Pimm of the University of Tennessee.[49] The researchers asked, "What does it take to arrive at an assembly of species that remain in equilibrium?" They did their experiments by adding species in various combinations to a glass tank to determine what would survive and in what ratio. What they found was that a biological community is both complex and persistent; the process of growing a community takes lots of time.

Drake and Pimm maintain that once you destroy a finished, complete community (e.g., a prairie), you cannot just plant those same species and expect to put it back together again. There is no such thing as an "insta-prairie." A prairie restorer must give the prairie a successional history (i.e., actually grow the prairie over a trajectory of years). Some plants will come in and others will drop out; however, as those facilitating species change, the soil, fauna, and flora around them make it possible for the final assembly. Drake and Primm state, "They warm up the crowd for the real act."[50]

One implication from this work is that our agricultural businesses may be following the wrong paradigms; this principle may even have implications beyond agriculture. This natural system alludes to the necessity of change and time. If this principle were more widely applied we would design our production systems differently.

Let us take another principle: nature runs on sunlight. This strategy is more straightforward (i.e., we should use the Sun's rays to fuel our planet). Not so obvious is that the solutions to harnessing the Sun's force might come from photosynthesis; thus, observing how this process works and mimicking the process for building solar technologies could be the next big push in solar research.

Benyus's work has been carried out by many scientists. This is an exciting area to explore when creating a sustainable corporation. Benyus ends her book with:

> the good news is that we'll have plenty of help [to use nature as a source of innovation] we are surrounded by geniuses. They are everywhere with us, breathing the same air, drinking the same round river of water, moving on limbs built from the same blood and bone. Learning from them will take only stillness on our part, a quieting of the voices of our own cleverness. Into this quiet will come a cacophony of earthly sounds, a symphony of good sense.[51]

This philosophy applies to individual actions, organizing teams of people, designing corporations, and learning how organizations fit within larger ecosystems (e.g., within industries cities, and society).

Service and Flow Economy

Another tactic calls for a radical change in the relationship between producer and consumer (i.e., a shift from an economy of goods and products to one focused on services and flows).[52] This organizational tactic calls for offering consumers the *service* of products rather than *the products*. Rather than producing goods that are sold and owned as assets, consumers obtain services by leasing or renting goods.[53] The frequently used example is the washing machine; instead of purchasing a washing machine, consumers could pay a monthly fee to obtain the service of having their clothes washed. The service firm would have a means of billing consumers; the manufacturer would maintain the machine. If the machine ceased to provide this specific service, the manufacturer would remain the property owner and be responsible for fixing the machine. Also, the consumer does not have to take responsibility for recycling goods. This technique provides incentives for companies to produce relevant, long-lasting, better, environmentally friendly products to receive steady returns, and it leads to fewer physical goods.

This service economy is focused on *material cycles*. Sometimes called *nutrient cycles*, material cycles describe the flow of matter from the nonliving to the living world and back again. As this happens, matter can be stored, transformed into different molecules, transferred from organism to organism, and returned to its initial configuration.[54]

Examples of material cycles are the carbon cycle and an oxygen cycle. The carbon cycle involves two chemical reactions, which are also important in energy flow: photosynthesis and cell respiration. Carbon enters the living world as carbon dioxide gas, which is "fixed" (made useful to life) into sugar molecules. Carbon is recycled to the nonliving world as carbon dioxide gas; oxygen is recycled as oxygen gas. Oxygen from oxygen gas is never "fixed" in the way carbon is; it is used to "burn" sugar for energy. Photosynthesis is usually pictured as light energy + carbon dioxide + water → sugar + oxygen. Cell respiration is sugar + oxygen → carbon dioxide + water + energy. The nitrogen cycle is in the nonliving world (in the atmosphere where it exists as nitrogen gas). Plants, animals, and most other life forms cannot use nitrogen gas. Certain bacteria, however, use nitrogen gas as a nutrient.

If a product lasts a long time but its waste materials cannot be reused in manufacturing and biological cycles, then the producer must accept responsibility for the waste. This analysis has been the basis of the "cradle-to-cradle" methodology and philosophy.[55] *Cradle-to-cradle* is described more fully in Chapter 9 and is a process of making a product, recycling it (when it is done being used), and using the recycled parts for a new product. As a corporate tactic, creating services (vs. goods) requires a new business model and a new relationship with consumers. We will revisit this idea in Chapter 9 when we discuss manufacturing techniques.

Finding New Markets: Blue Ocean Strategy

One interesting way to use the concept of *key success factors* is to consider the ideas of two researchers who coined the words "red ocean" and "blue ocean" (see Table 6.3). These metaphors refer to market opportunities using key success factors. *Red oceans* are existing market spaces and industry boundaries that are defined and accepted by industry players, with known competitive rules of the game. Companies try to outperform rivals to gain a greater share of existing demand. As the market space becomes mature and crowded, prospects for profits and growth are reduced. Products become commodities and "cutthroat competition turns the red ocean bloody."[56]

Blue oceans are defined as unexplored market space, demand creation, and the opportunity for highly profitable growth. Most blue oceans are created within red oceans by expanding existing industry boundaries; the key success factors are clues for this expansion. One example is Honda's fuel-efficient automobile; this Japanese automaker created a blue ocean in the mid-1970s with small, reliable cars. Their competitiveness in motorcycles was waning, and they were trying to find a new way to use their competencies to enter new market spaces. They used this blue ocean as a way to enter the United States.

The authors of this technique call for *value innovation*, which they define as *the region where a company's actions favorably impact both its cost structure and its value proposition to buyers*. Cost savings are made by eliminating and reducing the factors an industry uses to compete; buyer value is improved by raising and

Table 6.3 Comparison and Contrast of Red vs. Blue Oceans[57]

Red ocean strategy	Blue ocean strategy
Compete in existing market space	Create uncontested market space
Take margins from competition (or other industry players)	Make the competition irrelevant
Existing demand	Create and capture new demand
Generally value–cost tradeoffs	New ideas about value
Alignment, responses to environmental changes dominate strategic concerns	Realignment, new competencies, new opportunities to use competencies

creating elements the industry has never offered. Over time, costs are reduced further as scale economies come into play due to high sales volumes (which superior value generates).[58]

Thus, competition, based on red oceans, assumes that (1) an industry's structure is defined, and (2) firms are forced to compete within that structure. In contrast, value innovation can be based on the view that market boundaries and industry structure are not defined, and it can be reconstructed by the actions and beliefs of industry players.

The process of identifying a blue ocean may include some of the following steps:

(1) Design a "*strategy canvas*," which is a *diagnostic* framework for building a compelling strategy. It captures current key success factors in the known market space (remember this is what customers care about, and it is what it takes to compete). A value curve (the basic component of the strategy canvas) is a graphic depiction of a company's relative performance across its industry's factors of competition. For example, a typical strategy canvas for the wine industry can be found in Figure 6.3. This canvas shows the situation before some of the innovative wines (e.g., Yellow Tail and Concha Toro) entered the market.

(2) The next step is to reconstruct the key success factors in crafting a new value curve. Four major actions are to *eliminate, reduce, raise,* and *create key success factors.* For example, in the wine industry, Yellow Tail wines reduced or eliminated aging qualities, range, and vineyard prestige. They marketed themselves as "easy drinking and selection with fun and adventure," priced their wines in the low range (vs. comparable wines), and showed a kangaroo on their bottles (but did not otherwise add much information).

Thus, *simplicity* opened a new market space comprised of people who did not know much about wine. To most consumers, wine choices were overwhelming and intimidating. Traditional bottles looked the same, labels were complicated with all sorts of terminology, and the choices so extensive that even clerks were at a loss to make specific recommendations. Yellow tail changed that, reduced the range of wines offered, removed all technical jargon, and presented an unintimidating choice (see Figure 6.4).

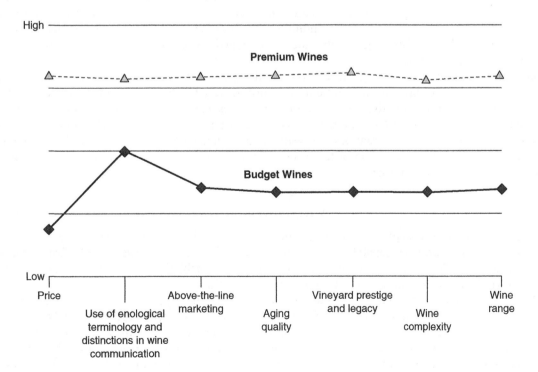

Figure 6.3 Traditional Wine Canvas

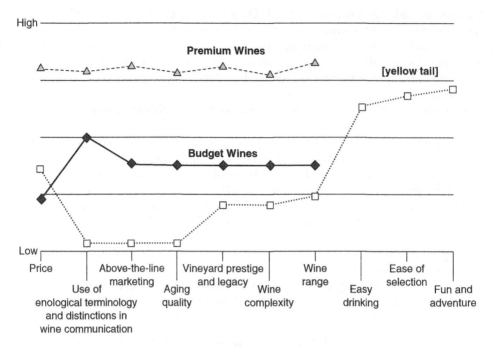

Figure 6.4 Innovation in the Wine Industry Using the Blue Ocean Concept

Relating Key Success Factors, Resources, and Capabilities

Key success factors and resources and capabilities as sources of competitive advantage are related. In brief, firms use certain methodologies to identify their resources and capabilities; a key one is identifying key success factors (which are eternal to the firm) and finding ways within the firm to meet these factors. For example, Yellow Tail wine created a fun image for its wine. It developed processes within its firm to present the wine to the public as a fun experience.

One could model the firm using the DuPont Model (described earlier in this chapter), or one could benchmark against other firms to determine if one's firm is truly best-in-class in a certain area or function. One then tries to gain competitive advantage from resources and capabilities. For example, the extent to which competing firms do not have the same resources and capabilities could provide a firm with a course of advantage. Also, if other firms cannot copy resources and capabilities then a firm is likely to maintain this source of advantage for a long period of time. Also, the more embedded the resources and capabilities are, the more a firm can gain from them.[59]

Chapter Summary

The main purpose of this chapter is to describe the resource-based view of the firm and the implications of this view for a firm's resources, capabilities, and competencies. Assessing these aspects of a firm is the process of internal analysis. This chapter described what are resources, capabilities, and competencies; how they are identified within a firm; and how they are used to gain competitiveness.

The key is that core competencies are few and that resources and capabilities are used to generate value. Competencies are found within a firm in the functional areas, value chains, and organizational routines. Firms entering a market might find that they are confronted with incumbent responses, and that the incumbent firms have certain competencies that have been developed in the context of markets that the new firms are entering. This chapter showed that firms can adopt new tactics to implement their strategies (e.g., new competencies that are suggested by the environmental sustainability point of view). This chapter presented three of these tactics: radical resource productivity, biomimicry, and service and flow tactics. Finally, we saw how new industries might come about, and how firms can apply their resources, capabilities, and competencies in developing new market spaces (i.e., blue oceans).

In subsequent chapters, we will discuss these ideas more specifically and explore how firms mount strategies and tactics (using a natural environmental lens) to gain competitive advantages. The next chapter suggests specific strategies for business lines and for corporations that have multiple business lines, called corporate strategy.

Case Revisited: What Can Cape Wind Learn about Competencies?

The Cape Wind project shows that more than technical capability is needed for a successful project; the Cape Wind Organization discovered their missing capabilities (and a source of competitiveness) were in the area of stakeholder management (a concept discussed in Chapter 2). This case illustrates how analysis of competition and customers does not always provide all of the key information for firms and illustrates how important it is to marry key success factors with firm competencies via an internal analysis.

Thus, projects such as Cape Wind clearly have stakeholder management as a major key success factor. Yet, the Cape Wind organization seemed to be wanting in this area. Also, when establishing a completely new type of industry (e.g., renewable energy), gaining legitimacy is critical. (This institutional view of the firm was discussed in Appendix 4.1.)

The Cape Wind project was still fighting for its initiation as of early 2015; it continued to experience delays due to stakeholder objections.

Terms to Know

Competitive advantage: when a firm earns (or has the potential to earn) a persistently higher rate of return on capital over its rivals

Entry: a new firm (or an existing firm, which wants to diversify its products) enters a new market

Exit: a firm withdraws products or services from a market by closing down, selling a product or service, or by focusing on other markets

Organizational capability: a firm's capacity to deploy resources for a desired end result

Strategic thinking: matching a firm's resources and capabilities to the opportunities that arise in the external environment

Profile: A Hot Commodity[60]

The fundamental source of natural capital on Earth comes from the Sun. A useful way to understand the Sun's economic value is to view the incoming solar energy as a budget. The average intensity of solar energy at the top of Earth's atmosphere facing the Sun is roughly 1,360 watts per square meter.[61] NASA estimates that about 40 percent of that energy is absorbed at Earth's surface.[62]

This solar energy budget is the basis of many new firms. One such firm is Sundrop Fuels, Inc. This organization utilizes the Sun's natural capital by making "green gasoline." The company uses concentrated solar power to convert cellulosic material and natural gas into fuel. The company's "drop-in" biofuels are fully compatible with modern engines, pipelines, and distribution infrastructure.[63] In June 2008, two months before the subprime loan market collapsed, Copernican Energy, Sundrop Fuels, and the National Renewable Energy Laboratory created a partnership.[64]

Supported by a $20 million PIPE investment from Oak Investment Partners and Kleiner Perkins Caufield & Buyers, the partnership wants to produce over a billion gallons annually by 2050 at a price of $2 per gallon.

Sundrop's processes and products reduce their consumer's lifecycle carbon footprints in comparison to petroleum based fuels.[65] In 2011, Sundrop Fuels received a $155 million venture capital infusion from Chesapeake Energy in return for a 50 percent stake in the company.[66] In 2013, Sundrop Fuels finalized the acquisition of 1,213 acres in Boyce, Louisiana to build a 15,000 barrel per day green gasoline facility.[67]

Heating Up. *This company is one of many examples of new entrepreneurial efforts to address the future environmental challenges we face in our world. Sundrop is taking a big risk by being a start-up, by needing large infusions of capital and by developing new technologies. New companies trying to do these things tend to face large challenges to become an established company. Given what you know about renewable energy, business, and new companies, can you suggest a few things you would advise the company to increase its chances of success? One format for this analysis can be the development of a potential business model.[68]*

Questions and Critical Thinking

1 When viewing firms from the perspective of resources and capabilities, every organization is unique with its unique capabilities to use resources; resources become unique when they are used. This perspective, however, makes generalizing "an excellent organization" difficult. To what extent can you point to a set of capabilities that every organization should develop to become excellent? What unique capabilities can you suggest for being best-in-class for environmental sustainability?

2 A section in this chapter points to some unique tactics for implementing strategy. Provide one example of an organization *not mentioned in this chapter* exemplifying each of the following tactics: radical resource productivity; biomimicry; service and flow economy.

3 Consider the concept of "blue ocean" as described in this book. Take a company you know well and develop a set of ideas about how to change their key success factors for the industry they are operating within, in order to develop a new business idea.

Notes

1 R. H. K. Vieter, "Cape Wind: Offshore Wind Energy in the USA," Harvard Business School Case 708-022 (Boston, MA: Harvard Business School, January 2008).

2 Ibid.

3 Ibid.

4 W. C. Kim and R. Mauborgne, *Blue Ocean Strategy: How to Create Uncontested Market Space and Make the Competition Irrelevant* (Boston, MA: Harvard Business School Press, 2005), 15.

5 The profits arising from market power are referred to as Monopoly Rents; those arising from resources and capabilities are Ricardian Rents. These Ricardian Rents are earned by a scarce resource over and above the cost of bringing it into production.

6 E.g., D. A. Vazquez Brust and C. Liston-Heyes, "Environmental Management Intentions: An Empirical Investigation of Argentina's Polluting Firms," *Journal of Environmental Management* 91, no. 5 (May 2010): 1111–1122.

7 G. Hamel and C. K. Prahalad, *Competing for the Future* (Cambridge, MA: Harvard Business School Press, 1994), 18.

8 Co-authored by Michael Aper, Master of Arts in Sustainability candidate at Wake Forest University.

9 "About," Nest Labs, 2015, https://nest.com/about/ (accessed March 1, 2015).

10 T. Fadell, "Thermostats? Yes Thermostats," Nest Labs, 2015, blog https://nest.com/blog/2011/10/25/thermo-stats-yes-thermostats/ (accessed March 1, 2015).

11 T. Fadell, "Welcome Home," Nest Labs, 2015, blog https://nest.com/blog/2014/01/13/welcome-home/ (accessed March 1, 2015).

12 M. LaMonica, "GreenBiz 101: What You Need to Know about the Internet of Things," GreenBiz, 2015, http://www.greenbiz.com/blog/2014/05/12/greenbiz-101-what-do-you-need-know-about-internet-things (accessed December 22, 2015).

13 S. Rothenberg, "Sustainability through Servicizing," *MIT Sloan Management Review* (Winter 2007): 83–91. Also, *The Economist*, "The Rise of the Sharing Economy," March 8, 2013, 9.

14 M. E. Porter, "What Is Strategy?" *Harvard Business Review* 61 (November 1996): 61–78.

15 J.-C. Spender, *Industry Recipes: The Nature and Sources of Managerial Judgment* (Cambridge, MA: Basil Blackwell, 1989); A. Huff, "Industry Influences on Strategy Formulation," *Strategic Management Journal* 3, no. 2 (April/June 1982): 119–131.

16 DuPont Analysis is an expression which breaks Return on Equity (ROE) into three parts.

17 Profitability is an efficiency measure.

$$\text{Profitability} = \frac{\text{Earnings before interest and tax (EBIT)}}{\text{Sales}}$$

The profitability measurement represents the operating performance of a business entity expressed as a return on sales. It also provides a measurement of operational efficiency in the profit and loss statement, void of finance costs. Activity is a measure of the efficiency.

$$\text{Activity} = \frac{\text{Sales}}{\text{Total net assests}}$$

The activity measurement reflects balance sheet efficiency in terms of the utilization of scarce resources.

ROCE is a measure of the return on capital employed:

$$\text{ROCE} = \text{Profitability} \times \text{Activity}$$

or

$$\text{ROCE} = \frac{\text{EBIT}}{\text{Sales}} \times \frac{\text{Sales}}{\text{Total net assests (TNA)}}$$

$$\text{ROCE} = \frac{\text{EBIT}}{\text{TNA}}$$

ROCE provides a measurement of the operational return on the investment in total net assets. This is also the return on net assets (RONA) or the return on investment (ROI) due to the equivalence concept derived from separating finance from operations.

18 M. D. Cohen et al., "Routines and Other Recurring Action Patterns of Organizations: Contemporary Research Issues," *Industrial and Corporate Change* 5, no. 3 (June 1996): 653–698.

19 R. Madhavan and D. Fogel, "How Organizational Routines Change," Working Paper, University of Pittsburgh, March 15, 1994.

20 D. Katz and R. L. Kahn, "Organizations and the Systems Concept," in J. R. Hackman, E. E. Lawler III, and L. W. Porter (eds.), *Perspectives on Behavior in Organizations*, 2nd ed. (New York: McGraw-Hill, 1983), 98–99; M. D. Cohen and P. Bacdayan, "Organizational Routines Are Stored as Procedural Memory: Evidence from a Laboratory Study," *Organization Science* 5, no. 4 (1994): 554–568.

21 Cohen and Bacdayan, "Organizational Routines Are Stored as Procedural Memory."

22 R. R. Nelson and S. G. Winter, *An Evolutionary Theory of Economic Change* (Cambridge, MA: Belknap, 1982).

23 M. Kilduff, "The Reproduction of Inertia in Multinational Corporations," in S. Ghoshal and D. E. Westney (eds.), *Organization Theory and the Multinational Corporation* (New York: St. Martin's Press, 1993), 259–274. Kilduff points out three key differences between March and Simon's (1958) first articulation of the concept of routines and Nelson and Winter's (1982) subsequent refinement. First, Nelson and Winter emphasized that routines may be opaque, rather than transparent; thus, people might not be able to precisely articulate even those routines that they are acting out. Second, Nelson and Winter were among the first to note that replicating routines across boundaries is problematic. Finally, they argued that routines are not only instruments of management control; in addition and more importantly, routines represent a negotiated settlement of competing political interests, historical precedent, and informal agreements among organizational actors.

24 C. J. G. Gersick and J. R. Hackman, "Habitual Routines in Task Performing Groups," *Organizational Behavior and Human Decision Processes* 47 (1990): 65–97.

25 S. B. Bacharach, P. Bamberger, and W. J. Sonnenstuhl, "The Organizational Transformation Process: The Micropolitics of Dissonance Reduction and the Alignment of Logics of Action," *Administrative Science Quarterly* 41, no. 3 (September 1996): 477–506; J. E. McGrath and J. R. Kelly, *Time and Human Interaction: Toward a Social Psychology of Time* (New York: Guilford, 1986).

26 McGrath and Kelly, *Time and Human Interaction*, 18.

27 D. J. Teece, G. Pisano, and A. Shuen, "Dynamic Capabilities and Strategic Management," *Strategic Management Journal* 18, no. 7 (August 1997): 509–533; D. J. Collis, "Research Note: How Valuable Are Organizational Capabilities?" *Strategic Management Journal* 15, no. S1 (Winter 1994): 143–152; B. L. Simonin, "The Importance of Developing Collaborative Know-How: An Empirical Test of the Learning Organization," *Academy of Management Journal* 40, no. 5 (October 1997): 1150–1174.

28 K. Cool and I. Dierickx, "Rivalry, Strategic Groups and Firm Profitability," *Strategic Management Journal* 14, no. 1 (January 1993): 47–59.

29 J. B. Barney, "Firm Resources and Sustained Competitive Advantage," *Journal of Management* 17, no. 1 (March 1991): 99–120.

30 Ibid.

31 R. M. Grant, "The Resource-based Theory of Competitive Advantage: Implications for Strategy Formulation," *California Management Review* 33, no. 3 (Spring 1991): 114–135.

32 However, as we have seen, such tight coupling makes it difficult to change any given routine, thus leading to reduced adaptability. From the adaptability viewpoint, loosely coupled routines are better. The best situation for an organization may well lie in the development of some modularity in the organization's routines. The designers of the organization should consider the domains in which adaptability is critical, and carefully design modular routines in those domains. Explicitly paying attention to the interfaces of a routine with meta-routines and specifying the interfaces in such a manner as to minimize the interdependencies is a way to develop modular routines.

33 APQC, "What We Do: Benchmarking," www.apqc.org/benchmarking (accessed December 22, 2015).

34 McKinsey & Co., "Forgotten Value: Streamlining Business Support Functions," www.mckinsey.com/Client_Service/Automotive_and_Assembly/Latest_thinking/Forgotten_value_Streamlining_business_support_functions (accessed December 12, 2011).

35 K. M. Eisenhardt and J. A. Martin, "Dynamic Capabilities: What Are They?" *Strategic Management Journal* 21, no. 10–11 (October–November 2000): 1105–1121.

36 For example, A. Capezio, J. Shields, and M. O'Donnell, "Too Good to Be True: Board Structural Independence as a Moderator of CEO Pay-for-Firm-Performance," *Journal of Management Studies* 48, no. 3 (May 2011): 487–511.

37 C. Bradley, A. Dawson, and A. Montard, "Mastering the Building Blocks of Strategy," *McKinsey Quarterly*, October 2013, http://www.mckinsey.com/insights/strategy/mastering_the_building_blocks_of_strategy (accessed October 8, 2014).

38 D. Leonard-Barton, "Core Capabilities and Core Rigidities," *Strategic Management Journal* 13, no. S1 (Summer 1992): 111–125.

39 D. J. Teece, *Dynamic Capabilities and Strategic Management: Organizing for Innovation and Growth* (New York: Oxford University Press, 2009), 34–37; Eisenhardt and Martin, "Dynamic Capabilities: What Are They?"

40 T. Dunne, M. J. Roberts, and L. Samuelson, "Patterns of Firm Entry and Exit in the U.S. Manufacturing Industries," *The RAND Journal of Economics* 19, no. 4 (Winter 1988): 495–515.

41 *The Economist*, "Bulletins from the Future," July 9, 2011, 9.

42 S. Bennett, "Tumblr, Facebook, Twitter, Instagram & Snapchat – How Teens Use Social Media [INFOGRAPHIC]," SocialTimes, October 18, 2013, http://www.adweek.com/socialtimes/teens-social-media/492148?red=at (accessed December 22, 2015).

43 Ibid.

44 P. Hawken, A. Lovins, and L. Hunter Lovins, *Natural Capitalism: Creating the Next Industrial Revolution* (Boston, MA: Little, Brown, 1999), 11.

45 M. Stacey, M. Taylor, and D. Legge, "A New Role for Natural Resources Companies," *Strategy+Business* (Summer 2012): 8–11.

46 J. Benyus, *Biomimicry: Innovation Inspired by Nature* (New York: Morrow, 1997), 3. Also, J. Benyus, "12 sustainable design ideas from nature," YouTube, May 17, 2007, www.youtube.com/watch?v=n77BfxnVlyc (accessed December 22, 2015).

47 Ibid.

48 "Janine Benyus: Biomimicry's surprising lessons from nature's engineers," TED, February 2005, www.ted.com/talks/janine_benyus_shares_nature_s_designs.html (accessed May 10, 2011).

49 S. L. Pimm, *The World According to Pimm: A Scientist Audits the Earth* (New York: McGraw-Hill, 2001).

50 Benyus, *Biomimicry*, 21.

51 Ibid., 297.

52 Rothenberg, "Sustainability through Servicizing," 83–91. Also, *The Economist*, "The Rise of the Sharing Economy," March 8, 2013, 9.

53 Hawken et al., *Natural Capitalism*, 16.

54 "What is a material cycle?" in Annenberg Learner, "Life Science: Session 8—Material Cycles," www.learner.org/courses/essential/life/session8/closer5.html (accessed December 23, 2012).

55 W. McDonough and M. Braungart, *Cradle to Cradle: Remaking the Way We Make Things* (New York: North Point Press, 2002).

56 Chan Kim and Mauborgne, *Blue Ocean Strategy*, 4.

57 Adapted from W. Chan Kim and R. Mauborgne, "Blue Ocean Strategy," *Harvard Business Review* (October 2004): 81.

58 Ibid., 16.

59 The following are key success factors

- Model the firm
- Functions analysis
- Routines identification
- Benchmarking
- Importance vs. strength
- Creating Competitive Advantage: Extent: scarcity and relevance
- Sustainability: durability, transferability (immobility), replicable, using isolating mechanisms
- Appropriate value: property rights, bargaining power, embeddedness

Adapted from R. Grant, *Contemporary Strategy Analysis*, 8th ed. (Hoboken, NJ: John Wiley & Sons, 2012): 111–140 (chapter 5).

60 Co-authored by Michael Aper, Master of Arts in Sustainability candidate at Wake Forest University.
61 "Incoming Sunlight," EOS Project Science Office, NASA, http://earthobservatory.nasa.gov/Features/EnergyBalance/page2.php (accessed January 24, 2015).
62 "Surface Energy Budget," EOS Project Science Office, NASA, http://earthobservatory.nasa.gov/Features/EnergyBalance/page5.php (accessed January 23, 2015).
63 "Benefits," Sundrop Fuels, Inc., http://www.sundropfuels.com/Benefits/renewable-biofuels (accessed January 23, 2015).
64 "Company History," Sundrop Fuels, Inc., http://www.sundropfuels.com/assets/white_papers/17.pdf (accessed January 23, 2015).
65 "Combining cellulosic biomass with natural gas to create affordable drop-in advanced biofuels," Sundrop Fuels, Inc., http://www.sundropfuels.com/assets/white_papers/16.pdf (accessed January 23, 2015).
66 Michael J. De La Merced, "Chesapeake Energy to Start V.C. Fund," *New York Times*, http://dealbook.nytimes.com/2011/07/11/chesapeake-energy-to-start-v-c-fund/?_r=0 (accessed January 23, 2015).
67 "About Us," Sundrop Fuels, Inc., http://www.sundropfuels.com/About%20Us/about (accessed January 23, 2015).
68 Business Model Generation, http://businessmodelgeneration.com/ (accessed January 23, 2015).

7

BUSINESS STRATEGY AND CORPORATE STRATEGY

Rohner Textil AG

The Swiss firm, Rohner Textil AG (Rohner), agreed to adopt a sustainability strategy in 2005. Rohner decided to utilize cradle-to-cradle principles as its guidelines; the result was a 30 percent increase in total output, a drastic reduction in costs, and the production of the first 100 percent biodegradable commercial fabric, which revolutionized the textile industry and set a precedent for responsive environmental design.[1] The Climatex® LifecycleTM fabric was designed as upholstery fabric for office furniture.

Rohner's initial intent was to use material constructed from cotton combined with polyethylene terephthalate (PET), which comes from recycled carbonated drink bottles. Rohner believed that by creating a product out of recycled waste material, the fabric would have inherent marketing appeal; however, it soon discovered all sorts of problems (e.g., PET opened the company up to liability since toxic chemicals in the PET could be inhaled by users). Additionally, cotton farmers typically use large quantities of pesticides on their crops; cotton is responsible for 20 percent of the world's harmful pesticide use. Finally, PET was not a compostable product (as it does not decompose).

Thus, the design failed on many fronts.[2] However, the company then partnered with Ciba-Geigy (a chemical company) and came up with materials that could meet stringent environmental sustainability criteria (e.g., using wool from free-range sheep to replace the PET). Today, Rohner's Climatex® LifecycleTM fabric is all-natural and 100 percent biodegradable. (One interesting byproduct of this new fabric was that the used water coming out of the factory [from the production of this fabric] was as clean or cleaner than the water coming in from the town's drinking water supply.[3])

Chapter Overview

This chapter builds upon our understanding of external and internal analysis (see Chapters 5–6) and provides a more in-depth look at strategy (see Chapter 4). In the last chapter, *cost* and *differentiation* were identified as two sources of competitive advantage; these forms were generic ways to describe critical parts of an organization's strategy. This chapter expands these strategies and frames them within the larger context of business and corporate strategy. Specifically, this chapter describes generic *sources* of competitive advantage and explains how environmental sustainability (as a lens on strategy) can enhance an organization's competitiveness. Two basic questions will be explored: *how can firms compete* (referred to as *business strategy*) and *where* should firms compete (referred to as *corporate strategy*).

At the end of this chapter, you should be able to:

1 distinguish between business and corporate strategy;
2 describe how *low-cost* and *differentiation* function to create competitive advantages for firms;
3 define *vertical integration* (and explain the reasons and methods for it);

The first question, related to strategy, is how can firms compete (which is the definition of a business strategy)? Managers involved in business strategy also make decisions about how their firms can compete within particular markets. Most companies are inherently preoccupied with costs; however, some firms use *cost advantages* as a means of gaining advantage over others. Still others, while cost conscious, tend to build into products and services factors that motivate consumers to pay a premium (e.g., superior quality and perceived added consumer benefits). Consider, for example, Nike products, which may sometimes be priced at a premium because of the brand; a similar piece of clothing could be functionally the same but not cost as much (as it is not branded). These are low-cost vs. differentiation strategies. The second set of questions, related to strategy, include:

- Where should we compete?
- What markets should we enter?

When firms decide to enter multiple markets, they are practicing *corporate strategy*, these decisions involve discerning the parts of the value chain most suitable for engagement. This technique is called *vertical integration*,

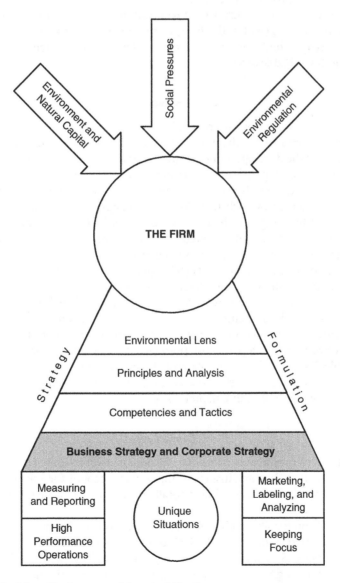

Figure 7.1 Strategy Model with an Environmental Sustainability Lens

and it has many facets (which we will explore in this chapter). Also, I will present some analytical tools used by managers to understand their various markets (and how they make decisions about whether to enter, enhance, or exit these market positions [building on the information in Chapter 6]).

Business Strategy: How Can Firms Compete?

This section helps clarify *how* to compete. Business strategy is a combination of *positioning* a firm's products and services in markets and then *supporting the positioning* to gain advantages over competitors. (We will address how firms determine their markets in the section on corporate strategy.)

Firms use all sorts of strategies to position themselves and support their positioning; however, our discussion will be more focused on identifying what are considered *generic strategies* (i.e., strategies that firms commonly use). The two that I will discuss are *low-cost* and *differentiation*. In brief, firms may position themselves in markets as the low-price leader; otherwise, differentiation implies that consumers have a reason to pay a premium for a particular product or service.

One main idea in this chapter is that firms tend to position themselves according to one of these generic strategies and then create activities (within the firm) to support the positioning. For example, low-cost strategies tend to be supported by high internal efficiencies. Differentiation tends to use advertising, unique product designs, and highly valuable service.

Cost Advantages

Cost cutting is a constant conversation in companies. In recent decades, the need to cut costs has been supported by the ability of firms to cut their costs dramatically by shifting production to emerging-market countries. Cost analysis (and the development of strategies based on costs) may vary according to the industry in which a firm operates; for example, firms in shipping, such as Maersk Shipping, have a constant preoccupation with efficient routes and low fuel costs. Manufacturers are constantly trying to find the leanest way to produce goods, often informed by such techniques as six sigma and lean manufacturing methodologies, which are two common methodologies to help firms identify variation and waste in their firms.

When considering costs, there are two related ideas that firms need to consider: *cost drivers* and *cost analysis*. Cost drivers are the components generating costs for a company, and cost analysis is the process of evaluating ways to lower costs. A company needs to be aware of cost drivers before it conducts analyses and, ultimately, before it develops strategy. In this chapter, I will describe some of the core cost drivers or determinants of a firm's cost per unit of output relative to competitors. We will revisit this topic in Chapter 11, which will present information about manufacturing processes and operations.

Cost analysis has many forms; however, in general, firms tend to analyze their cost position relative to competitors, identify ways to improve this cost position, and adopt process methodologies for continuous improvement. Table 7.1 has a list of sample cost drivers with examples associated with environmental concerns. I will cover three of these in depth in this chapter: *input costs*, *economies of scale*, and *product development*. I will cover *production techniques* in Chapter 11.

Input Costs

Input costs are costs related to resources used to make products. Every product or service has input costs that impact the overall cost structure. In some instances, input costs account for a majority of the overall product costs (e.g., software development costs are almost totally in the design of the software since production and distribution costs are minimal).

Although the cost of silicon for silicon chip manufacturing has been historically minimal, recently the cost has risen due to the scarcity of silicon, making U.S. chips much more expensive. Interestingly, Chinese silicon solar panels are cheaper than U.S.-made panels (and might even be cheaper than their production costs) due to a phenomenon called dumping.[4] *Dumping* is a term used when countries financially support their companies with international trade by making products much cheaper than other global competitors (i.e., product

Table 7.1 Cost Drivers

	Examples and ways to gain efficiencies
Input costs	Labor: have people work at home to cut carbon outputs
	Materials: decrease the need for certain materials; decrease the environmental footprint of inputs
	Location: locate in areas that are more environmentally friendly and promote easier access to inputs or customers
Economies of scale	Indivisibilities and the spreading of fixed costs: increase volumes so that fixed costs are spread over more products
	Increased productivity of variable inputs
	Inventories and capacity utilization
Economies of learning	Improved capabilities: increasing the expertise within the firm
	Increases in individual skills
	Processes to obtain knowledge about best practices
Product design	Using techniques such as cradle-to-cradle
	Life-cycle analysis to decrease products' environmental footprints
	Observing basic product design principles that improve environmental outcomes, decrease costs, and increase quality, such as using biomimicry for product design
Production techniques	Process innovation
Managerial input	Managerial effectiveness
	Cultural impacts: employee motivation to perform
	Increased flexibility to meet changing environment

pricing is below the variable cost to produce the product). This process is viewed as a violation of the WTO rules on trade.[5] Those who complain about some countries and their businesses say that the pricing of their products does not accurately reflect input costs.

Firms control input costs in several ways, mainly through changing the input sources (e.g., using labor from an emerging market or altering product design to enable cheaper inputs). An example of lowering costs through product design is modern computer hardware designs that require less storage due to the availability of storage in the cloud.

Certain inexpensive inputs can drive costs later in the production process. For example, the costs to build a house include the costs of materials, location, and the current market for housing; however, rarely do construction processes take into account the ongoing costs caused by the design of the house (e.g., energy efficiency, maintenance costs, and even the costs to renovate). Thus, even though input costs can be cheaper initially, the homeowner might be forced to absorb costs from inefficiencies later on that might exceed the initial savings.

Input cost planning requires a balance between upfront expenses and long-term expenses derived from initial decision making. Input costs are also only one of several cost drivers. Another cost driver is economies of scale.

Economies of Scale

Economies of scale are calculated as the quantity of a product that must be produced to achieve maximum returns. The production process, for a specific good or service, exhibits economies of scale over a range of outputs when the average cost (i.e., the cost per unit of output) declines over that range. If average cost declines as output increases, then the marginal cost of the last unit produced must be less than the average cost (see Figure 7.2). If average cost is increasing, then marginal cost is exceeding average cost (producing diseconomies of scale).

Economies of scale have often been associated with manufacturing operations; however, service organizations can also experience economies of scale. For example, a university faculty member's salary, location of classes, and administrative costs can be spread over more and more students; thus, a school's incentive is to have large class sizes to achieve these efficiencies. Of course, this benefit is often countered with the impact on educational quality. Therefore, multiple factors (e.g., quality control) must be considered when a firm is working toward economies of scale.

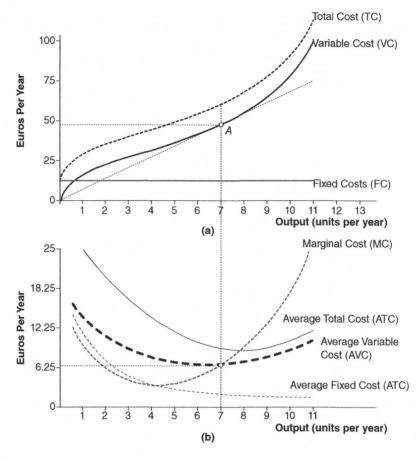

Figure 7.2 Cost Curves

Notes

a total cost TC is the vertical sum of fixed cost FC and variable cost VC.

b average total cost ATC is the sum of average variable cost AVC and average fixed cost AFC. Marginal cost MC crosses the average variable cost and average total cost curves at their minimum points.

Firms that produce multiple products may experience *economies of scope*, which is a variation of this concept. Economies of scope exist if a firm achieves unit-cost savings as it increases its variety of goods and services. For example, firms may be able to use similar distribution channels to obtain inputs or ship their products, cutting down on distribution costs for each individual product. Also, certain machines can be used for multiple products, increasing their efficiencies. Thus, critical scale advantages provide incentives for firms to become larger and larger.

Economies of scope can be achieved in many ways. For example, branded products may achieve these efficiencies through brand leveraging. The Hewlett-Packard Company (HP), the world's biggest computer maker, recently announced that it planned to spin off its computer products into a separate company;[6] analysts worry that this move could decrease the ability of HP to achieve economies in its purchasing. Many of the first PCs HP sold went to corporate customers that bought the computers along with tech services and server systems. Also, HP has had favorable deals with retailers because it also sold printers and ink through them; without these ties (economies of scope), the separate PC company might have a tougher time competing with low-cost vendors from Asia. Also, the new company could lose bulk discounts for components. Thus, HP (through its recent moves to economize) could be destroying the value it gets from being large and gaining economies of scale and scope.

Economies of scale and scope have limits. For example, some companies can get so big that they are difficult to manage—an inverse of the "too big to fail" mantra so prevalent in the financial sector from 2008 to 2011. In fact, there is a great deal of evidence that big players in the banking industry do *not* outperform smaller banks on profitability or costs.[7] An awareness of economies of scale and scope is a good way for a company to decrease cost drivers; however, as demonstrated here, economies of scale or scope do not directly translate into profits.

Product Development

Product development is another way to impact costs and competitive advantage. A product development strategy specifies the portfolio of new products that a company will try to develop. It also dictates whether the development effort will be made internally or externally. These decisions have dramatic cost implications.

Several techniques are key, here. One common technique involves life-cycle assessments (usually coupled with life-cycle thinking and management). Life-cycle analyses are systems for addressing the environmental consequences of entire product chains (from resource extraction to waste management). Life-cycle assessment (LCA) is a method for analyzing the environmental impacts associated with a product or service; this method includes studies of materials and energy flows throughout the production of a product or service (from raw materials to disposal).[8]

An LCA usually starts with a goal and scope definition, which specifies the product to be studied and the purpose of the study. For example, chemical companies often identify specific chemicals to study for the purpose of finding ways to substitute ingredients with environmentally friendly alternatives containing the same performance characteristics as the existing ingredients.

Analysts usually do an inventory to construct a life-cycle model of the product system (including a calculation of the amounts of emissions produced and the resources used in the product system). Emissions and resources are related to potential environmental outcomes (e.g., resource depletion or global warming). The significance of these impacts is weighted so that a total environmental impact can be calculated. The interpretation of these data then leads to action (e.g., declarations of environmental impacts, reengineering of products, or statements to suppliers to reduce their components' environmental impacts).[9]

Cradle-to-gate, *cradle-to-grave*, and *cradle-to-cradle* are other terms for LCA. These terms indicate the extent to which the product system is modeled in an LCA. For example, a furniture company, Herman Miller, decided to change its approach to LCA from cradle-to-grave to cradle-to-cradle when it designed its MIRA chair; instead of expecting consumers to recycle their chairs, Herman Miller reused parts from the discarded chairs to produce its new MIRA chairs. This technique meant that Herman Miller took responsibility for taking back its used chairs and reusing most of their components. The cradle-to-cradle techniques call for reusing all technical components and ensuring that the biological components are biodegradable.[10]

When companies engage in these processes, they are clearly deleting waste and costs from their products. Although we are discussing this technique within cost strategy, this type of analysis works well within the differentiation strategy (i.e., finding ways to make a product perform better).

In summary, we have introduced *low-cost strategy*, which some companies use to gain competitive advantage (by focusing on product development). This strategy calls for companies to position themselves within market spaces that reward low costs and do not require lots of features in products and services that would increase cost and functionality. This requires companies to engage in certain core activities (such as LCA) and gain competencies in areas such as manufacturing excellence, product design (for less cost and environmental impact), and economies of scale. I will now contrast this low-cost strategy with differentiation.

Differentiation

Every effective strategy is about being different from competitors and trying to find a positioning that is unique. Certain firms provide something unique and valuable to buyers simply by offering low pricing. *Differentiation advantage* happens when a firm is able to obtain a price premium in a market that exceeds the costs of providing the differentiation.[11]

For example, companies that produce paper products offer similar types of products; however, some firms (such as Avery) offer services that help people use the paper (e.g., templates for making resumes, labels, and report covers). One of the classic commodity products—steel—does not differentiate easily; however, some steel companies provide custom steel making and create steel products that can make the customer's tasks easier and less costly.

Analyzing differentiation is about product characteristics (supply side) and interactions between the firm and its customers (demand side). Firms that identify differentiation opportunities tend to offer enhanced value via unique product characteristics, services, and added benefits (not available from competitors). For example, PepsiCo expanded its portfolio beyond soda and potato chips when Indra Nooyi joined the company and took over as its CEO. Pepsi, as a drink, always offered customers a reason to pay a premium for a relatively simple drink; however, in recent years, it lost significant market share in the cola business (coming in third, behind Coke and Diet Coke);[12] this lost market share was a reason for diversification.[13] Pepsi brought Nooyi into the company to initiate its current strategy after the previous CEO failed to sufficiently increase Pepsi's profits. This new strategy included diversifying its portfolio by adding healthier brands and products that can be consumed all day long.[14]

The real benefit of pursuing differentiation strategies is that the associated variables (upon which a firm can differentiate) are limitless. The basis of differentiation includes every aspect of how a product is made and delivered. A firm's opportunities for creating uniqueness in its offerings can be found in many places within the firm. For example:[15]

1   product features and product performance;
2   the degree of vertical integration (which influences a firm's ability to control inputs and intermediate processes);
3   complementary services (e.g., credit, delivery, and repair);
4   the skill and experience of employees to respond to customer requests and to understand customer requirements;
5   intensity of marketing activities (e.g., the level of spending on advertising);
6   location (such as found with retail stores);
7   the quality of purchased inputs;
8   technology embodied in design and manufacturing;
9   the brand and its extensions.

I will now discuss two of these features: *product design* and *brand*.

Product Design

One obvious way to create differentiation is to design products in a manner that makes them unique. Many product features are designed in response to customer feedback. Firms conduct research to identify and analyze customer preferences; they can then determine how the firm might translate these preferences into product features. Common techniques (e.g., multidimensional scaling, conjoint analysis, hedonic pricing analysis, and value curve analyses) are indicative of the techniques most widely used by firms.[16]

Many firms utilize social and psychological factors as a means of product design. For example, Coke and Pepsi have claimed unique product designs; however, blind test tastes have shown that few people can tell the difference. Thus, the positioning of the products and response of the brand to psychological factors help define differentiation.

Brands

My purpose here is to highlight that brands differentiate products and services. A brand is a *name, term, sign, symbol,* or *design* (or a combination of these) intended to identify the goods or services of one seller (or group of sellers) and to distinguish them from those of the competition.[17] This definition refers mostly to brand elements; elements are any identifying feature of a product. For example, *Toyota* is attached to all of Toyota's products; however, Toyota assigns unique names to each car type (e.g., Corolla and Lexus). In a more general sense, a brand differentiates a product or service from other products or services designed to satisfy similar needs. These differences may be rationales or tangible (i.e., related to pre-purchase performance) or more symbolic, emotional and intangible (i.e., related to what the brand represents).[18] For example, some brands may align with larger issues in society, politics, or culture[19] (e.g., Patagonia, Whole Foods, and Starbucks). We covered Patagonia's branding efforts in Chapter 4's opening case.

Businesses have always been subject to various external factors (consider the SLEEP-AT model presented in Chapter 5). Today, companies can mobilize public opinion based on these factors. Nike's brand renovation is an example. They shifted their focus from elite athletes to human dimensions (i.e., competition and life) and offered a broader view of competition that suggested that overcoming barriers (e.g., racism, sexism, and global poverty) is much more impressive than success in sports.

A value chain analysis is a powerful method used to strengthen low-cost and differentiation strategies. This method has a rich source of identifying sources of low-cost or differentiation.

Using the Value Chain to Identify Sources of Costs and Differentiation

Studying the value chain is a powerful method of analyzing and making recommendations for cost and differentiation. Every business can be viewed as a chain of activities; the value chain illustrates the steps for making and selling a product and the value created at each step. In most value chains, each activity has a distinct cost structure (determined by cost drivers). They also have distinct benefits from the product or service design.

Analyzing costs requires disaggregating the value chain. Recall that we are focused here on a product or product group; thus, an organization might need to do several analyses if it has several products or services. Disaggregating the firm into separate activities requires judgments about the distinctiveness of an activity, the importance of an activity, and the extent to which activities are performed.

A generic value chain is often depicted as a set of primary and secondary activities. Figure 7.3 shows one example from a biotechnology firm.

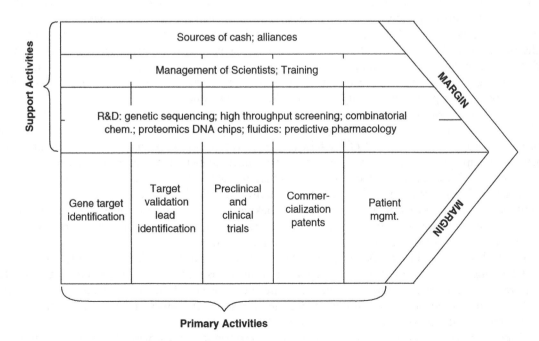

Figure 7.3 Biotechnology Firm's Value Chain

The primary activities of the value chain are those that are directly observable in the making and selling of a product. For example, input resources (e.g., raw materials and packaging) go into manufacturing that then create a product, which is sold to consumers. (They are ordered this way as it represents the order in which the activities occur.) Secondary activities support primary activities and occur throughout a firm (e.g., human resource management, technology, and legal services).

After determining distinct areas of a value chain, analysts typically establish major cost areas; this process involves an assignment of operating costs to each activity (often referred to as activity-based costing).[20] This analysis leads to the identification of cost drivers. For example, in some service industries, labor and marketing are major cost items. In manufacturing, input materials and manufacturing equipment might be major cost drivers. Essentially, activity-based costing reveals the activities that require the most financial investment.

The final step in analyzing a value chain is to identify where costs might be cut and where efficiencies can be gained. Some firms benchmark a particular activity against competitors and firms that have similar activities; benchmarking may find not only relative cost positions but also methods for reducing costs. For example, the biotechnology company pictured in Figure 7.2 found that its costs of doing clinical trials far exceeded other firms; it invested heavily in cutting these costs and in finding ways to speed up the process so that it could bring a drug to market more rapidly.[21]

Value chain analysis can also be used to determine differentiation strategies. When using a value chain to look at differentiation (vs. using it to analyze costs), an analyst might want to extend the value chain to include the customer's customer. For example, a food producer might want to consider not only its customer (the supermarket) but also how the purchaser of the food (the supermarket's customer) uses the product. This analysis can lead to excellent information about how to package a product and make it more appealing to the end consumer. This concept relates to what was discussed in the *input costs* section about the construction of a home. For example, when a window company is considering the development of an energy-efficient window, their value chain will not only consider the appeal of the window to the contractor building the home, but they will also consider the homeowner's long-term energy savings. Both entities are consumers of the same product, and the company could take measures to satisfy both to gain advantage over competitors with similar products and services.

The next step for developing a differentiation strategy with a value chain is to find *drivers of uniqueness* in each activity. Assess a firm's potential for differentiating its product by examining each activity in the firm's value chain and identifying the variables and actions through which the firm can achieve uniqueness (in relation to competitors' offerings). For example, the "toy of the century," Lego, did an analysis of their product and discovered several things. First, they were driving costs by having too many different products; thus, they decided to reduce the number of unique products they were producing. Also, they reaffirmed that the major activity that drove value for Lego was not the manufacturing but the packaging of Lego. Not only did they have high costs in this packaging activity, but they also had high value.

Similar to cost analysis, managers look for all sorts of ways to drive value; sometimes these value drivers are found in *secondary* activities of the value chain. For example, many car companies discovered that the provision of financing was a critical component of the sales process in the consumer market; thus, they mounted finance companies to help with car purchases. However, as consumer financial markets became more efficient, these financing methods became less valuable. Thus, differentiation strategy is a continual process of reevaluating value.

Moving from a cost strategy to a differentiation strategy can sometimes be challenging for a company. Dell Computers pursued a cost strategy when it started making the value proposition to consumers that it had cheaper computers than other companies. As people bought more and more Dell computers, they associated excellent, value-laden computers with Dell. Dell's reputation increased.

Although this strategy helped Dell to grow, there was skepticism that this trend would continue indefinitely. Changing strategies would not be easy for the company as it spent many years building competencies to support its key strategy (i.e., low cost) and would need to now switch to another strategy (i.e., differentiation). This change could cause some ambiguity for the firm; some Dell analysts believe this is one reason Dell has struggled to continue to grow and add value as a firm.

The lesson, here, is that firms need to remain flexible to continue to grow with changing times and markets. For a company like Dell, looking back at its value chain could be the first step toward a differentiation strategy.

Corporate Strategy: Where Should Firms Compete?

This section defines corporate strategy (i.e., the decisions firms make as to where they will compete). Corporate strategy is important to firms; they must decide on their markets and how they will balance their different product lines across different markets. Thus, corporate strategy decisions are those that define markets and how a firm will enter those markets. For example, a firm can vertically integrate, diversify its core into adjacent markets, or even decide to do transformational changes and enter completely new and untested markets. We will explore some of these strategic moves in the next section.

Vertical Integration

What determines the types of activities undertaken within a firm (vs. in the marketplace)? This is a fundamental question many managers routinely ask. One answer comes from the concept of *relative cost.*[22] Firms acquire costs whether they do an activity within a market or within a firm. Market costs can come from activities such as search costs, costs of negotiating and drawing up contracts, monitoring costs (to make sure suppliers are doing what they say they would do), and litigation costs (in the event these suppliers fail to deliver on their promises).

The decision whether or not to produce in-house versus in the market is often informed by transaction costs. Transaction costs are those costs of operating in the market. If transaction costs, associated with organizing across markets, are greater than the costs within a firm, then an activity will be done within the firm, and vice versa. This interaction is called *relative cost* or *"make-buy" decisions* because the firm must decide whether it is more cost-effective to operate a piece of the value chain itself or to purchase the services of other companies for that piece.

Appendix 9.2 has an extensive discussion of how managers analyze value chains to make these "make-buy" decisions. Also, we discussed this situation in Chapter 4. Here, I want to focus on *vertical integration* as a corporate strategy decision; this is the "make" aspect of the "make-buy" dichotomy.

Vertical integration refers to a firm's ownership of vertically related activities. The further a firm's ownership extends over successive stages of the value chain, the greater the degree of vertical integration. Vertical integration brings into the firm activities that could be risky to conduct in the market (e.g., if a firm finds that it needs a strategic input, such as a rare earth metal, to produce its product, it might want to ensure the availability of that input by buying a firm that produces the input). This approach can become problematic when firms absorb the costs of doing an activity in-house when cheaper goods could be found in the market.

Vertical integration can be either backward (the firm takes ownership of its inputs [e.g., manufacturing]) or forward (the firm takes over ownership and control of activities undertaken by its customers [such as distribution]). For example, some pharmaceutical companies do R&D, manufacture drugs, and market them; other drug companies might choose to buy the R&D on the market and only produce and market the drugs.

Table 7.2 Vertical Integration vs. Outsourcing: What to Think About[23]

- The fewer the firms, the greater the transaction costs (and the larger the advantage of vertical integration).
- Transaction-specific investments increase vertical integration advantages. For example, if organizations have only one supplier they might want to consider vertical integration or to support a new entrant into the supply chain.
- Information asymmetries produce a greater likelihood of opportunistic behavior and promote a greater need for vertical integration.
- Taxes and other market costs (e.g., regulatory costs) can sometimes be avoided by vertical integration.
- High uncertainties over costs, demand, supply, and the ability of a market player to deliver makes for difficult contract formation (making vertical integration more attractive).
- The greater the strategic similarity among various parts of the value chain, the greater the advantages of vertical integration.
- The greater the number of capabilities that must be developed, the greater the benefit from outsourcing. Developing capabilities can be expensive and uncertain in terms of outcomes. Thus, to reduce costs and uncertainty outsourcing might be preferred.
- The more that innovation is needed, the more likely it is that outsourcing has advantages over vertical integration.

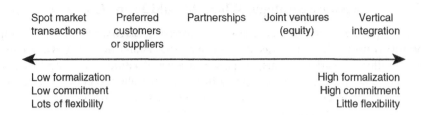

Figure 7.4 Options for Managing Vertical Integration Relationships

(Sometimes this is called *outsourcing R&D*). In each of these cases, the firm is deciding how much of the process (from concept to consumption) it wants (or can afford) to control.

Table 7.2 has a list of items to consider for vertical integration (vs. outsourcing the activities). This table shows that each decision has tradeoffs; also, certain situations are more conducive to one form of operating over another. For example, the table is clear that when only one or two firms produce inputs for a firm's products, the firm may be subject to a hold up (i.e., the supplier can charge a premium for the needed input). Under this situation, without effective contracts, a purchasing firm might consider producing the inputs instead of buying them.

One way to think about vertical integration is to consider different types of vertical relationships. We could place these relationships on a continuum. Figure 7.4 shows the various options available to firms. At one extreme, with a relatively low degree of formalization and low degree of commitment, the firm is buying items on the spot market (meaning the cash or physical market where prices are settled in cash on the spot at current market prices, as opposed to forward prices). This transaction-based purchase is a singular, independent purchase and does not commit the firm to future purchases. At the other extreme is complete vertical integration, which brings all activities within the firm. This complete integration creates a high degree of commitment.

Choosing the optimal vertical relationship for a firm requires the consideration of numerous factors in addition to those listed in Table 7.2. Most important are the following:

Allocation of Risk

How is risk spread by the firm and its market arrangements? Much of the risk depends on the bargaining power of the partner and on the efficiency of the relationship. For example, contracts offset risks by assigning responsibilities and expectations, and they are actively negotiated among partners. In the case of joint ventures, managers spend considerable time determining who will run the joint venture, how investment decisions will be made, who gains rewards, and various other daily decisions that contribute to the joint venture's success or failure. Because contracts have varying levels of risk (and each situation has unique factors), some are best formed as fixed-price contracts—others are best as performance-based.

Resources, Capabilities, and Strategy

What opportunities does a firm have in light of its competencies? Within the same industry, different companies will choose different vertical integration arrangements based on their particular resources, capabilities, and strategies. (See Appendix 9.1 and the description of the lumber business for examples of this difference.)

Incentives

How can arrangements be formed to provide incentives for people to behave according to the interests of the owners? This issue is most prevalent for firms that are vertically integrated along every aspect of the value chain. As a vertically integrated company usually has many disparate parts, it can be challenging to get all employees to act in accordance with the company's values and standards. Also, a firm that outsources all activities has to provide incentives for all of the market relationships to perform to its values and standards.

Thus, there are two key questions to frame the issue of vertical integration:

1   What types of activities will a firm undertake internally (and what will it outsource)?
2   How does a firm design vertical relationships with both external and internal suppliers and buyers?

These decisions are strategic, meaning they impact where a firm will compete and how it will compete. Firms within a given industry would make different decisions based on transaction costs, resources, capabilities, strategy, allocation of risk, and ability to design incentives for performance.

Vertical integration decisions are made about a specific market space; however, what if a firm decides to enter a variety of market spaces? What if it wants to enter adjacent spaces and diversify its businesses? How does it create a firm-level strategy that involves various business strategies? To answer these questions, the next section presents information on diversification and ways for firms to decide on their parenting advantage.

Diversification

Diversification occurs when a firm enters into new markets (e.g., international markets) with existing or new products or services. A firm's decision to diversify rests primarily on deciding whether or not to enter a particular market. This entrance decision requires the same analyses used in business strategy. Managers of a diversified firm must decide if operating in multiple businesses assists the firm in gaining competitive advantages.

General opinion toward diversification has shifted through time. Several periods in the U.S. economy, for example, saw several large companies diversifying for all sorts of reasons. After 1980, diversification trends declined. Companies had a tendency to shed noncore businesses.[24] This trend was prevalent in Europe, as well.[25] These changes occurred as a result of the increased focus on shareholder wealth, turbulence and transaction costs, and trends in management thinking.[26]

The motives for diversification fall generally into two major areas: growth and risk mitigation. In the absence of diversification, firms tend to grow only as much as their existing industries will afford; thus, some firms diversify to gain additional revenue. For example, Levi Strauss produced jeans for men, and it expanded to produce jeans for women and children (using its product manufacturing capacity). Google's expansion into the smart grid and even the development of cars is yet another example of diversification.

Some firms try to reduce risk by diversifying. They reason that if cash flows of different businesses are imperfectly correlated, then bringing them together under one owner reduces the variance of the combined cash flows. For example, while housing might do poorly when interest rates are high, investment bankers might do well. So, a firm might want to enter these two markets to ensure that at least one of these businesses is producing positive cash flows. Yet, the likelihood that one firm has capabilities in both businesses might be low at best. This reasoning is clearly straightforward for investors who can diversify their portfolios; however, the reasoning is less straightforward for companies. Acquiring other firms incurs high costs and usually involves paying a premium on the market value.

There are several different preferred rationales for diversification. The general rationale is that companies create economies of scope (a topic discussed earlier in this chapter). Economies of scope exist when cost reductions (or other benefits) are realized from producing multiple products. For example, food manufacturers investing in healthy ingredients might be able to leverage these ingredients across multiple food products. This rationale is not unlike economies of scale (i.e., cost efficiencies gained from producing a single product). Economies of scope come from tangible resources (e.g., distribution channels, research laboratories, and common technologies). Microsoft's bundling of software is an excellent example of economies of scope; in fact, it was so successful that government officials and competitors challenged Microsoft for its apparent monopolizing of certain product markets.[27]

An expected diversification comes with electric utilities. They will naturally extend into various sources of energy. Electrabel, Belgium's largest electricity group, announced in mid-2015 that they would build 25 new turbines in Belgium. This represented a €400m investment, half by Electrabel and by its partners, such as municipalities and the rail infrastructure authority Infrabel. This type of investment is happening all over the world by electric utilities diversifying their energy sources.[28]

Intangible resources (e.g., brands and knowledge) can offer economies of scope; organizational capabilities and competencies can also be transferred within the diversified firms. These same results could be achieved by other means, for example through licensing and franchising. Additional rationales for diversification can come from emerging markets and private equity firms. In the case of emerging markets, some firms argue that they can create more efficient internal markets than the available external markets. This argument is particularly salient in emerging markets, which reflect transactional arenas where buyers and sellers are not easily or efficiently able to come together; they have institutional voids that make for high transaction costs and operating challenges.[29]

As demonstrated, there are many reasons for diversification; regardless of how a company attains it, the bottom line is that the diversified product or service increases the value of a firm. However, sometimes even a profitable diversification strategy can result in conflict within the firm. For example, newer businesses tend to get more management attention and resources than older, more established businesses. This attention may be necessary to ensure new business success.

One way that firms can test their diversification motive is to ask three basic questions:[30]

1 Are the industries chosen for diversification attractive (or capable of being made attractive)?
2 Is the cost of entry such that future profits are possible?
3 Will the new unit gain competitive advantage under the new corporation (realizing the parenting advantage)?

The third question is essential as it challenges the long-term profitability and success of the venture. Companies can enter unattractive industries and still acquire unusual returns due to their competencies; however in some cases, they can destroy the value of the acquired companies (e.g., when Exxon bought furniture and consumer goods companies). In other cases, value is enhanced such as when VF Corporation, an apparel company, bought various brands that afforded it great market share in clothing (and the ability to leverage manufacturing and distribution channels).

Ultimately, it is how firms develop their strategies for diversification that can add value to the firm; thus, what works for one company might not work for another. Philip Morris, which specialized in tobacco, diversified away from its core business after anticipating that the cigarette industry would decline in the future. Philip Morris decided to diversify its product offerings and looked for acquisitions of unrelated products to decrease dependence on the future of tobacco.[31] In 1989, its tobacco products accounted for 40 percent of sales, food products accounted for 51 percent, and beer accounted for 8 percent.[32] The company is now a subsidiary of Altria.

Prolific research on diversification has resulted in inconsistent findings and, in most cases, little evidence of the benefits from diversification. Higher levels of diversification seem to be related to lower profitability.[33] Even in different institutional environments during relatively stable periods (as well as during recessions), diversification negatively impacts performance in more developed institutional environments while improving performance in the least developed environments.

Institutional voids refers to the absence of market intermediaries;[34] thus, emerging markets are those where specialized intermediaries are absent or poorly functioning. This definition implies that every market is emerging in some sense; however, markets where capital markets, labor markets, and product markets are less well-functioning than others are labeled "emerging." For example, some firms believe that their internal labor market is more efficient than the external labor markets; thus, they draw on their own employees when looking for management talent for new business ventures (instead of looking in the marketplace).

In emerging markets, firms diversify to substitute for the lack of external market efficiencies. Firms such as TATA and BIRLA in India, Wampoa of Hong Kong, and Carso of Mexico show high returns and are highly diversified where "relatedness" is hard to determine. In other words, they have vast arrays of types of companies under their ownership; the only common element is the name of the company.[35]

Private equity firms can reduce transaction costs of external capital markets. These firms raise money into a fund that is then used to buy businesses. This technique lessens the need to raise money each time a firm wants to make a transaction. These firms are unique in their structures and operations (aligning incentives with owners). Private equity firms close their money-raising at one point and thus need to make the best use of their existing capital. The major payouts for managers and owners are when the businesses are sold. Thus, this incentive causes managers to do their best to maximize returns.

Another way that firms can best realize returns from diversification is to stick with what they do best. Several researchers have found that companies that diversify into businesses closely *related* to their core activities were significantly more profitable than those that pursued unrelated diversifications;[36] however, the meaning of *related* and *unrelated* is determined by the individual firm. Some relatedness might come from operational areas (e.g., common distribution and manufacturing); however, relatedness can also come from strategic areas such as application of common competencies and resources. Operational relatedness is relatively easy to identify (e.g., exploiting common inputs); strategic relatedness is more difficult to identify. For example, General Electric claims that the firms it manages are better off with GE because of GE's capability to manage large businesses. This type of logic has been termed "dominant logic" or "mental model" and refers to managers' cognition of the rationale unifying different parts of the company.[37]

A firm is more likely to diversify into a new business when its existing business lines can potentially share more inputs with the new business; however, a firm is less likely to diversify when its existing business lines are complex and unique. Importantly, the firm's likelihood of diversifying into a new business decreases when its existing business lines do not share inputs with the new business. These results suggest that increasing coordination costs counterbalance the potential synergistic benefits associated with related diversification.[38]

Firms that do diversify tend to constantly question the value of the "parent." *Parenting advantage* comes from the resources and general management skills possessed by the parent company, holding company, or corporate center. Some researchers argue that *all* of the advantage from diversification comes from the parenting advantage since this is where the true management of the diverse businesses is accomplished.[39] Yet, some managers within companies complain that the "parent" puts too many restrictions on its associated businesses.

Major issues with diversification include whether or not the diversified businesses add value. Research shows that value-added comes usually from relatedness (i.e., from businesses within a firm that complement each other). Also, value can come from the parent of all businesses if that parent acts in a manner that adds value to all businesses. (The next section shows how firms map out their diversified businesses to make decisions about value-added outcomes.)

Portfolio Analysis

In the case of diversified or large companies, managers have a daunting task of keeping track of the firms' myriad activities, in addition to making decisions about what businesses to buy, sell, or hold. Portfolio planning methods help to show individual businesses within a company in a single graphic representation using a pictorial map. The most common representation is to form a bivariate map using two dimensions: *industry attractiveness* and *company capability*.

In the GE/McKinsey matrix (see Figure 7.5), industry attractiveness is defined by a combination of *market size, market growth rate, market profitability, cyclicality, inflation recovery*, and *market potential*. Business unit competitive advantage (or company strength) is a combination of *market share, return on sales* (relative to competitors), and *relative position* (in regard to areas such as distribution, marketing, costs, and technology).[40]

In Figure 7.5, there are five different business units plotted on the matrix. The business unit in the upper left quadrant is a clear winner in terms of being positioned in a highly attractive market and having high

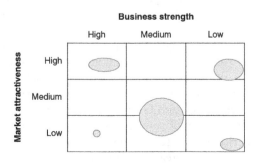

Figure 7.5 Sample GE Nine Cell Matrix for Portfolio Planning

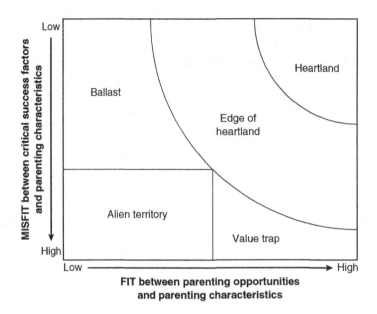

Figure 7.6 Ashridge Portfolio Technique

business strength. However, the business unit in the lower right hand corner is a candidate for harvesting; it is in an unattractive market and the firm is not strong in the unit. Although this example is simplified for the sake of the illustration, it shows how a firm can plot its various businesses to obtain information about the value of each of its units. This analysis often leads to strategy implications (i.e., whether to invest, hold, or harvest a particular business). These analyses are useful for picturing the entire company on one analytical framework and to determine relative tradeoffs when there are scarce investment funds.

A similar matrix is the Boston Consulting Group's Growth-Share Matrix. This matrix uses a single indicator for each dimension; *industry attractiveness* is the rate of market growth and *competitive advantage* is relative market share. The four quadrants of this matrix are often labeled with a "question mark" for high market growth and low relative market share, "stars" for high market growth and high relative market share, "dogs" for low market growth and low relative market share, and "cash cows" for high relative market share and low growth rates. This approach to strategy has some benefits; however, it is often flawed because market share can be gained unprofitably. Also, the analysis suggests that "cash cows" should be milked rather than given further investment; however, cash cows may be continued sources of profitability if they gain investment (for updating products and services). Thus, Boston Consulting Group's Growth-Share Matrix might be too simplistic to be used effectively.[41] A cynic would call this approach the animal farm analysis of strategy.

The Ashridge Portfolio Display takes into account the value-creating potential of the parent.[42] The focus is on the fit between a business and its parent company (see Figure 7.6). The vertical axis is "potential for value destruction from a misfit" and the horizontal axis is "potential for parent to add value to the business."[43] The analysis then results in various designations such as "value trap," "ballast"—the potential for adding value is seldom realized because of problems of management fit, or high fit but limited potential to add more value. These situational designations may lead to strategic decisions about harvesting, holding, or investing.

Creating value from a portfolio of businesses is often a difficult management task requiring analysts and managers to make tradeoffs using qualitative data. The Ashridge analysis is probably the most subjective, while the Boston Consulting Group (BCG) and GE matrices are a little more quantitative.

Organizations have an infinite number of ways to increase the effectiveness of each business within a corporate portfolio. Yet, managers tend to use a common set of tactics to increase the effectiveness of all businesses. Many of these tactics relate to increasing information flow and transference of skills. I will cover a few of these common tactics in the following section.

Methods for Increasing Corporate Effectiveness

One major challenge with managing a portfolio of businesses is creating a strategy decision process that balances the decentralized nature of individual businesses with a coordinated strategy across all of a firm's businesses. Top management spends considerable time balancing business-level autonomy with corporate-level guidance and discipline.

Strategic planning is one mechanism for achieving this balance; this planning includes collecting data about each individual business and aggregating it for decision making. Strategic planning has been widely criticized for various reasons. Included in the list of criticisms are:

1   The process is ineffective for formulating strategy because of the tendency toward rigid cycles, preoccupation with business-level plans, and insufficient corporate-level planning.
2   Planning systems tend to emphasize strategy formulation in lieu of strategy execution.[44]
3   Planning systems have an inherent assumption that the more formalized the plan, the better it is for directing the business. This preoccupation with formalization gives a false sense of security that the data are accurate and that the process should be maintained (even when the need for change is evident).[45]
4   Planners believe they can predict the future. For example, plans are often formalized using net present value (which forces the analyst to predict future cash flows). The myth is that this prediction, coupled with formalization, can provide managers and analysts with *certainty* about the future.
5   Planners push for objectivity and deny the subjective judgments of key managers. The lack of recognition of subjective data often deletes potentially valuable ideas and information that cannot be communicated in specific data points.
6   Planning takes so much time that managers are often preoccupied with getting the plan done (to the detriment of managing the business).[46]

These are just a few of the criticisms levied against formal strategic planning processes. Some companies have overcome the negative tendencies of strategic planning by emphasizing financial controls over planning; this emphasis tends to focus on business-level strategy formulation and short-term outcomes. Also, a firm may opt to be a holding company (with many businesses across a wide range of industries and little attempt at coordination).

Another means of modifying planning processes is to make them more flexible and less formalized (e.g., the utilization of frequent updates and ranges of outcomes, vs. specific targets or data points, increases a firm's flexibility). A viable mechanism for managing multiple businesses is *corporate services*. Corporate services are staff members who are nonspecific to a particular business; instead, they provide the same services to all businesses within a corporation. These include corporate management functions and business-level services (e.g., planning, purchasing, legal services, information technology, government relations, and internal audit). Many companies find this to be a cost-effective provision of these services, i.e., cheaper than can be obtained in the market.

The tendency of the corporate management unit to meld with shared services has been found to be inefficient; therefore, these are separated. For example, many multinational companies require their corporate management to share best practices across businesses as well as to help coordinate the activities of large customers across businesses. The effectiveness of these managers is determined by how well they can share information. On the other hand, shared services are measured against their efficiencies vs. market prices. A common difficulty with shared services is *transfer prices* (i.e., how to charge specific businesses for services provided). Business unit managers often argue that they can gain the same services more cheaply in the market.

Another means of managing across businesses is for managers to share skills, resources, and capabilities.[47] Creating value by sharing skills, resources, and capabilities requires that these activities are applicable to different businesses, and that they can be transferred in a manner that will provide returns on the investments. For example, a common practice is to use people to act as transfer agents (e.g., when domestic managers are asked to lead foreign operations). Providing education within a firm serves a similar function and is a notable part of many companies' strategies. Corporate management plays a critical role in transferring these skills, participating in strategy formulation and implementation across businesses, and in providing information so that unit managers can learn about best practices.

Some companies have attempted to adopt a unifying theme to guide business units. For example, Burt's Bees has stated that care of the environment guides all of its diverse products; 3M has stated that its core capabilities revolve round "things that stick." These common theme approaches are yet another way to unify diverse products units. (Chapter 5 contained information on a common set of principles that can be used to create this coherence across business units.)

A final means of managing multi-business organizations is to reach beyond incremental strategy initiatives to periodic corporate restructuring. This approach could be guided by a systematic approach to analyzing the potential for increasing the market value of a multi-business company through corporate restructuring.

The steps in this restructuring, as recommended by McKinsey & Co., are as follows:[48]

1   The starting point of the analysis is *current enterprise value*, which includes equity plus the value of debt. This value equals the net present value of anticipated cash flows over the life of the company.
2   The second step suggests that value can be improved by increased communication about the company (a point we will explore in depth in Chapter 8).
3   A third move is to increase value through internal improvements by reducing costs or increasing efficiencies.
4   A fourth move is to explore whether or not the current businesses are more valuable to other owners. A buyer might be able to add more value than the current business owner.
5   Fifth, where will the company find growth?

These steps form a process for value creation and are the constant preoccupation of corporate management. The ability to manage value is an essential part of developing sound corporate and business strategies.[49]

Profile: In for the Long Haul[50]

Chapter 7 explains how environmental sustainability can enhance an organization's competitiveness. In the automobile industry, the growing demand for alternative fuel-based vehicles has caused many automakers to enter multiple markets. Through the use of various technologies, automakers are pursuing different strategies to offset their CO_2 emissions and increase their competitiveness. Honda, Hyundai, and Toyota are all chasing fuel cell technology and a hydrogen economy.[51] Their strategies consist of plans to offset CO_2 throughout their vehicles' lifespans. Audi is taking a different approach by reducing their CO_2 footprint during production. The company, in partnership with Joule Unlimited, develops synthetically engineered bacteria to create e-fuel.[52] After being exposed to sunlight, the bacteria inhale CO_2 and hydrogen and secrete fuel.[53] The byproduct is either ethanol or alkanes which are key ingredients in diesel.[54]

Another one of Audi's e-fuels is called e-gas. In Werlte, Germany, the company owns the world's first industrial-scale power-to-gas plant which produces synthetic methane in a two-part process.[55] Wind turbines create a surplus of electricity used to split water into oxygen and hydrogen; a process known as electrolysis. CO_2 is then combined with the hydrogen to produce e-gas. The production of the company's A3 Sportback model offsets exactly as much CO_2 as the vehicle will later emit during operation.

Each strategy has unique and shared challenges. Honda, Hyundai, and Toyota are faced with the challenge of lowering costs and implementation. Pure hydrogen cannot be used in current infrastructure and is expensive to transport, unlike Audi e-gas which is fed into existing natural gas lines. Furthermore, a hydrogen economy is also dependent upon the energy efficiency of fuel cells which are needed to create electricity. Albeit, Audi e-gas still emits harmful pollutants whereas the combustion of hydrogen does not. In the U.S., the Department of Energy has been working on making hydrogen and fuel cell technologies more feasible. The agency's R&D efforts "have reduced high-volume manufacturing costs for automotive fuel cells by more than 35 percent since 2008 and more than 80 percent since 2002, while doubling their durability."[56]

Driving Success. Combined efforts between the public and private sectors are transforming the market of fuel cell vehicles and increasingly making a hydrogen economy more attractive. Although Audi has had success in Europe, their e-fuels-based vehicles have not successfully penetrated the U.S. market. With the challenges in mind, which strategy do you think is most competitive? In an attempt to commercialize fuel cell vehicles, Toyota released 5,680 patents to rival automakers.[57] Why is it more beneficial for Toyota to share information? Which technology-driven strategy, if any, will be the first to commercialize?

Smart Grid: An Excellent Example of Diversification

To illustrate many of the points in this chapter, I will use an example that is popular in many energy markets: the development of the smart grid. This term has had many meanings; in essence, it is the combining of time-based prices with technologies that enable users and providers to automatically control the use of electricity. The smart grid is a marrying of information technology with the electricity system.

The smart grid has many benefits. It can lower the overall costs of electricity, give more control to users, provide data on electric systems that can be used to innovate, and potentially promote a cleaner environment by using existing capacity more efficiently. The smart grid's development will involve various companies, each adopting various strategies. Some companies will be low-cost providers and develop appliances that can be used in various parts of the smart grid; others will provide devices that can help consumers manage home-based electricity use. Some companies will choose to be system integrators; others may vertically integrate to control the most lucrative parts of the smart grid.

New players will enter, and major technology firms will generate new smart grid technologies; these technologies will provide faster and better monitoring of our power lines, help forecast reliability problems before they occur, and provide diagnostics that are only dreamed about today.[58] The upstream impacts of the smart grid will be a reduced likelihood and severity of blackouts and more efficient operations. The downstream benefits for end users include how they control their power use.

Some observers believe the smart grid will go through a stage of exaggerated hype before it takes hold.[59] Much of the development will depend on public policy and clarity of pricing in addition to technology development.

Data analytics and seamless integration are all business opportunities with the smart grid. Companies will participate in this development in various ways, using strategies explained in this chapter. Existing incumbents will be challenged like never before with the entrance of new players, and the utility industry will likely change its behavior and partner with consumers (as these end users now have some control over the grid).

The smart grid could be the biggest development in environmental sustainability over the last 100 years. It also could set the precedent for other resources (e.g., how we handle water and waste). While the strategy principles are stable, the industries that use them are *not* stable. Companies that play in this risky game will find that technologies will change rapidly, market entrance and exit will occur often, and winners and losers will not be obvious. To play this game, firms will need many ways to offset risk. Chapters 10 and 11 will be most useful in helping managers to identify and use risk-mitigation tactics.

Chapter Summary

This chapter describes *business* and *corporate* strategy. Business strategy is concerned with *how* firms compete, and corporate strategy looks at *where* firms compete. A firm does not have to choose between these two strategies; instead, they provide managers with two different methods for developing competitive advantage. Managers will spend a significant amount of time analyzing and developing these strategies.

Two business strategy methods that are commonly used by organizations are low-cost and differentiation. When a firm follows a low-cost strategy, it can defend its market position by cost control. This strategy is effective when a firm faces increased competition, the product line becomes more of a commodity, or a firm must fight to maintain its competitive advantage. A firm follows a differentiation strategy when it wants to charge a premium for a product or service.

When firms have multiple product or service lines, they develop a corporate strategy, which defines not only how to play in a market but also the markets that a firm should play in; these decisions are aided by portfolio analyses. Also, top management must discover ways to increase value across businesses using techniques such as planning and knowledge transfer.

Case Revisited: The Future of Rohner and Their Products

Rohner Textil AG created a very successful product that sold widely. The Climatex® LifecycleTM was also a differentiated product that met strict standards and appealed to customers who wanted an environmentally friendly product.[60] It took Rohner about seven years to develop the material, and they realized that they were unique in their ability to produce a 100 percent safely biodegradable fabric. Despite this opportunity to have a truly unique product, they felt that, in the spirit of true sustainability, they would share their ideas with companies in the industry.[61]

This story is interesting because it clearly illustrates a differentiated product; however, it requires high costs to design and manufacture. A firm must consider every aspect of the value chain, and they need to determine whether such an innovation truly creates a competitive advantage. Rohner could argue that it now has a platform for generating new products; it has built a reputation for environmentally sustainable products in the textile industry. Yet, if the company cannot leverage the fabric's success, it might find that it will be challenged to generate future profits.

Terms to Know

Cost advantage: when one firm has an ability to control costs more efficiently than competitors

Differentiation: trying to find a positioning in a market (and support for that positioning) that is unique

Diversification: when a firm extends its products and services to different markets (these are decisions about what businesses a firm will be in)

Economies of scale: the number of a product that needs to be produced to achieve maximum returns

Value chain: chain of events from inputs to customer purchase of a product (and the relative costs and benefits of each stage of the process)

Vertical integration: a firm's ownership of vertically related activities (the greater a firm's ownership extends over successive stages of the value chain, the greater the degree of its vertical integration)

Profile: The War behind the Wall[62]

Looking at the Strategy Model, it is easy to see how important business and corporate strategies are to the success of the firm. Diversification is one method used to gain competitive advantage and reduce potential risks. When a firm decides to diversify they are also deciding to enter a new market. Trends in diversification have fluctuated over time, but the acquisitions of smart grid technologies by giant tech-firms, like Google's acquisition of Nest, suggests that a new era of diversification is well in-effect.

Corporations and businesses are ardently battling for position in the growing smart grid market. The U.S. Department of Energy estimates that the true value of the smart grid market will be $100 billion by 2020.[63] That's an attractive figure; however, the major incentive is the estimated 400 percent increase in Western countries' electricity prices in the next 30 years without smart grid technology. Needless to say, there has been an explosion of public and private investment into smart grid technologies.

The market consists of a large amount of household commodities that are now capable of internal monitoring, customized preferences, and communication with the larger network to maximize efficiency. However, smart grid technology has major commercial and industrial market applications as well. Eight out of the 25 companies highlighted by Bloomberg Business as companies to watch in 2015 were either smart grid products or services.[64] In December 2014, Forbes also released a list of 10 energy analytics companies to watch.[65] One such company, Fat Spaniel Technologies provides data-driven software products that manage renewable energy industries. In 2010, the company was acquired by a power inverters provider, Power-One, Inc.

Not all smart grid firms are finding it more advantageous to be acquired. Silver Spring Networks and GridPoint, instead, have both acquired companies. Silver Spring Networks delivers an open, standards-based networking software platform that can be used by "major utilities and cities worldwide to support multiple smart grid and smart city applications and services on a single, unified network."[66] On January 7, 2015, the firm announced that it had entered into an agreement to acquire utility data analytical solutions provider Detectent, Inc.[67] In a similar move GridPoint acquired several companies between 2008 and 2009. GridPoint, like other smart grid products and services, offers comprehensive, data-driven energy management solutions.[68] GridPoint also provides an aesthetic and streamlined interface for their customers. On their website, the company has a dashboard that monitors their total kWh reduced, energy costs saved, and pounds of CO_{2e} eliminated in real time.[69]

Into the Fray. One core question is why don't electric utilities dominate this "behind the wall" market? They have customer relationships, know a great deal about their customers, and have regulatory power on their side. Many U.S. utilities are monopolies. If electric utilities want to dominate the market should they acquire firms that enter this smart grid market or should they go it alone? At the least, what criteria would you suggest for this "make" or "buy" decision?

Questions and Critical Thinking

1 Some managers believe that they should follow a differentiation or low-cost strategy, but not both; they believe that each strategy demands unique sets of competencies. Other managers believe that they can pursue *both* low-cost and differentiation strategies. What do you think? Can firms support only one or the other type of strategy or can they do both? Support your ideas with specific examples of firms.

2 A common strategy when entering new markets is to enter using the most flexible organizational structure possible. If the market becomes more productive then firms can escalate their commitments (e.g., firms can sell into a foreign market and follow that with a joint venture as a means of escalating commitment). What criteria should a firm use to make these decisions?

3 Managing a portfolio of businesses can be tricky. One major decision is to harvest a business that is medium strength in a low market attractiveness situation. When might a firm want to maintain its ownership in a business such as this? Are there situations when even a very low strength and low market attractiveness business might still be valuable to a corporation?

4 Should homeowners be hesitant to allow electric utilities to monitor their homes constantly? The smart grid has the potential of helping everyone save money; however, monitoring homes could mean that public utilities have data on homeowners that might violate privacy. For example, the utility will know when a person is at home, which appliances are being used, and even collect data on visitors to the home. What ways can our society allow the smart grid to operate yet protect consumer privacy?

Notes

1 J. York and A. Larson, *Rohner Textiles: Cradle-to-Cradle Innovation and Sustainability*, University of Virginia Case Study UVA-ENT-0085 (Chesapeake, VA: Darden Publishing, 2006). Also available at www.iehn.org/publications. case.rohner.php (accessed December 15, 2015).

2 W. McDonough and M. Braungart, *Cradle to Cradle: Remaking the Way We Make Things* (New York: North Point Press, 2002), 165–186.

3 Ibid., 4.

4 C. Steitz, "China's Solar Elite Warns Duties Will Hurt Everyone," Reuters, June 13, 2012, www.reuters.com/article/2012/06/13/china-eu-solar-idUSL5E8H83RL20120613 (accessed June 13, 2012).

5 See WTO rules on trade: World Trade Organization (WTO), "Principles of the Trading System," www.wto.org/english/thewto_e/whatis_e/tif_e/fact2_e.htm (accessed August 30, 2013).

6 J. Scheck and J. S. Lublin, "Investors Rebel Against H-P Plan," *The Wall Street Journal*, August 20, 2011, 1–2.

7 M. Venzin, *Building an International Financial Services Firm: How Successful Firms Design and Execute Cross-Border Strategies* (New York: Oxford University Press, 2009).

8 J. Mandel, "2 Studies Target Sticking Points, Gaps in Life-Cycle Calculations of Biofuels," Greenwire, February 10, 2011, http://www.nytimes.com/gwire/2011/02/10/10greenwire-2-studies-target-sticking-points-gaps-in-life-69552.html?pagewanted=all (accessed November 29, 2014).

9 F. Consoli et al., "Guidelines for Life Cycle Assessment: A Code of Practice," in Proceedings of SETAC Workshop in Sesimbra, Portugal (1993); ISO, *ISO 14040:2006: Environmental Management—Life Cycle Assessment—Principles and Frameworks* (Geneva: International Organization for Standardization, 2006).

10 McDonough and Braungart, *Cradle to Cradle*, 103–115. Also, see W. McDonough and M. Braungart, *The Upcycle: Beyond Sustainability—Designing for Abundance* (New York: North Point Press, 2013).

11 M. E. Porter, *Competitive Advantage: Creating and Sustaining Superior Performance* (New York: Free Press, 1985), 120.

12 Ibid.

13 J. Seabrook, "Snacks for a Fat Planet," *The New Yorker*, May 16, 2011, www.newyorker.com/reporting/2011/05/16/110516fa_fact_seabrook (accessed June 15, 2011).

14 M. Esterl and V. Bauerlein, "PepsiCo Wakes Up and Smells the Cola," *The Wall Street Journal*, June 28, 2011, B1.

15 M. E. Porter, *Competitive Advantage*, 124–126.

16 T. H. Davenport, M. Leibold, and S. Voelpel, *Strategic Management in the Innovation Economy* (Germany: Publicis, 2006), 248–286.

17 Chicago AMA, Dictionary, https://www.ama.org/resources/Pages/Dictionary.aspx?dLetter=B (accessed December 20, 2015).

18 K. L. Keller, *Strategic Brand Management: Building Measuring and Managing Brand Equity*, 3rd ed. (Upper Saddle River, NJ: Pearson/Prentice Hall, 2008), 5.

19 D. Holt and D. Cameron, *Cultural Strategy: Using Innovative Ideologies to Build Breakthrough Brands* (Oxford: Oxford University Press, 2010), 15.

20 *The Economist*, "Activity-Based Costing," June 29, 2009, www.economist.com/node/13933812 (accessed December 1, 2011). Also, R. S. Kaplan and S. R. Anderson, *Time-Driven Activity-Based Costing* (Boston, MA: Harvard Business School Press, 2007).

21 M. Herper, "The True Staggering Costs of Inventing New Drugs," *Forbes*, February 10, 2012, www.forbes.com/sites/matthewherper/2012/02/10/the-truly-staggering-cost-of-inventing-new-drugs/ (accessed November 1, 2012).

22 R. H. Coase, "The Nature of the Firm," *Economica* 4, no. 16 (November 1937): 386–405.

23 Adapted from R. Grant, *Contemporary Strategy Analysis*, 7th ed. (Hoboken, NJ: John Wiley & Sons, 2010), 361.

24 R. P. Rumelt, "Diversification Strategy and Profitability," *Strategic Management Journal* 3, no. 4 (October/December 1982): 359–370.

25 R. Whittington, M. Mayer, and F. Curto, "Chandlerism in Post-War Europe: Strategic and Structural Change in France, Germany, and the UK, 1950–1993," *Industrial and Corporate Change* 8, no. 3 (1999): 519–550.

26 Grant, *Contemporary Strategy Analysis*, 405–406.

27 R. Chandrasekaran, "Microsoft Attacks Credibility of Intel Exec," *The Washington Post*, November 13, 1998, www.washingtonpost.com/wp-srv/business/longterm/microsoft/stories/1998/microsoft111398.htm (accessed December 7, 2011); J. Brinkley and S. Lohr, "Retracing the Missteps in Microsoft's Defense at Its Antitrust Trial," Law Offices of C. Richard Noble, PC, June 9, 2000, www.richardnoble.com/microsoft-trial.htm (accessed December 1, 2011).

28 P. Sertyn, "Wind Energy in Belgium's Flanders Region Booms" (*De Standaard*, July 17, 2015) http://www.standaard.be/cnt/dmf20150716_01779962 (accessed August 23, 2015).

29 T. Khanna and K. Palepu, *Winning in Emerging Markets: A Road Map for Strategy and Execution* (Boston, MA: Harvard Business Press, 2010).

30 M. E. Porter, "From Competitive Advantage to Corporate Strategy," *Harvard Business Review* 65, no. 3 (May–June 1987): 46–47.

31 It acquired Miller Brewing in 1970 for $227 million; at the time, Miller was the eighth-largest U.S. brewer with a 4.4 percent market share. Philip Morris increased Miller production, introduced new lines of products (Miller Malt Liquor, Milwaukee Ale, Miller Ale), acquired Meister Brau in 1972, and, in 1975, introduced Miller Lite. By 1972 (under Philip Morris), Miller grew to the third-largest brewer; in 1980, Miller became the second-largest brewer in the United States. Today, Philip Morris Companies is a holding company with diversified product offerings: Miller Brewing, General Foods (acquired in 1985), Kraft (acquired in 1988), Oscar Meyer (acquired in 1981), and Philip Morris.

32 Adapted from Grant, *Contemporary Strategy Analysis*, 132.

33 R. M. Grant, A. P. Jammine, and H. Thomas, "Diversity, Diversification and Performance among British Manufacturing Companies, 1972–1984," *Academy of Management Journal* 31, no. 4 (December 1988): 771–801; L. E. Palich, L. B. Cardinal, and C. C. Miller, "Curvilinearity in the Diversification–Performance Linkage: An Examination of over Three Decades of Research," *Strategic Management Journal* 21, no. 2 (February 2000): 155–174; J. D. Martin and A. Sayrak, "Corporate Diversification and Shareholder Value: A Survey of Recent Literature," *Journal of Corporate Finance* 9, no. 1 (2003): 37–57.

34 K. G. Palepu and T. Khanna with R. J. Bullock, *Winning in Emerging Markets: A Road Map for Strategy and Execution* (Boston, MA: Harvard Business Press, 2010), 14–15.

35 A. Chakrabarti, K. Singh, and I. Mahmood, "Diversification and Performance: Evidence from East Asian Firms," *Strategic Management Journal* 28, no. 2 (February 2007): 101–120.

36 R. P. Rumelt, *Strategy, Structure and Economic Performance* (Cambridge, MA: Harvard University Press, 1974).

37 C. K. Prahalad and R. A. Bettis, "The Dominant Logic: A New Linkage between Diversity and Performance," *Strategic Management Journal* 7, no. 6 (November/December 1986): 485–502; M. S. Gary and R. E. Wood, "Mental Models, Decision Rules and Performance Heterogeneity," *Strategic Management Journal* 32, no. 6 (June 2011): 569–594.

38 Y. M. Zhou, "Synergy, Coordination Costs, and Diversification Choices," *Strategic Management Journal* 32, no. 6 (June 2011): 624–639.

39 M. Goold, A. Campbell, and M. Alexander, *Corporate-Level Strategy: Creating Value in the Multibusiness Company* (New York: J. Wiley, 1994).

40 McKinsey & Co., "Enduring Ideas: The GE–McKinsey Nine-Box Matrix," *McKinsey Quarterly* (September 2008), www.mckinseyquarterly.com/Enduring_ideas_The_GE-McKinsey_nine-box_matrix_2198 (accessed September 15, 2011).

41 H. Quarls, T. Pernsteiner, and K. Rangan, "Love Your 'Dogs,'" *strategy+business* no. 42 (Spring 2006), www.strategy-business.com/article/rr00030?gko=6cbfe (accessed September 14, 2011).

42 Goold et al., *Corporate-Level Strategy.*

43 A. Campbell, M. Goold, and M. Alexander, "Corporate Strategy: The Quest for Parenting Advantage," *Harvard Business Review* 73, no. 2 (March 1995): 120–132.

44 L. Bossidy and R. Charam, *Execution: The Discipline of Getting Things Done* (New York: Crown Business, 2002), 197–201.

45 H. Mintzberg, "The Fall and Rise of Strategic Planning," *Harvard Business Review* (January–February 1994): 107–114.

46 M. C. Mankins and R. Steele, "Stop Making Plans; Start Making Decisions," *Harvard Business Review* (January 2006): 76–84.

47 Porter, "From Competitive Advantage to Corporate Strategy."

48 T. Koller, M. Goedhart, and D. Wessels, *Valuation: Measuring and Managing the Value of Companies*, 4th ed. (Hoboken, NJ: John Wiley and Sons, 2005), 23–45.

49 Ibid.

50 Co-authored by Michael Aper, Master of Arts in Sustainability candidate at Wake Forest University.

51 E. Pfanner, "Toyota Accelerates Rollout of Fuel-Cell Cars," *The Wall Street Journal*, June 25, 2014, http://www.wsj.com/articles/toyota-accelerates-rollout-of-fuel-cell-cars-1403700630 (accessed December 22, 2105).

52 M. de Paula, "Audi Says Synthetic 'E-Fuel' From Microorganisms Is Better Than Gas or Diesel," *The New York Times*, January 31, 2014, http://www.forbes.com/sites/matthewdepaula/2014/01/31/audi-tests-synthetic-e-fuel-derived-from-microorganisms/ (accessed April 1, 2015).

53 U. Irfan, "Scientists Engineer Bacteria to Make Fuel from CO_2," ClimateWire, *Scientific American*, August 23, 2012, http://www.scientificamerican.com/article/scientists-engineer-bacteria-to-make-fuel-from-co2/ (accessed April 1, 2015).

54 Audi, "We Live Responsibly," http://www.audi.com/corporate/en/corporate-responsibility/we-live-responsibility/product/synthetic-fuels-Audi-e-fuels.html#fullwidthpar__ah (accessed April 1, 2015).

55 Audi, "Vorsprung durch Technik" http://www.audi.com/content/com/brand/en/vorsprung_durch_technik/stream.html (accessed on December 22, 2015).

56 Office of Energy Efficiency and Renewable Energy, "Hydrogen and Fuel Cells," U.S. Department of Energy, http://energy.gov/eere/transportation/hydrogen-and-fuel-cells (accessed April 1, 2015).

57 Toyota, "Toyota Opens the Doors and Invites the Industry to the Hydrogen Future," USA Newsroom, http://corporatenews.pressroom.toyota.com/releases/toyota+fuel+cell+patents+ces+2015.htm (accessed April 1, 2015).

58 P. Fox-Penner, *Smart Power: Climate Change, the Smart Grid, and the Future of Electric Utilities* (Washington, DC: Island Press, 2010), 197–198.

59 "Wiser Wires," *The Economist*, October 10, 2009, 73.

60 York and Larson, *Rohner Textiles: Cradle-to-Cradle Innovation and Sustainability.*

61 Ibid.

62 Co-authored by Michael Aper, Master of Arts in Sustainability candidate at Wake Forest University.

63 E. van der Meer, "2 Minute Expert Briefing: Smart Grid Technology," United States Department of Energy, 2015, https://www.smartgrid.gov/all/news/2_minute_expert_briefing_smart_grid_technology (accessed April 4, 2015).

64 A. Aston, P. Engardio, and J. Makower, "25 Companies to Watch in Energy Tech," Bloomberg Business, 2015, http://www.bloomberg.com/ss/09/07/0714_sustainable_planet/1.htm (accessed April 4, 2015).

65 H. Clancy, "10 Companies to Watch in Energy Analytics," *Forbes Tech*, December 31, 2014, http://www.forbes.com/sites/heatherclancy/2014/12/31/10-companies-to-watch-in-energy-analytics/ (accessed April 4, 2015).

66 Silver Spring Networks, Inc., 2015, http://www.silverspringnet.com/ (accessed on April 14, 2015).

67 Silver Spring Networks, Inc., "Press Releases," January 7, 2015, http://www.silverspringnet.com/article/silver-spring-networks-to-acquire-detectent-inc-a-leading-provider-of-utility-data-analytics-solutions/#.VS3XFNzF8-A (accessed on April 4, 2015).

68 GridPoint, Inc., "About GridPoint," 2015, https://www.gridpoint.com/about-gridpoint/ (accessed April 14, 2015).

69 GridPoint, Inc., 2015, https://www.gridpoint.com/ (accessed on April 14, 2015).

Part III

SUPPORT FOR STRATEGY

8

MEASURING AND REPORTING ENVIRONMENTAL STRATEGY

Goldman Sachs and GS SUSTAIN

In 2003, Goldman Sachs (the investment banking and securities firm) joined a group of investors to form the Asset Management Working Group (a United Nations Environment Program Finance Initiative) "to identify environmental and social issues likely to be material for company competitiveness in the global energy industry, and to the extent possible, quantify their potential impact on stock prices."[1] They called this initiative GS SUSTAIN. Goldman Sachs also developed its own environmental, social, and governance (ESG) framework to evaluate any company's performance.[2]

Anthony Ling, the chief investment officer of Global Investment Research at Goldman Sachs, spoke about GS SUSTAIN in 2010 to investors:

> *When we look at the magnitude of change that we believe is going to shape the world over the next quarter of a century and beyond, it's something that we have never seen before . . . If company CEOs don't get it, they are going to fail. If investors don't get it, they are going to underperform the market.[3]*

Trends indicate that our population is growing in size as well as aging, urbanization rates are increasing globally, NGOs are focusing more on companies (and their social and environmental practices), and industry structures are changing rapidly. All of this change will accelerate in the future. As Ling indicated, if companies do not learn how to respond to these kinds of changes, it could be detrimental to their rates of success. This is why Goldman Sachs thought it was important to develop more sustainable practices.

In developing GS SUSTAIN, the company integrated financial and nonfinancial information. They took the view that ESG performances were good proxies for the management quality of companies relative to their peers. They stated that performance on all three dimensions identified the companies with the ability to be sustainable.[4]

The company developed a list of more than 80 global companies (across various industries) after it utilized models to collect and analyze the data. Today, GS SUSTAIN is a unique global equity strategy that brings together ESG criteria, broad industry analysis, and ROC to identify long-term investment opportunities.

Their analysis of mature industries includes diverse sectors (e.g., energy, consumer products, and banks); in looking at companies within these sectors, they analyze the ways that they manage their social and corporate obligations, ROC, and strategic positioning relative to sector competitors. They also focus on emerging industries (e.g., alternative energy technology and biotechnology); here, they look for differentiated business models and positive exposure to fast-moving structural trends.

Chapter Overview

GS SUSTAIN is one of many company schemes that measure and report on environmental sustainability outcomes. This chapter shows how companies measure their environmental outcomes and report on their findings.

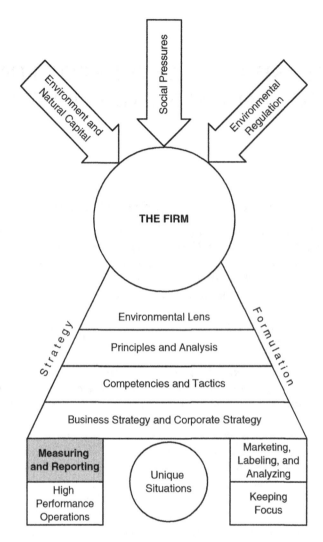

Figure 8.1 Strategy Model with an Environmental Sustainability Lens

At the end of this chapter, you should be able to:

1 specify how firms can measure whether or not they are creating value;
2 define a nonfinancial reporting method for recording a firm's environmental and social activities;
3 present a business case for a report combining financial and nonfinancial information.

This chapter includes extensive speculative material since the science and practice of measuring and reporting on environmental outcomes, related to company performance, is new and not yet standardized. However, changes are occurring rapidly and firms are increasingly paying attention to this important business function and more standardization is occurring.

Strategy as a Search for Value

Business is about searching for value from either production or services or investments. A product has value when (1) a customer assigns worth to a product or asset, and (2) this results in a profit for the producer or trader.

Goldman Sachs, as an investment firm, sees great value in maintaining a broad perspective with respect to their investments (vs. just focusing on economic returns); as a result, they take into account the social and governance performance of the companies they target for investments. This is an example of using *production* as a means of increasing value; Goldman Sachs is producing a better product by considering ESG.

Production, as a means of value creation, is one focus of this book; value is created this way by *transforming products that are less valued by consumers into products with increased value.* Companies may attain this value creation by taking raw materials (as an example) and transforming them into products used by consumers. Commerce creates production value through the arbitrage of environments (i.e., taking a product or service from one place and selling it with increased value in another place). Firms try to maintain *value-added*, which is the sales revenue from output minus the cost of material inputs (e.g., wages, interest, rent, royalties, license fees, and taxes). Gross profit must account for many material inputs, so actual value-added is sometimes difficult to obtain; however, it is critical (within this transformation) that firms try to ensure profit maximization.

Given that firms operate over time, profit maximization means maximizing the net present value of profits over the lifetime of the firm. The value of the firm is calculated in the same way as any other asset (i.e., it is the present net value of returns that the asset generates). The relevant returns are the cash flows *to* the firm.[5] The value of the firm's assets must equal the value of claims *against* those assets.[6] The discounted cash flow value of the firm is equal to the market value of the firm's securities, plus any other financial claims (e.g., debt and pension liabilities). Thus, shareholder value is calculated by subtracting the debt and other non-equity claims from the discounted cash flow value of the firm. This analysis is key for managers wanting to compare and contrast different investment opportunities and avoid a simplistic timeframe for payback of an investment. (The simplistic view does not take into account the full value of an investment because it only considers the time to get the investment back, not the total returns.)

Our strategy analysis for *maximizing value* is on a par with this. At times, stock markets are volatile; also, firm values are often difficult to determine. One big difficulty of using discounted cash flow for strategic thinking is predicting the future and correctly estimating the future cash flows that firms can realize.

Applying *enterprise value analysis* to business strategies involves several steps:

1   Identify strategic alternatives; the most straightforward way to do this analysis is to compare current strategy with possible alternative strategies.
2   Estimate the cash flows associated with each strategy.
3   Estimate the implications of each strategy for the cost of capital. (According to the risk characteristics of different strategies [and their financing implications], each strategy will have a different cost of capital.)
4   Select the strategy that generates the highest returns.

This analysis is easier on paper than in practice; the analyst needs to make all sorts of assumptions about a business's future. Also, given that we said strategy is emergent as much as it is a priori, we need to maintain flexibility in this analysis. Investments, based upon strategies, might be more appealing in the future when there is more information; the initial investment could be much more risky.

To resolve the issue of flexibility, some analysts think it is better to view strategy as a portfolio of options. An *option* is a right (vs. an obligation) to do something. Financial options, and their pricing, have been a source of much conversation among investors because they provide flexibility to investors so that they can acquire more information on the value of a security. Investors can purchase the right—but not the obligation—to invest in a particular stock.

This same logic has been applied to firms and their strategies—a field referred to as *real options*.[7] Given that the world of most companies contains a lot of uncertainty, flexibility is valuable. Instead of committing to entire projects (or strategic directions), firms break projects into phases and invest in each phase sequentially. At the end of a period of time, if the investment does not look like it will yield the expected returns, company managers can withdraw from the project (i.e., spend no further money on it).

For strategy formulation and implementation, our main interest is how we can use this logic to create firm value. Our focus is on using this logic as a means of maintaining the right to seek a strategic direction but not the obligation (e.g., many firms tend to invest small amounts in learning about emerging markets instead of making large investments in such uncertain environments). As an example, the use of real options is common in firms relying heavily on R&D as a source of competitiveness. R&D managers invest initial sums of money in various R&D projects. As the projects develop, some will look more promising than others. Management can then allocate resources to projects with more promise and less to projects with less promise. This topic is reviewed in more detail in Chapter 11.

Discounting for Natural Capital

One major challenge for sustainability thinking is how to bridge future impacts into present decision making. Managers, policymakers, and consumers are constantly making choices related to present needs and future impacts. They often ask themselves whether purchasing or investing today is better than waiting until the future.

One method discussed in this chapter for taking the future into account in present decision making is discounting. Firms apply discount rates based on a risk-adjusted opportunity cost of capital. This rate is several times higher than the social rate of time preference. Social rate of time preference is the basis of discounting in policies designed to enhance the well-being of society over time.[8] This is the rate at which society would be willing to substitute present for future consumption of natural resources. This rate is not only hard to measure when being used for decision making but calls for us to make ethical choices.

What do we owe the future? Should future people be treated equally with us and considered to have the same claim to natural resources as we do today? If we think this way, we should not put a lower weight on their utility and hence discount it. One author suggested that pure discounting is ethically indefensible.[9] This thinking leads us to act now. Not acting now to preserve natural capital would be to discount the utility of future people.

This argument brings ethical considerations into a debate about discounting which both informs it and confuses it.[10] Do we even treat all people equally in the present? No we don't. The argument is also complicated by taking into account the substitutability of nature with technology. I discussed this difference in Chapter 1 when I presented the difference between strong and weak sustainability. If we think we can substitute natural capital with other forms of capital, we are more likely to discount the future.

My stance in this book has been to consider natural capital as a form of capital and to consider how our society, at whatever level of analysis we take, can preserve that natural capital. This book attempts to show ways to invest in natural capital as a source of competitiveness. Future people matter. Their prospects are dependent on us and whether or not economic growth can be sustained. Some natural capital will be lost and we will probably have to substitute other forms of capital to preserve society's growth. Deciding on this substitution is critical. To accomplish effective decision making we must have accurate accounting of natural capital. This topic is discussed in this chapter.

Profit Maximization and Return on Capital Employed

Profit maximization is a good proxy (and reasonable assumption) for a measure of strategic effectiveness. If we extend our analysis over long periods of time, a firm's attempt to maximize profit is also a good proxy for maximizing enterprise value. However, the financial methods used to decide on strategies in the future are inherently flawed. Discounted cash flow valuation of enterprises presents challenges to estimating future cash flows. Thus, analysts will combine their financial analyses with nonfinancial information (e.g., their knowledge of industry history and trends) to make decisions about the future direction of a firm.

Once a direction is set, managers use various tools to assess a firm's attainment of its strategic goals. Public companies might use stock valuation (which represents the best-available estimate of expected cash flows in the future); however, this macro measure does *not* do a good job of diagnosing changes a company needs to make to increase cash flows (even though research shows that stock performance is a good proxy for overall firm performance).[11] To solve this problem, many companies do more in-depth analyses and adopt other measures to help them make decisions. One method is return on invested capital (ROIC) or the amount of money generated over an investment's span. "When executives, analysts and investors assess a business's potential to create value, they sometimes overlook the fundamental principle of value creation—namely that the value of a business depends on its ROIC and growth."[12] The higher a company can raise its ROIC (and the longer it can sustain a rate of ROIC greater than its cost of capital), the more value it will create. So, we should try to understand this analysis as critical to every strategic and investment decision.

Throughout this book, we have discussed sources of competitive advantage, which explain why some companies can have higher ROIC than others. Returns are driven by sources of competitive advantages that enable companies to realize price premiums, cost and capital efficiencies, or some combination of these. Industry structure or regulatory practices can also be a determinant of ROIC. Companies that find a means of being unique and making money can gain persistent returns.

Long-term revenue growth is a product of market growth and at times (at least in the short term) market share.[13] True innovation is the growth strategy with the highest potential for products and business models; however, attracting new customers to an existing product, persuading existing customers to buy more, and developing new products for existing and new customers are all ways to create additional value. One way to analyze where changes could be made to increase a company's value is to use the formula:

$$ROIC = \frac{NOPLAT\left[\text{Net Operating Profit and Loss After Taxes}\right]}{\text{Invested capital}^{14}}$$

or

$$ROIC = (1 - \text{Operating Profit Tax Rate}) \times \frac{EBITA\left[\text{Earnings Before Income Tax Added}\right]}{\text{Revenues}} \times \frac{\text{Revenues}}{\text{Invested capital}}$$

The preceding equation is one of the most powerful equations in financial analysis. It demonstrates the extent to which a company's ROIC is driven by its ability to maximize profitability (EBITA divided by revenues, or the operating margin), optimize capital turnover (measured by revenues over invested capital), or minimize operating taxes.[15]

An example can illustrate this process: Lowe's Home Improvement grew to become a formidable rival of Home Depot.[16] Figure 8.2 compares and contrasts the two companies according to their ROIC (and the components that make up this number). Both companies operate in the same basic markets and compete for roughly the same customers, yet the data in Figure 8.2 show some interesting differences in the effectiveness of their strategies.

In this example, Home Depot's ROIC lagged behind Lowe's. Why? In Figure 8.2, we see that Home Depot's operating margin was lower than Lowe's (i.e., 6.8 vs. 8.3); this lower operating margin is due primarily to Home Depot's higher selling and general and administrative expenses (SG&A) expenses. This added expense came from Home Depot's attempt to provide better customer service by adding people at its various locations. We see, however, that Home Depot's stores are probably more efficient than Lowe's since the revenues for invested capital are higher for Home Depot (vs. Lowe's). Yet, if we investigate further, we see that Lowe's has newer stores than Home Depot. This makes Lowe's operating margin more costly; however, newer stores may be more appealing to customers and, therefore, more profitable in the future.

When the new leadership entered Home Depot in 2008 they saw these challenges and mounted a set of tactics to improve ROIC. Recent outcomes show that Home Depot has improved ROIC within the last 8–10 years. Home Depot showed a 14.5 percent ROI over 10 years (2004–2014) while Lowe's showed 10.08 percent.[17]

My goal, here, is to show how this analysis can lead to many hypotheses about where to improve profitability within a company. Yet, we ultimately defer to the company's strategy when analyzing these results. This is why looking at ROIC alone is not sufficient; strategies cannot always be measured in financial terms.

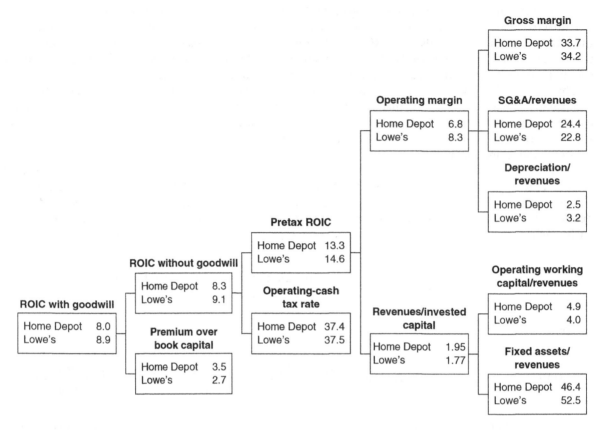

Figure 8.2 Home Depot and Lowe's ROIC Tree 2008

Additionally, firms seeking to integrate environmental strategies require unique approaches to measurement. While the ROIC of companies may point to environmental and social indicators of performance, the likelihood is that we will not find meaningful outcomes from financial analysis alone; thus, we need to do nonfinancial analyses as well. The remaining parts of this chapter will include information on this nonfinancial reporting. This chapter also provides advice about how companies can ultimately combine the two types of measures into one reporting framework.

Types of Reporting

Companies do all sorts of reporting. Sustainability reporting mainly occurs to:

- improve stakeholder relations;
- improve management of sustainability issues;
- protect the license to operate;
- enhance company reputations.

Company reporting can be categorized into internal, external mandatory, and external voluntary. Sustainability reporting largely occurs for internal purposes; however, external mandatory reporting is also done to comply with legislative mandates. The highest growth area is voluntary external reporting.[18] For example, many companies (especially in the United States and Europe) are producing CSR reports despite the lack of regulatory mandates.

Several typical internal reports can include sustainability information. For example, many companies track energy and water usage to compare various facilities on their usage patterns. Oftentimes, they will use a dashboard to capture critical success factors related to sustainability and report on these continuously; they can also use the dashboard to get a quick overview of performance. External mandatory reporting includes public disclosure requirements and the disclosure of information that is material to a firm's functioning. For example, the Emergency Planning and Community Right-to-Know Act (EPCRA) mandated annual public reporting of toxic pollutant releases that impact the environment. Many countries have national registers of environmental emissions (e.g., Poland, Japan, and the Netherlands).[19] The Communist Party in China implemented new rules on January 1, 2014 requiring over 15,000 Chinese firms to make public disclosures (some hourly) of all pollutants, heavy metals, and wastewater.[20]

NGOs compile information related to the environmental performance of companies, regions, and countries. Some of this information goes to investment clients. On a broader scale, the OECD supports the utilization of Pollutant Release and Transfer Registers (PRTRs) by its member countries. Also, several national and regional governmental organizations have developed systems to collect and disseminate data on environmental releases (and transfers) of toxic chemicals by industrial facilities. More PRTRs are under way, stimulated by the recommendations of the 1992 United Nations Conference on Environment and Development in Rio de Janeiro that affirmed the right of communities and workers to know about toxic chemicals impacting them and the need of firms to catalogue chemical inventories to meet that right-to-know. International bodies, environmental groups, industrial firms and associations, and other NGOs are involved in developing these systems.

PRTRs generally report on the releases and transfers of individual chemicals by individual industrial facilities.[21] These data are entered into a database and actively disseminated to the public. The aim is to improve environmental quality and promote cleaner technology. So little data is withheld from the public that firms are often concerned that trade secrets could be compromised. Nevertheless, this nonfinancial reporting is gaining momentum (as evidenced by Goldman Sachs' efforts to use this information for investing). Many companies are trying to find ways to collect and report on nonfinancial information. The next section captures this type of reporting in more depth.

Nonfinancial Reporting

The need for nonfinancial reporting has increased dramatically in the last two decades. This increase comes from several incentives. For example, many of a company's assets are intangible and are not shown on the company's balance sheet; also, many firms are searching for ways to communicate the environmental and social outcomes related to their performances. One challenge to nonfinancial reporting is that managers and analysts have few commonly understood (or used) definitions of nonfinancial information, given the breadth of the concept. A useful definition is a "wide-ranging term which can include both regulated and voluntary disclosure by companies. From a shareowner and investor perspective [sic], it is information, other than financial statements, which is relevant and material to investment decision making."[22]

The term "nonfinancial information" has become synonymous with CSR, sustainability and ESG performance. For our purposes, nonfinancial information refers to all information reported to stakeholders that is not defined by an accounting standard or derived from an accounting statement.[23] Nonfinancial information can be categorized into three key groups and might or might not be included in publically available reports:

1 intangible assets (including intellectual capital);
2 key performance indicators;
3 ESG.

Since 1998, several studies have shown that a firm's "book value" (i.e., worth on paper) is about 25 to 35 percent of a company's market value;[24] the remainder is attributed to intangible assets that do not appear on the balance sheet. A comprehensive study has suggested that companies consider *intangible assets* as being comprised of six categories: (1) R&D (and related intellectual property); (2) human capital; (3) advertising, brands, and related intellectual property; (4) customer loyalty; (5) competitive advantage; and (6) goodwill.[25]

Few companies currently report on intangibles in any meaningful or rigorous way. Although you can find statements about intangible assets in the Management Discussion and Analysis (MD&A) statements in annual reports, these statements are too general to be effective in evaluating a company. Several other countries do encourage organizations to report on intangible assets. For example, Austria has mandatory reporting for universities as a result of the Austrian Universities Act, administered by the Federal Ministry of Education, Arts and Culture.[26] Yet, efforts to have standardized and required reporting are still underdeveloped in most countries.

Key performance indicators (KPI) are a second category of nonfinancial information. These are metrics used by managers to implement and monitor strategy realization. One of the most well-known examples of a KPI format is the Balanced Scorecard.[27] This scorecard captures organizational performance from four perspectives: (1) financial, (2) critical business processes, (3) customers, and (4) learning and growth. These areas are associated with cause-and-effect relationships, performance drivers, and linkages to financial outcomes. The Balanced Scorecard approach has lagging indicators (financial performance and critical businesses processes) and leading indicators (customer satisfaction and learning and growth). The authors of the scorecard state that the Balanced Scorecard is designed to measure strategy and has three distinct dimensions:

1 Makes strategy the central organizational agenda. The Balanced Scorecard also requires organizations to describe and communicate their strategies in a way that can be understood and acted upon.
2 Aligns every resource and activity in the organization.
3 Provides a way to establish new organizational linkages across business units, shared services, and individual employees.[28]

The Balanced Scorecard has become a unique way to link financial outcomes with KPIs and to then link these to an organization's strategy. Figure 8.3 shows one organization's use of the Balanced Scorecard. Notice that this scorecard builds on the ROIC model we introduced earlier; however, it includes many nonfinancial measures. You can consider this a roadmap for performance in the organization. A roadmap such as this one guides managers throughout the organization to focus on specific actions.

Another KPI that has recently become popular is the Net Promoter Score (NPS). This simple yet powerful tool builds upon research that connects *profitable growth* to *customer loyalty*. This score is calculated by subtracting the percentage of customers who are detractors from those who are promoters based on one question (which is rated on a 10-point scale): *"How likely are you to recommend [x] to a friend?"*[29] This measure can be used by any organization type, including NGOs and government agencies.

ESG metrics, the third category of nonfinancial information, is key since our focus in this book is on environmental metrics. Several groups have been developing ways to measure and report on ESG including ASSET4,[30] MSCI,[31] Trucost,[32] the Society of Investment Professionals in Germany (DVFA), and the European Federation of Financial Analysts Societies (EFFAS).[33]

In contrast to intangible assets and KPIs, separate ESG and Social Responsibility (SR) reports are common for companies, particularly in Europe. One study concluded:

This increase in ESG reporting reflects the growing understanding on the part of major organizations around the world of the crucial relevance of this information not only to the financial community as it assesses [its] financial prospects but to society in general as it seeks to understand the impacts of these global firms on the environment working conditions and communities in general.[34]

Corporations use various names for this ESG category.[35] Among them are:

• financial, social, and environmental performance (Novo Nordisk);
• corporate social responsibility (Hitachi Group);

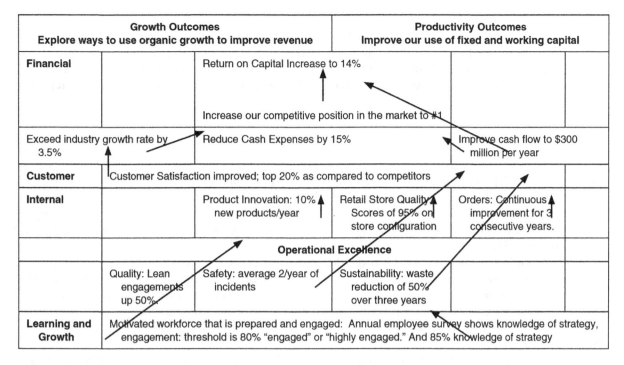

	Growth Outcomes Explore ways to use organic growth to improve revenue			Productivity Outcomes Improve our use of fixed and working capital		
Financial		Return on Capital Increase to 14%				
		Increase our competitive position in the market to #1				
	Exceed industry growth rate by 3.5%	Reduce Cash Expenses by 15%			Improve cash flow to $300 million per year	
Customer	Customer Satisfaction improved; top 20% as compared to competitors					
Internal		Product Innovation: 10% new products/year	Retail Store Quality Scores of 95% on store configuration	Orders: Continuous improvement for 3 consecutive years.		
			Operational Excellence			
	Quality: Lean engagements up 50%	Safety: average 2/year of incidents	Sustainability: waste reduction of 50% over three years			
Learning and Growth	Motivated workforce that is prepared and engaged: Annual employee survey shows knowledge of strategy, engagement: threshold is 80% "engaged" or "highly engaged." And 85% knowledge of strategy					

Figure 8.3 Sample Balanced Scorecard

- sustainability (Duke Power);
- corporate citizenship (Novartis);
- sustainable value report (BMW Group).

The rise of ESG has impacted capital markets. Some refer to this type of investing as socially responsible investing (SRI), valued at over $21 trillion.[36] This type of investing is defined as an investment that considers ESG criteria to generate returns and positive social impact. This term includes others commonly used by investors such as responsible investing, socially responsible investing, and impact investing.[37] (Chapter 12 contains more information on this type of investing.)

Accountability, transparency, and control are generally at the heart of reporting such information, which is provided by managers to those outside the organization (e.g., typically owners); formalizing reporting and regulation builds trust with information consumers. Several researchers have suggested that sustainability reporting will improve corporate behavior as long as the reporting follows agreed-upon practices for consistency, transparency, materiality, and other meaningful reporting characteristics.[38]

The Institute of Chartered Accountants in England and Wales suggested long ago that the long-term pursuit of shareholder value should be seen as closely associated with the preservation and enhancement of all types of capital.[39] Sustainability is such a concern that it must be considered at least as important as any other challenge facing businesses; thus, mandatory sustainability reporting needs to be further developed.[40]

Several organizations have dedicated their work to support initiatives on nonfinancial reporting. The International Integrated Reporting Council,[41] Climate Disclosure Standards Board,[42] International Institute for Sustainable Development[43] and the GRI are among them. I will cover just one such organization to illustrate their impact and processes. The GRI is one way to make this reporting consistent and to meet the various criteria demanded by investors. The description of this reporting process, which has gained global recognition, is the focus of the next section.

Global Reporting Initiative

The GRI is one of the most powerful and widely accepted reporting formats, and it helps set the standard for sustainability reporting. Robert K. Massie and Allen White designed its standards with the help of two U.S.-based organizations, CERES (formerly the Coalition for Environmentally Responsible Economies) and the Tellus Institute (which is supported by the UNEP). Their goal was to develop a framework for reporting sustainability information.[44]

What Is the GRI

The GRI is a network-based organization that pioneered the world's most widely used sustainability reporting framework. GRI is committed to the framework's continuous improvement and application worldwide, and its core goals include the mainstreaming of disclosure on ESG performance.[45] GRI's vision is to create a sustainable global economy with organizations managing their economic, ESG performances and impacts responsibly (which includes transparent reporting). Their mission is to make sustainability reporting standard practice by providing guidance and support to organizations.[46]

GRI's Reporting Framework has been developed via a consensus-seeking, multi-stakeholder process. Participants are drawn from global business, civil society, labor, academic, and professional institutions. Organizations register to become stakeholders with voting rights in the election of members for a Stakeholder Council (SC). The SC is GRI's formal stakeholder policy forum (similar to a parliament) that debates and deliberates key strategic and policy issues. The SC meets annually and includes various stakeholders from different geographic regions.[47]

The SC's key governance functions include approving nominations for the Board of Directors (Board) and making strategic recommendations to the Board (e.g., future policy or business planning activities). They are also the "eyes and ears" of the GRI network in their diverse locations and constituencies. Key supporting functions by individual SC members may include participating in technical working groups, advising, and actively helping to build the GRI network in their constituencies or regions. As of 2015 GRI had over 8,100 organizations represented in the GRI database of reports.[48]

The Reporting Framework sets out the principles and performance indicators that organizations can use to measure and report their economic, environmental, and social performances. The cornerstone of the Framework is the Sustainability Reporting Guidelines. Other components of the Framework include sector supplements (unique indicators for industry sectors) and National Annexes (unique country-level information). The individual indicators for economic, social, and environmental aspects of each organization come from various sources. For example, the energy indicators build on work done through the World Resources Institute and their GHG reporting formats and models.[49]

GRI Guidelines and Reports

The GRI's guidelines have several suggestions important to a complete report. The prescriptions include what should be included in a report (i.e., core and associate measures, items that reflect and influence the organization, and completeness) and the process for stakeholder involvement. Organizations are required to adhere to measurement standards such as:

- balance (positive and negative aspects of the organization);
- comparability for consistency in reporting;
- accuracy;
- timeliness;
- clarity;
- reliability.

A report that is aligned with the GRI guidelines contains four main parts:

- a section on the company's sustainability vision and strategy;
- a corporate profile;
- a section on governance structures and management systems relevant to sustainability;
- performance indicators.

The general guidelines have universal applicability (i.e., they are valid for all types of companies, irrespective of company size or industry affiliation); however, they do not account for specific sustainability challenges within different industries. Therefore, GRI working groups have created sector supplements, which are currently available for the energy utility, financial services, food processing, mining and metals, and NGO sectors. These supplements complement the general guidelines with industry-specific aspects.

GRI guidelines do not set performance goals (e.g., they do not establish CO_2 emission values that companies must achieve); they merely generate transparency in terms of current practices. In fact, the guidelines cannot set performance goals because of the very diverse nature of companies using the GRI guidelines. It is up to decision-makers in specific companies to define sustainability objectives. However, the reports contain information on reduction targets, which is often an indicator of a company's commitment to sustainability.

The previous version of the guidelines (i.e., "Third Generation [G3]") covered indicators relating to social, environmental, and economic aspects. These indicators range from material and water usage; the work force breakdown by country, region, and employment type (i.e., full-time and part-time); emissions and amount of waste; net employment creation; and average days of employee training. The current version (G4), release mid-2013, has improved on the reporting affording greater clarity and flexibility to organizations to produce quality reports.

Over 6,800 organizations filed their GRI reports in 2014 and posted them for public access.[50] The percentage of filers varies by sector. For example, only four universities submitted reports in 2014 (vs. sectors such as energy and energy utilities, which have about 250 reports). Also, the total number of reports submitted has dramatically increased over the years, as has regional representation. Fourteen organizations submitted reports in 1999 and 273 in 2005.[51] In 2010, 45 percent of these reports stemmed from Europe, followed by Asia (20 percent). Reports from North and Latin America made up 14 percent, while Africa lagged far behind with only 3 percent. However, looking at single countries, the United States accounts for 10 percent of the total number of reports worldwide. The leading European countries are Spain and Sweden, which account for 19 and 10 percent of the total number of reports in Europe, respectively.[52] These numbers have remained consistent in subsequent years.[53]

Reporting on sustainability issues can offer many advantages for companies. It is easier to track a firm's progress if it has established and published specific environmental or social targets. Also, publishing a sustainability report raises internal and external awareness of the topic. Furthermore, increased transparency can yield further credibility and reputational benefits (e.g., consumer recognition and a willingness of capital markets to provide capital to these companies).

Critiques of GRI

Users have several concerns about GRI. For one thing, the GRI stakeholder process may have become too responsive to too few stakeholder groups, thus narrowing its focus. For example, NGOs tend to be focused on specific issues such as water preservation or land conservation, and they tend to be more involved than most organizations in the design and implementation of standards. The GRI claims that this concern is unfounded as all stakeholder groups are involved equally.

Also, the GRI is not without its critics. Most firms utilizing the GRI generate documents that are separate from their general economic annual reports. While annual reports are subject to control and certification by independent third-party agencies,[54] the sustainability report is not subject to the same verification process when it is featured separately. Today, a considerable number of firms integrate sustainability reporting into their annual reports to show their honest commitments to sustainability. This, however, may deteriorate the transparency principle of the GRI, since integrated reports can no longer fully respect the GRI guidelines.[55]

Another criticism relates to the principles themselves. In an academic article published in 2006, researchers demonstrated that there was an overemphasis of the social dimension of sustainability. They found that 50 percent of all indicators were social indicators, followed by environmental (approximately 30 percent), and economic indicators (approximately 10 percent). To be truly sustainable, these indicators should be somewhat balanced. At a minimum, more indicators should be proposed for environmental sustainability.[56]

Another concern is the lack of adoption by the investment community. This industry tends to not get involved with the GRI because of the time investment required to work on standards and the concern that the GRI might not yield information relevant to their investment decisions. In general, the GRI has been challenged to demonstrate the financial relevance of their information. While some measures are related to financial outcomes (e.g., resource savings), others (e.g., diversity and social outcomes) are not as obvious. Also, organizations often find that the reported results are confusing from an investment standpoint. Given the myriad indicators, organizations are not certain where to invest to improve their sustainability. This "nonstrategic" reporting is of concern to most organizations, and it has encouraged many of them to alter their approach to the reports and include directly relevant indicators with respect to their strategies.[57]

Ultimately, some companies hesitate to publish sustainability reports because publishing reports, in general, requires significant time and money. Some large organizations, for example, have reported that as many as 100 people have been involved in the preparation of a GRI report.[58] Several organizations are also concerned that the resources involved in preparing the reports (especially data collection) provide few benefits to the organization's competitiveness. Also, publishing a sustainability report for the first time may focus attention where attention might not be wanted.

Additionally, the guidelines are constantly being updated and further developed. (The "Fourth Generation (G4)" was published in 2013.) Furthermore, so-called National Annexes are planned that customize the GRI to specific countries. As with the sector supplements, these do not take the place of the reports; they are used in addition to them, and they are to include specific country or regional issues or circumstances.

Profile: Materiality—The Core of Transparency

Information transparency is a key principle of any functioning market economy. Investors make decisions on company information disclosed in financial reports. Employees make employment decisions based on company declared information about its workplace. Customers make purchase decisions based on product information generated largely by company officials.

Regulators, stock exchange officials, investors, and customers increasingly demand nonfinancial information. These stakeholders are generating disclosure requirements or guidance for voluntary reporting so that companies can disclose information about environmental stewardship, governance, contributions to society, and KPIs.

The Sustainability Accounting Standards Board (SASB) reporting guidance for companies traded publically in the U.S. is one example of these requirements or voluntary guidance. The European Union 2014 Directive is a mandatory standard for environmental, social, and diversity company information.[59]

One critical component of all of these initiatives is to identify what is material to report. Information is material if it presents a substantial likelihood that the disclosure of the omitted fact would have been viewed by a reasonable investor as having substantially altered the total mix of information made available.[60]

Can we extend this definition to include other stakeholders? For example, can we call something material that will help communities make decisions about legislation on company actions? Can we call something material if it influences consumers or employees?

One suggested format is to take the aggregated views of the firm's perception of its role in society, because this perception determines the stakeholders it chooses to engage and stakeholder weightings. The challenge is to get a representative sample of the stakeholders.[61] Thus, the suggested method is for the firm to identify the stakeholders, their perceptions and then aggregate the perceptions as to how significant each issue is to the company.

Here is the idea: what if regulatory agencies required boards of directors to state this information (stakeholders, the material issues important to stakeholders, and the company's aggregated significance to the stakeholders for each material issue)? Could this disclosure and process be one significant step toward better disclosure and toward an integrated report as described in this chapter?

The Growth of Sustainability Reporting

So far, reporting on sustainability issues is mostly voluntary. Also, similar to financial reporting, international standards set the standard for sustainability reporting; the goal of the guidelines is to provide a framework and match financial reporting standards in terms of "rigour, comparability, auditability and general acceptance."[62] The GRI guidelines are currently the most prevalent ones worldwide with any competing system lagging far behind in terms of scope and diffusion.

Not all companies report to the same extent. Reports can be distinguished according to their application levels, which can either be self-declared by the companies or checked by the GRI. The levels (ranging from A [the highest] to C [the lowest]) indicate the number of indicators published and the scope of disclosure. A plus sign behind the level indication shows that the report content has been approved externally. We expect to see the number of corporate sustainability reports continue to grow as they have in recent years. For example, the number of reports generated in the United States has experienced steady growth over the past five years, and there is also international growth (e.g., Brazil has had an extraordinary growth rate of almost 50 percent).[63]

Calculating Various Footprints

Several organizations, municipalities—and even countries—use the metaphor of a "footprint" to capture their impact on the earth and as a way to report nonfinancial data instead of (or in addition to) using the GRI. A "footprint" is generally defined as a calculation of total impact by an entity (e.g., a person, product, or company). Associated analyses have been labeled variously: carbon footprint, environmental footprint, or ecological footprint.[64] For example, *ecological footprint analysis* compares human demand on nature with the biosphere's ability to regenerate resources and provide services; it accomplishes this analysis by using prevailing technology to assess the biologically productive land and marine area required to *produce* the resources a population consumes and then *absorb* the corresponding waste.

Footprint values are typically categorized for carbon, food, housing, and goods and services as well as the total footprint number of Earths needed to sustain the world's population at that level of consumption.[65] This categorization can also be applied to an activity (e.g., the manufacturing of a product, driving of a car, or living in a household). This analysis is similar to life-cycle analysis, wherein the consumption of energy, biomass, building materials, and other resources is converted into a normalized measure of land area. Viewing resource consumption in this way is useful when seeking to understand how much is actually being consumed.

An important analysis for organizations is the amount of CO_2 produced by a company; this is where we get the term carbon footprint. The amount of CO_2 output is important because carbon contributes to global warming (as discussed in Chapter 1). Analysis for testing carbon production can be carried out for various organizational units (e.g., departments, regions, or the entire corporation). Also, similar analyses have been carried out for cities, countries, and even individual households. A product's carbon footprint measures the CO_2 emissions at each stage of a product's life. The same analysis can be made for a service. In essence, this analysis is a specific type of life-cycle analysis.

The leading guidance and protocols for carbon analysis are:

1   CarbonTrust;[66]
2   BSI British Standards[67] PAS 2050;[68]
3   ISO 1400 series, especially 14064, 14040, 14044 and 14048l;[69]
4   WRI/WBCSD GHG Protocol.[70]

CarbonTrust is a nonprofit organization in the United Kingdom with the mission of accelerating attainment of a low-carbon economy. The organization provides specialist support to help businesses and the public sector reduce carbon emissions, save energy, and commercialize low-carbon technologies. For example, The Carbon Trust joined with the Department of Environment, Food and Rural Affairs (DEFRA) and the British Standards Institution (BSI). They formed the PAS 2050, which is a specification for the assessment of the life-cycle standardized GHG emissions of goods and services. This standard has been adopted by many organizations (e.g., it is Wal-Mart's primary standard for life-cycle analysis); to date, the organization has developed approximately 80 Product Category Rules.

One major benefit of the PAS 2050 is that it specifies Product Category Rules that could be used by all companies with similar products. Also, the standard specifies the emissions for all carbon footprint analyses including:

1   emissions resulting from all processes used in the transformation of raw material;
2   direct emissions from land-use change;
3   emissions associated with the production of consumables used during the life-cycle of the product;
4   operations such as factories, warehouses, supply centers, offices, and retail outlets;
5   storage of products and inputs (including raw materials) at any point in the product life-cycle;
6   biogenic and atmospheric carbon stored in the product.

Emissions *not* included in these analyses involve the production of capital goods used in the life-cycle of the product, human energy inputs, transport of consumers to and from the point of retail purchase, and transport of employees to and from their normal places of work.

The overall benefit of footprint analysis is that these calculations provide ways to compare and contrast various entities (e.g., organizations and their general impact on the environment). Yet, clearly much more work needs to be done before we can accurately identify specific footprints. This type of analysis tends to be more for communicating intent than accurate measurement of the impact. Would it be possible for a firm to combine all reporting to reflect the integrated information about organizational performance? The next section explores this question.

One Report

Charlotte-based Polymer Group Inc. (PGI) is a global innovator, manufacturer, and marketer of engineered materials focused on nonwoven products. The 2010 PGI Stakeholder's Report was a unique report as it combined social, environmental, and economic data in one report (vs. separate financial and ESG data reports). Veronica M. Hagan, CEO of PGI stated:

> This is PGI's first Annual Stakeholder's Report, which integrates our sustainability report, based on the Global Reporting Initiative (GRI) G3 reporting framework, with the qualitative and quantitative data from our annual report.

> This integrated report format allows PGI to communicate directly to our fellow stakeholders, employees, and customers about all areas of our business—incorporating financial reporting, organizational highlights, and sustainability initiatives in one standardized and easily accessible document.[71]

Another example is Smithfield Foods, a $13 billion global food company and the world's largest pork processor and hog producer. In the United States, the company has brands including Smithfield®, Eckrich®, Farmland®, Armour®, Cook's®, Gwaltney®, John Morrell®, Kretschmar®, Curly's®, Carando®, Margherita®, and Healthy Ones®. They introduced their report as follows:

> Welcome to the Smithfield Foods 2012 Integrated Report—our first to combine our annual financial results with our sustainability reporting. Our sustainability strategy is based on our core values and organized by five pillars that represent our key areas of sustainability focus: animal care, employees, environment, food safety and quality, and helping communities. In this summary report, we report on our progress and performance in each area. We have also identified and report on a sixth pillar—value creation—recognizing that this concept underpins our sustainability strategy and connects it with our business results.[72]

We will hopefully see greater adoption of this unique approach by firms as it has many benefits. The integrated report is a clear way to report on an integrated sustainability strategy, and it increases disclosure and transparency. Thus, the case for one report is compelling.[73] One study suggested a set of principles for sustainability reporting;[74] among the principles were:

1 fully integrated annual reports (and other corporate communications);
2 information embedded in a variety of hard copy, PDF, and web-based communications;
3 reporting, based on continuous stakeholder dialogue, linked to the business agenda (and fully reflected in the reporting).

Several organizations have suggested guidelines for one report: the International Integrated Reporting Council (IIRC), the Sustainability Accounting Standards Board (SASB), the UN-sponsored Sustainable Stock Exchanges Initiative (SSE), and the Corporate Sustainability Report Coalition (CSRC) are among the more important organizations.[75]

Despite the evidence that one report would improve transparency, little to no academic research exists on this topic. For example, while lenders need information to know if borrowers are trustworthy, few comparable guidelines exist for sustainability. One nonprofit organization, SASB, is trying to change this situation by developing standards for corporate disclosure with respect to stewardship, social policies, and corporate governance. The organization sees its primary stakeholder as the SEC.[76] The IIRC is viewed as the organization with the most promise to develop and monitor one report guidelines.[77]

Few companies are producing one report. The major criticisms for one report include:

1 The market's efficiency means there is no reason for companies to change their priorities.
2 If the benefits existed, companies would already be doing one report.
3 One report would create confusion.

Some responses to these objections are:

- Markets are not completely efficient; better information about company operations will improve capital allocation.
- Companies are not accustomed to thinking about sustainability and, until recently, the reporting procedures were not fully developed. Revealing nonfinancial information will improve management practices.
- Stakeholders do not necessarily have congruent interests;[78] a firm's ability to communicate as fully as possible about its operations is key for accommodating this diversity.

The one report concept is appealing for many reasons (despite the lack of current evidence as to its impact); among the reasons are transparency and connectivity. One report would increase transparency by detailing, in one place, information related to total company performance. More importantly, the information would enable relationships that might, in some instances, be unexpected. For example, information on new operational projects could include information related to environmental performance.

The next decade will likely see some exciting advances in this push toward one report.

Environmental Sustainability Corporate Rankings

Rankings have also resulted from the recent attention to sustainability. Various agencies, NGOs, governments, and journals have ranked companies, municipalities, regions, and countries according to their excellence in the environmental area. These rankings have been used for investment decisions, identifying best-in-class companies,[79] and identifying practices that can be used in various types of organizations.[80]

One recent ranking was *Newsweek*'s Green Rankings. It consisted of two lists—one that surveyed the 500 biggest companies in the United States and another of the 500 largest companies in the world. Both lists highlighted firms that are leading—or lagging—in environmental performance. Data were analyzed in cooperation with Trucost and Sustainalytics, two environmental-research firms that assess companies' environmental footprints (e.g., GHG emissions and water usage); management, including environmental policies, programs, and initiatives; and disclosure (e.g., via company reporting and involvement in transparency initiatives). The data were drawn from a variety of sources (including the companies) and vetted for reliability.[81]

The *Newsweek* rankings suggested that the United States was trailing other parts of the world in the sustainability arena. After IBM (No. 2 on the global list), there were 12 spots before the next U.S. company (HP, No. 15 globally). A number of European companies were in between, as well as firms from Australia, Brazil, India, Canada, Japan, and Mexico. Due largely to Europe's tighter regulatory environment, European companies tend to dominate these types of lists when they favor transparent disclosure.

IBM, in the No. 1 spot on the U.S. list, has been measuring, managing, and voluntarily reporting on its environmental impact for more than 20 years. It says it has conserved 5.4 million kilowatt-hours of electricity over that time (cutting its CO_2 emissions and saving the company more than $400 million in the process). Energy efficiency and conservation are a "business no-brainer," says Wayne Balta, a vice president who oversees sustainability at IBM. The company has extended its eco-savvy far beyond its own operations (e.g., by providing software to enable customers to identify energy-saving efficiencies in their workspaces).

So, are these rankings useful and accurate? One study shows some interesting results. It reviewed 108 of the ratings and selected 21 for deeper evaluation.[82] Table 8.1 shows the list of the 21 rating schemes it selected.

Table 8.1 Rating Schemes for Ranking Companies[83]

Access to Medicine Index[84] The Index 2010 report covers 27 pharmaceutical companies, comprising 20 originators and seven generics manufacturers. The ranking is based on 106 indicators that measure activities across four strategic and seven technical areas. The research and analysis for the Index 2010 was conducted by MSCI/Risk Metrics.

ASSET4 (Thomas Reuters)[85] provides relevant and systematic ESG information based on 250+ KPIs and 750+ individual data points along with their original data sources. Professional investors use this ESG data to define a wide range of responsible investment strategies and integrate it into their traditional investment analysis. Corporate executives (e.g., CSR and IR managers) use the corporation-focused solution to benchmark their own performance against peers and track relevant news. Quantitative analysts use the ESG data within the Quantitative Analytics solution to identify a new range of signals. Issues such as climate change, executive remuneration and employee rights are becoming as important as traditional metrics for companies and investors; that is why having access to objective and comparable database and analysis tools is so important.

Bloomberg ESG Disclosure Scores[86] brings together speakers from the U.S., Europe, and other important markets for targeted, practical discussion on pertinent themes of sustainable and responsible investment. Most importantly, it brings together practitioners from the field to debate, challenge and invigorate that discussion. Responsible Investor.com welcomes you to this year's conference.

Carbon Disclosure Project[87] was launched to accelerate solutions to climate change and water management by putting relevant information at the heart of business, policy and investment decisions. CDP furthers this mission by harnessing the collective power of corporations, investors, and political leaders to accelerate unified action on climate change. Over 3,000 organizations in some 60 countries around the world now measure and disclose their GHG emissions, water management, and climate change strategies through CDP, in order that they can set reduction targets and make performance improvements. These data are made available for use by a wide audience including institutional investors, corporations, policymakers, and their advisors, public sector organizations, government bodies, academics, and the public.

Climate Counts[88] is a collaborative effort to bring consumers and companies together in the fight against global climate change. CC scores the world's largest companies on their climate impact to spur corporate climate responsibility and conscious consumption. The goal is to motivate deeper awareness among consumers—that the issue of climate change demands their attention, and that they have the power to support companies that take climate change seriously and avoid those that don't.

CR Magazine *100 Best Corporate Citizens*[89] *Corporate Responsibility Magazine* (the new name of *CRO Magazine*) announces an annual "100 Best Corporate Citizens List," known as the world's top corporate responsibility ranking based on publically available information and recognized by PR Week as one of America's top three most-important business rankings.

CSRHUB[90] gives its users the information they need to evaluate corporate social values and sustainability. Once armed with ratings based on their own values, users can take action to both change their behavior and to change the world. CSRHUB gives consumers access to more than 125 sources of CSR information. The largest contribution of data comes from aggregating five of the eight leading ESG research firms. The CSRHUB database also aggregates information from publishers, NGOs, and three government agencies. Using a proprietary system for mapping and normalizing this broad range of information, CSRHUB provides consistent ratings on around 5,000 companies in 65 countries. CSRHUB does not provide the underlying ratings and only serves as a hub.

Dow Jones Sustainability Indexes[91] were launched in 1999 as the first global sustainability benchmarks. The indexes are offered cooperatively by SAM Indexes and Dow Jones Indexes, the marketing name and a licensed trademark of CME Group Index Services LLC. The family tracks the stock performance of the world's leading companies in terms of economic, environmental and social criteria. The indexes serve as benchmarks for investors who integrate sustainability considerations into their portfolios, and provide an effective engagement platform for companies who want to adopt sustainable best practices. The Dow Jones Sustainability Indexes comprise global and regional benchmarks including European, Eurozone, Nordic, North American, U.S., Asia Pacific, and Korean indexes. Subsets of these indexes allow investors to exclude certain sectors from performance measurement. Dow Jones Indexes and SAM together can create customized versions of the indexes to meet investors' specific requirements for their unique investment objectives.

EIRIS[92] is an independent, not-for-profit organization that works to help its clients develop the market in ways that benefit investors, asset managers, and the wider world.

They empower responsible investors with independent assessments of companies and advice on integrating them with investment decisions.

Ethisphere's World's Most Ethical Companies[93] is an international think-tank dedicated to the creation, advancement and sharing of best practices in business ethics, CSR, anti-corruption, and sustainability. Ethisphere's "World's Most Ethical Companies" designation recognizes companies that truly go beyond making statements about doing business "ethically" and translate those words into action. WME honorees demonstrate real and sustained ethical leadership within their industries, putting into real business practice the Institute's credo of "Good. Smart. Business. Profit." WME is awarded to those companies that have leading ethics and compliance programs, particularly as compared to their industry peers.

FTSE4Good Index Series[94] helps investors worldwide make informed investment decisions and benchmark the performance of their investments. FTSE calculates over 120,000 end-of-day and real-time indices covering more than 80 countries and all major asset classes. The FTSE4Good Index Series has been designed to objectively measure the performance of companies that meet globally recognized corporate responsibility standards. Transparent management and criteria make FTSE4Good a valuable tool for consultants, asset owners, fund managers, investment banks, stock exchanges, and brokers when assessing or creating responsible investment products.

GoodGuide[95] provides the world's largest and most reliable source of information on the health, environmental, and social impacts of consumer products. It provides authoritative information about the health, environmental, and social performance of products and companies. It helps consumers make purchasing decisions that reflect their preferences and values.

GS Sustain[96] is a global equity strategy that brings together ESG criteria, broad industry analysis and ROC to identify long-term investment opportunities.

(continued)

Table 8.1 (continued)

Maplecroft Climate Innovation Indexes (CIIs)[97] Climate change is one of the key business and economic issues of our time. Companies that successfully innovate and manage climate-related opportunities and risks are better equipped to operate in this future growth environment. Maplecroft's CIIs identify companies best-positioned to take advantage of these new opportunities due to their disruptive innovations and partnerships. The Maplecroft CIIs provide investors and stakeholders with insight into the activities of leading U.S. companies and address the compelling case for climate-related innovation and carbon management as leading indicators of future financial performance.

Murky Waters: Corporate Reporting on Water Risk (CERES)[98] is an assessment and ranking of water disclosure practices of 100 publically traded companies in eight key sectors exposed to water-related risks: beverage, chemicals, electric power, food, homebuilding, mining, oil and gas, and semiconductors. The report highlights best practices, key gaps, and trends in water reporting and lays out a set of recommendations for companies and investors.

Newsweek Green Rankings[99] compares environmental footprints, management (policies, programs, initiatives, controversies), and reporting practices of big companies.

Oekom Corporate Ratings[100] analyzes companies using the world's most comprehensive collection of criteria for the ethical evaluation of companies—the Frankfurt-Hohenheimer guidelines drawn up by professors Johannes Hoffman and Gerhard Scherhorn.

Sustainalytics[101] a provider of ESG research and analysis specializing in the RI and SRI markets.

The Global 100 Most Sustainable Corporations in the World (Global 100)[102] is an annual project initiated by *Corporate Knights*, the magazine for clean capitalism. In 2010, *Corporate Knights* collaborated with three strategic partners to identify the Corporate Knights Global 100 Most Sustainable Corporations in the World. The Corporate Knights Global 100 team included Inflection Point Capital Management—a sustainability-focused asset management venture founded by Dr. Matthew Kiernan, Legg Mason's Global Currents Investment Management, and Phoenix Global Advisors LLC (a consulting and technology platform focused on sustainability).

Trucost Environmental Impact Assessment[103] in collaboration with Unit4 has developed Sustain4 that makes use of Trucost's database and model to rapidly assess and benchmark an organization's environmental impacts based on readily available financial and business data.

Vigeo[104] is a European expert in the assessment of companies and organizations with regard to their practices and performance on ESG issues.

The research found too much overlap in the ratings, generality within their objectives, and many ratings failed to explain their uniqueness. The study also found inconsistencies between some raters' stated objectives (i.e., helping companies improve their performances and disclosures and their own lack of transparency and availability). So although these ratings are interesting, one should be skeptical about their accuracy. The reliability and validity of the measures are still evolving. In fact, the group that studied the ratings is now designing a report about how to improve the ratings.[105]

Global Environment Outlook Reporting

Reporting happens at national and global levels as well. The Global Environment Outlook (GEO), created in 1972, is a function of the UNEP (the leading global environmental authority) and sets the global environmental agenda. As such, it is responsible for keeping the world's environmental situation under review and promoting the acquisition, assessment, and exchange of environmental knowledge and information.[106] The GEO publishes reports, the first of which came out in 1997; the fifth GEO report was published in mid-2012 in time for the United Nations Conference on Sustainable Development (Rio+20).[107] The GEO's main reporting goal is to produce scientifically credible and policy-relevant assessments of the state of the global environment and to enhance the capacity of a wide range of actors to perform integrated environmental assessments.

The UNEP performs little direct monitoring and surveillance, unlike other international organizations (e.g., the World Meteorological Organization and the WHO). The UNEP collects, collates, analyzes, and integrates data from UN agencies, other organizations, and national statistical offices to form broader environmental assessments. GEO assessments thus compile and interpret scientific findings on the causes and consequences of environmental change, provide policy options to mitigate and adapt to the change, and engage a diverse range of experts (from all regions and professions) in the production process—linking science and policy by turning credible data into information that is relevant for environmental decision makers.

In integrated environmental assessments such as the GEO, *process* is critical to the quality of the product. Results are greatly impacted by how the assessment is conducted, who participates, and the associated conditions. Salience, credibility, and legitimacy all shape the impact of scientific assessments.[108] *Salience* means that scientific input is timely, focused, and addresses issues of current importance to policymakers. *Credibility* refers to the adequacy of scientific evidence, arguments, and the credentials of the scientists involved. *Legitimacy* of scientific assessments requires that the processes be perceived as free of bias, consider the views of stakeholders, and treat differing views fairly. GEO strives to deliver across all three dimensions.

To ensure these outcomes, the UNEP uses a consultative group comprised of member states and experts to help frame the report in a way that is responsive to policy needs. Governments also nominate experts to review the report, and they facilitate review meetings. By actively shaping the vision and process, the involved governments have transitioned from being a target audience to a functional stakeholder group. Yet, this engagement, some scholars note, could also lead to message dilution, politicization, and erosion of legitimacy in the eyes of the scientific community and the public.[109] The tension between the desire for governmental input and the fear of governmental involvement is present in other environmental impact assessment processes (e.g., the IPCC). Associated reports have been impacted by the conflicting perspectives.[110]

State-sponsored sustainability efforts have adopted the GEO methodology for the production and/or improvement of the State of the Environment or Integrated Environmental Assessment reporting.[111] The inclusion of a range of stakeholders in the process has increased its relevance by integrating various perspectives, priorities, and data sources.[112] In addition, the structure has fostered ongoing, inclusive dialogues between policymakers and stakeholders and has enhanced regional assessment processes. Global environmental monitoring and assessment is complex and requires a dynamic approach.

Other organizations have developed assessments and indices to fill this gap. Robust examples include the World Resources Institute's *Earth Trends Reports* and the *Environmental Performance Index*, a collaborative effort between Yale University, Columbia University, and the World Economic Forum. The Global Earth Observation System of Systems (GEOSS), created in 2005 as a partnership among governments and intergovernmental organizations, provides "comprehensive, coordinated and sustained observations of the Earth system" as well as "timely, quality long-term global information as a basis for sound decision making."[113] While GEO is intended to be an assessment process and GEOSS an observation system, the creation of GEOSS in the wake of the 2002 World Summit on Sustainable Development might be an indication that governments found the UNEP data analyses and information function inadequate.

Profile: China Can Be a Leader for Integrated Reporting

The Government Report delivered on March 5, 2015 at the Third Session of the 12th National People's Congress,[114] Premier of the State Council Li Keqiang noted that "China's economic development has entered a new normal, meaning China must adopt a new attitude." "New normal" means: Economic growth that makes more judicious use of limited resources, and to protect the country's vast natural capital from degradation while reducing negative impacts on the environment such as carbon emissions and air pollution.[115]

The "new attitude" that will support China's transition to sustainable development means revamping six forms of capital that comprise its economic system: financial capital, natural capital, manufactured capital, human capital, social and relationship capital, and intellectual capital, including:

- *Focusing on innovation and knowledge creation since the country can no longer rely upon low-cost, resource-intensive manufacturing jobs to provide employment opportunities and spur economic growth.*
- *Advancing national ecological security as the basis of economic development and social prosperity.*
- *Enhancing social and relationship capital among its people to, as Li put it, "improve our ability to communicate effectively with international audiences."*

Chinese executives are beginning to understand their role in the new normal, and might benefit from new ideas and tools to use the six forms of capital more judiciously. "Integrated reporting," is such a tool as it is a new form of corporate disclosure to demonstrate and reinforce a new attitude.

In the International IR Framework (IR Framework) developed by the IIRC, integrated reporting (IR) is defined as "a concise communication about how an organization's strategy, governance, performance and prospects, in the context of the external environment, lead to the creation of value over the short, medium, and long term." This reporting format was described in this chapter. At the core of the IR Framework are the six types of capital mentioned above.

When a company reports on how it uses and impacts the six types of capital, it creates visibility that affects resource allocation decisions. Traditional financial reporting can be very effective in highlighting a company's performance regarding financial and manufactured capital. IR includes performance measures regarding the other four types of capital and how all six forms are related to each other.

No Chinese company has yet issued an integrated report, but many are producing sustainability or CSR reports, which are a step in that direction.

IR is still in its early stages, with only one country, South Africa, having made it a requirement of all listed companies. This is a tremendous opportunity for China. As the world's second largest economy, the widespread adoption of IR in China would demonstrate to a skeptical world that China really is serious about sustainable development. This would then challenge other large countries, such as the United States, to rise to the occasion as well. No country needs IR more than China because IR is one of the few management tools in existence that can effectively address the scale and scope of environmental degradation in China.

Is China ready to become an example for the world about how to promote and enjoy sustainable long-term prosperity?

Chapter Summary

Unique to environmental sustainability is how to measure and report on outcomes. While ROIC may point to environmental and social indicators of performance, companies need to supplement these data with *nonfinancial analyses and reports*. This type of reporting is often voluntary, a combination of internal and external reports, and is often separated from financial reports. Nonfinancial reports include at least three key types of information:

1   environmental, social, and governance analyses;
2   intangible assets (including intellectual capital);
3   key performance indicators.

Ultimately, the goal is to have companies combine this type of reporting with financial reporting and create *one report*. As these data are disclosed, rating agencies will produce more rankings and external reviews that are transparent and useful to stakeholders.

Case Revisited: Goldman Sachs Sets the Model

Goldman Sachs provides one example of how nonfinancial measurement is influencing investment decisions; however, the standards by which these measurements are derived and used are far less uniform than for financial information. While the trend of using nonfinancial information is compelling and potentially useful, it can also be risky. As nonfinancial reporting standards are developed, analysts need to find ways to adapt these standards to specific company strategies. In essence, we may be better to adopt principles rather than exact standards; this is a discussion that is ongoing even for financial measurements.

Terms to Know

Footprint: A popularized term that refers to the aggregate of measurements of an entity's impact on the environment (e.g., a person's impact from various activities)

Nonfinancial information: All information reported to stakeholders that is not defined by an accounting standard or derived from an accounting statement

One report: Combining financial and nonfinancial information into one report (vs. reporting these activities separately)

Profile: Enlighted[116]

In November of 2012, the City of San Jose announced that it had reduced lighting costs in San Jose City Hall by 53 percent.[117] Appendix 8.1: Sustainability Frameworks identifies Leadership in Energy and Environmental Design (LEED) as an industry-specific framework. LEED is widely recognized as being one of the leaders in green building certification; however, the announcement was not about the building's LEED Platinum certification. The announcement was made to honor the success the City of San Jose had working with Enlighted, a smart lighting start-up out of Silicon Valley. Even after a rigorous lighting program had been in place, Enlighted was able to show significant energy improvements using their innovative sensor and analytics platform.[118]

Both the remote sensing technology and LED chips are digital and use similar semiconductors[119] allowing for fluent implementation. Enlighted's platform also works with fluorescent lighting. To match their innovative product, Enlighted has created a unique business model that will install at no initial cost and immediately guarantees energy savings of 5–20 percent.[120] Along with making a stir in the public sector, the firm's advanced lighting control system has rapidly penetrated the commercial real estate market. Enlighted has implemented their technology in 228 customer sites, including Fortune 500 companies, as well as 30 states with roughly 19.4 million square feet installed.[121]

Seeking Enlightenment. Chapter 8 highlights the tremendous growth of sustainability reporting. Today, firms that specialize in industry-specific types of reporting are creating value by providing unique services, improving energy use, and reducing risk along with many other benefits. Services for energy measurement and management are becoming increasingly competitive. Along with frameworks, Appendix 8.1 also identifies several widely used tools for measuring sustainability. How could start-ups like Enlighted use tools such as the Greenhouse Gas Protocol to increase the credibility and legitimacy of their product?

Questions and Critical Thinking

1   The reporting of nonfinancial information can be infinite and capture so much of what an organization does. In your opinion, what criteria should be used to select nonfinancial measures?
2   We discussed resources, capabilities, and competencies in Chapter 5. What competencies does a company need to report effectively via nonfinancial measures? (Consider the ability to both conceptualize and report on these aspects of a company.)
3   The Global Reporting Initiative has become a standard means of reporting nonfinancial information, especially as related to sustainability. Review the Global Reporting Initiative online.[122] What advice would you give to an organization trying to adopt this standard for the first time?
4   Choose a particular company of interest. Take a look at its various reports and comment on how effectively they report on the three nonfinancial aspects of the company: (1) environmental, social, and governance; (2) intangible assets; and (3) key performance indicators. What criteria did you use to determine *effective commentary*?
5   Consider the difference between *principles* and *standards*. Should reporting adhere to strict standards? Or should there be some latitude along with an adherence to a set of principles?

Appendix 8.1. Sustainability Frameworks[123]

Category	Name	Summary
Overarching Principles	The Three "Es"	This is based on the United Nations' work regarding what is needed for sustainable development. The Three Es are usually referred to as Economy, Environment, and social Equity.
	The Triple Bottom Line	Sometimes used interchangeably with the Three Es but different in subtle ways; often framed as Social, Economic, and Environment or as People, Planet, and Profits.
	The Natural Step Framework	This provides a planning framework in the form of four "system conditions" or principles based on science that guides decision makers of an organization or governmental body systematically toward sustainability.
	ICC Business Charter for Sustainable Development	Provides a basic reference for actions by individual corporations and business organizations around the world. The charter, which was prepared in 1990 for launching at the Second World Industry Conference on Environmental Management, has been signed by over 1,000 companies and organizations.
	CERES Principles	Created in response to the Exxon Valdez disaster, CERES offers a code of conduct and a credo for organizations to adopt. The principles address issues such as energy conservation, waste reduction and disposal, and management commitment.
	Conservation Economy	Ecotrust has put together a website that documents best practices for social, economic, and environmental practices. They have identified "patterns" (e.g., certification and labeling) that have application in many situations.
	Natural Capitalism	The four principles of natural capitalism were originally explained in the book of the same title by Paul Hawken, Amory Lovins, and L. Hunter Lovins. The four principles are built upon concepts of radical resource productivity, biomimicry, service and flow economy, and reinvestment in natural capital.
	Six "Es"	Trade unions in Europe are developing a working model that will support companies and organizations that wish to change their operations on the basis of the goals set for Agenda 21. This model is called 6E, which stands for ecology, emissions, energy, ergonomics, efficiency, and economics.
	Agenda 21	Created at the Rio Earth Summit through the United Nations, this lays out actions needed at a national and international level to reach sustainability. Talks about what needs to happen but provides no accountability to make it happen.
	UN Global Compact	Created by the United Nations to foster corporate citizenship. Puts forth 10 principles for business in three areas (i.e., labor standards, environment, and anti-corruption—in support of the Agenda 21 goals).
	Taillores Declaration	A set of principles for colleges and universities. Provides 10 principles. Signed by universities from all over the world.
	Equator Principles	Similar to Taillores but for financial institutions.
Industry-Specific Framework	Leadership in Energy and Environmental Design (LEED)	Provides a scoring system and certifications for evaluating the sustainability of buildings.

Environmental Management System/ISO 14001 and related standards	International guidelines for environmental management systems and their certification. Most often used by manufacturing and, to a lesser extent, government. Can provide a process for managing a sustainability effort but, by itself, does not provide sustainability targets.
Smart Growth/New Urbanism	Provides guidelines for land use planning and livable communities.
Hannover Principles	Developed by William McDonough Architects for Expo 2000 (held in Hannover, Germany). The nine principles focus on the design of "green" buildings (or the "built environment") and stress the interdependent relationship human society has with nature.
Biomimicry	Using nature as inspiration for human designs. Developed by Janine Benyus.
Industrial Ecology	Designing manufacturing systems so that the waste of one process is input to another.
Green Chemistry	Designing chemical processes to eliminate hazardous byproducts and improve the efficiency of the processes themselves.
Product Stewardship, Extended Producer Responsibility, Extended Product Responsibility (EPR)	These three terms are roughly synonymous, with subtle distinctions about who should bear responsibility. Preferred terms vary by country. The concept is to make manufacturers responsible for their products for their entire life-cycle, including end of life.
Global Reporting Initiative	Standards for sustainability reports. Created by CERES; it is intended to provide consistency across organizations.
Measurement-Related Tools	
Bellagio Principles	Provides criteria or guidelines for the selection of metrics.
Genuine Progress Indicator	Gross National Product adjusted so that spending on "bad things" (e.g., prisons and environmental cleanup) are deducted.
Greenhouse Gas Protocol	A standardized method of reporting climate impacts. Important to follow if you plan to trade carbon credits or make public claims about reductions in GHGs.
Life-cycle Assessment and Costing	A method of examining the impacts of a product or decision over its entire life-cycle (from raw materials and manufacturing to transportation, use, and disposal); a method of examining the costs of financial decisions (e.g., construction of buildings) over their lifetime (vs. first cost).
Ecological Foot Printing	The Biological Footprint approach shows one how to estimate the land needed to sustain a way of life.

Notes

1 Goldman Sachs, *Introducing GS Sustain* (New York: The Goldman Sachs Group, June 22, 2007), 5, www.natcap solutions.org/business-case/GoldmanSachsReport_v2007.pdf (accessed December 20, 2012).

2 Ibid.

3 Goldman Sachs, "Interview with Anthony Ling," *Crossing the Rubicon*, video, May 2010, http://www.goldmansachs.com/our-thinking/archive/crossing-the-rubicon-immersive/index.html (accessed December 22, 2011).

4 Goldman Sachs, *Introducing GS SUSTAIN*, 11.

5 For more information on firm valuation and discounted cash flow analysis, see T. Koller, M. Goedhardt, and D. Wessels, *Valuation: Measuring and Managing the Value of Companies*, 5th ed. (Hoboken, NJ: John Wiley & Sons, 2010).

6 F. Modigliani and M. H. Miller, "The Cost of Capital, Corporation Finance and the Theory of Investments," *American Economic Review* 48, no. 3 (June 1958): 261–297.

7 M. Amram and N. Kulatilaka, *Real Options: Managing Strategic Investment in an Uncertain World* (Boston, MA: Harvard Business School Press, 1999).

8 Steven C. Hackett, *Environmental and Natural Resources Economics: Theory Policy and the Sustainable Society*. Fourth edition (Armonk, NY: M.E. Sharpe, 2011).

9 F. Ramsey, "A Mathematical Theory of Savings," *Economics Journal* 38 (1928): 543–559.

10 For the strongest ethical argument, see N. Stern, *The Economics of Climate Change: The Stern Review* (Cambridge: Cambridge University Press, 2007), 35. A good critique of Stern's views is D. Helm, *The Carbon Crunch: How We're Getting Climate Change Wrong—And How to Fix It* (London: Yale University Press, 2013).

11 Koller, Goedhardt, and Wessels, *Valuation*, 26–35.

12 Ibid., 59.

13 Ibid., 99.

14 For an in-depth discussion of this process, see Koller, Goedhardt, and Wessels, *Valuation*, especially Chapter 8.

15 Ibid., 169.

16 This example is adapted from Koller, Goedhardt, and Wessels, *Valuation*, 169–172.

17 Calculated using Y charts. http://ycharts.com/dashboard/(accessed August 24, 2015).

18 W. R. Blackburn, *The Sustainability Handbook: The Complete Management Guide to Achieving Social, Economic, and Environmental Responsibility* (Washington, DC: Environmental Law Institute, 2007), 364.

19 Ibid., 317.

20 "Transparency in the Haze," *The Economist*, February 8, 2014, 44.

21 UN Economic Commission for Europe, "Welcome to PRTR.net," www.prtr.net (accessed December 15, 2012).

22 International Corporate Governance Network, *ICGN Statement and Guidance on Non-financial Business Reporting* (London, ICGN, 2008), https://www.icgn.org/sites/default/files/ICGN-IntegratedBusiness%20Reporting.pdf (accessed December 22, 2015).

23 R. G. Eccles and M. P. Krzus, *One Report: Integrated Reporting for a Sustainable Strategy* (Hoboken, NJ: John Wiley & Sons, 2010), 81–100.

24 A. Wyatt, "What Financial Non-Financial Information on Intangibles Is Value Relevant? A Review of the Evidence," *Accounting and Business Research* 38, no. 3 (2008): 217–256.

25 Ibid.

26 Organisation for Economic Co-operation and Development, *Intellectual Assets and Value Creation: Implications for Corporate Reporting* (Paris: OECD, December 10, 2006), 16 www.oecd.org/daf/corporateaffairs/corporategovernanceprinciples/37811196.pdf (accessed January 18, 2013).

27 Eccles and Krzus, *One Report*, 90.

28 R. S. Kaplan and D. P. Norton, *The Strategy-Focused Organization: How Balanced Scorecard Companies Thrive in the New Business Environment* (Boston, MA: Harvard Business School Press, 2001), 7.

29 F. F. Reichheld, "The One Number You Need to Grow," *Harvard Business Review* 81 (December 2003): 46–54.

30 Information about ASSET 4 can be found at: Thomson Reuters, ESG Research Data, http://thomsonreuters.com/esg-research-data/ and Thomson Reuters, AlphaNow: ASSET4, http://alphanow.thomsonreuters.com/solutions/asset-4/.

31 Information about MSCI can be found at MSCI, "Environmental, Social & Governance," www.msci.com/products/esg/.

32 Information about Trucost can be found at www.trucost.com/.

33 Information about DVFA can be found at the European Federation of Financial Analysts Societies' website, "DVFA: Society of Investment Professionals in Germany," http://effas.net/index.php?option=com_content&view=article&id=64:dvfa-society-of-investment-professionals-in-germany&catid=42:members. The EFFAS website is http://effas.net/.

34 Steve Lydenberg, quoted in Eccles and Krzus, *One Report*, 98.

35 One study found that fewer than 40 out of 157 companies has built models linking KPIs and strategic success. See Eccles and Krzus, *One Report*, 90.

36 "Executive Summary" (Global Sustainability Investment Review. 2014): 3 http://www.gsi-alliance.org/wp-content/uploads/2015/02/GSIA_Review_download.pdf (accessed August 24, 2015).

37 Ibid.

38 R. Gray, "Does Sustainability Reporting Improve Corporate Behaviour? Wrong Question? Right Time?" *Accounting and Business Research* 36, no. S1 (2006): 65–88.

39 ICAEW (The Institute of Chartered Accountants in England and Wales), "Professional scepticism and other key audit issues," www.icaew.com/en/technical/audit-and-assurance/professional-scepticism (accessed December 15, 2012).

40 Gray, "Does Sustainability Reporting Improve Corporate Behaviour?" 65.

41 Integrated Reporting. "The IIRC," www.integratedreporting.org/the-iirc-2/ (accessed August 24, 2015).

42 "About CDSB." Climate Disclosure Standards Board, www.cdsb.net/about-cdsb (accessed August 15, 2015).

43 "About IISD." International Institute for Sustainable Development, www.iisd.org/about/(accessed August 24, 2015).

44 Global Reporting Initiative, "What Is GRI?" www.globalreporting.org/information/about-gri/what-is-GRI/Pages/default.aspx (accessed August 12, 2011).

45 H. S. Brown, M. de Jong, and T. Lessidrenska, *The Rise of the Global Reporting Initiative (GRI) as a Case of Institutional Entrepreneurship*, Corporate Social Responsibility Initiative Working Paper No. 36 (Cambridge, MA: John F. Kennedy School of Government, Harvard University, May 2007), 20.

46 Global Reporting Initiative, "About GRI," www.globalreporting.org/information/about-gri/(accessed May 21, 2011).

47 Global Reporting Initiative, *The GRI's Sustainability Report July 2004–June 2007* (Amsterdam: GRI, 2007), www.globalreporting.org/resourcelibrary/GRI-Sustainability-Report-2004-2007.pdf (accessed August 20, 2015).

48 GRI. "Sustainability Disclosure Database." www.Database.globalreporting.org (accessed September 3, 2015).

49 World Resources Institute, "Greenhouse Gas Protocol," www.wri.org/project/ghg-protocol (accessed January 18, 2013).

50 Endnote: GRI, *Annual Activity Review* 2012/2013. 24, https://www.globalreporting.org/information/news-and-press-center/Pages/From-Information-to-Transformation-GRIs-20122013-Activity-Review.aspx (accessed September 21, 2015).

51 Global Reporting Initiative, "What Is GRI?"

52 Global Reporting Initiative, *GRI Sustainability Reporting Statistics* (2010), www.globalreporting.org/resourcelibrary/GRI-Reporting-Stats-2010.pdf (accessed September 14, 2015).

53 Endnote: GRI, Annual Activity Review.

54 W. R. Sherman and L. DiGuilio, "The Second Round of G3 Reports: Is Triple Bottom Line Reporting Becoming More Comparable?" *Journal of Business and Economics Research* 8, no. 9 (2010): 59–77.

55 L. Hartman and M. Painter-Morland, "Exploring the Global Reporting Initiative Guidelines as a Model for Triple Bottom-Line Reporting," *African Journal of Business Ethics* 2, no. 1 (2007): 45–57.

56 J. M. Moneva, P. Archel, and C. Correa, "GRI and the Camouflaging of Corporate Unsustainability," *Accounting Forum* 30, no. 2 (June 2006): 121–137.

57 A. Kolk, "A Decade of Sustainability Reporting: Developments and Significance," *International Journal of Environment and Sustainable Development* 3, no. 1 (2004): 51–64.

58 Personal correspondence, Bank of America, April 18, 2012.

59 Nonfinancialreporting.http://ec.europa.eu/finance/accounting/non-financial_reporting/index_en.htm.(accessed February 20, 2015). The plenary of the European Parliament adopted on 15 April 2014 the directive on disclosure of non-financial and diversity information by certain large companies and groups.

60 SASB U.S. Supreme Court case *TSC Industries* v. *Northway, Inc.* 426 US438 (1976).

61 R. C. Eccles and M. P. Krzus, *The Integrated Reporting Movement: Meaning, Momentum, Motives, and Materiality* (Hoboken, NJ: Wiley, 2014), 159–161.

62 A. Willis, "The Role of the Global Reporting Initiative's Sustainability Reporting Guidelines in the Social Screening of Investments," *Journal of Business Ethics* 43, no. 3 (March 2003): 233.

63 Global Reporting Initiative, *GRI Sustainability Reporting Statistics.*

64 M. Wackernagel and W. E. Rees, *Our Ecological Footprint: Reducing Human Impact on the Earth* (Gabriola Island, BC: New Society Publishers, 1996), 9.

65 N. Chambers, C. Simmons, and M. Wackernagel, *Sharing Nature's Interest: Ecological Footprints as an Indicator of Sustainability* (Sterling, VA: Earthscan, 2000), 25.

66 Carbon Trust, "Certification," http://www.carbontrust.com/client-services/footprinting/footprint-certification (accessed December 22, 2015).

67 BSI, the British Standards Institution, is a nonprofit organization that develops and publishes standards that oversee virtually every aspect of modern society. Headquartered in London, United Kingdom, BSI is the United Kingdom's national standards organization and its representative in the European CEN and the international ISO and IEC. The pioneer of standards for management systems, BSI is now the world's largest certification body.

68 British Standards Institution, *PAS 2050:2011 Specification for the Assessment of the Life Cycle Greenhouse Gas Emissions of Goods and Services* (London: BSI, 2011), http://shop.bsigroup.com/en/forms/PASs/PAS-2050 (accessed September 20, 2011).

69 ENLAR Compliance Services, Inc., "The ISO Environmental Standards," http://iso14000expert.com/iso14000.html#EnvironmentalStandards (accessed September 15, 2014).

70 The Greenhouse Gas Protocol, www.ghgprotocol.org/(accessed September 17, 2011).

71 Polymer Group Inc., *2011 Stakeholders' Report* (Charlotte, NC: PGI, 2012) www.polymergroupinc.com/pdf/en/PGI_2011_Stakeholders_Report.pdf (accessed January 18, 2013).

72 Smithfield Foods, *2012 Integrated Report* (Smithfield, VA, 2012), iv, http://files.shareholder.com/downloads/SFD/2317552797x0x590240/F33D665C-409C-4825-A50E-D7F90C10F399/smi_integrated_12.pdf (accessed February 29, 2014).

73 Eccles and Krzus, *One Report*, 148.

74 W. Bartels, J. Iansen-Rogers, and J. Kuszewski, "Count Me In: The Readers' Take on Sustainability Reporting," *Urban Affairs Review* 45, no. 3 (September 2008): 39.

75 R. G. Eccles and M. P. Krzus, *The Integrated Reporting Movement* (Hoboken, NJ: Wiley), xiii.

76 J. Doom, "New Group, 'SASB,' Wants to Help SEC Define Sustainability" (*Bloomberg*, October 5, 2012).

77 Eccles and Krzus, *The Integrated Reporting Movement*, 281–298.

78 Eccles and Krzus, *One Report*, 170.

79 E. Lowitt, *The Future of Value: How Sustainability Creates Value Through Competitive Differentiation* (San Francisco, CA: Jossey-Bass, 2011).

80 Ibid., 190; D. C. Esty and A. S. Winston, *Green to Gold: How Smart Companies Use Environmental Strategy to Innovate, Create Value, and Build Competitive Advantage* (New Haven, CT: Yale University Press, 2006).

81 Newsweek, *Green 2015*, http://www.newsweek.com/green-2015 (accessed December 22, 2015). These are the updated rankings from 2012. The website contains the older rankings as well.

82 SustainAbility, *Rate the Raters, Phase Three: Uncovering Best Practices* (Brussels: ARISTA, February 2011), www.aristastandard.org/content_files/rtrphase3report3.pdf (accessed October 24, 2011).

83 Adapted from M. Sadowski, K. Whitaker, and A. Ayars, *Rate the Raters, Phase Three: Uncovering Best Practices* (London: SustainAbility, February 2011), www.sustainability.com/library/rate-the-raters-phase-three#.TvwK_dRAZLc (accessed October 24, 2011).

84 Access to Medicine Index. http://www.accesstomedicineindex.org/(accessed September 15, 2015).

85 Asset 4. http://thomsonreuters.com/products_services/financial/content_update/content_overview/content_esg/ (accessed September 15, 2015).

86 Bloomberg ESG Disclosure Scores http://www.responsible-investor.com/images/uploads/reports/ESG_USA_2010.pdf (accessed September 15, 2015).

87 Carbon Disclosure Project. https://www.cdproject.net/en-US/Pages/HomePage.aspx (accessed September 15, 2015).

88 Climate Counts. http://www.climatecounts.org/(accessed September 15, 2015).

89 http://thecro.com/content/100-best-corporate-citizens (accessed September 15, 2015).

90 http://www.csrhub.com/ (accessed September 15, 2015).

91 http://www.sustainability-index.com/(accessed September 15, 2015).

92 http://www.eiris.org/ (accessed September 15, 2015).

93 The World's Most Ethical Companies, http://m1.ethisphere.com/wme2013/index.html (accessed December 22, 2015).

94 http://www.ftse.com/Indices/FTSE4Good_Index_Series/index.jsp (accessed September 15, 2015).

95 http://www.goodguide.com/ (accessed September 15, 2015).

96 GS Sustain, http://www.goldmansachs.com/our-thinking/archive/gs-sustain-2011/ (accessed December 22, 2015).

97 http://maplecroft.com/cii/ (accessed September 15, 2015).

98 http://www.ceres.org/resources/reports/corporate-reporting-on-water-risk-2010/view (accessed September 15, 2015).

99 Green 2015, http://www.newsweek.com/green-2015 (accessed December 22, 2015).

100 http://www.oekom-research.com/index_en.php?content=corporate-rating (accessed September 15, 2015).

101 http://www.sustainalytics.com/ (accessed September 15, 2015).

102 http://www.global100.org/ (accessed September 15, 2015).

103 http://www.trucost.com (accessed December 22, 2015).

104 http://www.vigeo.com/csr-rating-agency/en (accessed September 15, 2015).

105 SustainAbility, *Rate the Raters, Phase Four: The Necessary Future of Ratings* (Brussels: ARISTA, July 2011) http://odpowiedzialnybiznes.pl/public/files/Rate_the_Raters_phase_4_report_AccountAbility_2011.pdf (accessed October 24, 2011).

106 For a more extensive analysis of this reporting process and reports see D. S. Fogel, S. E. Fredericks, and L. M. Butler (eds.), *Berkshire Encyclopedia of Sustainability*, vol. 6: *Measurements, Indicators, and Research Methods for Sustainability* (Berkshire, MA: Berkshire Publishers).

107 United Nations Environment Programme, "About GEO," www.unep.org/geo/geo1/misc/about.htm (accessed December 22, 2015).

108 D. W. Cash, W. C. Clark, F. Alcock, N. M. Dickson, N. Eckley, D. H. Guston, J. Jäger, and R. B. Mitchell, "Knowledge Systems for Sustainable Development," *Proceedings of the National Academy of Sciences* 100, no. 14 (July 8, 2003): 8086–8091.

109 R. B. Mitchell, W. C. Clark, D. W. Cash, and N. M. Dickinson (eds.), *Global Environmental Assessments: Information and Influence* (Cambridge, MA: MIT Press, 2006); J. van Woerden (ed.), *Data Issues of Global Environmental Reporting: Experiences from GEO-2000, Reports UNEP/DEIA&EW/TR.99–3 and RIVM 402001013* (Bilthoven: National Institute of Public Health and the Environment; Nairobi: United Nations Environment Programme, 1999); M. T. J. Kok et al., *Environment for Development—Policy Lessons from Global Environmental Assessments, Report for UNEP* (Bilthoven: Netherlands Environmental Assessment Agency, April 2009) www.unep.org/dewa/Portals/67/pdf/Environment_for_Development.pdf (accessed December 21, 2014).

110 InterAcademy Council, *Climate Change Assessments: Review of the Processes and Procedures of the IPCC* (New York: InterAcademy Council, 2010), http://reviewipcc.interacademycouncil.net/report.html (accessed January 7, 2012).

111 L. Pintér, D. Swanson, and J. Chenje (eds.), *GEO Resource Book: A Training Manual Integrated Environmental Assessment and Reporting* (Winnipeg: United Nations Environment Programme [UNEP] and the International Institute for Sustainable Development [IISD], 2007).

112 United Nations Environment Programme (UNEP), *Global Environment Outlook (GEO): SWOT Analysis and Evaluation of the GEO-3 Process from the Perspective of GEO Collaborating Centres* (Nairobi: UNEP, 2004).

113 The Group on Earth Observations, *The Global Earth Observation System of Systems (GEOSS) 10-Year Implementation Plan* (Geneva: GEOSS, February 16, 2005), www.earthobservations.org/documents/10-Year%20Implementation%20Plan.pdf (accessed April 15, 2012).

114 Premier Li Keqiang, "Report on the Work of the Government. Delivered at the Third Session of the Twelfth National People's Congress on March 5, 2015 and adopted on March 15, 2015," March 16, 2015, http://news.xinhuanet.com/english/china/2015-03/16/c_134071473.htm (accessed March 24, 2015).

115 R. G. Eccles and G. Lee, "Integrated Reporting: Corporate Disclosure for China's 'New Normal.'" Big Idea: Sustainability Blog (MIT Sloan Management Review, March 24, 2015). http://sloanreview.mit.edu/article/integrated-reporting-corporate-disclosure-for-chinas-new-normal/?utm_source=WhatCounts+Publicaster+Edition&utm_medium=email&utm_campaign=SU+3%2f24%2f15+-+BP+Mastercard&utm_content=Integrated+Reporting%3a+Corporate+Disclosure+for+China%27s+%22New+Normal%22 (accessed March 24, 2015).

116 Co-authored by Michael Aper, Master of Arts in Sustainability candidate at Wake Forest University.

117 "San Jose City Hall Reduces Lighting Costs, Improves Comfort and Workplace Personalization with Enlighted," Enlighted, Inc., blog, November 14, 2015, http://enlightedinc.com/press/san-jose-city-hall-reduces-lighting-costs-improves-comfort-and-workspace-personalization-with-enlighted/ (accessed March 1, 2015).

118 "About Us," Enlighted, Inc., blog, http://enlightedinc.com/about-us/ (accessed March 1, 2015).

119 U. Wang, "Enlighted Raises $20M To Make Lighting Persona," Forbes, April 18, 2013, http://www.forbes.com/sites/uciliawang/2013/04/18/enlighted-raises-20m-to-make-lighting-personal/ (accessed Marsh 15, 2015).

120 "A Business Model as Innovative as Enlighted's Technology," Enlighted, Inc., blog, 2015, http://enlightedinc.com/geo/ (accessed March 1, 2015).

121 Enlighted, Inc., blog, October 30, 2015 http://enlightedinc.com/press/enlighted-launches-global-energy-optimization-geo-program-companys-first-market-energy-savings-service-model-verge/ (accessed March 1, 2015).

122 Global Reporting Initiative, www.globalreporting.org/ (accessed November 10, 2012).

123 This appendix was adapted from D. Hitchcock and M. Willard, *The Business Guide to Sustainability: Practical Strategies and Tools for Organizations*, 2nd ed. (Sterling, VA: Earthscan, 2009), 266–275.

9

MARKETING, LABELING, AND ANALYZING PRODUCTS

The Noisy Chip-Bag Dilemma

The success of "green" products is hindered when consumers perceive them as overly pricey, less effective or inconvenient. To succeed, experts say, they must offer benefits beyond saving the environment. "If they [consumers] don't see the product benefit and the cost is higher, it's just difficult for them to go the extra mile," said Magali Delmas, a professor at the Institute of the Environment and Sustainability at the University of California, Los Angeles.

The announcement in October 2010 stating that Frito-Lay North America would scrap its compostable SunChips bag highlights some of the difficulties that producers have in creating environmentally friendly products. Consumers perceived SunChips as more expensive than other brands; also, some criticized the compostable SunChips bag for simply being louder than the original. Shoppers even created various YouTube videos testing how noisy the bags were, and many joined a Facebook group called "SORRY I CAN'T HEAR YOU OVER THIS SUN CHIPS BAG."

The bag, made from plant-based polymer polylactic acid, took four years to research and develop; however, it was pulled from five of the six SunChips varieties after just 18 months on the market. "One of the biggest issues likely is that while the bag may be better for the environment, was it better for the consumer?" said Wendy Cobrda, president and co-founder of Earthsense a company that tracks the green market. "If they sold it based on 'What's in it for me?' I don't think they would have gotten the same . . . response," Cobrda added.

Thus, sustainable products are clearly only good for the environment if people are willing to buy them.[1] These products would not be placed on the market and they would not influence other producers to follow with their more environmentally friendly products.

Chapter Overview

When you consider environmentally sustainable products, it is important to understand that effective marketing is essential for persuading consumers to switch from conventional goods and services to "green" products; thus, this chapter considers marketing as an essential part of a firm's strategy (see Figure 9.1) and will focus on marketing more broadly as price, promotion, place, and product. The discussion will begin with a cursory overview of successes and failures of green products in the marketplace. We will then explore how green advertising adjusts to a changing consumer culture and the dangers of misleading advertising. The second half of the chapter focuses on different levels of labeling and how life-cycle analysis (LCA) can assist with developing and selling products that meet consumer needs—and are beneficial; to preserving natural capital.

By the end of this chapter, you should be able to:

1 identify the tension between *consumer-focused* and *earth-focused* marketing;
2 provide some examples of how green marketing approaches consumers differently;
3 explain greenwashing;
4 compare and contrast the three types of sustainable labeling;
5 explain how LCA can assist with creating products that comply with a cradle-to-cradle philosophy.

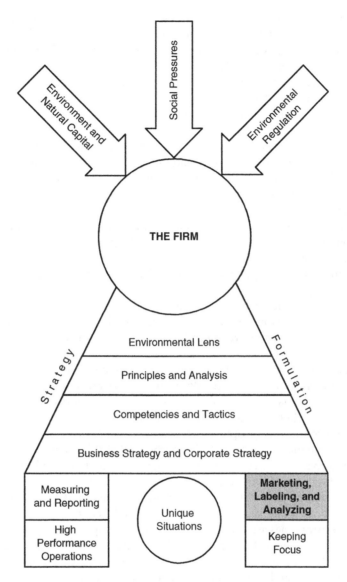

Figure 9.1 Strategy Model with an Environmental Sustainability Lens

Marketing is a cornerstone of business strategy. This chapter should help those interested in looking at strategy from an environmental lens to understand the unique characteristics of marketing "green" products and services.

Green Products

Similar to the issues experienced by Frito-Lay, ecofriendly cleaning products (and packaging) have all too often been criticized and/or rejected by consumers for not being as effective as "conventional" products. For example, some consumers have said that green dish detergents leave smears (because they lack phosphates). Consumers have also complained, online, that PepsiCo's "Eco-Fina" bottles (which contain 50 percent less plastic) are too flimsy and tip over too easily. Compact fluorescent light bulbs are considered, by some, as being "too bright."

One global study of more than 2,000 Americans showed that the United States ranks 24th out of 25 markets, worldwide, for cynicism.[2] For example, in addition to being one of the more environmentally cynical nations when it comes to pollution, the most recent study found that U.S. consumers are also skeptical about the costs and efficacies of green products and their impacts on the environment. Approximately two out of three Americans perceive green products as being too expensive and one-third believes that "green" products do not perform as well as "conventional" products.

One study of U.S. consumers revealed several themes:

1   The most surprising finding was that superior knowledge did not lead to an increase in willingness to protect the environment. One explanation could be that people do not have ownership of the environment. This is a classic tragedy of the commons (explained in Chapter 3).[3]
2   Environmental and economic uncertainty are both key issues for consumers; however, priority is given to economic uncertainty.
3   Fifty-eight percent of Americans say they recycle, 29 percent buy green products, and 18 percent commute in an environmentally friendly manner (e.g., by taking public transportation). These numbers are double those from 20 years ago.
4   Americans want companies to go green and believe that green practices are good for business.[4]

According to one report, consumers who previously purchased green products have decreased their green purchasing as a result of the recession. Forty-three percent of "light consumers" (i.e., those who buy some green products) reduced their usage of green products or switched to conventional ones.[5] Consumers who have yet to switch to green products are unlikely to do so, and most consumers do not seek out information on green products. Also, most consumers do not understand green certifications.

These and other data demonstrate the difficulty of marketing green and creating "green" products that appeal to consumers. Confusing labeling, confusion about terms, and uncertainty about the benefits of green products lead to these results. Furthermore, some researchers demonstrate what they call the "Prius effect." In one study, researchers found that people purchased a Toyota Prius not for environmental conservation but because it "makes a statement about me." The authors label this focus *conspicuous conservation* (i.e., seeking status through displays of austerity amid growing concern about environmental protection), which is a phenomenon related to conspicuous consumption.[6]

The market is obstructed by ever-changing definitions of green, and there is not one definition of the term, so consumers may be confused as to which environmental facet to support (e.g., clean air, BPA reduction, or clean water). Controversies are also a hindrance. For example, when plastic bottles got a bad name, many consumers switched to Nalgene bottles that could be reused—until studies began appearing that linked a key component of the bottles, bisphenol A (BPA), with cancer. So consumers switched again—often to bottles made by SIGG Switzerland AG. However, reports then claimed that the older SIGG bottles contained BPA, as well.

Fortunately, recent research, discussed in the next section, is proving to be useful in the marketing and consumption of green products. Companies are changing their message structure, creating product technology that better meets consumer needs, making products more accessible to consumers, and encouraging a culture that emphasizes green living and transparency. The next section will explain how companies use marketing to accomplish these goals.

Marketing Mix and Green Marketing

Marketing professionals refer to their "marketing mixes" (i.e., various components of the marketing function). These mixes include price, promotion, place (distribution and location), and product design. Our concern is with the unique marketing characteristics of "green" products and issues, often termed as green marketing.

Green marketing is a term that is poorly defined yet widely used. However, green marketing and green advertising may be defined as promotional messages that appeal to the needs and desires of environmentally concerned consumers.[7] These types of advertisements should contain at least one of three criteria:

1   addresses the relationship between a product/service and the biophysical environment;
2   advocates a green lifestyle with or without highlighting a product/service;
3   presents a corporate image of environmental responsibility.[8]

Advertising is a component of marketing and helps to promote products and services that support sustainability. Such products and services are often promoted via government and nonprofit organizations' social marketing campaigns to encourage sustainable behaviors. Thus, this type of advertising is specifically developed to appeal to the needs and interests of consumers concerned with sustainability issues (e.g., the environment and social justice).[9]

This type of advertising and promotion is viewed as social marketing because it uses commercial marketing approaches to influence voluntary behaviors of audiences in ways that are socially beneficial. One difference between *social marketing* and *socially responsible marketing* is that the former focuses on advertising and promotion to make sustainable behavior more likely, while the latter promotes products that are already regarded as sustainable.

Here is an example of how a social marketing campaign might change behavior: What if we wanted to conduct a promotional campaign to encourage people to consume less water?[10] This type of promotion could focus on the consumer's price and cost advantages (vs. emphasizing the environmental benefits). One study of such a campaign in Israel found that 75.6 percent of survey responders indicated that they were willing to save water after being exposed to the campaign promoting an average savings of 15 percent in water consumption. Yet, surveys conducted *after* the advertising campaign showed that only 38.1 percent of respondents thought they would continue to save water and money.[11]

In general, green marketing has not lived up to the hopes and dreams of many managers and activists. Although public polls consistently show that consumers would prefer a sustainable product over one that is less friendly to the environment, they tend not to act on this intent.[12] When consumers are forced to make tradeoffs between product attributes and helping the environment, the environment does not usually win. Some consumers perceive environmental benefits as costing more; others believe products are of lower quality or do not deliver on their environmental promises.[13]

One early study found that nine out of 10 U.S. consumers were concerned about the environmental impacts of their purchases. Seventy-nine percent of U.S. consumers say that a company's environmental practices influence the products and services they recommend to others.[14] A poll in British Columbia, Canada revealed that most British Columbians took a retailer's environmental record into account when deciding on where to shop. Three-quarters (77 percent) of British Columbians say that a retailer's actions, in helping to preserve and protect the environment, were "very important" (24 percent) or "somewhat important" (53 percent) in their overall decisions of where to shop.[15] Four in ten Americans said that they were willing to pay more for a product that was perceived to be better for the environment. Eighty-one percent of CEOs believed that companies should integrate sustainability throughout their supply chains; only 48 percent believe that their company has done so.[16] A survey of consumers in 17 countries (across five continents) found that 94 percent of Thai respondents and 83 percent of Brazilians were willing to pay more for environmentally friendly products (although only 45 percent of British and 53 percent of Americans surveyed were willing to do so).[17]

Consumers' recollections of advertising with green messaging are very high, with more than a third of consumers surveyed reporting that they frequently recall green messaging and an additional third recalling it occasionally.[18] Another study showed that 21 percent of consumers in the United States consider a product's reputation as the major factor when buying a product or service. Other factors were word of mouth (19 percent), brand loyalty (15 percent), and green advertising (9 percent).[19]

Climate change is a mainstream consumer issue. Consumers in the United States and United Kingdom are strongly concerned about global warming and are ready to take action. Sixty-six percent of U.S. and UK consumers agreed that everyone needs to take responsibility for their personal contributions to global warming. The majority of consumers have already made some easy, close-to-home changes such as reducing energy consumption at home (57.9 percent, U.S. and UK combined) and buying energy-efficient light bulbs (47.9 percent, U.S. and UK combined) or appliances (33.5 percent, U.S. and UK combined); however, very few have translated this into broader purchasing choices or more difficult behavioral changes. Furthermore, few planned to do so over the next six months. While 76 percent of respondents in the United Kingdom were able to identify an action as "the most important things that you can do" only 42 percent of respondents in the United States were able to do so (and few of these were specific actions recommended in the many top 10 lists of things to do on climate change).

There are not many who are completely unwilling to embrace a more climate-conscious lifestyle; however, a large proportion of people who are concerned about climate change do not feel motivated or empowered to take action. Only 42 percent of U.S. consumers (vs. 76 percent of UK consumers) were able to name a specific important action they could take.

Another study showed that 64 percent of U.S. consumers cannot name a single "green" brand, including 51 percent of those who considered themselves environmentally conscious.[20] Thirty-seven percent of consumers felt highly concerned about the environment; however, only 25 percent feel highly knowledgeable about such issues.[21] Only 22 percent felt they could make a difference when it comes to the environment.

Consumers want to know more about how businesses are addressing the climate impacts of their products. Sixty percent of U.S. and UK respondents want companies to provide more product-based information at the point of sale and half would rather do business with companies that are working to reduce their contributions to global warming.

The promotion of sustainable or environmental characteristics of a product or service tends to fall into one several categories, such as:

1   *Product or service claims.* These are focused on environmental or sustainable attributes that a product or service possesses (e.g., Whole Foods and Burt's Bees).
2   *Process claims.* These promote an organization's production processes, LCAs, or disposal methods that generate environmental or sustainable benefits (e.g., Herman Miller's Mira Chair).
3   *Image claims.* These associate organizations with sustainability or environmentally related causes or activities to generate consumer or public support (e.g., Patagonia).
4   *Social claims.* These are statements about socioeconomic impact, equity, society, a community (or its condition) in relation to some aspect of a product or service (e.g., Starbuck's fair trade outcomes on employment and social equity).

Several of these claims can be combined, and they can be impacted by advertising. Thus, the driving force behind consumerism may be the many multinational firms thriving in a capitalist system that perpetuate the consumer culture.[22] Advertising messages institutionalize consumerism and control messaging. A recent term that counters this trend (and attempts to develop a more democratic and sustainable form of advertising and consumption) is "cultural jamming."[23] "Jamming" is like a nonviolent resistance against ways we see the world.[24] The goal is to utilize advertising to promote less consumption rather than more.

Interestingly, consumers do not trust information from businesses on climate change; they are also skeptical of information imparted by the government, media, and celebrities; however, scientists, environmental groups, and family and friends in particular are seen as credible.[25] Consumers say they want more third-party verification of product information. Seventy percent of respondents in the United States and United Kingdom said that climate change claims should be proven by independent parties.

Consumers want to assume more responsibility in their lives, and they look to companies, NGOs, and government agencies for information about how to do so. Since consumers tend to do things that are easy, they want products and services that do not compromise price, performance, and environmental impact. However, green products tend to start with a deficit; they are perceived as inferior in terms of price and performance.[26]

These data begin to clarify the "gulf between green concern and green consumerism;"[27] this difference is what makes green marketing so challenging. Still, some consumers are willing to pay a premium for environmentally friendly products, especially when they believe a product (e.g., organic food or cotton) is healthier. Another reason is cost savings from a product's use; for example, many marketing campaigns promoting energy-efficient products have been successful in communicating the long-term savings to consumers. This approach is especially prevalent for energy savings. Table 9.1 shows various products and the percentage of increased cost consumers would be willing to pay for a green version of that product.

Table 9.1 Sample Price Premiums for Environmentally Friendly Products[28]

Percentage increase in price that consumers were willing to pay	Percentage surveyed	Product	Country/region
11.26	NA	Coffee	UK
13.00	33	Timber	UK
15.6	NA	Dishwasher	Spain
30.0	NA	Flowers	Netherlands
5–15	NA	Timber	Europe
10	37	Bananas	Europe
10	70	Bananas	Europe
10	64	All products labeled	Canada
5	NA	Green-labeled products	Singapore
6–10	34	Wood	USA
1–5	75	Wood	USA
10	60	Green products	USA
5	82	Green products	USA
5–7	NA	Food	USA

Consumers vary in their tendency to buy "green" by product category. For example, paper, packaged products, and disposable products for the home attract a relatively high percentage of consumers who buy green either all of the time or sometimes. However, travel, transportation, and financial services generate very few purchases of green products (even by those who systematically buy green).[29]

Despite any good that green marketing is attempting to do, it is not without drawbacks and critics. Some critics question whether advertising deliberately deceives consumers to generate sales or improve product or corporate images. Product claims have been a focal point for green critics; there are few standards or regulations monitoring this kind of advertising. When product claims are misleading, organizations are often considered *greenwashing*.

Greenwashing

Ultimately, marketing efforts help design products and services, create and use distribution channels, promote products and services, and enable firms to price items competitively. Many companies have been accused of "greenwashing" (i.e., creating false or misleading claims about "green" products, services, or activities). Greenwashing involves deceptive public relations or marketing claims about so-called ecofriendly products. Some research shows that this practice is widespread and leads to consumer distrust. For example, 73 percent of companies marketing products in this niche have been guilty of focusing on narrow sets of attributes while ignoring other possibly critical environmental issues. An example of greenwashing is a hybrid car that is advertised as "green" and "economical" but uses large amounts of electricity to recharge a battery that needs to be replaced within a short period of time.[30] Other greenwashing strategies may involve no proof of claims, vagueness in terms of using labels (e.g., "good for the earth" and "organic"), and false claims.

Environmental marketing is relatively young, and companies are legitimately struggling with finding the best ways to communicate what they are doing. In Chapter 1, we discussed the work that Coca-Cola is doing related to water management. In this case, the company has not actively communicated about their work in this area for fear of being accused of greenwashing. Also, because the company has the most valuable brand in the world, even good news could lessen the brand's value.

The consumer's perception of greenwashing is not something a company can always control; however, there are many ways a company can protect itself from these claims. Some of these methods have been discussed in this and other chapters. They include adoption of externally sanctioned standards, frequent audits, clear environmental management systems, and transparent reporting (and adherence to reporting guidelines).

Also, advertising is not the only way that a company can communicate how its product adheres to environmental standards. Labeling is another marketing effort that might be informative about a company's products and practices or might be misleading. These impacts are discussed in the next section.

Profile: The Coolest Company in Marketing[31]

When buying green products, American consumers are currently faced with the age old question: Cui bono? To the benefit of whom? Makower's analysis of the GOING Green Survey suggests that a knowledge gap exists between the number of American consumers who feel highly knowledgeable about environmentally conscious brands and those who feel they can make a difference when it comes to the environment.[32] In Patagonia's case, the firm has developed a business model that leverages high-knowledge consumers by providing the necessary information to ensure their consumers understand the firm's environmental impact and, in effect, the environmental impact of their purchase.

Interestingly, Patagonia's marketing strategy was not a marketing strategy at all. In the past, the firm has even asked consumers to consume less.[33] Patagonia has "never had to make a break from the traditional corporate culture that makes businesses hidebound and inhibits creativity. For the most part, we simply made the effort to hold to our own values and traditions."[34] In response to the age old question of cui bono, Patagonia's sales suggest; to the benefit of the planet.

In one example, Patagonia changed the way it manufactured wetsuits by distancing itself from the petroleum-based product neoprene.[35] Patagonia replaced the polychloroprene needed for wetsuits with a substance with rubber-like properties from the arid guayule plant, a shrub which thrives in the American Southwest. What has the firm done with the guayule proprietary rubber? They have made it available to the public because "when volumes go up, prices go down; and when more surfers can choose less harmful wetsuits, we all win."

The firm's sales increased 37.9 percent between 2011 and 2013. Today, the firm has used its success to create a venture fund called the $20 Million and Some Change fund.[36] Among other ventures, the fund has supported Patagonia Provisions which offers organic sourced foods and Patagonia Media which produces and sponsors media with an environmental lens. Patagonia's former COO and CFO Rose Marcario stated that most investments "will be in the $500,000 to $5 million range which include equity investments and minority and majority partners, as well as joint ventures."

Cool Points. *Consumer knowledge has always been an important aspect in marketing from the Ford's model-T to Apple's iPhone 6. In traditional marketing, effectively marketing information about a good's benefit to the customer has been essential to profitable sales. Mostly the benefits are utility-based incentives, but Patagonia is changing marketing and the line between green marketing and successful marketing is becoming increasingly blurred. Do you think that certified organic and sustainably procured and manufactured goods market themselves to some degree? How has Patagonia used their firm's ethos as a marketing mechanism?*

Environmental Labeling and Product Declarations

Eco-labels, environmental labeling, and product declarations represent a broad spectrum of "green" product-specific information in retail marketing. *Eco-labeling* involves the declaration of environmental information about a product. (*Product declarations* are similar but may include details beyond environmental declarations.) The overall goal of eco-labeling is to encourage the demand and supply of "green" and/or sustainable products and services. Consumers are often left to discern the verifiable, accurate, and non-deceptive information (i.e., information that accurately conveys the truly "green" aspects of environmental products and services).

Three types of labels have emerged as eco-labeling has evolved. Seals of approval (known as Type I labels) are labels awarded to products and services by third parties. They tend to compare the environmental characteristics of one specific good with the rest of the goods in the same range of products. Some of the best-known labels are Green Seal (USA),[37] Der Blaue Engel/The Blue Angel (Germany),[38] EU eco-label (Europe),[39] and the NF-Environnement Mark (France)[40] and DGNB (Germany).[41]

Type II labels are self-declarations (e.g., "carbon-neutral" or "organic") and are based on an organization's (self-declared) claims about its product's environmental performance. These labels do not require (or do not usually carry) third-party certifications. Yet, companies have learned that many consumers demand third-party certifications so some acquire independent verifications to support their claims. Also, many countries are now requiring that these labels carry third-party verifications before the company can use such a label. The third-party verifications may cause a shakeup in the types of labeling and push more and more companies to use Type III labels.

Type III labeling is an environmental declaration that is regulated by an organization such as the International Standards Organization standard 14025.[42] These tend to be product declarations providing environmental data about specific products. The different types of labeling vary by the level of stringency of criteria and use of third-party verification and development.

Table 9.2 shows examples of eco-labeling that are commonly used in various countries (varying by type). Some private companies monitor these labels. For example, the Ecolabel Index (one of the largest global directories of eco-labels) currently tracks over 425 eco-labels in most countries and 25 industry sectors.[43]

Some companies worry about the market impact of these labels and their impact on trade. While sales have increased moderately when labeling schemes have been used,[44] companies are worried that labeling might be used as a de facto trade barrier. (Those lacking specific labels can be prohibited from doing business in certain countries.)[45]

Today, there are a number and variety of eco-labels used in diverse contexts; this has diluted and fragmented the labeling process. Coupled with confusing and diverse standards, the consumer is left wondering what to believe when purchasing products. This issue (i.e., proliferation and confusion) will probably improve

Table 9.2 Worldwide Eco-Labeling[46] (GS = Government Sponsored; PS = Privately Sponsored)

Country	Labeling	Date initiated	Sponsor
Australia	Environmental Choice	1991	GS[47]
Australia	Good Environmental Choice	2001	PS
Austria	Hundertwasser Seal	1991	GS
Canada	Environmental Choice	1988	GS
China	Green Label		
China	Environmental Label	1993	PS
EU	EU Ecolabel	1992	GS
France	NF-Environment	1992	GS
Germany	Blue Angel	1978	GS
Global	International Eco-Certification Program	1991	PS
India	Ecomark	1991	GS
Japan	Ecomark	1991	GS
Netherlands	Stichting Milieukeur	1992	GS
Norway	Good Envrionment Choice	1991	PS
Scandinavia	Nordic Swan	1991	GS
Singapore	Green Label	1992	GS
South Korea	Ecomark	1992	GS
Taiwan	Environmental Seal		
United States	Green Seal	1989	PS
United States	Greenguard	2001	PS
United States	Cradle-to-Cradle	2005	PS
United States	STARS	2010	PS

in the future since only the more effective and scientifically sound measures are likely to survive. (There is a general feeling among many firms right now that eco-label providers launch with good intent but tend to devolve into struggling and ineffective organizations.)[48]

Labels such as organic and green technologies are either poorly defined or used in various ways. For example, one definition of green technology is "science-based applications that aim to protect the natural environment and resources by minimizing waste and toxicity, conserving energy, and reducing pollution and carbon emissions."[49] This broad definition can include so many products and applications as to make the category meaningless. One term that has had a great deal of scrutiny is organic. The next section explores this term's use.

Labeling "Organic"

A term often used in eco-labeling is "organic;" it has become very popular with companies and consumers and warrants a discussion about its emergence in the food industry.[50] There has been much debate over what is considered "organic"; as a result, the U.S. government has recently stepped in to regulate what can be labeled as such. The U.S. Department of Agriculture (USDA) now has national standards for the use of the word "organic." Other countries have similar standards.

"Organic," as a labeling term, is defined as a food or other agricultural product that has been produced through approved methods integrating cultural, biological, and mechanical practices that foster the cycling of resources, promote ecological balance, and conserve biodiversity. Synthetic fertilizers, sewage sludge, irradiation, and genetic engineering may not be used.[51] Consumers buying organic products (produced in the United States or abroad) can be assured that the foods are produced without antibiotics, hormones, pesticides, irradiation, or bioengineering. Organic farmers are required to adhere to certain soil and water conservation methods and rules about the humane treatment of animals.[52]

The USDA, for example, now uses private and state agencies to inspect and certify food companies that market organic foods. Small farmers with less than $5,000 in organic sales per year (e.g., those selling at small farmers' markets) are exempt from the certification process; however, they are still expected to be truthful in their label claims and comply with government standards. Individuals or companies selling or labeling a product as organic when they know it does not meet USDA standards can be fined up to $10,000 for each violation.

Currently, organic foods represent a small fraction of overall grocery sales in the United States, but the market is growing steadily. The new regulations are expected to help the organic industry as consumers become more confident in the labeling, and as larger corporations enter the organic foods market. U.S. sales of organic food and beverages (especially fruits and vegetables) have grown from $1 billion in 1990 to $26.7 billion in 2010 and then $39 billion in 2015.[53] Yet, organic food and beverage sales represented approximately 4 percent of overall food and beverage production and less than 0.5 percent of sales in 2012.

Acreage managed organically in 2009, worldwide, totaled 37.2 million hectares (up 2 million hectares from 2008).[54] Of the total area managed organically, 23 million hectares were grassland. Counted in the report were data from 160 countries. Countries with the largest areas of organically managed land were:

- Australia (12 million hectares);
- Argentina (4.4 million hectares);
- The United States (1.9 million hectares).[55]

The most significant growth in organic agricultural land occurred in Europe, with an increase of one million hectares. Regionally, the greatest share of organic agricultural land is in:

- Oceania (33 percent);
- Europe (25 percent);
- Latin America (23 percent).[56]

According to Organic Monitor estimates, global organic sales reached $54.9 billion in 2009, up from $50.9 billion in 2008 and continued to grow about 10 percent per year. The countries with the largest markets are the United States, Germany, and France. The highest per-capita consumption is in Denmark, Switzerland, and Austria.[57]

As new regulations are phased in, it is important to keep in mind that the term "organic" does not necessarily mean "healthier." The USDA makes no claim that organically produced food is safer or more nutritious than conventionally produced food. Consumers will still need to read nutrition labels and make wise selections to maintain an overall healthy diet. Keep in mind that the words "natural" and "organic" are *not* interchangeable; only "organic" food must meet the new USDA organic standards.[58]

Life-Cycle Analysis

You learned about LCA in Chapter 7. LCA is a process for assessing industrial, commercial, and institutional systems. The process enables the estimation of cumulative environmental impacts, usually through a value chain of events (see Appendix 9.2). The evaluation can be for cradle-to-gate (raw materials to product sale), cradle-to-grave (follows through to recycling), or cradle-to-cradle (product recycling to reuse in products).

The usual LCA is cradle-to-grave and includes analysis of raw material acquisition, manufacturing, product use or service delivery, maintenance, and final disposal. The usual environmental outputs analyzed are air emissions, water discharge, solid waste, co-products, and GHG emissions. Table 9.3 shows some examples of life-cycle approaches for different applications.

The concept stems from the World Energy Conference in the early 1960s; at the time, it focused mostly on energy use. This period followed with the process formalization and adaptation by companies such as Coca-Cola. The focus was generally on limits and eliminating product characteristics that caused high and harmful environmental impacts. The ISO 14000 series of standards formalized LCA, leading to other LCA analyses and procedures (e.g., product carbon footprinting, environmental preferable purchasing, and environmental declarations).

Today, LCA is both formalized and increasingly used to make decisions about product design. The decisions and analyses are supported by several excellent databases and software programs (e.g., SimaPro[59] and GaBi[60]) that can help model products and systems from an LCA perspective. For example, SimaPro uses databases for carbon footprint calculation, product design, eco-design, environmental product declarations, environmental impact of products or services, environmental reporting such as GRI, and the determination of key performance indicators. Users build complex models in a systematic and transparent way by utilizing the model's unique features, such as risk analysis (using Monte Carlo analysis). Risk analysis is part of every decision since firms are constantly faced with uncertainty, ambiguity, and variability. Monte Carlo simulation (i.e., the Monte Carlo Method) can produce all the possible outcomes of a decision and assess the impact of risk; this allows for better decision making under uncertainty.

The key benefit of LCA is the ability to develop a systematic evaluation of environmental consequences and a means of making environmental tradeoffs. Also, LCA has become an excellent means of quantifying

Table 9.3 Examples of Life-Cycle Approaches

Constituent	Focus	Uses
Public policy	Environmental policies	Government procurement; development of eco-labeling criteria
Industry	Supply chain; product development; building design	Purchasing; marketing communication; product declarations
Environmental NGOs	Campaign idea	Declarations; evaluation of policies and regulations
Consumers	Life-cycle choices	Eco-labeling

environmental releases from products (e.g., into the air, water, and land) and relating these releases to each stage of a product's development. LCA has been used to compare and contrast two or more products or processes and to assess the human and ecological effects of material consumption.

The usual LCA process involves four components:

1   goal and scope definitions;
2   inventory analysis;
3   impact assessment;
4   interpretation.

Analysts use LCA to compile inventories of materials, energy, water, and environmental releases; to evaluate environmental impacts; and to guide processes or product development. These are the main goals. The inventory analysis identifies data to be used in the LCA, the boundaries for analysis, the process flow, and the data-collection plan. Within this inventory analysis, one critical step is determining the functional unit. The purpose of the functional unit is to set a specified amount of a product or service that is delivered to the customer.

The boundaries of an LCA assessment relate to what will be included in the analysis and what will not be included. For example, many LCA analyses include only direct activities (e.g., manufacturing and raw materials). The analyst would take each part of the chain of activities and identify all impacts of each phase. For example, soy bean farming analysis might identify seeds, water, fertilizer, and the chemical compounds of each. After all analyses are completed the analyst would look for viable, feasible and desirable ways to improve the environmental outcomes.

The data are often difficult to obtain because it is challenging to obtain accurate assessments of the amount of resources that go into a functional unit as well as the environmental impact as a result of product use. Impact categories can include global warming, acidification, and toxicity. The assessed results of an LCA need to then be assigned to each category. For example, CO_2 emissions are assigned to global warming.

This link needs to be characterized (i.e., converted to show the exact impact of CO_2 on global warming). Across all linkages, the potential impacts need to be normalized so that all impacts can be compared and summarized. For example, impacts on global warming are often converted to CO_{2e} (the "e" referring to equivalent). Thus, the six major gases that impact global warming are all expressed in one measure.

The significant summaries of these data vary but include (1) the contribution of the life-cycle stages or groups of processes as compared to the total result, (2) dominance analysis that includes statistical tools or other techniques (e.g., quantitative or qualitative ranking) to examine significant contributions, and (3) looking for unusual or surprising deviations from expected or usual results.

LCA is a powerful tool. It leads to changes in the product, taking products out of production, increasing investments in environmental sustainability, and transparency of environmental sustainability claims. Also, LCAs can help product designers discover new ways to produce products and use substitute inputs that are more environmentally friendly. As a result of LCA, several people have discovered how to take the analysis beyond just the immediate firm to create larger positive environmental impacts. One such system is cradle-to-cradle analysis, which is the subject of the next section.

Cradle-to-Grave and Cradle-to-Cradle

A useful distinction when doing LCA is to look at a product from one of two perspectives: cradle-to-grave and cradle-to-cradle. *Cradle-to-grave* refers to analyzing a product from its raw materials to when it is recycled. *Cradle-to-cradle* refers to recycling materials from a product and using these materials again and again for producing new products.

The overarching presupposition behind these two perspectives is that our world is a closed system, and its basic elements are finite and valuable. This was the point of several sections of this book. Also, we have discussed environmental sustainability as a concern about eliminating waste from every possible aspect of production. To eliminate waste means to design products, packaging, and systems (from the very beginning) with the mindset that waste cannot exist.[61] The best way to accomplish this goal is a cradle-to-cradle mindset.

Products can be composed of materials that biodegrade and become food for biological cycles or of technical materials that stay in closed-loop technical cycles (i.e., they continually circulate as valuable nutrients for industry). In order for these metabolisms to "remain healthy, valuable, and successful, great care must be taken to avoid contaminating one with the other."[62] This also means that things that go into an organic metabolism must not contain mutagens, carcinogens, persistent toxins, or other substances that accumulate in natural systems to a damaging effect. Biological nutrients are not designed to be fed into the technical metabolism, where they would not only be lost to the biosphere but would weaken the quality of technical materials (or make their retrieval and reuse more complicated).

The cradle-to-cradle concept helps to remind us that our ultimate goal is not to populate landfills, create products that have waste (even after they are used), and generate harmful environmental effects. Thus, when doing LCA, analysis should move beyond product design and into a complete cycle of what happens to biological and technical nutrients.

Profile: Alternative Energy Cars—Does Tesla Have the Answer?[63]

In 1904, J.P. Morgan had decided to stop funding Serbian inventor Nikola Tesla's Waardenclyffe Tower. Major financiers were alarmed when they discovered that Tesla was planning on building the machine in an attempt to create free electricity using alternating current. The brilliant inventor had become distraught when he discovered that not only did J.P. Morgan stop their funding, but they also influenced other financiers to avoid supporting him as well. Although Tesla's alternate current never made it to the mainstream market, his namesake has.

Tesla Motors, co-founded by Elon Musk, is revolutionizing the automobile industry by using AC propulsion in their all-electric cars. The 2015 Model S powered by a lithium-ion battery is autopilot equipped, available with dual motor all-wheel drive, can travel up to 270 miles, and can accelerate from 0 to 60 mph in as little as 3.2 seconds.[64]

Table 7.2 shows the strengths and weaknesses of each corporate structure. All-electric cars struggling with high-costs and limited ranges have had poor market performance relative to their hybrid or petroleum-based competitors. The success of Tesla Motor's long-term growth depends on the widespread adoption of electric cars. In order to create this mass-market, CEO Elon Musk has partnered up with Panasonic to build a $5 billion[65] battery factory in the Tahoe Reno Industrial Center.[66] The new factory is estimated to double the world's lithium-battery production. Currently, Tesla Motors calculates that the production of their power-management and cooling systems cost less than $300 per kilowatt-hour (kWh). Sanford C. Bernstein, a research firm, estimates that battery powered cars will start to become competitive once costs drop below $200 per kWh.[67] Once fully operational, the Gigafactory will manufacture batteries for 500,000 vehicles.

Figure 9.2 Tesla Motors Model S. Photo Credit: Tesla Motors

By increasing the company's scale, Tesla estimates that the new factory will cut their production costs by as much as 30 percent.

Revving Up. *UBS bank notes that the raw materials needed to produce lithium-ion batteries account for 70 percent of their price. Reflecting on Chapter 7, do you think that Tesla Motors will be able to reduce input costs, increase scale and learning, and improve product design and production techniques enough to reach the $200 per kWh competitive threshold?*

Chapter Summary

Marketing is an important topic when discussing strategy as this function defines product, price, place, and promotion decisions. Consumers are becoming increasingly more predisposed to consider environmental criteria when making purchase decisions. Some research indicates that they might even pay premiums for environmentally friendly products; however, companies must often prove the product is beneficial to the consumer and justify its environmental claims before consumers are willing to purchase. This is where marketing can become very important to product success.

Firms have several tools available for making marketing decisions. Labeling is one of these tools. By determining which of the three types of labels to use with their products, firms are choosing the level of validation to pursue for their "green" products. One of the most important tools a company can utilize is LCA. When applying information gained through LCA, companies try to use sustainable design principles to help improve products (e.g., cradle-to-cradle processes). Ultimately, companies have to be careful that they are truly committed to product design to avoid being accused of greenwashing.

Case Revisited: Frito-Lay as a Cautionary Tale

Frito-Lay has a challenge, as do other companies that try to balance environmental outcomes, product quality, and cost; also, unintended consequences (as Frito-Lay found out) are numerous. Yet, this chapter supports the direction that these companies are taking and makes the case that continued analysis of a product's life-cycle can inform managers about how to improve product performance, lessen environmental degradation, and maintain efficient costs. The only way forward is to avoid greenwashing; this means making informed decisions based on scientific studies and by upholding integrity in marketing efforts. Frito-Lay can recover by reconsidering the entire marketing mix—from analysis to product design to advertising. Despite any good that came from their noisy chip bag, if it is not marketable to the consumer it cannot be successful. As product standards continue to improve, companies like Frito-Lay will gain valuable inputs.

Terms to Know

Cradle-to-cradle: recycling materials from a product and using these materials again and again for producing new products

Cradle-to-grave: analyzing a product from its raw materials to when it is recycled

Eco-labels: product declarations about the environmental footprints of specific products

Green marketing: promotional messages that might appeal to the needs and desires of environmentally concerned consumers

Greenwashing: creating false or misleading claims about environmental activities

Life-cycle analysis: a process that enables the estimation of cumulative environmental impacts (usually through a value chain of events)

Profile: Myco Board Is Not Just for Salads

Imagine a chair made from mushrooms. Savor is just the chair. It is manufactured by Gunlocke and designed by Alyssa Coletti of Nonfiction Creative, LLC.[68] Gunlocke introduced the chair to NeoCon in 2014.

Myco Board is made from corn stocks,[69] mycelium, and hemp (from Canada) and is Biodegradable Products Institute-certified for industrial compost. The Savor chair contains Myco Board. Eighty-six percent of the chair has renewable content. It takes about 80 minutes to make a chair which makes it an efficient chair to manufacture.

Roy Green, Director of Stewardship and Sustainability at Gunlocke explained the challenges in making such a chair. "The outside back of the chair, which would typically be made from a type of plywood, was very expensive because the back's shape was prone to cracking or splitting."[70] The company solved these problems by using solutions from a company called Ecovative Design.[71] The design firm came up with Myco Board which is grown, not glued, with natural, rapidly renewable mycelium technology.

Mycelium is a natural, self-assembling glue, digesting crop waste to produce cost-competitive and environmentally responsible materials. Mycelium (plural, mycelia) is an extension of the hyphae of fungi. A hypha is a thread-like, branching structure formed by fungi. As the hyphae grow, they become longer and branch off, forming a mycelium network visually reminiscent of the branches of a tree. The mycelium is the most important and permanent part of a fungus. The mycelia network that emanates from a fungal spore can extend over and into the soil in search of nutrients. The ends of some mycelia terminate as mushrooms and toadstools.[72] These mycelium features make it ideal for all sorts of products and applications.

Mushroom Materials from Ecovative Designs are Cradle to Cradle CertifiedCM Gold. Cradle to Cradle CertifiedCM is a certification mark licensed by the Cradle to Cradle Products Innovation Institute.[73] Ecovative uses the material for packaging, insulation, automotive applications, and even surf boards.

One author coined new terms using mycelium as the basis, such as mycorestoration through biotransforming stripped land, mycofiltration by creating habitat buffers, myco-remediation by healing chemically harmed environments, and mycoforestry by creating truly sustainable forests).[74]

The use of mycelium is a perfect illustration of using life forms, biomimicry, to design products.

Questions and Critical Thinking

1   Review the YouTube presentation by Melinda Gates entitled "What Non-Profits Can Learn from Coca-Cola."[75] Comment on her ideas that social marketing and social responsibility marketing (as discussed in this chapter) should use methods developed by the largest firms in the world. In this case, Gates describes the use of Coca-Cola-type marketing campaigns to increase the use of sanitary technologies to help people improve their levels of sanitation in developing nations.

2   Think about an advertisement you have seen supporting environmental sustainability. Evaluate this advertisement. What criteria would you use to determine its integrity? For example, are the claims supported by third-party organizations? Does the ad seem to be based on quality research?

3   Marks & Spencer is one the United Kingdom's largest retailers.[76] The company launched Plan A in 2007, which is a collection of 100 sustainability-oriented commitments to be achieved within five years. Marks & Spencer claims that Plan A has been a big success, producing brand enhancement and a decreased environmental footprint. This work has definitely strengthened customers' ties to the retailer. Marks & Spencer energy customers are incentivized to use less energy via the availability of discount vouchers that are useable in M&S stores throughout the country. Thus, Plan A has become fully integrated into the Marks & Spencer brand. Do some research on Plan A and make a note of how the company communicates its work. Also, make note of the relationships the company has with NGOs such as Oxfam and the tie-in with Marks & Spencer customers. For example, in return for bringing unwanted clothing to a local Oxfam shop (including at least one Marks & Spencer-branded clothing item), customers receive a coupon for £5 that can be used toward purchases at Marks & Spencer stores.[77]

Appendix 9.1. Sample Certification Schemes and Organizations

Name	Responsible agency	Scope	Intent
CATEGORY			
Agriculture			
National Organic Program (NOP)	U.S. Department of Agriculture, Agriculture Marketing Service	USA	Organic production is a system that is managed in accordance with the Organic Foods Production Act (OFPA) of 1990 and regulations in Title 7, Part 205 of the Code of Federal Regulations to respond to site-specific conditions by integrating cultural, biological, and mechanical practices that foster cycling of resources, promote ecological balance, and conserve biodiversity. The NOP develops, implements, and administers national production, handling, and labeling standards.[78]
Food Alliance	Food Alliance	USA	Food Alliance operates a voluntary certification program based on standards that define sustainable agricultural practices. Farms, ranches, and food processors that meet Food Alliance's standards, as determined by a third-party site inspection, use Food Alliance certification to differentiate their products, strengthen their brands, and support credible claims for social and environmental responsibility.[79]
Indocert	Indocert	India and international	Indocert is a nationally and internationally operating certification body established in India.[80]
Naturland	Naturland	Germany	Naturland issues certification for beekeeping, aquaculture, forest management, sustainable capture fishery, processing, textiles, cosmetic products, social responsibility, fair trade, and organic production.[81]
Pesticide Residue Free	SCS Global Services	USA	SCS's Certified Pesticide Residue Free program provides valuable independent recognition for growers whose products meet the most stringent residue standards in the marketplace today. Products certified to this premium standard are the answer for customers who want proof that there are no detected pesticide residues in their food.[82]
Leadership in Energy and Environmental Design (LEED)	Green Building Council	USA	LEED is an internationally recognized green building certification system, providing third-party verification that a building or community was designed and built using strategies aimed at improving performance across all the metrics that matter most: energy savings, water efficiency, CO_2 emissions reduction, improved indoor environmental quality, and stewardship of resources and sensitivity to their impacts.[83]
Buildings			
Comprehensive Assessment System for Built Environment Efficiency (CASBEE)	Japan GreenBuild Council (JaGBC); Japan Sustainable Building Consortium (JSBC)	Japan	CASBEE provides assessment of buildings and construction processes with a particular emphasis on problems peculiar to Japan and Asia.[84]

BRE Environmental Assessment Method (BREEAM)	BRE Global Ltd	UK	BREEAM is an environmental assessment method for buildings. It sets the standard for best practice in sustainable design and has become the de facto measure used to describe a building's environmental performance. BREEAM addresses wide-ranging environmental and sustainability issues and enables developers and designers to prove the environmental credentials of their buildings to planners and clients.[85]
Responsible Sourcing of Construction Products	BRE Global Ltd	UK	Responsible Sourcing of Construction Products provides a holistic approach to managing a product from the point at which component materials are mined or harvested, through manufacture and processing. Key areas of concern range across ethical, environmental, and societal issues including: Where do the materials come from? Have they been extracted and processed in an environmentally sensitive manner? Has the workforce involved in their extraction and production been treated fairly?[86]

Business management

ULE 880	UL	International	UL Environment, in partnership with GreenBiz Group, has developed an organization-wide sustainability standard that will be used to assess corporate policies and practices, known as the ULE 880: Sustainability for Manufacturing Organizations.[87]
Environmental Profiles	BRE Global Ltd	UK	The Environmental Profiles Certification Scheme provides ongoing, independent assessment and certification of environmental performance. The certification involves calculating the "cradle to grave" environmental profile of a building material, product, or system.[88]

Carbon offsets

VCS	Verified Carbon Standard	International	VCS quality assurance principles ensure all VCUs represent GHG emission reductions or removals that are real, measurable, additional, permanent, independently verified, conservatively estimated, uniquely numbered, and transparently listed.[89]
CAR	Climate Action Reserve	North America	The Climate Action Reserve encourages action to reduce GHG emissions by ensuring the environmental integrity and financial benefit of emissions reduction projects. The Reserve establishes high quality standards for carbon offset projects, oversees independent third-party verification bodies, issues carbon credits generated from such projects and tracks the transaction of credits over time in a transparent, publically accessible system.[90]
Climate, Community and Biodiversity Standards (CCB Standards)	Climate, Community, and Biodiversity Alliance (CCBA)	International	The CCBA is a unique partnership of leading international NGOs with a mission to stimulate and promote land-based carbon activities that credibly mitigate global climate change, improve the well-being and reduce the poverty of local communities, and conserve biodiversity. The CCB Standards evaluate land-based carbon mitigation projects from the early stages of development through implementation.[91]
The Gold Standard	The Gold Standard Foundation	International	The Gold Standard is a certification standard for carbon mitigation projects. They certify renewable energy, energy efficiency, waste management, and land use and forest carbon offset projects to ensure that they all demonstrate GHG reductions and sustainable development benefits in local communities that are measured, reported, and verified.[92]

(continued)

(continued)

Name	Responsible agency	Scope	Intent
Consumer products			
Green Seal	Green Seal	USA	Green Seal is a nonprofit organization that develops life-cycle-based sustainability standards for products, services, and companies and offers third-party certification for those that meet the criteria in the standard.[93]
EcoLogo	UL Environment	North America	EcoLogo provides customers—public, corporate, and consumer—with assurance that the products and services bearing the logo meet stringent standards of environmental leadership.[94]
Nordic Ecolabel	Nordic Ecolabel	Europe	The Nordic Ecolabel was established to provide an environmental labeling scheme that would contribute to a sustainable consumption. It is a voluntary, positive Ecolabeling of products and services. The Nordic Ecolabel was also initiated as a practical tool for consumers to help them actively choose environmentally sound products.[95]
Eco Mark	Japan Environment Association (JEA)	Japan	The Eco Mark Program is operated by JEA, founded in 1989, indicating product carrying the Eco Mark is certified as being useful for environmental preservation. The product information is provided with an environmental perspective.[96]
Blue Angel	The Environmental Label Jury; The Federal Ministry for the Environment, Nature Conservation and Nuclear Safety; The Federal Environment Agency; RAL gGmbH	International	The Blue Angel label is the German national environmental labeling program. Around 11,700 products and services in circa 125 product categories carry the Blue Angel eco-label and the number of product categories is constantly expanding.[97]
ENERGY STAR	U.S. EPA	USA	ENERGY STAR is a voluntary program of the U.S. EPA. Now in its 20th year, the ENERGY STAR program has boosted the adoption of energy efficient products, practices, and services through valuable partnerships, objective measurement tools, and consumer education.[98]
Fair Trade			
Fair Trade USA	Fair Trade USA	USA	Fair Trade USA is a nonprofit organization that certifies and promotes Fair Trade products in the United States. The leading third-party certifier, they work with more than 800 U.S. companies to audit and certify that the products they offer comply with international Fair Trade standards. To earn a license from Fair Trade USA to use the Fair Trade CertifiedTM label on their products, companies must buy from certified farms and organizations, pay Fair Trade prices and premiums, and submit to rigorous supply chain audits.[99]

Fish

Aquaculture Stewardship Council (ASC)	ASC	International	The ASC was founded in 2009 by WWF and IDH (Dutch Sustainable Trade Initiative) to manage the global standards for responsible aquaculture, which are under development by the Aquaculture Dialogues, a program of roundtables initiated and coordinated by WWF.[100]
Marine Stewardship Council (MSC)	MSC	International	The science-based MSC environmental standard for sustainable fishing offers fisheries a way to confirm sustainability using a credible, independent, third-party assessment process.[101]

Hotels

Green Seal	Green Seal	USA	Green Seal develops life-cycle-based sustainability standards for products, services, and companies and offers third-party certification for those that meet the criteria in the standard. Green Seal has 32 issued standards that cover over 375 product and service categories, including building and construction, consumer products, and service products.[102]

Natural resources

Recycled Content Certification	SCS Global Services		The SCS Recycled Content Certification evaluates products made from preconsumer or postconsumer material diverted from the waste stream. Certification measures the percentage of recycled content for the purpose of making an accurate claim in the marketplace.[103]
Biodegradable Certification	SCS Global Services		SCS Global provides certification for biodegradable liquid products such as cleaners, degreasers, detergents, and soaps.[104]
Recycling Program Certification	SCS Global Services		The SCS Recycling Program Certification is for recyclers and reclamation facilities who wish to make verified claims about their diversion strategies and recycling rates. The program helps to significantly reduce the amount of virgin materials consumed in the manufacturing process, reduce the volume of waste disposal, divert waste from landfills, and process materials at the end of their useful life and recycle them back into a similar product category.[105]
Environmental Claim Validations	UL Environment	International	With environmental claim validations from UL Environment, products come armed with third-party proof of their compliance with various green codes, standards, and procurement policies for recycled content, recyclability, landfill waste diversion, and rapidly renewable content.[106]
Sustainability Index	Wal-Mart		Wal-Mart has worked with some of their largest competitors and with The Sustainability Consortium (TSC) to develop measurement and reporting systems for product sustainability. This tool will help to improve the sustainability of the products; integrate sustainability into their core business; and reduce cost, improve product quality, and create a more efficient supply chain.[107]

(continued)

(continued)

Name	Responsible agency	Scope	Intent
Environmental management systems			
ISO 9000	International Organization for Standardization (ISO)	International	The ISO 9000 family addresses various aspects of quality management and contains some of ISO's best known standards. The standards provide guidance and tools for companies and organizations who want to ensure that their products and services consistently meet customer's requirements, and that quality is consistently improved.[108]
ISO 14001	ISO	International	The ISO 14000 family addresses various aspects of environmental management. It provides practical tools for companies and organizations looking to identify and control their environmental impact and constantly improve their environmental performance. ISO 14001:2004 and ISO 14004:2004 focus on environmental management systems. The other standards in the family focus on specific environmental aspects such as life-cycle analysis, communication, and auditing.[109]
Wood products			
FSC Certification	Forest Stewardship Council	International	FSC certification ensures that products come from responsibly managed forests that provide environmental, social, and economic benefits.[110]
SFI	Sustainable Forest Initiative (SFI)	USA	The SFI 2010–2014 Standard promotes sustainable forest management through 14 core principles, 20 objectives, 38 performance measures, and 115 indicators developed by professional foresters, conservationists, scientists, and others.[111]
Responsible Procurement Program	SCS Global	USA	The Responsible Procurement Program was conceived by the National Wood Flooring Association (NWFA) in conjunction with SCS Global, FSC, and the Rainforest Alliance TREES US Program, and is committed to producing and promoting wood floors that come only from environmentally and socially responsible sources, improving forest sustainability for future generations.[112]
Legal HarvestTM Verification	SCS Global		The SCS Legal Harvest Verification program is designed for responsible companies who are looking for a systematic way of demonstrating "due care" in sourcing forest products with the goal of eliminating illegally harvested wood from their supply.[113]

Appendix 9.2. Value Chain Analysis

This appendix suggests some ways that firms can create and capture value within and across value chains. We have covered many of these topics throughout the book, including LCA (which is essentially an analysis of a firm's value chain). In this Appendix, I will identify, but not focus on, factors that might affect potential industry earnings (e.g., substitutes, complements, and demand changes) so that we have an idea of whether an industry is likely to become more or less attractive as a result of changes in industry earnings. I will mainly focus on firms' strategies that can increase the share of potential industry earnings from the point of view of a value chain analysis.

Costs and benefits to buyers are the sources of competitive advantage within markets. Businesses attempt to push down costs and increase benefits delivered to customers to achieve advantages over competitors. Managers usually develop a firm's strategy by looking at costs and benefits from a cross-functional basis (and the way competition mediates between these costs and benefits and attainable margins). Thus, a firm's internal analyses (and its comparison with competitors) are important aspects of strategic approach.

To attain competitive advantage via cost reductions and increased benefits, the firm's management must make choices as to how to allocate resources. This allocation is more efficient when positive (i.e., mutually reinforcing linkages make the whole of the firm more than the sum of its parts). Thus, firms that attain competitive advantages tend to have functions or activities that are very tightly coupled with unique value propositions. This is not a static view but a dynamic one of constant discovery and development of a "path for continuous improvement rather than a position for all time."[114]

Industry analysis (from the perspective of firms active in an industry) is a useful means of understanding how firms create and capture value. Firms conduct industry analyses to determine the attractiveness of an industry and the profitability of the average industry firm. Industry analysis also helps to determine why firms are (or are not) profitable and suggests ways to cut costs or increase benefits.

Included in an industry analysis is an analysis of an industry's value chain. Every firm is part of a value chain, which is a method for breaking down industry activities into a chain of events (e.g., from basic raw materials to end customers). These strategically relevant activities are developed to understand the behavior of costs and sources of differentiation for participating firms. A value chain includes upstream firms and other suppliers that contribute inputs used by industry incumbents. Downstream from the incumbent firms are buyers (e.g., firms or final consumers who buy from firms in the industry). The entire chain (from raw materials to final consumers) is a "value chain" because each link in the chain has the potential to add value to its inputs by cutting costs or increasing benefits.

The logic of industry analysis is that parts of a value chain create some value and that participants in the chain will somehow divide that value among themselves. The greatest value the incumbents, as a group, could hope to capture is the entire value added by the chain (i.e., the value to the final buyers of the goods or services produced less the value of resources that are used to produce them).

However, value chain analysis is more than a simple value-added analysis. Value-added analysis ignores linkages with suppliers and customers and benefits of interdependencies within the firm. Whereas traditional cost analysis tends to emphasize across-the-board cost reductions, value chain analysis, by recognizing interdependencies, shows possibilities for increasing costs in one area to bring about lower costs in another (e.g., increasing the quality of inputs to improve manufacturing processes).

Industry earnings are the total value created minus opportunity costs of the resources required to produce that value. Anything that changes industry demand or the industry's opportunity costs of resources will affect the size of potential industry earnings, creating new value that can be captured by industry participants.

Quantity Produced by the Industry

Value creation is at the heart of using the value chain to gain competitive advantage. Whereas *value captured* is expanding one's position within a market space, *value creation* is expansion of the size of the market. This concept is not very different from the concept of *value migration* (i.e., that value migrates from ineffective to effective business designs).[115] This value movement occurs from company to company and industry to industry. Maximizing the share captured by a firm is done by reducing the share captured by other segments and firms within the chain.

A firm can use the same strategy to capture and create value; however, mostly capturing value has an adverse effect on value creation (e.g., monopolies). Also, as with most strategies, firms can both compete and cooperate to create and capture value. For example, low-cost strategies can lead a firm to compete on low prices at the retail level, thus increasing the firm's value capture within the industry. Yet, by cutting prices, the firm might not be able to invest in (or compete in) opportunities for value differentiation in other markets. Firms can overcome this inability by forming strategic alliances to combine competencies, thus generating opportunities to create value for both firms. Alliances can combine competencies and afford opportunities to firms not otherwise available to them separately.

Using the Value Chain to Gain Competitive Advantage: An Example

In early 1994, the U.S. ready-to-eat (RTE) breakfast cereal industry had reached a critical turning point in its evolution. In an industry historically characterized by stability and above-average profitability, slowing demand growth (which was partially due to a surge in nonbranded [or private label] sales) threatened to undermine the dominant positions of the Big Three (i.e., Kellogg, General Mills, and Philip Morris). The 1993 year-end statistics showed that industry sales growth had slowed to below 2 percent, while private labels had topped 5 percent market share by sales and 9 percent by volume for the first time. Price increases by the Big Three had widened the gap between branded and private-label products. The competitors had traditionally avoided destructive head-to-head competition; however, this mutual restraint appeared to be crumbling. Each of the firms faced major decisions going forward about whether to break with the industry's lock-step moves and how to deal with the threat of private-label competitors.[116]

Figure 9.3 shows the value chains of typical companies following these strategies. Private-label companies gained a competitive advantage by focusing on simpler cereals with less labor-intensive processes and containing fewer expensive fruits and nuts. Also, by eliminating marketing costs and relying on wholesalers and third-party distributors, private labels innovated in the value chain to create enormous value for themselves and the customer. Finally, private-label cereal companies used different types of outlets to sell their cereals, including large warehouse-like retailers (e.g., Sam's Club and Kmart). This rivalry continues today with the private labels making more and more progress at the expense of branded cereals (see Table 9.4).[117]

This example shows that firms can use value chain analysis to identify various activities contributing to competitive advantage, analyze these activities (for sources of cost and benefits), and change these activities (or their relationships) to increase competitive advantage.

Cost and Behaviors

To understand cost positions and behaviors, analysts split total costs into a limited number of economically meaningful activities and identify the forces (i.e., cost drivers) that cause costs to vary across different businesses or different strategic options. Thus, to begin a value chain analysis, the analyst must first identify the parts of the industry's value chain and then assign costs, revenues, and assets to these activities. Then the analyst can diagnose the cost drivers regulating each value activity.

Activity-based cost analysis helps provide a more accurate picture of how costs actually add value to the firm and the parts of the chain (see Table 9.5 for a comparison of value chain analysis vs. conventional

Supplying Firms → Incumbent Firm → Buying Firms → Final Consumer
Primary Activities: Inbound logistics → Operations → Outbound logistics → Marketing/Sales → Service
Support Activities: Infrastructure; Human Resource Management; Technology Procurement

Figure 9.3 The Generic Value Chain

Table 9.4 Cereal Value Chain (U.S. dollars per ounce)

	Branded	Private
Raw materials		
Cereals and other ingredients	.42	.38
Packaging	.19	.15
Cereal company		
Overhead	.40	.38
Manufacturing	.52	.47
Distribution	.14	0
Marketing	.75	0
Margin	.40	.07
Grocer		
12% of $3.20	.38	
Private label grocer		
Food wholesaler 10% of $1.61		.16
Private label grocer 15% of $1.90		.29
Total per pound of branded cereal	$3.20	$1.92

managerial accounting). In general, recurring costs and nonrecurring costs must clearly be distinguished from one another. Most interesting for strategic analyses, with respect to sustainable competitive advantages, are recurring costs. Also, cost categories are worth breaking out (instead of being lumped together) if they are expected to pick up significant differences across the businesses (or strategic options being compared), if they correspond to technically separable activities, or if they are individually large enough to exert a significant influence on overall cost positions. Activities should be isolated and separated if they satisfy any or all of the following conditions: (1) they represent a significant percentage of operating costs, (2) the cost behaviors of the activities or the cost drivers are different, (3) they are performed by competitors in different ways, and (4) they are likely to create differentiation.

Ask: "What would I have to pay for this activity outside of the firm?"

Table 9.5 Value Chain vs. Conventional Management Accounting

	Conventional	Value chain analysis
Focus	Internal	External
Perspective	Value added	Entire set of linked activities from suppliers to end-users
Cost-driver concept	Single driver: volume applied to overall firm level	Multiple cost drivers • Structural: scale, scope, etc. • Execution: plant layout, processes, etc. Each value activity analyzed separately
Cost containment philosophy	Cost reductions "across the board"	Cost containment as a function of the cost drivers regulating each value activity; exploit linkages; "spend to save"
Strategic issues	Not very many	• Identify cost drivers at the individual activity level and develop cost/differentiation advantages either by controlling drivers better than competitors or by reconfiguring the value chain • For each value activity, ask strategic questions pertaining to make vs. buy, forward or backward integration • Quantify and assess supplier power and buyer power and exploit linkages with suppliers and buyers

Not all strategic drivers are equally important all of the time; however, some drivers are probably more important to certain companies than others. For example, economies of scale are currently of minor importance to educational institutions whereas capacity utilization is critical to success. Few benefits accrue because a university is large and keeps getting larger; however, many benefits accrue to an institution that can manage class sizes and the use of facilities during the day. This driver accounts for the relative success of many universities, along with drivers that produce benefits (e.g., quality instruction and research productivity).

For each cost driver, a particular cost analysis framework can help to understand the firm's positioning. Also, different cost drivers influence different value chain activities. For example, the relevant cost driver for advertising is market share whereas promotional costs are usually variable. Coca-Cola can realize economies of scale in advertising because of its large market share. A coupon for cost reduction is strictly a variable cost/unit.

Analysts attach one or more of these cost drivers to each important activity. They start the analysis with a business's historical costs (or some other benchmark) and then use differences in leverage, vis-à-vis relevant drivers, to estimate the cost position of a competitor or of an alternative strategic action. In this analysis, activities or categories that account for larger percentages of costs should be given more attention. The analysis should focus on drivers that have the biggest impact on any particular cost category.

Analysis of Benefits

The analysis of benefits, in the value chain, tends to be harder to find. Benefits tend to depend more heavily on intangible assets than do costs. Also, while cost analysis can be conducted on the basis of relatively objective relationships, benefit analysis requires assumptions about subjective buyer preferences as well as objective information about products and services. The additive nature of these benefits may be more complicated than costs (i.e., they are not simply added together to get a total benefit of the chain).

An analyst can begin a benefits analysis by identifying the objective product attributes that drive buyers' choices. These characteristics are the physical and service-related attributes as well as complements that come with a product. The analyst tries to identify only those characteristics that have high impact on buyer choice and contribute significantly to overall value added. These benefits may include not only product elements but also such intangibles as image, brand, and product packaging.

Characteristics should be measured in terms of gross rather than net (of price) benefits to buyers. That is, price should be considered not as a characteristic but as a gross payoff per unit that is obtained from "serving up" a particular bundle of characteristics. To identify relevant characteristics, the strategist must understand how the buyer actually uses the product or service. This analysis may be elaborate and involve a long list of characteristics. Consider some principles to reduce the list:[118]

1   If the total contribution of a group of competing products relative to a particular characteristic is small in relation to the contribution from products outside the group, that characteristic can usually be neglected in the analysis of the small group.
2   A characteristic that is invariant over the group of competing products is irrelevant to the analysis.
3   Even if competitors within the group deliver different levels of a particular characteristic, such differentials can be ignored if they fail to have much of an effect on buyer choice.
4   The analysis should be made as simple and as quantitative as possible.

In many industries, analysts pay attention to the subjective components of buyer choice indicating signals of benefits.[119] Signals differ from characteristics in that they influence buyers' perceptions of a business's ability to satisfy their wants (vs. its actual ability to do so). They include factors such as image, cumulative advertising, length of time in business, customer databases, market share, and product appearance. The signals of benefits can be analyzed using a number of marketing techniques (e.g., direct surveys, attribute ratings, hedonic pricing analysis, and measures of willingness to pay).[120]

Principles of Vertical Integration

A firm can use value chain analysis to decide on "make or buy" transactions (i.e., the principles governing an organization's decisions as to how to structure its transactions or how deeply to vertically integrate). I introduced this concept in Chapter 7. Does the firm choose to make its resource decisions internally (using whatever management mechanisms are available)? Does it use a market to direct resources?[121] Figure 9.4 shows the different types of vertical integration relationships available to the firm according to the degree of formalization and degree of commitment needed to create the relationship. The various relationships demonstrate the large variety of options available to any firm.

Many incentives exist for firms to vertically integrate across the value chain. Value chain analysis can identify the set of activities needed for the firm to conduct its business; however, other forces determine whether the firm should do these activities internally or within the market. We will discuss several incentives to integrate vertically (e.g., asset specificity, competition, information access, market uncertainty, and transaction frequency).

What are the advantages of a firm using internal vs. market-allocation mechanisms? A nonintegrated firm experiences search and contracting costs when dealing with buyers and suppliers. These are transaction costs associated with using the market. If the firm, instead, internalizes the transaction and buys and sells within the firm, it bears a quite different set of transaction costs (e.g., the coordination of buying and selling activities within the firm and organizing and motivating workers). An optimal strategy, then, would involve trading off each of the available methods of organizing transactions to minimize their costs. Also, given that firms have core competencies that contribute to competitiveness, they tend to view some activities as necessary to achieving their goals (i.e., some core competencies are too risky to outsource).[122] Outsourcing increases the risk of imitation by other firms, thus eroding the sustainability of a core competency contribution to competitive advantage.

A hold-up issue arises when a firm is held hostage by either its suppliers or buyers. If a firm is reliant on a supplier for an input it might want to backward integrate to avoid a hold-up on the part of suppliers. The hold-up could take many forms, especially higher input costs or, in the extreme, input denial. Similarly, forward integration might serve to ensure access to scarce channel capacity. Thus, hold-up problems are a result of asset specificity.

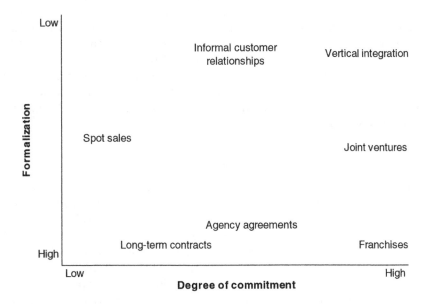

Figure 9.4 Examples of Different Types of Vertical Relationships

When there are low levels of competition within the supplier industry, firms are again faced with the prospect of hold-ups. Vertical integration can mitigate these circumstances by securing lower prices and more stable supplies.[123] How much vertical integration should there be? What form should it take? One means of approaching these questions is to use a matrix.[124] The matrix suggests that investment specificity and asset mix are the two dimensions that determine the degree of integration (and the form this integration should take). Occasionally, transactions with general assets call for market transactions; however, occasional transactions with specific assets call for contracts. If the transactions are more frequent and involve general assets then market transactions are still warranted; however, if the assets are specific and the transactions are frequent, then vertical integration is warranted.

A dimension that can change some of these prescriptions is when market uncertainty increases. What if I have an occasional transaction with specific assets but the market price is highly uncertain, or I cannot trust the supplier to follow through on commitments? I might want to vertically integrate to create higher input certainty. We are likely to see vertical integration when it is too costly and cumbersome for a firm to specify all contingencies. In general, the right level of vertical integration depends on the opportunities for specific investment, frequency of transactions across vertically linked units, and market uncertainty.

Entry and Incumbency Advantages

When incumbent firms are performing well (or are perceived as having the potential to perform well), other firms will want to join the industry. Incumbents try to combat this entry so that they do not have to share industry profits and can remain competitive. Thus, the incumbent firms try to mount entry barriers or conditions that make the industry less attractive to potential entrants. Scale advantages, cumulative investments (e.g., learning and innovation), reputation, consumer loyalty, and switching costs (along with demand-side increasing returns) are common examples of entry barriers. Some of these entry barriers relate to the industry's value chain.

One example of an entry barrier that relates to a firm's value chain may be economies of scope when a firm produces several product lines.[125] These are cost savings a firm achieves by having multiple products (since costs associated with producing and selling two products together are lower than the sum of the cost of producing or selling the two products separately). This barrier to entry is usually coupled with other entry barriers such as reputation.

Contracts and vertical integration could tie up channels of distribution (or potential entry areas) for competitors. Attempts to build entry barriers, if successful, increase market concentration and diminish competition. In principle, courts have viewed investments made to create entry barriers as predatory, even though no actual firm has been preyed upon because no entry had occurred. When Alcoa, a Pittsburgh-based firm, had a near monopoly within U.S. aluminum refining, it paid the primary suppliers of low-cost energy to withhold energy from any new firm that wanted to compete with Alcoa. The courts found that this practice violated antitrust laws.[126] Similar court actions occurred against the cereal companies for flooding the product space.[127] These are just some examples of potential entry issues and incumbency advantages when using value chain analysis as a basis of strategy.

Vertical Power: Buyer and Supplier Power

Value capture can occur in many places within the value chain. One major concern for firms is the vertical power of buyers and suppliers. Perfectly competitive firms charge a price equal to their marginal opportunity costs and thus cannot capture the value they create. The final consumers, in this case, capture all of the value (even though they have no market power and therefore no buyer power).

A single powerful supplier or buyer can change the situation in this example and set its output prices. No other type of firm in the chain has this luxury. For example, OPEC (Organization of Petroleum Exporting Countries) is an oil cartel in that its suppliers (e.g., firms that drill for oil or operate wells) are in competitive industries; the downstream buyers, oil refiners, distributors, and retailers are fairly competitive as well. Thus, OPEC is both a unique customer and a unique supplier (which can control prices and capture more value than other firms in the value chain).

One conclusion from this example is that large suppliers are powerful. Yet, "large" can have two meanings. First, it can mean that the purchasing firms buy only a small share of the supplier's output. Thus, the supplier will gain power since the buyer's purchase does not affect the supplier's profitability to a great extent. Second, "large" can mean that the supplying firm provides an input that represents a large share of the purchasing firm's cost. The power depends on the competitiveness of the supplier's industry (e.g., turbines represent a large portion of a windmill's costs but if the turbine industry is competitive, turbine firms will have no supplier power).

What happens when more than one segment of the chain has firms with some power? Two effects result: double marginalization or bargaining over transaction price. Double marginalization means that firms with supplier (or buyer) power will be better off when the other firms in the value chain are in perfectly competitive industries. Firms prefer to have market power in their own industries to mitigate the effects of competitors on value capture. Firms also prefer their buyers to have no supplier power. If a firm can increase its own supplier power (or reduce supplier power elsewhere in the chain), it can increase its profits. As for transaction costs, when a powerful supplier faces a powerful buyer, they can both influence associated transaction terms. They will bargain over the transaction price; since they both want the transaction to go forward, they will probably reach some solution to the pricing issues.

So far, we have been discussing *value capture*. Creating value depends on investments made by firms in the value chain. If complements and substitutes do not influence the industry, firms can invest in cost-reduction or product-development activities to increase the value they create. Relationships formed between (and among) firms in different segments can affect these investments and thus the value created. Creating additional value through relationships with buyers and suppliers can add more to firm profitability than value-extraction strategies. Thus, firms engage in joint ventures, strategic alliances, supplier and buyer contracts, and various relationships to increase the value for all participants. To more fully understand the ways to create value, a firm must address two key problems: *coordination* and *incentives*.

Coordination and Incentive Problems

We have already clarified that vertical relationships can add value by reducing transaction costs. Firms assess characteristics and prices of alternative inputs, sellers seek out buyers, and both firms must negotiate delivery schedules and other issues (e.g., handling delays, price disagreements, and product-related problems). All of these considerations consume resources. By forming relationships, firms can avoid having to constantly negotiate these issues and instead create routine means of deciding and interacting. These relationship-specific investments (i.e., investments that pay off only if the relationship continues) create opportunities for increasing value for all participating firms. To coordinate with other firms, some or all of the firms must make investments to facilitate coordination.

Even if these investments are made, firms have to solve an additional problem. Once one firm makes an investment, the other has an incentive to capture as much of the value created as possible. Except in simple cases, the formal contracts that govern a relationship will be incomplete. Contracts have problems because they cannot cover all contingencies and each party might not completely express its desires and information; also, the costs of forming and monitoring a contract can be very high.

Thus, firms have to find ways to provide incentives for all firms to continually not take advantage of the relationship and to act in a trustworthy manner. Firms usually try to create long-term relationships to create trust and incentives to operate in a manner that creates value for all participants. The trust relates not only to performance issues (e.g., whether a firm will do what it says it will do) but also relates to relationship issues (e.g., whether the firm will take its partner into account when making decisions).

Sometimes shifting profits around via vertical integration can increase those profits, typically by avoiding taxes and creating incentives to reconfigure the value chain. If an organization is paying very high taxes on its profits, it might be able to avoid some of those taxes by cosigning profits to a relatively less taxed product line. A good example of this shifting of the tax burden is provided by the oil business. Alaska taxes oil by collecting a fraction of its wellhead value. The wellhead is determined by the market price of oil minus its transportation costs. (In Alaska, this consists primarily of the rates charged in the Alaskan pipeline.) The same firms that drill the oil own the pipeline; thus, they pay the wellhead tax. Since pipeline profits are not subject to high state taxes, oil firms have an incentive to take their profits in the pipeline, by charging themselves high transportation rates (vs. in the heavily taxed extraction end). Firms would not be able to alter pricing as easily if they did not own the various lines of businesses.[128]

Similar opportunities exist for companies that do business across national borders.[129] Thus, firms that move up and down the value chain to create additional value try to increase competition in other value chain industries or try to create linkages across the chain, remaining aware of coordination and incentive issues.

Notes

1 This section is adapted from A. Peterka, "BUSINESS: Too-loud SunChips Bag Underscores Green Products' Problems," *Greenwire*, October 2010, http://www.eenews.net/Greenwire/2010/10/15/archive/23?terms=frito+lay (accessed January 15, 2012).
2 GfK Roper Consulting, "New Report: American Consumers Lead the World in Environmental Skepticism," PR Newswire, September 22, 2010, www.prnewswire.com/news-releases/new-report-american-consumers-lead-the-world-in-environmental-skepticism-103520764.html (accessed September 15, 2015).
3 G. Hardin, "The Tragedy of the Commons," *Science* 162, no. 3859 (December 13, 1968): 1243–1248.
4 GfK Roper Consulting, *The Environment: Public Attitudes and Individual Behavior—A Twenty-Year Evolution* (GfK, 2011), 5–7, www.scjohnson.com/Libraries/Download_Documents/SCJ_and_GfK_Roper_Green_Gauge.sflb.ashx (accessed January 23, 2013).
5 Integreon, "Grail Research's 'The Green Evolution' Report Reveals that Fewer Consumers are Buying Green Products," *Business Wire,* press release, November 16, 2011, http://origin-www.bloomberg.com/apps/news?pid=conewsstory&tkr=CXX:GR&sid=amB1G7tsI8fQ (accessed January 28, 2013).
6 S. E. Sexton and A. L. Sexton, *Conspicuous Conservation: The Prius Halo and Willingness to Pay for Environmental Bona Fides* (Berkeley: University of California, October 5, 2012) https://ncsu.pure.elsevier.com/en/publications/conspicuous-conservation-the-prius-halo-and-willingness-to-pay-fo (accessed December 22, 2015).
7 G. M. Zinkhan and L. Carson, "Green Advertising and the Reluctant Consumer," *Journal of Advertising* 24, no. 2 (Summer 1995): 1–4.
8 S. Banerjee, C. S. Gulas, and E. Iyer, "Shades of Green: A Multidimensional Analysis of Environmental Advertising," *Journal of Advertising* 24, no. 2 (Summer 1995): 21–31.
9 C. M. Hall, *Tourism and Social Marketing* (London: Routledge, 2012).
10 B. Jorgensen, M. Graymore, and K. O'Toole, "Household Water Use Behavior: An Integrated Model," *Journal of Environmental Management* 91, no. 1 (2009): 227–236.
11 A. Heiman, "The Use of Advertising to Encourage Water Conservation: Theory and Empirical Evidence," *Journal of Contemporary Water Research and Education* 121, no. 1 (2002): 79–86.
12 J. M. Ginsberg and P. N. Bloom, "Choosing the Right Green Marketing Strategy," *MIT Sloan Management Review* 46, no. 1 (Fall 2004): 79–84.
13 Roper ASW, *Green Gauge Report 2002: Americans Perspective on Environmental Issues* (New York: Roper ASW, March 2003).
14 Ibid.
15 Ipsos, "Environmental Actions Are a Differentiating Opportunity for BC Retailers," press release, April 16, 2008, www.ipsos-na.com/news-polls/pressrelease.aspx?id=3886 (accessed January 28, 2013). In another study, 70 percent of Americans and 64 percent of Canadians said that when companies call a product green or better for the environment, it is usually just a marketing tactic.
16 Accenture/United Nations Global Compact, *Towards a New Era of Sustainability in the Communications Industry: UN Global Compact-Accenture CEO Study* (2011), 9, www.unglobalcompact.org/docs/news_events/8.1/UNGC_Accenture_Communications.pdf (accessed January 28, 2013).
17 B. Robinson, "How Green Are We Really?" *Spirituality & Health Magazine,* January 2009, www.thefreelibrary.com/How+Green+Are+We+Really%3F-a0203133501 (accessed January 28, 2013).
18 MarketingCharts staff, "Consumers Recall Green Ads, but Often Skeptical of Them," April 24, 2008, www.marketingcharts.com/interactive/consumers-recall-green-ads-but-often-skeptical-of-them-4343/(accessed December 15, 2012).
19 Green Seal, *2009 National Green Buying Research* (Washington, DC: Green Seal, 2009).
20 E. Koester, *Green Entrepreneur Handbook: The Guide to Building and Growing a Green and Clean Business* (Boca Raton, FL: CRC, 2011), 33.
21 Joel Makower's analysis of Yankelovich's GOING Green Survey (2007). In J. Makower, *Strategies for the Green Economy: Opportunities and Challenges in the New World of Business* (New York: McGraw-Hill, 2009), 28.
22 See, for example, N. Klein, *No Logo: No Space, No Choice, No Jobs* (London: Harper Perennial, 2005).
23 V. Carducci, "Culture Jamming: A Sociological Perspective," *Journal of Consumer Culture* 6, no. 1 (March 2006): 116–138; M. Dery, *Culture Jamming: Hacking, Slashing, and Sniping in the Empire of Signs* (Westfield, NJ: Open Magazine Pamphlet Series, 1993).

24 A. J. Nomai, *Culture Jamming: Ideological Struggle and the Possibilities for Social Change* (Ann Arbor, MI: ProQuest UMI Dissertation Publishing, 2008), 5.

25 Two-thirds of respondents said that business needs to take global warming more seriously (combined 66.4 percent: U.S. 63.2 percent, UK 69.5 percent); and a similar number said that governments should take greater action (combined 64.1 percent: U.S. 59.4 percent, UK 68.6 percent). AccountAbility/Consumers International, *What Assures Consumers on Climate Change? Switching on Citizen Power* (Northampton, UK: June 2007), 9, www.consumersinternational.org/media/179823/what%20assures%20consumers%20gfsr.pdf (accessed December 15, 2012).

26 Joel Makower's analysis of Yankelovich's GOING Green Survey (2007). In J. Makower, *Strategies for the Green Economy*, 29.

27 Ibid., Chapter 6.

28 *Source:* Adapted from I. Galarraga Gallastegui, "The Use of Eco-Labels: A Review of the Literature," *European Environment* 12, no. 6 (2002): 316–331.

29 J. Manget, C. Roche, and F. Münnich, *Capturing the Green Advantage for Consumer Companies* (Boston, MA: Boston Consulting Group, January, 2009) http://www.bcg.com/documents/file15407.pdf (accessed August 25, 2015), 11.

30 N. Borin, "Greenwashing," in K. Christensen, D. S. Fogel, G. Wagner, and P. J. Whitehouse (eds.), *Berkshire Encyclopedia of Sustainability*, Volume 2: *The Business of Sustainability* (Great Barrington, MA: Berkshire Publishers, 2011), 256–257.

31 Co-authored by Michael Aper, 2015 Master of Arts in Sustainability candidate at Wake Forest University.

32 Joel Makower's "Analysis of Yankelovich's GOING Green Survey, 2007," 28.

33 Kyle Stock, "Patagonia's 'Buy Less' Plea Spurs More Buying," (*Bloomberg Marketing,* August 28, 2013) http://www.bloomberg.com/bw/articles/2013-08-28/patagonias-buy-less-plea-spurs-more-buying (accessed on March 15, 2015).

34 Patagonia, "Company History," 2015, http://www.patagonia.com/us/patagonia.go?assetid=3351 (accessed on March 15, 2015).

35 Patagonia, "Yulex®," 2015, http://www.patagonia.com/us/patagonia.go?assetid=93864_(accessed on March 15, 2015).

36 Patagonia, "Patagonia Works," 2015, http://www.patagoniaworks.com/#contacta (accessed on March 15, 2015).

37 Green Seal Weather USA, "About," www.greensealusa.com/about.html (accessed January 28, 2013).

38 The Blue Angel, "The Blue Angel—Eco-Label with Brand Character," www.blauer-engel.de/en/blauer_engel/index.php (accessed January 28, 2013).

39 European Commission, "The EU Ecolabel," http://ec.europa.eu/environment/ecolabel/(accessed January 25, 2013).

40 Association Française de Normalisation (AFNOR), "The NF Environnement mark," http://okocimke.kvvm.hu/public_eng/?ppid=2420000 (accessed December 22, 2015).

41 DGNB, http://www.dgnb.de/en/(accessed September 3, 2015).

42 International Organization for Standardization (ISO), *ISO 14040:2006: Environmental Management—Life Cycle Assessment—Principles and Frameworks* (Geneva: ISO, 2009), www.iso.org/iso/catalogue_detail?csnumber=38131 (accessed September 18, 2012).

43 Ecolabel Index, www.ecolabelindex.com/(accessed September 15, 2011).

44 Organisation for Economic Co-operation and Development, *Eco-Labelling: Actual Effects of Selected Programmes*, Report OECD/GD(97)105 (Paris: OECD, 1997); I. Galarraga Gallastegui, "The Use of Eco-labels: A Review of the Literature," *European Environment* 12, no. 6 (2002): 316–331; I. Galarraga and A. Markandya, "Economic Techniques to Estimate the Demand for Sustainable Products: A Case Study for Fair Trade and Organic Coffee in the United Kingdom," *Economia Agraria y Recursos Naturales* (Spanish Association of Agricultural Economics) 4, no. 7 (2004): 109–134.

45 S. Zarrilli, V. Jha, and R. Vossenaar (eds.), *Eco-labelling and International Trade* (Basingstoke: Macmillan Press, 1997).

46 Source: Adapted from I. Galarraga Gallstegui, "The Use of Eco-Labels: A Review of the Literature," *European Environment* 12, no. 6 (2002): 316–331.

47 Abandoned in 1993 due to industry opposition.

48 R. W. Seifert and J. M. Comas, "Have Ecolabels Had Their Day? The Truth Behind Sustainability Labels from the People Who Integrate Them," IMD article, May 2012, www.imd.org/research/challenges/sustainability-ecolabels-effectiveness-ralf-seifert-joana-comas.cfm (accessed January 28, 2013).

49 G. Day and P. Schoemaker, "Innovating in Uncertain Markets: 10 Lessons for Green Technologies," *Sloan Management Review* (Summer 2011): 39.

50 S. Strom, "Has 'Organic' Been Oversized?" *The New York Times*, July 8, 2012, BU1, BU5.

51 U.S. Department of Agriculture, "Welcome to the National Organic Program," www.ams.usda.gov/AMSv1.0/nop (accessed December 15, 2011).

52 Also, the Federal Trade Commission has guidelines for environmental marketing claims. See Federal Trade Commission, "Part 260: Guides for the Use of Environmental Marketing Claims," 15 U.S.C. §§ 41–58 (1996), http://www.ecfr.gov/cgi-bin/text-idx?SID=88c35ebd0c8024cff76f2601bde4cef3&mc=true&node=pt16.1.260&rgn=div5 (accessed December 22, 2015).

53 Organic Trade Association (OTA), "Industry Statistics and Projected Growth," June 2011, www.ota.com/organic/mt/business.html; citation from OTA, *2011 Organic Industry Survey* (Brattleboro, VT: OTA, 2011).

54 Ibid.; citation from H. Willer and L. Kilcher (eds.), *The World of Organic Agriculture: Statistics and Emerging Trends 2011* (Bonn: IFOAM; Frick: FiBL, 2011).

55 R. Cohen. "The Organic Fable," *The New York Times*, September 6, 2012, http://www.nytimes.com/2012/09/07/opinion/roger-cohen-the-organic-fable.html?_r=0 (accessed September 5, 2015).

56 Organic Trade Association (OTA), "Industry Statistics and Projected Growth," June 2011; citation from H. Willer and L. Kilcher (eds.), *The World of Organic Agriculture*, 40.

57 Organic Trade Association (OTA), "Industry Statistics and Projected Growth," June 2011; citation from H. Willer and L. Kilcher (eds.), *The World of Organic Agriculture*.

58 U.S. Department of Agriculture, "Labeling Organic Products," October 2012, www.ams.usda.gov/AMSv1.0/getfile?dDocName=STELDEV3004446&acct=nopgeninfo (accessed September 10, 2013).

59 SimaPro, "About SimaPro," www.pre-sustainability.com/simapro-lca-software (accessed October 1, 2014).

60 PE International, "GaBi Sofware," www.gabi-software.com/america/index/ (accessed October 1, 2014).

61 W. McDonough and M. Braungart, *Cradle to Cradle: Remaking the Way We Make Things* (New York: North Point Press, 2002), 92–117.

62 Ibid.

63 Co-authored by Michael Aper, Master of Arts in Sustainability candidate at Wake Forest University.

64 "Model S," Tesla Motors, http://www.teslamotors.com/models_(accessed January 13, 2015).

65 M. Maynard, "Tesla's First Gigafactory Site Will Break Ground Next Month," (Forbes, May 07, 2014) http://www.forbes.com/sites/michelinemaynard/2014/05/07/teslas-first-gigafactory-site-will-break-ground-next-month/(accessed January 13, 2015).

66 "The New Home of the Tesla Gigafactory!" Tahoe-Reno Industrial Center, http://www.tahoereno.com/ (accessed January 13, 2015).

67 *The Economist*, "Elon Musk's Gigafactory Assault on batteries," The Economist, June 14, 2014) http://www.economist.com/news/business/21604174-better-power-packs-will-open-road-electric-vehicles-assault-batteries (accessed January 13, 2015).

68 Nonfiction Creative, http://coletti.prosite.com/5866/about (accessed January 6, 2015).

69 Roughly 2.3 pounds per chair.

70 Roy Green, personal correspondence, November 20, 2014.

71 "About Ecovative," http://ecovativedesign.com/about/(accessed January 6, 2015).

72 Encyclopedia.com, "Mycelium," *World of Microbiology and Immunology*, 2003, http://www.encyclopedia.com. (accessed January 6, 2015).

73 "Get Cradle to Cradle Certified," http://www.c2ccertified.org/get-certified/product-certification (accessed January 6, 2015).

74 P. Stamets, *Mycelium Running: How Mushrooms Can Help Save the World* (New York: Ten Speed Press, 2005).

75 M. F. Gates, "What nonprofits can learn from Coca-Cola," TED Talks, YouTube video, October 12, 2010, www.youtube.com/watch?v=GlUS6KE67Vs (accessed December 10, 2011).

76 World Market Intelligence (WMI), *The UK Top 20 Retailers: Company Benchmarking Analysis*, 2010 ed. (London: WMI, January 2010).

77 Marks & Spencer, "Plan A: Doing the Right Thing," http://plana.marksandspencer.com/(accessed December 22, 2011).

78 Natural Resources Conservation Service, USDA, "FAQ: Conservation Planning with Transitioning to Organic Producers," November 2012, www.nrcs.usda.gov/Internet/FSE_DOCUMENTS/stelprdb1075372.pdf (accessed September 10, 2013).

79 Food Alliance, "About Food Alliance," http://foodalliance.org/about (accessed September 10, 2013).

80 Indocert, "Accreditations," www.indocert.org/new/index.php/en/accreditation (accessed February 23, 2013).

81 Naturland, "Standards," http://www.naturland.de/en/naturland/naturland-standards.html (accessed December 22, 2015).

82 SCS Global Services, "Certified Pesticide Residue Free," www.scsglobalservices.com/files/brochures/COM_FA_INF_PRF_V2-0_102512.pdf (accessed September 10, 2013).

83 U.S. Green Building Council, "LEED for Homes International Pilot" (n.d.), www.usgbc.org/Docs/Archive/General/Docs8679.pdf (accessed September 11, 2013).

84 Japan GreenBuild Council (JaGBC) and Japan Sustainable Building Consortium (JSBC), "An Overview of CASBEE," www.ibec.or.jp/CASBEE/english/overviewE.htm (accessed September 11, 2013).

85 BRE Global, "Why BREEAM?" www.breeam.org/about.jsp?id=66 (accessed September 11, 2013).

86 BRE Group, "Responsible Sourcing of Construction Products," www.bre.co.uk/page.jsp?id=1514 (accessed September 11, 2013); BRE Group, "Are you sourcing responsibly?" www.bre.co.uk/filelibrary/greenguide/PDF/KN4701_Responsible_sourcing_v2.pdf (accessed September 11, 2013).

87 UL Environment, "Frequently Asked Questions," www.ul.com/global/eng/pages/offerings/businesses/environment/about/faq/ (accessed September 11, 2013); GreenBiz.com, "ULE 880—Sustainability for Manufacturing

Organizations," http://www.greenbiz.com/blog/2010/08/02/introducing-ule-880-sustainability-manufactur-ing-organizations (accessed December 22, 2015).

88 BRE Group, "Environmental Profiles," www.bre.co.uk/page.jsp?id=53 (accessed September 15, 2013).

89 VCS: Verified Carbon Standard, "VCS Quality Assurance Principles," www.v-c-s.org/quality-assurance-principles (accessed September 12, 2013).

90 The Climate Action Reserve, "About Us," www.climateactionreserve.org/about-us/ (accessed September 12, 2013).

91 The Climate, Community & Biodiversity Alliance (CCBA), "About CCB," www.climate-standards.org/about-ccba/ (accessed September 12, 2013); CCBA, "CCB Standards," www.climate-standards.org/ccb-standards/ (accessed September 12, 2013).

92 The Gold Standard Foundation, "Who We Are," www.cdmgoldstandard.org/about-us/who-we-are (accessed September 12, 2013).

93 Green Seal, "About Green Seal," www.greenseal.org/AboutGreenSeal.aspx (accessed September 12, 2013).

94 EcoLogo, "About Ecologo," www.ecologo.org/en/ (accessed January 13, 2013).

95 Nordic Ecolabelling, "About . . . ," www.nordic-ecolabel.org/about/ (accessed September 12, 2013).

96 Japan Environmental Association (JEA), "Institution of the Eco Mark," www.ecomark.jp/english/ecomark.html (accessed September 12, 2013).

97 The Blue Angel, "The Blue Angel—Eco-Label with Brand Character."

98 U.S. Environmental Protection Agency (EPA), "About ENERGY STAR," www.energystar.gov/index.cfm?c=about.ab_index (accessed September 16, 2013).

99 Fair Trade USA, "Frequently Asked Questions," www.fairtradeusa.org/what-is-fair-trade/faq; Fair Trade USA, "Certification & Your Business," www.fairtradeusa.org/about-fair-trade-usa/who-we-are (both accessed September 16, 2014).

100 Aquaculture Stewardship Council (ASC), "FAQ: What Is the Aquaculture Stewardship Council?" www.asc-aqua.org/index.cfm?act=faq.faq&lng=1#antwoord1 (accessed September 16, 2013).

101 Marine Stewardship Council, "MSC Environmental Standard for Sustainability Fishing," www.msc.org/about-us/standards/standards/msc-environmental-standard (accessed September 16, 2013).

102 Green Seal, Inc., "About Green Seal," www.greenseal.org/AboutGreenSeal.aspx; Greal Seal, Inc., "Green Seal Standards," http://www.greenseal.org/GreenBusiness/Standards.aspx (accessed September 16, 2013).

103 SCS Global Services, "Recycled Content Certification," www.scsglobalservices.com/recycled-content-certification (accessed September 16, 2013).

104 SCS Global Services, *Biodegradable Certification Standard*, Version 5-0 (Emeryville, CA: October 2012) www.scs-globalservices.com/files/standards/SCS_STN_Biodegradable_V5-0_102212.pdf (accessed September 16, 2013).

105 SCS Global, "Recycled Content and Recycling Program Certification," brochure, www.scsglobalservices.com/files/brochures/SCS_Recycled_Content_Brochure.pdf (accessed September 16, 2013).

106 UL Environment, "Environmental Claim Validations," http://industries.ul.com/environment/certificationvalida-tion-marks/environmental-claim-validation (accessed December 22, 2015).

107 Wal-Mart, "Sustainability Index," http://corporate.walmart.com/global-responsibility/environment-sustainabil-ity/sustainability-index (accessed September 16, 2013).

108 ISO, "ISO 9000—Quality Management," www.iso.org/iso/iso_9000 (accessed September 16, 2013).

109 ISO, "ISO 14000—Environmental Management," www.iso.org/iso/home/standards/management-standards/iso14000.htm (accessed September 16, 2013).

110 Forest Stewardship Council, "Certification," https://us.fsc.org/certification.194.htm (accessed September 16, 2013).

111 *SFI 2015–2019 Standards and Rules*, http://www.sfiprogram.org/files/pdf/2015-2019-standardsandrules-web-lr-pdf/ (accessed December 22, 2015).

112 National Wood Flooring Association, "Responsible Procurement Program," www.nwfa.org/rpp.aspx (accessed September 17, 2013).

113 SCS Global Services, "Timber Legality Verification: FAQs," http://www.scsglobalservices.com/timber-legality-verification (accessed September 17, 2013).

114 P. Ghemawat and T. Khanna, "A Note on Positioning and Scope," Harvard Business Case No. 796180 (Boston, MA, 1996).

115 A. J. Slywotzky suggested that value migrates from ineffective to effective business designs. This value movement occurs from company to company and industry to industry. See A. J. Slywotzky, *Value Migration: How to Think Several Moves Ahead of the Competition* (Boston, MA: Harvard Business School Press, 1996).

116 K. S. Corts, "The Ready-to-Eat Breakfast Cereal Industry in 1994 (A)," Harvard Business School Case 795191 (1995; rev. 1997).

117 D. Canedy and R. Abelson, "Can Kellogg Break Out of the Box?" *The New York Times*, January 24, 1999, www.nytimes.com/1999/01/24/business/can-kellogg-break-out-of-the-box.html?pagewanted=all&src=pm (accessed January 13, 2013); R. Balu, "Kellogg Increases the Prices on Majority of Cereal Brands," *The Wall Street Journal*, December 15, 1998, B23; A. Kover, "Why the Cereal Business Is Soggy," *Fortune*, March 6, 2000, 74.

118 Ghemawat and Khanna, "Note on Positioning and Scope."

119 M. E. Porter, Competitive Advantage: Creating and Sustaining Superior Performance (New York: Free Press, 1985), chapter 3.

120 See, for example, J. P. Peter and J. H. Donnelly Jr., *A Preface to Marketing Management*, 8th ed. (Boston, MA: Irwin McGraw-Hill, 2000).

121 R. H. Coase, "The Nature of the Firm," *Economica* 4, no. 16 (November 1937): 386–405.

122 D. J. Teece, *Dynamic Capabilities and Strategic Management: Organizing for Innovation and Growth* (Oxford, UK: Oxford University Press, 2009): 130–131.

123 If there are structural reasons for the low level of competition in the supplier industry, a firm's ability to vertically integrate may be hampered.

124 O. E. Williamson, *The Economic Institutions of Capitalism: Firms, Markets, Relational Contracting* (New York: The Free Press, 1985).

125 See D. J. Collis, "The Scope of the Corporation," Harvard Business School Case No. 795139 (Boston, MA, 1995).

126 See *U.S.* v. *Aluminum Co. of America et al.* 148 F.2d 416 (2d Cir., 1945), http://myweb.clemson.edu/~maloney/424/alcoa.pdf (accessed January 15, 2013). On appeal, a circuit court found Alcoa guilty of monopolization, overturning a previous ruling of innocence. The second ruling used a narrow definition of the market for which Alcoa produced, claiming Alcoa had 90 percent of the market. Also, it used its monopoly power to produce excess capacity, dissuading competitors from continuing in and entering the market.

127 See Corts, "The Ready-to-Eat Breakfast Cereal Industry in 1994 (A)."

128 S. Oster, *Modern Competitive Analysis*, 3rd ed. (New York: Oxford University Press, 1999): 203–204.

129 P. Milgrom and J. Roberts, "Predation, Reputation and Entry Deterrence," *Journal of Economic Theory* 27, no. 2 (August 1982): 280–312.

10

HIGH-PERFORMANCE OPERATIONS

A.P. Møeller-Maersk: Setting the Standard in Transportation

A.P. Møller-Maersk is a diversified worldwide company that has 18 business units and does business in shipping and transportation for diverse markets (e.g., oil, supermarkets, and supply chain management). The company came under tremendous economic pressure in 2009. For the first time in its history, it reported a decrease in revenues and profits. Also, 2009 marked the first time the company filed its Sustainability Report, and it received a C+ on the GRI (a worldwide standard for environmental reporting). CEO Nils S. Andersen stated in the 2009 report, "We believe that sustainable development is essential for society and business to thrive and grow. We are committed to integrating sustainability into all of our business operations and making our performance transparent to our stakeholders."[1] Despite the CEO's intentions, the grade indicated that the company's performance was not meeting its own standard.

Maersk Lines, a unit of A.P. Møller-Maersk, is a shipping company serving customers and transporting containers all over the world. Its fleet consists of over 500 ships with 300 offices in over 125 countries. Its focus in 2009 was on reducing costs and "adjusting the company to new market realities."[2] Even with this focus, Maersk continued its efforts to save energy and improve its environmental performance through modifying its operations. Between 2002 and 2008, their efforts resulted in a 15 percent increase in energy efficiency per container shipped. Ninety-nine percent of energy usage and emissions came from ships (their own and time-chartered ships).

Starting early in the 21st century, the company instituted some effective changes in its shipping to reduce its energy use. They reduced the speed of their ships via a program called Super Slow Steaming.[3] Maersk won an award for this technique, which has become an industry standard.[4] Maersk Line won its second Sustainable Shipping Operator of the Year Award, showing a consistency in its accomplishments; the award was given to Maersk Line in recognition of its investments in sustainable growth, CO_2 reduction, and advancement in operating transparency.[5] Slowing ships actually resulted in not only better environmental performance but also in better overall performance (which has resulted in higher customer satisfaction). They lowered speeds from 22 knots to 16 knots, cutting fuel costs and CO_2 emissions and saving the company an estimated $300 million per year.[6]

Other innovations came from their Maersk Maritime Technology unit, which uses alternative energy sources (e.g., biofuels) in addition to new types of hull paint, optimized propellers, air lubrication, efficient fuel switches, and new voyage planning systems. Also, Maersk was part of many supply chains and has thus helped other companies achieve their environmental goals. For example, Nike set a goal of 30 percent absolute reduction in CO_2 by 2020 for transportation from factory to distribution, using 2003 as a baseline. Nike management stated:

> *Maersk has turned out to be our most willing partner in sharing information on projects, including details of project outcomes and transport solution's design. On top of that, they have really good innovation ideas for the future! Maersk has been a trusted partner for us.[7]*

These innovations and operations were not without challenges. Maersk realized that their innovations needed to be communicated to various stakeholders. For example, six Maersk Line ships were laid up near the community of Loch Striven in Scotland. The community was furious with Maersk because the ships were so noisy. Maersk made the mistake of sending the angry community leaders to the Clydeport harbor authorities with whom Maersk negotiated the permits for the layup of the ships. This action was a mistake as the residents wanted more involvement from Maersk in resolving the problems. Maersk learned that they could not turn these people away and thus engaged them directly. Subsequently, they held meetings to create dialogue with the community and conducted environmental studies (including acoustic surveys) to improve the sound impact of the ships.

Maersk was also constantly challenged to monitor its shipment of illegal and contraband cargo. They stated that when they receive sealed containers, they are not authorized to open them. They were able to solve some of these problems by dealing with recognized companies. For example, they screen bookings of tuna to ensure that they only accept bookings from shippers that are known to operate legally, using internationally recognized fishing practices.

By changing its operations, Maersk has become a paradigm for environmental sustainability in the shipping business. Yet one wonders whether or not this work is sustainable over the long term and whether these practices will produce the returns needed to compete with other shipping companies. These practices seem easily copied, further improvements could prove costly and harder to implement, and the easy part of their job may be behind them.

Chapter Overview

Companies can probably make the biggest impacts on their environmental footprints by evaluating the myriad operational areas under their control and addressing any problematic ones. This chapter provides examples of these operations (e.g., location decisions, supply chain management, and specific operational areas such as

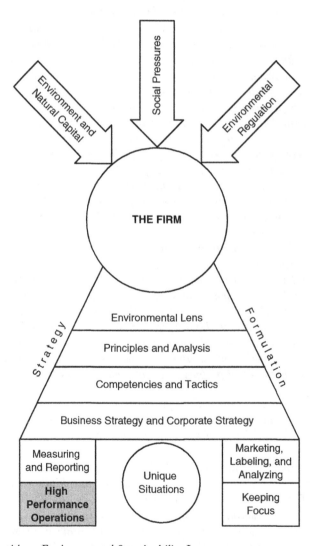

Figure 10.1 Strategy Model with an Environmental Sustainability Lens

transportation, construction, and purchasing). Each of a company's functions has a unique opportunity to decrease its negative environmental impacts and to increase its competitiveness.

At the end of this chapter, you will be able to:

1 define and describe how supply chain management can impact a company's sustainability efforts;
2 state, in your own words, how location influences a company's environmental impact;
3 analyze several company operations to determine opportunities for improving environmental outcomes.

The material in this chapter provides an understanding of how companies can change operations to decrease their impacts on the environment and increase their competitiveness. While the chapter only covers a few operational areas, you will quickly see how to generate other innovative and environmentally friendly changes within organizations to increase positive environmental outcomes.

Supply Chain Management

A *supply chain* consists of all parties involved (directly or indirectly) in fulfilling a customer's request. The supply chain encompasses the constant flow of information, products, and resources at different stages of a product's development. The components of the supply chain can usually be broken down into the following categories: suppliers, manufacturers, transporters, retailers, and customers. A typical supply chain can be depicted as follows:

Components/Raw Material Suppliers → Manufacturers → Distributors → Wholesalers → Retailers → Customers

The objective of every supply chain is to maximize the overall value generated by the firm. There are two main perspectives to maximizing value, and if a company can figure out how to utilize both of these perspectives, it will increase its competiveness. I presented similar information in Appendix 9.2 about value chains. The current section focuses on supply chains and their environmental and customer-focused characteristics applying the generic information from Appendix 9.2.

A *cycle view* of the supply chain defines the processes involved and owners of each process. This view is very useful when considering operational decisions as it specifies the roles and responsibilities of each member of the supply chain and the desired outcome of each process. For example, a company can specify that suppliers must provide inputs that meet a specific environmental standard when it wants to minimize its environmental impact. (This is the approach taken by Wal-Mart described earlier in this book.) In this case, the assumption is that if one component improves, the whole chain benefits.

A *push-pull* view of the supply chain categorizes processes based on whether they are in *response* to a customer order (pull) or *in anticipation of* a customer order (push). This view is useful when considering strategic decisions related to supply chain design. For example, some companies locate near customers so they can be more responsive and initiate actions in the supply chain promptly when orders are placed. This perspective prioritizes customer needs over discrete components of the chain.

Within firms, all supply chain activities belong to one of these micro processes:

1 Customer relationship management includes all of the processes that focus on the interface between the firm and its customers. For example, some firms have electronic data interfaces with customers so that the firm can provide just-in-time inventory to their customers. Just-in-time inventory decreases costs by avoiding expensive storage charges.
2 Internal supply chain management includes all of the processes that are internal to the firm, such as cost controls and efficiency efforts (e.g., lean management techniques).
3 Supplier relationship management (SRM) includes all of the processes that focus on the interface between the firm and its suppliers. For example, Volkswagen has a truck plant in Brazil where it manages seven suppliers located within a plant that manufactures small trucks. These suppliers each have a long supply chain, which is aggregated before entering the Volkswagen plant.[8] Volkswagen has learned, over time, how to manage its suppliers to ensure quality trucks are produced.

The two views and three processes present myriad opportunities to increase a firm's value. Zara, an apparel manufacturing and retail company, is a chain of fashion stores owned by Spain's largest apparel manufacturer and retailer, Inditex. Zara is an excellent example of supply chain management; its sales reflect efficiencies. In 2014, Inditek reported sales of €18.2 billion, and Zara represented €11.59 billion of that amount. In 2014, Zara had 2,085 retail outlets plus about 450 stores for other concepts (e.g., Zara Home). Inditek had 6,683 stores worldwide in 80 countries plus about 27 online markets. Thus, Zara was a significant part of the Inditek portfolio.[9]

The retail industry is known for its fickle customer demand and Zara distinguished itself by being responsive to customers. Its customer relationship management processes are excellent, showing in-depth knowledge of what customers want. The company has achieved unusual cycle times (i.e., times from design, manufacturing, and then to the stores) of four to six weeks; the industry average was over six months during this time.

Zara introduces new designs every week and changes 75 percent of its merchandise every three to four weeks. Zara's responsiveness presents a unique value proposition to its customers and allows Zara to charge full price for most items. Its supply chain management and SRM are integrated well and enable Zara to respond rapidly to changes in customer demand; these processes reflect use of excellent cycle and push-pull management of the supply chain.

Zara's manufacturing takes place at certain locations in Spain and Portugal for uncertain demand items and some low-cost locations (e.g., Asia) for highly certain items. Interestingly, more than 40 percent of its finished goods purchases (and most of its in-house production) occur *after* the season starts for particular types of clothes (competitors are at 20 percent). In order to enhance its responsiveness, the company has invested heavily in sophisticated information technology, distribution centers, and transportation so that delivery time is only 24 hours for European stores and 40 hours for stores in the United States and Asia.

Zara's environmental footprint and related social responsibility practices are impacted by these supply chain and management practices.[10] Thus, through its business model, Zara contributes to the sustainable development of society and the environments with which it interacts. (This commitment to the environment is a part of the Inditex group CSR policy.)

Zara is now developing eco-efficient management models for their already energy-efficient stores. This management model proposes measures that can be applied to all processes, from the design of stores; to lighting, heating, and cooling; to the recycling of furniture and decoration. Zara reduces the production of waste and encourages the recycling of hangers and security tags, which are collected in the stores and transformed into other plastic items. They have in-house communication campaigns and specific multimedia training plans to heighten employees' awareness of the need for sustainable practices. Also, Zara's stores use paper and biodegradable plastic bags (90 percent of the bags Zara gives out to customers are made of paper). Their fashion catalogues are printed on paper with the FSC/PEFP MARK, which is a certificate guaranteeing sustainable forest management.

Zara also supports ecological agriculture and uses organic cotton in the production of selected items of clothing (i.e., 100 percent cotton, free of pesticides, chemical agents, and bleaches). Petroleum derivatives or non-biodegradable materials are never used in producing their footwear. They have also introduced biodiesel fuel; Zara's fleet of trucks transports over 200 million items of clothing annually and uses 5 percent biodiesel fuel. This practice enables them to reduce CO_2 emissions by more than 500 tonnes. All of the animal products (including fur and leather sold at Zara) come exclusively from animals reared in livestock form and never from animals sacrificed for skin sale.

Environmental conditions can disrupt the efficiency of supply chains. For example, the following is from a sign I once saw at Best Buy:

> We apologize. Severe flooding in Thailand has resulted in inventory constraints on all hard drive products. At this time we must issue a purchase limit on hard drives to one per customer. We are sorry for any convenience this may cause.[11]

To purchase a 1-terabyte hard drive at Best Buy, the cost was $149.99 (vs. $139.71 on Amazon, $129.99 on Newegg, and $179.99 on CDW). The varied prices were a result of supply chain difficulties. Some companies were more harshly affected by the disruption than others. Also, this pricing difference is likely due to the efficiency and structure of each company's supply chain.

Thus, supply chain management is important to operational effectiveness and follows many of the concepts that apply to other chains of events discussed in this book (e.g., Chapter 9's presentation of LCA and cradle-to-cradle). These concepts refer to a chain of connected activities within and outside of a firm to ensure that products and services are produced and delivered (and in some cases are recycled and materials reused). Each of these concepts presents a different perspective on similar activities.

Firms tend to do extensive analyses of these chains, looking for ways to cut down on costs or increase value; one outcome is to more effectively manage specific resources that tend to impact the environment and create costs. Most important, for our purposes, is the management of environmental resources; one way to manage these resources is to carefully select locations based on environmental considerations (the subject of the next section).

The Importance of Location

Businesses must frequently make decisions about where to locate operations, home offices, and sales locations. These decisions impact the design of supply chains and the ability of companies to reach important customers, attract and retain employees, improve their environmental outcomes, and to manage their cost structures. Many firms must decide whether to centralize operations to gain economies of scale or to decentralize operations to become more responsive (by being closer to customers).

In this book, I have emphasized yet another factor: the impact of the natural environment on a firm's competitiveness. Many firms have the option of locating in areas where they have access to natural resources, resulting in the reduction of negative natural environmental impacts. For example, the North Carolina coastal area is eroding rapidly due to increases in sea levels; many of its businesses are contemplating moves to avoid the risk of having to halt operations and lose valuable property due to unusual weather events.[12]

The geographic scope of competition is a strategic variable. Geographic scope is a general measure of the number of different locations, regions, or countries in which a company operates. Companies often define their boundaries of competition by geography unless they operate in a global environment (or overcome location restrictions by reaching customers mainly through catalogues, the Internet, or mail). Given the dramatic decrease in costs of transportation and communication over the past 50 years, companies are finding that their breadth of competitive space is increasing rapidly.

- The cost of a phone call, for example, has become virtually free with systems like Skype.[13]
- Taking a flight from New York to Frankfurt, Germany, could cost as little as $500.[14] (Since passenger deregulation in 1978, airline prices have fallen 44.9 percent in real terms.)[15]
- Doctors in developing nations can watch new surgical techniques performed at a Los Angeles hospital live on the Internet and download supporting medical information in an instant.
  - If the local doctor were to lack the necessary medical tools to perform a surgery, the necessary items could be shipped in a day.
  - Some surgeries can be performed remotely via computers and robots.
- Multinational corporations can monitor operations throughout the world in real time and track shipments via GPS.

Couple these changes with three important principles of technological change and the capabilities of a modern company become sufficiently clear:

1 *Moore's Law*: computer-processing speed doubles every 18 months with transistor improvements.
2 *Gilder's Law*: communication bandwidth grows at least three times faster than computer power. (This means that if a computer's power doubles every 18 months [according to Moore's Law], the communication power doubles every six months according to Gilder's Law).
3 *Metcalf's Law*: the usefulness or value of a network rises exponentially with the number of users.[16]

These laws present a paradox about location. On the one hand, location matters greatly for access to resources and customers. On the other hand, technological advances and price changes make location somewhat irrelevant. Thus, the significance of location probably depends upon the type of business you have and the nature of the business model you use. For example, one can easily perceive that some retail operations could occur entirely online and not be dependent on location; however, other retail operations depend on location (e.g., small service companies that need to service appliances, barbers and hairdressers, and local food stores). Clearly, one would have a hard time imagining Starbuck's delivering its product totally online as much of what they are offering is the experience of the place, not just the coffee. For this reason, companies such as Starbuck's, McDonald's, and Lowe's Home Improvement spend unusual amounts of money on their real estate operations.

Companies are often called upon to make location decisions in foreign countries. This type of analysis is difficult at best. Motivations for choosing a location vary and include customer contact, resource availability, and whether outsourcing options will reduce costs or increase competitiveness. One useful analysis is to calculate the "distance" from a company's usual base of operations.[17] Distance refers to more than geographic distance and includes culture, administrative processes, and economic differences. For example, a business might be inclined to locate manufacturing operations in an emerging market due to cheaper labor costs; however, when taking into account the administrative process, cultural differences, and economic volatility of the location, the business might change its mind and locate in a less distant place.[18] China has proved to be one such location.

Thick Markets: A Method for Creating Location Advantages

Some location issues are overcome by clusters, innovation hubs, and economic agglomerations (terms that are used interchangeably). These location solutions derive from thick labor markets (with plenty of skilled workers), the presence of specialized suppliers and service providers, and knowledge sharing among various companies and universities located in the same geographic region.

The concept of clusters refers to having many competitors, suppliers, knowledge providers, customers, regulators, and supporting industries in one geographic region. Clusters are

> geographic concentrations of interconnected companies and institutions in a particular field. Clusters encompass an array of linked industries and other entities important to competition [and] include governmental and other institutions—such as universities, standards-setting agencies, think tanks, vocational training providers, and trade associations—that provide specialized training, education, information, research, and technical support.[19]

If a company locates within a cluster that is relevant to its business, it will typically increase its competitiveness. Some authors claim that clustering explains the divergence of certain geographical growth patterns over the past 30 years.[20] For example, some areas are thriving and can overcome even the worst recessions due to clustering activity.

Notable clusters in the United States are based on the location of natural resources (e.g., the oil industry, which is primarily located in Texas, Alaska, and Louisiana). The wine industry in California developed because of the region's ideal weather conditions for growing grapes. Innovation hubs, not dependent on natural resources, are somewhat harder to explain. For example, many high-tech companies are located in Silicon Valley although the area does not actually produce silicon. Companies such as Google, Facebook, Apple, and others locate in the same region because they can access labor markets, network, and carefully follow industry trends. Thus, Silicon Valley has become a hub for this type of business and attracts people who are interested in working in this field.

This is just one example of why some companies remain in seemingly illogical locations. Some companies pick enormously expensive places such as New York, Boston, and San Francisco; one observer cites the following example of this decision:

To hire a skilled worker with a college education, eBay and Adobe must pay that worker $87,033 a year in San Jose, but a similar company based in Merced would need to pay only $62,411. In fact, if eBay and Adobe moved to Merced, they would end up paying less to hire a college graduate than what they are paying now to hire a high school graduate, which is $68,009.[21]

While companies can cut costs by moving to less costly labor markets, they risk not finding the people and suppliers they need to develop their companies.

The growth of clusters and innovation hubs is dependent upon the populace of a location. Size matters; large population centers tend to have robust labor markets. Supply and demand for specific occupations are generally well balanced in highly populated locations. Labor markets that are thick (or have many buyers and sellers) are better at matching employers with workers; the ultimate match is generally closer to the ideal fit for both job seekers and those offering jobs. The economic returns of being in a thick labor market, as measured by increased earnings, are significant for professionals.[22] Also, thick markets tend to be somewhat less susceptible to recessions and their workers are generally more productive because of the competiveness for top jobs. Finally, thick job markets tend to benefit new firms because they can find skilled people to work in their firms more easily.

One research study found that well-educated professionals are increasingly gathering in larger cities; especially those in two-income households. In fact, some companies list a spouse's employment as the biggest reason that employees turn down jobs requiring relocation.[23] Thicker markets provide both partners with more opportunities.

Providers of specialized services also benefit from clusters; by moving to a cluster, firms can utilize specialized local suppliers. For example, high-tech firms can focus on what they do well without having to rely entirely on full-time employees. Geographic clusters reflect a virtuous cycle (i.e., the more you have, the more you get). Thus, firms relocating to clusters can take advantage of service offerings; simultaneously, the specialized services within the cluster benefit from the growth. This is the concept behind economic agglomeration.

Knowledge spillovers are yet another benefit of clusters. Innovation is not the product of the lone genius (despite popular press accounts to the contrary). The flow and diffusion of knowledge is facilitated by clusters, although these flows are somewhat invisible (i.e., leaving "no paper trail by which they may be measured and tracked").[24] Much research has shown that geographic proximity facilitates this tacit knowledge transfer. By clustering near each other, innovators promote each other's creative spirits and motivation.

Innovation hubs apply to environmental sustainability in several ways. First, they tend to have plenty of technology development and innovation. Companies working on wind and solar technologies in Germany, for example, tend to be located in similar locations.[25] However, clusters also create growth, which is an environmental challenge in any area. Growth in geographic locations calls for increased infrastructure, services, and the development of housing. For example, North Dakota[26] has been through a series of booms and busts over the past several decades. A boom happened in the late 1970s, driven by rising oil prices; however, in 1999, there wasn't a single rig drilling new wells in the state. By July 2012, monthly oil output reached almost 21 million barrels, making North Dakota the largest oil producer in the country after Texas. This recent boom has many environmentalists worried. For example, according to data obtained by *ProPublica*, oil companies in North Dakota reported over 1,000 accidental releases of oil, drilling wastewater, or other fluids (about as many as in the previous two years combined). Many more illicit releases went unreported, state regulators acknowledge, when companies dumped truckloads of toxic fluid along the road or drained waste pits illegally.[27] This rapid growth has made regulatory oversight of companies much more difficult.

An Example of the Environmental Risks Created by Location

Rising sea levels are considered a primary cause of the erosion along the United States' East Coast over the past century. As oceans start to rise faster, this will only get worse. Water is rising three times faster along the North Carolina coast than it did a century ago.[28] Sea level is expected to rise another meter by 2020. The low, flat northeastern shore (including the popular Outer Banks) is among the nation's most vulnerable places.[29]

North Carolina's insured property losses from hurricanes averaged $10.6 million a year (in 2005 dollars) from 1949 to 1988. Between 1989 and 2005, the monetary value of losses was almost 30 times greater than the previous period (at $296 million per year).[30]

One can only wonder who will pay for the remediation needed along the coast. For example, North Carolina state officials found that 68 percent of ocean beaches are eroding up to 15 feet a year. Sandbags now protect 352 homes and other buildings from creeping waters. Nags Head plans to split the cost of new sand (which is expected to last 10 years) between a county beach fund and a bond to be repaid by occupancy taxes. The necessary funds are still short $10 million.[31] Other solutions (e.g., moving homes and businesses) are too costly.[32]

With 325 miles of oceanfront and 5,000 miles of shoreline around its seven sounds, North Carolina has one of the most diverse coastlines. The Albermale and Pamlico Sounds form the second-largest estuary system in the lower 48 states, provide half of the nursery grounds for all saltwater fish between Maine and Florida, and nurture most of the state's economically important seafood. Thus, the environmental challenges threaten the core economic and social fabrics of these communities.

Furthermore, commercial fishing in 2009 brought about $77 million to North Carolina (sport fisherman took home an additional 12 million pounds of fish), coastal tourists spent $24 billion in 2009 (more than a third of that was spent in the vulnerable Outer Banks), and the tourism industry employs 30,530 people. Also, almost $133 billion of the coastal property is insured (which brings major dollars to the insurance industry).[33] The industry has about an $81 billion exposure in North Carolina.[34] Thus, coastal erosion has a major impact on the entire state of North Carolina.

The North Carolina coastline situation is one example of a cluster; participants in the food industry, tourism, recreation, and all of the supporting industries converge in a single location. As such, this is a good example of how environmental challenges play a role in business strategy and the potential of these challenges to upset industries, economies, and lives.

However, environmental challenges are much bigger than location. The management of specific operational areas is critical to decreasing a company's footprint, the subject of the next section.

Profile: Clusters and Energy—Can Charlotte Create a Cluster?[35]

Globalization has created opportunities for individuals, companies and whole industries to expand without the constraints of location. An individual can use the Internet to mount a business and have clients all over the world without ever meeting the clients face-to-face and without having a physical space other than where the individual's computer is located.

Yet, data show that companies co-locating together create more jobs than when they are separated from their related counterparts, a phenomena called clustering.[36] "By clustering near each other, innovators foster each other's creative spirit and become more successful . . . Location is more important than ever, in part because knowledge spillovers are more important than ever."[37]

Related firms locate close together in a cluster. Famous examples in the United States are steel in Pittsburgh, Silicon Valley, automobile manufacturing near Detroit, textiles and tobacco in North Carolina, and financial services in Charlotte, North Carolina. As evidenced by North Carolina, clusters do not last forever.

Research on clusters shows that at least a few factors are critical to the cluster's formation and ongoing success. These factors include human and social capital, educational institutions, research and innovation, capital resources, and favorable regulations and policies. Sometimes evidence of raw materials facilitates clusters such as the case of oil and gas in Texas. Clusters evidence a unique blend of these factors including an unusual number of trained people in related fields and unskilled workers who service the skilled labor. Also, many supporting firms and organizations such as accounting, banking, and educational programs have related skills and programs.

The issue confronting many regions is how to start a cluster. This is Charlotte, North Carolina's challenge as it finds its banking cluster is stagnant, textiles and tobacco are not prevalent in the state, and the city is growing in population. To sustain this growth the city is focusing on becoming an energy "hub," the word various stakeholders use for cluster.[38] Regional leaders point to Germany and the United Kingdom as prime examples where clusters thrive and yield the regional benefits that officials expect.[39] The European Union has a web tool to help develop clusters.[40]

For example, the German government passed a policy document outlining the Energiewende, or Energy Transition, that will phase out nuclear energy by 2022. The Energiewende's goal by 2050 is to supply enough energy to satisfy 80 percent of the nation's electricity needs with renewable energy sources.[41] Germany has various energy related clusters and has evidenced success by increased employment, achievement of energy goals, and worldwide recognition for its accomplishments.[42]

Another database related to the U.S. is the U.S. Cluster Mapping Project. The site analyzes over 50 million records to create a Location Quotient. The higher the LQ the more significant a cluster. Charlotte, North Carolina has an LQ of 2.76 for Electric Power Generation and Transmission, a relatively moderate LQ compared to other national LQs.[43]

So what would you tell Charlotte about establishing an energy cluster? What studies should they do and what steps should they take to get going? Review both the EU and U.S. clustering projects cited in this profile and create your own hypotheses about how these clusters start and are maintained.[44]

Organizational Forms to Address Environmental Challenges

Several commentators make distinctions among organizational forms that have different foci, have different roles to play in confronting sustainability challenges, and have different outcomes from taking a natural environmental lens. The organizational forms take on familiar and unfamiliar labels. Nongovernment, not-for-profit (discussed in Chapter 12), social enterprises, for-profit with a social overlay are just a few of the labels given to these organizational types.

The distinctions among the types are a matter of at least:

1 dominant intent;
2 governance structure;
3 profit distribution.

Organizational forms and purposeful designs can have impacts on organizational performance. Poorly designed organizations can create inefficiencies and can block effective strategy implementation. For example, some countries demand that foreign national companies organize as local joint ventures with a partner from the host country. This organizational form may not be effective in doing business and could create extra costs.[45]

Social enterprises and social entrepreneurship have addressed social and environmental challenges to complement not-for-profit and government organizations. These organizations are different from other organizational types by their dominant intent to address social and environmental issues, their tendency to be governed by for-profit types of boards and their distribution of profits to owners.[46] U.S. law, among other countries, do not recognize organizations that combine sources of funds and benefits from various organizational types. For example, organizations cannot currently receive tax deductible contributions in the U.S. combined with invested capital from markets and nonmarket rate loans.[47]

Some organizations declare themselves as for-profit yet declare a social mission as part of their strategies. Microfinance organizations such as SKS and textile manufacturer Patagonia are two examples. These organization structures are even more nuanced in some U.S. states.

Benefit corporations are for-profit corporations that declare their social benefit and are generally private companies. They make this declaration to signal to investors the organization's dominant intent and to protect themselves against investors who challenge the organization's expenditures on social causes and extending the fiduciary responsibility of the board of directors to make social expenditures that might lower shareholder returns. Over half the U.S. states have approved this corporate form, including Vermont, California, and Maryland among the earliest adopters.[48] A corporation that is labeled B-Corp has received a designation for this label from an accrediting organization called B Lab.[49] B Lab claims that B-Corps meet higher standards of transparency, accountability, and performance.

The Flexible Purpose Corporation is unique to California for companies seeking investment from traditional capital markets, hence they are public companies. L3C corporations (Low-profit limited liability companies) are yet another form seeking some investment from foundations. They, too, have a declared social mission.[50]

These organizational forms are new and have not been extensively tested in the courts and capital markets. They might be appealing from a public perception point of view yet they seem to add little value to an organization's effectiveness. Organizations are obligated to adhere to proven principles, as described in this book, to achieve competitive advantage. The next section describes some more of these proven principles and practices.

Management of Operational Areas

Specific parts of supply chains tend to provide opportunities to make large impacts on costs and competitiveness. One way to organize our thinking about management practices (in operational areas) is to use the types of capital introduced in Chapter 1. For example, manufactured capital is a firm's physical technology, plants and equipment, geographic location, and access to raw materials.[51] Management practices might include pollution control and prevention with process adaptations. Human capital would include environmental training, incentives, and reward systems. Thus, all environmental practices can be categorized according to these types of capital.

One could further classify the practices within each type of capital according to inputs, processes, or outputs.[52] For example, for investments in reporting structure, planning, and control processes, surveillance of the market for environmental opportunities would impact inputs, explicit environmental policies would impact processes, and environmental marketing would impact outputs. Thus, the number of different management practices is endless and emanate from inputs, processes, and outputs.

To manage our conversation, this chapter includes three specific operational areas that account for large environmental impacts and present significant opportunities for companies to manage environmental improvements and increase competitiveness: transportation, construction of buildings, and purchasing.

Transportation

Thirty-four percent of carbon emissions result from transportation.[53] More than a quarter of all U.S. driving is to and from work; 75 percent of this is performed in single-occupancy vehicles. Approximately 5 percent of the U.S. population uses public transportation to get to and from work (a figure that has been consistent since the 1980s).[54] If the United States continues this trend, the number of passenger miles traveled in cars will increase 80 percent by 2040.[55] Infrastructure, fuel, and raw materials needed to support this growth would generate up to four times more toxic and climate-changing emissions.

The world's love affair with the car comes at great costs. Consider some of these facts:

1 Transportation is the largest source of air pollutants.
2 As early as 2006, transportation was responsible for over half of the country's carbon monoxide emissions, over a third of its nitrogen dioxide, and almost a quarter of its fluorocarbons.[56]
3 Increases in maintenance, insurance, and fuel drive up the average cost of sedans to $9,122 yearly (i.e., 60.8 cents per mile).[57] Average income in the United States for 2013 rose to $52,100 in June, from its recent inflation-adjusted trough of $50,700 in August 2011.[58] Thus, the cost of a car averaged almost 20 percent of average income.
4 The vast majority of growth in traffic will occur in urban centers and surrounding suburbs where the U.S. population (and its economic activity) is overwhelmingly concentrated. The 100 largest U.S. metropolitan regions house almost two-thirds of the population and generate nearly three-quarters of our GDP.[59]

The above information is just a small sampling of the challenges we face as a nation and world with respect to transportation. Many people and companies recognize these challenges and are taking action. The opening of this chapter focused on the work that Maersk is doing to cut fuel and thus its environmental footprint. We see other industries also trying to decrease transportation's environmental impacts. For example, airlines are testing biofuels. The first U.S. biofuels flight was on November 7, 2011, and it used a 40 percent blend of biofuel made from algae.[60] Jet fuel is also now made from animal fat, garbage, shrubbery, and dozens of other substances.[61]

At least a dozen international airlines have flown commercial flights using biofuels. Many of these companies switched to biofuel on the heels of the EU announcing that it will charge airlines for certain levels of carbon emissions, while awarding credits for the use of biofuels that reduce emissions by at least 35 percent. Also, the airline industry has pledged to cut its emissions in half by 2050 (based on its 2005 levels).[62]

Biofuel is purchased in interesting places. Alaska Air purchased 28,000 gallons in November 2011 from Dynamic Fuels of Geisman Louisiana, a joint venture of Tyson Foods and Syntroleuma, a synthetic fuels company. Alaska Air Group estimates that its use of 20 percent biofuel for all of its flights in one year is equivalent to a reduction of 64,000 cars on the road.[63]

Transportation is key for most businesses; however, transportation is only one of several high-impact areas with respect to the environment. An equally important and impactful area of operation is the construction and use of buildings.

Constructing and Managing High-Performance Buildings

One powerful driver of negative environmental outcomes (especially with respect to global warming) is the energy used to construct and operate homes, offices, and industrial facilities. I can argue that the green-building movement (also referred to as sustainable construction, high-performance building, or environmentally friendly building) is the most powerful movement for influencing sustainable outcomes.[64] The energy used in buildings accounts for almost half of all energy consumption and half of GHG emissions. Globally, the percentage is closer to 76 percent when considering all power plant-generated electricity used to operate buildings.[65] The building industry consumes about 40 percent of the extracted materials and is responsible for 35 percent of CO_2 emissions.[66]

A solution for reducing the environmental footprint of buildings is to utilize high-performance, green, and/or sustainable construction (terms that are often used interchangeably). This has ecological, social, and economic implications and generally produces healthier indoor environments, resource efficiency, and ecological designs.[67] Seven principles inform this construction:

1   reduce resource consumption;
2   reuse resources;
3   use recyclable resources;
4   protect nature;
5   eliminate toxins;
6   apply life-cycle costing;
7   focus on quality.

These principles apply to all resources (land, materials, water, energy, ecosystems) and throughout the phases of a building's life (planning, development design, construction, use and operation, maintenance, medication, and deconstruction).[68]

Companies that construct buildings in a sustainable fashion have used certain standards that formalize these principles and ensure that their buildings are environmentally friendly. One of the most common standards in the United States is Leadership in Energy and Environmental Design (LEED).[69] LEED is an internationally recognized green-building certification system. Developed in March 2000, LEED provides building owners and operators with a framework for identifying and implementing practical and measurable green-building designs, construction, operations, and maintenance solutions.

LEED is a set of standards that promotes environmentally friendly building and development practices; a rating system recognizes specific projects adhering to these standards. There are different standards for new and existing buildings (see Table 10.1). The LEED-rating systems are developed through a consensus-based process with groups of knowledgeable volunteers.

Many organizations promote LEED and sustainable construction. In the United States, these include the U.S. Green Building Council (the originator of LEED standards), the Green Building Initiative (an organization that has the rights to Green Globes, a Canadian building standard used in the United States), the U.S. Department of Energy, the U.S. Environmental Protection Agency, the National Association of Home Builders, and numerous other government and nongovernment organizations. Several global organizations support environmentally friendly building such as the International Union for Experts in Construction, Materials, Systems, and Structures as well as the International Institute for a Sustainable Built Environment (a body responsible for the Green Building Tool).

Table 10.1 LEED Standards[70]

Standard type	Description and intent
New construction and major renovations	Addresses design and construction activities for both new buildings and major renovations of existing buildings, which include major HVAC improvements, significant envelope modifications, and major interior rehabilitation
Existing buildings	Encourages owners and operators of existing buildings to implement sustainable practices and reduce the environmental impacts of their buildings, while addressing the major aspects of ongoing building operations
Core and shell	For projects where the developer controls the design and construction of the entire core and shell base building (e.g., mechanical, electrical, plumbing, and fire protection systems) but has no control over the design and construction of the tenant fit-out
Commercial interiors	For tenants in commercial and institutional buildings who lease their space or do not occupy the entire building
Retail	New construction and major renovations: addresses specifics for the construction or major renovation of a retail building
Homes	Promotes the design and construction of high-performance homes—energy efficient, resource efficient, and healthy for occupants
Neighborhood development	Neighborhoods, portions of neighborhoods, multiple neighborhoods—there is no minimum or maximum size for a LEED for Neighborhood Development project
Schools	The design and construction of K–12 schools. Based on LEED for New Construction, it focuses on classroom acoustics, master planning, mold prevention, environmental site assessment, and other issues important to these buildings
Healthcare	Inpatient and outpatient care facilities and licensed long-term care facilities. It can also be used for medical offices, assisted living facilities and medical education and research centers.

Recent developments globally have helped define and enforce sustainable development standards across the world. The most advanced standards in addition to LEED can be found in the UK (BREEAM), Germany (DGNB) and Australia (Green Star).[71] Companies use these standards, most of which are optional, to support their building efforts. The concepts are obviously not new. Early civilizations benefitted from solar heating, careful positioning of buildings, and various combinations of water and building designs to heat and cool buildings. Persians made ice in the desert using wind catchers. (These structures used air baffles to cool the air.) The Anasazi people of the Southwest built passive solar structures. Thomas Jefferson invented a passive cooling system.[72] Thus, modern society seems to be "inventing" some practices that were used long ago.

Nevertheless, the impacts of sustainable practices are dramatic. For example, green-building practices are estimated to reduce energy use by at least 30 percent, carbon emissions by 35 percent, water use by 30 to 50 percent, and generate waste-saving costs of 50 to 90 percent.[73] In fact, green builders may even turn a profit from this type of construction. Rents on green buildings tend to run higher than on conventional buildings and green buildings are more intensively managed than non-green buildings; therefore, the total operating expenses are not that different.[74] In fact, green buildings typically use less energy and gas. A separately metered building (i.e., tenants pay for what they consume) will have lower energy costs (by 21 percent on average) even if the Energy Star score is the same. Green buildings, even if only Energy Star-labeled, tend to be occupied by above-average wage earners who generally feel more productive and take fewer sick days. Green leases and green operational practices are important to tenants.[75]

People spend most of their time in buildings so it makes good sense for these spaces to be pleasant, conducive to productive activity, and healthy. Indoor levels of pollutants, however, may be 10 times higher than outdoor levels.[76] Buildings can cause disease, such as the sick-building syndrome, which inflicts occupants with headaches; irritation to eyes, noses, and throats; and difficulties with concentration.[77] When buildings are built according to green design, they tend to show improvements in indoor air quality.[78]

Improving indoor air quality could save U.S. businesses $20 billion to $200 billion a year in energy costs and $58 billion in avoided costs related to sick time. Increased productivity could save another $200 billion a year.[79] Also, while construction has been harshly impacted by economic downturns, studies have reported that building green has not been significantly impacted. One study concluded that "green building has grown in spite of the market downturn. Green seems to be one area of construction insulated by the downturn, and we expect green building will continue to grow over the next five years despite negative market conditions to be a $96–$140 billion market" by 2013.[80]

The potential market is tremendous for green building. Also, more and more businesses are now following LEED standards and general green-building standards for new construction and renovated spaces. Showcase buildings often inspire builders and developers. For example, in 2002, ZEDfactory (formerly Dunster Architects) completed the Beddington Zero Energy Development (BedZED) in a London suburb. This was the largest mixed-use, carbon-neutral development in the United Kingdom and one of the first in the world. Dongtan, a development off the shores of Shanghai, is yet another inspiring project. The Chinese, helped by Western architects, are attempting to create a completely carbon-neutral island. Dongtan is conceptually an exciting venture, which may take five to 10 years to break ground. Unfortunately, at this point it is unclear if the city will ever be finished.[81]

One of the most ambitious green-building projects was established in 2006 by Masdar, a commercially driven enterprise focused on renewable energy and sustainable technologies. Masdar operated through five integrated units (including an independent, research-driven graduate university) and sought to create an advanced location in terms of positive environmental outcomes. Masdar is based in the United Arab Emirates (a global center of excellence in renewable energy and clean technologies) and is a wholly owned subsidiary of the government-owned Mubadala Development Company in Abu Dhabi, a catalyst for the economic diversification of the Emirates.[82]

High-performance buildings will remain important. Society is likely to learn a great deal more about how to construct buildings with decreasing amounts of impacts on the environment and many of these innovations will hopefully become standard practice. The next section contains some information about purchasing techniques that can contribute to better environmental outcomes for businesses and governments.

Environmental Preferable Purchasing

Environmental preferable purchasing (EPP) is an important operational area utilized by firms to impact environmental outcomes. The purchasing function in a firm manages all purchases made by a company, usually in response to the demands of operating units. EPP means garnering products and services that have a lesser (or reduced) effect on human health and the environment (when compared with competing products or services that serve the same purpose).[83] Acquiring green products can occur at any (or all) levels of production (e.g., raw materials, manufacturing, packaging, distribution, use and reuse, operation, maintenance, and disposal of the product).

EPP specialists seek the overall best value, taking into account price competitiveness, availability, regulatory requirements, performance, and environmental impacts. EPP involves being aware, in particular, of the environmental impacts of products and actions. The ideal products use minimal resources, have no ill effects on human health, and have no environmental impact. The availability of these types of products is significantly influenced by major buyers such as the U.S. federal government (which is one of the world's largest single consumers, spending yearly about $350 billion for goods and services).[84] The government's

EPP program works to ensure that the federal government's buying power is increasing the availability of environmentally preferable products, which helps minimize negative environmental impacts.

The government sets an example for businesses and its program has many other benefits (e.g., improved ability to meet environmental goals, improved worker safety and health, reduced liabilities [including reduced health and disposal costs], and increased availability of environmentally preferable products in the marketplace).

Most purchasing agents have clear sources of information on procurement and regulatory requirements and utilize established methods for evaluating price and performance. However, environmental factors in purchasing are less developed. Figure 10.2 is one model for an effective EPP. This model focuses on the purchasing function through a sourcing manager and the decisions he or she makes. Direct influences on these decisions vary and include purchasing criteria (e.g., product performance, pricing, and user demands).

Companies utilize LCA for making environmental determinations (already discussed in Chapter 9), and *system performance* refers to how efficient the purchasing function is within a firm. For example, several organizations have duplicative processes for purchasing and different ways of purchasing materials. This type of duplication is often wasteful.

A sourcing manager looks for various impact categories when making purchasing decisions with an environmental lens. An impact category is an area affecting environmental outcomes. Table 10.2 has a list of some of the more common impact categories that are considered by purchasers. For example, some managers might emphasize worker safety in their decisions while others focus on the environmental impact of raw materials.

Bank of America, as an example, focuses on specific product categories (e.g., paper goods, office furniture, and carpeting). This is from their purchasing policy:

> Bank of America has developed the following paper procurement policy because we recognize that paper is a key material used in providing financial services, that the majority of the paper we purchase is derived from forests, and that maintaining the ecological health of forests aligns with our commitment to environmental stewardship. Forests help regulate climate, support biodiversity, and provide other vital services that help sustain the cultures, local communities and economies relying on this resource.

The bank's paper procurement policy seeks to maintain the ecological health of forests through:

- Source Reduction and Recycling. The bank will build on its longstanding commitment to minimize consumption of paper products containing virgin wood fiber, in order to reduce demand on forests.
- Sustainable Forest Practices. When procuring paper products containing virgin wood fiber, the bank will require its suppliers to ensure that the source forests from which fiber is procured are managed using environmentally preferable practices.
- Protection of Endangered Forests. The bank will require its suppliers of paper products to identify and appropriately manage forests threatened by human or commercial activity.[85]

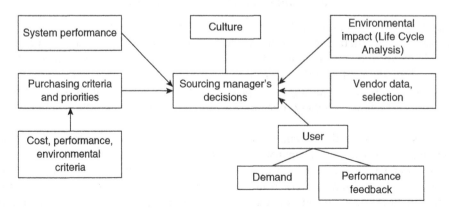

Figure 10.2 Model for Environmental Preferrable Purchasing

Table 10.2 Impact Categories for Determining Environmental Outcomes in Purchasing Decisions

Maximize	*Minimize*
Biodegradable	Product safety hazards such as flammability and corrosiveness
Recyclability	Noise
Recycled content	Odor
Durability	Radiation
Reusability	Waste, land, water, energy
Product performance	• Human health consequences; toxological and nontoxological such as carcinogens
	• Ecological consequences such as global warming; depletion of the ozone layer; acidification; eutrophication, photo-oxidant formation; habitat alterations, and biodiversity impacts

Bank of America has chosen to focus on the raw materials vital to their organization; by establishing companywide policies, they can ensure that they have a positive impact on the environment in this specific organizational operation.

EPP is becoming relatively widespread in companies and government organizations. North Carolina's Executive Order 156 (also called the Sustainability Initiative) requires state agencies to develop and incorporate policies and practices that preserve natural resources, conserve energy, eliminate waste and emissions, and lessen overall environmental impact. One of the major provisions (in the initiative) is for state agencies, whenever feasible and practicable, to increase their purchase and use of environmentally preferable products.

Purchasing can be a powerful influence on a company's environmental performance. Companies are discovering that they have many choices when purchasing products for use in offices and in production facilities. These alternatives are currently being viewed with an environmental lens (balancing costs, performance, and environmental impact) and can be challenging but rewarding in terms of competitiveness and environmental outcomes.

Transportation, construction, and purchasing all represent significant opportunities to influence the environmental impacts of organizations. Coupled with location decisions and supply chain management, firms can make significant changes in both their environmental outcomes and competitiveness. A simple idea is that by eliminating waste, a firm can become more competitive. The next chapter addresses how firms can keep their focus as they make these changes.

Chapter Summary

This chapter addressed some of the operational areas within companies and how these operations can be managed to impact competitive outcomes that also benefit the organization's environmental footprint. First, location decisions tend to be based on resource availability (e.g., raw materials and labor); however, environmental challenges (e.g., those on the coast of North Carolina) may not permit a firm to access certain locations. Location can also positively impact a company if firms choose to work in clustered areas, which create opportunities for knowledge spillovers, access to labor, and an ecosystem of suppliers, customers, and competitors.

Supply chain managers can also impact a firm's competitiveness and environmental outcomes, especially when they find ways to decrease waste through systematic analysis of how the chain creates value. Other operational areas of high impact are transportation, building construction, and purchasing. Each of these areas has standards and significant opportunities for improving a firm's competitiveness and environmental impact.

A common misconception is that by following "green" principles, a company will only increase expenses; in reality, by taking a closer look at operational areas and utilizing an environmental lens on operations, these practices can be profitable. Also, the environmentally friendly principles in this chapter can be applied to other areas of operations just as effectively as the ones mentioned in this chapter.

Case Revisited: A.P. Møeller-Maersk Develops a Standard for the Industry

A.P. Møeller-Maersk has been a leader in the transport business and developed new methods for cutting transport costs. Unfortunately, since most of its innovations can easily be copied by competitors, the company will likely have to continue innovating; however, continuing to focus on cutting its environmental impact (and finding ways to help customers do the same) may keep the company ahead of its competition.

Terms to Know

Clusters: having many competitors, suppliers, knowledge providers, customers, regulators, and supporting industries in one geographic region

Environmental preferable purchasing: a process by which the purchasing function within a company balances cost, performance, and environmental outcomes

Geographic scope: a general measure of the number of different locations, regions, or countries in which a company operates

Supply chain: the constant flow of information, products, and resources at different stages of a product's development

Profile: Cattle Can Help Fight Climate Change

Cattle get a bad rap when it comes to environmental and health outcomes. They are blamed for consuming lots of water (some say as much as 2,500 gallons of water for one pound of beef), for being unhealthy, for contributing to global climate change through their bovine burps, flatulence and even bad breath, and their trampling of plants and soils while eating precious grains.[86] Methane spews into the air from cattle!

Cattle replaced bison as the main beef source in the 19th century. Cattle were more cost effective to move from pasture to railhead and the yield was far greater from cattle than bison.[87] They are, in essence, more efficient converters of grass to food. This prevalence is what has called attention to them as potentially harmful to the environment.

Some facts may counter this view of cattle. U.S. agriculture accounts for 8 percent of our greenhouse emissions, the majority of which is from soil management practices. Methane from cattle can be mitigated by nutritional supplements and good pasture management. The cattle can restore carbon to the soil. Most cattle feed on grass causing "beneficial disturbances" through their waste and eating practices.

> *Research by the Soil Association in the U.K. shows that if cattle are raised primarily on grass and if good farming practices are followed, enough carbon could be sequestered to offset the methane emissions of all U.K. beef cattle and half its dairy herd.[88]*

The large water usage was challenged when some studies found that U.S. beef take about 441 gallons of water per pound (similar to rice).[89] Also, 85 percent of the land grazed by cattle cannot be farmed.[90]

> *The bovine's most striking attribute is that it can live on a simple diet of grass, which it forages for itself. And for protecting land, water, soil and climate there is nothing better than dense grass. As we consider the long-term prospects for feeding the human race, cattle will rightly remain an essential element.[91]*

Are vegetarians wrong in their approach to food?

Questions and Critical Thinking

1   Consider some of the building standards mentioned in this chapter. While these standards tend to help builders construct high-performing buildings, consider what they might do to the overall environment. For example, do they encourage new construction, cause existing buildings to lose value, and/or decrease environmental outcomes? Also, are there other ways to address some of these needs (e.g., sharing space within existing buildings or working at home)? Consider the harmful aspects of these standards, possibly using some recent articles about lawsuits against LEED.[92]

2   On January 12, 2010, California's Air Resources Board approved legislation setting carbon limits in the auto industry. California's Low Carbon Fuel Standard requires that transportation fuel producers and importers in California reduce the average carbon intensity of their fuel incrementally every year from 2010 to 2020. At the end of this decade, the fuels must reflect 10 percent less carbon intensity than the 2010 baseline. Some reports believe this will cut 16 million tons of GHG emissions in the state. Fourteen other states followed California's lead and implemented similar standards. The EPA followed this lead with recommended national standards. Do you think these requirements are a positive move? Consider the costs in making the transition as well as the need for dramatically changing emissions. The automobile industry has fought these changes. They claim these regulations will cause them to increase costs to consumers. What are your views?

3   What can be done to help transportation companies change to more fuel-efficient vehicles? For example, FedEx announced that they were testing hybrid vans and might convert their entire fleet to hybrids. By 2008, they had 172 hybrids in operation; by 2010, they had about 1,800. What can be done to get other carriers to follow FedEx's lead?

4   What can employers do to encourage people to increase their use of public transportation? At present, only 5 percent of the U.S. population uses public transportation to travel to and from work. What can we do to increase this percentage?

5   Consider a report entitled *The State of the Nation's Ecosystems*.[93] The website for the report states that the "Heinz Center's landmark interdisciplinary report is inspired by the belief that American citizens should have access to regularly reported, high quality, nonpartisan information on the state of our lands, waters, and living resources."[94] Also, this report can help companies identify the best locations for their operations. Choose a specific company and try to enhance the company's strategy using this report. For example, does the company have critical operations that are located in vulnerable ecosystem areas? If so, how would you recommend the company manage this type of risk?

Notes

1   A.P. Møeller-Maersk Group, *Sustainability Report 2009: In a Climate of Change* (Copenhagen: KLS Graphic House, 2010), 16, www.maersk.com/Sustainability/Documents/Maersk_Sustainability_Report_2009.pdf (accessed March 15, 2014).

2   Ibid., 75.

3   S. Laerke, "Super Slow Steaming From Idea to Implementation" (*Maersk Maritime Technology Ship Engineering*, November 14, 2001) http://www.skibstekniskselskab.dk/public/dokumenter/Skibsteknisk/Efteraar%202011/Slow%20steaming/IDA%20SSS%20Nov%202011.pdf (accessed December 11, 2014).

4   Maersk Line, "Weekly Highlights, 21 July 2009: Maersk Line wins award for super slow steaming initiative," www.maerskline.com/globalfile/?path=/pdf/advisories/09/20090721 (accessed September 18, 2013); J. Vidal, "Modern cargo ships slow to the speed of the sailing clippers," (The Observer, July 24, 2010) www.theguardian.com/environment/2010/jul/25/slow-ships-cut-greenhouse-emissions (accessed September 18, 2013).

5   Maersk Line, "Maersk Line wins Sustainable Shipping Operator of the Year Award," www.maerskline.com/link/?page=news&path=/news/story_page/11/Award (accessed September 18, 2013).

6   Ernst and Young, "The Perfect Blend," *Capital Insights*, America's Edition (January 2014): 18.

7   A.P. Møeller-Maersk Group, *Sustainability Report 2009: In a Climate of Change*, 77.

8   H. L. Corrêa, *The VW Resende (Brazil) Plant Modular Consortium SCM Model after 5 Years of Operation* (São Paulo: Corrêa & Associados Estratégia de Manufatura e Serviços, 2001), 3, www.correa.com.br/biblioteca/artigos/A06_Correa_The_VW_Resende_etc_POMS2001.pdf (accessed January 17, 2013).

9   Inditek, "About Us", http://www.inditex.com/en/our_group (accessed August 24, 2015).

10 Fiber2fashion, "Brand Story: Zara—Commitments," http://fashiongear.fibre2fashion.com/brand-story/zara/commitments.asp (accessed December 15, 2012).

11 Observed by the author, January 10, 2012, in Best Buy, Charlotte, North Carolina.

12 B. Henderson, "Rising Waters Threaten the Coast of North Carolina" (*The Charlotte Observer*, January 16, 2011): A1.

13 Skype, "What Is Skype?" www.skype.com/en/what-is-skype/ (accessed January 17, 2013).

14 For example, Lufthansa advertised cheap flights at this rate during the winter of 2012–2013. Lufthansa, www.lufthansa.com/us/en/homepage (accessed February 4, 2012).

15 According to the Air Transport Association, cited in F. L. Smith Jr. and B. Cox, "Airline Deregulation," in D. R. Henderson (ed.), *The Concise Encyclopedia of Economics*, 2nd ed. (Indianapolis, IN: The Liberty Fund, 2008), www.econlib.org/library/Enc/AirlineDeregulation.html (accessed March 15, 2011).

16 P. Marber, *Seeing the Elephant: Understanding Globalization from Trunk to Tail* (Hoboken, NJ: John Wiley & Sons, 2009), 51–52.

17 P. Ghemawat, "Distance Still Matters: The Hard Reality of Global Expansion," *Harvard Business Review* (September 2001), 3–11. Also, P. Ghemawat, *Redefining Global Strategy: Crossing Borders in a World Where Differences Still Matter* (Boston, MA: Harvard Business School Press, 2007).

18 A variation on this analysis extends the categories using an acronym SLEEP-AT: Social-Cultural (S), Legal (L), Economic (E), Environmental (E), Political (P), Administrative (A), and Technological (T). See Chapter 5 of this book.

19 M. Porter, "Clusters and the New Economics of Competition," *Harvard Business Review* (1998): 77–90.

20 E. Moretti, *The New Geography of Jobs* (Boston, MA: Houghton Mifflin Harcourt, 2012), 124.

21 Ibid., 122–123.

22 Ibid., 128.

23 D. L. Costa and M. E. Kahn, "Power Couples: Changes in the Locational Choice of the College-Educated, 1940–1990," *Quarterly Journal of Economics* 115, no. 4 (November 2000): 1287–1315.

24 Moretti, *The New Geography of Jobs*, 139.

25 H.-M. Henning and A. Palzer, *What Will the Energy Transformation Cost? Pathways for Transforming the German Energy System by 2050* (Fraunhaufer ISE, November 2015) https://www.ise.fraunhofer.de/en/publications/veroeffentlichungen-pdf-dateien-en/studien-und-konzeptpapiere/short-summary-what-will-the-energy-transformation-cost.pdf (accessed December 22, 2015).

26 C. Brown, "North Dakota Went Boom," *The New York Times Sunday Magazine* (February 3, 2013), 22–31.

27 N. Kuznetz, "North Dakota's Oil Boom Brings Damage Along With Prosperity," *ProPublica* (June 7, 2012), www.propublica.org/article/the-other-fracking-north-dakotas-oil-boom-brings-damage-along-with-prosperi (accessed February 3, 2013).

28 Henderson, "Rising Waters Threaten the Coast of North Carolina," A1.

29 Ibid., A12.

30 Ibid.

31 Ibid.

32 L. Montgomery, "On N.C.'s Outer Banks, Scary Climate-Change Predictions Prompt a Change of Forecast," *Washington Post* (June 24, 2011) http://www.washingtonpost.com/business/economy/ncs-outer-banks-got-a-scary-forecast-about-climate-change-so/2014/06/24/0042cf96-f6f3-11e3-a3a5-42be35962a52_story.html (accessed December 4, 2014).

33 Henderson, "Rising Waters Threaten the Coast of North Carolina," 5A.

34 S. Schallau and D. Wood, *Coastal Property Insurance, The Carolinas* (Appalachian State University, Brantley Risk Insurance Center, 2014), 5. http://www.aamga.org/files/whitepapers/2013wp/SchallauSteven_AppState_CoastalPropertyCarolinas.pdf (accessed August 24, 2015).

35 Thank you to Jennifer Loftin, Jessica Hamm, and Heather Hardman (Certificate candidates in Wake Forest University MA in Sustainability Program) for their background work on this profile.

36 E. Moretti, *The New Geography of Jobs* (New York: Houghton Mifflin Harcourt Publishing Company, 2012).

37 Ibid., 139.

38 "Leading the Charge" (Charlotte, NC, November 2015). http://charlottechamber.com/clientuploads/Economic_pdfs/Charlotte_Energy.pdf (accessed December 22, 2105).

39 European Commission, "Enterprise and Industry: European Cluster Observatory," http://ec.europa.eu/enterprise/initiatives/cluster/observatory/index_en.htm (accessed January 7, 2015).

40 http://www.clustercollaboration.eu/ (accessed January 7, 2015). Also see the work of the cluster observatory "Clusters at Your Fingertips," http://www.clusterobservatory.eu/index.html (accessed January 7, 2015).

41 D. Unger, "Germany's Aggressive Push for a Clean-Energy Future," *The Christian Science Monitor* (March 9, 2014) http://www.csmonitor.com/World/Europe/2014/0309/Germany-s-aggressive-push-for-a-clean-energy-future-video (accessed January 7, 2015).

42 Enterprise Europe Network, "Environment," http://een.ec.europa.eu/about/sector-groups/environment (accessed December 22, 2015).

43 U.S. Cluster Mapping Project, "U.S. Cluster Mapping—Industry Table Chart. 2014," http://www.clustermapping.us/cluster/electric_power_generation_and_transmission (accessed January 7, 2014).

44 http://www.clustermapping.us/cluster/electric_power_generation_and_transmissionwebsites# (accessed September 4), 105.

45 "Joint Ventures," (*Encyclopedia of Business*) http://www.referenceforbusiness.com/encyclopedia/Int-Jun/Joint-Ventures.html (accessed September 5, 2015).

46 M. Kelley, "Not Just for Profit, *Strategy+Business*, 54 (2009): 1–10.

47 A. R. Broomberger, "A New Type of Hybrid," *Stanford Social Enterprise Innovation Review* 9, no. 3 (2011): 49–53.

48 M. Lane, "Social Enterprises: A New Business Form Driving Social Change," *Young Lawyer* 16, no. 3 (2014) http://www.americanbar.org/publications/young_lawyer/2011-12/december_2011/social_enterprises_new_business_form_driving_social_change.html (accessed August 26, 2015).

49 B Lab, a nonprofit organization, certifies B Corporations. See http://www.bcorporation.net/ (accessed August 25, 2015).

50 A. Field, "IRA Rule Could Help the Fledgling LC3 Corporate Form," *Forbes* (May 4, 2012) http://www.forbes.com/sites/annefield/2012/05/04/irs-rules-could-help-the-fledgling-l3c/ (accessed August 25, 2015).

51 M. T. Lucas, "Understanding Environmental Management Practices: Integrating Views from Strategic Management and Ecological Economics," *Business Strategy and the Environment* 19 (2010): 543–556.

52 Ibid., 547–548.

53 "Carbon Dioxide Emissions: Transportation Sector," in U.S. Energy Information Administration, *Emissions of Greenhouse Gases Report*, Report No. DOE/EIA-0573(2008) (Washington, DC: December 3, 2009), www.eia.gov/oiaf/1605/ggrpt/carbon.html#transportation (accessed November 2, 2011).

54 U.S. Department of Transportation, Bureau of Transportation Statistics, *National Transportation Statistics 2012* (Washington, DC, 2012), Table 1–41, www.rita.dot.gov/bts/sites/rita.dot.gov.bts/files/NTS_Entire_0.pdf. (accessed September 15, 2015).

55 B. Milikowsky, *Building America's Future: Falling Apart and Falling Behind*, Transportation Infrastructure Report 2011 (Washington, DC: Building America's Future Educational Fund, 2011), 12, www.bafuture.com/sites/default/files/Report_0.pdf (accessed February 3, 2013).

56 U.S. Environmental Protection Agency, *Latest Findings on National Air Quality: Status and Trends through 2006*, Report No. EPA-454/R-07-007 (Research Triangle Park, NC: Office of Air Quality Planning and Standards, EPA, January 2008) www.epa.gov/air/airtrends/2007/report/trends_report_full.pdf (accessed September 18, 2014).

57 American Automobile Association, "Cost of Owning and Operating Vehicle in U.S. Increases Nearly Two Percent According to AAA's 2013 'Your Driving Costs' Study," news release, April 16, 2013, http://newsroom.aaa.com/2013/04/cost-of-owning-and-operating-vehicle-in-u-s-increases-nearly-two-percent-according-to-aaas-2013-your-driving-costs-study/ (accessed September 19, 2013).

58 R. Pear, "Median Income Rises, but Is Still 6% Below Level at Start of Recession in '07," *The New York Times*, August 21, 2013, www.nytimes.com/2013/08/22/us/politics/us-median-income-rises-but-is-still-6-below-its-2007-peak.html?_r=0 (accessed September 29, 2013).

59 Milikowsky, *Building America's Future*, 12.

60 UAL, "United Airlines Flies First U.S. Commercial Advanced Biofuel Flight," PR Newswire, November 7, http://ir.unitedcontinentalholdings.com/phoenix.zhtml?c=83680&p=irol-newsArticle&ID=1627061 (accessed September 18, 2013).

61 J. Nicas, "Frying the Friendly Skies: Airlines Test Biofuels but Costs are Hurdle; $17 a gallon," *The Wall Street Journal*, November 8, 2011, B1–B2.

62 Ibid., B2.

63 Ibid.

64 See C. J. Kibert, *Sustainable Construction*, 3rd ed. (Hobokon, NJ: John Wiley and Sons, 2013).

65 R. Gupta and A. Chandiwata, "A critical and comparative evaluation of approaches and policies to measure, benchmark, reduce and manage CO_2 emissions from energy use in the existing building stock of developed and rapidly-developing countries—case studies of UK, USA, and India," conference paper, 5th Urban Research Symposium: Cities and Climate Change: Responding to an Urgent Agenda, Marseille, France, June 28–30, 2009.

66 N. Subramanian, "Sustainability—Challenges and Solutions," *The Indian Concrete Journal* (December 2007): 43, www.thestructuralengineer.info/library/papers/Sustainability_Challenges_and_solutions.pdf (accessed February 4, 2013).

67 C. J. Kibert, *Sustainable Construction: Green Building Design and Delivery*, 2nd ed. (Hoboken, NJ: John Wiley & Sons, 2008), 7.

68 Ibid.

69 U.S. Green Building Council, "About LEED," http://www.usgbc.org/articles/about-leed (accessed September 18, 2013).

70 U.S. Green Building Council, "Leed Rating Systems," www.usgbc.org/leed/rating-systems (accessed February 23, 2013).

71 Kibert, p. 2.

72 These examples are cited in L. H. Lovins and B. Cohen, *Climate Capitalism* (New York: Hill and Wang, 2011), 104.

73 Secretariat of the Commission for Environmental Cooperation, *Green Building in North America* (Montreal: Communications Department of the CEC Secretariat, 2008), 4, www3.cec.org/islandora/en/item/2335-green-building-in-north-america-opportunities-and-challenges-en.pdf (accessed September 18, 2013).

74 T. A. Dorsey and D. C. Read, "Best Practices in High-performance Office Development: The Duke Energy Center in Charlotte, North Carolina," *Real Estate Issues* 37, no. 2/3 (2012): 38–42.

75 N. G. Miller and D. Pogue, "Do Green Buildings Make Dollars and Sense?" USD-BMC Working Paper 09–11, draft, November 10, 2009, 5, www.scribd.com/doc/24568098/Do-Green-Buildings-Make-Dollars-and-Sense-Draft-Nov-10-2009 (accessed September 18, 2013).

76 U.S. Environmental Protection Agency, "An Introduction to Indoor Air Quality" (2012), www.epa.gov/iaq/voc.html (accessed December 1, 2011).

77 U.S. Environmental Protection Agency, "Sick Building Syndrome," Indoor Air Facts No. 4 (revised), February 1991, www.epa.gov/iaq/pdfs/sick_building_factsheet.pdf (accessed September 15, 2015).

78 W. J. Fisk, "How IEQ Affects Health, Productivity," *ASHRAE Journal* (May 2002): 56–58.

79 W. J. Fisk, "Health and Productivity Gains from Better Indoor Environments and Their Relationship with Building Energy Efficiency," *Annual Review of Energy and the Environment* 25 (November 2000): 537–566.

80 McGraw-Hill Construction, *Green Outlook 2009: Trends Driving Change* (New York: McGraw-Hill, 2009); McGraw-Hill Construction, "Green Building Could Triple by 2013, Says McGraw-Hill Construction," press release, November 18, 2008, www.construction.com/AboutUs/2008/1118pr.asp (accessed September 18, 2013).

81 A. Williams, "Dongtan: The Eco-city that Never Was," *Spiked*, September 1, 2009, www.spiked-online.com/newsite/article/7330#.UjnfSNLYfvE (accessed September 15, 2011); S. Plottel, "Dashed Dreams of an Eco-City: The Failure of Dongtan Eco-City on Chongming Island," China, Global Site Plans, April 24, 2013, http://globalsiteplans.com/environmental-design/architecture-environmental-design/dashed-dreams-of-an-eco-city-the-failure-of-dongtan-eco-city-on-chongming-island-china/ (accessed September 19, 2013).

82 For background on Masdar, see Masdar, "About Masdar," www.masdar.ae/en/masdar/detail/launched-by-the-abu-dhabi-leadership-in-2006-with-the-mission-to-advance-re (accessed September 18, 2013).

83 U.S. Office of Management and Budget, "Instructions for Implementing Executive Order 13423: Strengthening Federal Environmental, Energy, and Transportation Management," March 29, 2007, www.whitehouse.gov/sites/default/files/omb/procurement/green/eo13423_instructions.pdf (accessed September 18, 2013).

84 U.S. Environmental Protection Agency, "Environmentally Preferable Purchasing," www.epa.gov/epp/pubs/about/about.htm (accessed January 17, 2013).

85 Bank of America, "Paper Procurement Policy," April 19, 2005, http://about.bankofamerica.com/assets/pdf/Paper_Procurement_Policy.pdf (accessed January 17, 2014).

86 N. Niman, "Raising Beef Is Good for the Earth," *Wall Street Journal*, December 20–21, 2014, c3.

87 P. Hill, "Are All Commons Tragedies? The Case of Bison in the Nineteenth Century," *The Independent Review* 18, no. 4 (Spring 2014): 485–502.

88 N. Niman, "Raising beef is good for the earth." The U.S. Union of Concerned Scientists found similar outcomes.

89 L. Roche, L. Kromschroeder, E. Atwill, R. Dahlgren, and K. Tate, "Water Quality Conditions Associated with Cattle Grazing and Recreation on National Forest Lands" (*PLOS|One*, June 27, 2013) http://www.plosone.org/article/info%3Adoi%2F10.1371%2Fjournal.pone.0068127 (accessed January 6, 2015).

90 N. Niman, *Defending Beef: The Case for Sustainable Meat Production* (White River Junction, VT: Chelsea Green Publishing, 2014).

91 N. Niman, "Raising Beef Is Good for the Earth." Also, Fact Sheet: The Environment and Cattle Production. http://www.beefboard.org/news/files/factsheets/The-Environment-And-Cattle-Producation.pdf (accessed January 6, 2015).

92 For example: T. Roberts, "USGBC, LEED Targeted by Class-Action Suit," BuildingGreen.com, October 14, 2010, www.buildinggreen.com/auth/article.cfm/2010/10/14/USGBC-LEED-Targeted-by-Class-Action-Suit/ (accessed January 15, 2013).

93 Heinz Center for Science, Economics, and the Environment, "The State of the Nation's Ecosystems 2008," https://islandpress.org/book/the-state-of-the-nations-ecosystems-2008 (accessed December 22, 2015).

94 Ibid.

11

KEEPING FOCUS

NASCAR: On the Road to Sustainability

When you think of environmentally prudent sports, NASCAR probably does not jump to mind. A typical NASCAR race includes 43 cars driving around a mile-long racetrack for three hours. However, in just under four years, NASCAR and its stakeholders have made substantial environmental improvements and technological advancements. NASCAR is not the leader in the sustainability among all companies but it has made substantial progress toward environmental sustainability, especially compared to other sports organizations.

NASCAR made this transition by focusing its mission on three key areas: waste, emissions, and power.[1] For example, NASCAR now has one of the largest recycling and environmental sustainability programs in sports entertainment. These power and waste efforts include the world's largest solar-powered sports facility and a tree-planting program that captures 100 percent of the emissions produced by on-track racing. NASCAR also has recycling partnerships with Coca-Cola Recycling, Coors Light, Safety-Kleen, and Creative Recycling to ensure the success of its recycling program.[2]

NASCAR targeted the reduction of emissions from vehicles by forming a partnership with Sunoco and the U.S. ethanol industry. The partnership launched a biofuels program to reduce emissions of fuel used during all of its racing events. Sunoco, the official fuel of NASCAR, manufactures renewable, low-carbon fuels emitting 20 percent less GHGs than unleaded gas. NASCAR's three national touring series began using Sunoco Green E15, a renewable fuel blended with 15 percent U.S.-made ethanol from U.S.-grown corn. After completing more than two million miles during NASCAR races using Sunoco Green E15, teams report an increase of up to 10+ horsepower.[3]

NASCAR has made numerous noteworthy efforts to reduce waste, produce alternative power sources, and cut down on emissions. Their strategies for tackling these three environmental problems can be easily categorized into three areas: overarching recycling initiatives, efforts directed toward the cars and race teams, and specific changes to facilities. I will discuss, here, some of NASCAR's accomplishments in each of these areas.

Recycling

Many of NASCAR's recycling initiatives focus on waste generated by consumers. At the tracks, Coca-Cola and Coors Light educate fans on the benefits of recycling and encourage them to drop plastic bottles and aluminum cans in designated bins. Bottle and can recycling has expanded to include the grandstands, concourses, suites, garages, and campgrounds at almost every track NASCAR visits. Freightliner provides a BlueTec-equipped, clean-diesel rig to pull the Coca-Cola Portable Processing Center, which processes 1,000 containers per minute at the venues.[4]

As title sponsor of NASCAR's national series, Sprint is committed to "Recycle for Victory," a wireless-recycling program that benefits a key NASCAR charity: Victory Junction. "Recycle for Victory" helps protect the environment by reducing the number of used cellular phones that end up in landfills. Fans who visit the Sprint Unlimited Experience (the company's mobile marketing display in the midway at every NASCAR Sprint Cup Series event) can pick up pre-addressed, postage-paid envelopes to recycle their used cellular phones, batteries, and accessories (from any carrier and in any condition). Since 2001, Sprint has recycled more than 24 million phones; this equates to more than 2,600 metric tons of material.[5]

In February 2012, Creative Recycling Systems (CRS) joined NASCAR as an official green partner. CRS provides NASCAR electronic asset disposition management and data security services by utilizing state-of-the-art processing and separation technology.[6] CRS prevents millions of pounds of electronics from entering the world's landfills each year.[7]

Cars and Teams

In addition to changing the type of gasoline used, NASCAR offsets the environmental impact of cars by safely disposing of the waste created by the vehicles. Safety-Kleen Systems, Inc. (the official environmental services supplier for NASCAR) provides oil recycling and re-refining services to more than 200 NASCAR-sanctioned races a year, ensuring that all oil and lubricants used in racing are recaptured and reused. Safety-Kleen collects and re-refines more than 200,000 gallons of race-used oil annually. The company also provides absorbent products used for cleaning fluid spills inside NASCAR garages.[8]

Goodyear, the official tire supplier of NASCAR's top three series, facilitates a responsible recycling program for tires used on NASCAR stock cars and trucks. After race weekends, tires are transported to Charlotte, North Carolina and receive first-phase processing onsite. The recycled material is sold to various industries for next-generation usage (e.g., for power generation and asphalt mixtures). Approximately 121,000 tires in NASCAR's top three national series, combined, are recycled each year.[9]

NASCAR has also started the largest tree-planting program in sports with its partners UPS and the Arbor Day Foundation. The NASCAR Green Clean Air Program plants 10 trees for each green flag that drops during the races. The trees that are planted by NASCAR are able to capture the equivalent of 100 percent of the carbon produced by the on-track racing; each race produces about 43 metric tons.[10] The program debuted at 11 tracks in the 2009 Sprint Cup season and, in 2010, planted more than 1,000 trees to balance the carbon produced by racing. In 2011, the initiative expanded to the NASCAR Whelen All-American Series and now encompasses more than 26 tracks nationwide.[11] NASCAR officials say they plant 80 to 100 trees each weekend and have planted over 6,000 trees since the initiative began in 2009. Trees are always planted within the local vicinity of that weekend's particular racetrack, and NASCAR typically works with city officials to determine the area of greatest need.[12]

Some of the racing teams have joined NASCAR's efforts. For example, Roush Fenway was the first team to equip their cars with 3M Novec 1230 Fire Protection Fluid, an environmentally sustainable fire suppressant. 3M researchers developed Novec-branded products to replace substances that have high global warming potential and undesirable toxicity. GE installed new lighting fixtures and bulb technologies in both their Concord, North Carolina, and Indianapolis, Indiana race shops. These changes equate to adding 93 acres of forest or removing 65 cars from the road for a year. Kyle Busch Motorsports opened a new 77,000-square-foot corporate headquarters that is on the path to LEED certification. This state-of-the-art facility houses the latest in geothermal heating and cooling, cocoon insulation, and LED lighting that reduces energy consumption.[13]

Facilities

NASCAR moved into two new LEED-certified office buildings. The 20-story NASCAR Plaza in Charlotte, North Carolina (certified Silver LEED) and the new International Speedway Corporation and NASCAR headquarters in Daytona Beach (certified Gold LEED) are both examples of NASCAR's commitment to green efforts in all areas of its operations.[14]

NASCAR has also inspired significant "green" changes at U.S. racetracks. Pocono's Raceway installed a 3 MW solar farm in 2010, which now serves as the track's primary energy source while also helping to power more than 250 homes in the surrounding area (and lowering CO_2 emissions by 2,370 metric tons annually). With 40,000 solar panels on 25 acres of land, it is the single biggest renewable energy stadium project in the world (and twice the size of the next-largest project).[15]

Darlington Raceway has planted 25 acres of switchgrass on its track property in conjunction with Clemson University. Switchgrass can be easily converted into bio-diesel and other types of fuel. The track also owns several acres of protected wetlands and fully complies with all government regulations in order to maintain the integrity of the wetlands and increase their positive environmental stewardship. Similarly, New Hampshire International Speedway has more than 520 acres of permanently protected conservation land located throughout the 1,200-acre facility. These habitats provide natural environments for many species of animal and plant life, which are native to the state.[16]

Infineon Raceway has nearly 3,000 sheep living on its property to maintain the grasses and fire lanes around the facility, and it built 15 owl boxes to encourage the birds to nest and hunt for gophers and other rodents, eliminating the need for pesticides. The facility also features nearly 1,700 Panasonic solar panels, which are capable of offsetting 41 percent of the raceway's energy use. Michigan International Speedway (MIS) was the first sports facility in Michigan to join the Michigan Business Pollution Prevention Partnership (MBP3) and is a member of the federal EPA program, WasteWise.[17] WasteWise is a voluntary EPA program, which enables organizations to eliminate costly municipal solid waste and select industrial wastes (benefiting their bottom lines and the environment).[18] A race weekend recycling program (with the help of Coca-Cola) has collected more than 71 tons of plastic, aluminum, and paper since 2008 at this track alone.[19]

Chapter Overview

One of the most important components of any strategy is the set of processes used to implement it.[20] I have claimed that strategy formulation is a result of pressures on the firm (e.g., the natural environment, social and institutional pressures, and government mandates). Firms respond to these pressures by focusing on their core resources, competencies, and the steps necessary to position the organization in a profitable or productive market segment.

Complexities surrounding strategy formulation are heightened by the array of daily organizational actions necessary to achieve strategic goals. This chapter has some of the more important considerations in this implementation process. The theme, throughout this chapter, is "focus" (see Figure 11.1). I chose this theme because organizations often struggle to maintain focus on goals and strategies as they deal with day-to-day challenges.

Executing strategy successfully involves a complicated array of choices based on history, logic, pressures, and principles. There is no magic bullet to strategy formulation, and the same is true for strategy implementation. Both formulation and implementation involve choices (i.e., tradeoffs that make an ideal impossible). To complicate matters, every business and industry is unique. This uniqueness is developed over time and, in many cases, is the source of competitive advantage (as discussed in Chapters 4–6).

By the end of this chapter, you should be able to:

1   identify various business models and understand how business models assist in keeping a firm's focus;
2   define flexibility and explain when to use its tactics;
3   describe tactics for creating flexibility (e.g., flexible planning and using real options);
4   understand how critical performance variables help a firm maintain focus.

The principles in this chapter come from trawling a large amount of literature on what makes organizations successful as they implement their strategies. I will specifically focus on a few core areas that are essential for all managers and are relevant to a natural environmental lens on organizational competitiveness.

Business Models

A **business model** defines how organizations create, deliver, and capture value.[21] Table 11.1 shows an outline of critical business model components. We have addressed many of these components throughout this book. In this chapter, I highlight how changing a business model can contribute to innovation and thus increase an organization's competitiveness; it relates to how the organization creates value for customers and other stakeholders, makes money, and can continually maintain focus on its strategies and goals to increase competitiveness.

One illustrative example of business model innovation is Daimler AG's implementation of its Car2go program. They recently invented Car2go, which complements Daimler's core model of manufacturing, selling, and financing a range of vehicle types. The purpose of this innovation was to find a new revenue source by

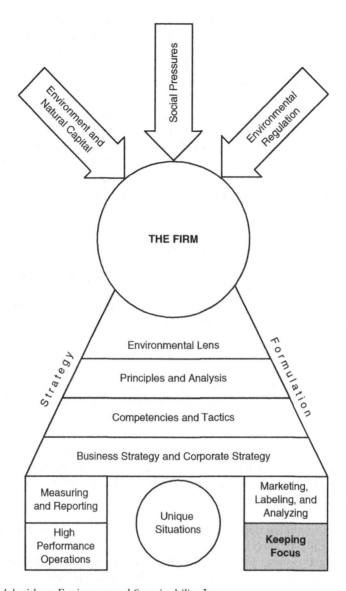

Figure 11.1 Strategy Model with an Environmental Sustainability Lens

targeting an untapped consumer. Car2go offers city dwellers mobility on demand via a fleet of Smart cars (an automobile product developed jointly by Swatch Watch and Daimler). The name Car2go is a creative way of stating "for two cars," which is a reference to the maximum seating of two in a Smart car.

The Car2go program offers convenience because cars are accessible at various locations, any time of the day. Customers complete a one-time registration process; after that, they can rent a car on the spot or with an advanced reservation. They use the cars as long as desired (after which they are billed monthly). This service is similar to the ZipCar, which is available in the United States. The Daimler's pilot tests in the United Kingdom started with internal employees and moved toward citywide residents in some of their operational bases (e.g., Ulm, Germany, and Austin, Texas). Each level of testing was viewed as a prototype, a process Daimler is attempting to adopt in their car manufacturing. This service complements their core business model while offering innovation; as it services the Car2go cars, the company can identify ways to improve its other products and services. Their business model can be summarized using the components listed in Table 11.1 (see Table 11.2).

Table 11.1 Business Model Components

Component	What is addressed
Customer segments	Who is served
Value propositions	Solves customer and stakeholder problems; presents points of difference and points of parity with other suppliers to the market
Channels	Communication, distribution, and sales methods to deliver the value proposition
Customer relationships	Relationships within each segment
Revenue streams	Results from value propositions successfully offered to customers
Key resources	Assets required to offer and deliver the value proposition. These can be tangible, intangible, and human resources.
Key activities	Core processes for using resources
Key partnerships	Who needs to help?
Cost structure	Costs to deliver the value proposition

Creating new business models, like Daimler did with Car2go, may give a firm a competitive advantage. Additionally, by aligning the new innovation with the company's overarching goals, it creates an opportunity for greater success because it does not require the firm to shift focus from its original aim: manufacturing, selling, and financing a range of vehicle options. In essence, Car2go helped Daimler to produce a better product in other areas of the company.

Business models help to implement strategy and identify ways to continue adding value to organizations by outlining the components that must be considered before making a change. Business models are relatively easy to change (vs. an organization's strategy). Also, business models, across organizations, tend to have patterns. For our purposes, I will highlight five patterns found in most companies: unbundling, the long tail, multisided platforms, free, and open.[22] These patterns can be used to create constant innovation, focus attention on important improvement areas, and find ways to better serve customers while adding organizational value.

Unbundling

Unbundling refers to three types of businesses: customer relationships, product innovation, and infrastructure. The three types may coexist within a single business; however, ideally they are unbundled into separate entities to avoid conflicts and undesirable tradeoffs.[23]

Table 11.2 Business Model Components for the Car2Go

Component	What or who is addressed
Customer segments	City dwellers
Value propositions	Individual urban mobility without car ownership
Channels	Car2go.com, mobile phones, Car2go parking lots, Car2go shops, pick up/drop off anywhere
Customer relationships	One-off sign ups
Revenue streams	Pay/minute
Key resources	Service team, telematics systems, Smart car fleet
Key activities	Fleet management, telematics management, leaning
Key partnerships	City management
Cost structure	Systems management, fleet management

Businesses that rely on customer relationships use business models to determine how to find, acquire, and retain customers. For example, banking has realized that *share of wallet* (i.e., gaining as much business as possible from an individual customer) is important for profitability. Therefore, many banks have invested large sums in obtaining customers and then offering them various products related to their initial purchases to promote the bank's services. As such, this type of business model develops core competencies in service and an ability to cross-sell various products and services. Cell phone companies are another example of this business model.

Businesses that rely on product innovation use business models to develop new and attractive products and services. For example, Newell Rubbermaid (building on Rubbermaid's product development competencies) creates new products continuously; some analysts say that it develops a new product every day. Building business models can assist companies, such as Rubbermaid, by helping them to focus on developing products that meet the criteria outlined in the model. Businesses also use business models to build and manage platforms for high-volume, repetitive tasks. Wal-Mart and Lowe's Home Improvement are examples of businesses that would utilize this type of business model (especially in the ways they manage large supply chains).

Some food companies attempt to use all three of the unbundled models. For example, a food broker can work to acquire supermarket customers (customer relationships) and then also attempt to expand its business with the supermarket itself by supplying various types of food (infrastructure). A company could also invest in R&D to innovate food packaging to increase customer convenience (food innovation), or a firm can create economies of scale and find ways to produce large amounts of food (infrastructure). The likelihood that one organization can use all three models is low and probably not desirable because the company runs the risk of getting away from its core competencies and creating a confusing internal environment that causes a loss of focus.

Long Tail

A second major business model pattern is entitled "the long tail." This model focuses on a large number of products that sell relatively infrequently. These models tend to have low inventory costs and strong platforms to make niche content broadly available to interested buyers.[24] For example, most of YouTube's videos are infrequently viewed; a very small percentage account for most of the traffic (especially when a video "goes viral"). Similarly, online video stores (especially Hulu and Netflix) have content unique to purchasers who tend to be niche-focused. A company such as Lockheed Martin might sell only a few large ships or fighter jets per year. These companies tend to make money through advertising or extensive, lengthy sales campaigns (vs. directly through service offerings) or create unique customer relationships.

Multisided Platforms

A third model is entitled a "multisided platform" because it brings together two or more separate (but interdependent) customer groups. Such platforms are of value to one group of customers only if the other group of customers is present. Value creation evolves from facilitating interactions among different groups and the creation of network effects.[25]

Platforms serving two-sided networks are not a new phenomenon (e.g., energy companies and automakers link drivers of gasoline-powered cars and refueling stations in a well-established network). However, multisided platforms have become more prevalent in recent years because they help companies save money, increase impact, and develop efficiencies with new products and services. Google, for example, links advertisers and web searchers. Also, traditional businesses have been reconceived as two-sided platforms, for example, consider retail electricity markets that match consumers with specific power producers and enable them to express their preferences for coal or renewable power at different prices.

Free

Free, another business model pattern, relies on at least one substantial customer segment that is able to benefit from a free offer. Nonpaying customers are financed by another customer segment.[26] Skype relies on this model.

Members of this network can make free Internet calls to each other; however, calls out of the network are not free. Another example is to offer free energy audits to identify energy efficiency opportunities. Customers might decide to improve the efficiency opportunities by purchasing services or products from the audit company. Similar approaches are taken by consulting companies who offer free seminars or retirement counselors who offer free retirement calculations hoping that they will be able to sell investments to the retiree.

Open

Open business models are used by companies to create and capture value by systematically collaborating with outside partners.[27] For example, companies buy and sell innovation to create value. A recent example is a company that evolved from an in-house venture by Eli Lilly; InnoCentive solicits various people in the market to participate in product development.[28] In this way, innovation comes from individuals outside of the company; however, InnoCentive retains the rights to use the ideas for their products and services.

As more industries begin using an environmental lens to look at their companies, this lens presents all sorts of opportunities to reinvent industries through developing new business models. Business models help organizations focus on how to make money and the customer value proposition (two critical components for implementing a competitive strategy). The development of business models sometimes involves changing existing processes and organizational arrangements. The next section discusses why people resist these changes and focuses on reasons most relevant to environmental sustainability.

Resistance to Taking Action

Organizations often need to change the ways they do business to create a more compelling strategy. They need to change all sorts of aspects of the organization (e.g., the organization structure, processes, and even the people who do the work). People resist these changes for all sorts of reasons. This change process and resistance makes keeping a focus on the new vision or goals difficult at best.[29]

Many commentaries have catalogued general ideas about resistance to change and how to overcome these resistances.[30] This section covers sources of resistance to change that are unique to supporting natural environmental outcomes. One way to organize our thinking about this resistance is to look at various levels of abstraction: global and national cultures, institutional arrangements, organizational factors, and individual mindsets.

At global and national levels, values tend to conflict with actions that support the environment. In the United States, the national culture tends to advocate that individuals can control everything, including the natural environment. This belief in individualism and individual control causes Americans to place an unparalleled emphasis on individual rights in every area of social life and to be suspicious of group rights.[31] It also encourages Americans to criticize government institutions (especially Congress and bureaucracies). This value leads Americans to believe they can create technological fixes to negative environmental outcomes, or that they can otherwise control most outcomes. Capitalism tends to support this view as well. Capitalism's private property and free market values and practices all too often do not promote caring for the natural environment.

Preservation of the natural environment applies only to those aspects of the environment and natural resources that have monetary value. While NGOs take on causes to preserve and conserve the environment, market mechanisms do not participate in this outcome unless the natural resources have specific value. Assigning property rights to these resources is often impractical; for this reason, we default to the right to use concept or what is called usufruct rights.[32] Change efforts that take away these rights to use are often resisted.

Other cultural issues tend to make us not pay attention to natural environmental outcomes. For example, some countries tend to have a current timespan, ignoring history or future outcomes. This focus is very different from countries such as Hungary which tend to have a focus on history and how it relates to the present and future. The U.S. timespan tends to be the present. This focus makes the long-term focus of environmental outcomes difficult to understand and value. Corporations tend to focus on short-term profits and discounted cash flows for project evaluations. Nature and markets function on different timescales and different bases for valuation.

A property system may have a false dichotomy of either private property or tragedy of the commons. Capitalism, for example, might not lend well to experimenting with other forms of ownership and steward-ship. For example, group ownership and socially enforced responsibilities do not tend to be used in the United States or valued as alternatives to private property.

Organizations tend to resist change for many reasons, especially when it comes to the natural environ-ment and the need to change organizational processes for better environmental outcomes. One reason is that most environmental costs are external to the organization, what economists call negative externalities (see Chapter 3). These are costs imposed on society (vs. associated organizations) as a result of the organizations' actions. For example, an organization that destroys an ecosystem is only held to its legal requirements for remediation. Thus, their penchant to act to save an ecosystem is minimal. Also, if they do act to preserve the ecosystem, they are likely to put competitors in a preferable position since those competitors do not have to absorb the costs of externalities.

Problem solving approaches are path dependent. This term means that common ways of doing things become dominant and end up constraining the development of more efficient and effective alternative approaches. (This was the same point made in Chapter 6 about organizational routines.)

As organizations, sectors, or even societies lock into certain ways of solving certain problems (e.g., pol-lution controls) these entities create costs (sometimes referred to as sunk costs) and become committed to a particular way of operating and solving problems. Thus, change is very difficult and alternative paths of operating become fewer. Path dependency often generates overwhelming resistance to change, even when the potential cost savings and environmental benefits of alternative approaches are large.[33]

At times, it can be difficult to represent environmental issues effectively. For example, the Earth art move-ment, starting around the 1960s, has sought to make visible the elusive presence of nature. Earth art is an art movement in which landscape and the work of art are inextricably linked. It is also an art form that is cre-ated in nature, using natural materials such as soil and rock, organic media (e.g., logs and leaves), and water combined with manmade materials (e.g., concrete and metal). Sculptures are not placed in the landscape; the landscape is the means of creation. The works frequently exist in the open, well away from civilization and are left to change and erode under natural conditions.

Though most often associated with monumental land-based sculptures, Earth art encompasses a wide range of media (e.g., sculpture, body-art performances, installations, photographic interventions, public pro-test art, and community projects). Diverse artists (e.g., Robert Smithson, Ana Mendieta, Andy Goldsworthy, and Ichi Ikeda) are connected through their representation of Earth as a domain of ethical concern. They take an ethical stance that counters both the instrumental view that seeks to master nature and the Romantic view that posits a return to a mythical state of unencumbered continuity with nature. By incorporating receptive surfaces into their work (e.g., film footage of glaring sunlight, an aperture in a chamber that opens to the sky, or a porous armature on which vegetation grows) Earth artists articulate the dilemma of representation that nature presents. Revealing the fundamental difference between the human world and the Earth, Earth art mediates the sensations of nature while allowing nature itself to remain irreducible to human signification.[34]

Dance has also been used to communicate about the environment. One production was with the North Carolina Dance Theatre's Innovative Works and included pieces such as "Higher Consciousness," "Kinetic Energy," "Time is of the Essence (Save the World)," and "Tree Hugger."[35] In these dances, the environment was portrayed as being abused by people and in need of protection.

People react to these representations and maintain images of the environment and role of humans as they interact with the natural world. These representations might or might not motivate them to act. Without these representations, we might have difficulty obtaining a visceral feel for our challenges with the natural environment. Also, many people do not experience the art forms; thus, their perceptions are not often chal-lenged. The point here is that ineffective representation of the environment may inhibit meaningful change.

At the individual level, we all face pressures to preserve, conserve, or otherwise care for the environment. Seven-in-ten Americans (70 percent) say scientists contribute a lot to the well-being of society; however, scientists hold generally negative views of the quality of news coverage of scientific issues. A large majority (83 percent) of scientists characterize television news coverage of science as only fair or poor. Their views of newspaper coverage are somewhat better, but a majority (63 percent) also rate newspaper science coverage as only fair or poor.[36] Politics and science have become entangled on numerous occasions over the past several years. Politicians have increasingly questioned the scientific evidence pertaining to human-induced climate change, even as climate scientists argue that this evidence is incontrovertible.[37]

Nearly half of all responding scientists (49 percent) said that U.S. scientific achievements rank first in the world. However, they might be failing to appreciate the full impact of the ethical, moral, political, and other perspectives with which the broader public filters scientific information. Just 17 percent of the public thinks that U.S. scientific achievements rank as the best in the world. (Clearly, the public is somewhat less confident in the United States' scientific prowess than are scientists.) Fewer Americans today (27 percent) offer scientific achievements as one of the country's most important achievements (vs. a decade ago [47 percent]).[38] Thus, engaging people more in the science of the environment might overcome resistance to change.[39] These findings are indicative of many countries throughout the world.

The data suggest that we might be experiencing a disconnect between scientists and society. This disconnect could mean that individuals will not act based on scientific evidence, especially when it pertains to the natural environment. Yet, the general public has a positive affect toward scientists and thinks that what they do is important to society.[40]

Two experimental studies demonstrated that feeling as though an object, such as an idea, is "ours" (i.e., experiencing feelings of psychological ownership) influences how people selectively adopt others' suggestions for change. Whereas feelings of ownership cause individuals to embrace the adoption of suggestions that expanded upon their possessions (referred to as additive change), it simultaneously made them reject the adoption of suggestions that shrank them (referred to as subtractive change). This means when we get confirming information, we accept ideas; when we get disconfirming information, we tend to reject ideas. Also, a sense of personal loss and negative affect mediate this joint effect of psychological ownership and change type on the adoption of others' suggestions for change.[41]

Finally, much research has been done on the ways individuals make decisions. Much of this research has supported the concept of System 1 and System 2 thinking. System 1 is an implicit (automatic), unconscious process and System 2 is an explicit, controlled, conscious process.[42] The implications for our focus, here, is that we often use System 1 thinking when approaching environmental issues. For example, we tend to view climate change and climate warming as unimportant when the weather is consistent in our region or when it is cold. Also, we use System 1 thinking when we use heuristics such as associating new information with existing patterns or thoughts (vs. creating new patterns for each new experience). For example, if we live in an area where we only see warm weather, we would experience a new climate with this lens. In a legal metaphor, a judge limited to heuristic thinking would only be able to think of similar historical cases when presented with a new dispute (vs. seeing the unique aspects of that case). This outcome may happen when environmental science suggests that historical legal cases might be flawed in their reasoning.

In summary, societies, organizations, and individuals have many reasons to avoid change. These resistances make organizational changes that pertain to improving environmental outcomes very difficult. Yet, several techniques can be used to overcome these resistances. The next sections of this chapter demonstrate some of these techniques.

Profile: Managing Risks—A Risky Business[43]

This chapter discusses the importance of flexibility during risk management. Flexibility requires thinking about alternative methods for implementation and requires the ability to adapt resources, direction, and processes to achieve organizational goals. To manage potential future risks, the U.S. military has begun implementing sustainable adaptive strategies. In a 2014 Pentagon briefing, U.S. Secretary of Defense Chuck Hagel stated, "Climate change may cause instability in other countries by impairing access to food and water, damaging infrastructure, spreading disease, uprooting and displacing large numbers of people, compelling mass migration, interrupting commercial activity, or restricting electricity availability."[44]

In response to the aforementioned threat multipliers, each military branch has committed to creating 1 GW of renewable energy by 2025,[45] moving toward their ultimate goal of net-zero impact. Sustainable strategies are also becoming part of the military's ethos. The U.S. Army's mission statement now includes "transforming for the future.[46] *In the Army's annual Sustainability Report to Congress, Vice Chief of Staff Lloyd J. Austin III wrote:*

> *Training, equipping, and supporting the Army's operations require land, resources, and people. Rising global demand for scarce resources, increasing regional unrest and the effects of climate change are just some of the trends that will affect our future security environment. The Army recognizes that incorporating sustainability considerations into our operations, acquisitions, and installations will help reduce our resource demands while preserving current and future operational flexibility.*[47]

In 2010, a team of Army research scientists from the Research, Development and Engineering Command (RDECOM) developed an improved surface-coating method for products that are free of hazardous air pollutants. The Sustainable Painting Operations for the Total Army (SPOTA) program has since developed 45 distinct technologies with more than 1,000 products affected.[48] The program focuses on paints, sealants and adhesives, solvents, and rubber-to-metal bonding. Their main goals are to eliminate organic hazardous air pollutants and reduce volatile organic compounds. The Army estimates that the improved surface-coating method will reduce air pollutant emissions by 4,000 tons and save the Army $1 billion of the next 15 years.

The Situation Room. Table 11.3 details the wide array of risks that a firm might experience. An asset is a resource (owned or controlled by the firm) that will yield future economic benefits. In the context of climate change, asset impairment can be a major challenge when developing risk management strategies. In what ways does asset impairment such as physical erosion or sea-level rise affect operations, cognitive, competitive, and franchise risks?

Flexibility

Every manager is well aware that strategy formulation, when implemented, effects changes in focus and details. The pragmatic realities of implementation require **flexibility** (i.e., the willingness and ability of the firm to consider and implement changes in elements of its strategy, either proactively or in response to changed circumstances [especially unmeasured risk]). The key elements of this definition are a willingness to consider and implement changes and an ability to consider and implement changes. Flexibility requires thinking about alternative methods for implementation and an ability to adapt resources, direction, and processes to achieve organizational goals.

Strategic Risks and Flexibility

Risk is part of every organization. Table 11.3 shows a list of risks that most organizations face and examples of each one. This table shows that as organizations implement their strategies, they are often confronted with several risks. Customer complaints could rise, defects in products become obvious, markets change, and unexpected regulatory changes may demand strategic changes. For example, many firms expected the Obama administration to implement a cap-and-trade system during its first term. Firms developed their strategies around this expectation, especially some of the energy utility companies. When the cap-and-trade legislation did not get passed, firms modified their strategies to adapt to that reality. Some companies had needlessly spent money in anticipation of this legislation.

Organizations experience certain pressures that make risks harder to manage; these pressures cause organizations to act more flexibly. (Some specific pressures were discussed in Chapters 1–3.) Some specific internal pressures on organizations (as they implement strategy) are rapid growth, strong organizational culture, and complexity of information management.

Growth puts pressure on firms because it makes for unclear direction and points out employee and managerial inexperience. For example, entrepreneurial firms often experience difficulties when they become larger firms. This growth often calls for different competencies, and the new realities are often difficult for the founders. Organizational cultures are often resistant to change. The paradox with organizational cultures is that stronger cultures tend to produce better results until they resist needed changes.

Table 11.3 Firm-Level Risks[49]

Operations	• System downtime • Errors • Unexplained variances • Defect rates; quality standards • Customer complaints
Political	The range of viable options that the firm can implement without attracting insurmountable political opposition from its stakeholders
Cognitive	Willingness of the firm's managers to seriously consider alternatives to current strategy An attitude has effect, cognition, and behavioral intent
Asset impairment (e.g., financial, intellectual property, intangibles, physical erosion)	• Unhedged derivatives • Tangible and intangible assets • Decline in market value • National risk; country risk • Loss or impairment of information An asset is a resource (owned or controlled by the firm) that will yield future economic benefits
Competitive	• Changes in competitive environment • Changes in outside influences
Institutional	The regulatory, mimetic, and social factors that impede or enhance the flexibility of a firm Unknown institutional pressures or lack of institutional structure (e.g., property rights)
Franchise risk, reputation risk	Consequence of any one of the other sources of risk

Information management is another area that puts pressure on firms and creates unusual risks. The complexity of transactions, especially for a firm that is diversified, creates a lot of uncertainty within organizations. Consider what information management is like in firms that have 100 employees. Now rethink this complexity within firms such as the U.S. Department of Defense at 3.2 million, Wal-Mart at over 2 million, People's Liberation Army at 2.3 million, and Indian Railways at 1.4 million. Couple these size effects with high-velocity changes and decentralized decision making and one can comprehend the difficulty of managing firms and their risks. Simply understanding when a firm's situation has changed is a big task when there are many people involved. Organizations, in this position, are forced to remain flexible when building strategies.

Conceptualizing Flexibility

Strategy analysts commonly view strategic decisions as being rare, consequential, recursive, and costly to reverse. Such a perspective implies a mode of strategy making with long periods of implementing strategy that are punctuated by infrequent bursts of strategic analysis and decision making. Once the elements of strategy have been determined, they are not usually subject to major change until the next cycle of strategic analysis.[50]

However, one difficulty with strategic plans and direction is that circumstances do not always work out as anticipated (recall the commentary in Chapter 7 about strategic planning). Changes in technology, customers, regulation, and competition are making it increasingly difficult for firms to draw up meaningful five- and 10-year strategic plans.[51] Responses to such difficulties fall into two broad groups.[52] The first option is to deal with the new situation through alterations to the formal plan (e.g., through strategic issue-management systems).[53] For example, managers realize that their direction is not working; their way of addressing the issue might look like shifting budgets, projects, and people (to adapt to the new reality).

269

An alternative approach employs the notion of strategic flexibility and stresses a continuous strategy-making process.[54] In a dynamic and turbulent environment, strategic decisions might need to be continuously re-examined in light of new conditions and often in the absence of complete information. This situation has been characterized as action without certitude (i.e., keeping open the possibility of recognizing past errors and changing course).[55] Because of the rapidness and frequency with which change occurs, there is usually little time to comprehensively develop a strategic response; hence the need for a continuous recalibration of strategy.[56] A similar reasoning is embodied in the conception of the firm as a "platform of capability," which can respond flexibly to unanticipated opportunities and threats.[57] This second approach suggests that ensuring strategic flexibility ought to be a crucial element of strategic management. Strategic flexibility is a broad concept with multiple components, though the exact components have yet to be specified because it has not been thoroughly researched.[58] Some of the responses to strategic flexibility might include adapting to environmental changes, continually reshaping the productive process, changing game plans, or managing capricious settings.

Failure to adapt can lead to organizational decline.[59] Paradoxically, even when faced with facts about decline, management may tend to fail to act.[60] The key ideas, in most studies, are that organizations that act with flexibility tend to be open to new ideas and have a recursiveness (i.e., they continually adapt and engage in constant improvement). The need for flexibility is impacted by many factors (e.g., competitive threat, organizational slack, heterogeneity of top management, and uncertainty of decisions).[61]

Strategic flexibility does not imply the absence of a strategy; rather, it is the capability to change that strategy at short notice (if required or desired). Some managers view the value of a strategic decision by the myriad ways they could revise it,[62] or the firm's ability to "dismantle" its current strategies.[63] The latter is often difficult because established firms tend to be "frozen" around dominant designs, making it difficult for them to adapt when paradigms change.[64] This suggests that organizations need carefully designed and managed mechanisms that provide and protect strategic flexibility.

Flexibility is approached differently internally than externally. (External flexibility has already been discussed as diversification in Chapter 7 [e.g., some managers use diversified businesses as a way to manage changes in any given business line so that profits are not dependent on a single entity].) In this chapter, I will focus on internal flexibility. Internal flexibility points primarily to the nature of an organization's assets. For example, as situations change, firms can allocate capital rapidly toward a new direction as long as the organization's resources (e.g., human and financial capital) are available and not otherwise employed.

Commitment and Flexibility

In a famous example from history, Hernan Cortes demonstrated the value of strategic commitment during his conquest of the Aztec empire. When he landed in Mexico, Cortes ordered his men to burn all but one of his ships. According to many, this was not a lunatic's move; it was a purposeful signal of strategic commitment. Since they had no way of retreat, Cortes' soldiers had no choice but to fight hard and win. As Bernal Diaz del Castillo wrote, "Cortes said that we could look for no help or assistance except from God for now we had no ships in which to return to Cuba. Therefore we must rely on our own good swords and stout hearts."[65]

This story shows how strategic commitments can appear to limit options but actually make a firm better.[66] This is because a firm's commitments influence its stakeholders' and competitors' expectations about how it will compete in the future. In general, strategic commitment is beneficial if it helps to change a competitor's behavior in ways that are advantageous to the organization. For example, consider an organization preemptively investing in capacity expansion; in order to maintain capacity utilization rates, it will be forced to price aggressively. However, such a move may also cut off growth opportunities for rivals, forcing them to abandon expansion plans; this is an example of what is known as the "top dog" strategy of commitment.

The value of strategic commitment needs to be balanced against the need for strategic flexibility under conditions of uncertainty. For example, in the "top dog" strategy illustrated above, the firm has to contend with the risk that the expected market does not materialize, leaving the firm with underutilized capacity. In such circumstances, managers might want to build strategic flexibility into their decisions, effectively giving the firm option value.[67] An option value is the monetary value placed on the option. For instance, option value exists if a firm is able to delay an investment and await new information that has bearing on its profitability.[68]

An interesting concept is the "learn-to-burn" ratio, which is a key determinant of option value.[69] This is the ratio of the "learn rate" (i.e., the rate at which relevant new information is received by the firm) and the "burn rate" (i.e., the rate at which the firm is investing in sunk assets to support the strategy). A high learn-to-burn ratio implies that a strategic choice is characterized by a high degree of flexibility (i.e., the rate at which relevant new information comes in is greater than the rate at which investments must be made). In this case, delay has less value because the firm can quickly accumulate information about its prospects before it is too heavily committed.

Tactics for Being Flexible

Flexibility can be achieved in numerous ways. One major way firms increase their flexibility is through the versatility and quality of employees' skills, experience, and cognitive makeup. Indicative of this type of flexibility are cross training, job rotations, and the hiring of people who can do versatile jobs. For example, some researchers show that building a quality executive team involves hiring people who have the "right stuff." It is important to select a person who fits with the organization and can do various tasks outside of the basic job description; to keep people like this and gain productivity, a firm could offer competitive compensation, incentives, and clear job responsibilities. Additionally, many authors believe that the best way to maintain the core success of an organization is for future leaders to be groomed by current successful leaders.[70]

Firms try to create partnerships that are effective yet flexible. Versatility and range of interfirm networks can help a firm greatly. For example, outsourcing manufacturing to a partner prevents a firm from having to purchase equipment and hire employees to do this work. Chapter 10 showed how firms are monitoring these partners to ensure they are following sustainability principles. Firms gain the benefits of their partners' behaviors without having to invest in extensive assets.

Another flexibility method (for gaining flexibility) is a tolerance for marginal activities. Several organizational researchers have shown that innovative and resilient companies allow employees to work on interesting problems outside of their job descriptions. Since a flexible company recognizes that it must learn to continuously adapt to its changing environment,[71] experimenting with new ideas and businesses (and giving them the organizational space to grow) paves the way for future adaptation.[72] Google is known for allowing employees to spend 20 percent of their time on their own projects with the hope of inspiring innovations. 3M is known for this type of work and flexibility as well. Major product breakthroughs (e.g., masking tape and post-it notes) came from this practice).[73]

The versatility and range of a firm's network[74] redeployed are useful for strategic flexibility.[75] Some design features include:

1 The larger the network, the more informational advantage it offers.
2 It is better to have unique partners (as this reduces the redundancy of network contacts and increases network power).
3 It might be better to have a few strong ties with carefully chosen partners than a larger number of weaker ties.

Another method is designing resources and technologies so they are mobile.[76] Resources that hold the potential to be rapidly redeployed are at the core of strategic flexibility. For example, money can be rapidly deployed elsewhere; however, a technology developed for a specific purpose might not be useful in any other application. Some key aspects to consider in making resources and technologies mobile are:

1 A debt-free capital structure since a debt-ridden company may have its options curtailed.[77] The servicing of debt is less flexible than having cash or equity.
2 Dependence on special inputs creates a lack of flexibility. For example, firms that can only use one type of chemical mixture to make a product are dependent on the input manufacturer (and its ability to continue to provide that input).
3 The use of platform technologies increases flexibility and has thus become more widely used. Car manufacturers, for example, are now creating more common platforms for their cars; everything not visible

in a car is the same and what is visible is made unique (to create product differentiation). This platform formation could be especially important for new renewable energy solutions.

4   Flexible manufacturing systems are common in most industries, allowing for multiple uses of machinery and plant layout.

5   Organizations try to leverage their resources and capabilities by servicing a number of markets. (This technique was discussed in Chapter 7.)

Making sure that organizational structures, a culture of creativity, and systems do not inhibit adaptive behavior, increases flexibility.[78] The strategically flexible organization is one that is able to reconfigure itself successfully to accommodate new opportunities and threats (e.g., Intel managers report such reconfigurations almost every six months).[79] Malleable organizational structures and systems might include small corporate headquarters, maximum autonomy (for operating managers), task forces that cross divisional boundaries, and informal networks that cut across departments and divisions.[80]

Planning systems that constantly monitor and assess environmental signals can powerfully increase flexibility.[81] Strategic flexibility is predicated on an ability to read weak signals of impending environmental change well before the effects manifest themselves. Effective environmental scanning systems[82] and strategic issue-management systems are critical in this regard. Below is a discussion of scenario planning, which is an excellent example of this scanning methodology.

While strategic flexibility ought to be an integral part of strategic planning, an overly rigid plan can inhibit flexibility. A strategic plan (if followed rigidly after circumstances have changed) may lead to disaster. The real value of strategic planning is in instilling a "foreseeing culture"[83] (vs. imposing a mechanistic management technique). As former U.S. President Dwight D. Eisenhower is reported to have said, "Plans are nothing; planning is everything" (see Chapter 7 for a further discussion of strategic planning). Strategic planning systems that encourage flexibility will typically have the following characteristics:

1   high involvement of those who do the work rather than staff members;

2   some elements of a "rolling plan" (e.g., each year, the plan is revised despite its five-year horizon);

3   a preponderance of techniques (e.g., scenario planning and contingency planning) with emphasis on complex forecasts.

This third characteristic is especially important for producing flexibility. A valuable tool for equipping business planners to cope with the potentially expensive unknowns lurking in the future is called scenario planning. Instead of just projecting the past into the future, it uses a scenario-based process to create possible future events that may affect businesses, thereby giving firms a chance to prepare for them. The origins of scenario planning in business are said to go back to the 1980s when Royal Dutch Shell created a scenario based on a seemingly impossible "what if," such as oil prices dropping by 50 percent. Because they worked through this question, they were prepared for it when it actually happened in 1986.[84]

Scenario analysis is the designation of plausible futures and consideration of different responses to each future. Scenarios are carefully crafted stories about the future, embodying a wide variety of ideas and integrating them in a way that is communicable and useful. Scenarios help managers link uncertainties about the future with present-day decision making. For example, Shell Oil's *Signals and Signposts*, considers how events have unfolded since the 2008 publication of its *Shell Energy Scenarios to 2050* and offers an understanding of the changes brought about by the global economic crisis.[85] Here is their introduction to the earlier scenarios written by former CEO Jeroen van der Veer (who retired in 2009):

To help think about the future of energy, we have developed two scenarios that describe alternative ways it may develop. In the first scenario—called Scramble—policymakers pay little attention to more efficient energy use until supplies are tight.

Likewise, greenhouse gas emissions are not seriously addressed until there are major climate shocks. In the second scenario—Blueprints—growing local actions begin to address the challenges of economic development, energy security and environmental pollution. A price is applied to a critical mass of emissions giving a huge stimulus to the development of clean energy technologies, such as carbon dioxide capture and storage, and energy efficiency measures. The result is far lower carbon dioxide emissions.

We are determined to provide energy in responsible ways and serve our customers and investors as effectively as we can. Both these scenarios help us do that by testing our strategy against a range of possible developments over the long-term.

However, in our view, the Blueprints' outcomes offer the best hope for a sustainable future, whether or not they arise exactly in the way we describe. I am convinced they are possible with the right combination of policy, technology and commitment from governments, industry, and society globally. But achieving them will not be easy, and time is short. We urgently need clear thinking, huge investment, and effective leadership. Whatever your role in this, I hope these scenarios will help you understand better the choices you face.

Notice that the scenarios have identified predetermined forces and critical uncertainties. These are then developed into stories representing extremes of outcomes. Shell executives would then explore the implications of these different scenarios for the purpose of strategic planning. Another use of scenarios is to monitor their development (i.e., look for evidence that adaptations are needed to current practices within the company). While Shell executives may have a preference for the Blueprints Scenarios, they are prepared for either one coming about.

The objective of scenario planning is to create a number of diverging outcomes by extrapolating from the forces that drive them. This is done using the collective power of a group of interested people. An example of how the scenario planning process could work is:

1   A comprehensive group discussion focusing on what the members feel are major and relevant issues with respect to the business developments about to happen in areas such as technology, society, economics, and politics.
2   The group then evaluates these developments and prioritizes them. Which are most likely to happen first?
3   Outlines of possible futures (based on these priorities) are created. Later planning will be based on these scenarios.
4   The group then works through how each of these possible futures will impact the business.
5   Identifiers are created so that the occurrence of each possible "future" will be recognized and the appropriate response can be applied.
6   Create strategic responses to deal with each of these scenarios (i.e., to plan for them).

Unlike forecasting, scenario planning views each scenario as equally likely. Unlike more familiar "scientific" means of forecasting (e.g., market research), scenarios are largely products of imagination. The objective is not to forecast precisely what will happen, it is to say what *might* happen and create a response based on that. Each scenario can be tested with critical criteria such as:

1   plausible and consistent;
2   creates prepared minds;
3   relevant to topic and issues faced by the firm;
4   indicators sensitive to current market;
5   challenge—explores ranges;
6   elements of surprise are indicated;
7   long-term perspective.

We see these factors within the two Shell scenarios described above.

An adaptation to scenario planning is to consider possible futures that call for certain organizational actions.[86] This analysis could supplement scenario planning and even be included within it. Clear futures are found in highly regulated environments, mature and stable markets, and where few pressures exist (and thus few risk factors). These situations tend to call for adaptation actions because little can be done to change the environment. This is the stance taken by highly regulated companies such as Duke Energy (and the discussion in Chapter 3 about its need to adhere to the North Carolina State Public Utility Commission's mandates).

A company like Duke might plan alternative futures, which are characterized by a defined set of futures with well-established probability distributions. One of the predominant actions prescribed for alternative futures is called shaping. *Shaping* is the firm's active involvement with (and influence on) the bodies that regulate it. Electric utilities, pharmaceutical companies, tobacco companies, and telecommunications companies spend unusual amounts of money on lobbying their regulators and legislators. The purpose of these expenditures is to influence policymaking and regulatory involvement. For example, in the face of new environmental regulation (e.g., cap and trade), large utility firms have active lobbying efforts to shape the direction of the system.

A range of futures, with varying degrees of knowledge about the futures, is another situation (with more uncertainty than alternative futures). Shaping is less risky in this scenario because of known probabilities. Firms focus on processes that keep them informed of these changes. For example, rapid technology changes call for these types of tactics.

True ambiguity exists when firms have no experience with present-day situations. For example, firms that operate in war-torn areas are not certain about what might happen in even the short term. They get involved because the potential rewards of being on the ground are high. They tend to take a shaping tactic (trying to influence directions of business); however, the situations could change rapidly, and they could lose their investment at a moment's notice. Monte Carlo techniques are key planning tools for handling uncertainty. Monte Carlo methods are broad classes of computational algorithms used to model highly uncertain situations.[87]

Using Real Options to Increase Flexibility

A final, popular, complicated technique to increase flexibility is the use of real options. **Real options** are the right—but not the obligation—to undertake certain business initiatives (e.g., deferring, expanding, or contracting a capital investment project). Real options are generally distinguished from conventional financial options in that they are not typically traded as securities and do not usually involve decisions on an underlying asset that is traded as a financial security.

Options give its holder the right (but not the obligation) to buy (call option) or sell (put option) a designated asset at a predetermined price (exercise price). Options have value because their terms allow the holder to profit from price moves in one direction without bearing (or limiting) risk in the other direction.

Real options analysis begins with asking: "Do I have enough information to assess the returns from an investment?" If the analyst believes that he or she can make a better investment decision in the future, he or she may use options. For example, let's say that a firm is looking at a new market to sell renewable energy devices; the next year will determine whether these devices are popular or unpopular in that market. The firm is looking at a single payoff in one year after entering the market. That risky cash flow will be $13 million in the "popular" outcome or $9 million in the "unpopular" outcome. The outcomes appear equally likely.

A project with this kind of risk calls for a discount rate of 10 percent. The Discounted Cash Flow (DCF) technique summarizes the risky cash flows by their expected values or probability-weighted averages. The expected value is $11 million, so the present value of the project, discounted at 10 percent, is $10 million. If the current investment cost is $9.7 million, then the Net Present Value (NPV) of the project is +$300,000 (NPV > 0); the project adds value and the firm begins entering the market. The problem with this analysis is that it does not deal with the management's ability to time its decisions to take maximum advantage of the risk in cash flows.

Does management have other ways to proceed? Management could wait a year (or more) before deciding on whether to enter. If these types of energy devices turn out to be unpopular, then it would make little sense to invest $9.7 million to make $9 million a year later. If, however, the market is attractive, then an investment of $9.7 million in Year 1 would assure a $13 million payoff in Year 2, giving an NPV of $2.12 million in that future outcome. Since there is a 50–50 chance of a good outcome (invest; $2.12 million at Year 1) and a bad outcome (don't invest; $0 at Year 1), the expected value at Year 1 is $1.06 million. Discounted back to the present, the NPV is $960,810 now if they wait and decide next year.

Table 11.4 Investment Choice

	Uncertainty		Invest now		Wait	
Now	Probability = 50%		–$9.70		0	
Year 1	Unpopular	Popular	$9	$13	0	–$9.70
Year 2	Unpopular	Popular	–	–	–	$13
			NPV = $300,000		NPV = $962,810	

The cash flows and project values are summarized in Table 11.4.[88]

Another example is a firm investing $600 million over the next two years ($250 million immediately and $350 million one year from now) to build a new solar panel factory that will last 20 years, generate revenues that start at $80 million three years from now, grow at 8 percent, and incur total costs of $60 million (that also start three years from now but grow at 6 percent). There is no salvage value, no working capital, no tax, and depreciation is expensed at straight line starting two years from now. The weighted average cost of capital is 10 percent. What are the cash flows according to the timeline in Table 11.5? The value of management's decision to wait was quite high, even higher than the positive-NPV project. By ignoring this valuable option, they could have invested too early and missed a chance to add considerable value.

Table 11.5 Timeline for Investments

Timeline for investments	Years							
	0	1	2	3	4	...	19	20
Investment	–250	–350						
Revenues			600/19	600/19	600/19	...	600/19	600/19
			0	80	80(1.08)	...	80(1.08)^{17}	80(1.08)^{18}
Costs			0	60	60(1.06)	...	80(1.06)^{17}	80(1.06)^{17}

NPV = –$1.44 million

NPV = –250 – (350/1.1) + PV(revenues) – PV(costs) + PV(depreciation)

$$PV(revenues) = 80 \times \frac{1-(1-0.8/1.1)^{18}}{0.1-0.08} \times \frac{1}{1.1^2}$$

PV (costs) = –6080 (1 – (1.06/1.10)^{18})/.10 – .08 × 1/1.1^2 = –603.25
PV (depreciation) = 600/19 (1 – (1.1)$^{-19}$)/.1 × 1/1.1 = 240.14
NPV = –250 – 318.18 + 929.85 – 630.25 + 240.14 = –1.44

The ultimate learning point from these examples is that management can make risk work for them. When managers *choose* what risks to take, rather than being locked into investment opportunities, one-sided payoffs may emerge (with bad outcomes left on the table). DCF techniques give an NPV that is a probability-weighting of a collection of potential NPVs (some negative and some positive) for all possible future outcomes. It assumes management's future role is passive (even in the most extreme outcomes) once the original investment decision has been made. However, if management can actively respond to new information and somehow avoid the NPV < 0 outcomes, the true value of its opportunities will be higher than the standard NPV calculated.[89]

NPV analysis presents several challenges when trying to make effective investment decisions in these situations.[90] NPV works best when a firm is faced with a large current investment; when primary uncertainties can be defined, these uncertainties have predictable resolutions and terminal value is not highly variable. NPV is less useful with high-risk situations (e.g., when regulatory uncertainty and high-growth markets are present).

NPV does not take into account intangible assets.[91] For example, a company could be faced with converting intangible assets into valuable intangible "capital." Start-up companies face this challenge trying to turn an entrepreneur's ideas or intellectual property into a business. Also, NPV is limited when making many small investments in test markets or when market characteristics are unknown. For this reason, NPV is not a useful analysis for breakthrough innovations. NPV analyses assume that capital is a scarce resource, so what happens when capital is more abundant? As cost of capital falls, companies can justify more projects; sometimes this leads to forgetting whether a project fits with the strategy. This can become a dangerous situation that can lead to taking on too much debt. For these reasons, real options add greatly to strategy implementation because they force managers to think through all of the positive and negative outcomes of a project.[92]

Six general categories of real options are (1) growth options; (2) the option to expand scale; (3) timing— the option to wait; (4) the option to switch inputs, outputs, or processes; (5) the option to contract scale; and (6) abandonment. These categories can be pictured on a spectrum; an option's place on the spectrum is determined by the amount of information available and the inherent value of the option (see Table 11.6).[93]

There are various contexts that call for different responses to options (see Figure 11.2). Abandonment options, for example, are important in capital-intensive industries when management would like to have flexibility to capture some resale value for assets if their value (to the company) falls. Also, in high-variable cost industries (e.g., manufacturing), the option to shut down is quite valuable. The option to contract (or expand scale) is a flexible means of dealing with changing demand; simple examples are the ability to slow the rate of mineral extraction from a mine or to easily add a temporary delivery route if a market opens up. The option to switch is the ability to change product mix, such as land-use flexibility (e.g., switching crops) and the ability of a plant to switch between coal and natural gas in response to changing input and output prices. Timing options (to wait or defer) are valuable in natural resource industries and with many capital investments (e.g., any place where the investment to begin operations is irreversible).[94]

In every scenario, the value of flexibility is greatest when the project's value without flexibility does not have a high return or only breaks even. Consider real options when there is a contingent investment decision, uncertainty is high (and waiting has a high likelihood of producing new useful information), the value seems to be captured in the possibilities for future growth options (vs. current cash flows), and project updates and mid-course strategic corrections are a way of doing business.

Characteristics of the underlying asset and the terms of the option have an impact on option value, in the direction shown in Figure 11.3. These impacts are primarily unambiguous except as a put (sellable) option as maturity increases (see Figure 11.3).[95] In this figure, a call (buy) option is the right to buy the underlying asset by paying the exercise (predetermined) price. A put option is the right to sell the underlying asset to receive the exercise price.

Table 11.6 Likelihood of Receiving New Information

Ability to respond	Low	High
High	Moderate flexibility value	High flexibility value • High uncertainty about the future: very likely to receive new information over time; • Room for managerial flexibility: allows management to respond appropriately to this new information; • Plus, NPV without flexibility near zero: if a project is neither obviously good nor obviously bad, flexibility to change course is more likely to be used and therefore is more valuable.
Low	Low flexibility value	Moderate flexibility value

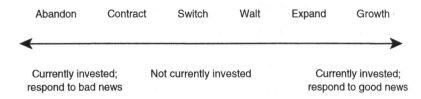

Figure 11.2 Options Choices

	As _____ increases,	
	Option Value	
	Call	Put
Asset price	↑	↓
Exercise price	↓	↑
Maturity	↑	↑
Volatility	↑	↑	(ambiguous)
Interest rate	↑	↓
Dividends	↓	↑

Figure 11.3 Option Value

Notice that as uncertainty goes up, options become more valuable. Also, managers can use their skills to improve an option's value before they actually exercise the option (making it worth more than the price paid to acquire or create it). The following list explains tactics managers could use to increase the value of real options.

1. Reduce the Present Value of Expected Operating Cash Flows

Reduce the present value of expected operating cash flows by cutting costs through economies of scale (cost per unit falls as the number of units increases) or leveraging economies of scope (using the same costs to do two different things). A company unable to perform these tactics alone could perhaps do it through partnership.

2. Increase the Present Value of Expected Operating Cash Flows

This is achieved as a result of increasing revenues by raising the price earned, producing more of the commodity in question, or by generating sequential business opportunities. In options language, this is called a "compound option."

3. Increase the Uncertainty of Expected Cash Flows

Greater uncertainty raises the value of an option by increasing the value of flexibility. This is perhaps the crucial difference between options and NPV analysis. When a company is fully invested (as NPV analysis assumes), uncertainty has a negative effect because returns are symmetrical (i.e., losing one's entire investment is as much a possibility as doubling its value). But when buying an option, a company has not bet the entire value of its investment; it is exposed to the upside but not the downside. It only pays a small fraction of the total investment, reserving its right to make future investments. As a consequence, an option holder wants to do everything it can to increase the uncertainty of expected returns and then invest fully or back out (depending on how things go). To decrease uncertainty, managers increase the quality of information through conducting research and collecting expert opinions.

4. Extend the Opportunity's Duration

This raises an option's value because it increases total uncertainty.

5. Reduce the Value Lost by Waiting to Make the Full Investment

The cost of waiting would be high if an early entrant seized the returns. When first-mover advantages are significant, the dividends are correspondingly high, thus reducing the option value of waiting. The value lost to competitors can be reduced by discouraging them from taking their options (e.g., by locking up key customers or lobbying for regulatory constraints).

6. Value of an Option Can Be Increased by Increasing the Risk-Free Interest Rate

This increase is not generally possible because no one player can influence the risk-free rate. But it is worth noting that, in general, any expected increase in the interest rate raises the value of an option despite the negative effect on NPV because it reduces the present value of the exercise price.

7. Use Real Options as a Signaling Device to Various Industry Players

This means that companies can signal to competitors and customers that they intend to introduce a product, enter a market, or respond to competitive pressures. The companies do not have to invest fully until they see the market reactions. If customers do not respond positively, then the company simply does not make the investment in the new market or product. If competitors ignore the company's overture, the company knows that it will not experience retaliation.

Real-options strategies are distinguished from other responses to uncertainty (e.g., forecasting and scenario planning). The shift in outlook from "fear, uncertainty, and minimize investment" to "seek gains from uncertainty and maximize learning" opens up a wider range of possible actions, and it is crucial to the usefulness of real options as a strategic (vs. a valuation) model.

Determining the right levers is dependent upon internal and external constraints on company operations. These constraints might be technical, or they might have to do with a functional area within the company. They would also concern investment factors (e.g., the delay between investments and payoffs and constraints on incremental investments).

Critical Performance Variables

There is a final technique to maintain an organization's focus and to gain signals when organizational changes are needed: using critical performance variables to track organizational performance. This concept was introduced in Chapter 8 and is explained more fully here. Many organizations have numerous measures to track performance. As discussed in Chapter 8, many of these measures are mandated by regulatory agencies; others are useful for internal purposes. For example, all public organizations have required accounting measures for accurately disclosing their financial situations. They also might have internal measures (e.g., individual employee productivity ratings) that inform compensation, promotion, and development decisions for those employees. Ultimately, the measures chosen by a firm (to evaluate strategy) are a reflection of their critical performance variables.

Firms can develop a list of success factors. Better yet is transforming a list of performance measures into a coherent whole (such as described by the balanced scorecard technique described in Chapter 8). This combination can be accomplished through developing a map of the value creation.[96]

Several organizations focus on employees. Well-known examples include Bill Marriott's widely communicated statement: "Take care of your employees and they'll take care of your customer."[97] Marriott's management knows that employees drive value in the hotels. It also knows that if it measures employee satisfaction, it will have a good idea of how to increase its occupancy in its hotels. This is their theory of value creation. Nordstrom and Disney have similar philosophies and metrics.

Some retail organizations tend to focus on adding stores in as many markets as possible as a way to create value. While this method might be helpful at times, a lack of focus on growth in existing stores can lead to destruction of value. This is the hard lesson learned by many organizations, such as Starbuck's and McDonald's.[98]

What if we wanted to create a measure for sustainability in an organization? The measurement of sustainability is complicated (as indicated within several chapters in this book). Yet, an organization could focus on one specific aspect of sustainability, such as "our products and services will be the most environmentally friendly in our market spaces." Building this kind of measure has wide implications because it clarifies the value of the organization and focuses employees' attention on this one metric. Some authors call these measures *key performance indicators* or KPIs.[99]

Several researchers have concluded that people cannot effectively pay attention to complicated measurement schemes. Therefore, focusing on a few key variables can have a more significant impact on behavior and help employees define how their work can support organizational goals.[100] One way to start developing measures is to focus on what can go wrong.[101] For example, firms must ask what could cause a strategy to fail? This can be accomplished by identifying things so important to the company's success that if the organization fails to pay attention to these variables, the entire strategy would fail or be at risk.

Critical success factors can help greatly to maintain an organization's focus, identify the strongest predictors of success, and leverage specific actions for large organizational impacts. This concept of focus has been the basis of the entire chapter and critical success factors are key for maintaining focus.

Chapter Summary

The implementation of strategy is key for organizational success. While many processes can be used to implement a strategy, this chapter covered the importance of staying both flexible and focused to achieve organizational goals. The specific techniques (discussed here) were building business models, overcoming resistance to change, practicing flexibility techniques, and carefully choosing performance variables.

The most important parts of a business model are the revenue–cost relationships and the customer value proposition. Business models tend to have patterns (e.g., unbundling, long tail, multisided, free, and open), which vary depending upon the desired emphasis.

While deciding the direction, organization managers want to be flexible so that they can respond to changing conditions. Risks inherent in external and internal conditions make analysis difficult (and thus require flexibility). Flexibility is both a willingness and ability to implement changes in the elements of a strategy. To manage flexibility, managers have myriad actions they can pursue (e.g., hiring people who have multiple skillsets, using unique planning techniques such as scenarios, and using real options).

Finally, implementation is best done with the use of performance measures that can track a firm's successes and indicate how an organization is progressing toward its intended goals. Performance measures often evaluate *key* or *critical performance variables*. Identifying these variables (and utilizing measures to study these variables) helps employees understand the key functions of a firm and keeps managers focused on their goals.

Case Revisited: NASCAR Stays on the Track

The NASCAR environmental effort gives hope to all. A sport that is unlikely to be considered best-in-class for environmental sustainability is making lots of efforts to be the best it can. Most impressive are the programs (and influence on all of its partners). NASCAR has found ways to impact every level of its chain (e.g., suppliers, teams, racetracks, and customers). They have become an excellent study of how a company can make environmental sustainability the focus by integrating it into its core strategies.

NASCAR has demonstrated that even an organization based on the consumption of fossil fuels can take steps to become more environmentally friendly. Yet, some commentators say that NASCAR has taken the easy steps and what must be done in the future (to continue improving their environmental performance) will be much harder. These changes include the redesign of cars, changing the fuel mix, and how races are conducted. Additionally, NASCAR's primary audience tends to travel long distances to get to the tracks (in larger cars and motorhomes) and might not be as aware of the environmental challenges facing our world. How will NASCAR impact the consumers of its sport?

NASCAR could use some of the techniques mentioned in this chapter to confront these challenges (e.g., developing scenarios for the future of racing, testing the strategies on different tracks, and revising its business model). Looking forward, key questions include:

- How could the entertainment value be preserved (or enhanced) as environmental outcomes are improved?
- Could NASCAR increase its partnerships beyond the EPA and vendors to improve environmental outcomes?

This organization is worth watching closely as it can teach other industries (e.g., trucking and shipping) about sustainable practices.

Terms to Know

Business model: describes the rationale of how an organization creates, delivers, and captures value

Flexibility: the willingness and ability of a firm to consider and implement changes in the elements of its strategy (either proactively or in response to changed circumstances—especially unmeasured risk)

Real options: an alternative or choice that becomes available with a business investment opportunity; the right (but not the obligation) to invest

Scenario analysis/planning: the designation of plausible futures and consideration of different responses to each future

Profile: Communicating about the Environment Using Performance Arts

Figure 11.4 "Homeless Children." Credit: Gary Chan Photography[102]

Usual approaches to communicating to the public about the environment and the challenges we are facing involve written essays, oral presentations, and documentary films. These communication venues include inter-pretations of science, moral lessons about human impacts on the environment, and adaptation and mitigation suggestions that individuals, organizations, and governments should follow. The McColl Center for Art & Innovation in Charlotte, North Carolina, includes four pillars of their Environmental Artist-in-Residence Program: art, science, community and education. Each year, three environmental artists-in-residence com-mence remediation projects in partnership with Charlotte Mecklenburg Parks & Recreation, Catawba Lands Conservancy, Charlotte Mecklenburg Schools, Queens University, Discovery Place and the Charlotte Nature Museum.[103]

Yet, visual and performance arts are not common ways to communicate about the environment. Three exam-ples are Richard Schechner's environmental productions Dionysus in 1969, Makbeth, and Commune performed in his Performing Garage on Off-Off-Broadway in New York City.[104]

Another performance art approach is dance. Karole Armitage, a New York-based choreographer, produced "On the Nature of Things," at the American Museum of Natural History.[105] The dance takes place on three stages in the Milstein Hall of Ocean Life at the Museum. The dance includes commentary from Paul Ehrlich's work by the same name.

This is not Armitage's first dance of this type. She produced "Fables on Global Warming," a ballet, and a family-oriented piece called "Four Seasons—A Spinning Planet."

An article quotes Armitage describing her dance:

What it's meant to do is to make the subject matter completely personal and emotional . . . you go from a sense of peace and balance to peril and turbulence and population pressures and stress; then you see a con-frontation and reckoning with that, which leads to a change in consciousness to rediscover equilibrium. To me it's a matter of changing how we think.[106]

Using the Arts. *Why don't we commonly use the arts to communicate science, especially the performance arts? Can you explain this lack of use? Do we tend to discount this type of communication because it does not conform to the scientific rigor that we are used to seeing in science? What are your beliefs about the arts as a means of com-municating about science?*

Questions and Critical Thinking

1   Refer to Table 11.1. Consider a book publisher (e.g., Routledge or Island Press). Design a few new business models to help the company make money and achieve positive environmental outcomes. You might consider altering the channels of distribution for the books or how the company relates to its customers.

2   This chapter highlighted NASCAR's use of environmental sustainability principles and practices. Consider other racing organizations and their environmental stances. For example, the American Le Mans Series (ALMS) has always been a leader of U.S. racing organizations with their interest in green technology. They comply with the Green Racing protocols of the U.S. Department of Energy, the U.S. EPA, and SAE International.[107] They also use the Michelin Green X Challenge to reward their teams' environmental practices.[108] What standards should be used in this industry to judge best-in-class racing organizations?

3   Strategy implementation invariably involves organizational change; however, by most accounts, chang-ing the ways organizations do their work is difficult. People resist change (as indicated earlier in this chapter), the change process is not always obvious, and competing interests (in a change process) make it difficult for managers to keep focused. Do some background research on organizational change and develop your own understanding of the change management techniques you might recommend for a specific organization. While this topic is vast, it might be worth the time to learn more about what researchers have suggested.

Here are a few references to get you started:

- D. Anderson and L. A. Anderson, *Beyond Change Management: How to Achieve Breakthrough Results Through Conscious Change Leadership*, 2nd ed. (San Francisco: Pfeiffer, 2010).
- B. Doppelt, *Leading Change Toward Sustainability: A Change-Management Guide for Business, Government, and Civil Society*, 2nd ed. (Sheffield: Greenleaf, 2010).
- J. P. Kotter and D. S. Cohen, *The Heart of Change: Real-Life Stories of How People Change Their Organizations* (Boston, MA: Harvard Business School Press, 2002).
- R. E. Quinn, *Deep Change: Discovering the Leader Within* (San Francisco, CA: Jossey-Bass, 1996).

4 As a means of understanding scenario analysis, use your own future and develop two or three scenarios. When you develop these scenarios, try to follow the prescriptions developed in this chapter and the referenced literature. Remember that scenarios are not probability statements about what is *most likely*, rather, they are equally likely outcomes (in terms of your future). Once you develop these scenarios, consider their usefulness with respect to making choices for jobs, where you live, and educational options.

Notes

1 NASCAR Green, "About: NASCAR—Leading Sport and Business in Sustainability," http://green.nascar.com/about (accessed September 24, 2013).
2 NASCAR Green, *NASCAR: The Sports Leader in Sustainability* (Daytona Beach, FL: NASCAR, 2012), 1, http://americaneg.vo.llnwd.net/o16/nascar/2012/Projects/green-white-paper-high-res-4-19.pdf (accessed September 24, 2013).
3 Ibid., 2.
4 NASCAR Green, "About: NASCAR."
5 NASCAR Green, *NASCAR: The Sports Leader in Sustainability*, 3.
6 E. Jones, "NASCAR: America's Green Sport," *Sports Business Digest*, October 31, 2012, http://sportsbusinessdigest.com/2012/10/nascar-americas-green-sport/ (accessed December 2, 2012).
7 In 2011, NASCAR's efforts saw some 12 million bottles and cans recycled, which is the equivalent of 300,000 gallons of gasoline. NASCAR's top three racing series (Sprint Cup, Nationwide, and Camping World) use approximately 450,000 gallons of gasoline throughout the NASCAR season. NASCAR's recycling program offsets the environmental impact of that gasoline. For the remaining 150,000 gallons of used gasoline, NASCAR's use of Sunoco Green E15 fuel helps to make up the difference in reducing the amount of emissions released by the racecars. September 2012 marked three million miles NASCAR racers had driven using E15, NASCAR Green, "About: NASCAR."
8 Ibid.
9 NASCAR Green, *NASCAR: The Sports Leader in Sustainability*, 3.
10 K. Wagner, "How NASCAR Is Going Green," CNN Money, April 19, 2013, http://tech.fortune.cnn.com/2013/04/19/nascar-green-mike-lynch/?iid=H_T_News (accessed May 3, 2013).
11 NASCAR Green, *NASCAR: The Sports Leader in Sustainability*, 1.
12 NASCAR Green, "About: NASCAR."
13 NASCAR Green, *NASCAR: The Sports Leader in Sustainability*, 5.
14 Ibid., 2.
15 Ibid., 4; NASCAR Green, "About: NASCAR."
16 NASCAR Green, NASCAR: The Sports Leader in Sustainability, 4.
17 Ibid.
18 U.S. Environmental Protection Agency, "Wastes: WasteWise," http://www.epa.gov/epawaste/conserve/smm/wastewise/index.htm (accessed February 24, 2013).
19 NASCAR Green, *NASCAR: The Sports Leader in Sustainability*, 4.
20 J. Pfeffer and R. I. Sutton, *Hard Facts, Dangerous Half-Truths, and Total Nonsense: Profiting from Evidence-Based Management* (Boston, MA: Harvard Business School Press, 2006): 135–158.
21 A. Osterwalder and Y. Pigneur, *Business Model Generation: A Handbook for Visionaries, Game Changers, and Challengers* (Hoboken, NJ: Wiley, 2010).
22 Ibid., 56.
23 J. Hagel and M. Singer, "Unbundling the Corporation," *Harvard Business Review* (March–April 1999). Also, see M. Treacy and F. Wiersema, *The Discipline of Market Leaders: Choose Your Customers, Narrow Your Focus, Dominate Your Market*, exp. ed. (Reading, MA: Addison-Wesley, 1997).
24 C. Anderson, *The Long Tail: Why the Future of Business Is Selling Less of More* (New York: Hyperion, 2006).

25 T. Eisenmann, G. Parker, and M. W. Van Alstyne, "Strategies for Two-Sided Markets," *Harvard Business Review* (October 2006) http://hbr.org/2006/10/strategies-for-two-sided-markets/ (accessed February 26, 2013).

26 C. Anderson, *Free: The Future of a Radical Price* (New York: Hyperion, 2009).

27 H. Chesbrough, *Open Business Models: How to Thrive in the New Innovation Landscape* (Boston, MA: Harvard Business School Press, 2006), 1–20.

28 InnoCentive, "What We Do," www.innocentive.com/about-innocentive (accessed February 4, 2014).

29 B. Doppelt, *Leading Change toward Sustainability: A Change-Management Guide for Business, Government, and Civil Society*, 2nd ed. (Sheffield: Greenleaf, 2010), 93–96 and 261–263.

30 J. P. Kotter and D. S. Cohen, *The Heart of Change: Real-Life Stories of How People Change Their Organizations* (Boston, MA: Harvard Business School Press, 2002), 103–124. Also see R. E. Quinn, *Deep Change: Discovering the Leader Within* (San Francisco, CA: Jossey-Bass, 1996), 133–145.

31 P. H. Schuck and J. Q. Wilson, "Looking Back," in P.H. Schuck and J.Q. Wilson (eds.), *Understanding America: The Anatomy of an Exceptional Nation* (New York: Public Affairs, 2008), 629.

32 British Dictionary, "usufruct" http://dictionary.reference.com/browse/usufruct (accessed December 12, 2014).

33 Doppelt, *Leading Change toward Sustainability*, 23.

34 A. Boetzkes, *The Ethics of Earth Art* (Minneapolis: University of Minnesota Press, 2010).

35 North Carolina Dance Theatre (Charlotte, NC), "Tree Hugger" performed by the North Carolina Dance Theatre, choreographers Mark Diamond, David Ingram, Sasha Janes and Dwight Rhoden, November 3–19, 2011, http://charlotteballet.org/about/history-mission/ (accessed December 22, 2015).

36 Ibid., 2.

37 Ibid., 33.

38 Ibid., 1–2.

39 Ibid., 56.

40 D. Jamieson, *Reason in a Dark Time: Why the Struggle Against Climate Change Failed—and What It Means for Our Future* (Oxford, UK: Oxford University Press, 2014), see Chapter 3.

41 M. Baer and G. Brown, "Blind in One Eye: How Psychological Ownership of Ideas Affects the Types of Suggestions People Adopt," *Organizational Behavior and Human Decision Processes* 118, no. 1 (May 2012): 60–71.

42 D. Kahneman, *Thinking, Fast and Slow* (New York: Farrar, Strauss, and Giroux, 2011).

43 Co-authored by Michael Aper, Master of Arts in Sustainability candidate at Wake Forest University.

44 Z. Schlanger, "Pentagon Report: U.S. Military Considers Climate Change a 'Threat Multiplier' That Could Exacerbate Terrorism," *Newsweek*, October 14, 2014, http://www.newsweek.com/pentagon-report-us-military-considers-climate-change-immediate-threat-could-foster-277155 (accessed January 19, 2015).

45 A. Sieminski, "Statement to U.S. House of Representatives Subcommittee on Energy and Power Committee on Energy and Commerce," Energy Information Administration, 2013, http://www.eia.gov/pressroom/testimonies/sieminski_02052013.pdf (accessed January 19, 2015).

46 "Organization," United States Army, http://www.army.mil/info/organization/ (accessed January 19, 2015).

47 "Sustainability Report 2012," United States Army, September 7, 2012, http://www.army.mil/e2/c/downloads/269536.pdf (accessed December 22, 2015).

48 D. Lafontaine, "RDECOM program wins SecArmy award," United State Army, April 1, 2011, http://www.army.mil/article/54271/rdecom-program-wins-secarmy-award/?ref=news-environment-title7 (accessed January 19, 2015).

49 *Source:* L. G. Zucker, "Institutional Theories of Organization," *Annual Review of Sociology* 13 (1987): 443–464.

50 J. C. Camillus, "Reconciling Logical Incrementalism and Synoptic Formalism," *Strategic Management Journal* 3, no. 3 (July/September 1982): 277–283.

51 R. A. D'Aveni, *Hypercompetition: Managing the Dynamics of Strategic Maneuvering* (New York: Free Press, 1994).

52 M. Jelinek and C. B. Schoonhoven, *The Innovation Marathon: Lessons from High Technology Firms* (San Francisco, CA: Jossey-Bass, 1993).

53 J. E. Dutton and E. Ottensmeyer, "Strategic Issue Management Systems: Forms, Functions, and Contexts," *Academy of Management Review* 12, no. 2 (April 1987): 355–365.

54 J. S. Evans, "Strategic Flexibility for High Technology Manoeuvres: A Conceptual Framework," *Journal of Management Studies* 28, no. 1 (January 1991): 75–76.

55 R. P. Rumelt, "Inertia and Transformation," in C. A. Montgomery (ed.), *Resource-Based and Evolutionary Theories of the Firm: Towards a Synthesis* (Boston, MA: Kluwer Academic, 1995).

56 Evans, "Strategic Flexibility for High Technology Manoeuvres," 77–78.

57 H. I. Ansoff and E. J. McDonnell, *Implanting Strategic Management*, 2nd ed. (New York: Prentice-Hall, 1990).

58 The various conceptualizations are taken from the following authors, respectively: R. Marschak and R. Nelson, "Flexibility, Uncertainty, and Economic Theory," *Metroeconomica* 14 (February 1962): 42–58; H. I. Ansoff, *Corporate Strategy: An Analytic Approach to Business Policy for Growth and Expansion* (New York: McGraw-Hill, 1965); K. Arrow, *The Limits of Organization* (New York: Norton, 1974); J. Rosenhead, "Planning under Uncertainty: 1. The Inflexibility of Methodologies," *The Journal of the Operational Research Society* 31, no. 3 (March 1980): 209–215; J. Rosenhead, "Planning under Uncertainty: II. A Methodology for Robustness Analysis," *The Journal of the Operational Research Society* 31, no. 4 (April 1980): 331–341; J. S. Evans, *Strategic Flexibility in Business*, Research

Report No. 678 (Menlo Park, CA: SRI International, 1982); M. J. Piore and C. F. Sabel, *The Second Industrial Divide: Possibilities for Prosperity* (New York: Basic Books, 1984); D. A. Aaker and B. Mascarenhas, "The Need for Strategic Flexibility," *Journal of Business Strategy* 5, no. 2 (1984): 74–82; K. R. Harrigan, *Strategic Flexibility* (Lexington, MA: Lexington Books, 1985); Evans, "Strategic Flexibility for High Technology Manoeuvres"; P. Ghemawat, *Commitment: The Dynamic of Strategy* (New York: Free Press, 1991); Y. Paik and R. Jacobson, "Flexibility-Based Competitive Advantage," paper presented at the 1993 Academy of Management Meetings, Atlanta, GA, 1993; R. Sanchez, "Strategic Flexibility, Firm Organization, and Managerial Work in Dynamic Markets," *Advances in Strategic Management* 9 (1993): 251–291; D. M. Upton, "What Really Makes Factories Flexible?" *Harvard Business Review* (July–August 1995): 4–84; D. Ulrich and M. F. Wiersema, "Gaining Strategic and Organizational Capability in a Turbulent Business Environment," *The Academy of Management Executive* 3, no. 2 (May 1989): 115–122.

59 M. P. Sharfman and J. W. Dean Jr., "Flexibility in Strategic Decision Making: Informational and Ideological Perspectives," *Journal of Management Studies*, 34, no. 2 (March 1997): 191–217.

60 M. L. Tushman, W. H. Newman, and E. Romanelli, "Convergence and Upheaval: Managing the Steady Pace of Organizational Evolution," *California Management Review* 29, no. 1 (1986): 29–44.

61 Y. Gong and M. Janssen, "From Policy Implementation to Business Process Management: Principles for Creating Flexibility and Agility," *Government Information Quarterly* 29, no. S1 (January 2012): S62.

62 Ghemawat, *Commitment.*

63 Harrigan, *Strategic Flexibility.*

64 R. M. Henderson and K. B. Clark, "Architectural Innovation: The Reconfiguration of Existing Product Technologies and the Failure of Established Firms," *Administrative Science Quarterly* 35, no. 1 (March 1990): 9–30.

65 R. A. Luecke, *Scuttle Your Ships Before Advancing: And Other Lessons from History on Leadership and Change for Today's Managers* (New York: Oxford University Press, 1994).

66 D. Besanko, D. Dranove, and M. Shanley, *The Economics of Strategy* (New York: John Wiley, 1996).

67 A. K. Dixit and R. S. Pindyck, *Investment under Uncertainty* (Princeton, NJ: Princeton University Press, 1994).

68 Besanko, Dranove, and Shanley, *The Economics of Strategy.*

69 Ghemawat, *Commitment*, 10.

70 J. C. Collins and J. I. Porras, *Built to Last: Successful Habits of Visionary Companies* (New York: HarperBusiness, 1994).

71 A. de Geus, *The Living Company: Habits for Survival in a Turbulent Business Environment* (Boston, MA: Harvard Business School Press, 1997).

72 E. P. Kelly, "The Living Company: Habits for Survival in a Turbulent Business Environment (Book Review)," *Academy of Management Executive* 11, no. 3 (August 1997): 95–97.

73 S. Berkun, *The Myths of Innovation* (Sebastopol, CA: O'Reilly, 2007), 58.

74 N. Worren, K. Moore, and P. Cardona, "Modularity, Strategic Flexibility, and Firm Performance: A Study of the Home Appliance Industry," *Strategic Management Journal*, 23 no. 12, (December 2002): 1123–1140.

75 R. Madhavan, "Strategic Flexibility and Performance in the Global Steel Industry: The Role of Interfirm Linkages," Ph.D. dissertation (University of Pittsburgh, 1996), 12.

76 Evans, "Strategic Flexibility for High Technology Manoeuvres," 82.

77 See, for example, J. A. Brander and T. R. Lewis, "Oligopoly and Financial Structure: The Limited Liability Effect," *American Economic Review* 76, no. 5 (December 1986): 956–970.

78 A. J. Bock, T. Opsahl, G. George, and D. M. Gann, "The Effects of Culture and Structure on Strategic Flexibility During Business Model Innovation," *Journal of Management Studies* 49, no. 2 (March 2012): 299.

79 Jelinek and Schoonhoven, *The Innovation Marathon.*

80 S. Nadkarni and V. K. Narayanan, "Strategic Schemas, Strategic Flexibility, and Firm Performance: The Moderating Role of Industry Clockspeed," *Strategic Management Journal* 28, no. 3 (March 2007): 187–206.

81 Evans, "Strategic Flexibility for High Technology Manoeuvres," 84.

82 F. J. Aguilar, *Scanning the Business Environment* (New York: Macmillan, 1967).

83 D. S. Fogel and R. Madhavan, "Strategic Planning Routines as Meta-Routines," working paper, University of Pittsburgh, 1998.

84 P. J. H. Schoemaker, "Scenario Planning: A Tool for Strategic Thinking," *Sloan Management Review* 36, no. 2 (Winter 1995): 25–40.

85 Shell Global, *Signals & Signposts: Shell Energy Scenarios to 2050* (The Hague: Shell International BV, February 2011) http://www2.warwick.ac.uk/fac/soc/pais/research/researchcentres/csgr/green/foresight/energyenvironment/2011_shell_international_signals_and_signposts_-_shell_energy_scenarios_to_2050.pdf (accessed December 22, 2015).

86 Schoemaker, "Scenario Planning: A Tool for Strategic Thinking."

87 C. P. Robert and G. Casella, *Monte Carlo Statistical Methods*, 2nd ed. (New York: Springer, 2004).

88 T. Copeland and V. Antikarov, *Real Options, A Practitioner's Guide* (New York: Texere, 2003), 4–5.

89 M. E. Edleson, "Real Options: Valuing Managerial Flexibility," Harvard Case Study No. 294109 (Boston, MA: Harvard Business School, 1994).

90 L. Bryan, J. Fraser, J. Oppenheim, and W. Rall, *Race for the World: Strategies to Build a Great Global Firm* (Boston, MA: Harvard Business School Press, 1999).

91

Knowledge (internal know-how, know what, know why, specific experience and information)	→ Intellectual Property (knowledge transformed through research and development with the investment in legal protection, into property that earns direct cash returns)
People (global pool of high-quality individuals)	→ Talent (development of high-quality people into world-class performers through investment and selection, who can create and exploit winning global value propositions)
Relationships (advantageous links between producers, suppliers, and customers)	→ Networks (privileged ownership of infrastructure that provides value to all connected parties through direct economic benefits and access to opportunities through "eyes and ears everywhere")
Reputation (superior value proposition in delivering goods and services)	→ Brands (concerted investment in definition, advertising, and promotion of distinctive reputation that lowers interaction costs with customers and results in recovery of higher prices)

92

Net Present Value (NPV)	*Real Options*

Consider all cash flows over the life of a project
Discount cash flows back to present
Use market opportunity costs of capital
Special case of real options approach; real options
   approach that assumes no flexibility in decision making

$$NPV = -1 + \Sigma_{t-1}^{N} \frac{E(FCF_T)}{(1+WACC)^t}$$

MAX (at $t = 0$) $[0, E_0 V_T - X]$; project accepted only at E_0 MAX (at $t = T$) $[0, V_T - X]$; if $V_T > X$ → accept
$t = 0$, $E_0 V_T > X$ the project.

93

Call option:	the right to buy the underlying asset by paying the exercise price
Put option:	the right to sell the underlying asset to receive the exercise price
In-the-money;	
out-of-the-money:	regards the relative asset value to the exercise price in each option setting
European options:	can be exercised only at maturity
American options:	can be exercised any time during the life of the option
Caps and floors:	boundary conditions that bound the value of the underlying asset
Deferral option:	an American call option found in most projects where one has the right to delay the start of a project
Option to abandon:	formally an American put
Option to contract (scale back):	selling a fraction of a project for a fixed price
Option to expand:	formally an American call
Switching options:	portfolios of American call and put options
Compound options:	options on options
Rainbow options:	options driven by multiple sources of uncertainty

94 L. Trigeorgis, "Real Options and Interactions with Financial Flexibility," *Financial Management* 22, no. 3 (Autumn 1993): 202–224.

95 The options concept is based on the Black-Scholes formula modified by Robert Merton, as follows:

$$Se^{-\delta t*}\{N(d_1)\} - Xe^{-rt*}\{N(d_2)\}$$

Where:

$$d_1 = \{\ln(S/X) + (r - \delta + \sigma^2/2)t\} / \sigma^* \sqrt{t}$$
$$d_2 = d_1 - \sigma^* \sqrt{t}$$

$N(d_1)$ is the proportion of shares required to replicate the call option, and $N(d_2)$ is the probability that the call option will be exercised on expiry.

Table 11.7 shows the real options equivalent of the financial options concept.

Table 11.7 Real Options Equivalent of the Financial Options Concept

Variable—Financial option value levers	Symbol	Real options equivalent	Effect on option value: + means an increase raises option value; – means an increase lowers option value
Stock price	S	The present value of cash flows from the investment opportunity on which the option is purchased; the value of the underlying risky asset.	+
Exercise price	X	The present value of all the fixed costs expected over the lifetime of the investment opportunity; expenditure required to purchase asset.	–
Uncertainty	σ	The unpredictability of future cash flows related to the asset; more precisely, the standard deviation of the growth rate of the value of future cash inflows associated with it.	+
Time to expiry	t	The period for which the investment opportunity is valid. This will depend on at least technology (a product's life cycle), competitive advantage (intensity of competition), and contracts (patents, leases, licenses).	+
Dividends	δ	The value that drains away over the duration of the option. This could be the cost incurred to preserve the option (by starving off competition or keeping the opportunity alive), or the cash flows lost to competitors that invest in an opportunity, depriving later entrants of cash flows.	–
Risk-free interest rate	r	The yield of a risk free security with the same maturity as the duration of the option; time value of money.	+
Cumulative normal distribution	$N(d)$		

$$NPV = S - X \text{ or Asset valuation} - \text{Expenditure}$$

96 R. Simons, *Seven Strategy Questions: A Simple Approach for Better Execution* (Boston, MA: Harvard Business Review Press, 2010), 70.
97 Marriott International, "J. Willard Marriott," www.marriott.com/culture-and-values/j-willard-marriott.mi (accessed September 20, 2013).
98 H. Schultz, *Onward: How Starbucks Fought for Its Life Without Losing Its Soul* (New York: Rodale, 2011).
99 PricewaterhouseCoopers, *Guide to Key Performance Indicators: Communicating the Measures That Matter* (London: PwC, 2007), https://www.pwc.com/gx/en/audit-services/corporate-reporting/assets/pdfs/uk_kpi_guide.pdf (accessed December 22, 2015).
100 Simmons, *Seven Strategy Questions*, 75.
101 Ibid.
102 This photograph of homeless children in a scrapyard in Nepal won the top honor in "Quality of Life" category. The children search scrapyards for usable items and sell them to buy their food and clothing, http://www.environmentabout.com/1244/best-and-award-winning-environmental-photos-of-2011 (accessed March 23, 2014).
103 McColl Center for Visual Art, *Environment*, http://mccollcenter.org/about/spheres-of-impact/environment (accessed March 23, 2015).

104 R. Schechner, *Environmental Theater*, exp. ed. (New York: Applause Theatre & Cinema Books, 1994).

105 G. Kourlas, "Tracing Steps for a Greener Path," *The New York Times*, Sunday, March 22, 2015, AR 11.

106 Ibid.

107 American Le Mans Series, "Green Story," http://energy.gov/eere/articles/cutting-edge-vehicles-take-center-stage-texas-green-racing-event (accessed December 22, 2015).

108 American Le Mans Series, "The Michelin® Green X® Challenge," booklet (2009), http://advancedbiofuelsusa.info/wp-content/uploads/2009/03/09_michelin_greenx_challenge_booklet.pdf (accessed September 20, 2013).

Part IV

UNIQUE SITUATIONS

12

ENVIRONMENTAL SUSTAINABILITY IN UNIQUE SITUATIONS

Habitat for Humanity

Habitat for Humanity was founded in 1976 with the goal of eliminating poverty-level housing conditions worldwide,[1] it and has been headquartered in Georgia since the organization's founding, with offices split between its birthplace in Americus, Georgia and a more recent corporate presence in Atlanta. Habitat for Humanity was organized upon four core tenets:

1   Houses are sold at no profit, and buyers are charged no interest.
2   Homes are built by the future homeowners and community volunteers (with trained supervision).
3   Individuals, businesses, and faith groups provide the financial support.
4   The homes are designed to be simple, affordable, and of good quality.

The organization has worldwide affiliates with outreach to over 90 countries.

In 2010, the organization began pushing two new strategies: neighborhood revitalization and environmental sustainability. "Neighborhood revitalization" was a generic term used for a combination of rehabilitation and repair programs that focused on existing housing. Habitat for Humanity had traditionally focused on new construction; this strategy broadened its mission to include other types of building standards and outcomes. The second push had been toward incorporating environmental sustainability programs with energy-saving design aspects.

Habitat quickly became a leader in sustainable building practices. Habitat offices (called affiliates) had a unique ability to pilot "green" programs without having their options limited by a cumbersome or overpowering headquarters mandate. Each affiliate (i.e., each local Habitat office) was not required to build homes above the standards of local construction codes, and affiliates had financial independence from the headquarters. So, in many cases, a local board of directors or affiliate directors decided what to build and how to build it.

This new sustainability direction created challenges for the organization and its affiliates:

- *The cost of sustainability was often more reasonable than most might expect; however, the start-up and training costs could be great.*
- *Habitat for Humanity International built national partnerships through programs such as Partners in Sustainable Building (funded by the Home Depot Foundation); however, the various national programs were brand new and often had too small an impact.*

Regional and statewide funding programs were common, as with the SystemVision program funded, for example, by the North Carolina Housing Finance Agency. This program provided $4,000 to participating North Carolina affiliates that incorporated a whole-house energy standard and a guarantee to the homebuyer that utility usage would stay below a guaranteed rate. If this guaranteed rate was exceeded for any reason, the program would reimburse the difference. The program promised consumer energy bills in the $50–$75 range or better by 2020. The benefit to the affiliate was excellent; the $4,000 more than covered the average expense—if executed properly.

Chapter Overview

The Habitat case illustrates some unique contributions to environmental sustainability through noncommercial organizations. The focus of this chapter is to look at situations outside of the usual business organization that can be impacted by applying a sustainability lens. These situations include entrepreneurship and four unique areas of society: government, NGOs, universities, and emerging markets. Strategies in these situations may have some overlap with the business strategies addressed in this book; however, each of these areas is set apart by rules and standards unique to its setting.

By the end of this chapter, you should have a basic understanding of what makes each of these situations unique in the realm of environmental sustainability. All of these entities work together to keep our world clean, safe, and productive for future generations. Also, at some point, all individuals will work for, work with, or be impacted by these unique situations.

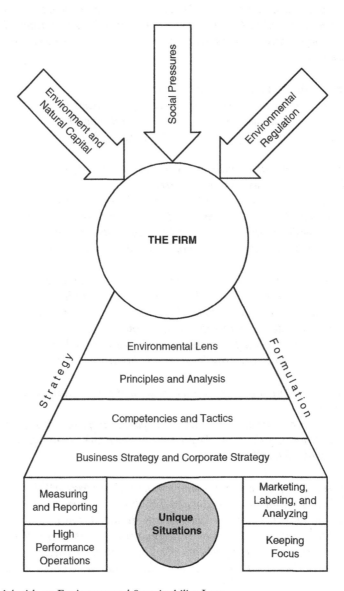

Figure 12.1 Strategy Model with an Environmental Sustainability Lens

At the end of this chapter, you should be able to:

1 define socially responsible investing and specify the data that support (or refute) the returns obtained from this investing criterion;
2 identify contexts when entrepreneurial firms have an advantage over larger, more established firms;
3 identify opportunities to address large social challenges through entrepreneurial efforts;
4 understand the unique attributes and sustainability opportunities for four types of organizations: government, NGOs, universities, and organizations in emerging markets.

This chapter will begin by discussing socially responsible investing. I will demonstrate how investors are combining their needs for returns with demands to support values related to environmental sustainability and social outcomes.

Socially Responsible Investing and Sovereign Wealth Funds

I introduced **Socially Responsible Investing (SRI)** in Chapter 8. The term refers to the use of socially responsible and environmentally and economically sustainable criteria for investments. This section highlights the use of SRI as an alternative to usual investment criteria and innovations in businesses that are evolving to improve their actions in support of the environment.

The SRI industry uses nonfinancial criteria, in public and private investment, to assist those who want their investments to be consistent with their values (and to join with others to change unethical corporate and government behaviors). SRI is applicable to anyone who makes investments, not just individuals who work within the realm of investment.

SRI usually refers to the process of exclusion, engagement, or positive investment at individual, institutional, or government levels. Social investment funds include Portfolio21, Highwater Global, Winslow Green Growth Fund, and New Alternatives.[2]

An example of *exclusion* is not investing in companies that create excessive environmental waste. An example of engagement and positive investment is when U.S. investors joined together (via their contributions to pension, state, and religious funds) to pressure U.S. businesses to end their implicit or explicit support of apartheid (i.e., systems of racial segregation). These types of engagement and investment forced a major turning point in the effort to end apartheid.

Governments have been components of (and greatly intertwined with) SRI. Some governments have even made retirement saving compulsory or have insisted on disclosure about whether funds are SRI (such has been implemented in Britain).[3] China has established the National Council for Social Security Fund for social security expenditures.[4] CalPERS in California (the largest U.S. public pension fund with $266.1 billion under investment) supports several investments considered SRI.[5]

This type of socially conscious investing is substantial in the United States. In 2014, $6.57 trillion was classified as SRI.[6] Canada, Australia, and Japan, along with the USA, accounted for most of the investment.

The U.S. contribution equated to 12.2 percent of total assets under professional management;[7] within SRI allocations, 82 percent of funds incorporated environmental, social, and governance factors mostly in the form of exclusions (e.g., tobacco, alcohol, and gambling). This means that they used environmental and socially responsible considerations as part of their investment decisions.

Currently, SRI is not standard practice; however, the need for sustainable SRI has never been more urgent.[8] Although there are instances of companies taking climate change seriously (e.g., Ingersoll-Rand and Google), and groups of shareholders actively working for change (e.g., the Interfaith Center on Corporate Responsibility and CERES), it is not likely that SRI will become mainstream in the United States in the near future.[9] Lack of clear terminologies and little history with investment returns are two reasons for this lack of mainstream use.

Similarly to SRI, Sovereign Wealth Funds (SWF) have social and environmental goals and are prevalent around the world; the 50 largest funds have nearly $5.855 trillion under investment and nearly 59 percent of this is oil- and gas-related.[10] Norway's SWF is currently the largest in the world and a leader in setting ethical requirements for its investments by avoiding investments in companies that cause severe environmental damage. It had about $737.2 billion invested in 2013.[11] Ironically, it was created through its Norwegian Petroleum Income. Its standards excluded Rio Tinto because of its investment in Freeport's mine in West Papua. China Investment Corporation is the largest Chinese SWF with $575.2 billion in 2013. China's four SWF investments totaled $1.309 trillion but have no ethical requirements.[12]

Many governments do not require their SWFs to be consistent with government policies and values. For example, New Zealand established a government fund for superannuation in 2002 with minimal ethical requirements. In fact, they invested in nuclear armaments, despite New Zealand having opposed U.S. and French nuclear weapons for many decades.[13]

These funds have mixed reputations and impacts given these criteria and actual investments. We can probably anticipate that the funds will improve as they become more transparent and accountable. They are a unique investment method. Another investment with unique characteristics is creating a new organization. This is the subject of the next section.

Entrepreneurship

Entrepreneurial activity is often supported by political leaders believing in free markets, championed by social groups, reinforced by infrastructure at universities, embraced by venture capitalists, and is integrated into local, state, and federal governments. The term "entrepreneur" could refer to anyone who starts a business; however, in this chapter, I prefer to use a narrower definition to mean somebody who offers an innovative solution to a problem without regard to resources currently controlled.[14]

Entrepreneurship requires different strategies from those utilized by established businesses. This section defines what an entrepreneur is, discusses key concepts for success, and explores the budding realm of social entrepreneurship. Social entrepreneurship, in particular, is a situation that has profound impacts on sustainability issues. Environmental sustainability can be a crucial component of an entrepreneurial process.

Entrepreneurship Defined

The **entrepreneur** is one who undertakes personal economic risk to create a new organization that will exploit new technology or innovative processes that generate value; thus, entrepreneurship is a process of creating a new organization that generates this value.[15] Entrepreneurship is a dynamic process of vision, change, and creation. Essential ingredients include the willingness to take calculated risks, formulating an effective venture team, generating the needed resources, building a solid business plan, and recognizing opportunity where others see chaos, contradiction, and confusion.[16] In addition to firm creation, entrepreneurs create new knowledge, form new institutions and industries, and promote public-private partnerships and social businesses. Celebrated contemporary examples of entrepreneurs abound with the likes of those who started Apple, Google, and Alibaba in China.

Researchers have attempted to explain the growth in entrepreneurship. Some researchers believe there is a new segment of individuals within society who are drawn to entrepreneurship by displacement from unemployment or due to their attitudes about the traditional employment system. Broken social contracts between companies and employees may further explain this growth in interest; for example, employees working with large organizations may come to realize that they are not as secure as they once thought. Thus, they might tend to want to work with smaller organizations and have more influence. Also, immigration policy could be a factor; immigrants might have difficulty securing employment and start their own firms simply to secure an income. Thus, we may have an "entrepreneurial class" of people in the United States.

Research has delved into certain myths about entrepreneurs. For example, entrepreneurs are often viewed as antisocial. This myth is dispelled by the fact that successful entrepreneurs have wide networks and use them to gain resources to support business growth. Another myth is that entrepreneurs are mostly young; however, this idea is not supported by data. In fact, most entrepreneurs are older and experienced. Entrepreneurs are viewed as having world-changing ideas; however, most new businesses are designed around mundane ideas or products that solve problems. Finally, the belief that most funds come from venture capital is a myth. As it turns out, most funding is from "the 'three fs'—friends, family, and fools."[17]

Table 12.1 Number of Firms, Number of Establishments, Employment, Annual Payroll, and Estimated Receipts by Enterprise Employment Size for the United States and States, Totals: 2012[18]

Enterprise employment size	Number of firms	Number of establishments	Employment
01: Total	5,726,160	7,431,808	115,938,468
02: 0–4	3,543,991	3,549,102	5,906,506
03: 5–9	992,716	1,005,042	6,527,943
04: 10–19	593,641	630,811	7,974,340
05: <20	5,130,348	5,184,955	20,408,789
06: 20–99	494,170	687,272	19,387,249
07: 100–499	83,423	360,207	16,266,855
08: <500	5,707,941	6,232,434	56,062,893
09: 500+	18,219	1,199,374	59,875,575

Despite these myths, this area in business has continued to grow (see Table 12.1). The United States had 27,281,452 small businesses and start-ups in 2008–2009; however, 21,351,320 of these businesses did not employ people. Of the remaining 5,930,132 firms, 3,617,764 (61 percent) had one to four employees whereas only 18,469 (0.3 percent) had 500 or more employees.[19] These data show a shift toward small business growth. Table 12.1 shows data from 2012, the latest year available.

With such variability and risk, there is an expectation of high failure rates; however, the data are clear that firm deaths for those with less than 20 employees are fewer than births (1,734,000 deaths vs. 1,945,000 births from 2006 to 2007).[20] In fact, the number of deaths of firms with 500-plus employees is greater than births (356,000 deaths vs. 229,000 births).[21] This trend has been consistent over a number of years.

In the United States, citizens value entrepreneurs and hold them in high esteem, especially when they succeed. Culture, receptiveness of the capital markets, and public policy are among the macro conditions impacting them. Micro explanations of success or failure include family traits and personality. Some research shows that an entrepreneur's tolerance for ambiguity defines his or her ability to be successful as an entrepreneur. Psychologists correlate entrepreneurial success with the amount of risk a person is willing to assume and to characteristics such as self-efficacy, the need for achievement and/or control, and a tolerance for ambiguity.[22] Others point to expertise or mentoring[23] or to the entrepreneur's intentions and related attitudes.[24]

These macro and micro conditions all contribute to the success of a venture; however, recent thinking is that success is largely based on engagement in venture seeking (i.e., looking for opportunities and finding ways to develop them). Successful entrepreneurs have a unique ability to identify and exploit opportunities. This constant searching is what leads to a person finding viable opportunities and producing a successful venture, the subject of the next section.

Advice for Entrepreneurial Success

In the next subsections, I will explore some key concepts that could help emerging entrepreneurs to be successful.

Finding Opportunities

An important first consideration is where aspiring entrepreneurs can find opportunities—what one author called "finding fertile ground."[25] An environment is favorable for entrepreneurial efforts if the price-cost margins are protected for at least some reasonable time period after commercialization of an innovation.[26] This protection can come in many forms such as patents, unique partnerships, and myriad actions that corporations use to keep ahead of the competition.

Certain knowledge conditions are favorable for start-up businesses. When knowledge is not complex (and not much new knowledge is needed to support a business), entrepreneurs can more easily create market opportunities. Also, the existence of large markets provides a better opportunity for entrepreneurs, especially if the markets can be served without much advertising or marketing expense, which can overwhelm a new business and use precious cash that is needed for other parts of the business.

Codification of knowledge enhances the performance of new firms because codified knowledge is more easily available to entrepreneurs than tacit knowledge. Entrepreneurs have a better chance of being successful if they use their information sources, develop networks, talk to everyone close to an innovation, and use any prior knowledge.

Technology characteristics influence the ability of the innovator to appropriate value; for example, knowledge embedded in an innovation may be tacit or explicit. *Explicit* knowledge can be written down and easily communicated. *Tacit* knowledge is less tangible, a product of someone's experience, and is thus difficult to transfer to another person by means of writing it down or verbalizing it. For example, stating to someone that Sydney is in Australia is a piece of explicit knowledge that can be written down, transmitted, and understood by a recipient. However, the ability to speak a language, use mathematics, or design and use complex drawing techniques requires knowledge that is not always known explicitly (even by expert practitioners). The more tacit the knowledge, the more protected the innovation.[27]

For new businesses, value-added tends to come from places other than manufacturing and marketing (since large companies have the advantage when these functions are required). New firms tend to perform better when they exploit general-purpose technologies (vs. specific-purpose technologies). A **general-purpose technology** is one that can be applied in multiple markets. Established firms tend to find general-purpose technologies hard to manage since they want technologies that create value in their current markets and at their stage of the value chain.[28] Consider that the best approach is with technology that already exists.[29]

Lead-time is the time it would take followers to catch up. The effectiveness and efficiency of innovators, with respect to lead-time, determines how much value innovators will obtain from the innovation. If others can copy an innovation quickly the original innovator will not reap large rewards.

Ultimately, it is most important for entrepreneurs to think constantly about challenges and solutions, and to see opportunities everywhere. Also, new firms tend to perform better when exploiting opportunities in new markets with unknown demand, since large firms generally rely on market research data based on large market samples. When looking for data, start with a customer problem identified by customer complaints, expressions of unfilled wishes, or your own observations and determine if customers are having difficulties with certain products or industries. Customers often have difficulties articulating the relationships between new products and services and their needs. So, you will have to act like an anthropologist to observe people and discover ideas.

Next, look at the role of dominant design or standards. For example, technology evolves through periods of incremental change, interrupted by radical changes in a dominant design—and then experiences converge again. Since current explorations of new renewable energy solutions are demanding new technology standards, the entrepreneur might be able to enter a market when these standards are not yet established. Lack of dominant design is generally best for new firms; at this stage, markets are fragmented and have less competition. Dominant designs are rarely cutting-edge technologies; thus, a new technology might cause a radical shift in a market yet not become the dominant design. The risk for the entrepreneur is that they will be working with a standard that does not become dominant.

Demand conditions that are favorable to entrepreneurs include large markets, high rates of industry growth (so that new companies do not need to steal customers from large competitors), and heterogeneity of markets (containing many segments).[30] These conditions provide new entrepreneurs with a customer base that is often not threatening to larger, more powerful companies. Entrepreneurial firms have advantages when the work is more labor-intensive, requires minimal advertising, involves fewer competitors, and the average firm size is small. Entrepreneurs can also have advantages in young industries, which generally have fewer competitors and diverse standards (as discussed earlier in this section).[31]

Another potential way to find opportunity is by exploiting established companies' weaknesses. This can be best accomplished through looking at R&D trends. R&D agendas come from client needs and the abilities within a firm.[32] Most R&D yields "usual" returns despite the celebrated examples of "spectacular" returns. Thus, investments in innovations are not guarantees of success and strategic choices in the area of R&D involve substantial uncertainty.[33]

Opportunities are greater when business appears marginal to larger companies or the product is something larger companies are not very good at producing. Look for innovations that were rejected by larger companies (e.g., when they were making investment decisions and rejected good ideas simply to narrow their scopes). You might use a current job as a means of identifying information that could lead to new opportunities; three-quarters of new businesses are related to their founders' former employers (either serving the same customers or offering similar products).[34]

When entrants design a new product that may threaten a monopolist using two mechanisms: replacement or efficiency. The **replacement mechanism** occurs when a monopolist has little incentive to innovate because a new entrant has a stronger basis for developing an innovation. In this case, monopolists gain little from innovation. Thus, an entrant can replace a monopolist with the innovation and weaken the established firm's incentive to innovate. The **efficiency mechanism** is when monopolist firms have an incentive to innovate to protect their positions. In this case, the new entrant can, at best, become a duopolist if it innovates (i.e., two suppliers control the market).

There are more opportunities for more players when an industry changes rapidly. In Chapter 6, I mentioned blue ocean strategies (which are created by combining, deleting, adding, and changing key success factors). Recall that key success factors answer two key questions:

1 What do customers want?
2 What does a firm need to do to compete?

Also, an entrepreneur needs to be considering the question: What industries will exist in the future that may be unknown today? For example, renewable energy is presenting all sorts of opportunities to invest in new ways of producing energy and consuming it using solar panels, unique building designs, and alternative ways to distribute energy. Water technologies are emerging opportunities across the world.

Entrepreneurs can exploit points when an industry is shifting from one basic technology to another. These inflection points provide uncertainty and a chance for new players to create market opportunities. Entrepreneurs should also pursue opportunities to create new products or services based on discrete technologies, such as a technology that can be exploited on its own (vs. a systemic technology that must be exploited as part of a larger system). For example, software that works with just one operating system can be limiting and subject to other software packages replacing it.

Established companies are generally better at exploiting established business opportunities (vs. new firms) due to experience, reputation effects, and scale economies. Each of these advantages might be difficult to overcome by a new firm. So, new firms should probably not start businesses in these conditions. To offset these advantages, new firms might exploit established capabilities, listen to customers, serve those who are underserved, and hire the employees of established competitors.

Big companies are generally focused on efficiency. They tend to be slower at innovation (despite their advantages) even though they may have incentives to innovate.[35] Larger firms tend to cut back expenditures on R&D to gain efficiencies. Established firms tend to use existing capabilities and find it more difficult to develop new capabilities. They have developed routines that serve them well; however, these routines are also core rigidities that prevent, at times, innovation. Thus, routines often lead dominant firms in an industry to dismiss or reject the value of new products or services.

Managing information is important. For example, if an entrepreneur wants to license technology to an existing manufacturer and have that company manufacture a product, the manufacturer needs to be told what the new technology will do. This discloses the information. Codified knowledge is easier for contracting. When technical standards exist, market-based mechanisms are more viable. This helps with coordination. When complementary assets are general, market-based mechanisms are good choices. (See Chapter 6 for a more complete discussion of this make-or-buy decision.)

Patenting and penalties are the best ways to mitigate the effect in this case. *Adverse selection* is another issue that entrepreneurs face. For example, potential employees misrepresenting their abilities to gain a job is a common problem in start-ups. Thus, to avoid this problem you could use franchising.

Before venturing into a business, it is important to explore a feasibility study. In other words, once you have settled on an idea, consider how feasible it is for a new business. Advice about feasibility studies is the subject of the next section.

Feasibility Studies

Once an idea is identified, the next step is to develop a feasibility study (prior to developing extensive organizational plans). A feasible idea is one that has a high potential of being implemented in a market. There are many ways to approach a feasibility study.

In essence, successful entrepreneurship is comprised of three critical elements: markets, industries, and one or more key people who make up the entrepreneurial team. Here are the core questions in a feasibility analysis:

1 Are the markets and industry attractive?
2 Does the opportunity offer compelling customer benefits as well as a sustainable advantage over other potential solutions?
3 Can the team deliver the results they seek and promise to others?[36]

These questions are the starting point. To complete a feasibility study, an entrepreneur must thoroughly explore multiple components of the potential business. Below is the list of components that could be included in a written feasibility study:

1 executive summary;
2 market assessment: segmentation;
3 market assessment: all segments;
4 industry assessment;
5 the technology;
6 team assessment;
7 sources of competitive advantage;
8 development strategy;
9 communicating your idea.

I have described in this book, in various chapters, technologies to do these assessments.

As can be seen, a feasibility study has many components. If a potential entrepreneur can effectively address all of these areas, the new business has a greater chance of success. One common mistake made by entrepreneurs is that they skip the study of the feasibility of an idea and try to develop a complete business plan. This process is not advised since many seemingly good ideas, when tested for feasibility, do not stand up to scrutiny. Therefore, entrepreneurs are advised to take their time before formalizing the business.

Entrepreneurial Mindset

A third consideration is developing an entrepreneurial mindset (i.e., learning to see opportunities, acquiring the right mindset, and training yourself in innovation processes). Think "new business" constantly and continually rework your ideas. Push yourself to see opportunities rather than risks and look for potential innovations within disparate life experiences. Finally, write constantly about your life goals and what you want out of life. Then constantly search for opportunities that satisfy these goals.

Large companies can be entrepreneurial, as well. If they want to act entrepreneurially they might want to consider the firm's product life-cycle. To find ideas in large companies, consider 15 types of innovation as represented in Table 12.2. A firm's resources and capabilities, competitor positioning, potential responses, and category maturity all determine what to pursue. For example, changes in a life-cycle of a product or industry could be caused by changes in demographic characteristics, preferences, power of the players, demand growth, creation and diffusion of knowledge, and dominant designs and standards that take hold.

As an industry matures, players become more concerned about the manufacturing process and selling products (vs. product design). Most of the innovations in Table 12.2 are not strategic; they are incremental improvements or applications of new knowledge about products or services. Also, outside factors can

Table 12.2 Types of Innovation with the Life-Cycle of a Product or Industry

	Growth Phase	*Maturity Phase*	*Decline Phase*	
Types of Innovation	1 Product or service leadership	2 Customer intimacy[37]	3 Operational excellence[38]	4 Category renewal Organic[39]
	Disruptive[40]	Life-extension[41]	Value-engineering[42]	Acquisition
	Application[43]	Enhancement[44]	Integration[45]	Harvest and exit[46]
	Product[47]	Marketing[48]	Process change[49]	
	Platform[50]	Change the experience[51]	Value-migration[52]	

influence a company's need to innovate (e.g., deregulation might increase demand and allow for more variance in ideas that may have been prevented previously [such as what recently happened in energy provision and telecommunications services]).

A large company that controls the standard gets high returns.[53] Standards can be set by government, agencies, for example, the American National Standards Institute, or are simply established by competitive markets. These standards can be proprietary or open. But why do standards emerge in some product markets and not in others?

To get standards adopted, there must be agreement among a group of firms, government mandates, or network externalities that create a dominant design. To achieve these results, entrepreneurs should work with producers of complementary technologies to make their technologies appealing. Use "increasing returns" concepts; when upfront costs are high and marginal costs are small, unit costs will drop dramatically as volume increases (as with drug and software production).

Network externalities result in the value of a product or service increasing with the number of people using it (e.g., email, dominant software, and the QWERTY keyboard). To achieve these results, consider the following actions:

- Launch beta versions to gain a share of the market. For example, solar energy companies may be best to try a few designs to tests their efficacy.
- Use a model that encourages consumers to constantly come back to you for products and services (e.g., buying razor blades from you for your razor).
- Offer upfront components very inexpensively.
- Provide incentives (e.g., cheaper subsequent version costs).
- Ensure that complementary products and services are developed.
- Attract customers first then make money; make large bets!
- First-mover advantage is important.

First-mover advantage can be a firm's competitive advantage when it is first in a particular market or first to use a particular strategy; to the extent that a market has other first-mover advantages, innovation can help a firm to exploit those advantages. Thus, first-mover advantages on either the demand or supply side create a favorable climate for innovation. Markets tend to favor innovation by allowing firms to rapidly exploit early leads;[54] the more that a product, service, or lead-time can be protected by property rights, the greater the advantage by first movers. Also, the greater the costs and risks of being first-to-market, the greater the importance of complementary resources. Finally, the greater the importance of product standards, the greater the advantage of being an early mover (to influence those standards [see Figure 12.2]).

Barriers to entry might come into play because they create a first-mover advantage within an industry. This consideration refers to entry into industries with incumbents earning high returns. New entrants could find themselves at a disadvantage relative to incumbents due to the existence of (1) pre-commitment contracts, (2) licenses and patents, (3) experience-curve effects, or (4) pioneering brand advantage. For example, new companies in sports equipment manufacturing have a hard time establishing brands for their products. So, they tend to produce for existing brands (e.g., Nike and New Balance).

If the industry has already converged on a dominant design and patent protection is weak, large companies can easily imitate a small firm. Success will depend largely on who has better marketing and manufacturing. This is where complementary assets are important. These are assets used along with your product (or a combination of assets) along the value chain and horizontal linkages.[55] Incumbent firms that have existing manufacturing and marketing will typically do better than new firms. New firms, if they need manufacturing or marketing, should contract for the service. If complementary assets are specialized, however, this strategy of contracting will not work.

In sum, entrepreneurs can be successful if they adhere to a few pieces of advice that stem from research and practice. Once the entrepreneur develops his or her idea, and conducts feasibility studies, seeking support is another step in the process of business formation. How entrepreneurs present their ideas could determine whether or not they gain needed support.

The next section in this chapter provides some advice about presenting ideas.

Profile: Is an Organic Product an Innovation?[56]

The Rodale Institute, a 501(c)(3) nonprofit,[57] is dedicated to pioneering organic farming by creating business innovations. The Rodale Institute, founded by J. I. Rodale, has been researching the best practices of organic agriculture since its founding in 1947. In 2014, the Institute partnered with St. Luke's Anderson Campus hospital in Pennsylvania to create one of the nation's first farm-to-hospital food systems.

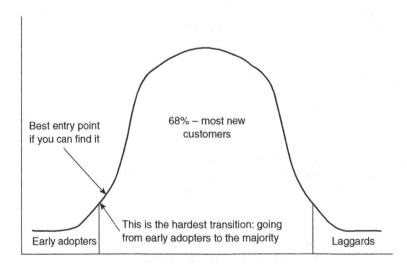

Figure 12.2 Product Life-Cycle Curve

Figure 12.3 Farm-to-Hospital Food System. Photo Credit: Rodale Institute

The Rodale Institute developed five acres on the hospital's 500-acre campus to locally grow organic produce for St. Luke's patients, visitors, staff, and volunteers.[58] Rodale Institute expects that the plot will produce about 44,000 pounds of fresh produce which will be distributed through the hospital's food services supplier Sodexo. The partners expect the operation to expand to ten acres where it will produce roughly 100,000 lbs. of produce. The farm will produce lettuce, broccoli, tomatoes, peppers, cucumbers, summer squash, Swiss chard, kale, garlic, cabbage, beets, and potatoes.[59]

Some critics of organic agriculture claim that buying organic produce is a "class-driven decision" dependent on the affluence of the customer.[60] In 2012, Stanford University published a 40-year study that concluded that fruits and vegetables labeled organic were no more nutritious than their conventional competitors.[61] However, Rodale Institutes 30-year side-by-side research program, Farming Systems Trail®, concluded that:

- *organic crops outperform conventional yields in droughts;*
- *organic systems replenish soil nutrients better than conventional agricultural systems;*
- *conventional systems produce 40 percent more GHGs.[62]*

The client-base for St. Luke's farm-to-hospital model has unique demographics and preferences due to their state of health. This change in demand has created a unique opportunity to create innovative new products in terms of the hospital food system's dominant design. By creating on-site, organic food production, the partners are attempting to meet the demand for healthy food while also cutting the horizontal expanse of their supply chain.

Food for Thought. Table 12.2 shows how demographic characteristics, preferences, and dominant design influence the firm's product life-cycle. In the context of product life-cycle, food systems are a unique market to apply the entrepreneurial mindset. For example, could food labeling policy be the reason organic produce was found to be no more nutritious than conventional food production? If so, what is the role of transparent policy in achieving a product's status as better than a predecessor product?

Is it possible that the healthier agricultural inputs (e.g. lower use of pesticides and fertilizers) of St. Luke's organic farm-to-hospital food system will appeal to consumers over the conventional modes of agricultural production and transportation?

Critical Ideas for Presenting New Businesses

Entrepreneurs must often present their businesses to other people (e.g., selling ideas to potential funders). The key components for a winning presentation can be summarized by the term "HOMA" (as shown in Table 12.3).

Table 12.3 Presentation of Business Ideas

Human (the people who perform the services or provide resources for the venture, directly or indirectly)

- Does the team have the right experience, skills, and attitudes given the idea? Do they have a good reputation? What are their relevant accomplishments?
- Does the opportunity make sense given the people? Can they pull this deal off? Are they committed to this idea?

Opportunity

- The idea—is it solid and clear?
- Does the venture try to solve a real need? A real problem?
- Is this an attractive industry with growth opportunities? Show me the analysis of the industry and how you know it is attractive.

Model

- Is the business model clear and compelling for making money? What drives costs and what drives revenues?
- What are the core assumptions behind the deal?
- What is the deal?
- Is there a balance—financials, operations, customer approach, and learning?

Activities

- Can the venture support the positioning? What are the core activities?
- Can risk be identified and avoided?

HOMA is one of many approaches; however, entrepreneurs can find many alternative sources for advice on how to present ideas. Also, the presentation format might vary according to context (e.g., venture capitalists may have different format needs than angle financiers). Banks and hedge funds will have other presentation ideas. One other format that might work in various contexts comes from an acronym entitled SUCCESC.[63] The letters stand for the following concepts:

- Simple: elevator pitch; what is the spine of the business? Tell the audience in one minute what need you are solving and about your solution.
- Unexpected: hook me in; give me a reason to be impressed. Possibly give the audience a startling fact.
- Concrete: solve real needs; give me analogies to relate to and make this visual.
- Credible: can you do it? Why you?
- Emotional: provide some basis for me to get excited and involved. Relate your idea, for example, to large societal issues such as disease or poverty.
- Story: what is the story you are telling? You are weaving a story for your audience that helps them to relate to your ideas.
- Context: know your audience and address their specific interests.

Whatever idea the entrepreneur pursues (and regardless of whether the innovation is social or traditional), he or she will inevitably need to make sure that others can understand the business idea and its likelihood of success. Thus, an entrepreneur who follows these principles and ideas and develops excellent presentation skills is more likely to succeed than one who does not.

Let us now explore how entrepreneurs can attack social problems using an entrepreneurial model. Also, can entrepreneurs successfully find new ways to address the environmental problems we are all facing?

Social Entrepreneurship

Entrepreneurs have always been the drivers of progress that act as engines of growth (i.e., they harness opportunities and innovation to fuel economic advancement). **Social entrepreneurs**, like their business counterparts, are similarly focused; they tap into vast reserves of ambition, creativity, and resourcefulness to solve large, intractable problems.[64] Social entrepreneurs pioneer innovative, effective, and sustainable approaches to meet the needs of the marginalized, disadvantaged, and disenfranchised.[65]

Social firms, like other types of enterprises, have dominant logics that guide their actions.[66] They are as old as time with renowned examples such as Marie Montessori who established unique schools and a pedagogy for impoverished areas. These organizations have a different dominant logic about how a manager conceptualizes his or her business.[67] (See Table 12.4 for a description of how social entrepreneurship is different from other types of entrepreneurship.)

Table 12.4 Types of Entrepreneurs[68]

	Conventional	*Institutional*	*Cultural*	*Social*	*Intra-preneurship*
Structure	Profit	Profit	Not-for-profit and profit	Not-for-profit and profit	Within an organization
Primary motive	Returns to shareholders	Institutional reform and development	Cultural diffusion and enlightenment	Social change and well-being	Returns to shareholders
Offering to consumers/ constituents	Product or service	Legitimacy	Support and establish norms and values	Promote ideology and social change	Products or services
Contemporary examples	Business services, software developers, tourism, new technology	Edison, Facebook, Google, Kodak, Apple	Museums, folk art festivals, orchestras, dance	Tom's Shoes, Grameen Foundation, Scojo Foundation	Compete with existing businesses within the firm

Tremendous business opportunities exist in addressing the world's most difficult challenges.[69] Microfinance, for example, provides accessible loans and other assistance to help people who would otherwise not have access to capital markets.[70] These finance businesses set up infrastructures to loan money and facilitate business. The most renowned attempt has been Grameen Bank, which is located throughout the world.[71]

Certain companies (e.g., Nutriset, which is a private company in France) have been selling food products to combat hunger and malnutrition since 1986. Nutriset is known for developing Plumpy'nut®, the first highly fortified, ready-to-use therapeutic food (RUTF) for the treatment of severe acute malnutrition.[72] Other examples are Scojo Foundation, which sells affordable reading glasses in developing nations such as India; Nicholas Negroponte's One Laptop per Child program, which tried to get computers into the hands of children;[73] WaterHealth International, which provided "off-the-shelf" technologies to purify water;[74] and Habitat for Humanity, which builds eco-friendly houses.[75] Belgian Bart Weetjens started Apopo, a company that trained giant African rats to sniff out landmines on former battlefields. The program was a modest success, with mine-clearing operations in Mozambique and a contract to expand into Africa's Great Lakes Region. Apopo wanted to expand its work and tried to get more funding to support its efforts.

Weetjans tried several fundraising techniques such as an adopt-a-rat program and CEO Christophe Cox hired a consulting group (specializing in social enterprises) to run the business using some known principles and practices. They developed strategic options such as expanding mine-clearing operations to the Middle East, getting into the cargo-inspection business, and utilizing the rats for disease detection.[76] Now Apopo is expanding its services into the medical community and is growing financially due to this new opportunity. Apopo serves as a prime example of using innovative thinking to address some of the world's problems.

While charity might be one solution to addressing the poverty challenge, many analysts point to its failure. Sub-Saharan Africa, despite receiving millions in aid, has not grown economically. Additionally, charitable giving is not a reliable financial source. Total estimated charitable giving in the United States increased just 3.5 percent in 2012 (from 2011) to $316.23 billion in contributions.[77] Giving to religion decreased an estimated 2.0 percent from 2011 to 2012. Inflation-adjusted giving to religious organizations is estimated to have declined over 4.7 percent from 2010. Some organizations (especially religious and foundations) do address world poverty; however, despite this charitable giving, the world is still filled with hunger, illness, and poverty.[78] So, some people argue that the wealthy can save the world by giving money to social entrepreneurs.[79]

Social entrepreneurs share a commitment to pioneering innovations that reshape society and benefit humanity. Whether they are working on a local or international scale, they are solution-minded pragmatists who are not afraid to tackle—and successfully resolve—some of the world's biggest problems.[80]

Four Unique Situations Outside of Business

This book has developed various concepts and frameworks that can be used in most organizations; however, a few types of organizations call for special considerations. This section contains comments on four organizational types: government, NGOs, universities, and organizations in emerging markets. Each of these contexts has unique sustainability requirements, opportunities, and impacts.

1. Government

Local, regional, national, and supranational governments have become increasingly sensitive and responsive to lessening their impacts on the environment. Governments are in a unique position to impact the environment as they can improve their own operations while also influencing the operations of others through regulations and incentives.

Governments have large footprints in terms of land and buildings. For example, the U.S. federal government has direct ownership of almost 650 million acres of land (2.63 million square kilometers), which is nearly 30 percent of its total territory. These federal lands are used as military bases, testing grounds, nature parks, reserves, and Native American reservations. They are also leased to the private sector for commercial exploitation (e.g., forestry, mining, and agriculture). The lands are managed by different administrations such as the Bureau of Land Management, the U.S. Forest Service, the U.S. Fish and Wildlife Service, the National Park Service, the Bureau of Indian Affairs, the U.S. Department of Defense, the U.S. Army Corps of Engineers, the U.S. Bureau of Reclamation, and the Tennessee Valley Authority.

The U.S. government is the nation's largest asset holder. It manages 896,000 buildings and structures with a total square footage of 3.29 billion that sit on more than 41 million acres of land. The General Services Administration, which acts as the federal government's landlord, owns or leases 9,600 assets and maintains an inventory of more than 362 million square feet of space.

A focus on sustainability creates efficiencies; thus, the U.S. federal government can cut costs and save millions of dollars by making relatively small changes. For example, Ray Mabus, President Obama's secretary of the Navy and the former U.S. Ambassador to Saudi Arabia, is pushing for greater use of renewable power and energy-efficient construction; running U.S. military ships on nuclear energy, biofuels, and hybrid engines; and flying military jets with biofuels. In October 2010, the Navy launched the USS *Makin Island* amphibious assault ship, which is propelled by a hybrid gas turbine/electric motor. On its maiden voyage from Mississippi to San Diego, it saved $2 million in fuel.[81] These types of changes will not only have a profound effect on the environment, but they will also save taxpayer dollars and possibly the lives of soldiers.

A smart city is one that promises a cleaner environment and tends to use fewer resources.[82] Smart cities can be identified (and ranked) along six main axes or dimensions: a smart economy, smart mobility, a smart environment, smart people, smart living, and smart governance. In particular, the axes are based on theories of regional competitiveness, transport economics, natural resources, human and social capital, quality of life, and participation of citizens in the governance of cities. A city can be defined as "smart" when investments in human and social capital, traditional transport, and modern communication infrastructure fuel sustainable economic development and a high quality of life with a wise management of natural resources through participatory governance.

There are other ways to evaluate whether a city is sustainable other than the "smart" criteria. In fact, there are several organizations that rank cities according to sustainability. For example, one credible ranking system is SustainLane U.S. City Rankings.[83] Their report benchmarks each city's performance in 16 areas of urban sustainability. These peer-reviewed rankings track cities working to improve quality of life. Some cities are becoming more self-reliant and better prepared for an uncertain future, while others have been slow to act on opportunities to "green" their municipalities.

Some of the top 10 cities on the SustainLane rankings might surprise you, such as Chicago and New York:

Portland, Oregon
San Francisco, California
Seattle, Washington
Chicago, Illinois
New York, New York
Boston, Massachusetts
Minneapolis, Minnesota
Philadelphia, Pennsylvania
Oakland, California
Baltimore, Maryland

The rankings for these cities were derived from many different sources, including NGOs that specialize in specific environmental areas. In a few cases, government sources and private organization data were part of the overall assessments.

New York City (NYC) is a particularly interesting example. Despite its skyscrapers and congested streets, it is one of the most sustainable cities in the country. NYC's per capita emissions are a third of those in the rest of the country because of public transit use, densely packed buildings, and smaller homes. Still, the city plans to slash GHG emissions by 30 percent by 2030. Mayor Michael Bloomberg unveiled one of the country's most comprehensive sustainability plans (dubbed PlaNYC), made up of 127 separate initiatives. These initiatives include revamping aging infrastructure, planting a million trees over 10 years, and making sure that all city residents live within a 10-minute walk of a park.

New York is also empowering pedestrians through "Summer Streets," a program that closes (either temporarily or permanently) portions of the city to traffic, creating "car-free recreation corridors." In addition to government action, the city boasts many grassroots and neighborhood organizations working to green the city. Sustainable South Bronx is one of the most successful of these. The group, centered in a low-income area of the city, is working on greenways, installing green roofs, and on green job training and placement.

Outside organizations, such as the International Council of Local Environmental Initiatives (ICLEI), often support governments with their sustainability efforts. ICLEI is an association of over 1,220 members who are committed to sustainable development. The members come from 70 different countries and represent more than 569,885,000 people. ICLEI's mission is to build and serve a worldwide movement of local governments to achieve tangible improvements in global sustainability with a special focus on environmental conditions through cumulative local actions. ICLEI provides technical consulting, training, and information services to build capacity, share knowledge, and support local government in the implementation of sustainable development at the local level. Its basic premise is that locally designed initiatives can provide an effective and cost-efficient way to achieve local, national, and global sustainability objectives.[84] ICLEI's general mandate is to build an active and committed municipal membership of local spheres of government (local and regional governments and authorities) as well as international, regional, national, and subnational local government associations.

2. Nongovernmental Organizations

Over the past 15 to 20 years, there has been a significant increase in NGOs that care for the environment as part of their mission. NGOs and not-for-profits have made significant impacts on our world. In general, they take on challenges that are not handled by for-profit businesses and government agencies. For example, they give voice to the poor and provide ways to feed those in need through kitchens funded by donations.

The overall not-for-profit sector is now worth over $1 trillion a year globally.[85] One report suggests that the U.S. nonprofit sector could free up at least $100 billion in additional value by changing its notions of stewardship and its operating practices.[86]

An NGO is a legally constituted organization created by private organizations or people. When NGOs are funded totally or partially by governments, the NGO maintains its nongovernmental status insofar as it excludes government representatives from membership in the organization. NGOs can function domestically or internationally.[87]

International NGOs have a history dating back to at least the mid-19th century. They were important in the antislavery movement and the movement for women's suffrage and reached a peak at the time of the World Disarmament Conference in Switzerland between 1932 and 1937. However, the phrase "nongovernmental organization" only came into popular use with the establishment of the United Nations Organization in 1945. In the United Nations Charter, there is a provision in Article 71 of Chapter 10 for a consultative role for organizations, which are neither governments nor member states; in this article, the term "nongovernmental organizations" was coined. There are numerous alternative ways to refer to NGOs (e.g., independent sector, volunteer sector, civil society, grassroots organizations, transnational social movement organizations, private voluntary organizations, self-help organizations, and non-state actors [NSAs]).

Globalization during the 20th century gave rise to the importance of NGOs. Many problems could not be solved within a nation, so outside organizations began emerging. International treaties and for-profit international organizations (e.g., the World Trade Organization) were perceived as being too centered on the interests of capitalist enterprises. Some argued that, in an attempt to counterbalance this trend, NGOs have risen as a solution to some of these problems. NGOs tend to emphasize humanitarian issues, developmental aid, and sustainable development. NGOs are a heterogeneous group; they exist for a variety of reasons, usually to further the political or social goals of their members or funders. Examples include improving the state of the natural environment, encouraging the observance of human rights, improving the welfare of the disadvantaged, or representing a corporate agenda. NGOs also vary in their methods. Some act primarily as lobbyists, while others primarily conduct programs and activities.

NGOs need healthy relationships with the public to meet their goals. Thus, foundations and charities often use sophisticated public relations campaigns to raise funds and employ effective lobbying techniques with governments. There is also an increasing awareness that business management techniques are crucial. NGOs mobilize public support, voluntary contributions, often have strong links with community groups in developing countries, and often work in areas where government-to-government aid is not possible. NGOs are accepted as a part of the international relations landscape and, while they influence national and multilateral policymaking, increasingly they are more directly involved in local action.

UN Secretary General Kofi Annan formed the Cardoso Panel to assess the integration between the United Nations and civil society organizations. The panel, chaired by former Brazilian President Fernando Cardoso, included a number of prominent people representing governments, private sector companies, NGOs, and academia. The panel recognized that over 2,000 NGOs have consultative status with the UN Economic and Social Council and about 1,400 with the UN Department of Information. This involvement means that NGOs are critical to the functioning of the UN.

Not all people working for NGOs are volunteers. Also, the reasons people volunteer are not necessarily purely altruistic; they might pursue such experiences to enhance their skills, experience, and contacts. For example, Habitat for Humanity volunteers can acquire new relationships and a visibility uncharacteristic of other work.

3. Universities

Universities are different from other organizations due to their power structure and educational mission. Their attention to environmental sustainability is relatively new and, until recently, was limited to the operations of facilities. Several organizations, such as the American Society for Sustainability in Higher Education, are developing quality assessments specifically for colleges and universities. These standards are designed to become more widely accepted and to create pressures on higher education institutions to act environmentally responsibly. If the assessments adhere to principles similar to the ones advocated in this book (and correlate to campus strategy), they will influence campus stakeholders and yield a more environmentally sustainable organization.

Universities are unique environments as they contain multiple power structures with faculty, administration, and students all involved in parts of the operations. Universities also tend to have decentralized decision-making processes that do not usually afford the opportunity to have centrally organized programs. This uniqueness calls for assessments that differ from other types of organizations. Additionally, many colleges and universities focus on sustainability and "green" initiatives for competitive reasons.[88]

Universities have tried to organize uniform agreements around commitments to sustainability. The Talloires Declaration (TD) was the first such attempt. It is a 10-point action plan for incorporating sustainability and environmental literacy into teaching, research, operations, and outreach at colleges and universities. It was initiated in 1990 at an international conference in Talloires, France, and has been signed by over 350 university presidents and chancellors in over 40 countries. The outcomes of these efforts are unclear and some data show that universities have not met their obligations.

Second Nature, a nonprofit organization, works with higher education leaders to incorporate sustainability into curricula and student and faculty practices. Second Nature was established in 1993 in Boston, Massachusetts. It is the primary supporter of the American College and University Presidents' Climate Commitment (ACUPCC). The ACUPCC provides a framework and support to help enable U.S. colleges and universities to implement comprehensive plans in pursuit of climate improvement through CO_2 reductions. The organization was officially unveiled in June 2007 and currently has 683 signatories on its commitment statement.

A partner with Second Nature, the Association for the Advancement of Sustainability in Higher Education (AASHE), was established in 2006 as the first professional higher education association for the campus sustainability community. AASHE works with all sectors of a campus, integrating sustainability in campus governance, education, and research. Other attempts to aid universities in their missions to become environmentally sustainable are:

- The World Resources Institute;
- The Consortium for Environmental Education in Medicine;
- The Association for University Leaders for a Sustainable Future.

Despite these attempts, sustainability programs are still in their infancy at most universities. For example, many of the important university commitments are less than 10 years old, as are the organizations listed in this section. Therefore, methodologies that measure sustainability have not been fully developed. The following shows a few methodologies for measuring sustainability on college and university campuses.

Sustainability Tracking, Assessment, and Rating System

STARS (Sustainability Tracking, Assessment, and Rating System) is a new, relatively pervasive approach used by universities in the United States. It is supported by the AASHE. STARS is a self-reporting tool that requires a university to collect sustainability information on a standard form that is submitted to the AASHE, which then assigns the university a quality rating.[89] STARS is currently used by over 250 colleges and universities.[90]

STARS has four analysis categories: education and research; operations; planning, administration, and engagement; and innovation. The ratings are highest to lowest (Platinum, Gold, Silver, and Bronze) with one category entitled "STARS reporter" for those that want to disclose information but not pursue a rating. These ratings are modeled after the LEED categories for buildings.

One of the benefits of STARS is that it allows universities to compare themselves to other universities and colleges and discover best practices among all of the STARS members. However, one of the drawbacks is its self-report format and lack of significant adaptation to a particular organizational mission.

National Wildlife Federation's State of the Campus Environment

The National Wildlife Federation (NWF) has issued reports based on results of surveys sent to every university in the United States. The stated goal has been to "track trends and advance knowledge about environmental stewardship, sustainability activities and related curricular offerings in higher education."[91] The survey contained assessments in three broad, overarching categories—management, academics, and operations—which were then divided into subcategories. The report provided enough information so that universities could compare their responses to other institutions and determine best practices for becoming sustainable. Therefore, while this report was not individualized, it did provide some suggestions for how schools might improve. This report eventually became known as the College Sustainability Report Card.

The College Sustainability Report Card claims to be the only independent evaluation of campus and endowment sustainability activities at colleges and universities in the United States and Canada. In contrast to an academic focus on sustainability in research and teaching, the Report Card claims it examines colleges and universities, as institutions, through the lens of sustainability. The Green Report Card.org website and the College Sustainability Report Card are both initiatives of the Sustainable Endowments Institute. The Institute is a nonprofit organization engaged in research and education to advance sustainability in campus operations and endowment practices.

What Makes for Effective Assessments

All of these methodologies have attempted to elevate the conversation about sustainability and to provide some insights with respect to campuses and their environmental sustainability efforts. These measurements require a lot of research before they are valid and reliable tools.

Effective measurement systems have specific characteristics to increase their usefulness. These characteristics should cover topics reflective of the organization's significant economic, social, and environmental outcomes, and they should substantively assess organizational practices from various perspectives. Thus, a quality assessment identifies associated stakeholders and explains, in the report, how it has responded to their reasonable expectations and interests. Assessments require a certain mass of data before they are considered valid representations of an organization's state of sustainability.

Quality reports happen in a context; thus, they are not divorced from the overall organizational strategy and its boundaries of operation. Unfortunately, this is where most current assessment tools fail. Clarity, timeliness, balance (positive and negative commentary), and reliability are other important factors in quality assessments.[92]

In sum, each of these methodologies needs much more rigorous analysis to accurately measure a campus's environmental sustainability.[93] Also, most of the current assessment tools are insensitive to the strategic directions of colleges and universities. Universities are unique environments, and they can influence future workforces, generate new knowledge, and be models and facilitators within their communities. As sustainability assessments improve, universities will have the potential to be models for other types of organizations and to increase their own sustainability efforts.

4. Emerging Markets

The term "emerging markets" was first introduced by economists at the International Finance Corporation (IFC) in 1981.[94] References to "emerging markets" since that time have been frequent; however, the associated definitions have varied widely.

- Some have poverty criteria (e.g., low-income country, below-average living standards, or not industrialized).
- Others refer to capital markets such as low stock market turnover.
- Still others refer to growth potential such as recent economic growth.[95]

A fundamental premise about emerging markets is that they reflect those transactional arenas where buyers and sellers are not easily or efficiently able to come together. Ideally, every economy would provide a range of institutions to facilitate the functioning of markets; however, developing countries fall short in a number of ways. These institutional voids make a market "emerging" and are a prime source of higher transaction costs and operating challenges. "Institutional void" refers to the missing market intermediaries. Thus, these markets operate differently from mature markets. For example, it would take you two to three times longer to start a new business in emerging markets (e.g., Brazil, Indonesia, and the Republic of Korea) than in the United Kingdom or the United States.[96] In Brazil, it would actually take you 10 times longer. Thus, markets can be placed along a continuum, from entirely dysfunctional to highly developed. This fact implies that every market has some degree of emergence.

While this might be a generalization, most emerging markets tend to have missing institutions and thus lack rules and regulations related to the environment; if these rules do exist, there is oftentimes no one to enforce them. The focus on economic growth (and creating the necessary economic institutions) can push environmental concerns to the bottom of emerging markets' priorities.[97]

Emerging markets are of great interest to corporate executives, scholars, governments, and supranational organizations. Many in business and government are convinced that a significant part of world growth will come from emerging markets. This growth will result from growing middle classes and from innovations from emerging market companies. Still, emerging markets and their high growth rates pose unique challenges, especially in relation to environmental outcomes as economies grow.

Some emerging markets are world-class innovators in attacking social and environmental sustainability. Brazil, for example, created Bolsa Família, a stipend for poor families paid on the condition that the family's children go to school and are vaccinated. Brazil influenced over 20 other countries to adopt similar schemes.[98] Brazil's Curitiba, a town in the state of Paraná, is another innovative example. The city's most famous figure, Jaime Lerner, led an effort to build parks instead of canals for flood control, made a walkable city, built rapid transit linked to a light rail system, and gave citizens money and vouchers for trash.[99]

Globalization has been a result of the liberalization of trade and movement of resources (e.g., labor and technological changes that facilitate ever-decreasing costs of communication) and a global economy tends to decrease poverty and increase opportunities for countries still considered as emerging. Because of these factors, markets are not only emerging within the first-world context but also in parts of the world that previously were unable to be competitive in the global market.[100]

U.S.-based Monsanto Company faced unique challenges in Brazil. It was a pioneer in developing biotechnology in the agricultural sector (creating products such as seeds that could increase crop yields). In the United States, the company relied on a sophisticated infrastructure to develop and protect its technology. This infrastructure included science, highly trained labor, and a court system that would protect the company's patents if needed. The company found that its successful soybean seeds (which comprise 50 percent of the market share in the United States) would be ideal for the Brazilian market; however, in 1998, it tried to enter the market and was impeded by court cases and local environmental opposition. Monsanto challenged the injunction but found that the courts in Brazil were delayed and unresponsive.

Also, mature-market companies often move production to emerging markets because they can cut costs by not following the rules and expectations that exist elsewhere. This is a major concern about emerging markets and is the reason environmental sustainability efforts should be strongly focused on these markets. For example, Apple has been singled out for pollution throughout its supply chain in China.[101] Apple's 2011 Supplier Responsibility Report showed violations from 36 audits. Another example comes from a recent report showing that Meiko Electronics Plants in Guangzhou and Wuhan produced several contaminates and were fined several times for pollution-generating activities. For example, the copper content in sediment samples taken from the Nantaizi Lake (where Meiko discharges its effluents) reached as high as 4,270 mg/kg. This is 56 to 193 times the amount found in the sediment in the major lakes in the middle of the Yangtze River.

Case Revisited: Habitat for Humanity and Its Future

Habitat for Humanity shows the potential of NGOs; it has had a tremendous impact on communities, has become one of the top 10 homebuilders in the United States, and provides innovative and affordable housing for people in great need. Habitat for Humanity's challenges are similar to other organizations (e.g., management, balancing local and global mandates, and funding). Yet, its ability to influence communities and engage volunteers to deliver its services makes the organization unique. Also, its sustainability innovations can be models for all homebuilders.

Although Habitat for Humanity is a mature organization, it continues to search for ways to innovate, grow, and maintain its entrepreneurial mindset. While the addition of sustainability into its mix of homebuilding and renovation work might help it to remain relevant and fulfill its social mission, it may ultimately need to completely remake itself as an organization. This transformation might mean exploring new avenues of growth such as developing a for-profit homebuilding arm. These changes need to be considered carefully so that Habitat does not lose it core constituents and support.

Chapter Summary

The purpose of this chapter was to explore unique situations for environmental sustainability work. **Business models** are expressions of how firms make money and the value proposition of a product or service to a customer. Most analyses of business models identify nine components: customer segmentation, value propositions, channels, customer relationships, revenue streams, key resources, key activities, key partnerships, and cost structure. A relatively new and unique business model includes responsible investing in socially, environmentally, and economically sustainable investments. These types of investments have a greater focus on social and environmental considerations. Funds related to these causes might be relatively new, but they are doing well compared to the overall market.

Entrepreneurs create new businesses and also provide a unique context for environmental sustainability. Relevant to our approach to strategy are social entrepreneurs who use business solutions to solve large, intractable problems in society. Their dominant logic is different from other businesses, focusing on social problems in lieu of returns to shareowners.

Governments, NGOs, universities, and emerging markets also create specific contexts for environmental sustainability. This chapter included information about municipalities, which have unique challenges related to their operations and setting standards for their communities. They can have profound impacts on their communities if they provide incentives, regulation, and support for businesses and homeowners. NGOs are unique in that they operate outside of the government, yet function as an influential bridge between domestic, national, and international entities. This provides NGOs with unique opportunities to influence sustainability.

Universities also play a unique role in generating knowledge and in educating the future workforce. They have recently engaged in significant work related to their own environmental sustainability; however, this work has been relatively slow compared to industrial organizations. Finally, emerging markets present unique challenges. One major issue is the push for sustainable development and the attempt to mitigate pollution as these markets develop. Government policy designers and business owners are trying to find ways to mitigate anticipated pollution without restricting access to raw materials and sources of energy, which are necessary for growth.

These contexts are unique, present unique challenges, and could be high leverage points for work on environmental sustainability. We may find that these unique situations (i.e., government agencies, NGOs, universities, and entrepreneurial firms) are where the most impactful innovations develop. They may develop solutions to our world's environmental problems that for-profit businesses are hard-pressed to both recognize and address.

Terms to Know

Business models: the specification of how an organization creates, delivers, and captures value

Entrepreneur: somebody who offers an innovative solution to an unrecognized problem, without regard to resources currently controlled

Nongovernmental organization: a legally constituted organization created by private organizations or people, with no participation or representation by any government

Social entrepreneurs: people who tap into vast reserves of ambition, creativity, and resourcefulness to solve large, intractable problems

Social responsibility investing: the use of socially responsible and environmentally and economically sustainable criteria for investments

Profile: Paul Hawken[102]

Chapter 12 defines the entrepreneur and discusses their importance within the firm. The dynamic, entrepreneurial process of vision, change, and creation are embodied by Paul Hawken. Throughout his life he has responded to many social and environmental pressures using the firm as a strategy model to create industry and perpetuate innovation. His story reflects the opportunities for entrepreneurial activity when supported by free markets, social groups, universities, and venture capitalists.

Figure 12.4 Paul Hawken, University of Portland Commencement Speech 2009. Photo Credit: ServiceSpace[103]

In 1965, it seemed that social pressures in the United States were nearing a tipping point. The war in Vietnam was quickly escalating, the Civil Rights Movement was emboldened by new leaders, and a new American generation was awakening; a generation that would challenge the status quo and forever change the country. That year a 19-year-old Paul Hawken joined Martin Luther King Jr.'s staff in Selma, Alabama where "he registered press, issued credentials, gave updates and interviews on national radio, and acted as marshal for the final"[104] March on Montgomery.

A year later, in 1966, Hawken responded to emerging environmental pressures by creating the United States' first natural foods company in Boston, Massachusetts; as the President and Founder of Erewhon, Hawken focused exclusively on selling organic produce, dairy, beans, eggs, juices, and condiments.[105] By 1973, the company had grown extensively obtaining contracts with farmers in 37 states on 56,000 acres that supplied Erewhon's 3,000 wholesale accounts.

Since 1979, Hawken has been a crucial part of growing seven successful firms including the Natural Capital Institute (NCI) which he began in 2000.[106] The NCI's mission is to "provide the highest quality research in the dynamics between society and the biosphere in order to move humanity to a just and environmentally benign existence." The Institute's research has shifted from environmental funding, water resources, and policy innovation to SRI and CSR. NCI is creating the world's first SRI mutual fund database which will develop and annotate a list of the 100 Best Companies around the world. Hawken is also a best-selling author. His books have been published in 27 languages in over 50 countries selling more than 2 million copies worldwide.[107]

Appendix 12.1. Relevant NGOs and IGOs

Organization	Headquarters	Summary
World Business Council For Sustainable Development (WBCSD)[108]	Geneva, Switzerland	WBCSD is a CEO-led, global association of some 200 companies dealing exclusively with business and sustainable development. The Council provides a platform for companies to explore sustainable development, share knowledge, experiences, and best practices, and to advocate business positions on these issues in a variety of forums; working with governments, nongovernmental, and intergovernmental organizations.
World Trade Organization (WTO)[109]	Geneva, Switzerland	WTO is a global international organization dealing with the rules of trade between nations. At its heart are the WTO agreements, negotiated and signed by the bulk of the world's trading nations and ratified in their parliaments. The goal is to help producers of goods and services, exporters, and importers conduct their business.
International Emissions Trading Association (IETA)[110]	Geneva, Switzerland	The IETA is a nonprofit business organization created in June 1999 to establish a functional international framework for trading in GHG emission reductions.
EURELECTRIC	Brussels	EURELECTRIC together with the International Electricity Partnership (IEP) has produced a roadmap as a global vision to be shared by electric power industries in various countries including developing countries.
Edison Electric Institute (EEI)[111]	Washington DC	The EEI is the association of U.S. Shareholder-Owned Electric Companies. Organized in 1933, EEI works closely with all of its members, representing their interests and advocating equitable policies in legislative and regulatory arenas.
Electric Power Research Institute Inc. (EPRI)[112]	Palo Alto, California	The EPRI conducts R&D relating to the generation, delivery, and use of electricity for the benefit of the public. An independent nonprofit organization, EPRI brings together its scientists and engineers as well as experts from academia and industry to help address challenges in electricity, including reliability, efficiency, health, safety, and the environment.
BUSINESSEUROPE[113]	Brussels	BUSINESSEUROPE plays a crucial role in Europe as the main horizontal business organization at the EU level. Through its 40 member federations, BUSINESSEUROPE represents 20 million companies from 34 countries. Its main task is to ensure that companies' interests are represented and defended vis-à-vis the European institutions with the principal aim of preserving and strengthening corporate competitiveness.
Nippon Keidanren		Nippon Keidanren (Japan Business Federation) is a comprehensive economic organization with a membership of more than 1,600 comprised of companies, industrial associations, and regional economic organizations. Its mission is to accelerate growth of Japan's and the world economy and to strengthen the corporations to create value to transform the Japanese economy into one that is sustainable and driven by the private sector, by encouraging the idea of individuals and local communities.
National Business Initiative[114]	Johannesburg, South Africa	The National Business Initiative which has just celebrated its 15th anniversary is a not-for-profit organization with a business membership base of 140 leading corporations. It plays a bridging role at strategic and programmatic level between business, government, international, and local partners to shape thinking and action toward a sustainable future. Focus areas include climate change, energy efficiency, water, skills development, enterprise development, and corporate citizenship.

Organization	Location	Description
Confederation of Indian Industry (CII)[115]	Delhi	The CII works to create and sustain an environment conducive to the growth of industry in India, partnering industry and government alike through advisory and consultative processes. CII is a non-government, not-for-profit, industry-led, and industry-managed organization, playing a proactive role in India's development process. Founded over 115 years ago, it is India's premier business association, with a direct membership of over 8,100 organizations from the private as well as public sectors, including SMEs and MNCs, and an indirect membership of over 90,000 companies from around 400 national and regional associations.
Federation of Indian Chambers of Commerce and Industry (FICCI)[116]	New Delhi	FICCI, the apex industry organization in India, is the leader in policy thinking and change and is in the vanguard of nation building. Established in 1927 and with a nationwide membership of over 1,500 corporate companies and over 500 chambers of commerce and business associations, FICCI espouses the shared vision of Indian businesses and speaks directly and indirectly for over 250,000 business units.
International Institute for Sustainable Development (IISD)[117]	Winnipeg	IISD is a non-partisan, charitable organization specializing in policy research, analysis, and information exchange. The institute champions global sustainable development through innovation, research, and relationships that span the entire world.
Carbon Disclosure Project (CDP)[118]	London	CDP is an independent nonprofit organization holding the largest database of corporate climate change information in the world.
California Climate Action Registry[119]	Los Angeles	California Climate Action Registry is a private nonprofit originally formed by the State of California. It serves as a voluntary GHG emissions registry to protect and promote early actions to reduce GHG emissions by organizations.

Visualizing: Chapter 12 explains the challenging process of entrepreneurial vision. How did Paul Hawken take his experiences with social and environmental pressures and use them to understand customer problems and the role of dominant designs or standards? Where could you look for data today that will help you understand future customer problems? Do you have an entrepreneurial vision that will change today's dominant designs or standards? How can identifying these components give you a competitive edge into today's markets?

Questions and Critical Thinking

1   Each of the unique contexts (discussed in this chapter) has special considerations when a firm's leadership mounts a strategy while utilizing environmental sustainability as a lens. Compare and contrast two of these contexts and the unique opportunities that they present for using environmental sustainability principles and practices.

2   Many NGOs support environmental sustainability and see partnerships with business organizations as one way to generate change and impact. Consider a large NGO (e.g., the Nature Conservancy, Sierra Club, or Environmental Defense Fund) and list its partnerships with businesses. Do these relationships seem to have a positive impact on both the NGO and the business organization? How would you measure this impact?

3   Who is responsible for the environmental impacts of businesses located within emerging markets? For example, is Monsanto and Bayer responsible for its suppliers and the suppliers' environmental outcomes? Should U.S. law hold Apple accountable for these impacts (even though these outcomes occurred in a different country)?

4   Consider other unique contexts for environmental sustainability strategies, such as (a) extremely poor nations and communities and (b) Antarctica, which has no government (although various countries have attempted to claim sovereignty in certain regions). How do organizations operate in these contexts? What environmental standards should be used in the absence of clear guidelines?

Notes

1   This case is adapted from M. Nestor and D. S. Fogel, *Habitat for Humanity: Implementing a Global Strategy Locally*, GlobaLens Case No. 1–429–170 (Ann Arbor: University of Michigan, William Davidson Institute, May 16, 2011).

2   Social Investment Forum Foundation, *2010 Report on Socially Responsible Investing Trends in the United States* (Washington, DC: U.S. SIF, 2010).

3   www.institutionalinvestor.com/Article/2862601/People/Research/4002/Overview.html#.UkQoINLYfvE (accessed September 26, 2013); J. Gittelsohn, "Calpers Invests in New-Home Project as Land Values Rise," Bloomberg, September 12, 2013, www.bloomberg.com/news/2013-09-11/calpers-invests-in-new-home-project-as-land-values-rise.html (accessed September 26, 2013).

4   S. Shen and G. Wildau, "China State Pension Fund Gets Local Mandates," Reuters, January 17, 2012, http://uk.reuters.com/article/2012/01/17/china-pension-idUKL3E8CH02Q20120117 (accessed March 23, 2012).

5   I. Rose-Smith, "CalPERS Readies New Responsible Investing Plan," *Institutional Investor*, July 10, 2011.

6   USSIF: The Forum for Sustainable and Responsible Investment, "Report on US Sustainable, Responsible, and Impact Investing Trends 2014," www.ussif.org/trends (accessed December 22, 2015).

7   Social Investment Forum Foundation, *2010 Report on Socially Responsible Investing Trends in the United States*, 15.

8   M. L. Wald and J. M. Broder, "Utility Shelves Ambitious Plan to Limit Carbon," *The New York Times*, July 13, 2011, www.nytimes.com/2011/07/14/business/energy-environment/utility-shelves-plan-to-capture-carbon-dioxide.html?_r=1&ref=johnmbroder (accessed January 5, 2012).

9   L. H. Lovins and B. Cohen, *Climate Capitalism: Capitalism in the Age of Climate Change* (New York: Hill and Wang, 2011), 9–10.

10 Sovereign Wealth Fund Institute, "Fund Rankings," www.swfinstitute.org/fund-rankings/ (accessed September 25, 2013).

11 J. Cosgrave, "Has the World's Largest Sovereign Wealth Fund Peaked?" (CNBC, October 27, 2015) http://www.cnbc.com/2015/10/27/has-the-worlds-largest-sovereign-wealth-fund-peaked.html (accessed December 22, 2015).

12 Sovereign Wealth Fund Institute, "Fund Rankings"; European Federation of Public Service Unions, "Chinese Sovereign Wealth Fund: Questionable Ethics Says EWC GdfSuez," news release, October 17, 2011, www.epsu.org/a/8056. (accessed September 25, 2013).

13 E. Steigum, "Sovereign Wealth Funds for Macroeconomic Purposes" (Centre for Monetary Economics, BI Norwegian Business School, Working Paper Series, 4/12, December 2012) http://www.bi.edu/cmeFiles/Working%20 paper%202012%2004%20combined%20v2.pdf (accessed December 22, 2015).

14 "Global Heroes: A Special Report on Entrepreneurship," *The Economist*, March 14, 2009, www.economist.com/ node/13216025 (accessed January 20, 2013).

15 C. J. Schramm, *The Entrepreneurial Imperative: How America's Economic Miracle Will Reshape the World (and Change Your Life)* (New York: HarperCollins, 2006), 4.

16 D. F. Kuratko and D. B. Audretsch, "Strategic Entrepreneurship: Exploring Different Perspectives of an Emerging Concept," *Entrepreneurship Theory and Practice* 33, no. 1 (January 2009): 1–17.

17 "Global Heroes."

18 Statistics of U.S. Business, "U.S. and States Totals," http://www.census.gov/econ/susb/ (accessed August 27, 2015).

19 U.S. Census Bureau, "Statistics of U.S. Businesses (SUSB): Latest SUSB Annual Data," data for U.S. & states, totals and U.S., all industries (Washington, DC, 2010), www.census.gov/econ/susb/ (accessed January 20, 2013); U.S. Census Bureau, "Nonemployer Statistics," www.census.gov/econ/nonemployer/ (accessed January 20, 2013); U.S. Census Bureau, "Statistics about Business Size (including Small Business)," www.census.gov/econ/smallbus.html (accessed January 20, 2013).

20 U.S. Census Bureau, *Statistical Abstracts of the United States: 2012* (Washington, DC: 2011): Table 765: Firm Births and Deaths by Employment Size of Enterprise: 1990 to 2007, https://www.census.gov/ces/pdf/2010-2011_Research_ Report.pdf (accessed December 22, 2015). U.S. Small Business Administration, "Firm Size Data," specifically, "Statistics of U.S. Businesses" and "Nonemployer Statistics" sections, www.sba.gov/advocacy/849/12162 (accessed January 15, 2012).

21 Ibid.

22 M. S. Cordon, J. Wincent, J. Singh, and M. Drnovsek, "The Nature and Experience of Entrepreneurial Passion," *Academy of Management Review* 34, no. 3 (2009): 511–532.

23 S. D. Sarasvathy, *Effectuation: Elements of Entrepreneurial Expertise* (Cheltenham: Edward Elgar, 2008).

24 J. Iversen, R. Jørgensen, and N. Malchow-Møller, "Defining and Measuring Entrepreneurship," *Foundations and Trends in Entrepreneurship* 4, no. 1 (2008): 1–63.

25 S. A. Shane, *Finding Fertile Ground: Identifying Extraordinary Opportunities for New Ventures* (Upper Saddle River, NJ: Wharton School Publishing, 2005).

26 Diffusion of new ideas is higher for profitable ideas requiring low levels of specific capital. Technologically complex, hard-to-articulate innovations favor innovators over imitators. Licensing may be a way to credibly commit to users a moderate price path to encourage adoption of a new product. Here are some alternative models and considerations important to technology development:

- Networks: using a firm's network as a basis of competitiveness, rather than creating an organization that is self-contained.
- Geographic clusters or agglomeration economies.
- Disaggregating the value chain.
- What is the role of the government? Should the government protect or invest in emerging technologies.

27 Most products develop dominant designs; some products go beyond this dominant design to the establishment of uniform technical standards. Network externalities are whenever the value of a product to an individual customer depends on the number of other users of that product (see discussion on demand-side increasing returns). These arise when products are networked together (telephone); availability of complementary products (lens and camera); and economizing on switching costs (widely used products decrease individual costs such as certain software). In the long-run, innovators in most markets are eventually displaced in a Schumpterian process of creative destruction. Creative destruction is the process whereby old sources of competitive advantage are destroyed and replaced with new ones. The essence of entrepreneurship is the exploitation of the "shocks" or discontinuities that destroy existing sources of advantage. Successful innovators invest in creative search. In most technologies, the minimum efficient scale for innovation is moderate. Inasmuch as managers are agents in the firm and not owners, they will not face the right incentives to innovate. In most organizations, management reward structures discourage innovation by punishing failure more than rewarding success. Creating financial and cultural ownership in the firm by managers will lead to more innovation. Shared responsibility for projects encourages risk taking. Innovators may license innovations to rivals who are expected to be more efficient in the exploitation of that innovation due to the presence of complementary assets. Licensing may increase the speed with which the innovation enters the market. Innovators faced with capacity constraints will typically find it profitable to license small innovations to a rival. Industries where competition centers on innovation and the application of technology provide some of the most challenging and complex situations for applying strategy concepts and analysis.

28 W. J. Baumol, *The Free-Market Innovation Machine: Analyzing the Growth Miracle of Capitalism* (Princeton, NJ: Princeton University Press, 2002), 3

29 Entrance strategy may vary according to the competitive situation. The issue for the entrant is how to avoid retaliation. Consider the following tactics:

- oligopolistic competition;
- routines at the firm level;
- productive entrepreneurship;
- rule of law;
- technology selling and trading;
- firms must innovate to survive;
- firms embed competencies in routine behavior—reduces the firm's risk.

The incumbent firms have the advantage because they can get large returns from small improvements and minor technical improvements; innovation is the primary basis of competition. The engine of growth comes from a surprisingly small number of countries and industries.

30 C. M. Christensen and M. E. Raynor, *The Innovator's Solution: Creating and Sustaining Successful Growth* (Boston, MA: Harvard Business School, 2005), 86–93.
31 G. A. Moore, *Dealing with Darwin: How Great Companies Innovate at Every Phase of Their Evolution* (New York: Portfolio, 2005), 13–28.
32 Shane, *Finding Fertile Ground*, 125–145.
33 Preemptive patenting may serve to reduce entry into a market. Patenting may reveal important information to rivals.
34 R. C. Young and J. D. Francis, "Entrepreneurship and Innovation in Small Manufacturing Firms," *Social Science Quarterly* 72, no. 1 (March 1991): 149–162.
35 Christensen and Raynor, *The Innovator's Solution*.
36 J. W. Mullins, *The New Business Road Test: What Entrepreneurs and Executives Should Do Before Writing a Business Plan*, 2nd ed. (New York: Prentice Hall/Financial Times, 2006), 245–253.
37 Customer Intimacy Innovations: these are in order of migrating from closest to the product to closest to the customer. In general, this zone is keeping the product basically the same and changing a few features or ways the customer experiences the product.
38 Focuses on differentiating the supply side; the benefits are lowered costs and faster time to market.
39 Using internal resources to gain an innovation. Generally, the company stays within the same sector but repositions its offering.
40 Disruptive: new market categories based on discontinuous technology change or a disruptive business model (e.g., Napster, Apple iTunes).
41 Structural modifications to an existing offering to create distinctive subcategories (e.g., minivan introduction, running shoes, and computers for children).
42 Extracts costs from materials and manufacturing of an established offering without changing external properties (e.g., TVs, PCs, and cell phones).
43 New markets for existing products by finding unexploited uses for them (e.g., use of fault-tolerant computers for ATMs and Apple computers for desktop publishing).
44 Changing features closest to customer experience with little impact on the actual product or service (e.g., navigation systems in cars and Teflon in frying pans).
45 Lowers the costs of integrating elements of a system or disparate parts (e.g., home entertainment centers and all-in-one printers).
46 Comparing and contrasting these two methods is critical. Most observers agree that companies ultimately have to use organic growth to be continuously innovative.
47 Differentiating through changes to features and functions. Must be fast to market (e.g., hybrid engines, cameras in cell phones, and flat-screen technologies).
48 Changes to the marketing mix other than products (e.g., new channels and pricing).
49 Usual Six Sigma approach or value chain analysis (e.g., Dell and Walmart).
50 Linking with other parts of the value chain or with complementary products and services (e.g., allowing PCs to be clones of IBM machines through software and chip designs).
51 Change the experience that the customer has (e.g., restaurants, business hotels, and coffeehouses).
52 Building away from commoditizing. Moving up the chain (such as with answering machines to voicemail and component companies becoming systems integration service providers).
53 L. Busch, *Standards: Recipes for Reality* (Boston, MA: MIT Press, 2011).
54 D. Besanko et al., *Economics of Strategy*, 3rd ed. (Hoboken, NJ: John Wiley, 2004), see pp. 465–477. "Early-mover advantages" are those that can be gained by moving early into a market: learning curve—can gain more learning than competitors; network externalities—when the more consumers that buy a product create demand-side increasing returns, hence creating an advantage to early movers; reputation and buyer uncertainty—once a firm's reputation has been crafted, the firm will have an advantage competing for new customers, increasing the number

of customers who have had successful trials, and thus, further strengthening its reputation; buyer switching costs—if buyers incur substantial switching costs, early movers can gain an advantage. Early movers may fail to achieve the expected returns because of the lack of complementary resources (as we saw in the digital imaging industry). Early movers may bet on the wrong technologies, even if they have a patent. Finally, if adoption rates are very slow, first movers may be at a disadvantage, having to sustain their presence without return. If adoption rates are rapid and imitation rates slow because of patents or other reasons, then early movers make more sense, as in the case of pharmaceutical companies. These companies try to speed up their patent process because the adoption rate is very rapid for many drugs, having proven their effectiveness in terms of impact and market in clinical trials. Finally, first movers are best when they can get their standard accepted—if they can't they might want to wait.

55 Some young companies are successful if a dominant design exists. If the industry has not yet converged on a dominant design, then it is hard to say whether or not a new firm will capture the returns from a new product or service introduction. Success before a dominant design is in place depends on what product designs are favored by different niche markets and what design ultimately becomes dominant. If you come up with a design that appeals to a valuable niche market or a design that ultimately becomes the dominant design, then you can capture the returns from the introduction of new products or services.

56 Co-authored by Michael Aper, Master of Arts in Sustainability candidate at Wake Forest University.

57 "About Us," Rodale Institute, http://rodaleinstitute.org/about-us/ (accessed January 17, 2015).

58 Megan, "Rodale Institute and St. Luke's University Health Network Partner to Provide Organic Produce to Patients, Staff, and Visitors," Rodale Institute®, July 18, 2014, http://rodaleinstitute.org/rodale-institute-and-st-lukes-university-health-network-partner-to-provide-organic-produce-to-to-patients-staff-and-visitors/(accessed January 17, 2015).

59 "St. Luke's Rodale Institute Organic Farm," St. Luke's University Health Network, http://www.slhn.org/organicfarm (accessed January 17, 2015).

60 R. Cohen, "The Organic Fable," *The New York Times*: The Opinion Pages, September 6, 2012, http://www.nytimes.com/2012/09/07/opinion/roger-cohen-the-organic-fable.html (accessed January 17, 2015).

61 K. Change, "Stanford Scientists Cast Doubt on Advantages of Organic Meat and Produce," *The New York Times*, September 3, 2012, http://www.nytimes.com/2012/09/04/science/earth/study-questions-advantages-of-organic-meat-and-produce.html?_r=0 (accessed January 17, 2015).

62 "The Farming Systems Trial," Rodale Institute, http://rodaleinstitute.org/assets/FSTbooklet.pdf (accessed January 18, 2015), 4.

63 For a discussion of this model, see C. Heath and D. Heath, *Made to Stick: Why Some Ideas Survive and Others Die* (New York: Random House, 2007) to increase your knowledge of some of these ideas.

64 J. G. Dees and B. B. Anderson, "For-Profit Social Ventures," in M. L. Kourilsky and W. B. Walstad (eds.), *Social Entrepreneurship* (Dublin: Senate Hall Academic Publishing, 2003): 1–26.

65 Throughout history such individuals have pioneered solutions to seemingly intractable social problems, fundamentally improving the lives of countless individuals as well as forever changing the way social systems operate. Among them are Florence Nightingale, who transformed hygiene practices at hospitals, dramatically reducing death rates; Maria Montessori, who created a revolutionary educational method that supports each child's unique development; and more recently, Muhammad Yunus, who began offering microloans to impoverished people in Bangladesh in 1976 to allow them to become economically self-sufficient, a model that has been replicated in 58 countries around the world. So while social entrepreneurship isn't a new concept, it is gaining renewed currency in a world characterized by a growing divide between the haves and have-nots.

66 J. G. Dees, "The Meaning of 'Social Entrepreneurship'" (Durham, NC: Center for the Advancement of Social Entrepreneurship, Duke University, 2001), https://entrepreneurship.duke.edu/news-item/the-meaning-of-social-entrepreneurship/ (accessed December 22, 2015); J. Austin, H. Stevenson, and J. Wei-Skillern, "Social and Commercial Entrepreneurship: Same, Different or Both?" *Entrepreneurship Theory and Practice* 30, no. 1 (January 2006): 1–22.

67 M. H. Morris, D. F. Kuratko, and J. G. Covin, *Corporate Entrepreneurship and Innovation*, 2nd ed. (Mason, OH: Thomson/South-Western, 2008).

68 *Source:* Adapted from P. A. Dacin, M. T. Dacin, and M. Matear, "Social Entrepreneurship: Why We Don't Need a New Theory and How We Move Forward from Here," *The Academy of Management Perspectives* 24, no. 3 (2010): 37–57; and S. A. Zahra, E. Gedajlovic, D. O. Neubaum, and J. M. Shulman, "A Typology of Social Entrepreneurs: Motives, Search Processes, and Ethical Challenges," *Journal of Business Venturing* 24, no. 5 (2009): 519–532.

69 C. Seelos and J. Mair, "Social Entrepreneurship: Creating New Business Models to Serve the Poor," *Business Horizons* 48, no. 5 (May–June 2005): 241–246; S. Hamm, "Capitalism with a Human Face," *BusinessWeek*, December 8, 2008, 48–53; S. Hamm, "Social Entrepreneurs Turn Business Sense to Good," *BusinessWeek*, November 24, 2008, www.businessweek.com/magazine/content/08_49/b4111048005937.htm (accessed May 12, 2011).

70 J. A. Phills Jr., K. Deiglmeier, and D. T. Miller, "Rediscovering Social Innovation," *Stanford Social Innovation Review* 6 (Fall 2008): 34–44.

71 M. Yunus, *Banker to the Poor* (New York: Public Affairs, 1999); M. Yunus, *Creating a World Without Poverty: Social Business and the Future of Capitalism* (New York: Public Affairs, 2007); C. K. Prahalad, *The Fortune at the Bottom of the Pyramid: Eradicating Poverty Through Profits* (Upper Saddle River, NJ: Wharton School Publishing, 2006);

P. Smith and E. Thurman, *A Billion Bootstraps: Microcredit, Barefoot Banking, and the Business Solution for Ending Poverty* (New York: McGraw-Hill, 2007).

72 Nutriset, "Plumpy' Nut®: Ready-to-use therapeutic food (RUTF)," www.nutriset.fr/en/product-range/produit-par-produit/plumpy-nut-ready-to-use-therapeutic-food-rutf.html (accessed September 26, 2013).

73 S. Stecklow and J. Bandler, "A Little Laptop with Big Ambitions," *The Wall Street Journal*, November 24, 2007, http://online.wsj.com/article/SB119586754115002717.html (accessed September 26, 2013).

74 WaterHealth International, "Our Solution," www.waterhealth.com/our-solution (accessed January 21, 2013).

75 D. Chiras, "Habitat for Humanity Builds Green Homes," *Mother Earth News,* April/May 2003, www.motherearth news.com/green-homes/habitat-for-humanity-builds-green-homes.aspx#axzz2g0tVOnbQ (accessed September 26, 2013); B. Wargo, "Habitat for Humanity Builds First Green Homes," *Las Vegas Sun*, April 30, 2010, www.lasvegassun.com/news/2010/apr/30/habitat-humanity-builds-first-green-homes/ (accessed September 26, 2013).

76 Hamm, "Social Entrepreneurs Turn Business Sense to Good."

77 *Giving USA: The Annual Report on Philanthropy for the year 2011* (Chicago: Giving USA Foundation, Executive Summary, 2012): 4–7.

78 Many organizations are addressing social problems through business. See, for example, the Skoll Foundation, http://www.skollfoundation.org/skoll-entrepreneurs (accessed September 15, 2015).

79 M. Bishop and H. Hall, "Donations Barely Rose Last Year as Individuals Held Back," *The Chronicle of Philanthropy*, 2014, www.philanthropy. com/artcile/Fundraisings-Recovery-Could/154701 (accessed August 27, 2015).

80 Ibid.

81 T. L. Friedman, "The U.S.S. Prius," *The New York Times*, December 18, 2010, 19.

82 R. Giffinger, C. Fertner, H. Kramar, R. Kalasek, N. Pichler-Milanovic, and E. Meijers, "Smart Cities—A Ranking of European Medium-Sized Cities," European Smart Cities (Vienna: Centre of Regional Science, 2007), http://www.smart-cities.eu/download/results_indicators.pdf (accessed August 31, 2011).

83 W. Karlenzig, *How Green Is Your City? The SustainLane U.S. City Rankings* (Gabriola Island, BC: New Society Publishers, 2007).

84 "About ICLEI," ICLEI—Local Governments for Sustainability, http://icleiusa.org/ (accessed December 22, 2015).

85 L. M. Salaman, H. K. Anheier, R. List, S. Toepler, S. W. Sokolowski, and Associates, *Global Civil Society: Dimensions of the Nonprofit Sector* (Baltimore, MD: Johns Hopkins Comparative Nonprofit Sector Project), 8, http://ccss.jhu.edu/wp-content/uploads/downloads/2011/08/Global-Civil-Society-I.pdf (accessed February 5, 2014).

86 B. Bradley, P. Jensen, and L. Silverman, "The Nonprofit Sector's $100 Billion Opportunity," *Harvard Business Review* (May 2003): 94–103.

87 For an interesting and complete list of NGOs related to environmental sustainability, see P. Hawken, *Blessed Unrest: How the Largest Movement in the World Came Into Being and Why No One Saw it Coming* (New York: Vintage, 2007).

88 D. Devuyst, "Introduction to Sustainability Assessment at the Local Level," in D. Devuyst (ed.), *How Green is the City? Sustainability Assessment and the Management of Urban Environments* (New York: Columbia University Press, 2001).

89 STARS "Sustainability Tracking & Rating System," https://stars.aashe.org/ (accessed March 20, 2011).

90 For a copy of the manual, see AASHE, "STARS Sustainability Tracking Assessment & Rating System Version 1.1 TechnicalManual"(February2011),http://www.aashe.org/files/documents/STARS/stars_1.1_technical_manual_final.pdf (accessed March 20, 2011).

91 National Wildlife Federation, "Campus Environment 2008: A National Report Card on Sustainability in Higher Education" (2008), 1, http://www.aashe.org/files/documents/STARS/stars_1.1_technical_manual_final.pdf (accessed March 20, 2011).

92 M. Shriberg, "Institutional Assessment Tools for Sustainability in Higher Education: Strengths, Weaknesses, and Implications for Practice and Theory," *International Journal of Sustainability in Higher Education* 3, no. 3 (2002): 254–270.

93 M. Everard, P. Johnston, R. Karl-Henrik, and D. Santillo, "Reclaiming the Definition of Sustainability," *Environmental Science Pollution Resources International* 14, no. 1 (2007): 60–66.

94 T. Khanna and K. G. Palepu, *Winning in Emerging Markets: A Road Map for Strategy and Execution* (Boston, MA: Harvard Business Press, 2010), 4.

95 Ibid.

96 T. Khanna and K. G. Palepu, *Winning in Emerging Markets*, 114.

97 Ibid.

98 "Casting a Wide Net," *The Economist*, January 10, 2015, 53.

99 Grist staff, "15 Green Cities," *Grist*, July 20, 2007, http://grist.org/article/cities3/ (accessed September 5, 2015).

100 FTSE "All-World Index Series Monthly Review," www.ftse.com/analytics/all-world/Home/Sample (accessed August 27, 2015). FTSE series of Indexes has over 35 different indexes. The FTSE Global 100 Index had 104 stocks in the portfolio and showed a 2015 total 12 month return of 10.90. The Emerging Index showed a 12-month 18.26

return rate, one of the highest recorded returns for the indexes except for Asia and Eastern Europe. The indexes indicate that emerging markets present good investment opportunities.

101 Friends of Nature, Institute of Public & Environmental Affairs, Green Beagle, Envirofriends, and Green Stone Environmental Action Network, "The Other Side of Apple II," 2011, http://www.metronews.fr/info/apple-la-pollution-est-dans-le-fruit/mkia!6P2HwsiBChDls/Report-IT-V-Apple-II.pdf (accessed December 22, 2015).

102 Co-authored by Michael Aper, Master of Arts in Sustainability candidate at Wake Forest University.

103 N. Mehta, "Paul Hawken's Commencement Address in Portland" (ServiceSpace, May 17, 2009), http://www.servicespace.org/blog/view.php?id=2077 (accessed February 2, 2015).

104 "Professional Work," Paul Hawken, "1965: March on Montgomery," 2007, http://www.paulhawken.com/paulhawken_frameset.html (accessed February 2, 2015).

105 "Professional Work," Paul Hawken, "1966–1973: Erewhon Trading Company," 2007, http://www.paulhawken.com/paulhawken_frameset.html (accessed February 2, 2015).

106 "Professional Work," Paul Hawken, "2000–Present: Natural Capital Institute," 2007, http://www.paulhawken.com/paulhawken_frameset.html (accessed February 2, 2015).

107 "Write," Paul Hawken, 2007, http://www.paulhawken.com/write.html (accessed February 2, 2015).

108 WBCSD, http://www.wbcsd.org/home.aspx (accessed February 5, 2013).

109 "The WTO In Brief," WTO, http://www.wto.org/english/thewto_e/whatis_e/inbrief_e/inbr00_e.htm (accessed January 22, 2013).

110 IETA, http://www.ieta.org/index.php?option=com_content&view=article&id=15&Itemid=114 (accessed January 22, 2013).

111 EEI, http://www.eei.org/whoweare/abouteei/Pages/default.aspx (accessed January 22, 2013).

112 EPRI, http://www.epri.com/Pages/Default.aspx (accessed December 22, 2015).

113 BUSINESSEUROPE, http://www.businesseurope.eu/Content/Default.asp? (accessed September 20, 2015).

114 National Business Initiative, http://www.nbi.org.za (accessed December 22, 2015).

115 CII, http://www.cii.in/ (accessed January 22, 2013).

116 FICCI, http://www.ficci.com/ (accessed January 22, 2013).

117 IISD, http://www.iisd.org/about/ (accessed January 22, 2013).

118 Carbon Disclosure Project, https://www.cdp.net/en-US/Pages/HomePage.aspx (accessed December 22, 2015).

119 http://www.climateactionreserve.org/about-us/california-climate-action-registry/ (accessed December 22, 2015).

INDEX

320

Hannover Principles 115, 125, 203
Hansen, James 62
harm prevention 34
Hawken, Paul 202, 311
hazardous waste 74, 79
healthcare 118
heat-related deaths 25
heat waves 24
Herman Miller 161, 212
Hewlett-Packard Company (HP) 160
high-performance operations xix, 239–258
Hitachi 188
HOMA approach to presenting new business 301–302
Home Depot 185–186
Honda 148, 172
Hong Kong 45, 168
horizontal segmentation 119
hotels 118, 225, 278
household products 118
housing 291, 309–310
HTC 94
Huggies 97
Hulu 264
human capital 5, 188, 199, 248, 304–305
human resources 90, 128
human rights 40, 306
hybrid vehicles 255
Hyundai 172

IBM 110, 196, 316n50
ice 24–25
IKEA 32, 115
imitation 142, 143, 231, 300
impact analysis 116–117
Impact, Population Size, Affluence and Technology (IPAT) formulation 43
implementation 96, 101, 129, 261
incentives 58, 59–60, 166, 233–234, 299
income statements 90
incomplete information 57–58
incumbents 121–122, 127, 145, 150, 173, 227, 232, 300, 316n29
India: carbon dioxide emissions 47; certification programs 222; diversification 168; eco-labeling 215; energy consumption 11, 13–14; NGOs 313
Inditex 242
individualism 265
Indocert 222
Indonesia 38, 39, 309
industrial ecology 203
industry analysis 117–121, 125, 126–128, 134, 137, 138, 181, 227
industry attractiveness 168, 169–170, 175, 298
industry earnings 227
industry recipes 137, 138

industry structure 100, 185
inequities 34
infant mortality 43, 45
information disclosure 70, 98, 278; see also reporting
information management 268, 269, 297
information sharing 171
InnoCentive 265
innovation 114, 185, 315n26, 316n29; business models 264; China 199; clusters 244, 245; entrepreneurship 297, 298–299, 315n27; first-mover advantage 299–300; outsourcing 165; value 148–149
input costs 158–159
Instagram 145
Institute of Chartered Accountants 189
institutional risks 269
institutional view 89–94, 105n10
institutional voids 168, 309
insurance 119
intangible assets 125, 187–188, 200, 230, 276
integrated reports 194–196, 200, 201
intellectual capital 5, 143, 187, 199, 200
intellectual property 188, 285n91
Inter-American Development Bank 21
interest rates 278
Interface Carpet 115
Intergovernmental Panel on Climate Change (IPCC) xxn9, 18, 28n82, 199
internal conditions 96, 100–101, 129
International Code of Conduct on the Distribution and Use of Pesticides (1985) 79
International Council of Local Environmental Initiatives (ICLEI) 305
International Emissions Trading Association (IETA) 312
International Finance Corporation (IFC) 308
International Institute for Sustainable Development (IISD) 313
International Integrated Reporting Council (IIRC) 195, 200
International Monetary Fund (IMF) 34
International Standards Organization (ISO) 194, 203, 215, 217, 226
Internet 119, 121, 137, 243, 246
intra-preneurship 303
investment: corporate rankings 196; Global Reporting Initiative 192; Goldman Sachs 183; net present value 274–276; real options 276–278, 286n95; socially responsible investing 189, 293, 310, 311
ISO 1400 standards 194, 203, 215, 217, 226
Israel 45

Japan: carbon dioxide emissions 47; certification programs 222; eco-labeling 215, 224; emissions register 187; energy consumption 11; Nippon Keidanren 312; socially responsible investing 293
Jefferson, Thomas 250

public relations (PR) 38
public trust doctrine 65
purchasing 251–253, 254
purposeful behavior 94
push-pull view of the supply chain 241

radical resource productivity 146
radioactive waste 75
Rainforest Alliance 32, 39
rankings 196–198
raw materials 112, 183, 218, 246, 253, 310
real options 183, 184, 274–278, 280, 285n92, 286n95
recession 123
recreation 112
Recycled Content Certification 225
recycling 148, 161; buildings 249; by consumers 210; cradle-to-cradle concept 218, 220; environmental preferable purchasing 252, 253; NASCAR 259–260, 261, 282n7; Rohner 156; Zara 242
Recycling Program Certification 225
"red oceans" 148, 149
refugia 112
regulation xviii, xix, 55–84, 113, 114, 274; antitrust laws 36, 232; Climate Change Act 8; common law 64–65; common pool resources 71; Companies Act 36–37; company responses to 69–70; cost-benefit analysis 63–64, 71; effectiveness of 68; emerging markets 309; environmentalism 59–62; institutional view 91, 93; market failure 57–59, 71; public opinion 57, 68; renewable portfolio standards 65–68, 69; RITE Project 68–69
Reich, Robert 38, 39
relatedness 169
relative cost 165
renewable energy 11–14, 20, 304; BrightSource Energy 110–111; Cape Wind 151; clusters 245; E+Co 30; entrepreneurship 296, 297; Germany 247; NASCAR 260, 261; regulation 65–68, 69, 71; RITE Project 69; strategic group analysis 121; tech firms 95; Wal-Mart 32, 107; see also solar energy; wind energy
renewable energy credit (REC) 65–67
renewable portfolio standards (RPS) 65–68, 69
replacement mechanism 297
reporting xix, 108, 181–182, 186–201; carbon dioxide emissions 59; China 199–200; Companies Act 36–37; corporate rankings 196–198; Corporate Social Responsibility 38; Global Environment Outlook 198–199; Global Reporting Initiative 37, 189, 190–192, 193, 194, 201, 203, 217, 239; integrated reports 194–196, 200, 201; materiality 192–193; sustainability 193–196
reputation xviii, 48, 57–58, 114, 285n91, 297, 316n54; barriers to entry 127, 145, 232; consumer attitudes 211; Dell Computers 164; reporting 186; reputational risk 269; Rohner 174; Wal-Mart 124

research and development (R&D) 117, 165–166, 184, 188, 264, 297
resilience xvii, 110, 116
resistance to change 265–267, 268, 281
resource-based view of the firm 109–110, 125, 136, 141
Resource Conservation and Recovery Act (RCRA, 1976) 58, 60, 74
resources (natural) xv, 6, 9, 129; buildings 249; certification programs 225; clusters 244; common pool 71; developed and developing countries 45; discounting 184; environmental preferable purchasing 253; exploitation of xvii; footprint analysis 193; life-cycle assessment 161; location 243, 253; population pressures 46; public trust doctrine 65; radical resource productivity 146; smart cities 304; see also energy; natural capital; water
resources and capabilities 109–110, 129, 135, 136–137, 144–146, 150; barriers to entry 122; competitors 138; definition of resources 125; diversification 168; entrepreneurship 299; evaluation of competencies 142–144; flexibility 271–272; identification of competencies 138–142; sharing 171; tactics 146–148; vertical integration 166
respiration 148
Responsible Procurement Program 226
Responsible Sourcing of Construction Products 223
restructuring 172
return on capital employed (ROCE) 139, 153n17
return on invested capital (ROIC) 118–119, 184–186, 188, 200
return on investment (ROI) 153n17, 185
return on net assets (RONA) 153n17
revealed preferences 64
revenues 185, 186, 263, 277
right-to-know laws 60
right-to-use concept 265
rigidities 144
Rio Tinto 32, 294
risk 89, 95, 279; Coca-Cola 3; diversification 167; entrepreneurship 294, 295; flexibility 268–269; impact analysis 116; risk analysis 217; risk management 37, 267–268; smart grids 173; vertical integration 166
RITE Project 68–69
rivalry 122, 126
Robb, Walter 38
Rodale Institute 300–301
Rogers, Jim 55, 72
Rohner Textil AG 156, 174
Rosling, Hans 43
routines 140–142, 144, 153n23, 154n32, 297, 316n29
Royal Dutch Shell 8, 144, 272–273
rule of law 90, 116, 316n29
Russia 11, 13–14, 47